The Stock Market

WILEY PROFESSIONAL BANKING AND FINANCE SERIES
EDWARD I. ALTMAN, Editor

The Stock Market
Fifth Edition

RICHARD J. TEWELES
EDWARD S. BRADLEY

A revision of earlier editions by
the late George L. Leffler and Loring C. Farwell

JOHN WILEY & SONS

New York • Chichester • Brisbane • Toronto • Singapore

Library of Congress Cataloging-in-Publication Data:

Teweles, Richard Jack, 1924–
    The stock market.

    (Wiley professional banking and finance series,
ISSN 0733-8945)
    "A revision of earlier editions by the late
George L. Leffler and Loring C. Farwell."
    Includes bibliographical references and index.
    1. Stock-exchange. I. Bradley, Edward S.
II. Leffler, George Leland, 1899–   Stock market.
III. Title. IV. Series.

    HG4551.T48   1987   332.64'2   86-33950
    ISBN 0-471-82044-X

Printed in the United States of America

10 9 8 7 6 5 4 3 2 1

Series Preface

The worlds of banking and finance have changed dramatically during the past few years, and no doubt this turbulence will continue through the 1980s. We have established the Wiley Professional Banking and Finance Series to aid in characterizing this dynamic environment and to further the understanding of the emerging structures, issues, and content for the professional financial community.

We envision three types of book in this series. First, we are commissioning distinguished experts in a broad range of fields to assemble a number of authorities to write specific primers on related topics. For example, some of the early handbook-type volumes in the series concentrate on the Stock Market, Investment Banking, and Financial Depository Institutions. A second type of book attempts to combine text material with appropriate empirical and case studies written by practitioners in relevant fields. Finally, we are encouraging definitive, authoritative works on specialized subjects for practitioners and theorists.

It is a distinct pleasure and honor for me to assist John Wiley & Sons, Inc. in this important endeavor. In addition to banking and financial practitioners, we think business students and faculty will benefit from this series. Most of all, though, we hope this series will become a primary source in the 1980s for the members of the professional financial community to refer to theories and data and to integrate important aspects of the central changes in our financial world.

EDWARD I. ALTMAN

Professor of Finance
New York University,
Schools of Business

Preface

Since the fourth edition of this book, there have been material changes in the investment markets and the climate which surrounds them. As in most industries, the advancement of electronic devices has changed the manner in which the securities business operates from a mechanical point of view. In addition, the ability to gather, digest, and organize information has had considerable influence on market efficiency with resultant effects on the value of fundamental and technical research. Volume and price levels have substantially passed previous records. Trading in indexes of many kinds and options on the indexes has become widespread and has great influence on the equity markets.

As with previous editions, this book is designed for investors, brokerage house employees, students, and others with an interest in how the market operates and functions. It is not intended to displace investment books which are available to describe modern portfolio theory and valuation in much greater detail than could possibly be attempted here. This is, however, more than a primer. There are few aspects of investing or trading that are not considered.

Despite the fact that this is the second edition of this work prepared by the present authors, credit is still due the original authors, George L. Leffler and, later, Loring C. Farwell, as well as those who helped us with our fourth edition. In addition to those credited in the body of this edition and in the preface to the fourth edition, we are grateful for the contributions of Barbara Najman and David L. Nudelman, who helped with the laborious search for obscure information.

RICHARD J. TEWELES
EDWARD S. BRADLEY

Long Beach, California
New York, New York
April 1987

Preface to the Fourth Edition

This is a study of the stock market as it operates and functions in the 1980s. The book is written for investors, members of brokerage firms, and college students. It is designed to fill a gap between the large number of excellent books on investments and those on capital market institutions. The former properly devote most of their attention to an evaluation of a broad spectrum of investments and the latter to descriptions of many market institutions other than the stock market. Although the reader will find in this book an up-to-date description of the stock market and its operations, the serious student of investing will need to supplement this material with additional reading in the areas of valuation and portfolio theory. Exhaustive discussions of all the subjects discussed here would require a five-foot shelf of books, but the reader will nevertheless find that all aspects of investing and trading in securities are considered.

This book was inspired by *The Stock Market* as originally written by Professor George L. Leffler and later revised by Professor Loring C. Farwell. Without the base provided by these stock market scholars and those who helped them write their material over twenty years ago, this book would not have been written.

In addition to the countless scholars and practitioners who educated us through their books and articles, we are grateful to Joann McLean and Terry Anderson for helping with the manuscript, Don Johnston and Philip Kiyokane, who performed such uninviting tasks as searching for obscure facts and helping with the index, and Jim Manor, of Drexel Burnham Lambert, who was never too busy to search for bits of information on the shortest of notice.

RICHARD J. TEWELES
EDWARD S. BRADLEY

Long Beach, California
New York City
June 1982

Contents

PART 4.   REGULATIONS   287

PART 5.   INVESTING PRACTICES AND SPECIAL INSTRUMENTS   329

GLOSSARY   491

INDEX   515

The Stock Market

1 Fundamental Information

1 Securities Markets and Securities Owners

This book is about stock markets and the way they work. The word "stock," at least in its North American usage, means equity or ownership in a corporation. There are many securities which are not stocks and which may be issued by corporations, governmental bodies, and other types of issuer. The emphasis in this book is on stocks. This edition devotes considerably more space than previous editions to instruments other than stocks, not because they are necessarily more important than stocks, but because the markets and the increased sophistication of investors have made the distinction between the two broad categories less meaningful than before. Prior to further discussion of market mechanisms and practices, however, the variety of securities markets and their typical participants deserve consideration.

First, a distinction should be made between *primary* and *secondary* markets. The initial sale of securities from the issuing corporation or governmental body to the investor, either publicly or privately, is called a *primary* distribution. The issuer uses the funds raised by the sale to expand production, further research, build bridges, and the like. Because few investors could be persuaded to tie up their funds indefinitely, most securities are negotiable, and the initial buyer may reoffer the securities to any interested party at whatever price is mutually satisfactory. This next transaction is said to be a *secondary* transaction in that the proceeds of the sale accrue to the previous holder, not the issuer. Thus, when 100 shares of General Motors (GM) are traded on the floor of the New York Stock Exchange, none of the proceeds are paid to GM. Rather, the previous owner of those shares will receive the entire proceeds of that sale.

Certainly, the issuance of securities is a critical function. This branch of the securities industry is called "underwriting" or "investment banking." The task of the investment banker when making an offering of new securities is inextricably interwoven with the behavior of prices in the secondary market. The function is so specialized, it deserves treatment of its own and, indeed, volumes have been devoted to it. In this book, a compressed but thorough discussion of the topic will be found in Chapter 14.

This book is concerned primarily with the secondary market for stocks in the United States. Markets abroad have grown greatly and continue to grow. New York may still be the world's financial capital by most measures, but developments in London, Tokyo, Zurich, and Frankfurt, to say nothing of Singapore and Sydney, have made a New York–only orientation not only parochial but also unprofitable. Investment managers who are unaware of foreign developments are no longer able to perform their duties responsibly. The major foreign markets are covered in some detail in Chapter 11.

KINDS OF MARKETS

Currently, the secondary market for securities in the United States is divided into two broad classes of market: the organized securities exchanges and the over-the-counter (OTC) market. Before the inexorable march of the semiconductor and the microprocessor, the distinction between these markets was quite clear. Computerized linkage between the markets has now developed to the point where distinctions are often hard, if not impossible, to discern.

National Securities Exchanges

Section 6 of the Securities Exchange Act of 1934 requires registration of all "national securities exchanges" with the Securities and Exchange Commission (SEC). In 1962 there were 14 such exchanges registered, but by 1986 active dealings were conducted on only seven:

New York Stock Exchange
American Stock Exchange (New York)
Midwest Stock Exchange (Chicago)
Pacific Stock Exchange (San Francisco and Los Angeles)
Philadelphia Stock Exchange
Boston Stock Exchange
Cincinnati Stock Exchange

In addition, active dealings in options are conducted on the Chicago Board Options Exchange and the exchanges listed, except for the Midwest, Boston, and Cincinnati exchanges.

Volume of Exchange Business

It will doubtless come as no surprise to most that volume on the New York Stock Exchange (NYSE) surpasses that on all other domestic exchanges both in number of shares traded and in dollar value. In fact, the NYSE surpasses all other domestic exchanges *combined*. The following are comparisons for 1985:

TOTAL VOLUME BY SHARES (IN MILLIONS)[1]

	Total Shares	Total (%)
NYSE	30,221.8	81.6
American	2,114.7	5.7
Other exchanges	4,709.1	12.7

MARKET VALUE OF SHARES SOLD ($ MILLIONS)

NYSE	1,023,202	85.3
American	26,332	2.2
Other exchanges	150,252	12.5

Also one should note that a very large proportion of the volume reported by the exchanges other than the American (Amex) is actually generated from trades involving stocks whose primary market is the NYSE but which are also listed elsewhere.

A final statistic may be even more revealing. At year-end 1985 the 614.6 million shares of International Business Machines (IBM) listed on the NYSE had a market value of about $95.266 billion.[2] The combined market value of *all* equity securities listed on the Amex as of March 1986 was $95.802 billion.[3] Indeed, were one to reassemble the fragments of the former American Telephone and Telegraph (AT&T) complex, the market value of those shares on January 31, 1985 would have totaled $98.942 billion, all listed on the NYSE.

Over-the-Counter Market

Securities transactions that do not take place on an exchange are said to be OTC. The market is huge, consisting in part of virtually all trading in U.S. government and agency securities and all municipal bonds—obligations of cities, towns, states, and the like. In addition, the great majority of corporate bond transactions and the trading of thousands of different stock issues not listed on exchanges takes place OTC.

By and large the issuing companies are smaller and less well known than the established listed corporations, although some appear in *Fortune* magazine's 500 largest industrial company list. Because of the prevalence of a great many small and obscure corporate stocks, however, the market has long had a speculative appearance, only partly justified. Almost all of the stocks of today's corporate giants were once traded OTC and were thought to be highly speculative purchases. In recent years the NYSE has permitted direct listing of a few established companies which went from initial public

[1]*NYSE 1986 Fact Book*, p. 74.
[2]*Ibid.*, p. 42.
[3]"Amex Stats—March 1986," The American Stock Exchange.

offering to exchange trading, bypassing the more usual OTC seasoning period. In fact, the National Association of Securities Dealers (NASD) stoutly maintains that there is no reason to list shares any longer on *any* exchange.

Nevertheless, the investor seeking to find the "new Xerox" or the "new Syntex" before the crowd does is well advised to scrutinize this market. The best time for share-price growth with most corporations is while the shares are still relatively undiscovered. By the time the stock has been listed the chances are that it has already become too visible; that is, analysts from major firms now begin following it closely and the pricing of the shares becomes dominated by larger, more sophisticated investors. The effect of this tends to make stock prices behave in a less explosive manner than when they traded OTC.

Traditionally, OTC has been a *dealer* (or principal) market in which dealers buy and sell from inventory, marking prices up and down just as any wholesale merchant would. Dealers are said to "make a market" by continuously quoting a price at which they are willing to buy a security ("bid") and a higher price at which they will sell ("ask" or "offer"). Commissions are not charged. The dealer's profit, if any, comes from the "spread," the difference between the bid and offer prices.

For many years the OTC market was an informal telephone network of competing dealers. Finding the best price was often laborious and not always practical. In 1970, however, the NASD introduced an automated quotation system called NASDAQ which electronically linked dealers via computer terminals and video screens, thus further closing the gap between the classic OTC "negotiated" market and the exchange "auction" process.

The NASDAQ system has proven an enormous success. Trading volume in this system was 20.7 billion shares, about 68% of NYSE share volume, in 1985. On the other hand, dollar value of trading lagged considerably behind the NYSE–$233,454 million to $970,500 million.[4] This total exceeds all equity markets except for the NYSE and the Tokyo Stock Exchange, and indeed was greater than the equity values traded on the London, Zurich, and Frankfurt exchanges combined. It should also be noted that a considerable volume (1.101 million shares in 1985) in listed stocks is traded OTC by NASD member dealers in what is called the "third market." The OTC market will be examined in more detail in Chapter 9.

STOCKHOLDERS

The most recent NYSE survey of periodic shareownership was released in December 1985.[5] Among the interesting results of this study is that 47.04 million Americans, nearly one in every five, now owns stock. The number of men and women shareholders was almost exactly even, 22.509 million

---

[4] *NASDAQ 1986 Fact Book*, p. 12.
[5] *NYSE 1986 Fact Book*, pp. 55–56.

women and 22.484 million men. There was an overall increase in shareowners from the 1983 survey of 4.68 million, an 11% gain.

The median age of shareholders declined slightly from the previous survey from 45 to 44. The current investors are a more affluent group than their predecessors. Household median income of the 1983 stockholder was $33,200 versus $36,800 for the 1985 survey. This increase of 11% is about the same as the national median, which rose from $20,200 to $22,400 during this same period.

The median portfolio of 1985 owners was $6,200. Persons who invest exclusively in NYSE-listed issues totaled 47.1%. Those who restricted their activities to other exchanges accounted for 2.4%, while OTC claimed only 8.6%. Investors who used more than one of these forms accounted for 24.8%. Probably the most interesting figure was the 6.2 million investors who owned only mutual funds. This represents a 67% advance in only two years, and such holders now make up 17.1% of all investors, testimony to the increased domination of the market by the institutional investor.

The NYSE estimates that in addition to the 47 million direct shareholders a considerable number benefit from indirect ownership of shares. Such individuals have policies or accounts with life insurance companies or mutual savings banks, or participate in some form of pension plan. This number was 133 million in 1980, the last year in which this estimate was done. The NYSE does not count a person in both categories, so that an individual who holds stocks *and* has a life insurance policy is only counted in the direct owner category.

Institutional ownership of stocks continues to accelerate. The 1975 edition of the survey put such ownership at $230.5 billion or 33.6% of NYSE market value. Although the current survey did not address this point, figures compiled by Salomon Brothers[6] indicate that institutional shareholders now account for about 60% of shares owned:

	Billions
Thrifts	$ 5.3
Life insurance companies	80.5
Property liability companies	53.8
Private noninsured pension funds	362.4
State and local retirement funds	136.8
Foundations and endowments	62.5
Taxable investment funds	108.9
Securities brokers and dealers	16.5
Foreign	115.4
Households direct owners	1,436.1
	$2,378.2

[6]Henry Kaufman and Jeffrey Hanna, *Prospects for the Financial Markets in 1986* (New York: Salomon Brothers Inc., 1985), p. 52.

Certainly some portion of the foreign ownership of shares is by individuals, but it is likely that the larger portion is also institutional.

Reasons for Stock Ownership

The NYSE carried out surveys in 1954 and 1959 to find out what people thought about stock ownership. Although conditions have changed, it seems likely that many who buy and hold common stocks still feel the primary reasons cited over 30 years ago are essentially the same today: long-term growth of capital, dividends, and a good hedge against inflation.

The inflationary-hedge rationale does not always seem to be borne out, at least in the short term. During the 1970s the American economy was bedeviled by high inflation *and* falling stock prices. Over the long run, however, the balance is usually redressed, and patient holders who rode out that period found their expectations more than fulfilled in the huge bull market of the 1980s. This situation is far from unique. Exhaustive research at the University of Chicago has demonstrated that common stock ownership is the most reliable long-term inflationary hedge readily available:

> The rate of return on an equally weighted portfolio of all NYSE stocks that was held from the end of 1925 through the end of 1976 was 9.0 percent per annum compounded annually. The rate on long-term governments for the same period was 3.4 percent. Both of their calculations are in current dollars.[7]

The study has been updated with results that are essentially similar.[8] There have been periods when gold, real estate, fine wines, and even the likes of baseball cards have outperformed stocks, but such periods are usually rather brief. Real estate partisans would doubtless maintain their favorite is the superior long-term investment vehicle, and well it may be for some investors. Certainly, the tax code has consistently favored real estate investment, especially in the form of the single-family home. Under the best of circumstances, however, real estate investments cannot be made as easily as stock purchases, nor are they as liquid. A significant common stock investment can be made without undue risk for $10,000–$15,000; rarely if ever is this the case with real estate in the 1980s.

Naturally, no investor can afford to buy a weighted portfolio of all NYSE stocks either, and there is always the risk that, with limited funds, the wrong stocks may be selected, even though the "market" performs well. Nevertheless the risk factor keeps many conservative investors from buying common shares. Of course, no investment is without some form of risk. The buyer of a U.S. Treasury bond receives two guarantees—one explicit, the

---

[7]Lawrence Fisher and James H. Lorie, *A Half Century of Returns on Stocks and Bonds* (University of Chicago Graduate School of Business, 1977), p. 1.

[8]Roger G. Ibbotson and Rex A. Sinquefield, *Stocks, Bonds, Bills and Inflation: The Past and The Future* (Charlottesville, Va.: Financial Analysts Research Foundation, 1982), p. 36. Actually Ibbotson and Sinquefield found the rate to be 9.1% compounded from 1926 to 1981.

other implicit. The Treasury agrees to pay a stipulated rate of return, say 10%, and to repay the principal amount upon maturity. The *implicit* guarantee, in contrast, is that the Treasury will *not* pay the investor 12%, or even 10¼%, and will *not* pay the investor one penny more than the principal amount. Thus the investor who must seek a higher rate of return may find he or she cannot afford the risk of *not* investing in common stocks. "Safe" though some bonds may be, these investments can only preserve capital already acquired. Over the long run their rates of return have not produced a satisfactory offset to the inflationary erosion of purchasing power of the dollar. Thus the investor seeking to build capital is virtually forced to consider common stocks no matter what risks may be involved. As will be noted later, there are ways to reduce these risks but none to eliminate them.

Ownership of even the best quality shares gives no guarantees of superior, or indeed of any, return. Recent years have seen the bankruptcy of such companies as Johns Manville Corporation and International Harvester, which were once included in the Dow Jones 30 Stock Industrial Average. The problems that befell Texaco, in attempting to take over Getty Oil, and Union Carbide in the Bhopal, India, disaster indicate that stock investors must be vigilant and cannot allow investments to be made solely on a company's past results. Nevertheless, if there are no guarantees against loss, neither are there any that the investor cannot double or triple the investment by buying common stocks today. Investors seeking greater than average returns must be ready for greater than average risk.

POPULAR STOCKS

As of December 31, 1985, the 10 American corporations with the greatest number of shareholders were:[9]

Company	Share Volume
AT&T	313,019,442
IBM	259,650,205
Phillips Petroleum	245,696,850
American Express	179,393,600
Unocal	165,214,000
Beatrice Companies	161,516,000
Exxon	151,913,800
Ford Motor	149,366,500
Mobil	148,392,800
Texas Oil and Gas	148,078,600

[9]*NYSE 1986 Fact Book*, pp. 41–42.

In 1980 the list included Exxon, General Electric, Texaco, Sears Roebuck, Ford Motor, Southern Company, and General Telephone and Electronics. The breakup of the AT&T complex by the Justice Department and the federal courts led to the spinning off of shares in the former operating subsidiaries of "Ma Bell." Thus all the corporations on the list between GM and IBM are former AT&T subsidiaries.

Other changes in the list are more gradual but give interesting insight into the way American industry has changed over the years. For example, the decline of the American steel industry can be observed by noting that the 1961 list of the 10 most widely held companies contained both U.S. Steel and Bethlehem Steel. By 1981, U.S. Steel had slipped to eighteenth and Bethlehem to forty-seventh. The 1985 list places U.S. Steel thirty-eighth, and Bethlehem does not even appear in the top 50.

Naturally, many shareholders are patient long-term investors who infrequently trade their shares. The list of stocks "popular" in trading activity is much more changeable. Of course, institutional investors favor positions in large companies because only those stocks can absorb large dollar volumes without disruptive price changes. It should, therefore, come as no surprise to find companies like AT&T and IBM on both lists. Other favorites are more transitory. In the following 10 most actively traded list, Phillips Petroleum, Texas Oil and Gas, Unocal, and Beatrice all made the list because of takeover attempts and arbitrage trading associated with them. They are unlikely to be repeated in 1986.

Company	Share Volume
AT&T	313,019,442
IBM	259,650,205
Phillips Petroleum	245,696,850
American Express	179,393,600
Unocal	165,214,000
Beatrice Companies	161,516,000
Exxon	151,913,800
Ford Motor	149,366,500
Mobil	148,392,800
Texas Oil and Gas	148,078,600

BONDHOLDERS

There is no accurate estimate of the number of bondholders in the United States. Part of the problem is that for many years the U.S. Treasury and governmental agencies, both huge issuers of bonds, issued securities largely in "bearer" certificates where the owner's name was not recorded. Similarly, municipal bonds were overwhelmingly sold in this format, partly to avoid the expenses of hiring a transfer agent to record ownership changes. Federal legislation has prohibited the issuance of bearer securities since July 1983 because they were widely believed to be used in "laundering" criminal funds. Billions of dollars' worth of such bonds, however, will remain outstanding for a number of years to come. Corporations also issue large quantities of bonds, but in the United States, at least, these are always in registered format. This type of bond has the owner's name and address officially recorded by a transfer agent and the owner's name printed on the certificate. "Eurobonds" sold abroad by American corporations and others are still largely in the bearer format.

Institutions are by far the major holders of bonds. Some of this stems from a traditional legal view that safety of principal is the paramount concern of a *fiduciary* (someone legally charged with the investment of funds for the benefit of another). Characteristically, then, portfolios of state and local employee pension funds, state university endowment funds, and the like have been heavily invested in bonds. Many of these institutions are tax exempt and thus prefer the higher yields of corporate bonds to those of U.S. government or municipal securities. Although fiduciary investment in common stocks has become widespread since the 1950s, many of these portfolios remain heavily invested in bonds and similar debt instruments.

Other large owners of bonds include commercial banks, thrift institutions, life insurance companies, fire and casualty insurance companies, and investment companies. Investment companies have grown rapidly in the period from the late 1970s to the mid-1980s. These funds now provide access to high yields and safety of investments that were once only available in large minimum amounts beyond the individual investor's reach—often $100,000.

At the end of 1985, the estimated total outstanding amount of debt securities by issuer was:[10]

Corporate bonds	$792.0 billion
Municipal bonds	$614.4 billion
U.S. Treasury debt (privately held)	$1,394.3 billion
Federal agency debt (privately held)	$620.6 billion

This estimated total of $3,421.3 billion exceeds the amount of stock estimated to be outstanding by $1,043.1 billion. The largest owners of each of these were:

Corporate bonds—life insurance companies	$269.6 billion
Municipal bonds—commercial banks	$188.5 billion
U.S. Treasury—households	$465.8 billion
Federal agencies—thrift institutions	$155.2 billion

[10]Kaufman and Hanna, *op. cit.*, pp. 49–55.

2 Corporate Securities

The analysis of investment portfolios is complex. Investment advisors, brokers,[1] and investors may spend years in mastering these subjects. This chapter can serve only as an introduction to a fascinating field. It can, however, be a basis for understanding the fundamental nature of the securities that investors may buy and from whose ownership they may (or may not) profit.

CORPORATION FINANCE

The stock market is a market for corporate securities. The rights of ownership in other forms of business organization are not marketable in the same sense. Although enormous numbers of securities are issued by governments (foreign, federal, state, and local), these securities are all bonds or similar debt obligations and not stock that connotes ownership or "equity." Corporation finance, then, is inseparable from the stock market. Indeed, at bottom, the stock market is little more than a pricing mechanism for used assets; that is, collective assessments of what the assets of a given corporation are currently worth. The future may show such judgments to have been overly generous or absurdly low. Differences of opinion about value (or speed) make for exciting markets (or horse races). Yet for all the parallels that may be drawn between stock market investments and gambling, there lies a fundamental difference. We may decide to spend a pleasant afternoon at the track and bet or not bet as it pleases us. We may also decide that such frivolity, or even immorality to some, is a useless pastime and stay home. In either case our life is unlikely to be materially different, whatever our decision. Likewise we may choose to invest or not to invest in securities; but we may *not* choose to not pay our utility bills, not shop at the supermarket, and not buy gasoline for our cars. Life is so centered around products

---

[1]The colloquial term *broker* is used here as most people use it; that is, a salesperson who provides advice for customers and enters their orders. The more precise term is *registered representative*, although many firms use, for image purposes, such terms as "account executive," "investment executive," "investment broker," or the current favorite, "financial consultant."

and services provided by corporations that they are inextricably interwoven with our lives. If we are to understand securities and investing, we must have some understanding of corporation finance. In what ways do corporations work? In the next several paragraphs an outline of this subject is sketched in broad strokes with more complete examination left to other sources.

Requirements for Funds

Business activity depends on the availability of goods and services under the control of business management. Raw materials and services with which to produce goods are purchased, for the most part, as they are needed. The money received from the sale of goods is used to pay for additional raw materials and services as they are purchased. In a successful business the flow of funds from sales matches most requirements for funds. Goods and services are combined in finished products whose sale produces receivables. The collection of the receivables produces funds to continue the cycle.

Some goods needed by business concerns, however, must be stockpiled; for example, sales require an inventory of finished goods on hand to meet deliveries. The very production of these goods requires inventories of raw materials. The manufacturing process requires machinery, tools, buildings, and transportation equipment, the useful life of which may span many years. Sales are almost universally made on credit, and some receivables must be held by a business concern pending collection. Good sense requires the holding of a certain amount of cash, the universal form of purchasing power, for use as unexpected events occur and unexpected needs or opportunities arise. Sound cash management requires that cash in excess of predictable needs be invested in revenue-producing, liquid securities such as Treasury bills. The overall allocation of a typical U.S. manufacturing corporation's assets is shown in the accompanying balance sheet.[2]

The amount of the land and depreciable fixed assets (basically plant and equipment) is typically the largest single asset entry on an industrial balance sheet. The plant and equipment account is reduced by reserves for depreciation and depletion before the net investment is shown in the totals column. These reserves are an accumulation of charges that companies have made in past periods against the income they derived from sales of the products made in these plants and with this equipment. The charge is included in the prices customers pay for the products of manufacturers to compensate for the use of these assets in the production process. Eventually, the full cost of individual assets is met by these charges against income. Maintenance of productive capacity requires the continuing expenditure of money to buy new plant, property, and equipment. Annual requirements for such purchases almost equal annual charges of cost against income. Average U.S. industrial

---

[2]U.S. Department of Commerce, *Quarterly Financial Report for Manufacturing, Mining, and Trade Corporations, Fourth Quarter, 1985* (Washington, D.C., 1986), p. 4.

corporations have net plant, property, and equipment investments equal to about half the purchase price of the items on their accounting records. As new items are continually added and older ones retired, a continuing need for funds to maintain net investment in plant arises.

Sources of Funds

The stockpiling of goods requires the use of funds as the amounts invested in assets indicate. Corporate management has three usual sources of funds: (1) short-term creditors, (2) long-term creditors, and (3) owners.

The principal kinds of short-term credits are shown in the first section of the Liabilities and Stockholders' Equity section of the balance sheet (see Table 2-1). The largest of these is ordinarily trade accounts and trade notes payable. Just as most concerns sell to their customers on credit terms, they buy on such terms. Nearly all industrial corporations have such trade credits ("accounts payable" on many balance sheets) on their books at any given time. Further credit may be obtained by borrowing from financial institutions like commercial banks and finance companies. Many corporations have adopted a practice once used primarily by financial institutions of issuing commercial paper to help generate short-term funds. Commercial paper, really unsecured promissory notes of 9 months or less duration, is generally cheaper and more flexible than bank borrowing, but it is not without its dangers. The role of heavy reliance on this type of borrowing can be seen in the amalgamation of the Pennsylvania and New York Central railroads into the Penn Central Railroad. It led to one of the classic failures in American business. Although the problems of the combined railroads were in fact monumental, they were exacerbated by an excessive reliance on the continuous sale of commercial paper and the hopes that buyers would always buy new paper upon the maturation of their current holdings. When they refused to do so, the company collapsed as it was unable to pay maturing debts. This happened despite the fact that the railroad owned enormous assets, particularly real estate. It was cash poor and simply could not pay its bills.

Students of securities analysis in the 1950s and 1960s were taught that a corporation's *current ratio* (current assets divided by current liabilities) should not be less than 2/1, or 200%. This level of liquidity allowed for substantial bill-paying ability, even if a major debtor or customer defaulted. The ratio for typical companies now is about 152% ($519,429 million divided into $789,426 million). Indeed, the fourth edition of this volume (1982), noted that the ratio then was about 168%. It becomes clear that modern corporations are more willing than ever before to try innovative and riskier short-term financing. This may be fine in boom times but becomes perilous when short-term rates rise sharply as they did in the early 1980s.

The balance of funds is obtained on longer terms. The sources of long-term loans are again the financial institutions—commercial banks, finance and insurance companies, pension funds, and individual investors. Corporate

Table 2-1 Balance Sheet (For Corporations Included in All Manufacturing and All Nondurable Manufacturing Industries)

	All Manufacturing [1]				
	4Q 1984	1Q 1985	2Q 1985	3Q 1985	4Q 1985
ASSETS	(million dollars)				
Cash and demand deposits in the U.S.	30,314	26,059	28,094	31,399	35,305
Time deposits in the U.S., including negotiable certificates of deposit	20,077	21,146	18,331	19,977	20,944
Total cash on hand and in U.S. banks	50,391	47,205	46,426	51,376	56,248
Other short-term financial investments, including marketable and government securities, commercial paper, etc.	57,066	53,938	54,613	51,763	57,121
Total cash, U.S. Government and other securities	107,456	101,143	101,039	103,139	113,370
Trade accounts and trade notes receivable (less allowances for doubtful receivables)	282,104	294,205	295,486	297,762	293,232
Inventories	323,585	331,444	328,569	322,218	319,754
All other current assets	54,836	58,043	59,830	62,625	63,072
Total current assets	767,982	784,835	784,924	785,744	789,426
Depreciable and amortizable fixed assets, including construction in progress	1,133,620	1,132,501	1,149,971	1,165,964	1,172,596
Land and mineral rights	97,959	95,428	95,819	96,099	100,669
Less: Accumulated depreciation, depletion, and amortization	527,470	524,359	536,564	547,596	552,105
Net property, plant, and equipment	704,110	703,569	709,226	714,467	721,160
All other non-current assets, including investment in non-consolidated entities, long-term investments, intangibles, etc.	381,364	377,565	386,401	401,664	423,256
Total Assets	1,853,455	1,865,969	1,880,551	1,901,875	1,933,842
LIABILITIES AND STOCKHOLDERS' EQUITY					
Short-term debt, original maturity of 1 year or less					
a. Loans from banks	36,942	39,640	38,865	38,204	36,119
b. Other short-term debt including commercial paper	30,788	35,964	36,397	33,455	34,998
Trade accounts and trade notes payable	162,901	159,519	159,035	156,314	168,952
Income taxes accrued, prior and current years, net of payments	30,485	31,138	28,631	30,762	28,025
Installments, due in 1 year or less, on long-term debt					
a. Loans from banks	9,314	10,453	10,012	10,739	11,051
b. Other long-term debt	16,369	16,254	16,590	16,264	17,696
All other current liabilities, including excise and sales taxes, and accrued expenses	202,288	209,425	212,183	219,270	222,588
Total current liabilities	489,087	502,393	501,713	505,007	519,429
Long-term debt (due in more than 1 year)					
a. Loans from banks	93,581	94,501	94,416	89,409	95,157
b. Other long-term debt	230,579	241,438	248,899	264,453	267,552
All other non-current liabilities, including deferred income taxes, capitalized leases, and minority stockholders' interest in consolidated domestic corporations	156,642	160,891	166,260	169,208	176,720
Total Liabilities	969,888	999,223	1,011,288	1,028,078	1,058,857
Capital stock and other capital (less treasury stock)	235,466	230,362	230,990	236,437	237,897
Retained earnings	648,101	636,383	638,272	637,361	637,088
Stockholders' Equity	883,567	866,745	869,263	873,798	874,985
Total Liabilities and Stockholders' Equity	1,853,455	1,865,969	1,880,551	1,901,875	1,933,842
NET WORKING CAPITAL					
Excess of total current assets over total current liabilities	278,895	282,441	283,211	280,737	269,998
SELECTED BALANCE SHEET RATIOS	(percent of total assets)				
Total cash, U.S. Government and other securities	5.8	5.4	5.4	5.4	5.9
Trade accounts and trade notes receivable	15.2	15.8	15.7	15.7	15.2
Inventories	17.5	17.8	17.5	16.9	16.5
Total current assets	41.4	42.1	41.7	41.3	40.8
Net property, plant and equipment	38.0	37.7	37.7	37.6	37.3
Short-term debt including installments on long-term debt	5.1	5.5	5.4	5.3	5.2
Total current liabilities	26.4	26.9	26.7	26.6	26.9
Long-term debt	17.4	18.0	18.2	18.6	18.7
Total liabilities	52.3	53.5	53.8	54.1	54.8
Stockholders' equity	47.7	46.5	46.2	45.9	45.2

[1] During the first quarter of 1985, a considerable number of companies were reclassified by industry. To provide comparability, the four quarters of 1984 have been restated to reflect these reclassifications.

borrowing increased substantially relative to equity financing in the 1970s, probably because the stock market was not attractive to many during this period. Corporations that borrowed infrequently often appeared as issuers of bonds. Most noteworthy of these was IBM, which issued $1 billion in notes and debentures in a single offering in 1979, the first public debt offering ever for the computer giant.

The investment by owners, the net worth of business concerns, is as long term as the business itself. It is the first to be drawn on at the formation of the corporation and the last paid out in a liquidation. The capital stocks of corporations are the instruments of greatest interest to the stock market. Over the past 25 years or so, capital stock has declined in importance in the supply of business funds. In 1962, capital stock funds provided 65% of the value of total corporate assets. By 1982 this percentage had shrunk to 50%, and, as the current balance sheet demonstrates, is now barely 45.2% ($874,985 million/$1,933,842 million). This deterioration in balance sheet quality is at best troubling, and at worst ominous. It is true that foreign corporations, especially Japanese ones, habitually rely more heavily on borrowed funds than do American companies. It is likewise true that the great bull market of the 1980s has once again made it attractive to own and, consequently, for corporations to issue, common stock. Still, if long-term trends prevail, American corporations appear to be mortgaging their future to creditors rather than encouraging more stock ownership. The great historic success of the American economy is largely due to the efforts of venturesome, risk-taking entrepreneurs—from Andrew Carnegie and Henry Ford to Steve Jobs and Steve Wozniak, the founders of Apple Computer. By their very nature, bondholders and other creditors cannot be expected to be either venturesome or takers of high risks.

Corporate Financial Policy

A principal problem for the financial management of a corporation is determining the amounts and kinds of long-term securities and short-term borrowings to use. In addition, it must decide on the ratio to be maintained between debt and equity. Policies adopted by management must affect the shareholder, but the shareholder usually has little recourse other than selling the shares if such policies are not agreeable. From management's viewpoint, debt increases risk but also increases control and income. Increased equity participation decreases income and control by management, but at the same time reduces risk.

At some point the ratio of debt to equity becomes too risky to justify the addition of more debt. In normally stable industries such as banking and finance, the debt portion of capital may be relatively high. This becomes a cause for concern when highly leveraged lending institutions such as commercial banks carry as assets loans to sovereign borrowers which may well be unwilling or unable to pay them off. Problems with Third World borrowers have the potential to cause chaos in the international banking system as massive defaults could well wipe out the shareholders' equity of some major banks.

Public utilities borrow heavily because of their enormous capital needs for construction. Because of their monopoly (or quasi-monopoly) status, such borrowings are ordinarily not considered risky. A number of utilities, however, have substantial risk with nuclear generating plants and their construction, among them Long Island Lighting, Public Service of New Hampshire, and General Public Utilities, owner of Three-Mile Island. With a debt to equity ratio of 50% or greater, these corporations put the common shareholder at severe risk of capital loss if these plants cannot be developed economically.

Speculative industries may find that debt cannot be sold at any reasonable interest rate because the high-risk-taking lenders will insist on a rate of return that may negate any profits derived from employing the loan proceeds. A number of previously sound enterprises have fallen into this trap in order to repel the unwanted advances of corporate raiders in the early 1980s. To cite only a few examples, Unocal (Union Oil of California), Phillips Petroleum, and Walt Disney Productions were forced to issue large amounts of debt in order to fend off market operators who wanted little more than a quick profit through the bidding up of stock prices, figuring, correctly as it turned out, that they would ultimately be bought off in one way or another. This is not to say that such concerns cannot recover or that their shares no longer have appeal to the speculatively inclined investor. It does indicate, on the other hand, that investment-grade equities enjoying a sound, well-managed business can become speculative shares when too much debt is added.

When a business is successful, there is another major source of funds not yet discussed—the customer. As customers pay for their purchases they provide funds in excess of the amounts currently disbursed to pay for the production of those goods. Once earned, these funds become part of the shareholder's equity—the net worth of the business. Management must then choose either to retain those earnings for reinvestment in the business, or to pay some of them out in the form of dividends.

Should management believe that growth can be financed most efficiently through internally generated funds, it would usually pay small (or no) cash dividends to stockholders. Most rapid growth companies follow this course of action. Among such corporations are Digital Equipment, Data General, McDonald's, and Wendy's International. Some of these companies may occasionally "reward" shareholders with a stock dividend or split, but rarely pay cash dividends in excess of 1 or 2%, if at all.

More "mature" companies are likely to generate new funds through new issues of securities. The buyers of these securities are usually looking more for steady returns than for pure share price appreciation. Thus it is normal to see blue-chip firms entering the new issue market periodically to tap capital sources for expansion funds. Even such a renowned growth company as IBM has found this method an attractive alternative to financing everything out of retained earnings, a policy it followed for decades.

In summary, corporate directors must decide (1) the amounts of funds that must be invested in assets to operate successfully; (2) the sources from which these funds are to be obtained; and (3) management policy on internally generated funds. These decisions involve the concepts of risk, income, and control. Although in theory management and the owners, that is, the shareholders, make these decisions together, in practice management makes them arbitrarily. The shareholder normally becomes involved in a practical sense only in the event of failure. The reader will find in the following paragraphs a discussion of the various types of securities management might choose to utilize in implementing corporate strategy.

COMMON STOCK

Nature

All corporations issue common stock. It is the first security to be issued and the last to be retired. Common stock represents the chief ownership of the corporation and has the greatest management control. It has the last claim on earnings; all other securities must be paid first. Likewise, common shares have the last claim on assets in the event of dissolution. Should a company be forced into bankruptcy, holders of senior securities such as bonds will have prior claims on the remaining assets. Indeed, if such creditors settle for less than 100 cents on the dollar, the common shareholders will almost surely salvage nothing from their investments, except possibly some shares in a reorganized successor corporation.

Par Value

Common stock may have a *par, face,* or *stated* value. Today such terms are purely accounting devices with no practical application for the investor. Historically, it was supposed that the corporate assets were a sort of trust fund to be protected by the directors and that par values reflected that fund. This has long since ceased to be the case, and par values are arbitrarily fixed at such levels as 10 cents, $1⅔, or even "no par." Among other reasons for low (or no) par stock is the practice in some states of charging incorporation fees based on the par value of stock registered. Hence fees can be kept minimal by assigning low par values.

Book Value

Book value may be defined as the stated value of the assets behind each share and may be found by adding the three common shareholder accounts found on the balance sheet—par value, capital surplus, and retained earnings—subtracting any "intangible assets" and dividing by the number of shares outstanding. (In the balance sheet illustration par value and capital surplus appear as a single entry—"capital stock.")

The significance of book value is debatable. For one thing, corporate assets on the balance sheet are carried at cost less depreciation allowances. There is no way to tell from such numbers what the replacement cost of those assets might be or what they might bring if sold. For another, most corporations expect to be going concerns with an indefinite life-span. The investor thus has little likelihood of ever extracting book value in cash, although it may be comforting to know that substantial assets lie behind each share. Of course, corporations are sometimes liquidated voluntarily, and in such cases, an investor who bought shares at a market price below book value could have a handsome profit, presuming that the assets were sold at a price close to or above book value. Some securities analysts, notably disciples of Graham and Dodd, employ book value as one of a number of tests to determine the investment value of a security. In any event, let us say that the book value per share of a corporation may have some significance to either the patient long-term investor who feels value will ultimately prevail, or to the speculator who feels that some raider may discover that this corporation has a market price substantially below the break-up value of its assets. The typical investor, on the other hand, would be better advised to study thoroughly earnings per share, dividend policy, and liquidity if he or she is to form a rational basis for investing capital.

The following chart compares par, book, and market values of several well-known companies and illustrates how little correlation there appears to be between them.

Corporation	Par Value	Book Value (approx.)	Market Price (range 6/85–6/86)
AT&T	$1.00	$ 16.50	$20–$26
McDonald's	none	$ 48.50	$62–$108
DuPont	$1⅔	$ 67.10	$55–$85
Exxon	none	$ 45.70	$48–$60
General Motors	$1⅔	$112.50	$64–$89
IBM	$1¼	$ 82.00	$117–$162

From this one might conclude that book value may provide a sort of "negative filter" in steering the investor away from stocks whose market prices had gotten far out of line with asset values, but it provides an opaque crystal ball at best when applied to price predictions.

Classified Common Stock

Investors occasionally encounter classified common stock, often in the form of Class A or B shares. The differences are often in voting rights, but there is no uniform format and each issue must be examined separately.

For example, the Ford Motor Company has 182,480,820 shares outstanding. About 16.42 million of those shares are Class B stock owned by key officers, directors, and the Ford family. These shares are not available in the open market for public purchase. The interesting aspect of the Class B shares is that they amount to only about 9% of the outstanding shares and yet control 40% of the votes in company proxy elections. Thus it is not surprising to find Ford family members elected to directorships and other positions of control for reasons that surpass sentiment.

A somewhat different example is that of the Adolph Coors Company, a major brewer. The Coors family retains all of the voting (Class A) shares, and also owns about 75% of the 34.5 million nonvoting (Class B) shares. Thus the family retains absolute voting control, but at the same time shares in the benefits of public ownership.

A unique situation developed when General Motors made two major acquisitions in 1984 and 1985, publicly owned Electronic Data Systems and privately owned Hughes Aircraft. Instead of issuing more regular common shares, GM created two new classes of stock, Class E and Class H respectively. Although each is part of GM outstanding common stock capitalization, the performance of each class is linked to the performance of the new division created by the acquisition. Each has its own dividend rate, voting rights, and earnings per share. Price ranges in the first four months of 1986 were: GM (regular shares) $68–$88; GME $36–$49; GMH $32–$49.

The NYSE does not admit nonvoting common shares to stock listing, but other exchanges and the NASDAQ system are not so restrictive. A plethora of hostile takeover attempts in the mid-1980s led to the development of various strategies to fend off unwanted suitors. One suggestion for "shark repellent" was the creation of shares with weighted voting rights, allowing entrenched management a defense against a raider who might thus acquire 51% of the common shares but not 51% of the votes. The issue of one share– one vote went as far as a congressional committee, but has not as yet led to the legal imposition of a national voting standard. All in all, nonvoting common shares compose a small portion of those publicly traded, whether listed or not.

Stock Splits

A stock split occurs when a company divides its shares. For instance, a corporation with 5 million outstanding shares might increase that number to 10 million by splitting the shares 2 for 1. The split has no effect on the company's net worth or the value of a shareholder's investment. Rather, it spreads the ownership over more shares. That is, the owner of 100 shares of a $50 stock would own 200 shares of a $25 stock after a 2 for 1 split. The customary reasons for splits are to lower share prices and also to broaden ownership. The latter reason may be necessary to qualify for an exchange listing.

Investors have historically evidenced a preference for low-priced shares. For example, IBM shares have usually sold at high dollar prices. Prior to its 4 for 1 split in 1979 the shares sold at about $350 each. At that price the individual investor with $9,000 could only buy a 25-share *odd lot*, the term for purchases of less than the standard 100-share unit of trading. The typical investor would usually prefer to buy 200 or 300 shares for that amount, reasoning that a 4- or 5-point rise means several hundred dollars of profit, whereas a 10-point rise on 25 shares yields only $250. Indeed, many analysts felt that IBM's decision was largely based on a desire to make the shares more popular with average investors, thus lessening the institutional dominance in trading its stock.

Although splits themselves are purely bookkeeping transactions, they are usually evaluated bullishly by the market. For one thing, dividend rates are frequently raised at the same time so that a rate of $1 per share might become, for example, $.54 per share following a 2 for 1 split. In addition, making a stock price lower tends to increase its "sponsorship." Brokers and analysts are likely to be more attracted to salable merchandise. No matter how attractive a $400 per share stock may appear, brokers know that their typical clients are unlikely to be interested in buying odd-lot positions and will direct their attention elsewhere.

Growing companies may split shares to diffuse ownership and ultimately qualify for exchange listing. The NYSE requires at least 1 million shares in public hands before listing and also requires at least 2,000 holders of 100 shares or more. Listing requirements on the Amex are somewhat less stringent.

"Reverse splits" *reducing* the number of shares are not seen as frequently as those just described. The usual reason for such splits is to increase the share price. The NYSE in particular discourages the continued listing of chronically low-priced shares because this tends to attract the "wrong" type of buying—either speculators taking large positions in hopes of relatively small dollar price movements or novice investors with a few hundred dollars hoping to double or triple their stakes overnight.

Dividend Policy

The dividends paid to common shareholders may be critical to investment decisions. The dividend policy adopted by a corporation reflects many factors. Among these are: cash position, growth prospects, stability of earnings, capital spending needs, and reputation for reliability. In general, older, more mature companies tend to be more generous with cash payments, whereas younger companies are more likely to pay small cash dividends, saving most of their earnings and cash flow for reinvestment in the growth of a developing business.

The market is often contradictory about dividend expectations and what they mean in relation to market prices. In the 1960s investors paid scant attention to cash payments and focused almost exclusively on price appreciation. Popular stocks of that time (Syntex, Xerox, Polaroid, and the remainder of the "nifty fifty" institutional favorites) paid little or nothing in cash dividends. Investors, however, concentrated on rapid, predictable growth in earnings per share which was quickly translated into price appreciation. The blue-chip components of the Dow Jones average, on the other hand, were largely ignored unless they also demonstrated strong growth characteristics, which a few—Sears Roebuck, Procter & Gamble, and Eastman Kodak—actually did.

The collapse of that market in 1969 led to a reassessment of investment strategies. Renewed emphasis on sound earnings and regular dividend payments came back in vogue. Potential growth and dividends at some indeterminate future date became less important than cash in hand. The market of the 1980s appears somewhat ambivalent on this point. The growth mystique has not regained its former popularity in full. Indeed, many would hope that that popularity, which verged on mania, never recaptures the minds of investors to the degree it once did, for that is the road to speculative excesses and ultimate self-correction.

In sum, dividends are an important factor in investment decisions but not the only one. A company paying a modest dividend, but with a record of regular increases, is likely to be favored over the erratic payer of occasional large sums. Companies which regularly pay out half or more of their net income in cash dividends are not likely to exhibit much in the way of growth (e.g., public utilities). Some companies pay such a small dividend that few would buy their shares for the dividend alone. McDonald's pays an annual dividend of only 66 cents on a share price of about $70, a yield of less than 1%. If, however, one bought McDonald's shares in 1966 and held them to this day, the share value, adjusted for splits, rose from 50 cents to $70. This is simply another way of saying that the investor can't have it both ways. The investment decision must favor either growth or dividends. It is possible to get a little of both from one company, but an attempt to get a lot of both is unrealistic at the very least.

Stock Dividends

Instead of cash dividends, corporations may pay dividends in additional shares of stock. As we have already seen, cash dividends are paid out of current earnings. Occasionally, corporate directors may pay a dividend in a quarter when the dividend is not actually earned, sometimes even when a loss is reported. The directors in such circumstances are probably more concerned with the corporation's reputation as a reliable provider of dividends than with the reduction in retained earnings from which such unearned payments must be made. Naturally, this practice cannot be repeated often without damaging the company's financial health, but it causes no great harm if done during a brief downturn in earnings.

Stock dividends are normally accounted for by capitalizing the company's surplus, so that the surplus account is reduced and the common stock account increased by equal amounts. In effect, the deck is reshuffled, but the assets and net worth remain the same. To all practical purposes, a stock dividend and a stock split produce the same results—more shares outstanding at a lower price.

The shareholder does derive one advantage from the stock dividend as opposed to the cash dividend. The stock dividend, like the split, merely reduces the holder's cost basis per share and defers taxation until the shares are sold, while the cash dividend is taxable in the year paid. For example, an investor who originally purchased 100 shares at $60 and later receives a 50% stock dividend marks his or her cost basis down to $40 and then owns 150 shares. Any sale of these shares at a price higher than $40 will result in a taxable capital gain.

The distribution of other forms of property, such as shares in another company, is much less frequent than either cash or stock dividends, but is seen occasionally. More commonly called a "spin-off," it usually involves shares of another corporation, often a wholly or partly owned subsidiary that no longer fits into the parent company's long-term strategy.

Transfer of Stock

Stock certificates issued by a corporation represent the number of shares owned by the shareholders. These certificates can be issued in any whole number amount and are evidence of ownership. In the United States all share certificates are *registered*, which means the owners' names are printed on the certificate and recorded by a transfer agent employed by the issuer.

After a purchase is made, the transfer agent records the change of ownership on the settlement day for the transaction. This is normally five business days after the date of purchase. The transfer agent, usually a commercial bank but sometimes the issuing corporation itself, cancels the certificate surrendered by the seller and issues a new one in the name of the purchaser. This change of ownership is confirmed by the "registrar," another bank which checks the transfer agent's work to ensure that a cancellation accompanies each issuance so that the corporation does not issue more shares than are supposed to be outstanding at any time. In due course, ordinarily a few weeks from purchase, the new owner receives his or her certificate if such was requested. The expenses for the transfer are borne by the issuing corporation.

Actually, there is no need for physical stock certificates except that American investors seem devoted to them. The Tokyo Stock Exchange, which moves greater share volume daily than does the NYSE, has virtually eliminated the stock certificate in favor of computer entries. The U.S. Treasury has not printed a Treasury bill in many years, and indeed stopped issuing negotiable note or bond certificates in June 1986. It seems likely that the physical stock certificate is ultimately going the way of the T-bill, but the date seems distant.

TREASURY STOCK

The average investor has little concern about treasury stock and may not even be aware of its existence. Such stock represents shares once issued to the public but later reacquired by the corporation, usually through the open market but sometimes through a tender offer. The shares have no voting rights, receive no dividends, and are not used in the computation of earnings per share. The corporation may use it for stock bonus plans, sell it back to the public, or use it as a vehicle for acquiring the assets of another corporation through an exchange-of-stock tender offer. In the 1970s, for example, the market prices of the shares of many corporations fell to prices below book value. It thus became possible for a company to purchase $1 of assets for less than $1. Many corporations announced major stock repurchase plans in 1985–86. Merrill Lynch and Company and IBM were two of the more prominent of these. Although it is unlikely that IBM fears a raid on its shares by some market operator (none is likely to have $94 billion of ready cash), many other corporations are looking to thwart the aims of financiers who figure that some companies are worth more dead than alive. That is, once control is established, the raider with little knowledge of and less concern for the operation of the existing company is likely to sell its assets off piecemeal to competitors. By salting away large amounts of treasury stock, corporate management becomes more in control of the stock because the treasury shares cannot be voted against them.

Investment Merits

Many years ago, as earlier editions of this book will attest, there was considerable dispute as to whether the purchase of common stock could *ever* be regarded as an investment. The prevailing attitude was that bonds represented true investments because they promised the return of the principal amount. The risks inherent in equities made them all appear speculative to one degree or another. Trust agreements and various forms of fiduciary legislation made it difficult for most institutions to buy stocks, or put such an onus on the trustee if such an investment failed that few wished to risk the consequences.

As is often the case, however, the law lags considerably behind reality. Being largely based on precedent, it has difficulty adjusting to new developments or knowledge. Investors placing their faith in bonds were ignoring the reality of the time-value of money. Particularly in inflationary periods, of which there have been many in our history, the supposedly safe bond investment returns principal at maturity worth much less in purchasing power than the principal invested 10 or 20 years earlier. The more venturesome stock investor, on the other hand, often builds the investment to an extent that offsets this decline in purchasing power of the dollar.

Thus it is appropriate here to discuss the differences between investment and speculation. Investment could be taken in a generic sense to cover the entire spectrum of funds placed with the expectation of a monetary return of more than the funds placed. In this sense a speculation is merely a kind of investment in which the actual return might vary substantially from the expected return. If they are considered to be separate forms of commitments of capital or money to produce a return, the difference would generally be regarded as a matter of degree without a clear line of demarcation. Some even misuse the word "investment" by applying it to any substantial purchase, a practice widely encouraged by the advertising media to justify the expenditure. One hears, for example, of someone investing in a new car or a stereo system. By almost any standard, this is not a true investment because the only returns are likely to be psychic. Sometimes in a severe inflationary spiral a physical asset may appreciate in worth, not because of its scarcity, but because its replacement cost is rising even faster. In such instances some actual monetary return may be achieved, although it is usually incidental to the reason for acquiring the asset in the first place.

Where investment differs from speculation is not easy to pinpoint. In ordinary financial usage, investment implies that safety of principal is the primary concern, and the investor seeks the highest rate of return commensurate with the degree of that concern. The speculator is more concerned with the profit potential and is willing to expose the principal to greater risk in order to receive greater return. But how much risk justifies how much return? Clearly, the individual investor must make the choice, and one person's investment is another's rank speculation. No one can say how much more likely a given stock is to rise or fall in price than a given bond.

When one considers the historical rates of "real" (i.e., inflation-adjusted) return cited in Chapter 1, it is apparent that stocks over the long pull are not only sound investments, but indeed the *only* reasonable choice in some circumstances. For ease of investment, liquidity, low transaction costs, and legal protection, common stock investment has no peer. The investor who still finds this case unappealing because of the potential risk is likely to sleep better and, ultimately, to be happier with money in a federally insured bank account.

It is easy to make an investment in common stock. The stock brokerage business is intensely competitive, and there are numerous broker/dealers actively seeking the investor's business. At the end of 1985 there were 5,876 NYSE member-firm sales offices in the United States and many more offices of firms which are members of the NASD only. Again, from NYSE records there were 72,376 full-time registered representatives servicing customer accounts. Customers are now also able to place securities orders through many banking offices as a number of banks have brokerage affiliates or subsidiaries.

The advent of the discount brokerage firm allows for order execution at rates that are extremely cheap by anyone's definition, and even regular brokerage commission rates are inexpensive compared with the more or less uniform 6% real estate commission charged on typical residence sales (for comparative commission rates, see Chapter 12). Markups on such items as "investment grade diamonds"—virtually a contradiction in terms—have often ranged upward of 25%.

By no means the least important advantage is the visibility of most securities transactions and the legal safeguards afforded by a huge body of federal and state securities statutes. Stocks are openly traded and public information on the issuer's financial condition, as well as on the trading of its securities, is widely available. Indeed, in the United States, full disclosure of relevant financial data is required by law, and the American markets have earned a worldwide reputation for fairness and integrity. The insider trading scandals of 1986 notwithstanding (see Chapter 17), no foreign market enjoys such a reputation. In fact, these scandals ultimately enhance the credibility of the markets precisely because they *are* uncovered, the guilty *are* punished, and more stringent policies to deter a recurrence are established. No other country possesses a government agency with the experience, prestige, and authority of the SEC. The self-regulatory nature of American exchanges gives an additional measure of protection. Obviously, frauds can and do happen, and will continue anywhere large sums are at stake. Given the size of the domestic securities markets, however, they remain minimal.

PREFERRED STOCKS

Nature

The very term *preferred* connotes something more than perhaps it ought. Preferred stock is clearly *equity* in a corporation, and its holder is in no way a creditor in the event of a bankruptcy. If a corporation fails to pay dividends on either common or preferred stock, the holder has few if any legal recourses similar to what the least secured bondholder would have. Likewise, if a corporation went into an involuntary bankruptcy, the fact that one held preferred shares as opposed to common shares would offer scant consolation if the creditors were receiving back less than 100 cents on the dollar. With creditors not "made whole," the owners of preferred and common stocks could be likened to passengers occupying first class and steerage sections of a sinking liner.

The superiority of preferred over common rests in two areas—dividends and liquidation rights. Although the preferred shareholders have no *right* to receive dividends, they must receive the stated rate prior to any dividends being paid on the common stock. Also, if a corporation is placed in liquidation, the preferred shareholder has a preferential claim on remaining assets when compared to common shareholders, but distinctly inferior to bondholders. Preferred stock thus becomes something of a junior bond without the basic protection of a bond issue, but also without the appeal of common stock, namely, the ability to participate in the growth of a successful enterprise. If of good quality it gives the opportunity for generous dividend return with no opportunity for "growth." Price appreciation is indeed possible for the preferred stock, but *growth*, meaning a piece of a growing shareholder's equity, is not, unless the preferred is convertible into common stock, or has one of the quite rare "participating" features.

Par Value

Unlike common stocks, a preferred stock's par value may have considerable significance. At one time it represented the amount of money received on the initial sale ($100, $50, or $25 par values were common, with $100 probably the most usual). Dividend rates were normally linked to this par value so that a $100 par preferred stock with a $10 annual dividend rate was referred to as a "$10 preferred" or a "10% preferred." Rates were fixed, which meant preferred share prices moved inversely with interest rates, rising when the latter fell and vice versa. The volatility seen in interest rates in the late 1970s–early 1980s period threw the preferred-share market into turmoil, as investors would not buy an item that would be sharply discounted in price in a short time.

Adjustable Rate Preferreds

The instability of the fixed income market quickly brought forth the adjustable-rate preferred. Similar in nature to the floating-rate debt instruments discussed below, the adjustable-rate preferred features a dividend whose rate is periodically revised according to some formula. This would typically be set in line with a standard measure such as the 90-day T-bill rate, so that the dividend might be set at something like 1% over the T-bill rate for a certain period, or on a certain date. Indeed, the concept was carried to the extent of offering a "money market" preferred stock whose return reflects that of short-term debt instruments like commercial paper. For all intents and purposes, this type of preferred stock is really a short-term debt security, but has attractive tax features that one associates with equities. The market for preferred shares was dominated by these types of shares throughout the early 1980s, and they continue to be the most common form of new issuance. The return of some stability in interest rates brought back some of the more conventional preferreds in 1986.

Tax Advantages

At one time it was generally presumed that preferred stocks, being inherently riskier than bonds, ought to yield perhaps 1 to 2% more than debt of the same issuer. The tax code, however, has altered this presumption. With some exceptions, dividends paid on a domestic equity issue to another domestic corporate holder are 80% tax free. With a corporate tax rate set at 34%, it follows that the effective tax rate to another corporate holder is about 6.8% on preferred shares (the 20% taxable portion times 34%). This is far better on an after-tax basis than fully taxable bonds, so that, paradoxically, an apparently more risky preferred share carries a lower yield than a debt obligation of the same company.

The major market for such shares is thus corporate, not individual buyers. Fire and casualty insurers are the major buyers, but other large buyers include other financial and industrial corporations. Because individual buyers get no special tax advantage from preferred shares, they are not major purchasers, but the relatively generous yields and safety make them attractive to the individual who has limited funds and cannot participate in the bond market because of the large minimum purchases often required. The small investor can therefore get an attractive yield for an investment of perhaps $5,000 in preferred shares whereas the corporate bond market is more or less closed to such investors.

Cumulative Stock

Virtually all preferred stocks issued today carry the cumulative designation. If a dividend is passed on a cumulative preferred, no dividends may be paid on junior classes of securities. Furthermore, passed dividends accumulate and form an "arrearage" that must be made up before dividends can be paid on junior shares. Note that this is not the same right possessed by a bond-holder in the event of a skipped interest payment (a default). This latter situation involves the breach of a legal promise to pay and hence is grounds for a lawsuit. A corporation must clearly have its back to the wall in order to be forced to omit a preferred dividend. Although in theory their arrearages may ultimately be paid off, there is no guarantee that they will, and, in fact, history indicates that long-standing arrearages are progressively less likely to be collected. It is also possible to have noncumulative preferred stock, but it would be difficult to market such shares. Few potential buyers would be willing to risk a dividend cut or an omission with no recompense.

Sinking Funds

Because they are not bonds and do not represent borrowed money, preferreds have no maturity date when the principal will be repaid. They do, however, frequently have sinking funds similar to many debenture issues. These require a corporation to put aside money every year for the eventual retirement of these shares at par or a slight premium. Rather than a sinking fund, some corporations establish a purchase fund that allows for the repurchase of the shares in the open market rather than through a call provision that would be typical of sinking-fund redemptions.

Voting Rights

There is less uniformity concerning preferred stock voting rights than common stock. Whereas the common law generally presumes common stock votes (unless this right is explicitly restricted), no such presumption applies to preferred issues. The buyer must carefully read the terms of the offering to determine what voting rights may exist. In recent years preferred stocks have been offered without voting rights except in the case of a failure to pay the required quarterly dividend for a specified period (four consecutive quarters, for example). When the issue is a convertible into common stock, it usually has voting rights commensurate with the terms of convertibility. The investment merits of convertible securities are discussed in Chapter 23.

BONDS

General Form

A *bond* is an evidence of a loan extended by a creditor (the bond owner) to a corporation or other borrower. It calls for the repayment of a specific amount of money on or before a specific date and normally also calls for the periodic payment of interest for the use of the borrowed funds. The "zero-coupon" notes and bonds described below are exceptions to the interest payment requirements. To fulfill the terms of the loan the borrower gives a binding legal promise in the form of a trust indenture or deed of trust wherein a trustee, usually a commercial bank, is appointed to represent the interests of the bondholders. Should the corporation fail to make timely payments of interest or principal as required by the indenture, the trustee is empowered to bring legal action against the defaulting borrower. This promise-to-pay clause in the indenture ultimately separates bonds from stocks. The holder of any bond is a creditor, the holder of any stock is an owner. Equity conveys only limited rights and few, if any, legal obligations. Although the holders of bonds lack voting rights in corporate affairs and have no participation in net profits, they may demand satisfaction of their legal claims, even to the extent of forcing a corporation into bankruptcy.

Bond denominations vary widely, but by far the most common principal (par or face) amount is $1,000. The next most common bonds are baby bonds with $500 or $100 principal amounts. The trading market for corporate bonds usually calls for a round lot of $100,000 principal amount or multiples thereof. The primary buyers of corporate debt obligations are institutional investors to whom purchases of $1 million or more at a time are commonplace. Most important corporate bond buyers are either tax-exempt institutions (foundations, pension funds, endowment funds) or property-casualty insurers.

Bonds have been issued in four different forms: fully registered, registered as to principal amount only, bearer, and book entry. In the United States corporate bonds are almost always in fully registered form, although some older issues may be found with interest coupons. Fully registered bonds have the owner's name printed on the certificate and recorded with a transfer agent, very similar to the way corporate stocks are issued. Interest payment checks are mailed to the holder every six months, typically on either the first or the fifteenth of the month. Bearer bonds, as the name implies, belong to the bearer and ownership is not otherwise recorded. Interest payments are claimed by clipping off coupons attached to the certificate and presenting them to the paying agent of the issuer. Such bonds must be handled with extreme care because if lost or stolen they are costly and difficult to replace. This format was widely used by the U.S. Treasury, government agencies, and municipalities. Federal law no longer permits the issuance of bearer securities, but billions of dollars of such securities will remain outstanding until well after the year 2000. Registered-as-to-principal-only bonds are hybrids betweeen bearer and fully registered bonds, having coupons but also having the owner's name on the certificate. They are rarely seen today. Finally, book-entry bonds are never issued in physical form at all, being recorded only as computer entries. This format is widely used in municipal bonds and in U.S. government securities. From mid-1986, in fact, *all* U.S. Treasury obligations will be so issued. So far few corporate bonds have been issued in this form, but it is clearly the wave of the future.

Interest Rates

The interest rate on a bond is a fixed charge for the debtor corporation and is always paid as long as the corporation is solvent. This "coupon rate" depends on many things: the issuer's credit standing, the length of maturity, current interest rate conditions, call provisions, and so on. Debt issues may have relatively short maturities less than 10 years, or can extend to as long as 30 years. Under normal interest rate conditions, bonds with long maturities will bear higher coupon rates than bonds issued at the same time with short maturities.

Triple A bonds, the highest quality, bear the lowest rate of return when compared with others of similar issue dates. The rates of these bonds fluctuated widely but rarely exceeded 5% until the late 1960s. Runaway inflation and tight monetary policy propelled rates to over 15% in the early 1980s. Under these circumstances there can be little doubt about the difficulty lower quality issuers were confronted with. Many found themselves either completely "crowded out" of the market or forced to pay such exorbitant rates that their long-term viability was threatened.

Maturities

The investor has a wide variety of choices of maturity. Bonds purchased in the secondary (after issuance) market, of course, are readily available with any maturity from several months to nearly 30 years. In the initial offering, bonds are usually divided into these three major categories.

Short Term Maturities range from one to five years. Industrial corporations do not make many public offerings in this range, relying largely on bank borrowings or private placements with institutional investors. Financial corporations make a greater use in this maturity range primarily by issuing unsecured *notes*.

Intermediate Term These bonds have maturities between 5 to about 10 years. Much more common than shorter-term obligations, intermediates are also favored by banks and other financial organizations. As with short-term bonds, unsecured notes or debentures predominate.

Long Term These bonds have maturities of more than 10 years from original issue, but 15–20 years are the most common. Actually, the typical bond of this type is rarely outstanding for its full maturity, as most are retired through the operation of a sinking fund (see the following discussion). Although debentures are by far the most common bonds in this maturity range, a considerable number of secured issues are also sold. The major issuers of long-term secured bonds are public utilities.

Debentures

Debentures are issued on the general credit and good faith of the issuer. No specific assets back debentures, and in the event of a default a holder of this kind of bond becomes a general creditor of the issuer. Nevertheless, such bonds may be secure and many carry AAA ratings. Modern industrial corporations rarely issue any other form of long-term debt. If the corporation's earnings are adequate to service the debt, the investor need not be concerned about safety. Investors readily snap up new debenture issues of the likes of General Motors Acceptance Corp., AT&T, and the former Bell subsidiaries which now issue bonds as independent corporations. On the other hand, debentures issued by marginal borrowers could be extremely risky in times of economic distress, such as a recession.

Debentures are clearly superior to any type of equity security for safety of principal. They may even prove superior to some kinds of "secured" financing by weaker issuers. That is, IBM's pledge of its good faith to make timely payments of interest and principal is evaluated as more secure by the market than the mortgage bonds offered by some public utilities with sizable regulatory and construction problems.

Debentures may be "subordinated" to the claims of other creditors, either to bank loans or to other securities. They are also issued as convertible bonds which can be exchanged for the issuer's common stock at the request of the holder.

Sinking-Fund Bonds

These bonds do not form a separate category. Rather, the sinking-fund feature may be part of any bond indenture, but it is most frequently seen with debentures. The corporation agrees to set aside a certain sum annually for the eventual retirement of the issue. After a specific period, redemptions may commence and bonds will be "called" away from the holder utilizing these funds. This brings about the shortening of the average life of the issue, so that even if an issue of bonds started with a 20-year maturity, the average life of a typical bond might be only 10–15 years. Because the sinking-fund deposits are to be utilized only for the purpose of retiring outstanding bonds, the existence of a "sinker" tends to increase a bond's safety and marketability. Still, even a sinking fund is no guarantee that a default might not occur. The holder is still exposed to considerable risks.

Mortgage Bonds

In the early years of this century, mortgage bond financing was considerably more widespread than it is today. When the country's industrial plant was in its formative stage, heavy industry dominated the scene. This meant that companies with a need for large amounts of new capital were also those that acquired a large physical plant in the growth process. This was particularly true of the railroad and steel industries. Because these industries possessed substantial collateral in the value of their real property, it was logical that it be used for subsequent borrowing as expansion continued. The mortgage provision, however, gave investors a false sense of security with some of these issues, and when bankruptcies or defaults occurred, bondholders frequently found their claims on the collateral were not adequate to save them from substantial loss of principal. Today, most industrial corporations have abandoned the mortgage bond in favor of the sinking-fund debenture and other forms of noncollateralized borrowing.

Mortgage bond financing survives today principally in the gas and electric utility industry. Generally speaking, the indentures of a first mortgage bond places a first lien on all fixed property owned by the issuer. Another normal feature is an "after acquired property" clause that subjects to the terms of the indenture all property acquired subsequent to the issuance of the bonds, thus maintaining the collateral value as older collateral (buildings, facilities, etc.) depreciates. Numerous different series of bonds may be issued under a single indenture. For example, Michigan Consolidated Gas Company bonds issued in November 1981 and due in November 2001 were the twenty-third different series of bonds issued under the original indenture in 1944.

Mortgage bonds may also have sinking funds and are usually callable (redeemable) after a given period of protection, frequently about 5 years. The investor's security is probably better protected by the earnings of the utility rather than by any theoretical collateral value. There is scant possibility that a utility would actually be liquidated to satisfy bondholder's claims. This occurrence would be politically unacceptable to the utility's customers and state regulatory commissions.

Equipment Trust Certificates

This form of borrowing has been extensively used by railroads and occasionally by other transportation companies, particularly airlines. The loan proceeds are used to purchase rolling stock, but the issuing corporation does not acquire title to the property until the issue is redeemed. Until then title is vested in a trustee, giving the bond unusual security. Should the issuer default, the trustee may liquidate the rolling stock collateral without forcing the company, the railroad, into bankruptcy proceedings because the trustee, not the railroad, technically owns the equipment.

There are several variations, but the most common for railroad equipment is the "Philadelphia plan." Such offerings differ from the usual corporate debt sale in two ways. First, they are often made through a competitive bid rather than through negotiation. Second, they usually have *serial* maturities; that is, a portion of issue is redeemed each year after issuance. Both features are commonplace in municipal general obligation bonds but are unusual in corporate bonds. In a typical offering the issuer makes an initial down payment of 20% and borrows the remainder of the equipment costs through the certificates. The securities are then paid off in 15 equal installments and are usually noncallable. Title passes to the railroad only upon completion of all payments.

Because the certificates are redeemed faster than the collateral depreciates, the longer they are outstanding the safer they become. Interest payments are referred to as "dividends" for technical reasons, but are treated as true interest for tax purposes.

Income Bonds

Sometimes referred to as "adjustment bonds" these instruments are rarely issued any longer, but those still outstanding have similar characteristics. The bonds resemble a cross between a low quality debt instrument and a high quality preferred. They were most commonly issued during the reorganization of bankrupt railroads. A good example is the Missouri Pacific Railroad General Income A issue (4¾% of 2020). Trading in these bonds is relatively inactive, but they have wide price swings. Their trading range between 1972 and 1986 ranged from a low of 29½ to a high of 58⅝ (par 100%). Income bonds trade "flat" (without accrued interest), and the lack of certainty about payments probably exaggerates price swings. In the case of these Missouri Pacific issues, payments have been made annually since their issuance in 1956.

Collateral Trust Bonds

Once rather common, these bonds have become rarities. For example, the May 1986 issue of Standard & Poor's Bond Guide gives details on approximately 2,250 different corporate issues and includes fewer than 20 collateral trust issues. These bonds are secured by other securities owned by the issuer and pledged with a trustee. The value of the collateral ordinarily exceeds the amount borrowed by about 30%, so that a sudden deterioration in market value of the collateral will not unsecure the issue. In the past they were frequently used by railroads and public utilities as a means of consolidating debt, with the pledged collateral usually being secured debt of subsidiary companies.

Mortgage-Backed Securities

Not to be confused with mortgage bonds, these securities have been issued in huge numbers during the 1980s and appear to be a never-ending source of new corporate issues. Actually, the concept first found popularity as a government-guaranteed security, the GNMA pass-through (described in more detail in the following chapter). Quickly copied by various commercial, financial, thrift, and building companies, mortgage securities have become a major component of corporate debt issuance. They are usually backed by residential mortgages, and the repayment of these obligations is such a high priority to homeowners that default is a very last resort. The most popular type of new issue in this market is the Collateralized Mortgage Obligation (CMO), a security backed by other mortgage-backed securities, giving a high degree of safety as well as yields above those of comparable quality conventional corporate issues.

Junk Bonds

The name "junk bond" has been applied to corporate issues of less than investment grade. They are rated BB or lower, and carry high yields along with considerable risk. A number of them have been issued to fund "leveraged buy-outs," a strategy whereby a company is acquired either by a management group or a hostile raider. The funds realized from the bond sale are used to pay for the acquisition and retirement of the outstanding common stock, usually leaving a former publicly held corporation a private company. The Federal Reserve has placed some limitation on the issuance of such bonds when sold for this purpose. Despite the high yields, the typical investor should give these obligations a wide berth. Various studies have shown them to have a higher default rate than better quality issues, but also have shown that the additional risk appears less than the risk premium provided by the higher yields. All of which is fine to the investor able to diversify his junk holdings, but potentially disastrous to the individual who puts all his eggs in a junk basket. A possible alternative to the individual investor might be the junk bond mutual fund, several of which are available and are usually called by the more tasteful (and somewhat less pejorative) term "high yield bond funds."

Floating Rate Bonds and Notes

These were the predecessors of the adjustable rate preferred previously mentioned. Floating rate securities never stray far from par value, because their interest rate is periodically altered according to some predetermined formula. The rate often reflects some standard measure such as the 90-day Treasury bill rate or LIBOR (London Interbank Offered Rate). Citicorp was the first seller of these "floaters" in the domestic market, but they were also issued by a number of other borrowers. The stabilization of interest rates at lower levels in the mid-1980s has lessened the appeal of these issues and the market has swung back toward fixed rate issues.

Bonds with Warrants

Bonds with warrants attached for the purchase of equity issues have long been issued. This type of bond acts much like a convertible bond and reflects the performance of the underlying stock to a large degree. Conventional convertible bonds and warrants are discussed in detail in Chapter 23. A new type of bond with warrants made its appearance in the early 1980s. The innovation was to attach warrants to the bond calling for the purchase of additional bonds at the same coupon rate. Hence, if rates declined after issuance, the buyer could exercise the warrants and purchase more bonds at a rate not available for that issuer in the current market. Likewise, a rate decline would cause the warrants to rise in value so that the holder could sell them for a profit. This feature allows the issuer to sell bonds more cheaply than more conventional issues. Among issuers who have sold such bonds in the United States are New York's Municipal Acceptance Corporation and also the Kingdom of Sweden.

Bonds with Puts

These are conventional bonds with an unconventional feature. The "put" is an option to sell the bonds back to the issuer at par prior to maturity. In other words, the "call" option of the issuer has been reversed and granted instead to the buyer. If rates rise and the bond price falls, the holder may exercise the put and sell the bonds back to the issuer for the face amount, allowing the holder to reinvest the proceeds at current rates. This feature, therefore, keeps bond prices closer to par, since the likelihood of exercise increases as bond prices fall.

Exchangeable Debentures

These securities are much like convertible bonds, but they are convertible into shares of a corporation different from the issuer. There are only about 12 such issues actively traded. One interesting example is the National Distillers and Chemical 6% subordinated debenture convertible into 20.41 shares of Cetus Corp., a firm in the biotechnology field. The investor obtains a debt instrument plus a 6% coupon along with a speculative play in a high technology field with a company that itself pays no dividends. Some other exchangeable bonds are: Cigna Corp., exchangeable for Paine Webber; InterNorth, exchangeable for Mobil Corp.; and General Cinema, exchangeable for RJR Nabisco.

Commercial Paper

Commercial paper is the shortest-term corporate debt obligation, with maturities ranging from 30 to 270 days. It is an unsecured promissory note issued mainly by financial corporations, but more and more often also by industrial companies. It is almost always issued at a discount from par like a Treasury bill, although dealers occasionally create interest-bearing paper on specific customer request. Historically the major issuers have been companies like General Motors Acceptance Corp. (GMAC), Ford Motor Credit, and Household Finance Corp. In more recent years, however, usual issuers have been joined by such companies as Citicorp, Merrill Lynch, and Salomon Inc. Commercial paper is offered either directly to the buyer by the issuer itself, or through large dealer firms that make markets in the paper. The market is not very liquid, and buyers should be prepared to hold to maturity, which is never more than 9 months away. Commercial paper is usually sold in round-lot denominations of $1 million and up, although odd-lot pieces of as little as $25,000 periodically appear.

3 U.S. Government and Municipal Securities

The United States has become the most prodigious—some would say profligate—borrower in history. Federal expenditures regularly exceed tax and other revenues by staggering sums. By 1985, for example, the federal government owed more than $2 trillion (2,000 billion) and was running an annual budget deficit of an additional $200 billion. Such borrowings have a significant effect on the stock market and its investors, to say nothing of their impact on the entire economy.

Large federal deficits tend to drive interest rates up as the government competes for the investor's dollar. High interest rates, especially on the essentially risk-free securities issued by the Treasury, divert funds from the equity markets as well as from more productive forms of savings such as business and mortgage loans. Stock market history indicates that high stock prices cannot coexist with high interest rates for any appreciable length of time. During much of the period ranging from the 1970s to the mid-1980s, rates on U.S. Treasury securities ranged from 10 to 15¾%. With such returns guaranteed by the U.S. government, there was little incentive for sustained stock market investment, particularly considering the historic overall 9% return on common stocks indicated by the previously cited study by the University of Chicago Business School (see Chapter 1).

The extent of the debt is of great concern to current taxpayers, economists, and, ultimately, to future citizens who will have to service it. Some insist that the annual deficit is currently only 5% of the gross national product and hence no great danger. The existing trend, however, clearly is. Ten consecutive years of $200 billion deficits will double the current aggregate debt of $2 trillion, a debt it has taken 200 years to accumulate. Although Congress has yet to face up to the problem, the passage of the Gramm-Rudman Act in 1985 showed the first formal signs of serious concern. The act mandates automatic budget cuts if Congress cannot produce them. Although a key provision of the act was struck down by the Supreme Court in July 1986, Congress has shown more responsibility in facing up to the fact that "business as usual" has outlived its time. In any event, the huge deficit requires a huge mechanism to finance it, and the U.S. government securities market has thus become the world's largest and most liquid securities market—a market where millions of dollars in value routinely change hands in single transactions, often at prices equal to, or close to, the previous sale.

If one excludes those who trust in tangible assets such as real estate or more mystical ones such as gold, investors whose foremost concern is safety of principal should buy U.S. government securities. Because the payment of principal and interest is unequivocally guaranteed by the Treasury, there is no *default* risk in owning them; that is, the money *will* be repaid. Naturally, the government's ability to monetize the debt through inflation may lead to reduced purchasing power of the dollars invested when they are returned at maturity, but there is no question that they will indeed be repaid. There is no safer guarantee in the investment world.

Most investors, however, are concerned about more than default risk. They also seek generous returns (commensurate with whatever risk they are willing to undertake) and, where possible, tax advantages. Treasuries typically yield less than high quality corporate bonds, but not so much less that an investor might not be willing to forgo some of the yield advantage for increased safety. For example, long-term Treasury bonds yielded about 7.20% in mid-1986. The yield on AAA-rated corporate bonds at this time was about 8.85%. Although this yield spread is historically rather wide, the actual dollars received might not appear so consequential. An investor with $20,000 to invest would receive $1,440 annually in interest on the Treasury bonds and $1,770 on the corporate issues. Although $330 annually is not an insignificant sum, it might well be worth the price if it allows one an evening's sleep unperturbed by sundry financial demons.

In addition, there are possible tax advantages in owning Treasury securities. The interest paid on them is fully taxable at federal income tax rates but exempt from state and local levies. Consequently, an investor subject to state and city income taxes in addition to federal taxes may well find that the *after-tax* yield on a government bond closely approximates the yield on a less secure corporate obligation, stripped two or three times by the taxing authorities.

TREASURY BILLS

Treasury bills are the shortest-term Treasury securities, having maturities of 3 months, 6 months, and 1 year from issuance. Unlike longer-term debt securities they carry no "coupon" rate of interest. They are sold at a "discount," meaning that they are offered at a dollar price less than their value at redemption. For tax purposes this price difference, or discount, is treated as if it were received in interest payments. For example, an investor might buy $100,000 par value of 1-year Treasury bills yielding 6%. The dollar value of the investment is $94,000 and at maturity would be worth the par value (or face amount).

The popularity of bills soared along with interest rates in the latter 1970s and early 1980s. Although interest rates have since returned to more usual levels, the number of outstanding bills remains high. At the end of 1985 it was estimated that about $390.1 billion were outstanding, about 27% of the total publicly held marketable Treasury debt. Because some governmental entities such as the Federal Reserve Bank also hold large numbers of bills, the actual percentage may be higher. In fact, the word "hold" is used only in the sense of owning the obligation. The Treasury has not issued actual bill certificates in many years. They are issued only as computer notations called book entries.

The Treasury auctions new 91- and 180-day bills each Monday and 1-year bills once monthly. Secondary market trading is active, with most interest centering on the most recently auctioned issue. Because the standard "round lot" for trading is $1 million, it is virtually impossible for the typical investor to trade bills actively, nor is it desirable for such a person to attempt it. Virtually risk-free short-term investments may be made by investing in money market mutual funds, most of which are large buyers of bills, or in a money market bank account. Such investments may often be made for as little as $1,000 (funds) or $2,500 (bank accounts), and offer the safety and liquidity of bills without the trading problems. An investor, however, could purchase as little as $10,000 worth of bills directly from his or her nearest Federal Reserve Bank, although such purchases must be held until maturity. Few commercial banks or brokers will handle so small an order.

Treasury bills are quoted on a yield basis rather than on a dollar or percentage of par method. A typical quotation might appear: 5.63–5.59, indicating a discount bid to yield 5.63% and an offer to sell at a yield of 5.59%. Because higher yields mean lower dollar prices, the "bid" (what a buyer is willing to pay) appears to be less than the offer (what a seller is willing to accept). Translated into dollars, however, the bid is less than the offer. For example, if the bills quoted had a 1-year maturity and a $100,000 principal amount, the dollar price of the bid would be $94,370 ($100,000 − 5,630) while the offer would be $94,410 ($100,000 − 5,590). Traders refer to quotation changes in terms of "basis points," or hundredths of each percentage point of yield. Hence the spread in the quote given is 4 basis points. On the $100,000 principal amount illustrated, the spread between bid and offer is $40 (.0004 × $100,000). For the more common 3-month bill, each basis point is worth about one-fourth that amount (91/365 × .0004 × $100,000).

Treasury bills are generally regarded as the most nearly risk free of all securities and are thus extremely popular with institutional investors seeking temporary havens for funds awaiting reinvestment elsewhere. Foreign investors have been especially fond of Treasury bill investments. For one thing, the market for bills is the only one large enough to absorb a massive infusion of new funds without severe price disruption and the only one liquid enough to permit ease of large-scale withdrawals. Indeed, the flow of "petrodollars" from Organization of Petroleum Exporting Countries (OPEC) in the 1970s was largely recycled through investment in Treasury bills, although economists had feared major commitments (and concurrent disruptions) to the markets for other assets such as gold, real estate, and stocks. This illustrates another factor in the assessment of U.S. government securities as an investment—political stability. Being accustomed to it, Americans tend to take the continuity of the political process for granted. Many non-Americans, however, are more cautious and, having lived with or experienced threats of nationalization and expropriation of wealth, desire to safeguard assets where they are beyond the reach of such actions. This, coupled with the liquidity and size of the market, makes government securities in general, and Treasury bills in specific, the ultimate investment for the security-conscious investor, domestic or foreign.

TREASURY NOTES

About 57% of the current outstanding marketable debt of the U.S. government is in the form of Treasury notes. At year end 1985, notes composed $820.6 billion of the $1,421.6 billion of such government debt. Notes are issued with original maturities from 2 to 10 years, making them fitting for the intermediate-term investor. Because they are noncallable (cannot be redeemed prior to maturity by the Treasury) the holder is assured of the stipulated yield from purchase date.

Notes are issued at par and quoted as a percentage of par basis like corporate bonds. Because of the enormous size of each issue, however, the ⅛% ($1.25 per $1,000 par) quotation variation customary with corporate bonds is too wide for efficient trading. In a market where $100,000 is considered a small trade and multimillion-dollar trades commonplace, bid–asked spreads must be narrower; that is, if a bond is quoted at 98¼ bid–98½ asked, the dollar differential on a $1 million par bond transaction is $2,500 (.0025 × $1,000,000). Treasury notes and bonds, therefore, are quoted in minimum variations of 1/32 of par. Because each 32d is worth only $0.3125 per $1,000, quotation spreads may be made much narrower, benefiting both buyer and seller. Each 32d is shown as an apparent "decimal" in the standard quote display. Thus a price of 99.24 does not mean $992.40 but rather $997.50 (.9975 × $1,000).

Notes pay interest semiannually by coupon, check, or credit, depending on the format. In June 1986 the Treasury ceased the issuance of actual certificates for notes. All new issues from that date will be in book-entry (computer) form only. However, a large number of registered and bearer notes will remain outstanding until 1996. Holders of registered notes receive checks directly from the Treasury, while holders of bearer notes must clip and forward coupons to the Treasury, usually through a bank or broker/dealer intermediary.

Notes are available in denominations of $1,000 or $5,000, depending on the issue. Most brokers stipulate a minimum order of at least $5,000 for notes. Reflecting generally high interest rates of the time, 7-year notes yielded 12½% in 1984. By mid-1986 that rate had declined to a more normal 7% but is still not far distant from the return on high quality corporate obligations with similar maturities.

TREASURY BONDS

The Treasury's longer-term financing needs are met by issuing bonds. Technically, Treasury bonds may have any maturity the Treasury desires, but in recent years the practice has been to issue bonds with either 20- or 30-year maturities. Bonds have decreased in popularity over the past decade, doubtless due to the extreme volatility of interest rates during that period.

Although all bond prices fall when interest rates rise, the extent of the drop is greatly magnified on distant maturities compared to shorter ones. For instance, if new government issues were yielding 11% in all maturities (a hypothetical but useful illustration) and rates were to rise to 12%, 1-year obligations would decline from 100 to 99.08%. The decline on 30-year bonds, on the other hand, would be to 91.2%. Furthermore, if rates were to increase further to 14%, 30-year bonds would fall to 78.94%. Rate changes of this magnitude in fact occurred in the early 1980s, and investors holding long-term bonds actually saw such price declines. Although there was no real concern that the bonds would be repaid at maturity, investors forced to sell prior to maturity suffered severe losses. Naturally, this experience engenders a good deal of caution when investing new funds, and many investors have turned away from all long-term commitments including Treasury bonds. As of December 31, 1985, there were $210.9 billion outstanding, only about 15% of the Treasury's marketable debt.

The characteristics of bonds are similar to those of the previously described notes. One significant difference between notes and bonds other than maturities is callability. A number of longer-term bonds are redeemable by the Treasury prior to maturity via a call provision. Close to half of all bonds maturing from 1995 onward have a call provision. Such bonds can be readily identified by their newspaper listing. For example, the U.S. Treasury 13¼% of May 2009–2014 indicates a bond that will mature in May 2014 but is callable by the Treasury any time from May 2009 onward. If interest rates are significantly lower at that time, one should expect the bonds to be called so that the Treasury could refinance that debt at lower rates. If rates are still 13% or higher, there will be no incentive for the Government to redeem the issue prior to maturity. Noncallable issues do not have a hyphenated maturity but rather a single date, such as the 12⅜% of May 2004.

AGENCY SECURITIES

In addition to the securities described previously, there are numerous quasi-governmental issues which are generally lumped together under the overly elastic title of "agencies." Most are issued by associations or agencies created by Congress, and many are either government sponsored or guaranteed. In general, they are considered only marginally inferior in safety to direct obligations of the Treasury and tend to yield a bit more to compensate the buyer for the added risk, however small. Some possess the same tax features of Treasuries, but most bear no specific exemption from state or local taxes.

Agencies are generally regarded as extremely high quality obligations. Over $249 billion of these issues (exclusive of mortgage pools) were outstanding at year-end 1985, about 17% as great as the direct Treasury debt. Most of these organizations are self-sustaining and draw their operating revenues from the conduct of their businesses. Thus, while their governmental backing is either explicit or implicit, they do not drain funds from the Treasury.

Congress has created a wide variety of agencies authorized to issue securities. A partial listing may give some idea of this diversity:

Farm Credit System
Federal Home Loan Bank Board
Maritime Administration
Federal Home Loan Mortgage Corp.
Government National Mortgage Assn.
Student Loan Marketing Assn.
Tennessee Valley Authority
Washington Metropolitan Area Transit Authority
United States Postal Service

Maturities range from as short as 3 months (e.g., Urban Renewal Project notes) to debentures and bonds with maturities of 20 or 30 years. Thus an investor has a wide variety of choices in agency securities, and can often gain significantly better returns than those available on Treasury securities, without exposing his or her principal to much additional risk.

MORTGAGE BACKED SECURITIES

Banks and other mortgage lenders have long traded residential mortgages with investors and other lenders as a means of adding liquidity to their portfolios. Mortgages have a security rarely equaled in nongovernmental investments. Most Americans consider home ownership a sacred right and a failure to make the monthly mortgage payment as bad as, if not worse than, sin. Also, generally escalating home prices have for years protected the lender as the collateral value of the asset financed (the house) rose even faster than the principal amount was repaid.

The problem with mortgage trading is that every loan is unique—tailored specifically for a certain person, a certain property, a certain locality, and a certain rate. This has made for a general lack of liquidity and led to the immobilization of huge amounts of money tied up in mortgage investment. At the end of 1985, for instance, there were over $2.2 trillion of outstanding mortgage debt in the United States, or about $400 billion more than the entire U.S. national debt.

The key to unlocking this financial treasure was supplied by the Government National Mortgage Association (GNMA)—or "Ginny Mae," from its acronym. Mortgage bankers can now assemble pools of similar mortgages, usually in multiples of $1 million, and submit them to GNMA. The association guarantees the pools and packages them into a "pass-through" security which is then resold to investors in unit multiples of $25,000. The buyer becomes in effect a pro rata holder of numerous government guaranteed mortgages—either Veterans Administration guaranteed or Federal Housing Administration insured. The investor receives a monthly check "passed through" from the pool, representing his or her share of the interest and repaid principal of the loan. This is an extremely attractive investment for both institutional investors and individuals, particularly those who want security and a cash flow higher than that provided by regular government securities.

The mortgage banker, on the other hand, receives cash from the GNMA sale and can immediately start to make new mortgage commitments. The process seems to have created a situation with no losers. Investors received a high-yielding, government guaranteed payout; mortgage bankers received cash to expand their loans; the building industry received funds for new construction which otherwise would have been unavailable; and, naturally, security dealers received a new trading vehicle.

Small wonder, then, that GNMA's success has been emulated. Outstanding GNMA securities rose from $250 million in 1970 to over $100 billion by June 1981. Other government agencies as well as commercial interests also began issuing mortgage-backed securities, so that by the end of 1985 over $380 billion in mortgage pool securities were outstanding.

The original GNMA concept has been expanded and altered so that new, rather different securities have evolved from this base. Despite its attractiveness, the "pass-through" security has some significant drawbacks. The primary one is unpredictability; one simply cannot tell when mortgagors are going to prepay their loans. In fact, the sharp fall in interest rates in 1985–1986 led to massive refinancing of mortgage loans taken out at rates of 15% or even higher. This, in turn, led to the paying down of the principal in many mortgage pools years ahead of even the most conservative projections. With principal repaid so quickly, yields thought likely to prevail for years on mortgage securities were drastically reduced, upsetting many investment projections.

This problem has been addressed with the Collateralized Mortgage Obligations (CMO). Instead of simply packaging the mortgages for collateral, the CMO packages the pools themselves. Each CMO has several different maturities, with the cash flows from the pools being first directed to service the nearest maturity until it is paid off, then to the next maturity, and so on. The effect of this is a predictable semiannual interest coupon and the return of the invested principal in a known year. As noted, each CMO has several maturities from which the investor may select the most attractive choice. So popular has the CMO format become that it now represents close to 75% of all new mortgage backed security issuance.

LIONS AND TIGRS AND . . . CATS

The roller-coaster interest rate pattern of recent years not only brought forth complex new types of securities, it also rekindled interest in an extremely simple type of security: the zero-coupon bond. The "zero" is issued at a deep discount, possibly as low as 20% of its redemption value. In the interim the holder receives no interest payments but in turn has no concern about reinvesting his or her money at lower rates should they come about. In other words, if a zero is held to maturity, the original yield to maturity is locked in, even if interest rates fall sharply. Both corporate and municipal issuers have made great use of these securities to date. However, the steep decline in rates in 1986 has sharply raised bond prices and reduced the popularity of new zero issuance. Holders of outstanding zeros, however, have enjoyed price appreciation even better than that of stocks in the bull market occurring at that time.

Government agencies have been large issuers of zero-coupon securities. Two of the largest have been the Federal National Mortgage Association (FNMA) and the Federal Home Loan Mortgage Corporation (FHLMC). The Treasury resisted the idea for some time but finally started its own zero program in March 1985 when it introduced its Separate Trading of Interest and Principal (STRIPS). Its success has greatly slowed the further creation of the packages fashioned by astute investment bankers who seized on the demand for zero-coupon government securities by creating artificial ones through "stripping" the coupon from long-term Treasury issues.

The resulting components were packaged into two separate securities: (1) the coupons, representing a future cash flow stream received in a lump sum at maturity, and (2) the "corpus," or principal amount, also representing a lump sum payment at maturity. Investment bankers found that they could, in fact, price the two parts at a combined level higher than that of the bond itself, thus creating an arbitrage profit in the creation process.

Merrill Lynch was first to offer its Treasury Investment Growth Receipts (TIGRS). Only a few days later Salomon Brothers introduced its CATS, an acronym for Certificates of Accrual on Treasury Securities. There are other feline-named competitors, COUGARS and LIONS, as well as Easy Growth Treasury Receipts. Although all have essentially similar features, CATS appear to have taken the largest share of the non-STRIP market. In fact, the name has already become the generic word for stripped Treasury bonds, much like "xerox" or "scotch tape."

CATS are particularly attractive investments for long-term oriented, tax-sheltered vehicles: pension funds, IRA and Keogh accounts, and the like. They lock in the yield at purchase for the entire maturity period. The investor is thus relieved of worry that, should interest rates fall, his or her yield to maturity will be reduced because the coupon income will be reinvested at lower rates. With no coupon at all, zeros avoid this problem.

Stripped bonds provided spectacular value in the light of hindsight. For example, in September 1984 10-year CATS were priced at $302.53 per $1,000, yielding 12.5% to maturity. A $10,000 investment will be worth $33,000 if left undisturbed for 10 years. The subsequent decline in interest rates on Treasury securities have made 12% yields little more than a fond memory for some, but for the buyer of the CATS described, that yield is still being produced.

It should be noted that CATS are not attractive investments when not sheltered in a plan like an IRA or a Keogh retirement account. This is because the IRS will tax the holder on the interest "imputed" annually. That is, the discount is presumed to have been received on a pro rata basis even though no funds have actually been paid out. Because the zero-coupon municipal bond's imputed interest is paid by a tax-exempt payer, the increase in value of these securities is nontaxable (see the discussion under "Municipal Bonds").

GOVERNMENT AND AGENCY TRADING

Trading in U.S. government securities is virtually all done OTC. The OTC market (see Chapter 9) is in fact not a central location like a stock exchange but rather a web of competing dealers linked by telephone. The market is largely institutional in nature and is dominated by 36 large, officially recognized "reporting dealers" who are linked directly by wire with the Federal Reserve Bank of New York, the implementation arm of the Fed's Open Market Committee. The Federal Reserve helps regulate the nation's money supply through large purchases and sales of government securities, and these dealers play an integral role in the policy by buying when the Fed sells and selling to the Fed when it wishes to buy.

These dealers are either commercial bank or nonbank dealers. The bank dealers are all large "money center" banks such as Citicorp, Morgan Guaranty, or First Chicago. The nonbank dealers are mostly large securities firms such as Merrill Lynch, Salomon Brothers, or Goldman Sachs, plus a leavening of smaller specialty firms not well known to the public. In fact, many of these smaller firms have been acquired by banks and are operated as subsidiaries (e.g., Carroll, McEntee and McGinley, now a division of Marine Midland Bank).

Government securities trade in round lots of from $100,000 to $1 million, depending on the issue. Major dealers like Salomon Brothers or Goldman Sachs must maintain inventories running into billions of dollars. Obviously there is enormous risk in holding such positions in a volatile interest rate climate. As in any OTC transaction dealers "make markets" by standing ready to supply firm bids and offers—prices at which they will buy or sell. Their profit comes from a "spread," which is the difference between their bid and the offer, or asked, prices. For example, a dealer quoting Treasury notes might quote a spread of 97.16–97.20, a price difference of 4/32, or 1/8%. On a $100,000 order the dealer stands to make $250 (.0025 × $100,000) if prices do not change. There is, however, no assurance that the market will be so accommodating, and a trader may well find that, having bought notes at 97.16, the trader finds no buyers willing to pay more than 97.12, a loss on that trade of $250. Government trades are almost always reported to customers on a "net" basis, which means the customer pays or receives only the reported price. Commissions are not charged; the dealer's compensation being included in the markup on the buy side or markdown on the sell side.

Price reports of most government issues can be found in *The Wall Street Journal,* which has a particularly comprehensive listing of Treasury issues, and *The New York Times,* as well as some other daily papers. Agency securities, on the other hand, are less well covered, although *The Wall Street Journal* has extensive listings of FNMA, Federal Farm Credit, and Federal Home Loan Bank issues.

MUNICIPAL BONDS

While the federal government's debt burden has grown enormously in the past decade, that of state and local government has risen even faster. For instance, such debt was about $360 billion in 1980; by 1985 it was estimated at $614 billion. The securities issued by such governmental units are generically referred to as "municipal bonds," although the actual issuer might be as small as a local school district or as large as the state of California.

The preceding discussion of Treasury securities noted that interest payments on those securities are exempt from state and local taxation. The reason for this is a long-standing doctrine called "reciprocal immunity," which exempts federal and lesser governmental units from each other's taxes. The reverse of this coin is that the interest payments on municipal bonds cannot be taxed by the federal government. The doctrine is hardly immutable, as it is based largely on Supreme Court precedent in specific cases. Congressional legislation could alter this, but Congress has thus far met with little success in addressing the matter. Indeed, there is substantial disagreement that the doctrine should be changed at all. But because it seems to favor wealthy investors over less fortunate folk, the doctrine is likely to be a point of contention for some years to come.

To show the effect of tax-free interest versus taxable interest, assume two investors—one in the 28% federal income tax bracket and one at a 15% rate. If each invests $10,000 in the bank, the after-tax return on a 10% yield is $720 annually for the former, $850 for the latter. On the other hand, the same investment in municipal bonds at the same interest rate lets each retain the full $1,000 annual interest. This represents a 17.6% gain to the lower-taxed individual whereas it is a 38.8% gain to the higher bracket investor. Put differently, the 28% bracket investor would have to achieve a pre-tax return on a taxable investment of about 13.8% to retain the same after-tax dollars provided by a 10% municipal bond.

In addition to this benefit, most states exempt the bonds from state and local taxation when the holder resides in the state of issue. Some states have a fairly steep income tax (about 10% maximum in New York), which means the bonds may possess an even greater appeal to a high-bracket investor in one of those states. In general, this state and local exemption does not extend beyond the state borders, so that investors in Pennsylvania could shelter federally taxable income with California issues but would still be subject to state tax on this income.

GO AND REVENUE BONDS

"Municipals" have a somewhat mixed record on the issue of safety. There are two broad categories of bonds, "general obligation" and "revenue." Actually, it might be better to say that there are bonds that are general obligation (GO) and those that are not, because the term "revenue" is too imprecise to cover the numerous forms usually lumped under that heading. Of the two, GOs have an admirable—but not perfect—record of timely interest and principal payments. Defaults have been exceedingly rare, at least for major issuers, and have almost always been repaid. Some recent cases in point involve New York City and Cleveland, Ohio. New York's failure to pay in 1975 was euphemistically called a "moratorium," but every bondholder knew that meant "default." Ultimately the city was bailed out by a mammoth rescue operation involving a new superagency, the Municipal Acceptance Corporation, or "Big Mac" as it is known on Wall Street. Cleveland's default in 1978 was less visible to the public because the notes at issue were all held by banks. Nevertheless, the financial community was well aware of the problem, and Cleveland's credit rating suffered accordingly.

These, however, are clearly the exceptions. General obligation bonds are always backed by taxing power—personal and/or corporate income, sales, estate, and highway use taxes at the state level; real property taxes at the city or town level. Furthermore, new bond issues almost always have to be preapproved by voters. If taxes begin rising too sharply and borrowing becomes excessive, voters have historically evidenced the good sense (rarely exhibited by Congress at the national level) to reject new borrowings until old debt has been retired, or to place limits on debt or annual tax increases (e.g., California's well-known tax revolt embodied in Proposition 13). Overall, then, the GO bond has an outstanding record for safety of principal, second only to U.S. government securities among domestic issues.

Revenue bonds are another story. Although the vast majority of revenue issues have been trouble free for many years, there have been a few spectacular failures. The most recent of these were projects #4 and #5 of the Washington Public Power Supply System, known to Wall Street somewhat grimly as "Whoops." The default on some $2.25 billion of these issues has sent these bonds from a price near par to about 14% of par (bid in July 1985). In other words, the holders of such issues (1) receive no interest at all; (2) could realize only about $1,400 on a sale of $10,000 face amount; and (3) have scant hopes of ever seeing the principal amount or any substantial portion of it repaid.

How is it that the State of Washington's GO bonds are rated AA −, just a small degree below the very top, whereas *these* WPPS issues (not all WPPS defaulted) were a catastrophe to investors? Without going into detailed particulars, one should note a simple fact. Revenue bonds are almost *never* obligations of a state or city. Rather, they are obligations of an agency, authority, or system which has no ability to tax. These agencies issue bonds to be repaid by the profitable operation of the facilities constructed with the proceeds of the offerings. Therein lies the rub. What if the facilities cannot be operated profitably? With no other source of revenue, the issuing authority may be forced to suspend interest payments; that is, it defaults.

With this type of risk potential one would expect generous returns, and revenue bonds normally yield about 50% more than GOs of comparable rating and maturity. Before one condemns all revenue issues, however, it would be prudent to note the long list of such bonds that have provided reliable tax-free income for years and promptly repaid principal when due. Among these issues are:

New York State Thruway
Intermountain Power Supply System
New Jersey Turnpike
San Francisco Bay Area Rapid Transit

In addition to these huge projects, hundreds of hospitals, university dormitories, civic centers, stadiums, and the like have been constructed with funds so generated.

Revenue obligations typically have *term* maturities, meaning a single maturity for the entire issue. Usually the bonds are "callable," meaning that after a certain period the issuer can redeem the bonds prior to maturity. Revenue bonds often have maturities of 20 to 30 years from issue. Of course, there are exceptions to all of these "typical" cases, and it is not particularly unusual to see a noncallable revenue bond with 15-year serial maturities.

SHORT-TERM MUNICIPAL SECURITIES

States and cities also have short-term cash needs. Tax revenues are rarely collected more frequently than quarterly, and often only annually. But municipal cash needs for payroll and other expenses are constant. To bridge the gaps between receipts and daily municipal expenses, local governments often issue short-term paper usually called "notes." These are frequently sold in anticipation of more regular funding revenues and are thus sometimes known as tax anticipation notes (TANS), revenue anticipation notes (RANS), or bond anticipation notes (BANS). They are almost always issued at par with a stated coupon rate, payable in 6 months if the note has a 1-year maturity. If the maturity is less than a year, the note usually has a single coupon payable at maturity. In addition, there is a growing market for municipal commercial paper, a continuously offered security sold at a discount from par and redeemed at maturity for the par amount. These securities are usually backed by a letter of credit obtained from a local bank.

In general, the municipal note market is illiquid, and buyers should be prepared to hold such notes to maturity. A few large dealers make markets in notes, particularly those underwritten by their firms, but the market is far short of the Treasury bill market in providing continuous two-sided (both bid and offer) quotations.

MUNICIPAL TRADING

Like U.S. government securities trading, municipal bond transactions take place entirely OTC. The major market makers are the large broker/dealers and banks mentioned earlier in connection with Treasury securities. The major buyers are banks, insurance companies, bond funds—particularly unit trusts sponsored by retail brokerage firms—and individuals. Foundations and pension and retirement funds, which are large buyers of both corporate stocks and bonds, are rarely interested in municipal securities because they pay no taxes anyway, and the tax-free advantage (and correspondingly lower yields) of municipals are not attractive to them.

The market, despite its size, is not noted for its liquidity. A major problem is the multiplicity of issuers, which number nearly 40,000. The variety can be best seen by taking a glance at the *Blue List,* a national listing of secondary market (i.e., already outstanding bonds) offerings being made by dealers. It lists alphabetically (first by state, then by city) current issues for sale, indicating the size of the offering, the yield or price, and the dealer. Included in the October 5, 1984, edition, a rather ordinary day, were *15 different* issues of GO or revenue bonds from Cobb County, Georgia. One can imagine how many different State of California or State of Pennsylvania issues were also listed in this same issue of 173 pages. Likewise, one can imagine how much interest in a Cobb County bond is likely to be evinced by a prospective buyer in New York City

The market is large but fragmented, with few dealers making coast-to-coast markets. With most interest centered in local or regional areas, the business tends to favor small local firms or banks. Spreads between bid and asked prices are generally wide, and quotes are not readily available to the public. Indeed, even *The Wall Street Journal* carries no more than about two dozen listings of municipal issues, mostly revenue bonds.

4 Reading the Financial Page

The stock market reflects the news and the reactions of people to the news and their anticipation of impending events. The financial pages of general and specialized newspapers are an important source of information for many people. This chapter indicates some of the material that appears on such pages and in a broad sense what uses can be made of it.

STOCK PRICES

Daily Stock Transactions

The daily report of the stock market occupies more space and attracts more interest and attention than any other part of the financial section of the newspaper. The report is presented in two parts: the stock table and a summary of high points. Most leading financial pages cover New York Stock Exchange composite transactions, American Stock Exchange composite transactions, leading OTC stocks, and mutual funds. The composite transactions on the New York and American exchanges include stocks that are listed on one or more regional exchanges in addition to the larger exchange. Some newspapers may also list stocks listed only on certain regional or foreign exchanges for which local interest is perceived.

Readers of stock data may be interested in other tables found on many financial pages dealing with bonds, options, futures, money market instruments, and currencies.

Points

Several types of securities are quoted in the principal markets in points, but the term may be used differently for various securities.[1] In stocks, rights,

---

[1]The Constitution and Rules of the New York Stock Exchange defines a stock quite broadly by including "voting trust certificates, certificates of deposit for stocks, rights, warrants, and other securities classified as stocks by the Exchange."

and warrants a point means \$1. For stocks selling at \$1 or more per share, there are seven fractional points: ⅛, ¼, ⅜, ½, ⅝, ¾, and ⅞, with each ⅛ point variation being 12½ cents. Thus a stock selling at 25⅝ is valued at \$25.62½. Active stocks fluctuate between ⅛ and ¼ point between sales; larger fluctuations occur in periods of rapid change, such as those that might occur after important unexpected news items.

For stocks selling below \$1 per share, smaller fractional points are permitted. The smallest fractional point recognized by the commission schedules of the NYSE was 1/256 of a point. Actually, few stocks on the Exchange ever sold below one point and none so low as 1/256. Most exchanges now establish minimum variations on low-priced stocks at 1/32, although they reserve the right to alter variations for specific stocks if deemed desirable. In practice minimum variations apply primarily to stock rights which often sell for fractions of a point.

A Day's Transactions

To help gain a better understanding of the stock report, a sample section from the market report of *The Wall Street Journal* of July 12, 1985, is presented in Table 4-1. This tabulation is a complete record of the significant facts about the previous market day's transactions in all stocks listed on the NYSE.

Fifty-Two Week Range

Complete stock tables formerly began with a column indicating the high and low prices of the calendar year to date; this, however, was of small help

Table 4-1 New York Stock Exchange—Composite Transactions

Friday, July 12, 1985

Quotations include trades on the Midwest, Pacific, Philadelphia, Boston and Cincinnati stock exchanges and reported by the National Association of Securities Dealers and Instinet

52 Weeks High	52 Weeks Low	Stock	Div.	Yld %	P-E Ratio	Sales 100s	High	Low	Close	Net Chg.
		– A–A–A –								
23½	16	AAR	.48	2.2	16	102	21⅝	20½	21½	+ ¾
17⅜	9⅜	AGS		..	14	27	16½	16⅜	16⅜	− ¼
16½	9⅝	AMCA		..	..	1	11	11	11	.....
21½	13	AMF	.50	3.8	40	24048	13⅜	13	13¼	+ ⅛
13⅜	12⅞	AMF wd		..	..	1032	13⅜	13¼	13⅜	+ ⅛
49⅞	24¼	AMR		..	12	5890	u50½	48⅝	50⅜	+ 1⅞
22⅞	18⅝	AMR	pf2.18	9.6	..	11	22¾	22½	22¾	+ ¼
25⅞	22⅞	ANR	pf 2.67	11.	..	1	23½	23½	23½	+ ⅛
14¼	7⅝	APL		..	..	108	8⅛	8	8⅛	+ ¼
61⅛	44⅜	ASA	2	4.0	..	207	49⅝	49	49⅝	+ ⅝
27	12½	AVX	.32	2.5	10	51	13¼	13	13	− ⅜
28⅛	16	AZP	2.72	9.8	8	620	28	27⅝	27⅞	+ ⅛
60	36¾	AbtLab	1.40	2.4	17	731	59½	59⅛	59¼	+ ¼
29	16½	APresd	s.12i	.6	4	412	21⅝	21⅛	21⅜	− ⅛
13⅞	5	ASLFla		..	6	12	7	6⅞	7	+ ¼
18½	12¼	ASLFl	pf2.19	15.	..	106	14¼	14¼	14¼	.....
16	10⅜	AShip	.80	5.5	11	296	14½	14	14½	+ ⅛
35⅜	24⅛	AmStd	1.60	5.2	10	154	30⅝	30	30⅝	+ ½
67½	31⅞	AmStor	.64	1.0	12	274	66⅞	66⅝	66⅝	− ¼
78	46⅛	AStr	pfA4.38	5.7	..	35	78	77½	77½	.....
57⅜	51	AStr	pfB6.80	12.	..	61	57⅜	57⅛	57⅜	+ ¼
24⅝	16⅝	AT&T	1.20	5.2	17	9537	23⅜	23⅛	23¼	− ⅛
41⅜	31	AT&T	pf3.64	9.2	..	350	39½	39¼	39½	+ ⅛
42	31⅞	AT&T	pf3.74	9.3	..	259	40¼	40	40¼	− ¼
27¾	15⅛	AWatr	s 1	4.2	8	227	23⅞	23	23⅝	+ ¼
12¾	10	AWat	pf1.25	10.	..	z150	12½	12¼	12½	+ ¼
12¾	10	AWa	5pf1.25	9.6	..	z200	u13	13	13	+ ¼

SOURCE: *The Wall Street Journal*, July 12, 1985.

early in the year to market observers attempting to decide whether a stock was relatively cheap or expensive relative to where it had been in the past. Accordingly, the first two columns now usually indicate the highest and the lowest closing prices for a stock during the preceding 52-week period. Both columns are adjusted to reflect stock payouts of 10% or more.

The careful reader of stock tables should be alert to the many explanatory notes provided to clarify the numbers indicated. For example, if the letter "s" appears in the table just to the left of the indicated dividend, there has been a stock split or stock dividend of 25% or more within the past 52 weeks which will result in an adjustment in the indicated range. The letter "u" indicates a new 52-week high, and a "d" indicates a new 52-week low. The letter "n" indicates the stock was issued during the past 52 weeks.

In the case of AAR Corporation in Table 4-1, its high was 23½ and its low was 16. Since no qualifiers are indicated, this was its range for the past 52 weeks, including the current week to date but not the current trading day.

The significance of this column is that it shows how a stock stands on a given day compared with recent months. Some believe that this information permits determination of current strength or weakness. This column also makes clear when a given stock makes a new high or low for the year. Finally, the column can be used to compare a given stock's behavior with that of the rest of the market. If a stock makes a new low while many others are making new highs, some might find value in the comparison.

Stock

This column indicates the name of the company, which is frequently abbreviated in the interest of saving space. Although most readers are familiar with the designations for stocks in which they are interested, a stock guide available from a brokerage house indicates the complete names of all listed and many unlisted stocks.

If no other qualifiers appear between the name of the stock and the next column in the table, the listing can be presumed to be for a common stock. The letters "pf" are the most frequent qualifier and indicate that the listing is for a preferred stock. A company may have warrants outstanding that trade separately from its other securities, and, if so, these are designated with the letters "wt." If a company has a privileged subscription to new shares, they have rights outstanding that will trade in whatever market the company's common shares trade. Rights are designated with the letters "rt." If "ut" appears, it indicates that there is a combination of securities outstanding that trades together as a package.

Dividend Rates

The abbreviated name of the issue is usually followed by the dividend rate being paid on the stock. This is always in dollars and never in percentages and represents the annual dividend. This apparently simple figure is the most difficult part of the stock table to compute and is only an approximation. In some cases the newspaper or the financial service can state the rate with finality and authority. Such a statement may be made of any company that has paid a regular dividend for some time, such as $.75 per quarter. The editor of the table merely multiplies the quarterly dividend by four. In companies that have an irregular or an interim dividend policy, the problem becomes complex: no one knows from quarter to quarter what the dividend will be. Let us suppose that a given company last year paid these dividends by quarters: $.50, $.50, $.75, and $1.25. In the first quarter of the current year it paid $1. What is the annual dividend? There are at least four possible answers. First, take the total dividends paid for the past 12 months; this is $3.50. Second, report the amount of dividends paid last year; this is $3. Third, give the dividend for the first quarter of the current year only and state that this is the amount paid so far this year; this is $1. Fourth, multiply the dividend for the first quarter by four; this is $4. Each has some weakness.

Most newspapers indicate the annual disbursement based on the most recent quarterly or semiannual declaration, but this requires various explanatory notes to cover a long list of inputs and adjustments to the indicated dividend rates. These include payments in foreign currencies, extra or stock dividends, adjustments for stock splits, liquidating dividends, and omitted dividends. A guide to the explanatory notes is usually provided by a letter following the indicated dollar amount of the dividend.

Stocks are quoted "flat"; this expression means that the buyer pays nothing additional for accumulated dividends. It is presumed that anticipated dividends are reflected in the price. This is unlike most bond transactions in which the buyer pays any interest accumulated to the date of purchase.

Percent Yield

The percentage of current yield provided by a stock is calculated by dividing the annual cash dividend paid on one share of stock by its current price per share. Most financial publications utilize the most recent closing price in making this calculation. To whatever degree the annual cash dividend is inexact, the percentage of yield will also be inexact. Analysis of yields may be further complicated by the payment of stock dividends or other special distributions.

Percent yield should not be confused with stockholders' expected yields on their investments, which usually include and, indeed, emphasize the anticipated appreciation in the values of the shares as well as receipt of cash dividends. The percent yield, however, may be useful in comparing one stock with another or a stock with some other investment such as a bond.

Price–Earnings Ratio

The price–earnings (P–E) ratio of a stock is computed by dividing its current (or closing) price by the company's annual earnings per share. The latter figure is usually taken to be the sum of the company's most recent four quarterly earnings reports, although some analysts use the earnings from the latest reported year. If only outstanding shares are considered in this calculation, the result is often designated as primary earnings per share. If all possible additional shares, such as those that would result from the exercise of executive stock options or convertible bonds, are also considered, the figure yielded is usually designated as "fully diluted earnings per share." Generally, similar problems arise in trying to calculate a precise P–E ratio as was noted in the comments on computation of percent yield.

The P–E measure is sometimes considered to be a measure of a stock's value, but care should be taken to consider all of the inputs. A high P–E ratio can reflect buyer optimism, but it can also result from an extremely low earnings figure. (A deficit results in an infinitely high P–E ratio.) A low figure might indicate a bargain, but it may also indicate a widespread lack of confidence in the company's ability to maintain its earnings or the expectation of some dilution of the stock. If one is making comparisons between companies, it may be necessary to compare their accounting practices to search for inconsistencies. Different companies may be perceived as offering widely disparate risks. For example, one company's earnings may be far more variable than those of another's.

There is no standard P–E ratio, although one can use as a general guideline the average ratio for a group of stocks such as those that make up the Dow Jones industrial averages.

The Day's Sales

Sales volume is usually indicated in hundreds in order to save space. Thus, sales of 12,500 shares would be indicated as 125. The figure of 125 represents the number of reported shares sold and not the number of separate transactions; for active stocks the number runs from 100 shares up. For inactive stocks, such as those traded in 10-share units on the NYSE, volume is often reported as the day's total, such as 10, 20, or 50 shares.

The day's sales are reported both for the market as a whole and for each stock issue traded. A long-standing record for total day's sales on the NYSE dating from its formation on May 17, 1792, was established on October 29, 1929, when 16,410,030 shares traded hands. This record was not exceeded until April 10, 1968, when the volume was 20,410,000 shares. The dollar volumes for the two days, however, were far from statistically comparable because the average share price in 1968 was still only about one-half that in

1929. Since 1968, of course, the volume record has been exceeded many times, culminating in a climactic 302,390,000 shares on January 23, 1987.[2]

The average daily volume in 1984 was more than 91 million shares—far exceeding the approximately 5 million daily shares of 20 years earlier. The daily volume as an indication of its technical condition is of considerable interest to students of the market, some of whom are convinced that "volume goes with the trend." Briefly, this theory maintains that a meaningful rise or fall in prices is accompanied by a substantial increase in the volume of shares traded. Brokerage firms also have an interest in daily volume. It was once a common practice to regard a given average daily volume as a reliable indicator for the break-even point of such firms, but the increasing diversification of most brokerage firms has lessened their dependence on listed volume.

Unusual situations often create records in volume for individual stocks. When Allegheny Corp. was engaged in a proxy battle in 1961, the trading of 941,000 of its shares broke the record of the NYSE. This record has since been broken many times, culminating in the trading of 10 million shares of Superior Oil on June 21, 1984.[3]

Spectacular volume figures in individual issues are typically caused by surprise news announcements of unexpected increases or decreases in earnings or dividends, changes in key personnel, new product development or old product failure, or the impending acquisition of one company by another. There have been any number of isolated instances caused by more unusual events such as market tips by widely followed news commentators, changes of opinion by financial services, cornering of shorts, or government actions such as filing or withdrawing antitrust suits or making drastic changes in regulatory policy.

Some stocks, mostly high-priced preferred issues or inactive common stocks, receive special treatment on some exchanges. Some are sold in smaller units such as 10 or 25 shares. Some such issues trade at Post 30 on the NYSE although others trade elsewhere on the floor. Total volume in such stocks is, of course, relatively small and is usually reported in full rather than expressed in hundreds of shares.

The Day's Prices

There are four of the day's prices in most stock tables. The "open" represents the first sale of the day without regard to the time of day when it was made. The "high" is the highest price at which the stock sold during the trading session. A "u" (for "up") printed next to the "high" indicates that figure to be a new high for the year. The "low" is the bottom price for the day.

---

[2]The lowest volume day in NYSE history was March 16, 1830, when only 31 shares traded: 26 shares of United States Bank and 5 shares of Morris Canal and Banking Co.
[3]Considerable interesting historical data are available from the annual Fact Books published by the NYSE, ASE, and NASDAQ.

A "d" (for "down") printed next to the "low" indicates that figure as a new low for the year. The "close" or "last" is the last sale made during the trading day whether it occurred near the closing hour of the market or not.

Net Change

The term "net change" is often misunderstood. It is the difference between the closing price of a given day and the close of the last session in which the stock was sold. For the majority of stocks the net change represents a 24-hour change, or from the close of one session to the close of the next previous one, but in less active stocks it may represent a change over several days or weeks, even a month. The direction on change is indicated by a plus or minus sign, such as $-\frac{1}{2}$, which indicates that today's close was \$.50 under that of yesterday. No change is indicated by two periods (..).

Measurement of change is affected by dividend payments. When directors of a corporation pay dividends, a certain date is set as the "date of record" or the day that "the books are closed." Stockholders of record on that date will receive the next dividend on the stock. Technically, the stock is traded ex-dividend, according to the rules of the NYSE, on the fourth full business day before the list of stockholders is taken off. Hence, if the dividend was payable to stockholders of record on Friday, March 16, the stock would be sold ex-dividend on Monday, March 12. The reason is that the Exchange uses "five-day delivery," which means that a stock is not delivered until five days after it is sold. Hence, it is not possible to get a new stockholder's name on the books if the stock is sold four days before the date established by the directors—in this case March 16.

When it goes ex-dividend, a stock falls in price by the amount of the dividend. If a stock paying a \$.50 quarterly dividend sells at 45 before it goes ex-dividend, it will sell at 44½ on the day it goes "ex," because it is worth \$.50 less at that time. The stock is reported as showing "no change" if the price falls by the exact amount of the dividend. In the example just cited, "no change" would be reported if the stock closed on the ex-dividend date at 44½, but would be reported " $-\frac{1}{2}$" if it closed at 44. A stock paying a dividend between ⅜ of a point (\$.375) and ½ (\$.50) is rounded off to the higher figure of ½.

THE GAUGES

Market Statistics

In addition to the stock tables, financial publications offer a large amount of information in tabular form that some investors find interesting and sometimes useful.

Typical of such tables are those offered daily in the Stock Market Data

Bank in *The Wall Street Journal* and weekly in Barron's *Market Laboratory*. Large metropolitan newspapers offer similar information in their business sections, although in smaller quantity.

A sampling of data typically offered follows.

Number of Issues

Most, but not all, of the stocks listed on the NYSE are traded every day. The percentage of total stock issues traded each day or each week was formerly considered by some technicians to be an indication of the market's strength of interest and, therefore, an indicator of the market trend. Some few still consider it superior to the averages as a reliable indicator. Others consider volume in any form to have little or no significance and the trend to be an indicator only of where the market has been and not where it is going. The increasing importance of over-the-counter trading and the composite tapes has lessened interest in the percentage of issues traded.

Tables presented daily, weekly, or for longer periods summarize the activity of the approximately 2,300 issues trading on the NYSE, 900 on the ASE, and 4,700 on NASDAQ.

Various such tables are presented to summarize information that may be of interest to various readers. The diaries indicate the breadth of the market, compare advances with declines, compare advancing volume with declining volume, indicate the number of new highs and new lows established for that day for the past 52-week period, and the number of block (10,000 shares or more) trades.

The most actively traded issues are listed to help those traders who believe that they can learn about possible large accumulations or distributions from such data. Percentage gainers and losers indicate changes relative to the previous closing prices of various issues.

Table 4-2 indicates this information for July 15, 1985.

For those interested in minimum activity as a guideline, lists are available indicating bid and asked prices for stocks which did not trade at all for a day or a longer period. Perhaps 100 issues might not trade on the NYSE on a typical day. Generally this list consists of thinly traded preferred or when-issued (WI) stocks. *The Wall Street Journal* prints a list of such stocks each Monday which did not trade during the previous week.

Other Indicators

Although technicians are usually most interested in price and volume statistics, the list of data deemed to be useful is almost endless. Some analysts are particularly interested in odd-lot information. They may have concluded somewhat cynically that the small trader is destined to be wrong more often than not. An unusually high or low volume contributed by the odd-lot trader may be an indication that a market is at or near an interim top or bottom.

Table 4-2 Stock Market Data Bank

Most Active Issues

NYSE	VOLUME	CLOSE	CH
Amer T&T	3,617,500	22¼	− 1
Am Hospit	2,967,800	46	+ 3⅞
Crown Zell	2,631,000	41	− 1
Meril Lyn	1,732,200	34¾	+ ¼
Clev Elec	1,626,800	23½	− ⅛
IBM	1,557,700	125½	+ 1¼
Eastn AirL	1,420,800	9⅞	+ ½
Nor Ind PS	1,258,000	12¾	+ ¼
Times Mir	894,200	58⅛	+ ⅛
Pan Am	822,700	7⅜	+ ⅛
Gen Motors	816,200	67½	− ⅞
Baxter Trav	811,800	14	− 1¾
Eckerd Jk	792,600	26⅜	− 3⅛
Am El Pw	770,800	24½	− ⅜
SFe Sou Pac	769,000	34⅛	− ½

NASDAQ	VOLUME	CLOSE	CH
MCI Comm	1,596,800	10¼	− ¼
Triton	634,000	1¾	+ 1/16
Intel Cp	554,600	27⅛	+ ⅝
Intergraph	443,100	31½	+ 1
Apolo Cptr	420,800	18½	+ ½
Ft Fdl Mich	395,900	18¾	− ¼
Peop Expr	390,800	10⅛	− ¼

AMEX	VOLUME	CLOSE	CH
BAT Ind	735,100	4¼	+ 1/16
Wang LabB	345,200	17¾	− ⅛
Texas Air Cp	166,600	18¼	− 1½
Echo Bay g	158,200	12⅛	+ ¼
Tie/comm	140,500	4¾	....
Total Petl g	128,800	13⅛	+ ⅛
Amdahl	121,500	13¼	+ ¼

Diaries

NYSE	MON	FRI	WK AGO
Issues traded	2,024	2,041	2,025
Advances	875	873	658
Declines	691	670	917
Unchanged	458	498	450
New highs	184	186	125
New lows	12	11	17
Adv Vol (000)	47,354	63,767	29,118
Decl Vol (000)	43,145	43,005	44,135
Total Vol (000)	103,920	120,260	83,670
Block trades	2,082	2,459	1,619

NASDAQ	MON	FRI	WK AGO
Issues traded	4,144	4,144	4,146
Advances	879	1,092	780
Declines	850	705	942
Unchanged	2,415	2,347	2,424
New highs	199	237	155
New lows	46	42	55
Adv Vol (000)	25,984	36,873	15,467
Decl Vol (000)	20,082	13,891	23,531
Total Vol (000)	69,167	78,653	63,568
Block trades	926	1,032	776

AMEX	MON	FRI	WK AGO
Issues traded	791	786	771
Advances	278	296	232
Declines	233	242	305
Unchanged	280	248	234
New highs	33	36	29
New lows	14	16	13
Adv Vol (000)	2,787	3,022	1,764
Decl Vol (000)	1,862	2,132	2,106
Total Vol (000)	6,070	6,430	5,130
CompVol (000)	7,011	7,484	6,145
Block trades	38	75	50

Percentage Gainers . . .

NYSE	CLOSE	CH	% CH
Myers LE	2⅝	+ ⅜	+ 16.7
Rep Air wt	2½	+ ¼	+ 11.1
Goldn Nug wt	2¾	+ ¼	+ 10.0
Am Hospit	46	+ 3⅞	+ 9.2
Anacomp	3	+ ¼	+ 9.1
GTFl 1.25pf	13¼	+ 1	+ 8.2
Allied Prd	19¾	+ 1⅜	+ 7.5
Danaher	9½	+ ⅝	+ 7.0
Robrtsn H	30¾	+ 2	+ 7.0
EAL wtO	3⅞	+ ¼	+ 6.9
Pub Svc Ind	9⅞	+ ⅝	+ 6.8
Equifax s	34½	+ 2	+ 6.2
Hall Frank	32	+ 1⅞	+ 6.2
Fox Sta Phot	10⅞	+ ⅝	+ 6.1
NiaM adj pf	26	+ 1½	+ 6.1
Nwst Stl W	8¾	+ ½	+ 6.1
Payless Cash	17½	+ 1	+ 6.1
vjSalant Cp	4⅜	+ ¼	+ 6.1
Lamaur s	9	+ ½	+ 5.9

OTC	CLOSE	CH	% CH
Hlth Info	3	+ ½	+ 20.0
Fed Ntl Rsc	3⅛	+ ½	+ 19.0
EAL wtj	2⅝	+ ⅜	+ 16.7
Ponce Fedl	11⅝	+ 1⅝	+ 16.3
Repco Inc	6½	+ ⅞	+ 15.6
Hytek un	5¾	+ ¾	+ 15.0
Am Cabl	3⅛	+ ⅜	+ 13.6
Pancret	6¼	+ ¾	+ 13.6
Termflx un	4¾	+ ½	+ 11.8
Inmar	6 15/16	+ 11/16	+ 11.0
FMG Tele	2 9/16	+ ¼	+ 10.8
Medinet un	3⅞	+ ⅜	+ 10.7
Seeq Tch	2⅝	+ ¼	+ 10.5

AMEX	CLOSE	CH	% CH
Rch Tnk pf v	3½	+ 1	+ 40.0
Mcrae Ind a	4⅝	+ 1⅛	+ 32.1
Mcrae Ind b	4½	+ ¾	+ 20.0
Icee USA	7¼	+ 1	+ 16.0
Plym Rub b	3⅝	+ ½	+ 16.0
Atlas Cp wt	4	+ ½	+ 14.3
Cohu Inc	9⅜	+ 1	+ 11.9
Comp Con	5⅞	+ ⅝	+ 11.9
Weldtrn	12⅜	+ 1¼	+ 11.2
Mount Med	5⅛	+ ½	+ 10.8
Verit Ind	7	+ ⅝	+ 9.8
Laser Ind	11⅞	+ 1	+ 9.2
Tubos Mex	3	+ ¼	+ 9.1

and Losers

NYSE	CLOSE	CH	% CH
Baxter Trav	14	− 1¾	− 11.1
Eckerd Jk	26⅜	− 3⅛	− 10.6
Mngt Asst	2⅛	− ¼	− 10.5
Alberto Cul s	22	− 2	− 8.3
Texas Intl	3⅜	− ¼	− 6.9
Galvst Hou	3½	− ¼	− 6.7
Massey F	2	− ⅛	− 5.9
Mexico Fd	2	− ⅛	− 5.9
Gen Refrac	10⅞	− ⅝	− 5.4
Un Jersy Bk	44⅝	− 2⅜	− 5.1
Fst Penna	7¼	− ⅜	− 4.9
Banc Texas	2½	− ⅛	− 4.8
Katy Ind	15¼	− ¾	− 4.7
Brock Htl	2⅝	− ⅛	− 4.5
Sparton Cp	16¼	− ¾	− 4.4
Amer T&T	22¼	− 1	− 4.3
Castl Cke pfA	14	− ⅝	− 4.3
Maxxam Gp	13⅞	− ⅝	− 4.3
Noble Afll	13⅞	− ⅝	− 4.3

OTC	CLOSE	CH	% CH
Trillng Rs un	2¾	− ¾	− 21.4
Imunmed un	3	− ¾	− 20.0
BC Tx cvpf	8½	− 2	− 19.0
Rynco Sci	6⅜	− 1⅜	− 17.7
Equine	2⅜	− ½	− 17.4
Billings Cp	3	− ⅝	− 17.2
Cryo un	2½	− ½	− 16.7
Phrmknt	2¼	− 7/16	− 16.3
Hlthmate un	3⅞	− ¾	− 16.2
CS Televisn	4⅛	− ¾	− 15.4
Tera Corp	2⅞	− ½	− 14.8
Brock Exp	2¼	− ⅜	− 14.3
Utd Bk Sf	3	− ½	− 14.3

AMEX	CLOSE	CH	% CH
Cryst Oil	2¼	− ¼	− 10.0
Acton Cp	2½	− ¼	− 9.1
Casablanca	3¾	− ⅜	− 9.1
Lee Pharmc	6⅞	− ⅝	− 8.3
Russell	17⅜	− 1½	− 7.9
Texas Air	18¼	− 1½	− 7.6
Wstbrg Cap	6¾	− ½	− 6.9
Bush Ind	8½	− ⅝	− 6.8
Weathfrd	3½	− ¼	− 6.7
Am Royalty	12⅝	− ⅞	− 6.5
Clopay Cp	14½	− 1	− 6.5
Synaloy	3¾	− ¼	− 6.3
T Bar	5¾	− ⅜	− 6.1

SOURCE: *The Wall Street Journal*, July 15, 1985.

The number of shares sold short is considered meaningful by some, although their conclusions differ. Some believe that a large short position must be covered and thereby lends strength to the market. Others believe that short sellers are a particularly knowledgeable breed and that heavy short selling is an indication of weakness. Still others pay particular attention to odd-lot short sales in the belief that when large numbers of small traders are convinced that the market must go down it will certainly go up. Positions held by specialists are sometimes believed to be good indicators of where the market is going because the specialists might have the power to make their projections come true. Similarly, some are interested in the activity of professional floor traders although this is much less important than in past years.

Still other traders purport to find value in the number of new issues offered during a period or the number of secondary offerings. Selected data measuring trading in investment trusts or bonds may offer guidelines to future prices or, at least, explanation of past prices. There are those who watch for a listing of companies who intend to make presentations to meetings of securities analysts perhaps in the belief that such companies might impart some new information making it possible to project a significant movement in their stock values.

Given the number of people avidly seeking information and the number of financial publications avidly trying to provide the data, it is not too difficult to find as much statistical information about the markets as one could wish. The reader searching for sources not mentioned herein need only visit a well-stocked library or indicate to a service-minded broker what is needed.

Market Averages and Indexes

Most followers of the market pay particular attention to the "market averages." These are computed from prices of selected lists of representative stocks. Some have been computed over many years by financial services and newspapers. Such averages may reflect market direction as well as day-to-day fluctuations. When plotted on charts, market averages may indicate more clearly the course of the market than do the basic figures from which the averages are derived. Most services do not wish to calculate averages based on all stocks listed on an exchange, so they use the expedient alternative of choosing representative industrial, transportation, or public utility stocks and combining them into averages or indexes. Such lists may range from a handful to 1000s of issues.

One of the broadest market measures is the Wilshire 5000 Equity Index that is based on the total dollar value of 5,000 common stocks, including all those listed on the New York and American Stock Exchanges as well as others traded over the counter.

The major exchanges provide indexes of stocks traded on their floors in total or in groups. The New York Stock Exchange Composite Index offers a weighted average of all stocks traded on that Exchange weighted by their market value. The Exchange also provides indexes of industrials, utilities, transportations, and industrials. The American Stock Exchange provides similar figures as does NASDAQ for over-the-counter stocks.

Standard & Poors computes a weighted index of 500 selected stocks and another of 400 industrials. Lipper Analytical Services indicates the performance of mutual funds subdivided into various types.

Among the best-known market averages and indexes appearing daily or weekly have been those offered by the Dow Jones Company. These appear in its own publications, *The Wall Street Journal* and *Barron's,* and in a large number of daily newspapers. The company prepares averages of 30 industrial stocks, 20 transportations, 15 utilities, and a composite of all 65. It also offers such bond averages as 10 public utilities, 10 industrials, and 10 government bonds.

A small number of newspapers and some brokerage firms also prepare averages or indexes. Many leading financial pages offer tables of market averages and indexes. One of the most complete is that carried in *Barron's.* A more detailed examination of averages and indexes is made in Chapter 18.[4]

BOND PRICES

Bond Points and Prices

Bonds are quoted in points, but the bond point is 1% and not $1 as in stocks. This reduces all bonds, regardless of denomination, to a common measure of price. All are quoted as though they had a $100 denomination (see Table 4-3), although actually most bonds have a $1,000 denomination. A price of 95 would mean 95% of par; this would be $475 on a $500 bond, $950 on a $1,000 bond, and so on. For other than U.S. government bonds, the fractional bond points begin at $\frac{1}{8}$ and go up to $\frac{7}{8}$; no smaller fractional points are used to indicate changes in price. On federal obligations quotes are in fractional points of $\frac{1}{32}$. For example, if U.S. Treasury 4¼s were quoted 103.12, this might read 103$\frac{12}{32}$ or 103⅜. In dollars the bid is $1,033.75 on a $1,000 par value bond (see Table 4-4).

Maturity dates are always given for bonds, for example, "88," which means that the bond matures in 1988. In government bonds the call date is also shown; it is the earlier of the two dates. The obligor has the privilege of calling in and paying off the bond at the call date but not before. If no call date is indicated, which applies to most corporate bonds, the company may be allowed to call in the security at any time. An examination of the

[4]Both *Barron's* and *The Wall Street Journal* offer educational editions which explain the structure and use of the kind of information discussed here. These provide excellent sources for teachers and students of this subject.

Table 4-3   Corporate Bond Quotations

CORPORATION BONDS
Volume, $44,800,000

Bonds	Cur Yld	Vol	High	Low	Close	Net Chg.
AMR 10¼06	10.0	15	102¼	102¼	102¼	+ ¼
Advst 9s08	cv	36	109	109	109	...
AirPr 14⅝87	13.8	200	105⅝	105⅝	105⅝	...
AirbF 7½11	cv	6	107	106½	106½	+ 5⅜
AlaP 7⅞s02	8.6	10	91¼	91¼	91¼	+ ¼
AlaP 8⅞s03	9.1	6	97¼	97¼	97¼	− ½
AlaP 9¾s04	9.6	15	102	102	102	...
AlaP 10⅞05	10.1	10	108	108	108	...
AlaP 10½05	9.9	10	106¼	106	106	− ¼
AlaP 8⅞06	9.2	40	96⅜	96¼	96¼	− ¼
AlaP 8¾07	9.1	40	96	95⅞	95⅞	+ ⅛
AlaP 9½08	9.5	1	100¼	100¼	100¼	− ¼
AlaP 9⅝08	9.5	22	101¼	100⅞	101¼	+ ⅞
AlaP 12⅝10	11.9	21	106⅞	106⅛	106⅛	− ¾
AlskH 16¼99	14.2	14	114⅜	114⅜	114⅜	− ⅛
AlskH 17¾91	15.1	31	118½	117¼	117¼	− 1¼
AlskH 18⅜s01	18.1	207	102	101½	101½	− ½
Alco 8½10	cv	27	115	114½	115	− 1
Allgl 10.4s02	13.8	25	75¾	75¼	75½	− ¾

SOURCE: *The Wall Street Journal*,
November 7, 1986.

basic indenture, or contract, agreement must be made to ascertain just what the company's privilege is.

Bonds usually are quoted "with interest." The purchaser pays the quoted market price *plus* the interest on the bond at the time of purchase. Interest payments typically occur at six-month intervals; interest accumulates between such payment dates and must be paid by the new owner to the date at which the owner assumes ownership. Bonds may be quoted flat if they are income bonds or in default. In this case the purchaser's price is the quoted price.

Bond Yields

Computation of bond yields is mysterious to most laypeople. They can be computed in a few minutes, but an untrained person is unlikely to get the right answer. The best ways to ascertain yield on a given bond are to look it up in a bond table, some form of which is available in most brokerage offices, or to use a financial calculator. The reason for complexity in computation is that the formula for finding a bond yield takes into account five separate factors: maturity date, market price, coupon rate, deviation of price from par, and investment value of coupons remaining for payment before maturity. Yields, therefore, are seldom identical with coupon rates. A 12% bond is unlikely to be a 12% investment for a buyer. It may yield more or less, and the buyer should investigate before acting.

Quotations by Yield

Most bonds are quoted in terms of points, such as 100, 101½, or 102.22. In certain types of debt instruments, however, such as T-bills and railroad trust

Table 4-4   Treasury Bond Quotations
TREASURY ISSUES
Bonds and Notes

Monday, September 9, 1985

Representative mid-afternoon. Over-the-Counter quotations supplied by the Federal Reserve Bank of New York City, based on transactions of $1 million or more.

Decimals in bid-and-asked and bid changes represent 32nds; 101.1 means 101 1/32 a-Plus 1/64. b-Yield to call date. d-Minus T/64. k-Non U.S. citizens exempt from withholding taxes. n-Treasury notes. p-Treasury note; non U.S. citizens exempt from withholding taxes.

Treasury Bonds and Notes

Rate	Mat.	Date	Bid	Asked	Bid Chg.	Yld.
10⅞s,	1985	Sep n	100.5	100.9		5.19
15⅞s,	1985	Sep n	100.13	100.17	.1	5.24
10½s,	1985	Oct n	100.11	100.15	.1	6.76
9¾s,	1985	Nov n	100.11	100.15		6.85
10½,	1985	Nov n	100.17	100.21		7.24
11¾s,	1985	Nov n	100.22	100.26	1	6.83
10⅞s,	1985	Dec n	100.30	101.2		7.12
14⅛,	1985	Dec n	102	102.4	.2	6.75
10⅝s,	1986	Jan n	101	101.4	.2	7.53
10⅞s,	1984	Feb n	101.11	101.15	.1	7.61
13½s,	1986	Feb n	102.20	102.24	.1	6.80
9⅞s,	1986	Feb n	100.24	100.28	.2	7.70
14s	1986	Mar n	103.8	103.12	.1	7.65
11½s,	1986	Mar n	101.27	101.31	.2	7.79
11¾s,	1986	Apr n	102.7	102.11	.2	7.91

SOURCE: *The Wall Street Journal*, September 10, 1985.

Table 4-5   Quotations on U.S. Treasury Bills

Maturity Date	Discount Bid	Asked	Yield	Maturity Date	Discount Bid	Asked	Yield
1985				1986			
9–12	6.82	6.74	6.83	1–2	7.30	7.16	7.43
9–19	7.37	7.33	7.44	1–9	7.24	7.20	7.48
9–26	7.00	6.94	7.06	1–16	7.34	7.30	7.60
10–3	6.96	6.92	7.05	1–23	7.37	7.33	7.64

SOURCE: *The Wall Street Journal*, September 10, 1985.

certificates, quotations are in terms of yields (see Table 4-5). Buyers want low prices, so they make high-yield bids. Sellers want high prices so they quote low-yield offers. Those who deal in such issues become accustomed to thinking in terms of yields rather than the prices of the issues. Several examples are given in Table 4-5.

THE NEWS

The Averages and Indexes

A careful student of the market usually follows one or more of the leading stock averages or indexes just discussed or others. One's choice may depend on the financial sources of information utilized or the type of average or index considered best fitted to one's needs. Some might even devise their own measures of the market, but considering the amount of data available, it would hardly seem worth the time and energy required for most people to perform this kind of laborious chore.

Individual Stocks

Some believe it is wise to select a small but representative list of stocks and to follow them regularly. Most stockholders will always follow the prices of their own investments, but this is not necessarily the best list of stocks to follow in keeping abreast of market changes. Some analysts believe that it is wise to follow a list of such market leaders as GM, IBM, and GE. Some believe that a good picture of market action can be gained by watching GM alone. Still others might devise a list of stocks which they believe reflect the price action of the type and quality of stocks in which they choose to invest such as high technology stocks.

There is such a bewildering flow of business news items that the average market follower finds it hard to make an intelligent selection. There are, however, a number of basic indicators that are of value in interpreting business conditions. Because the stock market is heavily influenced by traders and investors who attempt to forecast business conditions, a careful study of the economic situation will do much to reveal basic causes of stock market trends.

Steel production figures are highly significant statistics. Released each week by the American Iron and Steel Institute, they cover the tonnage produced for the week. Their great importance is indicated by the fact that about 40% of all manufactured goods employ steel as a raw material.

Automobile and truck production figures are also highly important, because the automobile industry is one of the key industries of the country, not only as a leading consumer of steel and a leading employer but also as an indicator of consumer demand. These figures are released weekly by *Ward's Automobile Reports* and *Automotive News*.

Retail sales figures are gathered and released weekly by the Census Bureau. There are also surveys of consumer spending released periodically both by the federal government and by the University of Michigan.

The Association of American Railroads issues various data weekly including carloadings and rail freight traffic measured in ton-miles. Such figures may be useful as guides for appraisal of the volume of traffic moving in industrial and commercial channels, as well as possible indicators of earnings of railroads.

The F. W. Dodge Corporation releases data on building contracts awarded in 50 states each month. In a basic industry that is greatly influenced by business fluctuations and that, in turn, has a tremendous influence itself, this series is highly important, because the industry employs millions of workers and furnishes a great demand for building materials, appliances, furnishings, and equipment. Extremely important are the data on contracts for industrial or heavy construction, because these reflect the planning of thousands of corporations and are therefore a sign of either business confidence or the lack of it on the part of the country's corporate leaders. Building permit data are no longer significant.

Both McGraw-Hill Publishing Company and the SEC provide data on business plans for capital spending. These data give an opportunity for anticipation of changes likely to occur in construction and sales of durable goods.

Electric power production figures are compiled by the Edison Institution and issued weekly. These figures show changes in the kilowatt-hour output of the country. They have shown a strong growth for many years. Because they reflect industrial, commercial, and consumer demands, they need extremely careful interpretation when used as an index of business activity.

Periodic information concerning the petroleum industry is released by the American Petroleum Institute. Paper and paperbound statistics may be obtained from the American Paper Institute. Lumber production figures are issued weekly both by the Western Wood Products Association and the Southern Forest Products Association. *Metals Week* makes available current production figures of copper and aluminum among other metals.

The *Federal Reserve Bulletin,* issued monthly, contains myriad figures concerning important basic industries. The *Survey of Current Business* published monthly by the Department of Commerce also provides statistics on such industries as chemicals, food, electrical equipment, and metals.

The quantity of and variety of reports issued by various government agencies are far too long to be enumerated here, but it is not too difficult to learn what is available for anyone interested in particular data. In addition to the Bureau of Labor Statistics and the Census Bureau, information can be obtained from the Departments of Commerce, Labor, and Agriculture. Widely watched figures include those pertaining to inventories and the analyses of prices and production available from the National Association of Purchasing Agents. The Finished Goods Price Index and the Consumer Price Index are closely watched indicators of the degree of inflationary pressure.

In 1959 the Federal Reserve Board began publishing quarterly summaries of the major flows of funds and savings in the United States. This addition to the volume of information about significant factors in general economic activity is a basis for improved and amplified analysis of business conditions. Among other Federal Reserve figures that receive widespread attention are the prime commercial paper rate, the Eurodollar rate, money supply figures, commercial, industrial, and agricultural loans, free bank reserves, and installment credit outstanding. The credit and rediscount policies of the Federal Reserve system should be watched with great care because these are generally considered to be powerful weapons for control of business activity.

Corporate earnings fill many columns of the financial page over a period of time. Each day brings a stream of individual corporate reports, which becomes a flood during periods when quarterly reports are being released. These should be watched carefully in view of the popular belief that stock prices are influenced heavily by changes in earnings and dividends.

All experienced readers of the financial page realize the interdependence of business news. No one industry operates in a vacuum. The prosperity of one industry spreads to many others like ripples from rocks thrown into a mill pond. The prosperity of the automobile industry affects the demand for steel, rubber, glass, paint, accessories, parts, copper, nickel, and aluminum. Employment and trade are affected over wide areas. Similarly, a decline in construction means a reduced demand for lumber, paint, brick, cement, tile, steel, electrical equipment, appliances, glass, furnishings, and many other products. A drop in farm prices and in income lowers the demands for farm machinery, consumer goods, automobiles, mail order sales, fertilizer, and the many other products and services sold to farmers. Such phenomena explain why so many groups of stocks tend to move up and down in sympathy.

Political News

The reader of the financial page who overlooks the political news of the day will have a decidedly unbalanced picture of the stock market. The market is swayed today much more than it was many years ago by political developments which may greatly influence business conditions. Central governments today in all countries have a major influence upon the economic life of their nation through taxation, expenditures, and monetary policies. The theory that the central government is largely responsible for the prosperity of the country has grown so strong in recent years that it is doubtful if government will ever again play a minor role in the nation's economic existence. Hence, policies of the president, acts of Congress, federal court decisions, regulations of commissions—all must be properly weighed in an analysis of the stock market.

War, both "hot" and "cold," has been of vast importance for years. With the likelihood of a continuous struggle between the communist and free worlds for many years to come, the reader of the financial page must be ever watchful of the reaction of the market to political news. Often it even overshadows the economic developments of the day.

Source of News

The news that appears on the financial pages of a newspaper comes from many and varied sources. It is gathered largely by the great press associations, and by Dow Jones and Company, which publishes *The Wall Street Journal,* and the Dow Jones news ticker service. Many of the larger metropolitan papers have extensive business newsstaffs of their own. These agencies, in turn, gather their financial and business news from corporations, trade associations, research organizations, business executives, and government agencies. In general, such agencies do an excellent job of compiling, editing, classifying, and sorting out the most useful items in the endless stream of such reports. No paper can hope to publish all the material released today.

Much of the news is purely factual and presents no problem; it can be accepted at face value. The problem here is selectivity and interpretation. Readers, however, must be constantly on their guard against certain kinds of news stories. These are often called "inspired" by the gentlemen of the fourth estate. These stories are released by interested parties to show the favorable side of a picture, to convey an impression favorable to the source releasing the report, to impress the readers, to conceal unfavorable facts, to cover up a premature rumor, or to sway an audience to an unexpressed point of view. A corporation president in his report will seldom play up the unfavorable prospects of his company; rather, he will stress the hopes for the future or the profits of the past. A financier will deny rumors of a merger until its final details have been approved. A labor leader will present only his side of a labor dispute. Never in history have business leaders been so acutely aware of the importance of favorable public relations. The desire to present to the public at all times a "good story" of company affairs has become a major objective of management. The intelligent reader will do well to evaluate corporate reports at all times to see if they are complete, unbiased, and objective.

Market Reaction to News

A reader may cram with endless facts, statistics, statements, reports, and forecasts; the person may be well informed through a careful, continuous, and systematic study of the financial page and the numerous other reports of economic conditions. What then? The most difficult job in reading the financial page is not the finding of news; it is in interpretation.

Students of the stock market must realize that they are not dealing with a machine; one does not feed a mass of statistics into the market and see a reaction similar to pressing one's foot on the starter of a well-maintained automobile. The market is not an automaton. Rather it is a composite of all the hopes, fears, generalizations, forecasts, guesses, and analyses of the thousands upon thousands of individuals, firms, and corporations that deal in the market each day.

The market may or may not react to news as expected. A good piece of news may affect the market days or weeks before it reaches the news tickers; it may influence the market the instant it becomes known; it may produce results a day or two afterward; or it may never make the least difference in the price of the stock. All this is mysterious to the layperson. There is no easy road to interpreting financial or political news in terms of stock market trends.

The easiest way to interpret the market is to assume that it reacts only to so-called spot news. Some stock market commentators fall into this superficial method of analysis. If the market falls today, it is because the bad news outweighs the good news of the day; if the market is buoyant, the good news forces prices up. For example, a major coal strike is in the making: if the market breaks, there is pessimism about its settlement; if the market rises, the speculators are hopeful of a quick adjustment; if the market does nothing, traders are adopting a "wait and see" attitude. Too often such an analysis proves spurious, because many underlying forces influence the market. These forces are often as obscure to brokers close to the market, even on the floor of the Exchange, as they are to the outside observer. An underlying bull market may be in progress; but the most mature analysts do not perceive its growth until some time has lapsed and then opinion may be strongly divided as to when it will terminate. To interpret such a trend purely on the basis of "spot news" is likely to lead one to many false conclusions and financial losses. One of the most remarkable things about the market is its ability to absorb bad news without damage during strong markets and its inability to recover on good news during bear markets. This tendency has resulted in the creation of many Wall Street axioms, for example, "Buy on the rumor, sell on the news."

Many spot news stories are used to explain the daily changes of individual stocks after the fact. The one given the most prominence by many editors of the daily columns interpreting the market is on dividend actions, especially if the action taken was not expected. During some periods, news about rumored takeover actions may result in spectacular price movements.

Discounted News

Certain important news items cause substantial changes in the level of stock prices; others of equal importance cause no change. The explanation in many cases is based upon the principle of *discounted* and *nondiscounted news*.

Discounted news is that which has been successfully forecast or discounted before it reaches the ears of the general public or the financial pages of the daily paper. For example, well-informed traders and investors may predict the increase or reduction of a dividend, a stock split, a favorable or unfavorable earnings report, a rate increase, a change in prices, or a corporate merger. Acting on this forecast, often reinforced by inside information not available generally, a substantial amount of buying or selling of stock in the company affected takes place. The stock mysteriously rises or declines. By the time the news has reached the press, the market has fully discounted the news and nothing happens. If the news was good, the stock may have risen 5, 10, or 15 points before there was full realization of what was taking place. The amateur trader is apt to buy too late in such a situation. The market has already advanced as far as the situation justified.

In contrast to discounted news there is nondiscounted news. This news was not forecast at all or, in some cases, wrongly forecast in advance. It comes without warning, like the proverbial "bolt from the blue." Or the news story may be in direct contrast to the expectations. The stock may then react sharply; this depends on whether or not the news is good or bad. For example, a corporation may announce a stock split, a change in dividend, a merger, or a large order. A government official, judge, or commission may announce a significant policy or decision. A highly important political event may take place unexpectedly. Because the news story was carefully concealed until public disclosure to the news services, the market reacts at that time in accordance with the weight of opinion as to the ultimate effects of the news upon stock values.

The ability of the market followers to discount the news successfully can prove to be very profitable. Rare, indeed, is the trader who can do it well and consistently.

Optimism and the Market

The stock market and those who make a living from it, directly and indirectly, thrive on optimism. Almost everyone likes to hear good news about the market, whether one is trader, investor, stockholder, newspaper editor, broker, politician, business owner, housewife, farmer, or the well-known "person in the street." Hence, there is a great tendency for all those who produce, gather, edit, and distribute the news to look for the favorable side of the news and to minimize the unfavorable. The "bulls" in the market usually outnumber the "bears." For this reason, many readers of the financial page and many followers of the market tend to be carried away by the rosy glow of false hopes. No greater error can be made by the intelligent trader or investor.

The Market Can Do Anything

Students of the market who try to explain everything in terms of rational causes will find much to mystify them. No truer characterization has been made of the market than that it can do anything. On occasion it can show sharp gains with no discernible cause. At other times it will break widely with no news event to justify such action. No full explanation of market action exists.

2 Work of the Stock Exchanges

5 The New York Stock Exchange: Its Functions and History

This chapter deals first with the functions performed by the NYSE that exemplify the functions performed by all of this country's stock exchanges. The New York Stock Exchange has been selected because of its dominant position among listed markets. The Amex and the regional stock exchanges perform much the same functions in their respective spheres of operation. Brief discussions of these other exchanges are presented later in this book.

FUNCTIONS OF THE NEW YORK STOCK EXCHANGE

Creation of a Continuous Market

Without question, the creation of a continuous market for individual security issues is one of the most important functions of the stock exchanges. In a continuous market securities are bought and sold in volume with little variation in current market price as trades succeed one another. Four tests may be used to indicate continuity in the market for a given stock: (1) frequency of sales; (2) narrow spread between bids and offers; (3) prompt execution of orders; and (4) minimum price changes between transactions as they occur.

What makes a continuous market? Several conditions tend to create it. A large number of stockholders in a given company will do so, although some companies with large stockholder lists have less continuous markets than do companies with smaller lists. The size of the company also has significance, but many large companies have a less continuous market than do some smaller ones. Speculative interest in a given company undoubtedly makes a market more continuous. Heavy speculation implies frequent, fast sales and, usually, narrow spreads. In many cases this factor is more important than the number of stockholders or the size of the company in making a continuous market, especially over short periods. Margin buying and short selling increase the volume, frequency, and speed of sales, and probably make for smaller fluctuations between sales.

The benefits of a continuous market are principally two, although minor benefits may be added: (1) it creates marketable, liquid investments; and (2) hence, it facilitates collateral lending. Investors may place and withdraw funds rapidly. An institution, such as a bank, an insurance company, or a mutual fund, may keep its funds invested at all times; it may switch investments, and it may withdraw such funds immediately upon need. Similar advantages accrue to the individual who may have funds to invest or may need to withdraw them for personal or business use, for payment of taxes, or to meet emergencies. Other things being equal, listed stocks are usually better collateral for security loans than unlisted ones. They have a higher collateral value, which benefits the borrower; the lender also benefits by having behind the loan a liquid security which may be quickly sold if the loan becomes jeopardized.

The question of how continuous the market in stocks really is cannot be answered simply. Some stocks, such as the 50 most active stocks on the NYSE, have a remarkably continuous market. These stocks on the average provide about 25% of all sales on the Exchange. The first 20 leaders alone provide over 10% of all Exchange activity. Over one third of Exchange sales are concentrated in the 100 most popular issues.

Presently, there are over 2,000 stocks listed on the NYSE. During a typical day, it is unusual for as many as 100 stocks not to be traded. Typically, about 50 issues are not traded during a calendar week. Stated another way, over 85% of all issues are traded daily and over 95% are traded weekly. How continuous has the market been? The issues sold daily enjoyed a continuous market. But what about the issues not sold even weekly? It is true that these issues did not enjoy frequent sales. They failed, therefore, one of the tests of a continuous market. On the other hand, because of the system of specialists on the Exchange, any stock may be sold or purchased at any time, and quickly, if there is a demand for a transaction. In this sense, therefore, every stock on the Exchange may be said to have a continuous market to some degree. On the less active issues, however, the spread between bid and asked prices and the fluctuations between sales are likely to be greater (for some, much greater) than those of the 50 market leaders.

Three criticisms have been made in the past of the performance of this function on the Exchange. The first has been that sales for many issues are not frequent enough to assure a close, continuous market. This situation has just been reviewed. In fairness to the Exchange, it is doubtful whether activity in the less popular issues should be stimulated merely to create a more continuous market. A stock does not become a fundamentally better investment simply because some shares are sold daily rather than weekly.

A second criticism of the performance of this function has been that the Exchange, in creating a continuous market, permitted excessive activity detrimental to the best interests of the market. This criticism was voiced strongly many years ago when speculation in certain issues ran to extreme lengths. For example, in 1931 the entire capital of J. I. Case Company was turned over 68 times.[1] Again, in 1929 when the pool in Radio Corporation of America was at its peak of activity, sales of the stock in one day were equal to 10% of all listed shares of the corporation. There is no doubt that in the old, unregulated market of the past, market activity in certain stocks exceeded all necessary requirements for making marketable, liquid investments. This was particularly true when there was so much manipulation in the market and artificial market activity was an important implement in attaining a pool objective of higher prices. With today's substantial controls over the market by the SEC and the Exchange, it is unlikely that another J. I. Case situation of 1931 or a Radio Corporation of America operation of 1929 will again take place. Manipulation and pool activity are largely ghosts of the past. However, excessive speculation can and does still have its effect on the market from time to time.

Although turnover of individual stocks in any given year might feature turnover of 100% or more, the turnover of stocks as a whole was in a range of 15–25% for many years until quite recently. In 1928, when speculation was rampant, the turnover of stock was 132% and in 1929, 119%. The latter levels have not been approached in more than a half-century. Even the turnover rates of between 30–50% in the early 1980s were considered to be remarkably high when compared with the years from 1930–1980.

A third criticism of the performance of this function made in the past has been that the continuity of liquidity in the market was more apparent than real. If everyone tried to liquidate one's investments, this characteristic of the market would disappear; there would not be enough buyers and the market would collapse as in 1929. Although there may be liquidity as long as there are only a few sellers disposing of their securities, this characteristic may disappear under pressure. It is, of course, true that in severe market breaks, buying power is weaker than selling pressure and liquidity may vanish temporarily. The rapid responses to selling pressure after shocks to the market such as President Eisenhower's heart attack, President Kennedy's assassination, and the Chinese attack on American forces in Korea, among others, suggest, however, that the argument is not too strong. Delays in trading in most issues seldom exceeded two hours, and most orders in the market were executed before the ends of such days. Buying power was found quickly; sellers found liquidity in the sense that they were able to exchange their securities for cash with little delay.

In fairness to the exchanges, too, we should point out that lack of liquidity is not a characteristic unique to the stock market in times of crisis. The same situation in the past has prevailed in banking, commodities, and real estate.

---

[1]John T. Flynn, *Security Speculation* (New York: Harcourt, Brace & World, Inc., 1934), p. 303.

At the depth of the Great Depression of the 1930s, our entire banking system collapsed; 40% of the banks disappeared in the process. Basic raw materials and real estate found few buyers even at drastic price reductions.

Under normal conditions, the stock exchanges provide for stocks of established companies a reasonably continuous market. The ability of the exchanges to provide a continuous market for seasoned stocks, thus creating marketable, liquid issues, is one of the two outstanding functions that they perform. All things considered, they probably do a better job with this function for stocks than does the over-the-counter market. With the improvement of electronic information facilities in recent years, the differences have been considerably reduced.

The NYSE specializes in making a market for strong, nationally known companies backed by substantial assets and earnings; the shares are seasoned before being listed. The American Stock Exchange, regional exchanges, and over-the-counter markets do more to create a market for the newer, "unseasoned" issues, although there are notable exceptions. Continuity of liquidity in some of these markets is sometimes deficient but still generally usual.

Fair Price Determination

The function of a fair price determination is as important as creating a continuous market. Prices are not fixed by the exchanges or by their members; prices are determined on the exchanges by matching buy and sell orders.

The stock exchanges facilitate the bringing together of buyers and sellers from all over the nation and often from foreign countries. Bids and offers of these buyers and sellers in an auction market determine the prices as of the moment. Specialists on the exchanges play a temporary, facilitating part in this determination; through time, however, prices are fixed only by the effective demand and supply from the investing public and securities issuers. The result is as near a market for free competition as can be found in this country; the commodity markets, of course, are similar in operation. In a day when price fixing or price control by private business or government agency is a dominant factor in price determination all over the world, the exchanges still create one of the most free markets in existence.

Two criticisms have been leveled at the performance of this function of the market. One has been that, in the past at least, prices were not determined fairly but were manipulated; they were driven up by pools and manipulators who used every trick in the business to create artificial valuations; they were pushed down by "bear raiders" without regard to fundamental values. There is, of course, truth in the indictment that much manipulation did exist in the market, and that the markets have been largely free of such operations only within comparatively recent years.

Price determination by manipulation is indefensible without doubt. It is not in the best interests of the exchanges in the long run nor in those of the public. An organized exchange today that permitted manipulation, even if the SEC did not stop it, would be rendering a great disservice to the securities market.

A second criticism made of the performance of this function is that speculation tends to send prices above investment worth at times and below it at other times. It is true, of course, that prices do show large fluctuations. Perhaps they were too high in 1929, too low in 1932. It is all very well to say that stocks should sell at "investment values" or "intrinsic worth," but what do these terms mean? There is no recognized standard for measuring the investment value of a stock. As we saw in Chapter 2, for example, there is little obvious relationship between book value, par value, and market value for many stock issues. Investment value reflects opinions of people about a future that is not clearly seen and that no person has predicted with certainty.

It is sometimes stated that stock prices should be capitalized on the basis of earnings; for example, stocks should sell at, say, ten times earnings. We know that the market has never operated under any such precise formula. From 1939 to 1985, the Dow Jones industrial stocks sold at an average price-earnings ratio of about 12:1. The ratio, however, has soared to more than 23:1 and fallen to less than 8:1 in that same period. Similarly, current yields averaged about 4% during this period but ranged from a high over 7% (1974) to a low below 3% (1968). What then is the "real value" of a typical Dow Jones industrial average in terms of price-earnings and yield? There is no exact standard.

About all that we can conclude under these conditions is that a stock is worth what it will bring. If it sells below net quick assets, as many did in 1932, that is what it is worth; if it sells at 20 times earnings, that is its value. Stock prices are not fixed by mathematical rules and ratios; they are determined by what buyer and seller are willing to bid and offer. Perhaps the most important factor is public confidence, and this cannot be measured.

Stock prices should be influenced neither by manipulation nor by speculative excess. They are not so influenced to any considerable extent today. Other than this, fair price determination is accomplished by matching what buyers bid and sellers offer in a free market and agree upon as reasonable.

Aid in Financing Industry

Industry receives most of its new capital by retention of earnings and sales of securities off the stock exchanges. The exchanges render a different service for the most part.

Insofar as industry raises capital by selling securities, it usually does so through the over-the-counter market. New bond and stock issues typically are underwritten by securities houses. Only after the issues are sold by the underwriting houses and have become publicly held are they listed on an exchange. New companies may wait for many years before their issues are listed. Hence, raising capital for new or old companies by the sale of new bond or stock issues depends more on effective action in the over-the-counter market than on the stock exchanges.

Actually, corporations tend to raise only a small fraction of their corporate funds by the sale of new securities issues. With few exceptions the source of well over one-half their funds typically is derived from such internal sources as retained profits plus depreciation allowances. Net new security issues have not provided more than 10% of funds from external sources in many years. Such external sources as long-term debt provide considerably more funds and even such debt sources as an increase in accounts payable exceed the funds received from new stock issues by a considerable amount.[2]

Our conclusions at this point, therefore, are (1) the exchanges are not the primary market for new securities; (2) new security issues are underwritten in the over-the-counter market, as a rule, before being listed on any exchange; and (3) most of the new capital of corporations comes from internal sources and external sources other than the sale of new securities.

The organized exchanges, however, do make a real contribution to the financing of industry, although it is an indirect and secondary one. This is in the sale of rights of listed companies. Corporations may sell common stock and convertible bonds in either of two ways: (1) through the use of rights issued under a privileged subscription and (2) through sale in the over-the-counter market at either public or private sale. A corporation listed on an exchange frequently sells new stock or convertible bonds to its present stockholders on the basis of a privileged subscription. In this procedure, described in detail in Chapter 23, the stockholders are given rights permitting them to buy the new stock or bonds at attractive prices. These rights have an immediate and wide market on the exchanges. Many stockholders, in some cases over one-half, dispose of these rights by sale rather than by surrender to the corporation in the purchase of the new securities. Here the exchanges perform their services. By creating a continuous market for these rights during the period of the privileged subscription, the exchanges have enabled the company to market the new stock successfully.

In case stockholders do not wish to invest additional capital in their company, they can sell the rights to investors who do wish to do so. Thus the corporation secures new funds from the capital market. In this instance the exchanges, in a real sense, do aid corporations in their financing and enable them to secure additional new money on favorable terms. It is true that a given corporation, not listed, could issue rights and raise capital from its stockholders or others, but it is believed that this would be a more difficult operation than if the rights enjoyed a wide market on the exchanges.

Listed companies can sell their securities more readily than those that are not listed, either through underwriting syndicates or directly to stockholders;

[2]Specific figures may be obtained from such Federal Reserve publications as the *Federal Reserve Bulletin* and the *Flow of Funds Accounts*.

this facilitates new financing. The fact that a new security is to be listed improves its initial sale. The market prices of the listed company securities indicate trend of growth and earnings in such companies; this condition does enable the successful companies to raise capital more easily because of this publicity if they decide to raise additional money through the capital market. The listed stock, but not necessarily the listed bond, has a better and wider market than the unlisted issue. These gains are substantial; they cannot, however, be used to justify the broad assertion, occasionally found in books, that the exchanges furnish the primary market for new capital to industry.

Discounting Function

In earlier years it was generally believed by careful students of the stock market that stock price movements preceded business activity moves. The stock market was said to discount business conditions a number of months in advance. The term *discount* as used in this discussion means anticipation of change. The theory was that stock traders anticipating better business and higher earnings would buy stocks. When a decline in activity and profits was anticipated, traders would dispose of stocks. Their ability to do so resulted from their unusually well-informed position and knowledge of production, sales, and business conditions in general. It was assumed they were able to trade advantageously on this knowledge. Since many corporate "insiders" were in the market in these early years, weight was given to the view. Their knowledge of bookings or advance orders, rates of production, purchasing inquiries, and similar matters gave them invaluable background facts with which to speculate.

This notion about the ability of the stock market to forecast business conditions was stated many years ago by Huebner in these words: "Without exception every major business depression or boom in this country has been discounted by our security markets from six months to two years before the dull times or the prosperity became a reality."[3]

A number of studies have been made of the relationship between stock price changes and business conditions. Ayres, who examined 25 business cycles from 1829 to 1938, concluded that in the typical cycle the peak of stock prices was seven months in advance of the peak of business, and that the low of stock prices was five months in advance of the low in business.[4]

A study made by the Cleveland Trust Company covered the period from 1871 to 1953.[5] During this period there were 39 cyclical turning points in business. The conclusion was that in 29 of the 39 cases, stock prices turned ahead of business; in two cases they turned in the same month, in four cases in a later month, and in four cases there was no satisfactory comparison.

[3]S. S. Huebner, *The Stock Market* (New York: Appleton-Century-Crofts, 1934), p. 39.
[4]L. P. Ayres, *Turning Points in Business Cycles* (New York: Macmillan, 1940), p. 67.
[5]*The Cleveland Trust Bulletin*, April 16, 1954, p. 3.

The average lead was found to be six months, but leads ran as high as 21 months and lags as much as three months.

Another thorough investigation was made by Geoffrey H. Moore and his colleagues at the National Bureau of Economic Research.[6] In a study of 26 business cycles from 1899 to 1958, they found that the Dow Jones industrial average of stock prices led the change in business activity in 31 out of 52 turns. The average lead was four and one-half months. This appears impressive. However, he also found that stock prices ran as much as 21 months ahead of the cycle change in one instance and as far behind as nine months in another instance. With this tremendous range of variation, the average lead of four and one-half months loses much of its significance as a reliable indicator of turning points in business conditions. The group did decide to retain stock price movement as one in a series of measures of economic activity to be used to indicate business conditions. A later study by the same organization, published in 1975, concluded that in the preceding 100 years stock price movements anticipated 33 of 44 business cycle turning points, but the average lead time was extended to 5–9 months.

However satisfactory stock prices may have been in discounting changes in business conditions in many years, they certainly have been less reliable on many other occasions. In 1929, the big break in stock prices came in late October. The Dow Jones industrial average, however, reached its peak in September. It was already a laggard in predicting the depression. Construction contracts had reached their peak in June 1928; wholesale prices, in July 1929; and industrial production, in August 1929. Only after a preceptible weakening of the economy took place did the stock market make its resounding crash in October. Only in signaling the severity of the depression did the market show real forcasting ability.

Since 1939 the market has been quite erratic in its discounting ability. Industrial production rose steadily from 1939 to 1942; in the same period, industrial stock prices fell consistently. Industrial production reached its war peak in December 1943, and then fell until January 1946; industrial stocks rose during this interval. The year 1946 has been called "the year of the depression that never came." In anticipation of this depression, stock prices broke sharply in August of that year and were down in 1947; industrial production, however, rose in both 1946 and 1947. Industrial production rose from 1949 to 1953; industrial stock prices also rose in that period. A small recession in production began in 1953 and continued into 1954; industrial stock prices, however, did a good job of discounting the subsequent recovery in production by reaching a trough and turning upward 11 months in advance of the index of industrial production. Out of these five movements in production, stock prices failed in three distinct instances to discount the trend of the business cycle, as measured by industrial production.

Anyone who seeks to forecast business conditions on the basis of stock

---

[6]Geoffrey H. Moore (ed.), *Business Cycle Indicators* (2 vols.; Princeton, N.J.: Princeton University Press, 1961), for example, vol. I, 56.

market behavior is certain to have disappointments. Little reliance can be placed on the theory that stock prices alone anticipate changes in business conditions by four and one-half months. This is true of all series that are used to forecast business changes when taken individually. As two authorities on the business cycle once said, " . . . no sequence of average leads of time series in past cyclical revivals can tell what the exact sequence will be at the next revival."[7]

Other Functions

Four important functions of stock exchanges have been discussed previously in some detail. Three other functions are now mentioned briefly. First, the exchanges provide accurate and continuous reports on sales and quotations, superior to those of any other type of market. Second, they cause the release of much information on the listed companies, particularly in regard to financial conditions. Finally, the exchanges attempt to protect security owners through regulations designed to eliminate dishonest and irregular practices in the brokerage business.

HISTORY OF THE NEW YORK STOCK EXCHANGE

A complete and authentic history of the NYSE and Wall Street is yet to be written. Unfortunately, in the formative years of the Exchange no one ever seriously attempted to write a systematic, thorough, and unbiased account of its development. Few writers, in fact, were at all interested in the early financial history of the nation, in spite of the great importance of its financial institutions in promoting its growth. This brief report can outline only a few of the significant developments in this long and eventful chronology.

The First Market in Stocks

There is considerable doubt as to when the first securities market in New York began to function. Some dealings in securities were probably transacted as early as 1725. These operations grew out of an auction market in lower New York at the foot of Wall Street. The market dealt in commodities, such as wheat and tobacco, as well as securities; even slaves were bought and sold until 1788. Certainly the market for securities was of little importance.

The earliest mention of any definite market for securities in the newspapers to be found in the *Diary,* or *Loudon's Register,* published in New York in March 1792. A brief item on that date indicated that dealers in stock met each noon at 22 Wall Street; sales were conducted by a joint arrangement

---

[7]Cited by F. L. Eames, *The New York Stock Exchange* (New York: Thomas G. Hall, 1894), p. 13.

of auctioneers and dealers.[8] New York at that time boasted of one chartered bank—the Bank of New York; the city's population was only 35,000.

Speculation in Revolutionary War Bonds

The securities market first achieved prominence when the federal government was established. Alexander Hamilton, one of the great financial minds of American history, was selected as the first Secretary of the Treasury. In his "Report" of January 1790, he recommended that the newly created government should fund all of the Revolutionary War bonds—those of both the Continental Congress and the 13 colonies. The holders of these issues were to get new 6 and 3% stock. Great speculation swept the country as bankers, brokers, governors, congressmen, and speculators scoured the nation to buy up the heavily depreciated bonds. Vast fortunes were made in the process.

Hamilton was able to fund the Continental bonds without great opposition, but met with stubborn resistance from Jefferson and others in his proposal to fund the colonial bonds. In a final congressional battle he lacked one vote in the Senate and five in the House. Hamilton and Jefferson then made one of the most remarkable "deals" in American history.[9] Hamilton was to get his refunding bill; Jefferson was to obtain his wish that the national capital be moved—first to Philadelphia for 10 years and then to the South. Great was the rejoicing in Wall Street.

Second in importance only to the speculation in war bonds was that in the stock of the First Bank of the United States. This bank, chartered in 1791, issued stock at 100. Immediately, great interest developed in its shares not only among financiers and brokers but also among public officials. Within a year they had climbed to 195; the shrewd speculators then took their profits and the stock plummeted to 108 in one short month. Indignation ran high as the large profits of speculators and politicians became known.

The Buttonwood Tree Agreement

The first dealers in securities were not brokers so much as they were merchants and auctioneers. Trading in securities did not become a specialty of those men until speculation in government securities began in 1790. The commodity dealers and the securities brokers now began to separate; the latter took up trading under a buttonwood tree at 68 Wall Street. Eventually the brokers became tired of the monopoly of the auctioneers who sold the stocks, and sought to create an organization of their own. In March 1792, they met secretly in Corre's Hotel to discuss the maneuver. On May 17, 1792, they drew up and approved in bold script the first document in the history of what was later to be the New York Stock Exchange. Its text was short, its intent unmistakable:

[8]*Ibid.*
[9]R. I. Warshow, *The Story of Wall Street* (New York: Greenberg, 1929), p. 30.

We the Subscribers, Brokers for the Purchase and Sale of Public Stock, do hereby solemnly promise and pledge ourselves to each other, that we will not buy or sell from this day for any person whatsoever, any kind of Public Stock, at less than one quarter of one per cent Commission on the Specie value and that we will give preference to each other in our Negotiations. In Testimony whereof we have set our hands this 17th day of May at New York, 1792.[10]

In brief, the agreement had two provisions: (1) the brokers were to deal only with each other, thereby eliminating the auctioneers, and (2) the commissions were to be 0.25%.

The Period 1792–1817

Comparatively few records are available about this formative period. Although the Buttonwood Tree Agreement centralized the market, there was no great volume of trading other than in government stock. In 1793 the Tontine Coffee House was erected; it was the most elaborate structure in Wall Street and became the first indoor headquarters of the newly formed brokers' organization. Actually, this structure was a merchants' exchange, and many kinds of business were conducted there, including that of brokerage, which was conducted in a room "high up under the eaves." On sunny days the brokers still met on the open pavement.

After speculation in the war bonds and in the stock of the First Bank died down, the business sank to a low level. The tactics of the speculators brought no little criticism upon the business, and public interest shifted to other commercial activities. Newspapers gave scant attention to securities prices and did not resume quotations until 1815. On March 10 of that year the *New York Commercial Advertiser* carried a complete list of 24 stocks.[11] Nearly all were government securities and bank stocks; only one manufacturing company graced the list. The small amount of trading at that time was confined largely to a few federal issues and the leading banks. There were few stocks except those issued to finance banks, insurance companies, canals, turnpikes, toll bridges, and water companies.

Brokers in that period were strictly brokers; they did not act as dealers. Hence, transactions in the market originated outside the small group of brokers.

The Indoor Exchange: 1817

A significant step toward a more formal organization was effected by the brokers in 1817. At that time there were 8 firms and 19 individuals engaged in the business. Business was improving as more and more corporations were organized in the country, and the nation increased in economic stature.

[10]Eames, *op. cit.*, p. 14.
[11]Warshow, *op. cit.*, p. 59.

Accordingly, it was decided that a change was in order. The New York brokers at that time were far behind their rival organization at Philadelphia. The latter group had been operating as an organized board of brokers since 1790; it had a president, secretary, and a complete organization with rules. So, in early 1817 the New York group sent a delegate to visit the Philadelphia Exchange and return with a complete report. Immediately upon the return of this one-man delegation, the New York group formally organized its association in very much the same way as that at Philadelphia.[12]

The new organization adopted the name New York Stock and Exchange Board. A constitution was drawn up and officers were elected. Rules were established; one of them forbade "wash sales." Commissions which ranged from 0.25 to 0.50% were introduced. The group decided it was no longer proper to meet in the office of Samuel J. Beebe in the old Tontine Coffee House, so it rented a room for its exclusive use at 40 Wall Street at $200 per year with janitor service furnished.

Trading procedure from that period took on greater regularity than it had in the past. The president of the Exchange called the stocks in order; there were about 30 on the list at the time. As each issue was called, the brokers made known their bids and offers. Business began about 11:30 A.M. and was usually completed by 1 P.M. Discipline was maintained by fines. Contracts were settled by 2:15 of the day following the transaction—a practice continued for more than 100 years.

From 1817 on, the Board became an exclusive organization. Members were voted in with great reluctance; three blackballs kept out an applicant, although there were many applications. In 1817 the initiation fee was the not exorbitant sum of $25; this was raised to $100 in 1827.[13]

The Period 1817 to the Civil War

In the years immediately following the formal organization of 1817, the Exchange Board moved a number of times seeking better quarters. Ten years later it was located in the Merchants' Exchange. Business, however, was still dull. It reached its all-time low of 31 shares on March 16, 1830; only two issues, whose total value was $3,470, were traded.

From this period on, trading on the Board improved steadily. The Mohawk and Hudson Railroad was the first railroad stock listed; trading started in August 1830. Other important stocks were to follow. Millions of dollars' worth of stocks and bonds began to be issued for transportation companies and internal improvements. By 1838 $175 million in securities had been issued by railroads, banks, canals, and turnpikes; many of them found their way to the Exchange Board.[14]

A great fever of land speculation developed in the country in the mid-1830s. Throughout the nation everyone bought and sold land at ever-in-

[12]J. K. Medbery, *Men and Mysteries of Wall Street* (Boston: Fields, Osgood, 1870), p. 288.
[13]Eames, *op. cit.*, p. 85.
[14]Medbery, *op. cit.*, p. 292.

creasing prices. Banks loaned huge sums on real estate; large quantities of credit poured in from Europe. Farmers neglected their crops in the wild craze. Speculation even reached the Exchange Board; a number of railroad and canal shares doubled and tripled in a few months between late 1834 and early 1835. At last the bubble burst; a crop failure of 1836 was followed by the collapse of land prices in the following year. Although the crisis was largely commercial, the financial district of New York was severely shaken. Many states repudiated their debts; bank failures were on every hand. Speculation again fell to low proportions.

The Exchange Board was burned out of its headquarters by the big fire of 1835. After various attempts to establish a permanent location, one of which was the temporary occupancy of a hayloft, it secured in 1842 a room in the new Merchants' Exchange Building, which was located on the present site of Citibank. At the same time it created the office of a paid president; the salary was to be $2,000 per year. Dues were also raised. In the 1840s telegraphic communications began; New York was greatly aided thereby in becoming a national securities market. It had long surpassed Philadelphia as the leading financial center.

The country and the Exchange recovered eventually from the panic of 1837. Nothing of great importance seems to have taken place in the history of the Exchange during the 1840s. By 1848 its membership had grown to 75. Both morning and afternoon sessions were held. After hours much trading was done in the street in front of the Merchants' Exchange. Perhaps 5,000 shares were turned over daily.

By 1848 the Exchange was reporting its financial condition; it appeared to be in excellent shape. Receipts were $10,396 per year and expenditures only $9,317, which left a modest surplus of $1,079.

The volume of outstanding securities grew rapidly in the 1840s and early 1850s. It was estimated that in 1854 there were outstanding securities in the country in excess of $1,178 million. State issues accounted for $111 million alone. Perhaps 18% of the grand total was owned by foreign investors.[15]

In the early 1850s money became more plentiful as wealth poured in from California. Speculation again was rife as the public flocked to the board rooms. So great was speculation that an "outside" board sprang up with even more brokers than the regular exchange. It leased quarters in the room below the Exchange Board, and constant communications were carried on between the two markets. Banks aided the speculative craze with a liberal hand. Brokers were known to deposit $1,500 in cash and then draw checks of $100,000–$300,000 that were promptly certified. A popular magazine reported that the 12 months that ended June 1853 had never been equaled in prosperity since the formation of the new nation.[16]

Suddenly the picture darkened. London began to sell American securities; banks called loans; deposits fell; the market crashed. In late 1853 it was said that Wall Street was as somber as a plague-stricken city and that brokers

[15]Secretary of Treasury, *Report on Foreign Holdings of American Securities*, 1854.
[16]Medbery, *op. cit.*, p. 306.

flitted in and out like uneasy ghosts. The Exchange almost ceased to exist. By the summer of 1855, however, prosperity was back again. Money was plentiful, crops were excellent, railway earnings were high, and speculation was again profitable. This pleasant situation was only of short duration; in 1857 the market declined abruptly. Erie stock fell from 64 to 18, and New York Central from 95 to 53. An irresponsible banking system had again created chaos in the nation's economic organization.

It is worth noting that the Exchange Board showed a marked strength in the crisis of 1857. Although its securities fell sharply, the decline was less than for unlisted ones, which had no market at all. The value of a seat became apparent to all brokers, and many applications were presented in 1858. The Board, however, was in no mood for new members. It had become, in great measure, an exclusive club, a situation of which the brokers were very proud. They wore silk hats and swallowtail coats during business hours. It was a genteel business as well as a profitable one. The entry of young men was frowned upon. To this end, initiation fees were raised to $1,000—a hard fact that kept many young men from joining the organization, even when they were able to overcome the hurdle of five blackballs for membership. As one broker of the period described it: "The old fellows were united together in a mutual admiration league, and fought the young men tooth and nail, contesting every inch of ground when a young man sought entrance to their sacred circle."[17]

Before the Civil War the call money market in New York had grown to extensive proportions. It enabled speculators to carry newly issued securities with bank credit and played no small part in keeping control of the railroads in the hands of American rather than foreign interests. Brokerage firms often advanced large sums to aid in the construction of railroads.

The volume of speculation showed a substantial increase in the late 1850s. In one month of 1856 trading reached 1 million shares; in one day of 1857 the volume was 71,000.

Certain changes in the administration of the Exchange Board were made in 1856.[18] The use of a paid president was discontinued; the position was made honorary. It was not until after the reorganization of 1938 that a salary was again paid to the head of the Exchange. Salaries, however, were paid to the first and second vice presidents, who conducted the "calls" of securities. The income of the organization was now supplemented by annual dues of $50 per member.

During the period of 1817–1860 Wall Street knew a few great market operators, but not as many as in later years. An outstanding example was Jacob Little, one of the greatest of all "bear operators." In 1837 he founded his own firm of Little and Company. Always consistently bearish, he capitalized on the Panic of 1837. He made and lost four fortunes; from his last defeat he never recovered. Caught short 100,000 shares of Erie stock in late 1856, he failed for $10 million. He had sold short too soon.

[17]Henry Clews, *Fifty Years in Wall Street* (New York: Irving, 1908), p. 7.
[18]Eames, *op. cit.*, p. 37.

The Civil War

The Civil War witnessed a wave of speculation in the nation that had never before been equaled. Securities, gold, and commodities were all subject to unbelievable activity. Solid business owners, brokers, lawyers, clergymen, society ladies, politicians—all were burned with the fever of speculation that continued from early morning to late hours of the night.

No fewer than four exchanges operated during the war. The New York Stock Exchange adopted its present name in 1863. In addition, there was an open air exchange, the forerunner of the present American Stock Exchange. It traded in the same stocks sold on the floor of the New York Stock Exchange and operated during those hours when the Exchange was not in session. In 1862 the "Coal Hole" was established. This was in a basement at 23 William Street; it was operated by a shrewd individual who charged an admission fee for its use. Still another exchange was formed in the room next to the New York Stock Exchange; it traded on what news it could get from the leading exchange.

Trading in gold on the NYSE began on the floor in 1861 as soon as the country refused to redeem its greenbacks in specie. Gold soon went to a premium and greenbacks sold at a discount. It was not long before trading in gold became so important that it overshadowed security trading. The Exchange authorities, mindful of this fact as well as the unpatriotic implications of such activity, banned the sale of gold; the activity was immediately transferred to other exchanges, notably the "Coal Hole" and later the Gold Exchange. Gilpin's news room at William Street and Exchange Place was also transformed into a gold market with a $25 a year admission fee. A vast amount of gold speculation took place in these two markets. In 1864 speculation became so rampant that still another group, the Gold Board, was organized. The "Gold Room" was established, and the major part of this gold trading activity left the "Coal Hole" and Gilpin's to center there.

Greenbacks heavily depreciated during the war and fluctuated with every news story of the war's progress. Gold sold at heavy premiums in terms of the inconvertible paper currency. News was carried to the gold exchanges with greater rapidity than the Associated Press could bring it to the newspapers. Gold first sold at a premium in April 1862. As Confederate successes mounted, premiums advanced. On July 11, 1864, gold was selling at 285; greenbacks were worth 35 cents on the dollar.

The government made many fruitless attempts to stave off the steady depreciation of its currency. In February 1863 Congress made it a penal offense to offer loans on bullion above par; the law was ineffective. In April 1864 Secretary Chase attempted to sell gold at 165; the only effect was a sharp break in the market and a number of bankruptcies and the attempt was abandoned when the Treasury was unable to release a sufficient supply of gold. Congress passed the Gold Bill on June 21, 1864, which prohibited speculation in gold; gold rose from 210 to 250 and the act was repealed in two weeks. Even the successful termination of the war did not eliminate this curious speculative activity.

The Exchange suffered from two serious defects in the Civil War period: (1) its failure to provide a continuous market and (2) its lack of an effective administrative organization.

Black Friday

The most remarkable episode of the entire era of gold speculation developed in late 1869, four years after the close of the Civil War.[19] Jay Gould, called "the smartest man in Wall Street" by no less a personage than Commodore Vanderbilt, attempted to corner the entire gold market. The country was not yet back on a hard money basis; the government was not selling gold. Gould, with close relationships to leading political figures in Washington, including President Grant's son-in-law, was confident that the government would not sell gold. With his associate, Jim Fisk, he began to buy all the gold offered for sale in the Gold Room; it was then quoted at 130. Gould bought not only for his account, but also for that of Grant's son-in-law and the President's private secretary, although the latter refused the transaction. Confident that his scheme was politically secure, Gould accumulated through several firms contracts to deliver gold totaling $50 million. As there was only $20 million in gold on the market, more gold had been sold than could possibly be delivered on the future contracts. Grant's son-in-law, now thoroughly alarmed, withdrew from the deal, and this ended Gould's political ties with the government. In a short time the manipulator had accumulated $100 million in gold contracts. This had to be unloaded before the government would sell the precious metal. In order to do this he ordered his own associates, Jim Fisk and Albert Speyer, Fisk's chief broker, to buy gold. On Thursday, September 23, 1869, he was able to sell his entire $100 million in gold at the top of the market because of Fisk's support.

Friday, September 24, will always be known as "Black Friday." Fisk continued his buying as gold went to 145, 150, 155, 160, 161, 162. Then came from Washington the incredible news: the government was selling gold! Indescribable chaos took possession of trading as frenzied brokers in wild shouts sought to sell gold. Fisk and Speyer in futile attempts bid 160, 170, and 180 for gold; no one paid any attention to them as gold dropped to 140; as the gong sounded the close of the market, it stood at 135. Gould had failed to corner the market.

Thousands of failures resulted from "Black Friday." Gould's profits had been great, but Fisk and his two brokers, Belden and Speyer, were hopelessly involved. In a day when political corruption was commonplace and justice a travesty, Gould devised a simple plan. Fisk, who had made no commitments on paper, repudiated all of his transactions. Belden and Speyer assumed all legal responsibility for them and went into bankruptcy. As a reward Gould pensioned the two brokers for life. Despite endless lawsuits the creditors could not and did not reach Gould. And thus ended one of the most bizarre manipulations in American history.

[19]Clews, *op. cit.*, p. 181.

The Great Operators

During the period from 1860 to 1900, some of the greatest manipulations in the history of the stock market took place. Daniel Drew, Commodore Vanderbilt, Jim Fisk, Jay Gould, Sam Hallet, W. R. Travers, Leonard W. Jerome and his older brother, Addison, Anthony Morse, Jay Cooke, James R. Keene, Russel Sage—to mention only a few—were truly giants in their day. Each made great fortunes in securities; many of them died in bankruptcy. Giving no quarter to their opponents and asking none, they fought for fortune in the market with every weapon at their command. The only law they knew was the law of the jungle; their ethics, however unsavory they may appear today, were the ethics of their day. They played the hard game of business as the rules were known in that kaleidoscopic, but historic, epoch. Space prevents an adequate description of their many operations; a few are related briefly in Chapter 16.

The Exchange Expands

As the Civil War ended, the NYSE began a period of rapid expansion. The West was opening up rapidly; railroads were spreading "like measles at a girls' boarding school," as Daniel Drew described it; manufacturing was achieving new records in mass production; and the securities market was growing apace. The vast development of the railroads was particularly important to the Exchange, since those corporations were the chief issuers of securities in the trading market. About 70,000 miles of lines had been completed by 1873; their outstanding stocks and bonds totaled $3,780 million.

As the volume of trading on the Exchange improved, the system of "calls" was abandoned; this was about 1867. By 1871 the market was definitely operating on a continuous trading basis and the present auction method was in full operation.

New inventions greatly aided the mechanical efficiency of the Exchange. In 1867 the electric stock ticker facilitated the transmission of quotations and popularized trading. The telephone was installed in 1878 and linked the trading floor with the brokerage offices. An expansion of the telegraph system linked New York with brokerage offices in other cities. Seats were definitely declared salable in 1868; at that time they were worth $7,000–$8,000.

In 1869 the Exchange made far-reaching changes in its organization; the 533 members of the Exchange joined with the 354 members of the Open Board of Brokers and the 173 members of the Government Bond Department. The Exchange then had 1,060 members. The number was limited; a membership or "seat" became salable personal property, and from that date a membership could be obtained only by an applicant's buying the seat from a retiring member.

At the same time the Exchange changed its form of administration. Until then policies of management were submitted to a vote of members. As this was no longer practical, a new constitution was adopted. The Exchange was to be managed by a Governing Committee with executive, legislative, and judicial powers. An elaborate committee system was set up, which continued to function until the reorganization of 1938. The Governing Committee of 28 members was subdivided into seven standing committees, which were responsible for such matters as admissions, stock list, commissions, arbitration, and finance. The president continued to serve without salary and was an active broker.

Membership was increased by 40 to 1,100 in 1879. The proceeds of the sale of the new memberships were used by the Exchange to expand its physical plant at Broad and Wall Street. The number remained unchanged until 1929.

The Exchange introduced a number of much-needed regulations in 1869. Among them were certain listing rules. Listed companies were required to maintain both transfer agents and registrars as a safeguard to prevent over-issue of stocks; this was a prevalent practice in the easygoing days of Drew and Schuyler.

Trading in 1870

The character of trading in the post-Civil War period is well described by Medbery.[20] He relates that in 1870 trading on the Exchange was divided into two lists: a Regular List of 278 securities, which consisted of railroad stocks and bonds, city stocks, state bonds, and miscellaneous issues; and a Free List, which consisted of any issues that brokers desired to trade in. The trading in government bonds was in a separate room; all other securities were sold in the Regular Room. Discipline was maintained by fines, for example, $5 for smoking a cigar, $10 for standing on a chair, $.50 for knocking off a man's hat, and $10 for throwing a paper dart. The call method was still used, the Regular List being handled first. Rules permitted cash, regular way, buyer's option, and seller's option deliveries; the first two types were used most. No sale could be made for less than 5 shares; 10 shares was the real unit. Stocks were quoted in the same fractional points as today.

Nearly all of the trading was for speculation; few bought stocks for investment. Bank credit was abundant; a broker could deposit $5,000 and have checks certified for as much as $200,000. Brokers carried stock on margin for customers at interest rates of 6 or 7%; they allowed interest on margin deposited. Margins were very low; a good customer, properly introduced and financially responsible, could buy $1,000 in stock with a $50 margin. On active, speculative stocks, the banks would lend up to 80 to 90% of selling value.

The Period 1870 to World War I

The post-Civil War expansion, which was particularly outstanding in railroads, came to an abrupt halt in 1873 as panic gripped the country. In several

---

[20]Medbery, *op. cit.,* chaps. 2–5.

years improvement was again observable. From 1875 to 1879 about 51 million shares were traded on the NYSE annually; by the next five years activity had doubled to 104 million per year.[21]

In 1873 the Exchange was forced to close down for the second time in its history; the first time was in 1835, when a fire forced the organization to cease operations for a week until it found new quarters. This time the cause was the failure of Jay Cooke and Company, promoters of the Northern Pacific Railroad. Panic gripped Wall Street as the Exchange remained closed for 12 days. Fifty-seven Exchange members and several important banks failed. Exchange business became depressed for several years.

Several noteworthy changes were made in this period in the operation of the NYSE. In 1885 the Exchange provided for an Unlisted Department. This new department was created to permit greater trading in the ever-expanding number of industrials; it was to continue until 1910. Although railroad stocks were still the chief center of activity, the growth of giant trusts and combinations whetted the public's interest in these new industries. The Sherman Antitrust Act of 1890 had been passed to stem the flood of monopolies; it did little to curtail the growth of gigantic consolidations.

The Exchange, after a number of informal and voluntary attempts, all of which ended in failure, established a successful clearing house in 1892. The new plan met with immediate success, but it was to be 28 years before the present Stock Clearing Corporation was organized.

As the century drew to a close, the old manipulators were largely gone and a new group of financial leaders rose to power in Wall Street. These men were great railway magnates, bankers, and industrialists. They were builders rather than destroyers, even though their methods were often as ruthless as any employed by the early manipulators. Among them was J. Pierpont Morgan, a man of tremendous prestige in banking, railroads, and industrial combinations; his firm became the most powerful in Wall Street. Jacob H. Schiff of Kuhn, Loeb and Company was also a highly influential investment banker. Hill and Harriman were outstanding names in railroading. Rockefeller and his associates, Rogers, Pratt, and Flagler, held the controlling interest in the Standard Oil Trust. Andrew Carnegie and Charles Schwab were leaders in the steel industry. Many of these men, such as Rockefeller and Carnegie, never were in the stock market; others, such as Harriman, operated in it constantly. In this period the great investment banks dominated the securities markets more and more.

As the great industrial combinations rose to prominence, speculative activity took place in them. This first wave of speculation ended in the Panic of 1893. The depression of that year was one of the most severe in the nation's history. Railroads as well as industrials were hard hit. One-fourth of the railroads in the country were in bankruptcy courts, including such giants as

---

[21]H. P. Willis and J. I. Bogen, *Investment Banking* (rev. ed.; New York: Harper & Row, 1936), p. 228.

the Union Pacific, Santa Fe, Northern Pacific, and Reading. The economic distress of the country was extreme. Those were "hard times" indeed; the term "depression" had not yet entered the popular jargon. The stock market was similarly stricken.

The second speculative wave in industrial combinations ran from 1897 to 1903. During that period J. P. Morgan, then at the peak of his power, organized the first billion dollar corporation, the U. S. Steel Corporation. Its stock, although entirely "water" at the time, became a dominant stock market leader at once, a position it has retained ever since. Many of the other consolidations, however, proved to be disappointments, and speculative interest after 1903 turned elsewhere.

The turn of the century saw a pronounced expansion in trading on the NYSE. The annual stock volume, which had been only 57 million shares in 1896, rose to 265 million in 1901. The bond volume increased from $394 million to almost $1 billion in the same period. Huge amounts of new capital were authorized. In 1899 industrial corporations alone issued $2,244 million in new securities. New railroad issues totaled $107 million in the same year and increased to $527 million three years later.[22] Henry Clews estimated that $6 billion was the total capitalization of new combinations from 1897 to 1902.[23]

After the nation had decided unequivocally to go on the gold standard in 1900, the country began to undergo a monetary inflation. Prices by 1907 were up 16% from those of 1893. For ten years a continuous growth in production, corporation earnings, and dividends had taken place; and the market rose. In late 1906, however, signs of distress began to appear; new securities were not selling and the market weakened as big operators unloaded $800 million in securities. In March 1907, panic broke out in Wall Street both on the Exchange and in banking. All leading stocks showed severe declines. Many leading trust companies came under suspicion; the Knickerbocker Trust Company closed its doors, and bank runs became general. Banks all over the country partially suspended specie payments. Call money rose to 125%. The "rich man's panic" was short but severe.

The Exchange came under fire in two investigations before World War I. The first was the Hughes Committee investigation of 1909. Although highly critical of certain speculative practices, the committee did not press for legislation but recommended that the Exchange itself adopt a more vigorous program of self-regulation. The Pujo investigation in 1912, although authorized to study the stock market, was noted largely for its scrutiny of the so-called money trust.

There were only 145 stocks and 162 bonds listed on the "Big Board" in 1869 when the Exchange was consolidated. By 1914 those had grown to 511 and 1,082, respectively. The market, however, was still a professional one when the war broke out in Europe, although many members of the public

---

[22]*Ibid.*, p. 233.
[23]Clews, *op. cit.*, p. 772.

were attracted during peak periods of activity. The *New York Times* in 1914 was carrying only two pages of financial news, and one column was sufficient for stock quotations. The *New York Herald Tribune* had only three persons in its whole financial department. About 150 million shares were listed on the Exchange contrasted with more than 6½ billion today. The typical stockholder of the newspaper cartoonist was the pudgy banker with the silk hat and striped trousers.

Corporations did not boast of vast stockholder lists before World War I. Much of the stock of the giant industrials was carried in "street names" for speculation. American Telephone and Telegraph had 8,000 stockholders in 1901 and U.S. Steel 14,000. DuPont had not yet gone into industrial chemistry; it had only 2,800 stockholders as late as 1922. The vast Standard Oil empire was still closely held; Standard Oil Company (New Jersey) reported only 8,300 stockholders in 1920. The public was not yet "in the market."

In 1910 a corporation that has been eclipsed only recently and briefly by AT&T as a money maker and seldom as a stock market leader was formed from 24 corporations, many of them worthless. It was General Motors, promoted by W. C. Durant, one of the greatest bull market operators since Commodore Vanderbilt. He lost control of the company to New York bankers in 1911, but ousted them from power in 1916. At that time the company had only 473 stockholders. By 1919 Durant had rolled up a large fortune. In the following year the market fell and General Motors stock sagged to 12; Durant was bankrupt. In the 1920s he attempted to regain his position but his new automobile company was not a success. Reentering the stock market, he produced another large fortune by 1929; again, market reverses destroyed his fortune and he died a comparatively poor man. His creation, General Motors, however, enjoyed brilliant industrial and financial management and went on to unprecedented growth and prosperity. Over a 40-year period it has been a market favorite.

World War I

The opening of World War I brought with it a great crisis. In the early summer of 1914 war clouds loomed ominously over Europe. Security selling by European interests developed rapidly, as attempts were made to convert values into gold in anticipation of needs at home. Stocks dropped about 20 points on July 31, when the London Stock Exchange closed down. A hasty meeting of leading bankers and New York Stock Exchange officials was called. When convincing evidence was presented of a new avalanche of selling orders from Europe, it was decided to shut the Exchange indefinitely. It closed the next morning and remained closed until December 12, 1914; this was the first such closing since the collapse of Jay Cooke and Company in 1873. Trading was resumed on a restricted basis, but was not satisfactory for months. Eventually war orders poured in from Europe and prosperity began to stimulate industry. Speculation in some favored industries, known as "war brides," became pronounced; the market was again functioning in normal stride.

One important effect of the war was the great public participation in government bond buying. For the first time in the country's history the general populace became security conscious. The government, with every resource at its command, pushed the distribution of Liberty bonds. The taste for security ownership was stimulated; it developed with extreme rapidity in the next decade. Before the war it was estimated that there were only 200,000 security owners in the country; afterward there were 20 million, including those who owned government bonds.[24]

The New Era

The fabulous 1920s were called the New Era by some who had more imagination than foresight. The country witnessed a short but severe deflation in 1920 and 1921. There were great speculative losses in securities, commodities, and land. In several years, however, prosperity was again blanketing the nation as industry boomed. The world was at peace "for all time," it was hoped; factories were humming; prices were stable; the banking system was sound; the market was better and better. It was generally believed that depressions were a thing of the past and that the nation was on a permanent plateau of sustained and stable prosperity.

An unusual set of favorable circumstances paved the way for the market boom of the late 1920s. Our nation had emerged from the conflict the strongest and soundest nation in the world, with an incomparable productive system. We were now a great creditor nation and began to pour millions abroad; these great loans, which totaled $15 billion in a decade, sustained our foreign trade in no small measure. The government was friendly to big business and combinations grew on every hand—in banking, public utilities, automobiles, foods, motion pictures, and soon petroleum, electrical equipment and so on. Promising new industries, such as radio and aviation, stimulated investment. Other industries, such as motion pictures, chemicals, automobiles, and electrical equipment, made remarkable progress. Investment bankers perfected the art of wide security distribution. Common stocks achieved wide popularity, not only those of well-established companies on the NYSE, but also those of newly promoted corporations. The terms *holding company* and *investment trust* became magic terms. To further the boom, the Federal Reserve banks initiated an "easy money" policy in 1927.

Common stocks became "the thing" for both investment and speculation. The number of new stock issues floated in the capital market increased from 1,822 in 1921 to 6,417 in 1929. In the latter year, 62% of all new security issues were stocks, contrasted with only 15% eight years earlier. The year 1929 saw the capital market absorb $5,924 million in new stock issues, con-

[24]Willis and Bogen, *op. cit.*, p. 235.

trasted with only $1,087 million three years before. Stock prices rose in the same remarkable degree. The market value of all listed stocks on the Exchange increased from $27.1 billion in early 1925 to $89.7 billion in September 1929. The *New York Times* industrial average, which had reached a low of 66.24 in 1921, closed at 180.57 in 1925; after a short decline in 1927 it skyrocketed to the all-time high of 469.49 on September 19, 1929, or seven times its 1921 low.

With all of this expansion the volume of trading on the Exchange grew rapidly as the public entered the market in greater and greater numbers. Never had brokers had so many customers; never had the trading floor witnessed such activity. From an annual volume of 171 million shares in 1921, trading rose to 450 million in 1925 and in 1926, 920 million in 1928, and 1.1 billion in 1929. Brokers' loans were up to $8,549 million. Probably a million Americans were carrying 300 million shares on margin.

Then came the storm. On Wednesday, October 23, 1929, the market cracked. On a 6-million-share volume, the *New York Times* industrial average dropped 31 points. On the next day, the market dropped again as the ticker ran hours behind on a new record total of 12,895,000 shares. On October 28 the industrial average fell another 49 points, followed by 43 points on October 29 when 16,410,000 shares changed hands. That volume figure would not be exceeded until 1968. The New Era was over.

From 1929 to mid-1932 security values melted away as the country slid into its longest and worst depression. Consumer demand, industrial production, and security prices all eroded severely. The Dow Jones industrial average fell over 89% from 386 to 41. The 386 level would not be reached again until 1954. The listed value of stocks on the Exchange slumped from $89.7 to $15.6 billion. U.S. Steel dropped from 262 to 21; AT&T from 310 to 70; New York Central from 256 to 9; GM from 92 to 7; and RCA from 115 to 3. Seldom in all its turbulent history had gloom been so impenetrable on Wall Street. Grave troubles, however, were still ahead.

The Senate Investigation of 1933–1934

The most exhaustive investigation ever made by the federal government of the securities market and the Exchange was that of the Committee on Banking and Currency of the Senate in 1933 and early 1934. Like many investigations of that day, it had two purposes: (1) to uncover real or alleged flaws and irregularities in our economic system and (2) to build up a strong political support by extensive publicity for the forthcoming legislation that was to follow the investigation.

The Pecora investigation, as it was often called because Ferdinand Pecora served as chief examiner for the committee, ran for 17 months. It examined many of the most powerful figures in Wall Street: bank presidents, exchange officials, prominent brokers, investment bankers, and utility executives. When the investigation was over, 12,000 pages of testimony, which filled 20 volumes, had been taken. Many irregularities, unethical practices, and often cases of outright fraud were uncovered by the inquiry, which was highly publicized by the press.

Four federal laws developed from the investigation: the Banking Act of 1933, the Securities Act of 1933, the Securities Exchange Act of 1934, and the Public Utility Holding Company Act of 1935. The Securities Exchange Act of 1934 subjected all stock exchanges to extensive government control for the first time. Temporarily, power to enforce the Act was given to the Federal Trade Commission. Shortly thereafter a new and powerful federal agency, the Securities and Exchange Commission, was established to enforce the Act. Its work is described in detail in Chapter 17.

The Exchange Reorganizes

Although the Securities and Exchange Act and the SEC compelled the NYSE to make a number of changes in rules, for a while there was no significant change in its organization. As early as 1935 the chairman of the SEC had suggested to the Exchange administration that a reorganization was in order. A discussion of the proposal revealed divided reactions from Exchange members. Many of the commission firms believed some change was in order; the floor members, who owned most of the seats, opposed any such plan. A stalemate existed between the SEC and the Exchange until 1937, when the new chairman of the SEC, William O. Douglas, determined that a thorough reorganization of the Exchange was in order, whether it received a majority endorsement by Exchange members or not. In a very strong statement, dated November 23, 1937, Douglas stated in part:

> Operating as private membership associations, exchanges have always administered their affairs in much the same manner as private clubs. For a business so vested with public interest, this traditional method has become archaic. The task of conducting the large exchanges (especially the New York Stock Exchange) has become too engrossing for those who must also run their own business . . . Their management should not be in the hands of professional traders but in fact, as well as nominally, in charge of those who have a clearer public responsibility.[25]

The implications of the statement were clear. The Exchange must reorganize; there must be full-time paid executives to run the Exchange; there must be public representation in Exchange affairs; the club method of operation was archaic and undemocratic. To this many of the Exchange members agreed; others, often labeled the "Old Guard" by the press, were strongly opposed.

After some reluctance the Governing Committee gave the president of the Exchange power to appoint the so-called Conway Committee, which

---

[25]*The New York Times*, November 24, 1937.

was composed of five members of the Exchange and four prominent outside representatives and headed by a well-known manufacturer. The actual writing of the report was largely the responsibility of a rising young member of the Exchange, William McChesney Martin, Jr., who was thoroughly in favor of the reorganization plan; he had been named as secretary of the committee and was destined to be the first president of the reorganized Exchange. The committee was appointed on December 10, 1937, and made its report on January 27 of the following year. Specific recommendations were made for a thorough reorganization; among them were (1) a full-time paid president; (2) an entirely new Board of Governors with representation for nonmember brokers and out-of-town members; (3) public representation on the Board; and (4) a drastic revision of the committee system.

The committee report, which embodied most of Chairman Douglas's ideas on reorganization, was strongly praised by him as a sound step in the right direction. The great majority of the membership of the Exchange favored the recommendations of the report, but a few of the "Old Guard" counseled delay. Then a remarkable incident occurred. At 10:05 on March 8, 1938, the gong of the Exchange sounded and the president announced: "Richard Whitney and Company suspended . . . conduct inconsistent with just and equitable principles of trade." The leader of the Old Guard was not only bankrupt but guilty of dishonesty; his defalcations were extensive and could neither be concealed nor made good. The battle for reorganization was over. On March 17 the Governing Committee expelled Richard Whitney, former President of the Exchange; on the same day, by an overwhelming vote, it adopted the new plan of reorganization. The Whitney scandal was a bitter dose. Out of the reorganization fight, however, the Exchange emerged an organization with greater public responsibility than ever before and with rules that should make another Whitney scandal impossible. The new Board of Governors was voted into office in May 1938. The first President, Mr. Martin, took office shortly afterward.

History: 1939–1970

Many chapters in this book cover the changes in the operation of the NYSE since 1939 and the events that have affected its affairs. They will be only summarized at this point.

Despite the world-shaking events that developed in this period, the Exchange has operated in an atmosphere that has been quiet compared with many of the turbulent episodes that colored its career in earlier years.

World War II broke out in the late summer of 1939. Hitler's legions stormed into Poland on September 1. The *New York Times* 50-stock average gained a full point. On Sunday, September 3, England and France declared war on Germany. Monday was a holiday. On Tuesday the market rose sharply by six points. It continued to rise and by the end of the month there was an increase of another seven points. Industrial stocks were especially bullish during September and climbed 25 points as traders dreamed of luscious war profits. A period of pessimism and doubt, however, engulfed the market in May 1940 as the allies suffered heavy reverses. By April 1942, industrial stocks were down by one-third from their best levels at the opening of the war. A bull market then began; it did not end until August 1946, when fear of a phantom depression that never appeared unsettled the world of finance.

Stocks remained in the doldrums from late 1946 to 1949, and then began the longest bull market on record. Although the shock of the Korean War brought an immediate and drastic break in prices, the decline ran its course in two months. Recovery then became pronounced and the bull market re-emerged. There was a slight decline in early 1953 as a mild recession began. This was reversed in late 1953. The rise in the *New York Times* industrial average from September 1953 to December 1955 was 292 points, or 107%, one of the most amazing bull markets on record. The only hesitancy in this rise took place in September 1955 when the President of the United States suffered a heart attack. The ensuing break caused the widest one-day liquidation in points since 1929 and the greatest dollar loss in history. The market made a sharp recovery the following day and reached a new all-time high before the close of the year. These levels were maintained to mid-1957 when a second break in the market occurred. Between July and December of that year the *New York Times* average fell about 140 points, or 20% from its high point. Through 1958 and 1959 the market rose rapidly again; the *New York Times* average rose 200 points. A dip in 1960 was offset by a rise in 1961.

During the period 1939–1962 there was a minimum of criticism of the Exchange and its operations as compared with earlier years. The regulations of the SEC and the Exchange on manipulation and irregular practices were effective in shielding the Exchange from the bitter criticism that was so common from 1929 to 1933. Few incidents of irregularity ever appeared in the press.

There were two major investigations of the stock market during the latter part of this period: the so-called friendly investigation of early 1955 and the broad study begun in 1961. The first was conducted by the Senate Committee on Banking and Currency and was known as the *Fulbright investigation* because the Committee was headed by Senator Fulbright. The investigation was prompted by the uneasiness at Washington about the continued rise in stock prices and the fear that "another 1929" might be imminent.

The investigation began by mailing questionnaires to some 5,500 brokers, dealers, investment advisers, and others and to 113 economists. The study started on March 3 with the calling to the witness chair of many highly placed individuals in the field of finance and government. The investigation was at first concerned with the problem of whether stocks were too high in relation to earnings, dividends, and future prospects. There was no unanimity of opinion. Naïve opinions were expressed by supposedly well-informed persons, such as the one that book values are a key factor in determining stock prices. This line of investigation ceased in a few days.

The examination of the market then proceeded to a study of the possibility that the country might be surging into a period of overoptimism and over-speculation. The views of one economist were so pessimistic in this regard that a sharp break in the market took place after his testimony. Whether or not this was actually the cause of the break was disputed; the U.S. President announced at the same time that he had asked Congress for a new Negotiation Act that would affect the profits of airplane companies. Subsequent testimony was very conflicting as to the credit situation, some viewing it with alarm and others with composure. Few found the market or credit situation at a dangerous level. There was no mention of possible manipulation.

During the investigation no one, not even the investigating committee, appeared eager to cause any disturbance of the market. Actual criticism of the operations of the Exchange was scarcely voiced during the investigation. In fact, the most bitter part of the investigation appeared when political leaders of one party accused those of the other that they were trying to wreck the inquiry. The investigation closed in late March. No new laws grew out of it nor were any new regulations put into effect. The market and the public soon forgot the whole matter. The final report of the Senate Committee made no drastic recommendations.

The second investigation was an intensive inquiry by the SEC into the ways in which different operations were performed in the exchange market and by the brokerage community. The primary purpose of this investigation, which was known as "The Special Study," was to isolate and quantify the cause of the erratic behavior of the stock market in the recent past, particularly in May of 1962.

The Dow Jones average had ranged over more than 100 points over a period of one and one-half months until on May 29 it surged to close at 604. Most observers blamed the violent market movements upon the Kennedy Administration's enforcing of a U.S. Steel recision of a price increase rather than upon widespread manipulation or illegal conduct.

The remainder of the 1960s did not involve any great changes in exchange operation except for such mechanical improvements as the installation of a high-speed stock ticker in 1964.

History Since 1970

The decade of the 1970s saw changes in the structure and operations of the Exchange unequaled since the 1930s. The approval of public ownership of member firms in 1970 was followed a year later by the listing of the stock of a member organization (Merrill Lynch) on the Exchange.[26]

The first of the major developments of the 1970s began when the Exchange Board of Governors appointed former Federal Reserve Chairman William McChesney Martin, Jr. to conduct a study of the constitution, rules, and

---

[26]The first member corporation of the Exchange was Woodcock, Hess & Co. admitted in 1953.

procedures of the Exchange to determine how the public and financial community could best be served. His conclusions were published in August 1971 in his "Report with Recommendations." Included in the report were 14 recommendations, six of which could be implemented by the Exchange and eight by the government or other organizations. The changes included greater use of modern communication systems, development of a national exchange system, and development of a consolidated exchange tape.

Following the study, a reorganization of the NYSE was approved in 1972. The 33-member Board of Governors was replaced by a Board of Directors consisting of 10 public directors, 10 securities industry directors, and a full-time salaried chairperson. In August 1972, the first salaried chairman, James J. Needham, took office.

The increasing pressure by the SEC to develop a Central Market System was implemented in 1972 with a system of competing quotations. The thought behind such competing quotations was that bid-and-ask quotations exchanged among the NYSE and regional exchanges would provide investors with the fairest possible prices. A major step in advancing the central market concept was the consolidated tape that indicated the prices, volumes, and quotations for securities in all markets in which such securities traded. The pilot version of the consolidated tape was introduced in October 1974, and the full version of the tape went into operation in June 1975.

The development of the National Market System became a reality when President Ford signed the Securities Acts Amendments of 1975, which represented the most comprehensive securities legislation in over 40 years. Major provisions dealt with the development of a national securities market system and expanded regulation both by the exchanges and by the SEC.

The design of the National Market System was left to the securities industry, but Congress mandated a competitive environment that would result in maximum efficiency and liquidity. In pursuit of this goal, the NYSE developed the Intermarket Trading System (ITS) in 1977. This was a major contribution toward development of the National Market System.

The ITS is an electronic linkage designed to connect all competing markets. It enables brokers at one market center to connect into another market center electronically to obtain a better price for their customers. On April 17, 1978, the ITS began pilot operations on the New York and Philadelphia Stock exchanges. It was soon expanded to include the American, Boston, Cincinnati, Midwest, and Pacific exchanges to link all seven major exchanges in a nationwide trading and communication network designed to enable brokers to execute orders wherever the best price was indicated by the Composite Quotation System. The system was further expanded in 1982 to include a small group of listed stocks traded over-the-counter.

Changes in the commissions charged by the Exchange occurred from time to time as the volume of trading increased and as costs rose. Although changes were made in 1953, 1958, and 1972, the entire commission concept was changed on April 30, 1975, when the SEC required exchanges to abolish the practice of requiring fixed or minimum commissions. The competition in commissions ended a history of fixed commissions that extended back 183 years. The first serious price competition which followed resulted in the advent of discount houses which in turn encouraged old-line wire houses to expand into other areas of financial merchandise such as insurance, real estate, and tax shelters. Increasingly expensive costs of competition hastened the mergers of many firms and the absorptions of others into financial conglomerates.

The age of automation affected the NYSE just as it did other businesses. The Exchange introduced the leased-wire system of operation of its ticker service in 1952. Late in that same year, a system of tape recorders was installed in the Quotation Department to speed up the quotations in active stocks. Increasing volume required far more dramatic changes in the years that followed. In 1973 Market Data Systems Two was launched. This was designed to capture and display worldwide the trade and volume information from the trading floor. It was the core of the Exchange's worldwide communication network.

In March 1976, the Designated Order Turnaround System (DOT) began operation. It was originally designed to transmit 100 share market orders electronically from member firm offices to the trading posts. By the 1980s this system had grown to the point at which it handled an average of more than 35,000 orders per day, or about 50% of all transactions executed on the Exchange.

Availability of more sophisticated electronic equipment, aggressive competition from the over-the-counter markets, the entrance of the NYSE into such new areas as options and futures, and an increasing number of high-volume periods all combined to render improvements quickly obsolescent. The DOT system evolved into SuperDot 250 designed to handle market orders up to 5,099 shares, limit orders up to 30,099 shares, and even to store open orders until filled or canceled. The Opening Order Automated Report Service (OARS) was integrated with SuperDot to collect and store opening orders sent to the floor each day to enable the specialists to note imbalances between buying and selling interests and thereby help them to determine the day's opening prices. Given the fact that opening orders may account for as much as 20% of a day's volume, OARS represented a major reduction of the specialists' burdens.

Part of the pressure caused by increased volume began in 1952 when the NYSE began closing on Saturdays. This change, which was made despite anticipation of much higher volume, was forced primarily by the adoption of a 5-day week by other financial institutions in New York and elsewhere. Partially offsetting the reduced length of the trading week was an increased length of the trading day Mondays through Fridays. The market closed at 3:30 P.M., EST, rather than 3:00. This move caused considerable consternation among the business editors of evening newspapers who were able to print closing prices only with great difficulty or not at all. In 1974 trading hours were further expanded by one-half hour per day when the Exchange decided to remain open until 4:00 P.M. Another half-hour was added in 1985 by opening a half-hour earlier. This latter move was not greeted enthusiastically by employees of brokerage houses on the West Coast who had to be in their offices by 6:30 A.M. if they were to observe the market's opening.

A decade of low market volume had encouraged several proposals to reduce the number of Exchange memberships. In 1952 the members approved a plan to purchase seats for permanent retirement at a specified minimum price. Improvement in market volume caused seat prices to rise above the figure chosen after only nine seats had been retired. The reduced level of 1,366 seats remained unchanged after 1953.

Also 1953 was the year in which the decision was made to admit member corporations. This was a marked break with the traditional practice of admitting only individuals and partnerships. By 1961, 78 corporations were members. The number grew rapidly to 271 by 1972, remaining at about that figure until the end of the decade, but then turned upward again reaching 326 by 1980 and 452 by 1984.[27]

Many sweeping changes occurred during the 1970s and 1980s caused by competition, new products, and social changes. The Securities Investors Protection Corporation (SIPC) was created by Congress in 1970 to supplement the Special Trust Fund of the Exchange which was designed to protect customers' assets. Women who had formerly been employed only as clerks became Exchange members, brokers on the floor, and senior officials of member firms. Foreign brokers were allowed to become members of the Exchange for the first time in 1977.

The most obvious changes were physical. The first step of a major facilities upgrade program was undertaken in 1980 at a cost of $24.5 million. The 50-year-old trading posts on the floor were replaced with 14 new and larger ones designed to accommodate the data processing and communication equipment. Further improvements to both the facilities and the communications to and from the trading floor were made in 1981.

The NYSE had provided a market for stocks and bonds throughout its long history. In recent years, it has taken steps to broaden and diversify its product line. In 1970, warrants were admitted to trading for the first time. In 1977, a fully automated bond system went into effect. In 1978, the Ex-

---

[27]Member organizations include both corporations and partnerships; member partnerships have at least one general partner and member corporations have at least one voting stockholder who owns a seat on the Exchange. The number of partnerships belonging to the Exchange fell from 649 in 1930 to 176 in 1984. The total of member organizations dropped from 667 in 1960 to as low as 473 by the end of 1977, but by 1983 the figure had again risen to a historically high area of 639. The number of member offices, 5,876, and the number of registered personnel, 69,960, both exceeded prior record levels.

change developed a plan for creating a financial futures market in an effort to compete with the burgeoning commodities futures markets. Trading on this Exchange began in 1980, but competition proved more difficult to overcome than had been anticipated, and the venture proved to be disappointing. The Exchange was apparently somewhat slow to realize the potential of the stock options market and allowed other stock exchanges as well as the Chicago Board of Trade to gain a considerable lead in this business while plans were being developed.

The NYSE has poured immense amounts of time, effort, and money into examining its security market, stockholders, and the public transactions. Outstanding among these were the investigations of the number and characteristics of stockholders of publicly owned corporations. The first such investigation was conducted by a well-known research organization. It was the first serious attempt ever made to determine the number of stockholders.[28] Several such succeeding studies have been made by the Exchange staff since the early 1950s and it seems certain that future such censuses will continue to provide a flow of information on this subject. One of the more elaborate surveys in this area was released in 1978. Entitled "Public Attitudes Toward Investing," it was designed to determine the changes in the public's perceptions toward stock and bond investing that had occurred in the 18 years that had elapsed since the previous similar survey.

Today's management of the NYSE differs widely from that previous to 1939. Its management has changed from the old committee system to one resembling the modern corporation with a paid, professional staff in direct control. Of the 21-member Board of Directors, 20 are elected by the general membership of the Exchange for two-year terms, 10 are representatives of the public and have no affiliation with security brokers or dealers. The chairperson of the Board is chosen by the Board, but cannot be a member of the Exchange or be affiliated with a broker or dealer. The chairperson appoints the president and other officers of the Exchange.

The Exchange has opened its doors to the public for the first time in recent years, and hundreds of thousands of visitors now annually observe its operations. An extensive campaign by a staff highly conscious of the importance of public relations in business has been conducted to educate the public about the functions, about investing on a sound basis, and about share ownership. The Exchange no longer considers itself an exclusive club, but rather an institution with a public responsibility; its operations are no longer concealed by an impenetrable screen of secrecy so characteristic many years ago. As J. Pierpont Morgan once observed, "The market will continue to

---

[28]For example, *Shareownership in America: 1959* (New York Stock Exchange, 1960) and *1962 Census of Shareowners in America* (New York Stock Exchange, 1962).

fluctuate," but it is no longer dominated by the manipulative actions of pools and great operators as it once was. The stock market may be less colorful, but public protection is greater than ever before. The opportunities and risks provided by bull and bear markets are present now just as they have always been, but efficiency, competition, and sincere efforts to ensure fair practices are the order of the day.[29]

---

[29]Additional information about Exchange history may be obtained from many sources including Robert Sobel, *N.Y.S.E.: A History of the New York Stock Exchange* (New York: Weybright and Talley, 1975). The annual reports of the NYSE provide excellent updates of recent developments. Interesting statistics are available in the annual *Fact Books. Marketplace: A Brief History of the New York Stock Exchange* (NYSE, 1982) includes not only a well-written history of the Exchange but also some excellent photographs and illustrations from the Exchange archives.

6 The New York Stock Exchange: Its Organization and Membership

The NYSE was for many years organized as a "voluntary association," neither a corporation nor a partnership. In 1972 it was reorganized as a New York State not-for-profit corporation. The previous Board of Governors was replaced by a Board of Directors. Also in that year, the Exchange appointed the first salaried Chairman of the Board of Directors. Prior to that time, the post of Chairman of the Board of Governors was unsalaried, although it conveyed enormous influence and prestige. It was always held by a senior executive or partner of a major member firm.

In 1985 the NYSE's Constitution underwent its most comprehensive revision since 1938. The Board of Directors was expanded to 27 members, 24 of whom are elected by the members and 3 "ex officio." The latter are: the Chairman of the Board, the Executive Vice Chairman, and the President. The 24 member-chosen directors are divided into two broad categories—industry directors and public directors.

The public directors must include at least one associated with an issuer of NYSE-listed securities, but not affiliated with a financial institution. Another must be associated with a financial institution which is a significant investor in equity securities.

The industry directors must include 7 from firms dealing with the public, 3 specialists, and one floor broker. An additional industry director must be from a firm not dealing on a national basis, for example, a "specialty" company such as an arbitrage firm or research "boutique." Half of the industry directors representing public firms must be affiliated with firms based outside New York City. The distribution of industry directors thus ensures that parochial interests cannot dominate the formulation of Exchange policies.

QUALIFICATIONS FOR MEMBERSHIP

The NYSE provides the facilities for trading securities which are listed on it. The Exchange itself neither sets the prices of such securities nor in any way influences what those prices "ought" to be. It *does* set rules and policies, in compliance with the Securities and Exchange Act, to ensure that whatever prices are arrived at are determined by a fair and open market. Access to that market is restricted to members of the Exchange. Because this number is limited to 1,366, the NYSE may appear to be a club, excluding those not fortunate enough to have been admitted. Actually, membership is not that restrictive. There is always a membership available for purchase by anyone who meets the basic criteria of having reached the age of "majority required to be responsible for contracts in each jurisdiction in which he conducts business" (NYSE Constitution, para. 1402), sponsorship by two current members, and no impediments caused by violations of securities law or any felonies. Despite the lack of restrictions on female membership, the first woman was not admitted until December 1967. Since that time the number of female members has increased steadily. In 1985, 12 new female members were admitted to full equity membership.

Prices of memberships, or "seats," fluctuate with market conditions. Since 1978, members who own seats may lease them to others who meet the Exchange's requirements for regular membership. Seat prices frequently respond to forecasts of market activity in exaggerated fashion. For example, at the crest of the great 1960s bull market, memberships traded for as much as $515,000 in both 1968 and 1969. In anticipation of the adoption of negotiated commission rates in 1975, seat prices sold as low as $55,000, and continued a decline to touch a modern low of $35,000 in 1977. Fortunes of seat prices have since improved markedly. The 1985 price range was between $310,000 and $480,000, and in 1986 prices went over $500,000 for the first time since 1969. The highest price yet recorded was $625,000, not surprisingly in 1929. In relative terms that price was far in excess of current levels because of the much greater purchasing power of the 1929 dollar compared to the dollar of the 1980s.

Leased Memberships

As previously noted, members who own seats are allowed to lease them to persons who meet the Exchange's standards. At year end 1985, 418 of the 1366 memberships were leased. From the owner's point of view, the lease may represent an attractive way of earning a rate of return on the investment while awaiting a satisfactory price level to sell. Thus, some seats are actually purchased largely as investments, or speculations. The lessee, on the other hand, gets access to the Exchange market without the necessity of raising the capital required to buy a seat outright.

PHYSICAL AND ELECTRONIC

Access Members

The NYSE has a small number of "partial" memberships in the form of physical and electronic access members. The former are limited to 24, but there is no express limit to the number of electronic access members. The physical access members may trade on the Exchange floor in all securities like regular members, but may not perform specialist functions. The electronic class has access to the NYSE floor through direct telephone line or, alternately, through the SuperDOT system. There are currently 79 such members. Both classes of member pay a basic fee and an annual fee to maintain the status.

Options Trading Rights

In an effort to give some support to its options business (which to date has not been very impressive), the NYSE created "options trading rights," which are included in each membership. Should a member choose not to use these rights, they can be leased to others. The intent is to create a number of options traders who will fulfill a function similar to that of the American Stock Exchange's option principal members. If successful, the plan should increase liquidity and make NYSE-listed options more attractive than previously. Thus far, the only really successful and liquid contract traded on the NYSE is the option on its own Composite Index.

TYPES OF MEMBERSHIP

Membership is technically the personal property of the seat holder who purchased it. In some cases it is literally that. Seats are often passed along from fathers to sons, or willed to an heir. The vast expenses involved make it practically impossible for all but the wealthy to afford a membership. Most memberships are actually financed by the sponsoring member organization which nominates a candidate from among its employees. Because membership is the personal property of the owner, title may be vested only in an individual's name. Hence, when a member firm such as Merrill Lynch transfers a membership from one of its employees to another, the new member signs what is commonly called an ABC agreement that covers the disposition of the seat should the member decide to leave the employ of the sponsor or take up a different position.

   Members perform different functions depending on their type of business. The largest number are registered as "commission brokers." These members represent firms that deal with the public and handle only orders which originate off the floor, either from a customer through a registered representative or from the firm's trading desk. Their primary function is to get the best possible price for the customer by meticulously following the instructions on that order. The number of commission brokers fluctuates but is generally around 500 or so out of the total 1366 full members.

The next largest number of members are those registered as specialists. Their function is to be both market makers in listed stocks and also to provide a brokerage function when orders for those stocks are not capable of immediate execution. At the end of 1985 there were 409 individual specialists and 55 specialist units, ranging from as few as 2 specialists to large units handling markets for over 100 different issues.

Next most numerous are floor brokers, often called "$2 brokers." The name stems from a commission they once charged to execute orders left with them by other brokers. Thus they are "brokers' brokers," meaning that they derive their business from handling orders other members are incapable of handling at that moment. In busy, high-volume trading this can be a lucrative occupation—in slow markets, it is a difficult way to make a living. In recent years, much of their order flow has been siphoned off by the growing use of the DOT system and its successor SuperDOT. As member organizations may route orders directly to the specialist through this system, the $2 broker is often bypassed. A recent development giving them significant new business has been "program trading," which involves simultaneous execution of a wide variety of stock orders, often near the close. Whether this is merely a temporary stimulus or a longer-lasting permanent part of market trading remains to be seen.

There are a small number of registered traders, members who trade for their own account. Because the privileged status of a member with no responsibility to others seems unpalatable to the SEC, the NYSE introduced a variation on this role called "registered competitive traders." Such traders are expected to make a substantial portion of their trades to facilitate the execution of public orders.

Finally, some members are seldom (or never) present on the floor. Rather, they devote their attention to customer accounts, corporate finance, and nonfloor business. Orders entered by such members or their firms are usually executed through the SuperDOT or $2 brokers. These members are usually referred to as "office members," and their firms are often at some distance from New York. Their business normally does not justify a full-time presence on the floor, a costly proposition in addition to the expense of buying the membership.

Allied Members

Persons who are either general partners or member partnerships or principal officers of member corporations must be registered with the NYSE as "allied members" if they are not members. Allied members have the same responsibilities as members but do not have the privilege of trading on the floor. Allied members generally head major divisions or departments such as sales, trading, syndicate, or corporate finance. The number of allied members is not limited, and a member organization might have only one member but a dozen or more allied members. Allied membership is not purchased as a regular membership is. It is instead a registration that follows the function its holder performs.

Member Organizations

At the end of 1985 there were 599 member organizations, 435 of which were corporations with the remainder set up as partnerships. There were 667 member organizations in 1961, an indication of how, over time, the smaller entities have been squeezed out by the larger, more heavily capitalized ones. Of these firms, 381 dealt with the public while the other 218 confined their activities to trading with other members on the floor.

Until the 1950s member firms were always organized either as partnerships or as sole proprietorships. Corporate organization was introduced in 1953, but the incorporated member firms were still much like partnerships. Voting shareholders were very much like general partners except for the limited liability conferred by their stock. The first member organization to offer its stock to the public was Donaldson, Lufkin, and Jenrette which had made a name for itself by concentrating in the lucrative institutional equity business that grew dramatically in the 1960s (Donaldson has since been acquired by the Equitable Life Assurance Society, the large mutual insurance company). On July 27, 1971, the common stock of Merrill Lynch, Pierce, Fenner, and Smith was listed, the first member organization to achieve that status. Many others have since followed, including E. F. Hutton, Paine Webber, A. G. Edwards, and in 1986, Bear Stearns and Morgan Stanley. Another trend has been the acquisition of brokers, publicly owned or otherwise, by large, diversified financial service organizations. Among such transactions have been: Shearson Loeb Rhoades by American Express; Bache Halsey Stuart Shields by Prudential Insurance; Dean Witter Reynolds by Sears Roebuck; Kidder, Peabody by General Electric Credit; Tucker, Anthony, and R. L. Day by the Travelers Insurance Companies; and the previously mentioned Donaldson, Lufkin & Jenrette purchase.

Partnerships and Private Corporations

There are still 164 member partnerships, but only one of really significant size (Goldman Sachs and Company, which in 1986 sold a 12½% interest to a large Japanese bank, The Sumitomo Bank). General partners are required to be either members or allied members. Limited partners, who contribute only capital without a management role, must qualify as "approved persons." In fact, the typical limited partner is a retired general partner leaving his or her capital at work in the business. A number of others are simply wealthy investors looking for an attractive rate of return (few businesses can produce a rate of return on equity like investment firms in good markets). The ability of any partner to withdraw funds from the firm is closely regulated by NYSE rules so that a sudden removal of capital will not jeopardize the firm's finances and expose its customers to loss.

If the firm is instead organized as a closely held private corporation, voting shareholders must be either members or allied members. The status of a nonvoting shareholder is similar to that of a limited partner. Nonvoting shareholders, however, may be participants in some management activities, whereas limited partners may not be so involved.

Exchange Membership

Every member organization must have at least one general partner or voting stockholder who is a member of the Exchange. Of course, in a publicly held corporation any shareholder is a voting shareholder if the shares are listed on the NYSE. The number per firm varies—some specialists and $2 brokers, for example, are essentially one-person operations. The larger retail-oriented brokers and some of the large specialist units may have from 15 to 30 members on the floor at one time.

CAPITAL REQUIREMENTS

Every member organization is required to be in compliance with Section 15c,3-1 of the Securities Exchange Act of 1934, plus additional requirements specified by NYSE Rule 325. These rules specify a minimum amount of net capital plus a maximum ratio of net capital to aggregate indebtedness. A member organization's net capital may be loosely defined as its liquid net worth. Excluded from net capital would be such nonliquid items as: buildings, office equipment, and even exchange memberships. Even though most of these items have some liquidity, they are removed from the computation as their liquidation under duress might provide less value than expected. A broker is in adequate financial health if its total liabilities do not exceed its liquid assets by more than 10 times. Each firm is required to make regular reports of its capital status to the NYSE. If the ratio rises above 10 times, an early warning alert is issued and the firm is not allowed to expand business. If higher than 12 times, steps must be taken to reduce business. A ratio of greater than 15 times would force the firm into liquidation and cause the SIPC to become involved in the liquidation.

Audits

Exchange rules require an annual audit of net capital by independent public accountants to ensure accurate computation. In addition the Exchange also requires supplementary monthly and quarterly reports referred to as FOCUS reports. The 1934 Act also specifies a net capital report be sent to all customers at least semiannually. This is usually enclosed with a monthly statement every six months.

Fidelity Bonds

Rule 319 of the NYSE requires every member organization doing business with the public to carry fidelity bonds covering all employees of the firm, as well as partners, officers, and directors. The bond protects the public from dishonest acts by the broker's employees. Specific coverage is provided for check forgery, security forgery, fraudulent trading, and misplacement of securities. The size of the coverage is largely determined by a member's net capital requirement.

REGISTERED REPRESENTATIVES

The terms "account executive," "investment executive," and the like have replaced the term "customer's man" (a vaguely sexist term, anyway). Indeed, the current term in vogue appears to be "financial consultant," and is being used by at least two major brokers, Merrill Lynch and Shearson Lehman. From the NYSE's standpoint, however, all such persons are "registered representatives." In order to become such, an employee of a member firm must submit a detailed application accounting for his or her business and educational experience and pass a difficult six-hour examination with a score of 70% or better. Unless the candidate possesses considerable related experience in banking, finance, securities, or a related field, a minimum 4-month training program is required before becoming registered. This test (Series 7) is the same as prescribed by the NASD for full registration. Although all self-regulatory bodies have representation on the committees which structure and write the test, the NYSE has the primary role in its construction.

In 1985, the 599 member organizations had 6,144 sales offices and employed a record total of 75,011 full-time producing registered representatives. That is more than double the number of 10 years earlier. The development of banking- and insurance-controlled brokerage firms is likely to expand this number even more in the years ahead. For example, Merrill Lynch has more than 10,000 registered representatives. Larger financial firms, such as Citibank, will need even larger numbers of registered representatives when they are allowed full access to the securities industry in the future, a development which seems inevitable.

EXCHANGE ADMINISTRATION

The following is a brief sketch of the administration of the NYSE. Although it is true that the members own the Exchange, the NYSE's employees are insulated from undue influence by members or member organizations. They perform their regulatory tasks free from harassment, and a number of members would doubtless prefer them a little less zealous in the pursuit of their duties. As in all bureaucracies, there is a tendency at the NYSE and other self-regulatory organizations for employees to justify their jobs by producing mounds of reports and data. Although largely unavoidable, regulation can be overdone, and the costs to members of complying with such requests are truly large.

In 1985, the NYSE restructured its Regulatory Services Group into three divisions: Enforcement and Regulatory Standards, Member Firm Regulations, and Market Surveillance Services. The first-named division is responsible for setting regulatory standards within the Exchange community. It deals with all questions concerning standards for registered personnel and their qualifications, sales practices, and compliance with margin rules. The Member Firm Regulation Division applies the standards set by the Enforcement Division to reviews of member-firm selling and trading practices. The Market Surveillance Division monitors all trading activity in NYSE-listed securities done on the NYSE floor. The aim of this division is to make sure the markets provide continuous, fair, and orderly prices. Also, within this division is a special new Mergers and Acquisitions unit, designed to keep close watch on such activity involving NYSE-listed shares. Particular attention is paid to "insider trading."

The NYSE's other administrative units have less impact on member organizations. The NYSE provides services for companies wishing to list securities, in addition to those already listed. It also provides a wide variety of public relations and educational services, as well as being heavily involved in industry automation through its two-thirds-owned subsidiary, the Securities Industry Automation Corporation (SIAC).

7 Stock and Bond Lists, Tickers, and Quotations

This chapter deals with the listing of stocks and bonds on the NYSE, the requirements for listing, and some of the benefits of listing shares. Shares may also be listed on the Amex and other stock exchanges, as well as on the NASDAQ system. The requirements for such listings are covered in Chapters 7, 9, and 10. Another topic covered in this chapter is the "tape" reporting system through which trades of NYSE-listed shares are reported, even if the actual execution took place at some other location.

THE LISTS

Stock List

At the end of 1985 the shares of 1,541 different issuers were listed on the NYSE. These represent 1,503 different common stocks and 795 other issues for a total of 2,298 total equity issues. The 795 "other" issues are largely preferred shares, many of which are multiple listings of preferred shares by the same issuer. For example, Illinois Power, a major public utility, has listed not only its common stock but also seven different classes of preferred shares—Classes B, G, H, K, L, M, and N. Each has different dividend rates and features.

There were 52,427,000,000 shares listed with a total market value of $1,950,332 *million*. For purposes of comparison, 33.7 billion shares were listed at the end of 1980 and less than half that number in 1970. The NYSE-listed corporations are elite American companies. As of September 30, 1985, there were 11,121 corporations which were required to report quarterly and annual financial data to the SEC under federal legislation. These are publicly held corporations with at least $1 million in assets and 500 shareholders (there are thousands of other companies with publicly traded stock but with fewer shareholders and assets below those levels). Included in those "reporting" corporations were 4,784 NASDAQ-listed issues as well as the NYSE and other exchange listings. A glance, however, at the list of the 50 leading NYSE-listed companies ranked by market value reveals such names as: IBM, AT&T, GE, Coca-Cola, Procter & Gamble, Sears Roebuck, Eastman Kodak, and Exxon. It's hard to imagine how the typical American could go through an entire year without using or needing a product or a service offered by a listed corporation.

New additions are made to the list each year. In 1985 the NYSE approved the listing of 97 new common stock issues, the greatest number of new listings since the 98 that were admitted in 1973. Delistings because of failure to maintain minimum standards are rare, but some shares are delisted each year because of mergers and acquisitions. Among the well-known companies whose common shares disappeared from the NYSE rolls for this reason in 1985 were: Revlon, Inc.; Scovill, Inc.; American Hospital Supply; and Donaldson, Lufkin, and Jenrette, Inc. The last-named is of particular interest as it was the first NYSE-member organization to offer its shares to the public (1970), and in 1985 was acquired by the Equitable Life Assurance Society, a large mutual insurance company.

Recent years have also witnessed a new phenomenon—the delisting of shares because a once publicly held corporation reverted to private ownership through a process called a "leveraged buy-out." Among the companies that have followed this path in recent years are: Levi Strauss & Company, Denny's Inc., Beatrice Companies, and National Can. In this strategy, a management group borrows large sums in order to purchase a majority of the publicly held shares and retires them. The great revival of stock prices in the 1985–1986 bull market lifted share prices to a level where the leveraged buy-out lost some of its appeal. In addition, there were some regulatory and tax law changes which helped the leveraged buy-out wave to crest. In all, there were 105 removals for all reasons in 1985, leaving the stock list with a net decline of eight issues for the year.

Foreign Shares

The world's financial markets have become increasingly less parochial. Money now seeks out the most attractive investment no matter where the opportunity exists. The term "globalization" has been coined to describe the international capital flows in the securities markets. This is well illustrated in the continuing addition of foreign shares to the NYSE list. At the start of 1986, 54 foreign stock issues were listed there. This compares with only 38 such issues in 1980. The largest number of these were Canadian, as has long been the case. Many major Canadian industrial corporations trade as actively in New York as they do in either Toronto or Montreal. Well-known Canadian listings on the NYSE include: Bell Canada, Inco Ltd., Alcan Aluminium, Canadian Pacific, Hiram Walker, and Seagram Ltd.

The continued stunning growth of the Asian economies is reflected in the listing of eight Japanese corporations, most of them producers of goods well known and respected in the U.S. Among these are Sony, Honda Motor, and Matsushita Electric (Panasonic).

Interest in British companies is increasing. For a number of years several large British corporations have had shares listed on the Big Board. British Petroleum, Shell Transport and Trading, and Unilever PLC are some of the older listings. In 1985, however, the list was augmented with the successful "privatization" offering of the previously government-owned British Tele-communications PLC. This enormous offering (9 billion shares) was nearly as popular in the United States as it was in the United Kingdom. The shares of another large British corporation, Imperial Chemical Industries PLC, regularly trade more actively on the NYSE than at home on the London Stock Exchange.

All told there are $67.66 billion in market value of foreign shares listed on the NYSE. Current trends seem to favor additional listings, especially from Asian issuers, but with more European shares also. As the world's markets move towards globalization and 24-hour trading becomes common, it seems likely that the NYSE will increase its percentage of foreign share trading.

Bond List

There are in fact more bond issues listed on the NYSE than stocks, 3,856 to 2,298 in 1985. The bonds had a face amount of $1,327,375 million versus a market value (late 1985) of $1,339,298 million. These figures are almost double the values listed as recently as 1981, when they were $681,237 million and $573,893 million respectively.

Although most listed bonds are corporate issues, a number of foreign government issues are also traded on the NYSE. United States Treasury issues are listed even though the government does not pay any listing fees. The major market for Treasury securities, as noted in Chapter 3, is OTC. Many foreign fiduciaries, however, are prohibited from buying other than listed securities, and the listing of these issues facilitates trading and foreign ownership of U.S. government debt. In early 1986, there were 724 U.S. Treasury issues, 90 foreign government bonds, and 144 different international bank (e.g., World Bank) issues.

Once listed, a bond is likely to remain so until redeemed, even if inactively traded. This leads to such occasional curiosities as

The Kingdom of the Serbs, Croats, and Slovenes 8%, due in 1962 or

Republic of Poland (Pre-Socialist) 6%, due in 1940.

The debts were repudiated by the socialist governments that took control of Eastern Europe under Soviet aegis after World War II. Consequently, though long since matured, these obligations have never been redeemed nor has settlement been made to the bondholders. Listing is likely to continue until some settlement is made, which could be a very long time.

LISTING AND REGISTRATION

A distinction should be made between listing and registration. *Listing* refers to the procedure by which a company applies for and qualifies a stock for trading on an exchange. Before a stock is approved, a company must meet certain standards set by the NYSE and must also agree to meet certain terms and stipulations for listed corporations in subsequent years.

Registration, on the other hand, refers to the submission of certain financial and business information to the SEC under the provisions of the Securities and Exchange Act of 1934. All equity issues and corporate bonds, as well as foreign securities, listed on the NYSE must also be registered with the SEC. Registration does not imply approval of the company or its securities by the SEC.

THE VALUE OF LISTING

To Corporations

Corporations list their stocks for one or more of a variety of reasons. First, listing tends to make a security more marketable. The Exchange provides a ready, continuous market, thereby making the security more attractive to public investors. Next, listing tends to create lower financing costs when additional capital is raised in the future. Third, listing aids in the sale of rights.[1] Many stockholders, when they receive rights to buy new shares of an issue that they own, sell these rights rather than exercise them. If the stock is listed, there is a ready market for the rights, which helps to make the privileged subscription a success. Again, a company obtains a certain amount of publicity and advertising from having its securities listed. Consumers associate the company's product with its stock. Frequent sales on the Exchange keep the company's name before the public. In many cases, however, the brand name bears no relationship to the company name and the publicity value is nonexistent. A fifth reason would be the desire to obtain more stockholders. Many corporations consider this one of their most important reasons. More stockholders tend to create more customers, improve public relations, aid future financing, diversify the company ownership, and advertise the organization. Finally, listing helps to determine fair prices for the company stock. It is believed that the auction market for the stock will give to it a fair value based on effective interaction of demand for and supply of the stock.

[1]A discussion of rights is offered in Chap. 23.

Not all large corporations—even when clearly eligible—desire to list their stocks and they find many reasons for this attitude. Inability to meet listing requirements would, of course, prevent a company from listing, even though it might desire to do so. Many companies, however, do not believe that the expense of listing is justified by the benefits received. Some managements dislike the required disclosure of financial affairs and other information imposed on all listed companies. In other cases, they dislike the regulations by the SEC of "insiders" (officers, directors, and large stockholders) in their securities transactions. Rules of the SEC, such as proxy requirements, that accompany Exchange requirements, also have been criticized. Finally, numerous companies believe that the market for their shares in the OTC market is adequate for both the company and its shareholders. Certainly, the advances in visibility that have accompanied the refinement of the NASDAQ system, especially its National Market System, have produced far more liquid OTC markets than was previously the case. Furthermore, a number of chief executives have expressed displeasure with the specialist market-making system used on domestic stock exchanges, and have indicated a strong preference for the competing market makers which are a feature of the OTC markets. The NASD itself has waged a strong and effective propaganda war on behalf of its method. Nevertheless, it can't be denied that investors who think "stock" first logically think NYSE, and in this they find support in the news media which are still far more likely to report NYSE activity than any other.

To Investors

A number of advantages of listing have been or can be indicated. The Exchange provides a continuous market for stocks. Listing, therefore, tends to provide greater liquidity as it tends to encourage greater order flow, closer bid-ask prices ("spreads"), and quicker sales. This advantage should not be minimized. The Exchange auction market requires a specialist to maintain a market at all times in every listed stock. The OTC market allows for competing market makers, but does not compel anyone to make continuous markets. Market makers can enter and leave NASDAQ as they choose, provided they observe system requirements for notification. Indeed, they can simply abandon a stock altogether, something that cannot happen on the NYSE. This advantage is rather more notable for stocks than bonds. The OTC market for bonds is extremely liquid, provided the investor is dealing with the customary institutional quantities.

At one time the Exchange had a clear-cut advantage in the requirements forcing listed companies to provide regular financial information to the public. Most major OTC-traded corporations now provide similar coverage. Another advantage that still favors listed shares, but not as decisively as at one time, is the extension of margin credit. All NYSE and other exchange-listed stock is automatically marginable under Regulation T (see Chapter 13). This means the shares have collateral value for loans from broker/dealers or banks. Over-the-counter shares in the NASDAQ National Market System have had this privilege since 1986. Stocks not on this system must be on the Federal Reserve's "OTC Margin Stock List," and even though many shares are on this list, a large number are not.

Finally, there is the "tape." The sequential reporting of trades as they occur gives unparalleled visibility to the investor. The electronic reporting of the National Market System still does not approach the tape for clear visibility, actual retail pricing, and widespread dissemination. It is only on the tape that investors can actually witness their reports of executions.

Evolution of Listing Standards

The evolution of listing requirements of the NYSE furnishes an interesting chapter in the history of American business practices and ethics. Directors of U.S. corporations in the early years of the republic shrouded the affairs of their organizations in an almost impenetrable cloak of secrecy. What they did, what they earned, how many assets they controlled, and similar matters were considered to be purely private affairs. To permit the public, or even their own shareholders, to know any details of their financial affairs was considered unthinkable. Such attitudes changed slowly, and this secrecy constituted the basis for an almost continuous struggle between the Exchange and its listed companies from 1869 to 1933.

In 1869 the NYSE consolidated with the Open Board of Brokers and the Government Bond Department. A number of organizational features developed at that time continued until the Exchange reorganization of 1938. One of those features was a Committee on Stock List that set down a number of rules intended to safeguard securities owners. Among these were rules requiring transfer agents and registrars. Others set engraving standards to make counterfeiting of certificates more difficult. In general, these standards were well received by both the exchange community and the listed corporations.

In 1869 the Exchange began the formulation of a policy on information on company financial condition. It was the hope or expectation that listed companies would supply with their listing application a statement of financial condition. In that early day such a policy was a dream, a Utopia, a case of wishful thinking. The mere suggestion was looked upon with horror by all right-thinking business managers. Corporations did not publish financial statements; they had no intention of doing so; and they believed that such information was no one's business but their own. They certainly had no policy of giving out such facts to anyone, including the Exchange.

A classic example of the attitude of corporations, prevalent shortly after the Civil War, as to the release of corporate information on affairs is cited by Shultz.[2] The letter was written to the NYSE in 1866 by a railroad in answer to a request for a report on the company's affairs:

[2]B. E. Shultz, *The Securities Market* (New York: Harper & Row, 1946), p. 9.

The Delaware Lackawanna & Western R. R. Co. make no reports and publish no statements,—and have not done anything of the kind for the last five years.

A. C. Odell
Treasurer

It can be said that before 1900 little success was achieved by the Exchange in obtaining agreements by the companies to submit annual reports of condition. However, about that time applications began to be made to the Exchange that showed that the policy of making annual reports of condition was evident for some corporations and that the Committee on Stock List was "cautiously attempting to get industrial companies to agree to publish annual reports and include in them a balance sheet and income statement."[3] Utilities and railroads were very slow to accept such a policy. In fact, not a single railroad or public utility listing between 1900 and 1910 made an agreement to submit annual reports or, in fact, agreements of any sort.

It should be noted that up to 1910 the Exchange maintained an Unlisted Department in which most of the industrial stocks were traded. This department, of course, did not require listing; hence no agreements were forthcoming. It was abolished on April 1, 1910, and most of the companies in that category applied for full listing. After 1910 slow but steady progress was made by the Exchange in securing agreements by companies to furnish reports on financial condition, to maintain transfer and registry offices in New York, not to speculate in the company's securities, to notify the Exchange about issuance of rights and subscriptions, and not to dispose of stock interests in subsidiaries without notice. The agreements were by no means uniform; the railroads were particularly slow to accept those designed to protect investors.

By 1928 the corporate attitude toward publicity on its financial affairs had shown a considerable change from earlier days. It was therefore decided by the Exchange to establish a new policy of corporate publicity. It urged that all annual financial reports be made from audits prepared by independent certified public accountants. The Exchange could not force listed companies to do so, but it could urge them to do so. The policy, pursued over a five-year period, was largely successful and marked an important forward step in listing standards. By 1931 83% of all listed companies had accepted the policy. A few companies, however, were adamant in opposing it.

In April 1932 the Exchange made the 1928 policy of independent audits mandatory for all new companies applying for listing. There were certain exceptions. The railroads were exempted, since they were already operating under a system of uniform accounting reports, prescribed by the Interstate Commerce Commission. It was impractical to insist on such a procedure in certain cases; for example, a government applying for listing of one of its bond issues or companies already listed.

In 1933 there occurred an important test of the listing standards of the

[3]*Ibid.*, p. 17.

Exchange. The Exchange decided to make a test case of one large industrial company which had been particularly hostile to the 1928 policy of complete financial reports of condition. The campaign to secure complete disclosure from the company began in 1930. The company, at that time, was a great financial mystery to the general public. It did publish a balance sheet and income account, but these were not satisfactory either to the Exchange or to investors. The company resented to an acute degree any suggestions that it should give complete disclosure on its affairs. The attitude of the company was stated in a letter to the Exchange in the following language: "The management of the Exchange is neither responsible to the company's stockholders in respect to information to be published regarding its affairs, nor in any position to determine what are the best interests of the stockholders in that regard."[4]

The Exchange, however, was equally firm in its attitude. It refused to accept the argument that disclosure would mean injury to the company or to its stockholders or that it would mean the revelation of trade secrets to competitor companies here or abroad. In a final showdown the company met the demands of the Exchange and the stock was retained on the stock list. Today that corporation is a model in supplying information on its affairs. Within a few months the new Securities and Exchange Commission (SEC) made mandatory the submission of independently certified reports of financial condition for all companies registered on a national securities exchange. The SEC, a governmental body, completed overnight what the Exchange, a private institution, had been working toward for years.

Another significant listing standard of the Exchange concerns the voting rights of stock. Since 1926 the Exchange has refused to list common stocks that do not carry voting rights. During the 1920s a decided trend in corporate financial policy was to issue classified common stock, the so-called Class A and Class B stock. Class A stock, owned by the general public, carried no voting rights. Class B stock, owned by management and bankers, carried all the voting power, often without a capital commitment. That is, shares were often awarded to officers and the company's bankers without cost. Thus, the public furnished the capital but was excluded from the voting process. The Exchange ultimately forbade the listing of such shares although some may still be found in the OTC market and on some other exchanges.

The Exchange has also taken steps to require listed corporations to provide shareholders with regular financial reports, both quarterly and annual. In addition, listed corporations are required to use accounting standards that are reasonable and logical. While this may not seem particularly eventful, at the time of its adoption (1938), the policy was considered revolutionary.

In hindsight, such standards may appear minimal and unexceptional. The reason for that appearance is the fact that the federal government through the SEC and powers given it in the Securities and Exchange Act of 1934 has

---

[4]New York Stock Exchange, *Supplement to the Special Report of the Committee on Stock List,* April 26, 1933.

made even more stringent requirements for publicly held corporations. The NYSE, however, has demonstrated a long history of concern for the investor, and such concern, to a large extent, antedated the legal requirements.

LISTING REQUIREMENTS

The NYSE has specific minimum requirements that any corporation desiring listing must meet. There are a number of somewhat subjective criteria that are also important, although not nearly so important as the basic numerical ones. These subjective criteria include: (1) how much national interest is evidenced in the shares; (2) the company's position and stability within its industry; and (3) the nature of the industry it is in—is it expanding? Can relative position within the industry be maintained? The Exchange has shown little interest in the brief, often meteoric careers of some companies, particularly those in the high-technology areas where staying power is notoriously suspect.

Earnings

The company must demonstrate earnings in either of two ways. First, it must have earned $2.5 million (pretax) in its most recent year and at least $2 million in each of the two preceding years. The alternate method is to have aggregate earnings for the last three fiscal years of at least $6.5 million together with a most recent year minimum of $4.5 million. All three most recent years must be profitable, but the alternate method allows a profitable company the "luxury" of one off year.

Market Value of Publicly Held Shares

Subject to adjustment, the market value of such shares should be between $9 million and $18 million. The Exchange has no problems welcoming new listings of companies which exceed the upper end of these limits, for example, British Telecommunications. The adjustment mentioned links market value to changes in the NYSE Composite Index. If an applicant had the misfortune to have filed just prior to a severe market drop, an otherwise eligible corporation might suddenly be ineligible for listing. Some protection against this contingency is afforded by reducing the $18 million threshold in proportion to a market decline. If the index declined by 6%, the threshold value would be reduced to $16.92 million, although the $9 million floor would be maintained in all circumstances.

Net Tangible Assets

The corporation is expected to demonstrate net tangible assets of at least $18 million. Greater emphasis, however, is allocated to market value of listed shares, so that a shortage in the asset area might be offset by share values in excess of the minimum.

Numbers of Shares

A minimum of 1.1 million shares is required. All listed shares must have reasonable voting rights, and weighted voting shares may not be listed (in the Ford Motor case noted previously, the weighted voting shares are not listed). Preferred shares need not possess voting rights, except in the case of certain dividend defaults. Some preferreds, especially convertibles, do have voting rights.

Share Distribution

There must be either: (1) 2,000 holders of at least 100 shares, or (2) 2,200 total shareholders *and* an average monthly trading volume in its previous market of 100,000 shares for the most recent 6 months.

Foreign Share Listing Requirements

Foreign shares have been welcomed to list on the NYSE. Alternate listing requirements for these shares give recognition to the differences in international business conditions. Outside of relative size considerations, foreign shares are often in bearer format, making it difficult to ascertain the diffusion of ownership the Exchange requires. In such cases, the Exchange will accept an attestation by a member organization that a liquid market exists for the shares.

The basic requirements are the following:

Round-lot shareholders (at least 100 shares)	5,000
Market value of shares	$100 million
Net tangible assets	$100 million
Pretax income	$100 million (cumulative three most recent years; minimum $25 million any of the three most recent years)

These figures are on a worldwide basis.

With the exception of Canadian shares, foreign shares are likely to be listed in the form of American Depository Receipts (ADRs) or American Depository Shares to assure ready negotiability. If actual shares are to be listed, the NYSE requires that such shares have the transferability, dividend distribution rights, and general characteristics equal to the ADRs.

Warrants

If the common stock is already listed, the NYSE may also permit the listing of warrants for the purchase of those shares. Prior to 1970 the NYSE did not list warrants on the general presumption that they were inherently too speculative. Warrants may be listed if they have maturities from 3 to 10 years and have ownership distribution similar to the underlying shares. The exercise price may not be "substantially above" the common stock price at time of issue. They may not exceed 20% of the outstanding shares unless approved by stockholders. As of the end of 1985, there were 22 issues of warrants listed on the NYSE. These amounted to a total of 123 million warrants with a market value of $575 million.

Delisting

Delisting is never an automatic process. The Exchange reserves the right to suspend or delist shares at any time when continued dealings are not "considered advisable." This could conceivably happen even though minimum requirements were met. Grounds for delisting are:

Fewer than 1,200 round lot shareholders
Fewer than 600,000 shares in public hands
Market value less than $5 million

Additionally, any violation of the listing agreement with the Exchange is grounds for delisting. Such violations could include failure to make prompt reports of earnings and financial data, failure to solicit proxies, or the creation of a class of nonvoting common stock.

If the corporation commits any of these violations, the Exchange will send it written notice of a hearing to discuss the matter. If the evidence at the hearing indicates that continued listed trading is not in the interest of the shareholders, formal notice is sent to both the corporation and the SEC.

THE CONSOLIDATED TAPE

The method of reporting trades in NYSE-listed shares is still sometimes referred to as the "ticker," or, more commonly, as the "tape." In actual fact, ticker tape is no longer used. What is pitched from lower Broadway windows during a "ticker tape" parade is not brokerage ticker tape; it is imported from a computer center in Connecticut for the occasion. Indeed, ever resourceful Wall Streeters shower the streets with various forms of refuse, including order ticket forms and even toilet paper. An example would be when the New York Mets baseball team won the World Series and was honored with a ticker tape parade. Still, the idea has much appeal. One still sees cartoons of portly gentlemen in three-piece suits nodding sagely as they run a ¾-inch tape through their fingers, all the while puffing on enormous cigars. If the conventional perception of a stockbroker is a bit silly today, the perception of the tape is outmoded. Nevertheless, the tape does have an interesting history as well as a vital presence, even if that presence is entirely electronic.

The Origin of the Ticker Tape

The stock ticker was developed in 1867 by E. A. Calahan, an employee of the NYSE.[5] The reason for its development was somewhat obscure; one authority believes that it was because of a demand by customers for a check-up on the skill and speed with which brokers executed orders on the floor of the Exchange.[6] Prior to the use of the ticker, the Exchange permitted visitors to the gallery, and speculators were given an opportunity to watch the brokers execute their orders. This was obviously an unsatisfactory method.

Another expedient was also tried before 1867. This was the interesting practice of "pad-shoving"; a number of messenger boys would collect sales figures from the Exchange and hurry from one brokerage house to another shouting the latest prices. The invention of the stock ticker created technological unemployment for this group of harried individuals.

The first stock ticker was slow and crude, and even the "pad-shovers" were able to view it with scorn. Its breakdowns were frequent and embarrassing. On one occasion the ticker on the Gold Exchange broke down. A youth of 22, recently fired from his job as a railroad "newsbutcher" because of his unorthodox habit of operating a home-made chemical laboratory in the baggage car, was making his living quarters temporarily in the boiler room of the Exchange. He was able to fix the ailing ticker and was promptly hired at $300 a month by the owner of the ticker service to manage the shop that made the stock tickers. In a short time this young mechanic increased the efficiency of the ticker and received the then princely sum of $40,000. He was Thomas A. Edison, later to become one of the greatest of American inventors.

Ticker Improvements

The first tickers were able to carry their load tolerably well, but were crude by modern standards. They became totally inadequate to handle the 4-million-share days of the late 1920s, although repeated efforts were made to increase efficiency and cut down on the material appearing on the tape.

---

[5]J. E. Meeker, *The Work of the Stock Exchange* (New York: Ronald Press, 1930), p. 596.
[6]*The Security Markets* (New York: Twentieth Century Fund, 1935), p. 251.

A new ticker system was then developed with a maximum speed of 500 characters per minute, in contrast to the speed of 285 characters for the old machine. The new system was installed in late 1930, but unfortunately too late to handle the enormous markets of 1929, including those of the hectic days of October when the market closed. An all-time record for the tape's being late was reported on October 24, 1929, when the tape ran four hours and eight minutes late. The volume on that day was a new record, until then, of 12,880,900 shares. Five days later, when the market broke all records with 16,388,700 shares sold, the ticker ran only one hour and 31 minutes behind. Even the new high-speed ticker, when installed, was not always able to handle excessively active markets. In July 1933, the ticker ran one-half hour behind on a day's volume of 9,573,000 shares. The present ticker system is geared to handle markets of probably 200 to 250 million shares per day if the volume is well distributed. Sudden bursts of selling, however, cause the ticker to run late.

Ticker improvements over the years have increased the ability of brokers to give their customers up-to-the minute prices. The 500 characters-per-minute printer introduced in 1930 remained standard until the early 1960s. Sharply increasing volume during that period led to some experiments, including one that could print 900–1200 characters per minute on a vertically moving tape. The NYSE unveiled a 900 character-a-minute printer in December 1964. The ticker by that time had about reached the limits of electro-mechanical processing ability. Finally, on January 19, 1976, the Exchange introduced a new computer-directed system capable of handling 36,000 characters a minute. Volume, however, was accelerating rapidly and it is thus still necessary to drop digits or volume reports when the market runs at a torrid pace.

The tape is no longer the sole source of current information. Any broker sitting at his or her desk can tap a few keys on a desk-top terminal and instantly call up on a television screen the last sale, the current bid-ask quotation, and the current volume. Many of these units also feature a continuous display on the top of the screen. Most newer brokerage offices have completely dispensed with the tape and the "board," which is an electronic (or mechanical) display of popular stocks and that is situated in the front of each office. The offices customarily had a few rows of chairs in front of these displays where customers could sit and watch the activity. Of course, in the days before such "boardrooms," the board really *was* a board—a blackboard upon which young "board markers" chalked up recent price changes. A number of Wall Street veterans had their first brokerage experience as board markers.

In 1974 the Exchange first began a tape showing trades of 15 selected stocks when they traded on one of the regional exchanges as well as on the NYSE. Full consolidation began on June 16, 1975. The tape at that time identified a regional exchange trade of a stock whose primary market was on the NYSE by using an ampersand followed by a symbol connoting that exchange. For example, a print showing IBM & M indicated a trade of International Business Machines on the Midwest Stock Exchange. In later years, reporting capacity had improved so much that such identification was no longer needed and it was dropped.

Stock Symbols

The NYSE-listed shares may have one- to four-letter symbols to represent them on the tape. Common shares have one, two, or three letters, but some preferred stocks are classified by different letters in addition to the corporate symbol. Thus the Class M preferred shares of Pacific Gas and Electric (PCG) are identified on the tape as PCG Pr M to distinguish them from the 20 other PCG preferred issues currently listed.

A small number of companies have long maintained a distinctive one-letter symbol. Certainly, the most familiar of these is T for American Telephone and Telegraph, with almost 3 million shareholders still the most widely owned American corporation. Nearly as well known are: X (U.S.X. Corp.), S (Sears Roebuck), C (Chrysler), F (Ford Motor), and Z (Woolworth).

Sometimes a two-letter symbol clearly identifies the company, even to a novice. Not many would find difficulty identifying the "prints" GM or GE, or even VO (Seagram). Often, however, there is no immediately recognizable connection with the company, as with DD (DuPont), CZ (Celanese), or WX (Westinghouse Electric). The number of one-letter symbols is obviously limited, but the number of two-letter ones in use is much larger, probably around 200.

Most listed shares have three-letter symbols. This type has been popular for newer listings because it establishes a stock's market identity. Investors quickly noted the appearance of Anheuser Busch by its symbol BUD when it finally listed on the NYSE after many years in the OTC market. Such recognition also attaches to well-known major issuers represented by the following: DOW, IBM, XRX, CBS, MMM, and XON, although market veterans fondly recall the last-named's previous symbol J for the Standard Oil Company of New Jersey.

Occasionally, the symbol is retained even after a corporation has undergone a name change, so that the symbol appears to have little relevance to its current name. Unless one has a long memory there appears to be little connection between the symbol TGT and Tenneco. At one time the company was the Tennessee Gas Transmission Company, basically the owner of a natural gas pipeline. As the company became involved in other businesses, the name was changed but the widely known symbol remained. Much the same could be said for the symbol FNB used by First Chicago Corp., formerly simply the First National Bank of Chicago.

Trading and Volume Reports

All major company common shares on the NYSE trade in 100 share "round lots." The execution of a 100-share order is reported on the tape by the company symbol followed by the price, for example, GM 80. Multiple round lots of fewer than 10,000 shares are reported by dropping the last two zeroes and replacing them with the letter s. Hence, IBM 50s 147 is a report of 5,000 shares of IBM at $147 per share. A trade of 10,000 shares or more is reported in full, retaining the letter s, which now simply serves to separate the volume from the price—UTX 25.000s 53 is, therefore, 25,000 shares of United Technologies at 53. Note that dots are used instead of commas on the tape.

A repeated fraction following an execution report indicates another 100 shares at that price, executed immediately after the first report. For example, MO 2s 60½. ⅜ reports 200 shares of Phillip Morris at 60½ followed by 100 at 60⅜.

Post 30 Stocks

A number of relatively inactive stocks are traded at Post 30 on the NYSE floor. Because of their lack of turnover, specialists are allowed to make markets in *10 share* round-lot units. When such shares are reported on the tape they carry an explanatory print ss, to indicate trading in the 10-share unit. Consequently, ED PrC 2ss 53 identifies 2 10-share round-lot units of Consolidated Edison Class C preferred stock. The Amex has a few stocks which trade in 25- or 50-share round lots and are likewise identified on the Amex tape.

Delayed Reports

When a trade is out of its proper sequence on the tape, it must be reported with the symbol code SLD. This alerts traders that this transaction report is not in its correct spot, which might be significant for the trader looking for a "plus tick" to sell short, or one looking for the execution of a limit order. Because NASD Third Market traders are allowed to print as long as 90 seconds after execution, a number of their trades are so reported. A typical print of a "sold sale" appears as V. SLD 48, meaning Irving Bank trade of 100 shares reported at 48 and not in its proper sequential location on the tape.

Ex-Dividend Trades

On days when a stock goes ex-dividend, its market price on the opening sale is reduced by the amount of the dividend or the next higher one-eighth point, if the dividend should not be in one of the customary 12.5-cent trading variations. On ex-dividend date the marked-down share price is indicated as follows: FNB.XD 6s 29 (First Chicago Corp. trading ex-dividend 600 shares at 29).

Corrections

Considering the typical day's trading volume, the number of errors is small. Most errors are caught immediately and corrected in the following manner:

COR. 2.SLS.BK EK 10s73 WAS 8s73. The 1000-share execution of Eastman Kodak reported two sales previously was actually for 800 shares.

Miscellaneous Symbols

Other abbreviations seen on the tape occasionally are RT (rights), WT (warrants), and WI (when issued). When rights are exchange-traded, the trading period is brief, rarely more than a few weeks. Warrants, as noted earlier, are sometimes seen on the NYSE, but the Amex usually has many warrant issues. The WI is used during those periods when shares of one company are available at two different prices. This usually happens for a brief period between the record date and ex-dividend date for a stock split or a stock dividend, the WI identifying the new, lower priced shares. After the payable date for the new shares, the designation is dropped as all shares are then at a single price.

Consolidated Reporting

The tape is actually composed of two "networks," A and B. The latter reports all trades on the Amex. Relatively few Amex shares trade regularly anywhere else. When a stock is listed on the NYSE, however, it may well trade in substantial volume on any other domestic exchange (except the Amex), and even OTC in the so-called third market. All trades in NYSE-listed common stocks must be reported on the consolidated tape no matter where the actual execution took place. In fact, there is no way to tell from the tape alone where a trade took place, and from the investor's viewpoint, it matters little. This consolidated tape is a major step in the direction of the unified National Market System Congress proposed (without defining) in the Securities Act Amendments of 1975.

8 Trading Procedures

KINDS OF ORDERS AND THEIR USES

Skilled investors, traders, or brokers in the stock market may use only a few kinds of orders to buy and sell, but familiarity with all kinds is useful. They should know their rights and liabilities and the kinds of results to expect from different orders. They should understand how orders are processed in the market. Such knowledge is not only profitable, but also helps to avoid much misunderstanding.

Classification

There are many kinds of orders. Some are so rarely used that there is no merit in discussing them in detail here. Note that individual exchanges sometimes do not allow the use of certain types of orders. Sometimes a type of order is forbidden temporarily because heavy market activity does not allow it to be handled properly. Although not complete, the following classification covers all types of orders in common use:

1 Size of order
   (a) Round lot
   (b) Odd lot
2 Type of transaction
   (a) Buy
   (b) Sell
      1 Long
      2 Short
3 Price limits
   (a) Market
   (b) Limit or limited

4 Time limits
   (a) Day
   (b) Week
   (c) Month
   (d) Open or GTC
5 Special types of orders
   (a) Stop
   (b) Stop limit
   (c) On open
   (d) On close
   (e) Discretion

5   Special types of orders (contd.)
    (f) Immediate or cancel   **(m)** Scale
    (g) Fill or kill   **(n)** Cash
    (h) All or none   **(o)** Cancel
    (i) Do not reduce   1 Straight cancel
    (j) Alternative   2 Cancel former order
    (k) Contingent   6 Other orders for odd lots only[1]
    (l) Switch

SIZE OF ORDERS

Round Lots and Odd Lots

All trades in stocks on the floors of exchanges are divided into round lots and odd lots. The factor that differentiates the two is the so-called unit of trading. A *round lot* is one for the unit of trading or some multiple thereof. An *odd lot* is one for less than the number of shares required for the unit of trading.

The floor of the NYSE has 15 active trading posts. At these posts the unit of trading is 100 shares for nearly all issues. Approximately 1,500 active stocks are traded at these active posts. Although 100-share transactions are the most common type, orders often run into hundreds or thousands of shares.

For the inactive stocks the unit of trading is 10 shares. These are usually preferred stocks that experience a relatively inactive volume of trading and most of them are handled at Post 30. Because of the high price and slower turnover, the Exchange permits a unit of trading of 10 shares.

On the NYSE, an odd lot for 100-share-unit stocks is from 1 to 99 shares. For 10-share stocks the odd lot is from 1 to 9 shares. On other exchanges, round lots are sometimes designated as 25 or 50 shares and, in these cases, odd lots would be defined as 1–24 and 1–49 shares, respectively.

Exchanges can permit only the larger or round-lot orders to enter the continuous auction markets on their floors. In order to assure reasonably orderly, rapid market operation, it has become necessary to establish mechanical rules to handle the execution of odd-lot orders.

Stock buyers who trade in odd lots normally do so because the size of their investment funds precludes round lots, but sometimes buyers who usually deal in round lots buy odd lots of high-priced shares in order to keep their portfolios in balance. Odd-lot customers typically find that their cost of trading on a per-share basis runs higher than that of the round-lot customers. This is true partly because the commission structures of most brokers

---

[1]In addition to passing over such obscure orders as sell plus, sell minus, and participate but do not initiate, no mention is made of special orders used in the futures area, such as market if touched, sell and retender, and others.

favor round lots and partly because odd-lot customers are in weaker positions when it comes to negotiating commissions with their brokers.

TYPE OF TRANSACTION

Buy and Sell Orders

A buy order is usually placed by a customer who anticipates a rise in price. Such an order may represent the establishment of a new position, or it may cover a short position that may be proved successful or has become uncomfortably unsuccessful. In the first case, the customer's position is said to be long and in the second, the position has gone from short to flat.[2]

Customers who place a sell order are selling either long or short. If they are selling long, they are liquidating a long position. They may have reached their objective, may be cutting their loss on an unsuccessful investment, or may merely believe that the funds realized from the sale are better used elsewhere. Those selling short usually anticipate a price decline although there are other motives for selling short which will be discussed later in this chapter.

PRICE LIMITS

Market Orders

A market order is to be executed at the best possible price at the time the order reaches the floor.

Market orders are usually the most common of all orders and probably outnumber all other orders combined. They are more popular with larger traders, professional investors, brokers, and institutions than they are with the odd-lot public. They are also more common in executing selling orders than in buying orders, the reason apparently being that sellers want to sell quickly, but buyers are less eager to buy at current prices. On some occasions during which there has been heavy selling in the market, 85% of the orders have been market orders.

The greatest advantages of the market order are speed and certainty. Customers specify no price on this type of order. They merely instruct their broker to buy or sell immediately at the best possible price, that is, the highest price in the case of a market order to sell and the lowest price in the case of a market order to buy. Such orders are usually given top priority on the communications systems of most brokers. Any delay during which a price change occurred adverse to the customer's interest would be deemed "miss-

---

[2]One sometimes hears the term "buying short." This is incorrect and meaningless. A short position is liquidated by "covering" or "buying-in."

ing the market" and would be an error chargeable to the brokerage house or to the floor personnel responsible. Normally, unless an order is "stopped" by a specialist for the benefit of the customer, market orders can be executed within a few minutes after being given to a broker.

The other advantage of the market order is that it is certain to be filled barring such rare circumstances as suspension of trading in the stock or on the exchange.

Limit or Limited Orders

The chief characteristic of a limit order is that the customer decides in advance on a price at which he desires to trade. He believes that his price is one that will be reached in the market in a reasonable time and that will be advantageous to him. He is willing to wait to do business until he has obtained his price, even at the risk that his order may not be executed either in the near future or at all.

In the execution of a limit order, the broker is to execute it at the limit or better. A limit order to buy is executed at the limit or lower; a limit order to sell, at the limit or higher. If the broker can obtain a more favorable price for his customer than the one specified, he is required to do so.

For example, a customer wants to buy 100 shares of XYZ. The price has been fluctuating between 50 and 55. He places a limit order to buy at 51, although the current market price is 54. It is possible that within a reasonable time the price will fall to 51 and his broker can secure the stock for him at that price. If the broker can purchase the stock at less than 51, he must do so, because the customer is entitled to the best possible price.

Or take another example. A customer wishes to sell 100 XYZ. The market is 54. A limited order to sell is placed at 56. As soon as the market rises to 56, the broker will execute it at 56 or higher, if it is possible. In no case will the order be executed at less than 56.

The advantage of the limit order is that the customer has a chance to buy at less or to sell at more than the market price prevailing when the order was placed. The customer assumes that the market price will become more favorable in the future than it is at the time the order is placed. The word "chance" is important. There is also the chance that the order will not be executed at all. The customer, just mentioned, who wanted to buy at 51 may never get his order filled, because the price may not fall to that level. The customer who wanted to sell at 56 also may never get his order filled, because the stock may not rise that high during the time the order is in effect.

In a narrow, fluctuating market, when the stock is said to be "making a line," some believe it profitable to place limit orders. Making a line is a situation in which a stock moves within narrow limits, such as three or four points, over a period. If the trader believes the market trend to be upward (a bull market), the trader would fear missing the market. In a bear market the potential seller similarly would be disinclined to place limit orders to sell above the market.

An obvious objection and disadvantage to limit orders is that danger of missing the market. For example, in a bull market, if a buy order were to be placed several points below the current market price, it might never be filled because the market would continue upward. Similarly, in a falling market, if a sell order were to be placed above the current market price, the market might continue to fall and the order might never be executed. It is difficult to set a satisfactory limit. If the limit is close to the current market price, the order has little advantage over a market order; if too far away, it is unlikely to be executed. Setting a satisfactory limit takes much more skill than is generally supposed. In a rising market, for example, just how far below the market is it wise to set a limit on a buy order?

Prices on limit orders have a definite relationship to market price. A limit order to buy usually is placed below the current market price, whereas a limit order to sell is placed above the market price.

A limit order never becomes a market order, even after the stock sells at the limit. The broker must always observe the limit and cannot execute the order, regardless of price, merely because the market has touched the limit price. This is one difference between the limit and the stop order, which will be described shortly.

How is a limit order to be executed if the broker cannot buy or sell at the limit at the time he receives the order on the floor? The broker, immediately upon receipt of the order on the floor, attempts to execute it at the limit or better. This is often not possible, although it may happen that the limit has been reached or passed by the time the order is on the floor if the limit is not too far away from the market price at the time it is entered. In the event that the order cannot be executed immediately, the broker places the order with a specialist, who enters it in the "book." Brokers themselves cannot stand by to handle one order; they have others to execute. It can, however, be left with the specialist in readiness for execution at the first possible opportunity. The broker is now freed to execute other orders that can be taken care of at once.

Note that all limit orders may obviously be filled at better than their limits from time to time, but the expression "or better" should not be included on the order. This expression indicates that an order is correct when it might not look correct relative to the market. For example, assume that a stock closes at 65. A customer expects a sharply higher opening in the morning, but is still willing to buy the stock at 70. In this case, the broker might properly enter the limit order at "70 or better" in order to indicate to the floor broker that it is correct. Otherwise, there is some risk that the floor broker might return the order believing that the price is wrong or that it was mistakenly marked "buy" rather than "sell." The same applies to a limit sell order in which the limit is markedly below the last sale.

Limit orders are the most popular types of orders aside from market orders, and they account for almost one-half of all orders entered both in round lots and in odd lots.

TIME LIMITS

Day Orders

A day order is one that expires automatically at the end of the day entered. All orders are considered as day orders unless otherwise specified by the customer. They are good for the day of entry only, or such portion of the day as remains after the order is entered. Market orders are usually day orders, but there are exceptions. An order may be designated "market open" if trading has been suspended and trading in the stock which is to be bought or sold may not resume before the end of the day. Odd-lot orders that need a round-lot transaction to occur before execution may also be marked "market open." Limit orders, however, are frequently not day orders, although an order not marked otherwise is presumed to be a day order.

The theory of the day order is that the customer believes the conditions, as of today, are such that either buying or selling is justified. Tomorrow the market may change and other factors may indicate a different course of action.

Some customers like to enter an order good until a given time of day or a given date and may do so if their brokers choose to accept such orders. Most limit orders, however, are entered for a week, month, or are open.

Week Orders

These are orders that expire at the end of the calendar week, which is 4:00 P.M. on Friday. Specialists may not accept them on the floor of the Exchange. However, brokers may accept them if they care to do so. They are rare. There is no particular advantage in placing them; most find the open order preferable.

Month Orders

This is an order that expires after the last trading day of the month. Specialists may not accept them on the floor. Brokers may accept them and a few are placed. Again, there seems to be no particular advantage to them over open orders.

Open Orders

Open orders, also known as GTC orders, are good until canceled. They remain in force until filled or canceled or until the broker fails to confirm them to the specialist on the check dates. This type of order is used when customers believe that the action of the market is such that it will eventually give them their stock at their specified price. They are reasonably sure of their judgment and are in no hurry to have their orders executed. They know what they want to pay or to receive and are willing to wait for an indefinite period.

Under earlier exchange practices such orders were carried for long periods without confirmation. This was unsatisfactory for all parties concerned. A customer might sell a stock at the market while an old open order is in. If both the customer and broker forget to cancel the open order it might well be filled at a later date at which time the customer might accuse the broker of negligence by failing to cancel the open order, whereas the broker might assert a belief that the customer had additional stock and meant the order to be kept in. In other circumstances the broker may assume that the open order should be canceled and do so only to find that the customer does have additional stock, the order should not have been canceled, and the market was missed. Under present regulations members must confirm open orders with the specialists at regular intervals. If they are confirmed, the orders retain their priority on the books of the specialist. If they are not confirmed, they are canceled, must be reentered, and thus lose their priority.

Confirmation is of two types. The Exchange requires that open orders be confirmed by the close of business on periodic confirmation days designated by the Exchange. Such orders will automatically expire unless they are confirmed or renewed with the specialist at that time. Brokers may, and usually do, ask their customers to confirm such orders at frequent intervals, such as once a month or quarterly, which may be more frequently than is required by the Exchange.

Open orders to buy stock and open orders to sell stop are adjusted automatically when the stock goes "ex-dividend." A stock is considered to fall in price by the exact amount of the dividend on the date it goes ex-dividend. For example, if a stock is selling at 80 and pays a dividend quarterly of $1, it would be assumed to fall $1 in price on the day it goes ex-dividend. Accordingly, limit buy or sell stop prices on all such open orders are reduced by the amount of the dividend on the day the stock goes ex-dividend. If the dividend is not divisible by the minimum fluctuation of a stock, usually 12.5 cents, the fall in the price of the stock is deemed to be the next highest and not the closest increment. For example, if the dividend were 26 cents per share, open orders to buy or sell-stop orders would be reduced by three-eighths and not one-quarter. There is no such reduction of prices on open limit orders to sell or open stop orders to buy.

If a broker chooses to accept highly unusual time orders such as, good for two or three days, good until a specified time, or good until a specified date, the broker has the responsibility of monitoring them because the floor specialist will accept only market, limit, and stop orders. The monitoring requires not only noting the expiration instruction but also the possible price adjustments required by ex-dividend dates.

SPECIAL TYPES OF ORDERS

Stop Orders

An important type of order is the so-called stop order or stop-loss order. There are two distinct types of stop orders. One is the stop order to sell, and the other is the stop order to buy. Either type is in the nature of a *suspended* market order; it goes into effect only if the stock touches or passes by a certain price. The fact that the market reaches or passes the specified stop price compels the broker to obtain execution as a market order at the best possible price thereafter obtainable.

A stop order to sell becomes a market order when the stock sells at or below the stop price.

A stop order to buy becomes a market order when the stock sells at or above the stop price.

The price used on a stop order bears a relationship to current market price that is exactly opposite to that on a limited order. A stop order to sell is placed at a price below the current market price. A stop order to buy is placed at a price above the current market price.

There are six well-established uses for stop orders. Two of these might be called protective:

1 Protection for the customer's existing profit on a long purchase.
2 Protection for a short seller's existing profit on a short sale.

Let us illustrate the first protection. A trader purchases a stock at 60. It rises to 70. On a 100-share trade he has made a paper profit of $1,000, disregarding expenses. The trader believes that the market may reverse itself through either technical or fundamental conditions. The trader therefore gives the broker a stop order to sell at 69. If the reversal does occur and the price drops to 69 or less, the order immediately becomes a market order. The broker disposes of the stock at the best possible price. This may be exactly 69, or it may be above or below that figure. Let us suppose that the broker obtained 68½. The customer thus made a gross profit of 8½ points on the original purchase from which, of course, commissions and taxes had to be paid. If it had not been for the stop order, however, the stock might have fallen much below the stop price of 69 before an ordinary market order to sell could be placed and executed, and the trader's profit might have been further dissipated.

A similar situation arises in protecting a profit on a short sale. A stop order to buy is placed above the market price. For example, a short seller sells a given stock at 80. This judgment is correct and the stock declines to 72. The gross profit is 8 points. To protect the paper profit against an adverse price change, the trader places a buy order above 72; for example, at 72½, and the broker "covers" for the short seller at the market price. Let us suppose that the order is executed at 72¾. The short seller then makes a gross profit of 7¼ points.

Two other uses of the stop order may be called preventive:

1 Prevention or reduction of a loss on a long purchase.
2 Prevention or reduction of a loss on a short sale.

The first may be illustrated in this way. A customer purchases 100 shares of a stock at 30. This analysis of the issue leads him or her to believe that the price will rise in the near future. The trader realizes, however, that this judgment may be faulty and therefore immediately places a stop order to sell at a price below his or her purchase price of 30, for example, at 29½. As yet there has been neither profit nor loss; the trader is merely acting to prevent a loss that might follow from an error in judgment and against a fall in price. If the price does go down, the trader is closed out at about 29½ with a gross loss of ½ point or thereabout. It might, however, have been more.

The second use of the stop order involves a short sale. A short seller sells 100 shares at 110 in the belief that the market is going to decline. He or she then places a stop order to buy at 111, for example. If this judgment about the market is wrong and the stock goes up, the broker covers at 111 or near that price. The trader acts to prevent the greater loss that might accrue in a rising market through a less rapid and effective way for placing a market order to buy.

The final two uses of the stop orders are technical:

1 Entry of a market on strength on a long purchase.
2 Entry of a market on weakness on a short sale.

Let us assume that a technician has observed the market making a significant line (forming a base) between 70 and 75. He or she is not certain whether the market will break out on the upside and does not wish to tie up capital unless it does. The technician might enter an order to buy 100 shares of stock at 76 stop. If the stock reaches this level, 100 shares would be bought at the market, precluding the necessity of being called by the broker with the chance of missing a rapid upward move. Of course, had the technician been certain that the market would go up, the trader could have saved money by buying between 70 and 75. There is also the risk, of course, that the market will not go far before retreating, thereby illustrating a false breakout.

The mirror image is illustrated by entering an order to sell short at 69 stop to take advantage of an expected downside breakout. This is much like the buy stop except that it is somewhat complicated by the necessity to sell short on an up-tick so that the market may go down more than was hoped for before the order can be filled.

Two basic differences between stop orders and limited orders should be noted. First, they are placed on different sides of the market, and the limited order to buy usually is placed below the market. The reverse is true of orders to sell. Second, the limited order never becomes a market order when the limit is reached. The stop order always does.

Stop orders have three inherent dangers or weaknesses. First, there is the danger that they will cause avoidable losses. The trader may place the order too close to the market. A temporary reversal of trend will "touch off" the order, and the market will then move as expected. In the meantime the trader must bear a needless expense of getting back into the market again. In retrospect the trader should have placed the stop order farther away from the market. Of course, the farther away from the market the stop order is placed, the less the profit that can be salvaged or the greater the loss that will be incurred.

The second inherent limitation of the stop order is the fact that it may be executed at some distance away from the stop price. In a rapidly changing market the broker may not be able to execute at the stop price, but may have to execute at a price several points from it. There is no certainty of the exact price obtainable.

A third weakness is the possibility that accumulated stop orders will cause a sharp break in the price of an issue and an exchange will suspend stop orders under the very conditions that the trader had anticipated when he or she entered his or her stop order. Exchanges in the past have temporarily suspended stop orders in particular issues and even in all issues.

Many uninformed stock traders overestimate the value of the stop order. It has undeniable advantage, but it is no "sure-fire" profit maker. If a stock is declining steadily, the order will merely sell the customer out of the market with, perhaps, a small loss, but with a definite overhead cost. If the market is rising, the profit is made because of advancing stock prices and not because of stop orders. The profit comes from knowing when to sell in a rising market. If a speculator analyzes the market badly, all the stop orders in Wall Street will not bring penny's profit. They only limit losses. Stop orders in and of themselves do not constitute a trading technique.

Stop Limit Orders

Stop limit orders are rarely used. The trader who uses this type of order wants to obtain the advantage of the stop order, yet wants to be sure at what price the stock will be purchased or sold. The trader is not satisfied with the market price that results when a stop order becomes a market order, but seeks the advantages of both the stop order and the limit order.

A stop limit order to sell is effective as soon as there is a sale at the stop price or lower, and then it is executed, if possible, at the limit or higher.

An example will illustrate the rule. A customer owns 100 shares of a stock selling at 74 and feels that the price may break, but is not sure. There are two ways to place this order. One is to specify a stop and limit figure, which is the same in both cases. The order may state: "Sell 100 shares at 72, stop and limit." As soon as the stock falls to 72, the broker attempts to execute the order at 72 or higher, but in no case at less than 72. If the stock cannot be sold at 72 or better, there is no sale.

The order can be placed in another way. The order reads: "Sell 100 shares at 72 stop, limit 71." When the stock falls to 72, the broker immediately attempts to dispose of the 100 shares, but under no circumstances can the broker sell for less than 71. This has an advantage over the first method of stating the order, because in a falling market the order has more chance of execution under the stop price than at the stop price or higher.

A stop limit order to buy is executed as the reverse of a stop limit order to sell. As soon as there is a sale at the stop price or higher, the order is elected and executed, if possible, at the limit or lower. These orders may be used by short sellers, whereas the stop limit orders to sell are ordinarily used by stock owners.

In spite of its apparent attraction, this type of order must be used with extreme caution. If the trend of the market is definitely downward, a speculator or investor must be realistic and act accordingly. It is not time to quibble over price. Delayed action increases the danger of a sharp loss. The best policy under such circumstances usually is to get out of the market rapidly. The stop order will do this. The stop limit order will allow a trader to exit a market if it pauses before going too far or if it retraces its move. If the move is precipitous, a stop limit order is quite likely to be unfilled. As a result traders might find themselves out of the market when they wish they were still in it, and in when they wish they were out. Sometimes traders use stop limit orders because exchanges for brief or extended periods will not accept straight stop orders for fear that concentration of stops at "chart points" during active periods might cause unduly sharp price movements.

On the Opening

A market or limited order might be restricted to an execution on the opening only. The opening refers to the first sale of the stock being bought or sold and not to the opening of the exchange itself.

The purpose of entering such an order is primarily tactical. The trader believes that a stock will move in an anticipated direction immediately after the opening and that if it does not, the position should not be taken. The number of people, of course, who think that they can predict a stock's price direction this precisely is quite small. The number of those who can actually do it is far smaller. This type of order, therefore, is not used too frequently.

On the Close

This type of order is almost always a market order because there would be little purpose, technical or otherwise, in requiring a limited order to be filled on the close. Such an order may be utilized for one of several reasons. An obvious reason is that the trader believes that the stock will close on a strong note. Another is that the trader wishes to try for the highest price possible during the day, but if the trader fails to get the order filled, he or she would rather sell at the market on the close than remain in the market until the next day.

Unlike the order filled on the opening, the order filled on close is not limited to one particular sale. The broker might, in good faith, wait until 10 seconds before the close of the market to fill an order only to find that a broker who is a little more agile manages to fill an order with 5 seconds to go. In order to avoid disputes, exchanges specify a closing period, typically of 30 seconds, during which any order marked "on close" can be filled and deemed to be handled properly.

Discretionary Orders

In a *discretionary order* the customer grants the broker a certain amount of discretion in filling the order. The amount of discretion may be complete or it may be limited. It is assumed that brokers, using their knowledge of the market, can secure greater profits for the customers than the customers can for themselves by relying on their own judgment.

Under a completely discretionary order, the broker or broker's representative would decide on the stock, the number of shares, whether the order should be buy or sell, the price, and the time of execution. A completely discretionary order is regulated by Rule 408 of the Exchange. The rule requires that such an order be clearly marked as "discretionary" to enable supervisors to exercise control sufficient to avoid trades that are excessive or otherwise unsuitable for a customer's account. In addition, the customer must give prior written authorization.

Under an order involving limited discretion, the broker or broker's representative has discretion only as to price and time of execution. Such orders may be marked "Broker's Discretion," "NH" (not held) or "DRT" (disregard the tape). Rule 408 does not apply to such orders.

Whether or not a customer should ever use a discretionary order is debatable. Of course, one should have considerable confidence in the broker; nevertheless, the wisdom of the action even then is open to question. Can a busy broker or the broker's registered representatives with their many orders and customers give much individual attention to such orders? Is it not possible that they will fill the order at the first opportunity, when the market looks fairly good, rather than wait an indefinite time in the hope that it may get better?

It is doubtful whether any broker really wants discretionary orders. The commission is the same for a discretionary order as it is for any other kind of order. If the broker gets a good price, there will probably be only a casual "thank you" from the customer. If the execution proves to be timed badly and the customer loses money, the customer might blame the broker and may even sue. It is human nature to credit oneself for all favorable events and to shift the blame to others for one's misfortunes. Discretionary orders are no exception. Some brokers are so opposed to discretionary orders that they have standing rules prohibiting any employee from accepting them.

Probably the only people who should use discretionary orders are those who are incapacitated or on a prolonged vacation. In such cases it is perhaps advisable to place them with a trusted investment counselor. Customers sometimes give their bankers discretion in handling securities.

Discretionary orders were once used widely in manipulative operations. Pools would give such orders to specialists. The orders enabled the pool managers to use the services of specialists to ensure the success of their operations. Specialists, by their intimate knowledge of the market, were able to buy and sell at a time that ensured the greatest profit to the pool. Such actions, however, are no longer permitted.

Immediate or Cancel

When a customer enters an order marked "Immediate or Cancel," it specifies a price at which the order should be filled, but demands an execution or cancellation immediately. This differs from most limit orders that are usually entered for an entire trading day or are good until canceled.

An immediate or cancel order is for multiple trading units. The broker may fill as much of it as possible and cancel the remainder. This type of order is rarely used because there is seldom a reason for demanding such speed.

Fill or Kill

At first glance, this type of order might appear identical with the immediate or cancel, but there is a difference. A fill or kill order must also be filled or canceled immediately, but may not be partially filled. If a price is specified, all of the order must be filled immediately at the specified price or better.

A customer who wants an immediate execution of a 100-share order would always use a fill or kill rather than an immediate or a cancel in that a partial execution of a trading unit is not possible in any case.

Like immediate or cancel orders, the fill or kill is rarely used. When communications were slower, some customers entered fill or kill limit orders well away from the market as a means of getting a fast quote from the floor and thereby avoiding the lower priority regular request for a quote. Such customers, who were aware that a canceled fill or kill order was accompanied by a quote direct from the specialist, did not particularly endear themselves to busy floor personnel who were diverted from trading to give quotes.

All or None

All-or-none orders are used by traders in multiple units of trading who specify a price on their order, but also indicate that they want the entire order filled or none of it. This differs from the fill or kill in that the floor broker is given time to fill the order just as on any limit order.

In that the floors of most exchanges permit only market, limit, and stop orders, the all or none, like all special orders, involves skilled handling by the brokerage house that chooses to accept it because of its liability if the order is deemed to be mishandled. The broker with an all-or-none order would enter the crowd on the trading floor and obtain a "quote and size" from the specialist. Assume that the broker had an all-or-none order to sell 500 shares at 42 and the quote was given as 42 (bid) at 42½ (offered) 3 by 3. That would mean that only 300 shares were wanted at 42 and the broker would merely remain silent. If the bid were for 500 shares or more, however, the broker would immediately sell the 500 shares, thereby meeting the obligation to the client without violating floor procedure.

It will be noted that all-or-none, immediate or cancel, and fill or kill orders are somewhat similar, but do have marked differences. None of the three types is widely used, but of the three, all or none is probably most common.

Do Not Reduce

A limited order to buy or to sell stop is reduced automatically when a stock goes ex-dividend. A client who bid 50 for a stock that was about to pay a $1 quarterly dividend might not wish to have the order filled merely because the price dropped $1 on the ex-date. The customer with an open sell stop-loss order might feel even stronger about the matter.

It is possible, however, that a customer feels that 50 is a significant point and is not concerned about how the stock reaches that price. Such a customer would ask that his or her order be marked "DNR" or "Do Not Reduce."

Alternative

There are two types of alternative orders, one of which is rare, but the second is common and used by many disciplined traders.

In the first case, a customer might instruct the broker to buy one of either of two specified stocks at limits below the current market. The customer might do this because he or she is hunting for bargains but has insufficient funds or no inclination to buy both stocks. Although this seems quite efficient, it is not too popular because no broker can accept responsibility for canceling the second half of the order if the first half is filled. In a falling market, both prices could be touched at about the same moment, but the stocks might be traded on different areas of an exchange floor or even on different exchanges.

The second and far more useful type of alternative order involves no such problem because even though it also has the "either-or" characteristics, it cannot result in two fills. Assume that a customer has bought a stock at 40 with a price objective of 60 and does not wish to lose more than about 10 points if wrong about the outlook for the stock. The customer could enter an alternative order instructing the broker to sell at 60 (limit) or 30 stop, OCO ("order cancels order" or "one cancels the other"). This precludes having to watch the price action carefully because the trading plan will be carried out through these orders. The problem of the double fill does not exist in this case because only one stock is involved and the two prices vary considerably. Obviously, if one part is filled, there would be no problem in canceling the other in time.

Contingent

Whereas the alternative order instructs brokers to do one thing or another, the contingent order instructs them to do something only after something else has been done. For example, a broker might be told to sell a stock at one price and, when sold, immediately to buy another. The purpose of the order would be to make certain that funds were available for the purchase. The order would involve a limit order for the sell side and either a market or limit order for the buy.

Switch

A switch or swap order is a variation of the contingent order, but usually specifies a price difference rather than one or more price levels. A customer might own 100 shares of XYZ, but notes that ABC, which the customer regards as good or better than XYZ, is selling for $3 per share less. To take advantage of what is perceived to be a bargain, an order can be entered to sell 100 XYZ and to buy 100 ABC at a specified price difference of $3 per share or more with XYZ at a premium. Like all special orders, brokers who accept orders of this type are responsible for filling them properly.

Scale

Customers who wish to buy multiple lots of a stock in a market that they regard as "bottoming out" might put in a series of bids at specified differences. For example, if the market was currently 75, a client might place an order to acquire 100 shares at 70 and another 400 each one point down to 66, thereby giving a total of 500 shares with an average price of 68. In the event the stock did not reach 66, of course, the order would not be completely filled; but at least the client would have part of the position and it would be near the bottom of the market, for the moment.

Of course, the same could be accomplished by entering five different orders at five specified prices, but this would entail additional record keeping both for the broker and the customer. In addition, it is possible to scale the order down from an initial market order and, in such a case, the limits on subsequent orders could be established only after the first unit was filled. For example, the customer could order 100 shares at the market with an additional 100 shares to be bought at one point below the first and a second 100 shares at two points below the first. Limits could not be set on the second two units until the first order of 100 shares was confirmed by which point the market might have dipped and recovered and there would be no time to enter the second two orders at the desired points.

Scale orders to liquidate positions on strength may also be used, and the same two variations are available in this case; that is, all the orders may have specified points or subsequent orders may be priced on a scale up from the fill that is received on the first unit.

As in all limit orders, scale orders may be filled at a price better than that specified. Because this is always considered desirable by all but the most peculiar customers, it is not necessary to mark the order "or better."

Cash

A stock may be sold for cash rather than the regular way. This means generally that the stock must be delivered and funds received the same day rather than on the usual fifth day.

Sometimes cash transactions are utilized to avoid ex-dividend or ex-distribution dates, but such trades are not usual.

Sales made for cash may differ in price somewhat from the current regular-way market because of the inconvenience to the buyer or seller of giving up the five-day settlement privilege.

Cancel Orders

These are orders placed by customers that cancel other orders previously given to the broker. They are of two types: the straight cancel order and the cancel former order.

The *straight cancel order* cancels a previous order; no other order replaces it. The customer has changed his or her mind and is no longer willing to buy or sell the stock under present conditions.

The *cancel former order* (CFO) also cancels a previous order, but is replaced by a new order with some alteration in character. This alteration, as a rule, is a change in price. For example, a customer orders the broker to buy 100 shares at 36. The customer now cancels this order and reduces the limit to 35.

A cancellation is effective when it reaches the market in which an order was placed and not when it is given to the broker. The broker should use every effort to cancel the order as quickly as possible.

Market orders are rarely canceled unless they have been placed after the close of the market for execution the next day or if trading has been suspended and the order not yet filled. Canceling an order after it has been filled ("breaking" or "busting") is quite difficult. Brokers will make a serious effort to break a filled order only in cases of errors, serious emergencies, or significant misunderstanding.

ODD LOTS

Orders for less than the unit of trading on the NYSE were formerly handled by special odd-lot firms that specified carefully contrived rules and procedures for handling virtually any type of odd-lot order. Today, the odd-lot firms are gone and so is the uniformity. Although it is not possible to cover every aspect of odd-lot trading, a general discussion will prove useful.

Odd-lot orders today are usually handled by the same exchange specialists on the floors who handle round lots of the same stocks, but even here there is an exception. Some large brokerage firms handle odd-lot orders internally as dealers without transmitting the orders to an exchange. Such firms believe that either they can give better service or make more money or both. Other firms do not believe the expense of such an operation to be worth the cost of the investment and prefer to use the specialists.

The Odd-Lot Differential

A specialist or brokerage firm handling odd-lot orders is acting as a dealer and not as a broker. They therefore incur an inventory risk for which most believe that a commission is inadequate compensation. It is therefore common to add a markup to all odd-lot purchases and a markdown to all odd-lot sales. The markup or markdown is typically ⅛ point, but might be less for stocks selling at very low prices or more for those selling at high prices. On the NYSE, for example, the ⅛ applies only to stocks selling above 5/32. On the Amex, stocks selling at $40 or above are subjected to a differential of ¼ point.

On market orders this generally means that ⅛ is added to a purchase or subtracted from a sale. Because the odd-lot order itself does not become part of the auction market, the question arises as to the price to which the ⅛ is added or from which it is subtracted.

An odd-lot price is usually based upon a round-lot sale called the *effective sale*. In the case of a market order, the effective sale is the first sale (or next sale) to occur after the specialist receives the odd-lot order. For a limit order, the effective sale is the first sale that allows for the odd-lot differential. An order to sell at 35½, for example, would require an effective sale of 35⅝ or more. An order to buy at 68 would require an effective sale of 67⅞ or below.

There are some exceptions to the differential requirement. Orders on the opening of the market are not subject to a differential because the specialist can consider odd-lot orders together with round-lot orders in determining where to open a stock and thereby adequately protect against the risk of having to buy or sell substantial amounts of stock affecting the specialist's inventory.

Some firms belong to the New York Stock Exchange DOT system (Designated Order Turnaround system), which was initiated in 1976 for quick transmission and handling of orders up to 200 shares. If an odd lot is transmitted as an addition to a round lot through a firm which utilizes this system, the entire order is filled at one price. An odd lot submitted alone is still subject to a differential. The maximum order involving a combination of a round lot and an odd was initially 299 shares, but as increasingly sophisticated equipment was incorporated, first into the DOT system and later into SuperDOT, the maximum size of acceptable orders was periodically increased and will undoubtedly increase further.

The firms that handle odd lots in their own trading departments may or may not charge a differential. Some firms that usually charge differentials do not do so for orders on market openings.

Odd-Lot Stop Orders

If a customer enters a stop-loss order for an odd lot, the specified price refers to the effective sale and not the odd lot. For example, a customer orders 45 shares sold at 32 stop. The stop loss is said to be elected (hit) when there is a round-lot sale at 32 or below. The effective sale, however, is the next transaction, rather than the one that elected the stop. The reason for this is that if the electing sale were to be the effective sale, as was formerly the case, an odd-lot customer could never be filled at a price better than the designated stop as can a round-lot customer.

Odd-Lot Transactions on Quotations

Recall that a round-lot customer who is in a hurry to get an execution can enter orders such as fill or kill or immediate or cancel. It would seem that odd-lot customers could not have a similar opportunity because they have to wait for a round-lot transaction to act as an effective sale, but such is not the case. An odd-lot customer can elect to sell long (but not short) on the current bid minus the differential or buy on the current offer plus the differential. This, of course, is usually not too good a trading strategy, because the next round-lot sale would be unlikely to be either less than the current bid or more than the current offer, but would be quite likely to be between the two.

An odd-lot limited transaction may be marked "With or Without Sale" (WOW). For example, a customer may enter an order to sell 35 shares at 56 WOW. If a round-lot transaction took place at 56⅛ or above, the order would, of course, be filled on that transaction. If before an effective sale took place, however, the bid for the stock rose to 56⅛ or above, the odd-lot order would be filled on the quotation.

Odd-Lot Transactions on the Close

Odd-lot orders designated to be executed on the close of the market are executed on the final quotation rather than on the final sale. The reason is that a round-lot order can participate in the floor auction, but the odd-lot order requires a round-lot effective sale. The final round-lot sale could take place three hours before the close of the market and the specialist would have no way of knowing that it was the final sale.

It is rather common for an odd-lot order on the close to be part of a contingent order. For example, a customer might order a stock sold at a given price or on the close just as a round-lot customer might do. In addition, however, the odd-lot customer might also enter an order to sell at the market or on close to make certain that this position is liquidated by the end of the day. There is no need for a round-lot customer to use this type of contingent order, because the customer's market order suffices to create a transaction.

Bunching and Splitting

It is possible to combine odd-lot orders of two or more customers into one or more round lots with permission from all the clients. Commissions would still be figured on the basis of the various odd lots, but any differentials would be avoided.

Some clients with large positions have attempted to avoid influencing the market unduly by splitting their orders into a large number of odd lots, thereby having all of them executed at one price on only one effective sale. This is, however, considered quite unfair to the dealer, who must supply or absorb the stock and hence is regarded as an infraction of Exchange rules.

Odd-Lot Basis Price Transaction

In the case of an inactive stock, especially a high-priced stock, the odd-lot customer is at a distinct disadvantage to the round-lot customer. For example, assume that a customer wishes to trade 15 shares of a stock that is 85 bid and offered at 95. A round-lot customer could enter an order at about 90 with some reasonable hope of having the order filled. The odd-lot customer could only sell on the bid (at 84⅞) or buy on the offer (at 95⅛).

In order to avoid this, the exchange specialists set a reasonable basis price between the bid and the offer on which odd lots can be traded after the close. For example, the basis price for the stock cited in the previous example might be set at 90. Any order entered at least 30 minutes before the close of the market and marked to sell on the basis would be filled at 89⅞ and all orders to buy on basis would be filled at 90⅛. An order might also have been entered on a contingent basis. It might, for example, be marked to sell at 91 or on basis OCO. This would obviously be far better than selling on the quote. Orders may be filled on basis only for stocks with a 100-share unit of trading. The stock must not have traded during the day, and the spread between the bid and asked must be two points or more. The basis price is not necessarily set midway between the bid and offer but rather reflects the specialist's judgment as to where it would most likely trade depending on the tone of the market at the moment. The specialist's judgment must in turn be approved by a floor official to ensure fairness.

Other Odd-Lot Orders

Subject to exchange and brokerage house restrictions, most other odd-lot orders are handled similarly to round-lot orders. It is usually possible to use stop limit, opening, discretionary, do not reduce, alternative, contingent, switch, scale, cash, and cancel orders. Immediate or cancel and all-or-none orders would, of course, not apply and the fill or kill orders would apply to the current quote rather than to the next sale.

Because some brokerage houses handle their own odd lots and others do not and some houses belong to the DOT system and others do not, the odd-lot customer must learn what services the selected broker offers. If a broker does not charge odd-lot differentials, the customer is further advised to check the commission schedules to make sure that the savings on differentials are not lost through higher commissions. Wall Street has long been known for offering no free lunches.

SHORT SELLING

Short selling is a practice of particular importance to specialists, arbitragers, and other professionals. It is, however, used to some extent by the general public, sometimes as a speculative device and sometimes for tax purposes. Like floor trading, short selling has historically been subject to considerable criticism. Some discussion of the procedures and regulations pertinent to this technique follows as well as some discussion of its history and importance.

HISTORY AND IMPORTANCE

Early History

Short selling in the stock market is the practice of selling stock, delivery of which is to be effected by borrowing shares for the delivery. This has been a practice in the markets since their earliest days. Records show that the Dutch tried to forbid it as early as 1610. Although the London Stock Exchange was not formally organized until 1773, the use of short selling had already become so prominent in the unorganized market that as early as 1733, anti-short-sale legislation was introduced in Parliament.[3]

A study of the American securities markets will show that short selling attained a major importance early in the history of the NYSE. Jacob Little, often called the first great manipulator on the Exchange, operated from 1835 to 1857; he was a heavy and consistent short seller. In the early 1860s short selling became a major speculative tool of such great traders as Drew, Van-

[3]J. E. Meeker, *The Work of the Stock Exchange* (New York: Ronald Press, 1930) p. 607.

derbilt, Fisk, and Gould. One of the most spectacular displays of short selling was reported in 1901, when the famous struggle of the Hill–Morgan and Harriman–Kuhn, and Loeb interests for the control of the Northern Pacific resulted in great advances in the price of that stock.

The influence of short selling was recognized during World War I, when members were required to report secretly to the Exchange such sales in order to prevent "bear raiding" by irresponsible speculators or enemy agents.

1929 and After

There are no accurate figures on the amount of short selling in the 1925–1929 bull market, for data were not being tabulated at that time. No figures show what the short interest was in October 1929 just before the break. However, a president of the Exchange, in testifying before the House Committee on the Judiciary, stated: "At that time the short position was relatively small, and when the panic started, there were comparatively few persons who had sold short at higher levels and were ready and willing to buy stocks."[4]

On November 12, 1929, three weeks after the crash, the Exchange gathered figures on the short interest. The short interest, we should mention, means the number of shares carried in short accounts of brokers. About 1,692,000 shares were in the short interest on that date. No more figures are available until May 25, 1931, when short selling was heavy. By then, the short interest had risen to 5.6 million shares. The highest figure ever reported was 82.7 million shares in 1980.

It is generally recognized that short selling was heavy in 1931. The exact ratio of short selling to total trading is not known for that year, but it was estimated to be less than 5% by the president of the Exchange.[5]

Present Importance

The present volume of short selling is easily obtainable from the reports of the SEC, published monthly, or from some of the annual fact books published by the major exchanges. In 1984 short sales in round lots on the NYSE amounted to 2.022 billion shares, which was a new record for one year. The specialists' short sales amounted to 36.7% and those of other members were 45.6%, thus the public accounted for only 17.7%. Public short sales of odd lots totaled 520,000 shares.

The 2.022 billion shares of stock sold short in 1984 represented 8.8% of the total of 23.1 billion shares of the reported 1984 volume on the exchange.

---

[4]J. A. Ross, *Speculation, Stock Prices, and Industrial Fluctuations* (New York: Ronald Press, 1938), p. 200.
[5]R. E. Whitney in a public address on "Short Selling and Liquidation," December 15, 1931; quoted in Ross, *ibid.*, p. 265.

The level of short selling remains in line with this activity since World War II when it has typically ranged between 3 and 8%, with the figure being at the high end of the range in most recent years.

Another way to relate short selling to market activity is to examine the ratio of short interest, that is, the total number of shares that have been sold short and still have not been covered by a purchase at a given date, to the total number of shares in listed issues. In recent years this figure has ranged between .05 and 12%. In 1984 it was about 4.5%.

A third way to measure the importance of short selling is to compute the ratio of the short interest to the daily volume on the Exchange. For example, in 1984 average daily volume was about 91 million shares. The short interest varied from a high of 229.2 to a low of 182.7 million shares, so the ratio varied from 252 to 201%. It was once generally believed that the sustained influence of short interest that does not exceed 1½ day's volume was not overly significant, particularly if the short interest is concentrated among a few issues for technical reasons, such as arbitrages or short sales against the box. The liquidation of such positions need not result in the kind of market strength that comes from the covering of speculative short positions over a broad number of issues. The increased popularity of arbitraging stock positions against options in those same stocks or index options has enabled the ratio to be over 200% without causing much excitement.

TECHNIQUE

Meaning of Short Sales

A short sale has been precisely defined by the SEC under Rule 3B-3 in this language: "The term 'short sales' means any sale of a security which the seller does not own or any sale which is consummated by the delivery of a security borrowed by, or for the account of, the seller."

A similar definition is given by the NYSE. Its significance is that it covers two possibilities: (1) a sale of a security that the seller does not own; and (2) a sale effected by the delivery of a security borrowed by, or for the account of, the seller. These would appear to be two definitions of the same thing, which they certainly are not. In one case, the seller must borrow the stock because he or she does not own it; in the second, the seller may own the stock, but prefers to sell it short. These latter transactions are called *sales against the box* in that the sellers have the securities in their safety deposit box or account and can actually deliver them at the time of sale but choose not to.

At one time the "box short sale" was not considered to be a genuine short sale. Such sales were often made by important stockholders, executive officers, or directors in order to protect themselves against the loss of stock values; yet they did not desire to divest themselves of ownership of particular shares, either because of position, prestige, or need for control.

Reasons for the Short Sale

The short sale may be made by a speculator in anticipation of a price decline in a stock. In the speculator's opinion, the stock may be nearing the end of a substantial rise or be on the downgrade. In either case, the trader believes that in the near future the stock will decline enough to permit the sale to be covered at a satisfactory profit after all expenses are deducted. This is the so-called speculative short sale, which is probably the usual public conception of this type of transaction.

There are a number of technical short sales, which may or may not have anything to do with speculation in anticipation of a price decline. Many of these are made regardless of the possibilities of a price decline in the stock sold short. They will be described in detail later in the chapter.

Tax selling in recent years has accounted for a substantial amount of short selling. Before 1951 the short sale could be used to stretch short-term capital gains into long-term ones; this is no longer important because of changes in the tax law. It is still possible, however, to carry a capital gain over from one year into the next year.

Borrowing Stock

The short sale is possible because a trader can borrow stock from a lender and then make a delivery of it. The stock never belongs to the short seller. The first problem of the short seller, therefore, is to borrow the stock from someone who is willing to lend it.

The stock to be borrowed and delivered against a short sale is obtained through the cashiering department of the broker who handled the sale. In most cases, stock to be delivered is borrowed from the margin accounts of other clients of the same firm. Customers who sign margin agreements with most firms also routinely sign loan-consent forms. Frequently these are part of the margin agreement itself. Stock may not be borrowed from cash accounts without permission and may not be borrowed from margin accounts even with permission unless the customer has a debit balance equaling or exceeding the value of the securities borrowed. In a few instances, securities are borrowed from the accounts of partners of a brokerage firm or from voting stockholders of a brokerage corporation. Such accounts are known as *proprietary accounts*.

If a firm cannot find the needed securities among the accounts of its principals or its customers, it turns to other brokerage houses that might have available securities from one of the same two sources. In return for the securities, the lending firm is given the current market value of the security as collateral.

Another method of borrowing stock is possible although quite unusual. In this method, the firm approaches institutions that maintain portfolios and that are permitted to lend them under their corporate charters and the laws under which they operate. In most cases, such loans are not popular because of substantial expense and onerous procedures that are often involved. At one time financial institutions such as banks and investment funds routinely loaned stock by way of the "loan crowd" operating at the "money desk" on the floor of the NYSE. In fact, at one time, this was the source of practically all borrowed stock. However, stock is no longer loaned in this way.

Reasons for Lending Stock

The firm that borrows stock for its client receives the obvious benefit of the commission received for its service. The lending firm, however, benefits too. In most cases the money it receives in return for its stock is a "flat loan," that is, no interest is paid to either party. In addition, the firm lending the stock might in turn need to borrow stock one day to support a short sale made by one of its own clients, so it is wise to have established reciprocal relationships.

When conditions are unusual, the loan may benefit either the lender or the borrower so much more than it benefits the other party that a flat loan is considered unsatisfactory by one side or the other. If the stock is in short supply, it may lend at a premium. If the stock is readily available but money is tight, the stock might lend at a rate. These uncommon terms are further discussed below.

When stock loans are made from a restricted margin account, the customer has no use of the money received for the stock loan. The loan of stock in this instance provides a way for the broker to finance the customer's debit balance without paying interest to a bank. The customer still pays interest to the broker at the regular rate. Thus brokers can reduce their costs by lending customers' stock.

The normal procedure for bookkeeping is to continue to show the customer's account "long" the stock and at the same time show a credit for stock loaned in the "stock borrowed and loaned" account of the brokerage firm.

Lending Terms

Stock is loaned under one of three kinds of terms: (1) at a rate, (2) flat, and (3) at a premium.

When stock is loaned at a rate, as it was frequently done before 1930 and more recently when money again became tight, the lender receives a cash deposit equal to the value of the stock. In addition to the stock, however, the lender of the stock also pays to the borrower daily interest on the money received; the rate is slightly below the current call money rate. In that the use of the cash received is unrestricted and its cost may be 3–5% below the rates charged by commercial banks, stock loans provide an attractive alternative to other sources of cash. Not only would the banks charge more interest, but would demand securities equal to perhaps 133⅓% of the loan in order to cushion themselves against the risk of a drop in the value of the collateral.

When stock is loaned flat, no compensation passes either way between the lender and the borrower. The lender receives no compensation in the way of premiums, whereas the borrower receives no interest on the cash deposit received. Nearly all stock loans today are made this way.

When stock is loaned at a premium, the borrower must pay to the lender a charge based on the number of shares and the number of market (not calendar) days during which the loan was in effect. In such situations the stock is scarce relative to the demand by short sellers and the lender can take a profitable advantage of this to demand not only a 100% cash deposit as a protection, but also a daily fee for the use of the stock. This is an attractive situation to the lender if the premiums are high.

The premium is not interest and is not figured on a percentage basis. It is figured as so many cents or dollars per day for the life of the loan. In earlier years the premium was calculated on a fractional point basis. For example, a given stock might have been loaned at ⅛ point per share per day. In some instances it might have been loaned at a full point or more for short periods, such as when there was danger of a corner (see Chapter 16).

Premiums are now negotiated between buyer and seller and are usually based on a certain number of dollars per share. Until 1975, Rule 157 of the NYSE required that premiums must be based on a certain number of dollars per share and only at the following rates: 1, 2, 3, 6, 10, 15, and 20; higher rates had to be in multiples of $10. Suppose that a trader borrows 100 shares at a dollar premium for 45 market days; the trader would pay 45 times $1, or $45 in all, because the premium is a daily rate and does not include holidays or weekends.

Premiums have varied greatly in the past. Probably the all-time record was made in 1927 when for a short period the stock of the Wheeling and Lake Erie Railroad was loaned at $7 per share, or $700 per round lot, per day.[6] Several companies at that time were trying to buy control. Brisk bidding forced the price up beyond reasonable limits, which resulted in extensive short selling. In August 1918, General Motors stock commanded a premium of 1½ points per day for a time. During one week of January 1932, U.S. Steel common was loaned at ½ point per day. Such situations, however, are unusual. In 1931 and 1932, when a considerable number of stocks were being loaned at a premium, the average premium on such stocks was probably about $3 per 100 shares per day; on several occasions the average exceeded $5; at one time it was almost $12.

Stock lending at a premium has been infrequent the past few years. In many years, only one or two stocks are loaned this way and in some years none at all.

---

[6]J. E. Meeker, *Short Selling* (New York: Harper & Row, 1932), p. 198.

Protection to the Lender

As has already been indicated, the short seller must protect the lender of the stock by depositing an amount of cash equal to the market value of the stock. Where does this money come from? It comes from the proceeds of the sale of the borrowed stock. After the stock is sold, it is delivered to the purchaser through the National Stock Clearing Corporation on the day it is paid for. The proceeds are then used by the broker to protect the stock loan.

Mark to the Market

It is a practice in short selling for the loan to be secured at all times by approximately 100% of the market value of the stock. If the stock moves up by even a few points, more cash must be deposited with the lender by the short seller upon demand; if it declines, the lender must return cash. Thus full protection is always present regardless of the fluctuations in the price of the stock.

In order to be certain that the cash deposit is no more or no less than required, a notice is used by either lender or borrower. This formal notice is called a *mark to the market*. If the stock goes down, the broker representing the short seller sends a mark to the market to the lender's broker; it demands that cash be returned. If the stock goes up, the lender's broker sends the notice for more cash to be deposited. This demand is sent either directly or through the offices of a qualified clearing agency. The money must be paid directly or cleared through the agency immediately; there is no 5-day settlement rule.

In case either party fails to comply with Rule 165 of the Exchange for marking to the market, the other party can close the contract. This is done by giving notice to the offending party. After a short time lapse, the contract may be closed the same day by an officer or employee of the Exchange who is authorized to do so. The right to close the account protects both parties to the stock against irresponsibility.

Cancellation of Loan

A stock loan resembles a call loan in that either party may terminate the transaction by notice. Rule 160 of the Exchange, in describing the proper notice required, states:

> Unless otherwise agreed, notice for the return of loans of securities shall be given before 3:45, and such return shall be made on the fifth business day following the day on which such notice is given.

The borrower of the stock might cancel the loan because the customer covers the short position or because the stock has become available elsewhere on more favorable terms.

The lender of the stock might be forced to cancel the loan because the customer to whom the stock belongs might sell it, pay off a debit balance, or request the certificate. Under such conditions, the short seller's broker must either find another certificate within five days or require its customer to secure the stock from some other source. If the borrower of the security cannot deliver the certificate for any reason, the lender has the privilege of buying the security in the open market with any costs being borne by the defaulting borrower. Except under unusual circumstances the borrower has sufficient funds on deposit to cover any expenses of a buy-in.

Short Covering

Short covering or *to cover* is used for the act of buying in the stock that has been sold short. The shares so purchased are then returned after notice to the lender, together with any dividends or premiums that remain due.

Cash Dividends

The question is often asked: What happens to dividends declared to stock-holders of record during the time that a short sale is open? The answer is that dividends are charged to the short seller's account on the record date and go to the lender of the stock. The lender would have received the dividends if the stock has not been loaned; it is thus logical to be reimbursed for them. Such dividends would not be paid by the issuer of the stock, of course, because while the short sale is open, there is, in effect, more stock in the hands of the public than has been issued by the company.

Payment of the dividends by the short seller usually creates no hardship because the stock will usually drop enough in market price to approximate the dividend at the time it goes ex-dividend. The short sale will therefore be normally covered at a lower price than it would have been if the stock had not gone ex-dividend.

A similar procedure is followed in the case of bonds; that is, the short seller of a bond must pay any interest due on bonds that is paid while the seller is short.

Preemptive Rights

If preemptive rights are issued while a short sale is open, the borrowing firm buys sufficient rights in the open market to give the lending firm's customer a fair subscription privilege. The cost of the rights is debited to the short seller's margin account in the same manner as are cash dividends or bond interest.

Voting

It is, of course, impossible to create more votes for common stockholders merely because someone has chosen to sell a company's stock short. In that many stockholders, like voters everywhere, do not choose to exercise their franchise, it is usually no problem for a brokerage firm to provide voting proxies for all its customers who choose to vote.

In the rare, but highly publicized cases, where there are battles for control and almost every stockholder chooses to vote, it may be necessary for a short seller to cover this position merely because a proxy cannot be found. Like all corners, such circumstances are interesting but not usual.

Expenses

The short seller, in making the sale and short covering, will pay the usual buying and selling commissions. At the time of the sale, there will also be transfer taxes as well as the SEC fee to pay.

An old expression in Wall Street is: "The bull pays interest, but the bear does not." This is true, of course, because the margin buyer pays interest on a debit balance, whereas the short seller borrows no funds and hence pays no interest. However, if a short sale is marked to the market and a debit balance is created in the seller's account, interest expense will be incurred. The short seller must, of course, pay the lender any dividends on the stock during the period of the loan. In actual practice, this may be no expense at all, because as previously noted the stock usually falls by the amount of the dividend when it goes ex-dividend, and can thus be purchased at a lower price than prevailed before it went ex-dividend. Even if later the price rises and the sale is completed at a loss, the loss presumably is less than it would have been had no dividend been paid.

Example of Expenses and Profits

In order to show the expenses and profits from a short sale, an example of a transaction is shown.

Let us assume that Mrs. A., anticipating a decline in the price of stock XYZ, has decided to sell short. The stock is selling at 45. She sells 100 shares at that price and covers in 30 days at 35 after a decline of 22% in the price. The stock was borrowed flat.

Short sale: 100 shares at 45		$4,500.00
Selling expenses:		
Commission	$ 82.98	
SEC fee	.09	83.07
Net proceeds		$4,416.93
Add margin (assume 50%)		2,208.47
Total credits to account		$6,625.40
Covering purchase: 100 shares at 35	$3,500.00	
Commission	71.17	3,571.17
New credit balance		$3,054.23
Deduct margin deposit		2,208.47
Net gain on transaction		$ 845.76

Mrs. A., successfully forecasting the trend of the market, makes a net gain of $845.76, or about 38% on her original investment of $2,208.47.[7] A more precise analysis, of course, would consider such additional factors as the opportunity cost of the interest lost on the investment that could have been utilized elsewhere, the time required to make the 38%, which might be quite spectacular for six months but not too good for three years, and the risk attached to the investment.

KINDS OF SHORT SALES

The following classification is commonly found and serves as a basis for discussion:

1 Speculative sales
2 Hedges
3 Technical sales
   (a) Against the box
      1 For tax purposes
      2 For hedging purposes
      3 For future deliveries
   (b) For arbitrage purposes
      1 Between different markets
      2 Between equivalent securities
   (c) By security dealers and brokers
      1 By specialists
      2 By odd-lot dealers
      3 By investment bankers

Speculative Short Sales

The popular concept of the short sale is the speculative short sale; the seller owns no stock but borrows it and sells. The expectation is that the stock can be sold at a higher price than that used to cover or close the transaction. The initial impact of the speculative short sale is to increase the supply of stock offered for sale and thereby slow down a price rise. On the other hand, the effect of covering is to support or raise the price. The speculative short seller has one purpose only—to sell at one price and to cover at a lower price for a trading profit. In this the seller may or may not be successful.

---

[7]Commissions in the example provided may vary somewhat because commissions are negotiable among brokers. There were formerly small taxes to be considered on the sell side of the transaction, but the federal tax on par value was repealed and the New York State tax on number of shares involved phased out over a period of years.

The Hedging Short Sale

In this type of sale the short seller fears that there will be a decline in the market or in business conditions. Being a security holder, one does not want to take a loss on one's portfolio. This seller would therefore hedge against the anticipated decline by selling stock short, presumably market leaders, which lend themselves well to this purpose. The trader is not selling against the box, an operation to be described shortly, because the trader does not own the stock being sold. If the forecast is correct, the hedging operations will tend to protect the trader against losses caused by the drop in the security market or in business activity. How much activity of this sort takes place is not known; it is probably small.

Technical Short Sales

These short sales include all those in which the short seller either owns the securities sold or will come into possession of them shortly. In earlier years such transactions were not even considered as short sales. Rulings of the SEC, however, have placed them in the short sale category.

Short Sales Against the Box

The "box" used in this connection means the safe deposit box or account of the short seller. The trader actually possesses the security that is short sold. Delivery is made, however, by borrowing stock rather than delivering personally owned stock. The sale may be covered either by delivering personally owned stock or by buying stock in the market.

There are three important examples of short selling against the box. The first type is short selling for tax purposes. Prior to the changes in the Revenue Acts of 1950 and 1951, it was possible to obtain substantial tax reductions by selling securities short that had been purchased long for a price rise. Once a profit has been made on the transaction, the buyer would sell the stock short. The purpose was to stretch a short-term capital gain into a long-term capital gain, thereby securing the benefit of the reduced tax rate on long-term capital gains. Once the six-month period had passed, the speculator could cover the short sale by delivering the stock that had been bought long.[8] Substantial tax savings were thus effected. This, however, is no longer possible.

Subsequent tax law, however, still gave the taxpayer an advantage. One could use the short sale to carry over a profit from one year to the next. For example, in November of a given year a trader bought 100 shares of

---

[8]The length of the holding period needed to establish a long-term capital gain varies with current tax law. Indeed, the Tax Reform Act of 1986 eliminated any distinction between taxes on long or short term capital gains.

XYZ at 40. In December the stock was selling at 50. The trader wanted to retain the $1,000 profit, but did not want to report it as taxable income that year. Accordingly, the trader sold 100 shares short at 50 in December. In January the broker was instructed to deliver the long stock to the lender of the stock. Both the long and short positions were then closed out. The taxpayer now reports a $1,000 profit for the current year instead of in the previous year. Exactly how much of this is done is not known; there does appear to be a considerable amount near the end of the year.

A short sale may also be made against the box for hedging purposes. For example, a stockholder possesses a considerable block of stock and fears a market decline. Not certain of this judgment, however, the stockholder prefers to hedge rather than to make an outright sale. The hedging is done by short selling the amount of stock owned. If the stock falls, the gain on the short sale exactly offsets the loss on the long stock, disregarding taxes and commission. If the stock goes up, the gain on the long stock offsets loss on the short sale. The hedge has been successful. This type of short selling in earlier years was often done by corporate insiders who did not want to sell outright stock that might represent a substantial controlling interest in the company. They therefore did secretly what they dared not do openly. Today, insiders may not sell the stock of listed companies short.

Occasionally, a stockholder may sell stock short that cannot be delivered immediately. For example, the stockholder may be on vacation and the stock is not immediately accessible. In this case the trader sells short and then covers with the stock in the box.

Sales for Arbitrage Purposes

Two types of arbitrage transactions are possible. The first is between different markets. A stock may be sold in two markets, for example, New York and Los Angeles. A professional trader, seeing an opportunity to sell in New York at a higher price than that in Los Angeles, would make a short sale in New York and a purchase in Los Angeles. The short sale would be necessary because stock could not be delivered in a regular way in such an operation. A stock selling on several exchanges tends to have nearly the same price on each exchange, and communication equipment has become increasingly efficient; hence, there is little opportunity for profitable arbitrage of this type.

Arbitrage between equivalent securities is far more common. This may take place between common stock and other securities into which it is convertible, such as bonds or preferred stocks. It may be profitable to buy a convertible bond which is underpriced relative to the stock into which it is convertible, sell the stock short, convert the bond into stock, and deliver the stock against the short sale for an overall profit after commissions and other costs. It may also occur between stocks and rights, warrants, or options. Groups of stocks may be arbitraged against various stock index futures contracts and options on such indexes.

Virtually all such arbitrage opportunities are in practicality limited to professional traders who have available sophisticated communications equipment and sufficient capital to trade on a scale to make worthwhile the attempt to take advantage of small short-lived aberrations. Furthermore many arbitrage "opportunities" may involve substantial risk, for example, trading stocks involved in rumored or even announced mergers. The arbitrager might buy the lower-priced stock involved in an anticipated merger and sell the higher-priced stock short only to find that the terms of the merger change or that the merger fails to occur. Such "risk arbitrages" can lead to substantial losses.

Sales by Security Dealers

Brokers and dealers might utilize short sales for various purposes. Specialists frequently need to use this type of transaction in order to make an orderly market in the stocks in which they specialize.

Those who deal in odd lots, such as large commission houses and specialists, may also engage in short selling when the public buys on balance and the dealers have inadequate inventories to supply the demand.

Investment bankers bringing out new issues or holding substantial inventories might find it advantageous on occasion to sell short. The covering of such short sales tends to stabilize the market and thereby protects them against inventory losses that they would suffer in a market decline. In the case of new issues, covering short sales may help the new market get off to a good start by preventing significant price drops immediately after the issue, drops that might induce new public buyers to sell.

REGULATION

Criticisms and Defenses

Short selling has been the subject of many studies. The idea of selling short, of selling something not owned, is outside the experience of people used to ordinary retail and manufacturing practices. It is easy to find analogies in common experience—such as accepting prepayment on an order to deliver manufactured goods—but these are not usually thought to be the same kind of operation. Thus it is easy to criticize the practice.

Opportunities for abuse are evident too. If a number of traders made short sales in substantial volume of a given stock, their action obviously would increase the supply of that stock on the market. It might increase the supply significantly. If at the same time the price of the stock was falling because a tendency for the supply to exceed the demand at given prices already existed, the action of short sellers would accelerate the price decline. Similarly, if traders who had made short sales covered their transactions by purchasing in a rising market, their action would accelerate the rise. In these instances, short selling would thus reinforce both booms and recessions; it would undoubtedly draw criticism.

In contrast, of course, if traders sold short when prices were rising (in anticipation of a turn down) and covered their sales by purchasing when prices were falling (in anticipation of a turn up), their actions would add to the stability of the market. Observe that the regulations imposed on short selling as described below are designed to make this kind of action more likely.

Most significant to evaluating the usefulness of short selling in the market is the preponderant use of the technique by professionals for technical reasons. With the arguments in favor of the technical short sale there is little quarrel. These, in summary, are (1) it enables owners of securities to sell with a minimum of risk and delay when it is not possible to effect immediate delivery; (2) it permits both individual and institutional security holders to avoid the risk of price fluctuations; (3) it aids in the operations of dealers in odd lots; (4) it facilitates the work of specialists; and (5) it makes arbitraging possible.

Present Criticism

There is less criticism today of short selling than at any other time in many years. In fact, little comment on it—pro or con—appears in the press. The Senate investigation of the market in 1955 did not concern itself with short selling at any time, and the final report makes no mention of this aspect of speculative activity. The regular midmonthly reports on the short interest continue to appear in the press, but few are able to attach much significance to them.

Rules Prior to 1931

Before 1931 the NYSE had three rules on short selling. The substance was that no short sale should be made that would demoralize the market. In other words, members were not to effect such sales either for their own account or for customers if such transactions created a disorderly market. The rules were not definite in application, however well intentioned they may have been; they certainly did not result in effective control of short selling.

The 1931 Rule

In 1931 the Exchange made a rule that required all sales to be marked as "long" or "short." The purpose was to enable the Exchange to detect the amount and source of short selling. This was only a publicity regulation; in no way did it deter the rights of speculators to sell short.

The 1935 Rule

Although the rule of 1931 did not actually restrict short selling, brokers still did not allow short selling at a price lower than that of the last sale; such an operation was considered to "demoralize the market." Under this unofficial code a short sale could never be made at a given price until a long sale had been made at that price or below. Hence the brokers, by interpretation of the 1931 rule, made some attempt to prevent excessive selling on a declining market. At the suggestion of the SEC, the practice was officially incorporated in 1935 as a rule of the Exchange in this language: "No member shall use any facility of the Exchange to effect on the Exchange a short sale of any security in the unit of trading at a price below the last 'regular way' sale price of such security on the Exchange."[9]

Although this rule tended to eliminate a succession of short sales at continuously declining prices, it did not entirely prevent excessive short selling.

The Securities Exchange Act

The Securities Exchange Act of 1934 neither abolished short selling nor made any specific regulation about it, in spite of a rather considerable body of lawmakers who would have liked to eliminate or severely restrict it.

Only three references were made to the short sale. First, Section 7 gives the Federal Reserve Board the power to fix margins on such transactions. Second, Section 10, in relation to the use of manipulative and deceptive devices, states that it is unlawful on a national securities exchange to effect a short sale in contravention of such rules and regulations as the SEC may prescribe as necessary and appropriate in the public interest or for the protection of investors. Third, Section 16 forbids short selling by directors, officers, and principal stockholders of stock of the companies in which they hold this position. The Act therefore gave the SEC complete power to eliminate or regulate such transactions in whatever way it saw fit.

Under powers given by the Act, the SEC has formulated Rules 10A-1 and 10A-2, which now govern short selling on any national securities exchange.

The 1938 Rule

The first regulation of short selling by the SEC was introduced on February 8, 1938, after the Commission had examined the market decline of 1937 when a substantial amount of short selling took place in certain market leaders. Regulation was through Rules 10A-1 and 10A-2. Both are essentially the same today as when written in 1938 except for the provision that states when a short sale can be made. We are concerned at this point only with that part of Rule 10A-1 that stated: "No person shall . . . effect a short sale of any

---

[9]Chapter xiv of the *Rules of the Governing Committee,* 1935.

security at or below the price at which the last sale thereof, regular way, was effected on such exchange."

This rule meant that no short sale could be made at or below the price of the last sale; that is, all sales must be made at least ⅛ point above the last sale. As long as the market continued down, no short sale could be made.

The result of this rule was that the short interest dropped sharply and short selling was almost wiped out. For a time a loophole existed; the SEC rule had exempted odd lots. As a result, short selling through odd lots rapidly increased. The Exchange closed the loophole by putting both round and odd lots on the same basis (Rule 435). The SEC admitted that its rule was impractical, but did not change it.

In time the Committee on Floor Procedure of the Exchange worked out a proposed change in the rule and presented it to the SEC. After an investigation it was quickly adopted. The amendment became effective on March 20, 1939.

Other Sections of the 1938 Rule

The 1938 rule has several other provisions worthy of note. No sale may be executed unless it is marked "long" or "short." This is, of course, merely a continuation of the 1931 rule the Exchange established many years ago.

No sale shall be marked "long" unless the security to be delivered after the sale is actually carried in the customer's account or is owned by the customer and will be delivered as soon as is possible without undue inconvenience and expense. If available securities are not to be delivered on the sale, it is a "sale against the box" and must be marked "short."

Certain short sales are exempt from the up-tick rule, including sales by the owner of a security who intends to deliver it as soon as possible without undue inconvenience and expense, balancing sales by specialists and other dealers in odd lots, and sales by arbitragers involving equivalent securities.[10]

The 1939 Rule

The regulations of the SEC on short selling as amended in 1939 have been changed only in minor detail since that year.

Section (a) of Rule 10A-1 is so vital to understanding present regulations on short selling that we quote it in part:

> No person shall, for his own account or for the account of any other person, effect on a national securities exchange a short sale of any security (1) below the price at which the last sale thereof, regular way, was effected on such exchange, or (2) at such price unless such price is above the next preceding different price at which a sale of such security, regular way, was effected on such exchange.

[10]An expanded version of this subject may be found in NYSE Rule 440B.

It is always possible to sell short at a higher price than that of the last sale. Hence, if a stock last sold at 50, one can sell short at 50⅛. Under the 1938 rule this was the only type of short sale allowed.

No short sale may be made below the price of the last sale, regardless of the trend of the market. This eliminates "hammering of the market" when it is on the decline.

One may sell short at the price of the last sale under only one condition—that such price is above the next preceding different price.

As long as prices are stable and the last change in price is upward, an endless number of short sales may be made at the same price.

A minor part of Section (a) should be mentioned at this point. In case a stock goes ex-dividend, all sale prices prior to the "ex" date are reduced by the amount of the dividend. For example, assume that a stock may be sold short at 50. The company declares a dividend of $1 per share; after the stock goes ex-dividend, the stock may be sold short at 49.

Brokers and customers who are familiar with the operations of the short selling rule have a special terminology in place of the legalistic expression "at such price unless such price is above the next preceding different price." They use the terms *plus tick, minus tick,* or *zero plus tick.*

A plus tick takes place when a given sale on an exchange is made at a higher price than the previous transaction. Television screens over each post on the trading floor indicate the price of the last sale of each stock. Plus and minus signs indicate whether the figure represents a "plus tick" or a "minus tick." The SEC allows exchanges to use either the consolidated tape or trades made on their own floors as the basis for determining whether a tick is plus or minus. Both the New York and American Stock Exchanges have chosen to utilize the trades that take place upon their own floors.

A minus tick occurs when a sale is made at a price lower than that of the previous sale. For example, let us take three sales: 35, 34⅞, and 34¾. Both the second and third sales are minus ticks in sequence; a short sale may not be made on a minus tick. Of course, a short sale may be made after a minus tick if it can be made against a bid at least ⅛ higher than that that produced the minus tick.

A zero plus tick takes place when a given sale is at the same price as that of the previous sale, but the last change in price was upward. To illustrate, let us take three sales: 50, 50¼, and 50¼. There was no change in price between the second and third sales; this was the zero. However, 50¼ was above the sale at 50, giving us our plus. The third sale was level with the second sale, but above the first sale. A short sale can always be made on a zero plus tick.

THE SHORT SELLERS

Short sellers are primarily professional traders, usually members of exchanges. Typically, 80–90% of short positions are held by such professionals as specialists and arbitragers and the remaining 10–20% by the trading public. Of this amount, a substantial percentage is accounted for by short sales against the box for tax purposes.

It is not unusual that a few short sellers account for a large part of the short interest and that the short interest is concentrated in a relatively short list of stocks. This is probably caused by the concentrated interest in arbitraged issues.

The odd-lot public in general is unfamiliar with short selling and is reluctant to use it. Typically being an on-balance buyer of stocks, the public distrusts short selling. In most years, the percentage of short sales to all sales made by the odd-lot public runs well under 1%.

THE WORK OF THE SPECIALIST

Specialists are members of the Exchange who engage in the buying and selling of one or more specific issues of stock on the floor. Their work is central to the maintenance of a free, continuous market in the issues in which they act as specialists. Specialists on most exchanges usually are members of firms that engage primarily or exclusively in this activity. There are about 60 such firms on the NYSE.

Specialists may act as brokers or as dealers in transactions. In their capacity as brokers they execute orders for other brokers on a commission. In their capacity as dealers they act for their own accounts, profits, and risks. In this latter capacity they buy from the public when it offers stock for sale but other public bids for purchase are not available, and sells to the public when it bids but other public offers to sell are not available at or near the price of the last transaction. In other words, they maintain markets by purchasing stock at a higher price than anyone else is willing to pay at the time, and by selling stock at a lower price than anyone else is willing to take at the time. The customers of the specialists are other members of the Exchange; as specialists, they do not transact business directly with the public.

NATURE AND IMPORTANCE OF WORK

Origin

The origin of the specialist is somewhat obscure. Tradition has it that a certain Mr. Boyd, about 1875, suffered a broken leg. Upon returning to the floor, he conducted his trading while seated in a chair. Because of his limited mobility, he confined his operations to Western Union stock, a very popular issue at the time. This plan proved so successful that he continued this practice, even after he became well again. The specialists' function, however, grew rather slowly and it was not until about 1910 that it became of much importance. During World War I it fully justified its expectations and proved of great value in handling the active war stocks of that period.

Importance of Work

Specialists are willing and required to quote a stock and to buy or sell the stock, either for their book or for their own accounts. They are leading figures on the floor. As a rule, no one is eager to trade in stocks in which there is a poor market. Because specialists' commission income depends on their ability to maintain a good market for the stocks in which they are specializing, it is in their self-interest to maintain as continuous and close a market as possible.

In recent years, specialists acting as dealers in their own accounts were responsible for between 10 and 12% of all Exchange reported volume of purchases and sales. Actually their importance has been greater than this figure indicates because it does not include the transactions in which specialists acted as brokers. These brokerage transactions in any given year typically exceeded the dealer transactions.

There has been a rapid growth in the number of registered traders in recent years, many of whom act as market makers off the floor and who compete with the specialists who are on the floor. The activity of such registered competitive market makers is combined with that of the specialists statistically. The student of exchange activity should be alert to the dramatic increase of off-floor trading in recent years. Nevertheless, the floor specialist remains a key figure in the market.

THE SPECIALIST'S BOOK

Nature of Book

Historically the chief tool of the specialist was his or her book. Once used for all issues the book has been replaced by an "electronic book" screen for active issues. The old-fashioned ringbinder with pages 4 by 11 inches is still used, however, for many inactive issues. The pages are ruled and are usually printed with fractional stock points at regular intervals to permit easy insertion of orders. The left-hand page holds the bids or buy orders with the lowest bids at the top of the page, whereas the right-hand page contains the offers or sell orders with the highest offers at the bottom. If the orders are not too numerous, two pages will contain all the orders at a given full point, for example, all orders from 60 to 60⅞. In active markets, it was sometimes necessary to have several books to contain the orders for a given stock. The orders are entered in the book by the specialist according to price and in the sequence in which they are received at the post. The specialist notes the number of shares, putting down 1 for 100 shares, 2 for 200, and so on; and also notes the name of the member placing the order and the time limit, such as GTC. Stop orders are so indicated. When orders are executed by a specialist, they are executed in the sequence in which the names were recorded in the book at the price. This is the sequence in which the orders were received from brokers on the floor.

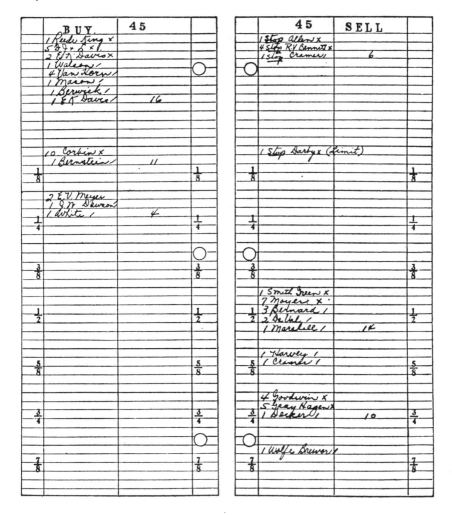

Fig. 8-1 Two pages from a specialist's book.

For purposes of illustration, Figure 8-1 shows two pages of a specialist's book, employing hypothetical firm names. Orders from 28 members or firms are indicated in the illustration. There are 13 buy orders, 11 sell orders, and 4 stop orders. Open orders are identified by crosses and day orders by short dashes. Let us now examine how these orders would be handled.

Handling a Buy Order

Let us suppose that Broker A comes to Post 2 where the specialist is handling XYZ. Broker A would first ask for the quotation on the stock. The specialist can quote from the notebook and will therefore reply, "45¼ to ½." This represents the highest bid and lowest offer in the book. At that time the specialist does not know whether Broker A wants to buy or sell, or is merely asking for information.

Broker A, however, has a buy order for 100 shares. Noting that the quotation is 45¼ to ½, the broker will not expect to pay less than 45½, but must attempt to get as good a price for the customer as possible, so the broker bids 45⅜ for 100. If no other member of the "crowd" is willing to do business at this price, Broker A will raise the bid to 45½. The specialist immediately calls out "Sold!" and allocates the sale to the first order on the book at that price. It was entered by Smith & Green. The specialist "gives up" the name, "Smith & Green," to Broker A and sends a report of the execution to Smith & Green. Meyer has now moved into the first position at 45½ on the book of the specialist, and if the specialist sells additional stock at that price, Meyer will be the first to receive a report of the execution.

Handling a Sell Order

Let us suppose that Broker B comes to the post and wishes to sell 300 shares. After inquiring as to the quotation, Broker B begins to offer the stock at a price higher than the best bid on the specialist's book in the hope of obtaining a higher price for the customer. Since the best bid at the moment is 45¼, there is not much sense in making more than two offers. Accordingly, Broker B offers 300 shares at 45⅜. Receiving no acceptance, the offer is lowered to 45¼. The specialist calls, "Take it!" or "Take them!" The specialist now notifies E. V. Meyer, the ranking bidder, that 200 shares were bought at 45¼. The other 100 shares goes to J. W. Dawson, next in priority. The names of these members are "given up" to Broker B when the transaction takes place.

Handling a Stop Order

A stop order to sell is one that becomes a market order when the stock sells at or below the stop price. The reverse is true of a stop order to buy. On our book being illustrated, the specialist has Darby's stop order to sell 100 shares at 45⅛. In order not to complicate matters, let us assume that the buying and selling orders just discussed were never put into effect and the book contains all of the original orders.

Let us assume that trading in the stock becomes active and that the specialist has bought for his book 500 shares. This cleared all the buy orders at 45¼ and 100 shares at 45⅛. Since there has now been a sale at 45⅛, it is possible to execute the stop order of Darby; it has now become a market order. The specialist now offers the stock at 45¼ to see whether a better price is offered. If this is not forthcoming, the specialist proceeds to cross an order for 100 shares between Darby and Corbin and so notifies both brokers.

Stopping Stock

Stopping stock is a practice by which a specialist or another member on the floor guarantees purchase or sale of a specified number of shares of a given issue at a given price. This amount of stock is reserved for another broker but not earmarked for any particular account. The stop may be given for the specialist's, or member's, own account. At no cost to the broker asking the favor, the specialist or member, by this "stop," gives that other broker a definite reservation.

Let us suppose that a broker comes to the specialist's post with an order to buy 100 shares "at the market." In our hypothetical book the best price that the broker could expect at the moment would be 45½. The broker, desiring to get the customer as good a price as possible, would like to buy it for less than 45½, but at the same time does not want to "miss the market" and pay more than that price. So the broker requests the specialist, or another member in the crowd, to stop 100 shares at 45½. It is possible that in the next few minutes stock may be offered on the floor at less than 45½. If the 100 shares can be bought at 45⅜, the broker will do so and then say, "The stop is off."

However, if our broker cannot buy the stock at 45⅜ and a transaction takes place in the crowd at 45½, this immediately puts into operation the buy order of the broker. The specialist or member who granted the stop now sells the stock and so informs the customer's broker by some phrase, such as "You are elected," that indicates the broker has bought the stock at 45½.

The amount of stock that a specialist will stop for a public order at a given price depends not only upon the amount of stock at a given price there is on the book, but also on the size and number of orders and what is reasonable. The specialist will not stop any part of the biggest order at a given price. In the hypothetical book under consideration, the specialist would probably be willing to stop 200 shares on the buy side and 700 on the sell side.

The practice of "stopping stock" allows an active floor broker an opportunity to obtain the best price possible for customers. A broker with several orders to execute has assurance that the price on the order for which stock was stopped will be the best in the market at the moment if a transaction occurs while the broker is handling another order and before returning to try to get a still better price a few minutes later. This privilege is not similarly available to members themselves. Stock offered may be stopped for them at the offer price and stock bid for them may be stopped at the bid price, but not the reverse. A member's order may not go ahead of public orders.

Opening the Market

The most difficult period of the day for the specialist is usually at the opening of the market. At that time many orders have piled up, some at the market, some limited, and some stop orders. It is the specialists' duty to open the market at a price that will permit all market orders to be executed, and yet at a price as close to the previous day's close as possible, so that the market may be as orderly as the situation permits. They do this by considering all orders and establishing as fair a price as possible. They must make adjustments for cancellations and other changes and enter the orders received before the opening. This situation may permit a specialist to arrive at an equilibrium price between buyers and sellers. It may, however, be necessary to obtain buyers when sellers predominate, or the reverse may be true. In many cases it may be necessary to supply stock or buy stock for his or her own account in order to equalize the volume of buying and selling.

The services of the specialist under trying circumstances are well illustrated also by action in the market of Monday, September 26, 1955, on the frenzied first day of business following President Eisenhower's heart attack on September 24. At the opening of the market on that day all specialists were carrying a total inventory of 1,651,000 shares, valued at nearly $50 million on the previous Friday. Because of the great liquidation at the opening on September 26, it was necessary for the specialists as a group to buy another 1,099,000 shares at a cost of $49.1 million to help stabilize the market. During the day purchases by specialists accounted for 23% of all purchases. At the close of the day specialists held 2,246,524 shares with a market value of $73.4 million.

Spread on Listed Stocks

In order to maintain an orderly market in stocks, specialists attempt to keep spreads in quotations and the size of variations between sales reasonable. The difference between the bid and the ask price should not be too great. For the active stock the spread in the quotation is usually very small. In perhaps 86% of the cases the variation between sales is ¼ point or less. For the less active stocks the spread is likely to run from ⅝ to a full point.

FUNCTIONS OF THE SPECIALIST

Services as Broker

There has, from time to time, been considerable criticism leveled at the specialists and their work, but the volume and intensity of such criticism have been sharply reduced in recent years. The place of the specialist appears secure based on two major services to the market: as brokers and as dealers in making orderly markets.

As a broker the specialist serves in somewhat the same capacity as a floor broker. In this function the specialist executes limit, stop, and market orders for other members of the Exchange. If we assume that these duties are performed rapidly and efficiently, a very useful purpose is served. This work saves time for other members, thus permitting them to operate more effectively for their customers and with a smaller investment in floor memberships. It seems questionable whether a more efficient system of handling limit and stop orders could be devised. The specialist also serves a useful function in maintaining an orderly market at the opening, as well as at other times.

Services as Dealer

The function of specialists when acting as dealers is to maintain an orderly market in the stock in which they specialize. The Board of Governors of the Exchange has defined the function as follows (Rule 104):

> The function of a member acting as a regular specialist on the floor of the Exchange, includes, in addition to the effective execution of commission orders entrusted to him, the maintenance, in so far as reasonably practicable, of a fair and orderly market on the Exchange in the stocks in which he is so acting.

The interpretation of this requirement, backed by numerous rules, is that the specialist should maintain a continuous market with price continuity and close bid and asked prices, and minimize the effect of temporary disparity between public supply and demand. To the extent that the specialists maintain a better, more stable, and orderly market, they are performing a useful function. The criticisms of the specialists that have been made in the past have stemmed from beliefs, fair or not, that in their capacity as dealers, they did not always place the interests of the public ahead of their own. Whether or not this was true, it seems clear that the specialists have enough economic incentive and are sufficiently bound by exchange and government rules to motivate most of them to perform their functions efficiently and adequately most of the time. A sampling of some of these restrictions follows.

REGULATIONS UNDER THE SECURITIES EXCHANGE ACT

Maintaining an Orderly Market

The Securities Exchange Act requires that the SEC make such rules and regulations as may be reasonably necessary to permit the specialist to maintain a fair and orderly market. Note that the intention of Congress was to limit the specialist's function to maintaining an orderly market rather than to trading for one's own profit.

Disclosure

Specialists may not disclose the contents of their books to any person other than an official of the Exchange, an authorized visitor to the floor, or a specialist who may be acting for such specialist. The SEC, however, may require disclosure when necessary in the public interest. There is, of course, little doubt that at times a specialist's book contains information that might be very useful to a few speculators. It is not considered disclosure of the book for specialists to state the number of shares involved in the best bid and offer. However, they are not compelled to do so if they believe such action would be inadvisable.

Discretionary Orders

Specialists may execute only market or limited price orders. In other words, the specialist must be instructed as to the issue, the type of order, the total amount, and whether purchase or sale. There can be no discretion given the specialist in these matters. Rules permit, however, a certain amount of brokerage judgment on such things as whether the specialist should stop stock, bid for, or offer the full amount of the order, and bid at or below or offer at or above the price of the order.

Manipulation

Any form of manipulation of security prices by a specialist is made unlawful by Sections 9 and 10 of the Act. This prohibition also applies to all other members of the Exchange. It should also be noted that manipulation is prohibited by the Constitution of the Exchange and by its rules.

REGULATIONS OF THE STOCK EXCHANGE

A body of rules was drawn up originally in 1938, and amended from time to time, by the NYSE in regard to specialists. The purpose has been to assure efficient and honest service by the specialists for their customers at all times.

Registration

Under Rule 103 all specialists must register with the Exchange. This permits the Exchange to check on the activities of members acting in this capacity. No specialist activity is possible without registration.

Trading for Orderly Market

Probably the most important rule of the Exchange is Rule 104, which states that no specialist shall buy or sell for his or her own account, or for one in which the specialist is interested, unless such dealings are reasonably necessary to maintain a fair and orderly market. The rule is similar to Section 11 of the Securities Exchange Act and has as its purpose the prevention of excessive trading for profits. In principle, the rule is very clear. In practice, the determination of what constitutes trading to maintain a fair and orderly market becomes complex. There can be no exact answer. The rule does not prevent specialists from trading for profit; they may also incur a loss in such activity. It is not practical to believe that a specialist would engage in trading without the objective of making a profit. The rule, however, seeks to prevent excessive and unreasonable trading for a specialist's own account to the possible disadvantage of the investing public served by the market.

Pools and Options

Rule 105 provides that neither the specialist nor the specialist's organization nor a participant in that organization shall have any direct or indirect interest in any pool dealing or trading in the stock in which the specialist is registered, nor shall these parties directly or indirectly hold, acquire, grant, or have an interest in any option in the stock in which the specialist is registered. As will be noted in Chapter 16 on manipulation, options played an important part at one time in the manipulation of security prices by pools.

Quotations for Own Account

A specialist may quote a stock for his or her own account and not from the book in order to maintain closer prices and incur proper price continuity.

At what price may the specialist quote a stock for a personal account? The specialist may and should quote the stock either when there are no bids or when there are no offers on the book. When there are bids and offers on the specialists' book, they may quote the stock, but may not compete with their book. They may bid and offer for their own account within the bids and offers on the book in order to improve the market. However, they cannot buy at or below the price of any order on their book to buy unless they have executed the orders of their customers at these prices, nor can they sell at or above the price of an order on their book to sell until they have executed the orders of their customers at these prices. For example, let us suppose that the quotation from the book is 25 to 25½. The specialist could offer the stock under 25½, such as ⅜, ¼, or ⅛. The specialist could bid for stock at 25⅛, ¼, or ⅜. In none of these examples does the specialist compete with bids and offers on the book, but is merely making a better and closer market.

In the illustration just given, if the last sale were 25⅜, the specialist would not be allowed to bid 25½, since regulations prohibit buying above the price of the last sale in the same session, except as noted below.

Deals for Own Account

Specialists may deal for their own accounts only if the transactions are necessary for the market, to achieve a position adequate for immediate or anticipated needs of the market or to cover a short sale. Except for transactions reasonably necessary to render a position adequate, specialists are not permitted to purchase shares at a price above the last sale in the same session.

Again, specialists are not permitted, unless it is necessary to render their

position adequate to meet the needs of the market, to purchase all or substantially all the stock offered on the book at a price equal to the last sale
when the stock so offered represents all or substantially all the stock offered
in the market. For example, let us suppose that the last sale of XYZ was 25
and the specialist had 1,500 shares in his or her book at that price on limited
orders. The specialist could not clear the book, except as noted, of these
1,500 shares for his own account, since this would leave the market with no
offers at 25. Similarly, with the same exception, the specialist may not supply
all, or substantially all, the stock bid on the book where the stock so bid
represents all, or substantially all, the stock bid in the market. Such a trade
would clear the market of all available bids at that price.

The specialists are forbidden to buy for their own accounts when they
have an unexecuted market order to buy; they are also forbidden to sell for
their own account when they have an unexecuted market order to sell. To
permit this would mean that they would be competing with their own customers and would not be performing their duties as agent in the interest of
their customers.

While on the floor they are also forbidden to buy stock for their own
accounts at or below a price at which they have a limited order to buy. For
example, let us suppose that the quotation is 25 to 25½ from the book. The
specialist could not buy for a personal account at 25 or less, since this would
be in direct competition with the specialist's own book. In 1953 an exception
to this rule concerned only with off-board trading was put into effect. The
specialist unit with prior approval of a floor governor may purchase off the
floor a block of one of the stocks in which the specialist is registered, without
executing purchase orders on the book, at prices at or above the per-share
price paid by the specialist for such stock. In other words, if the Exchange
believes that the regular market on the Exchange floor cannot within a reasonable time and at reasonable price or prices absorb a given block of stock,
the purchase of this stock off the floor is permitted if this purchase will aid
the specialist in maintaining a fair and orderly market.

Finally, specialists may not sell stock for their own account, except in a
similar manner as a block off the floor, at or above a price at which they
have a limit order to sell. To do so would be competing with the customer.

Crossing Orders

If a specialist has a buy order for 100 shares at 40 from Customer A and
another order to sell at 40 from Customer B, the specialist might cross the
orders by selling B's stock to A at 40.

Two rules govern such action. One rule requires that when a specialist
has an order to buy and an order to sell the same security, the specialist
must publicly offer the security at the minimum variation higher than the
bid. Since nearly all stocks sell above $1 per share, the minimum variation
in practice means ⅛ point. In our example, the specialist would first offer

the stock publicly at 40⅛. If there was no sale, the specialist could then cross orders and collect the usual commission from Broker A and Broker B. A second rule prevents the specialists from trading for their own account whenever it is possible to cross orders.

There are several reasons for these rules. One is to assure the customer the best possible price; another, to make the transaction publicly in the open market; a third, to protect the rights of the bidders and offerers in the "crowd" of that stock; and finally, to prevent the specialist from crossing orders merely to get the double commission that would result.

Crossing for Own Account

Crossing for own account is used to describe a transaction in which the specialist sells personally owned stock to the book or buys from the book for a personal account. Let us suppose that a specialist has a bid of 30 for 100 shares of stock on the book. By selling one's own stock for 30 to the book, the specialist would be crossing for a personal account.

There are three restrictions on such activity. First, the specialist must offer the stock at ⅛ higher than the received bid before crossing. Second, the price must be justified by the market. Third, the broker who originally gave the order to the specialist must accept the trade after proper notification. When crossing orders for one's own account, the specialist receives no commission.

Stopping Stock

Specialists are prevented from stopping stock on their own book or in the book of a competing specialist for their own account. Such an action would give an undue preference over orders of their customers. The specialists may give the privilege to others, but may not accept it for themselves. When a specialist desires to buy or sell stock for their own account, they must bid for or offer it in the open market.

TRADING FLOOR PROCEDURES

Although the basic auction-market rules governing stock trading on the NYSE have remained unchanged for many years, the NYSE floor changed vastly between the late 1970s and early 1980s. In 1980 the Exchange completed the replacement of the 50-year-old trading posts with 14 new and larger posts. Each of the new posts is surrounded by video display terminals and other electronic gear. To veteran floor personnel it probably appears a bit futuristic. Those who remember a time when 10 million shares daily was considered huge and barely manageable now consider a 10-million-share hour routine and even a little on the dull side.

In the early 1970s the daily volume averaged 14–16 million shares. By the mid-1980s this figure had grown to 80–90 million. This does not mean that floor personnel are handling 5 or 6 times as many orders as they once did. In addition to electronic and procedural advances, there has been a great increase in the size and volume of large block (10,000 shares or more) transactions.

Before attempting to indicate how virtually the same number of members on the floor as were there a decade ago can handle efficiently a greatly expanded volume, a brief review of the basics of auction-market trading is in order. Although the mechanism may seem a bit cumbersome, at root it is both fair and efficient. On no other exchange do so many large value trades change hands at prices so close to the last sale. About 90% of all transactions occur with no change or the minimum variation of ⅛ point. The bid and asked quotations are ¼ point or less about 65% of the time. Even more remarkably the average stock shows no price change or only ⅛ between 85 and 90% of the time. Much of the credit for such smooth price transactions must be given to specialists who continuously stabilize markets by selling from their own accounts when markets are strong and buying when markets are weak.

EXECUTION OF ORDERS

The Double-Auction Market

All orders on the Exchange are transacted on the basis of a free, double auction. In every transaction stock is sold to the highest bidder and purchased from the lowest offerer. The Exchange fixes no prices, although this misconception of Exchange activity has been held at times by many persons. Prices are determined through a process of bidding and offering. Most bids and offers are made by the outside investing and trading public, although a substantial volume of buying and selling is done by members of the Exchange. In 1980, for example, members accounted for 26.5% of the volume of shares purchased and sold on the Exchange. The public accounted for the balance.

PRIORITY OF BIDS AND OFFERS

The present rules on the priority of bids and offers may be divided into two classes: first, those covering bids and offers originating off the Exchange, and second, those initiated on the floor by floor traders.

Regulations on bids and offers cover about six pages in the *New York Stock Exchange Guide*. In the discussion that follows, only the chief principles of bidding and offering stock will be considered.

Highest Bid

Rule 71 of the Exchange states that the highest bid shall have precedence in all cases. For example, let us suppose that a broker bids 40 for a given stock; no other broker may bid in the crowd for that stock at 39⅞ or less.

Lowest Offer

Rule 71 also states that the lowest offer shall have precedence in all cases. For example, let us suppose that a broker wishes to offer stock at 50; no other broker may then offer in the crowd to sell the stock at more than 50.

Equal Bids

The problem of determining which broker is to buy stock becomes complicated when there are two or more bids at the same price. Because price is not involved, all bids being the same, priority must be determined by some other rule.

There are two methods of determining which broker is to buy. The first is that when bids are equal in price but enter the market at different times, the bid with time priority has precedence over later bids.

Rule 72 states that when a bid is clearly established as the first made at a particular price, the maker shall be entitled to priority and shall have precedence on the next sale at that price up to the number of shares specified in the bid. The term "first made at a particular price" means that the member clearly established the bid before any other member could do so. In this connection it should be noted that (1) a new auction starts with each new sale and (2) the priority of bids does not carry over from one auction to the next or from day to day.

In our first example, all bids and offers are at the same price:

Bids	Offers
A—100 shares	X—100 shares
B—100 shares	

A made her bid first. She therefore gets the 100 shares, whereas B receives nothing. A had a time priority.

In our second example, A entered her bid first, followed by B, who in turn was followed in time by C. All bids and offers were made at the same price:

Bids	Offers
A—100 shares	X—200 shares
B—100 shares	
C—100 shares	

In this example, A secures 100 shares and B secures 100 shares. C obtains nothing since he was behind both A and B in time priority and bid for an amount equaling the excess after A's bid had been filled.

The second situation occurs when all bids are equal in price but at least one is for a larger number of shares than the others. No bid has time priority. Precedence here is determined by Rule 72, which may be stated, in substance, as follows:

> On bids entered simultaneously, the larger ordinarily has priority with the following exception:
>
> > On bids entered simultaneously, each equal to or larger than the amount of stock offered at the bid price, the bidders toss a coin and the winner of the "match" purchases the entire amount of offered stock.

Simultaneous bids or offers usually come into existence when a transaction has occurred, some bids or offers in the market at that time remain unfilled, and bids or offers for these unfilled orders are reentered in the new auction following this transaction. Under these conditions the bids and offers on the unfilled orders are considered simultaneously made. Similarly, since there is a new auction at the start of each trading session, bids or offers entered at the opening are all considered to have been simultaneously made.

Let us start with the simplest possible example. Two bids are entered simultaneously for 100 shares each. Only 100 shares are being offered:

Bids	Offers
A—100 shares	X—100 shares
B—100 shares	

In this case, A and B match and the winner receives the 100 shares.

In our second example, there are three bidders wishing 100 shares each, but only 100 shares are being offered. All bids are entered simultaneously:

Bids	Offers
A—100 shares	X—100 shares
B—100 shares	
C—100 shares	

In this example, A, B, and C match and the winner receives the 100 shares being offered.

In our next example, there is the problem of unequal bids entered simultaneously:

Bids	Offers
A—300 shares	X—500 shares
B—200 shares	
C—100 shares	

No broker wishes to buy the entire 500 shares, but A has precedence, based on size. A receives 300 shares. There are now 200 shares left. B receives the entire amount since B's bid was equal to or greater than the amount offered. C obtains nothing.

In our fourth example, 400 shares are being offered. There are three simultaneous bids:

Bids	Offers
A—300 shares	X—400 shares
B—200 shares	
C—100 shares	

On the basis of size A has precedence and receives 300 shares. One hundred shares are left. Both B and C can buy this stock since each has a bid equal to or greater than the amount offered. Accordingly, B and C match and the winner receives the stock.

In our fifth example, 300 shares are being offered:

Bids	Offers
A—300 shares	X—300 shares
B—200 shares	
C—100 shares	

Because only A has a bid equal to or greater than the amount of stock offered, A obtains all 300 shares.

In the next example, 200 shares are being offered:

Bids	Offers
A—300 shares	X—200 shares
B—200 shares	
C—100 shares	

A and B match because each has a bid equal to or greater than the amount offered. C receives nothing.

In our final example, only 100 shares are offered:

Bids	Offers
A—300 shares	X—100 shares
B—200 shares	
C—100 shares	

All three bids are equal to or greater than the amount offered. All three bidders must match and the winner receives the 100 shares.

Equal Offers

It is unnecessary to illustrate the manner in which equal offers are handled. The principles that govern equal bids apply to equal offers.

Stock Ahead

The phrase "stock ahead," which is often heard by customers, indicates that a customer's stock was not bought or sold on a particular sale, even though the transaction may have been made at the customer's limit price. *Stock ahead* means that the customer's order was not executed because other orders had a priority in the market on the basis of time entered.

Matched and Lost

This term also arises from the rules on floor procedure. As indicated in the discussion of equal bids, if there are two or more bids of equal or greater size than the offer, the brokers match to see which one gets the stock. A broker who loses such a match reports to the customer that the broker has "matched and lost." The same principle applies to offers. When a broker has "matched and won," a report of execution is sent but no report of the match.

All-or-None Bids and Offers

Under Rule 61 the Exchange does not permit the making of a bid or offer in which there is a specification that the bid or offer must be accepted for the entire amount of stock or no business will be done. For example, a broker cannot offer to sell 1,000 shares at 30 specifying that the buyer must take "all or none." The Exchange considers that all bids or offers for more than the unit of trading shall be considered to be for the amount thereof or any less number of units. For example, an order for 500 shares can be considered as five orders of 100 shares each. Hence, if 1,000 shares were to be offered, a buying broker, bidding for only 100 shares at 30, could effect a contract for 100 shares.

Customers may enter "all-or-none" orders with brokers, but bids and offers, except in bonds where the number specified is 50 or more, may not be made this way on the Exchange floor. The broker may endeavor to execute the "all-or-none" order if an opportunity presents itself, without making a bid or offer, but by selling on a bid or by taking an offer equal to or greater than his order.

BIDDING AND OFFERING STOCK

Buying and selling stock on the floor follow a rigid routine. Certain procedures must be adhered to in trading or the utmost confusion would result. Let us follow through the execution of a buy order for AT&T common, placed by a customer with a firm which does not utilize the DOT system.

Bidding on Stock

A broker receives the order from the home office to buy 100 shares of AT&T common "at the market." The order may have come originally from an office, say in Chicago. The broker will go immediately to the Post where the stock is traded, going to the "Telephone crowd," and inquiring about the market. It should be explained that a so-called crowd in any given stock may run from as many as two specialists and a number of other members to one lone specialist. The broker inquires about the market in "Telephone," and glances up at the screen to see that the last sale was made at 25. The broker knows, therefore, that the stock will sell at close to that price.

The broker asks for the quotation on the stock by using some such phrase as "What's Telephone?" or "How's Telephone?" So far, there has been no indication of whether the broker wants to buy or sell. In response to the inquiry, the broker will receive the quotation from the specialists or one or more interested brokers or dealers. Let us say that the quotation is "25 to ¼." Our broker now knows that the best offer is 25¼, and it is doubtful, at the moment, that the stock can be bought for less. Nevertheless, the broker attempts to get a lower or better price. Since there is already a bid at 25, a bid at that price would not be made; hence the bid will be 25⅛. It is given in the shortest possible phraseology, namely, "25⅛ for 100." What this really says in effect is, "I will bid 25⅛ for 100 shares of AT&T common." This laborious statement is unnecessary. Everyone knows that the broker wants AT&T common; otherwise he or she would not have inquired about it. It is certain that the bidding is on the stock since the price preceded the preposition "for," which is always used in bidding. Bidding always follows an ironclad rule: State the bid first, followed by the preposition "for," followed by the number of shares bid. If a selling broker wants to accept this bid, the response is "Sold."

Our broker has placed the bid ⅛ below the best offer, and has tried to get the customer a better price. It is possible that some other member may enter the "crowd" at this exact moment and sell our broker the stock at

25⅛. However, if this does not happen, our broker obtains no response to the bid of "25⅛ for 100," and must bid higher; the new bid will be "¼ for 100." The member who has priority on the offer will make the sale; or members, on parity, if there is no priority, will "match."

As soon as the sale has been made, our broker and the other member of the Exchange verify one another's identity. This is done through badges worn by each member, which show the name, number, and firm represented. A member who executes a transaction for another may at this time "give up" the name of the member represented. In that case the further work of comparison and clearance on the contract becomes the responsibility of the member whose name is "given up."

No contract or paper changes hands at the time the transaction is completed. The only thing necessary is that each party to the transaction note the exact details of the deal. As soon as our broker has purchased the stock, the transaction is reported to the home office. The customer, in this case in Chicago, is then notified by a confirmation. The entire execution of the order may take only a few minutes.

As soon as the sale is completed, an employee of the Exchange, called a "reporter," writes out a sales slip that is entered on the tape electronically. If there is a change in the price of the stock, the reporter posts the price on the screen and indicates whether the price was higher or lower than that of the last different price.

Offering Stock

The process of offering stock is identical with that of bidding on a stock, except that the phraseology is changed. The rule for offering stock is: State the number of shares first, followed by the preposition "at," followed by the price. For example, let us suppose that a broker with a market order wishes to offer 500 shares of General Motors at 67½. The broker would state this offer by saying, "500 at ½." The response of the buying broker or dealer would be "Take it." If possible, a selling broker would try to get a higher price for the stock than the prevailing bid; if not possible, the selling broker will lower the offer to the level of the current bid.

Execution of Other Orders

It is often not possible to execute orders with the same dispatch as the market order to buy that was just described. The type of order may not permit fast execution, or the broker may be too busy. In the case of limit and stop orders the broker is apt to turn the order over to a specialist, who will execute it when the market permits. The broker who is especially rushed may call in the services of a floor broker, who will execute it as agent.

Post 30

Post 30 is a small countertop filing cabinet with space behind it for about a half-dozen Exchange members and employees to transact business. The chief equipment consists of the filing drawers.

The issues at Post 30 are inactive. For this reason a separate trading location with a concentration of issues is justified. For the most part the stocks are investment-grade securities, mostly preferred stocks. All price ranges are found at the post. The spread between bid and ask prices is higher than for active stocks, with some of the stocks showing a spread of between one and two points.

These stocks are known as 10-share-unit stocks. In other words, the trading unit is 10 shares, not 100. Not all of the 10-share-unit stocks are traded at Post 30; 25% of them are traded at the active posts.

The unit of trading, as indicated, is for 10 shares, orders from one to nine shares being considered as odd lots. The great majority of orders are GTC. Perhaps one-fifth of them are day orders.

Most trading is done through the cabinets. Orders are filed in the trays in time and price sequence on special cards. These colored cards indicate whether the order is a bid or an offer, the name of the broker placing the order, the name of the stock, the number of shares, and the time limit. Bids and offers so filed become binding as soon as accepted by other brokers. A bid or offer is accepted by the action of removing the card from the tray.

Post 30 trading goes on in a quiet way in contrast to much of the activity at the other active posts. In its own way, however, the post serves in a useful capacity in making a market for the slow-moving investment stocks.

The DOT System

The Designated Order Turnaround (DOT) system is an automatic electronic order execution mechanism used on the NYSE.

DOT was initially designed to handle market orders up to 299 shares consisting of round lots up to 200 shares and odd lots up to 99 shares, either separately or in addition to a round-lot order in the same stock. Its capacity and flexibility rapidly increased. Soon market and limit orders of 599 shares could be accommodated. By being transmitted directly to posts, DOT orders reduced the need for telephone clerks and freed commission house brokers and $2 brokers from carrying orders to the posts and executing routine small orders. Confirmations of completed transactions are sent rapidly back to the branch offices through the same system.

By 1980 the DOT system handled about half of all orders executed on the NYSE, and there was little doubt that the proportion would grow substantially as the system expanded and as more firms subscribed to it. Although entering an order into the system does not guarantee execution, Exchange figures in 1980 showed that 85% of DOT orders were executed and confirmed to the entering member firm within 5 minutes.

By 1984 the Exchange had developed SuperDot 250. This expanded system delivered market orders up to 1,099 shares and limit orders up to 30,099 shares from member-firm order rooms to the floor and returned reports of executed orders. The system continued to handle round lots, odd lots, or combinations of both. Turnaround times for the execution and reporting of routine market orders were reduced below one minute.

SuperDot 250 incorporated the Opening Automated Report Service (OARS) which was designed to handle preopening market orders of up to 5,099 shares. Because the system paired buy and sell orders, specialists were enabled to compare imbalances quickly with limit orders on their books and thereby open stocks far more quickly than would otherwise be possible. Considering that 15–20% of a typical day's orders are executed on the opening, this system which allows stocks to open quickly and then reports most executions within seconds after a stock open is remarkable indeed.

There is little doubt that the DOT system will expand to all exchanges and that competition will force most firms to utilize it. It also seems clear that related electronic systems will affect other exchange information and handling systems. The electronic workstation will even eliminate one of the Exchange's most venerable institutions, the specialist's book.

Block Positioning

In the 1960s several member firms began acting as "block positioners." These firms buy all or part of large blocks sold to them by customers, hold them in inventory temporarily, and then resell the block to other customers. Floor executions are usually by means of a "cross." The business is risky because of the large amounts of capital that must be committed and the possibility that the shares might be down in price before they can be resold. Nimble traders, however, can generate very large profits, especially in a generally rising market in which the risks of positioning are lowered. Block-positioning activities are regulated by the provisions of NYSE Rules 97 and 127. As with other NYSE rules, these are designed to ensure that the blocks crossed by block positioners do not put at a disadvantage customer orders either in the "crowd" or entered on the specialist's book.

Whereas the trading of large blocks was infrequent until only a few years ago, the recent growth of large trades has been spectacular and breaks new records almost every year. In 1965 there were 2,171 large block transactions which was an average of 9 per market day. The 48.3 million shares marketed in this way represented 1/3% of the total Exchange volume. In 1975 a new height was reached with 34,420 block transactions averaging 136 per day. The 779 million shares traded in blocks had grown to 16.6% of the volume. Tremendous annual increases took place every year until by 1984 there were 433,427 such transactions averaging 1,713 per day. The 11,492 *billion* shares had grown to only a fraction below 50% of total volume. Blocks of 10,000 shares once attracted excited attention from those watching the tape, but in recent years there have been many blocks of millions and even of 10 million shares.

The growth of block positioning reached the point where off-floor member transactions exceeded specialists' trading by 1979. Some positioning off the floor is done by registered competitive market makers who report their transactions as specialists. Specialists' trading on the floor has diminished rapidly in recent years despite the dramatic increase in volume.

Exchange Distribution or Acquisition

For large blocks, the Exchange established a procedure known as a distribution or acquisition. An Exchange Distribution is accomplished by obtaining sufficient buy orders from customers of one or more firms beforehand to permit a cross of the buy and sell order on the floor in the usual auction market. Interest in buying is stimulated by offering the stock within the current quotation free of commission. The seller may pay a special commission to the broker to add to the incentive to obtain the buy orders. Success for the distribution depends on the ability of member firms to obtain these buy orders in sufficient quantity in a fairly short period. An acquisition of a substantial block of stock of an issue may be accomplished by the obverse of this procedure.

An Exchange Distribution, or Acquisition, like the Specialist Block Bid, or Offer, must be approved by Exchange authorities before it is executed to assure conformance to trading practice. Notice of execution is given on the tape only after the orders have been obtained and they are crossed on the floor in the auction market.

Other methods of block trading reduced the growth of this once rather popular method to the point where there were only two in 1980 and none at all in the years following.

Special Offering, or Bid

Blocks of stock may also be sold through the Special Offering procedure. In this instance, a price for the shares is predetermined, taking into account the current quotation in the auction market. For the buyers the price is net. They obtain stock at the offering price without paying the usual commission. They may also obtain stock at a price slightly below the best offer in the auction market at the time of the offering. Selling brokers are offered a special incentive commission, perhaps two to two and one-half times the usual commission on a sale. The offering is published on the tape in the following way:

$$\text{SP} \quad \text{OFF} \quad \text{XYZ} \quad \text{COM}$$
$$100 \qquad\quad 40 \qquad\quad \tfrac{1}{2}$$

The offering must remain open for at least 15 minutes after this announcement, unless the announcement is made at least one hour before the offering becomes effective. When buy orders have been received on the floor, they are filled at the offering price until the entire block has been sold. A Special Offering must be approved by Exchange authorities before it is announced.

A Special Bid may be made by an investor seeking to acquire a large block of stock of an issue.

Increased member block-positioning activities as well as greatly increased institutional trading has sharply reduced the use of special offerings. There was only one such offering of 53,000 shares in 1980, one of 117,000 shares in 1982, and none since. Another special method, the secondary distribution, is still utilized a few times a year although much less than formerly. This method is discussed in Chapter 14.

Odd Lots

For many years odd lots were almost all handled through two specialized firms that split this business—Carlisle & Jacquelin and DeCoppet & Doremus. In the late 1960s these firms consolidated as Carlisle, DeCoppet. In 1976 Merrill Lynch received Exchange permission to make its own odd-lot markets and, in one stroke, removed about 20% of the business from Carlisle. Shortly thereafter Carlisle disbanded and specialists assumed the odd-lot function. The Exchange also ended the Monthly Investment Plan (MIP) at this time because Carlisle had been servicing the plan for other members.

An odd lot is any number of shares less than a full unit of trading; that is, for stocks which trade in 100-share units, an odd lot is 1 to 99 shares. For stocks which trade in 10-share units, an odd lot is 1 to 9 shares. Although most orders for odd lots are accommodated through the DOT system, such orders are actually being executed for the accounts of the specialists in the stocks traded.

Some individual member firms handle their own odd-lot orders through their own trading accounts in varying ways. Some handle all such orders and others, only some of them. Some handle orders only of a given type, particularly market orders.

Intermarket Trading System (ITS)

The answer of various exchanges to Congress's call for a National Market System has been the electronic linking of various markets in which the same stocks are traded. This began in 1978 with a pilot program involving the New York and Philadelphia stock exchanges and initially provided for the trading of only 11 issues. Periodically other markets were added. By 1985 the electronic communications system linked eight markets. In addition to the New York, American, Philadelphia, Boston, Cincinnati, Midwest, and Pacific stock exchanges, the NASD was added in 1982. The latter allowed users of the system to take advantage of favorable markets made off the floor by member firms.

The system grew rapidly from the original 11 issues to over 1,000 by 1982 and stabilized at something over that figure in the years which followed. Daily volume approximates 5 million shares.

The ITS is used not only for customer orders but also for specialists and market makers trading for their own account. The ITS allows, for example, a floor broker in New York to "hit" a Pacific Stock Exchange specialist's bid showing on the ITS terminal. The ITS should not be confused with the consolidated tape, which merely reports executions of NYSE (or occasionally Amex) listed stocks no matter where they occur. That is, a trade of a NYSE dually listed issue on the Philadelphia floor may be made between two Philadelphia members and reported on the tape without involving the ITS. A trade whereby a Philadelphia market maker buys shares from a Midwest specialist is both made through ITS and also reported on the consolidated tape.

Floor Traders

The position of independent exchange members trading for their own accounts has long been viewed with considerable suspicion by some regulators. The NYSE has attempted to justify their existence by requiring their registration as either *registered competitive market makers* or as *competitive traders*.

In the former case those so registered are required to accommodate public orders by making a bid or offer that will narrow the spread and give a better price to that order. Competitive traders, on the other hand, are required to execute "stabilizing transactions" much as the specialist does when trading for one's own account. Thus the competitive trader must be a buyer on sales below the last sale and a seller on sales above the last sale at least 75% of the time. The specific rules governing these activities are Rules 107A, 111, and 112.

BOND TRADING

For many years the NYSE maintained a "bond room" adjacent to the main trading area. In the late 1970s the bond trading facility was moved to a room located beneath the main trading floor. This move was made in anticipation of an imminent initiation of trading in listed equity options following the successful introduction of such trading on the Chicago Board Options Exchange (CBOE). The anticipated initiation, however, occurred almost 10 years after the room was moved.

9 The Over-the-Counter Markets

The OTC markets are far more important in the United States than in other countries, where activity tends to be concentrated on exchanges. Indeed, such trading is not even permitted in some countries, and major securities traders (e.g., some foreign pension funds) are not allowed to buy securities except on exchanges. In the United States, OTC can be best described as the market for all transactions which do *not* take place on an exchange, hence the expression "off board." With minor exceptions this includes all trading in: U.S. government and agency securities, money market instruments, municipal bonds, and mutual funds. In addition, it is by far the major arena for trading in corporate bonds, although exchange bond trading is occasionally relatively active. In 1985 average daily bond trading on the NYSE was a record $35.9 million (par value), a sum easily surpassed by the off-board trading of some of the major bond-trading firms alone. It is, however, the OTC stock market that is best known to investors. There are between 30,000 and 40,000 different common and preferred stocks traded OTC. Most of these are shares of small companies, traded locally with inactive and sporadic markets. A growing number of companies, on the other hand, are traded on the highly automated NASDAQ system, which comes close to exchange trading standards in many ways.

ORGANIZATION

The OTC market is not "organized" in the same sense that stock exchanges are; that is, there is no focal point like an exchange floor in which competing buyers and sellers assemble. Rather, it is an electronic marketplace linked by telephone, and it exists wherever two traders decide to trade. As with all other securities trading in the United States, New York is by far the most important center. Considerable OTC volume is also generated by traders in Chicago, Los Angeles, and San Francisco. In fact, virtually every major city has an OTC market where trading tends to feature local bank, insurance, and industrial shares, although some trading in national issues also occurs.

In the early 1980s an active and highly speculative market developed in Denver where trading largely involved "penny stocks," low-priced speculative oil and mineral exploration issues. The collapse of the world oil price structure dealt this market a harsh blow from which it has not yet recovered.

It is generally assumed that the expression "over-the-counter" derives from the long defunct practice in which corporations sold new shares directly to customers from the counter window at the treasurer's office. The term has little relevance today. In actuality, the OTC market of today is a model of electronic technology. The participants are primarily *dealers* who buy and sell on an inventory basis. In most transactions no commissions are charged; the dealer's profit, if any, is derived from marking up customer purchase orders and marking down the sale orders.

Almost all active participants are members of the NASD. This important self-regulatory organization governs its members in much the same manner as an exchange. In fact, almost all major NYSE members are also NASD members. The NASD and its functions are discussed in more detail in the following pages.

SIZE OF THE MARKET

A great many of the companies whose stocks trade OTC are small and no accurate recording is kept of trades, except perhaps by the transfer agents for the individual companies. The NASDAQ market, however, has grown to a size which rivals the NYSE in trading volume, even though it still falls substantially short of the NYSE's dollar value. At the end of 1985 there were 4,784 different securities issues in the NASDAQ system. During that year 20.7 billion shares traded through this system and represented a dollar value of $233.5 billion. The NYSE in that year had a volume of 27.5 billion shares with a dollar value of about $970.5 billion. In terms of dollar volume of trading, NASDAQ ranked third to the NYSE and Tokyo ($315.6 billion), but ahead of the *combined* equity trading totals of the London, Zurich, Toronto, and West German exchanges ($215.8 billion). With a total market value of $306.3 billion in listed securities, NASDAQ has become a major component of world securities trading.

TYPES OF SHARE TRADED

Historically, OTC was the major market for the shares of banks and insurance companies, as well as for the smaller industrials and recent issues. In the 1960s and 1970s, most of the major "money center" banks defected to list their shares on the NYSE. These included Chase Manhattan, Citicorp, First Chicago, Bank of America, and J. P. Morgan, among others. However, many banks remain OTC, including the preponderance of local banks without a national market. Likewise, a number of the largest stock insurance companies listed their shares on the NYSE. In this group one finds Aetna Life, Travellers, Cigna, and others. Many large insurers have chosen to stay OTC. Among these are Kemper, Safeco, Saint Paul Companies, Provident Life, and Farmers Group.

This is also the market for the new, growing company. Many great growth issues have emerged from the OTC market over the years: McDonald's, Wendy's, and Xerox are only three of the many familiar names that started their public trading in the OTC market. Although these companies and others ultimately listed their shares on the NYSE, their growth was most spectacular from the time of the initial public offering until the time of listing—in other words, when traded OTC. Current favorites in the market include such high technology issues as: Apple Computer, Apollo Computer, Intel Corp., and Convergent Technologies.

Another feature of this market is the ADR. The stringency of American securities laws makes it difficult to offer foreign shares for sale legally in this country. With the exception of Canadian stocks, most foreign shares are traded in the United States through this ADR mechanism. The foreign share problem is effectively solved by not trading the actual shares here, but rather issuing a receipt for the shares which may then be registered to comply with domestic laws. The ADR is typically issued by a foreign branch of a U.S. bank, most usually the Morgan Guaranty Trust, one of whose predecessor banks, The Guaranty Trust, invented the vehicle in the 1920s. The receipt entitles the holder to the same rights as the shareholder would ordinarily possess in the country of origin. In more recent years, many ADRs have been listed, breaking the OTC market's monopoly on these issues.

Particularly popular with U.S. investors have been Sony Corp., Matsushita Electric, Honda Motor, and Hitachi Ltd., all indicative of the growing worldwide importance of the Japanese economy. For many years a staple of ADR trading was the South African gold-mining company. The frequent correlation of declining stock prices with advancing gold prices made these issues popular hedge vehicles for some years. Political problems in South Africa, however, have made the ownership of these shares more speculative than usual, and in recent years American investors have not accorded them their usual status.

There are thousands of companies, mostly small, which may still make interesting investments but which do not qualify for (or do not desire) exchange listing. Many of these companies are closely held with few shares available to the public. Others may have nonvoting common stock which normally precludes NYSE listing. The OTC market offers a trading mechanism for these shares which might not otherwise exist. Although such issues may lack the liquidity and visibility associated with listed issues, the venturesome trader may find interesting possibilities here.

Finally, of course, there are thousands of virtually worthless shares regularly traded in the OTC market in an atmosphere not far removed from either Monte Carlo or Las Vegas. These include the likes of bankrupt corporations, companies with mysterious "secret" processes (almost always fraudulent), Tsarist bonds, and other similarly obscure instruments. Such securities often trade in cents per share, hence the name "penny stocks." Serious investors should avoid these shares as they rarely live up to the touted promises, and substantial (or total) losses are not uncommon. For the well-heeled risk taker, an occasional flier might be in order, as long as it is recognized that this is not investment but rather an outright gamble.

THE NASDAQ SYSTEM

Before February 1971 the OTC market operated in a manner that had prevailed for many years. Upon receipt of a customer order, the receiving firm would "shop the street" requesting quotations from dealers willing to buy and sell shares on a continuous basis for their own account. Such dealers were said to be "making a market." Normally, three different dealers were called and asked a question like "How's ABC?" or "How do you make ABC?" The market maker might have replied "20 to ½," meaning that he was willing to buy 100 shares, paying $20 per share, or sell 100 shares and charge $20.50. Another might have replied "20 to ⅜," the same bid price to a seller but a better (cheaper) offer to a prospective buyer. Note that the inquiring broker indicated neither a decision to buy nor to sell. If the customer had placed a buy order, the dealer with the offering at 20⅜ made the best price, and the order would be placed with him. Naturally, the business would flow toward the firm making the high bid or the low offer. This allowed for negotiation of prices, rather than the open-outcry auction markets which characterize exchange transactions.

There were both advantages and disadvantages associated with this system relative to that employed by the stock exchanges. The NYSE assigns each stock to a specialist responsible for maintaining a *continuous* market in the shares. This means that there is always a bid and an offer price on every listed stock, something not required of OTC market makers. The NYSE records every transaction on the tape, showing each investor the last sale and the timing sequence of the trade. The OTC market still cannot offer this visibility, although it has made great strides in that area. On the positive side, the NASD allows any firm to make a market in OTC securities, provided that firm can meet the specified capital requirements the NASD mandates to ensure ability to perform on contracts undertaken. This means there may be 10 or more market makers quoting prices in the more active NASDAQ issues. Such competition tends to produce narrower "spreads"—the difference between bid and offering prices—and gives better executions to the customer.

In 1971 the NASD introduced NASDAQ. The system uses video display screens to illustrate each market maker's "firm" (i.e., binding) quotation on a particular stock. The quotes are updated on a real-time computer system as the market changes, so that only up-to-the-minute quotations are displayed.

To illustrate, suppose a customer places an order to buy 100 shares of Apple Computer, a favorite NASDAQ issue. The broker's OTC trader will enter the symbol AAPL into his or her terminal, and the screen will instantly display firm quotations of all registered market makers in Apple and also the best bid price and the best offer (not necessarily being made by the same dealer). The trader then selects the best offer and telephones the firm indicating that price to consummate the sale.

In 1982 the NASD introduced a refinement of NASDAQ called the National Market System (NMS). This blatant usurpation of a term used vaguely by Congress in the Securities Act Amendments to define a long-term national goal caused a good deal of consternation at the exchanges as it appeared, quite correctly, that a proprietary service was being represented as what Congress had in mind for the securities markets of the future. Nonetheless, the term has stuck, and the NASD's ploy has become an entrenched part of the market.

The NMS is composed of the most active stocks in the NASDAQ system. At the end of 1985 these stocks accounted for 2,125 of the 4,784 NASDAQ issues and about 64% of total NASDAQ volume for the year. National Market System stocks are characterized by a last-sale reporting mechanism somewhat like the exchange tape. The system is not exactly like the tape in that traders are allowed 90 seconds to report a trade, whereas the NYSE tape is virtually instantaneous. Furthermore, the exchange tape reports all transactions sequentially, but NMS only reports the last sale in a particular issue. The listing criteria for an NMS stock are more stringent than for regular NASDAQ stocks but lower than the NYSE's. For example, NMS stocks require at least 4 market makers versus 2 for regular NASDAQ issues, and 500,000 outstanding shares versus 100,000. In addition, the NASD succeeded in persuading the Federal Reserve to grant automatic credit extension potential on NMS stocks in 1985. This put these issues on a par with exchange-listed securities in this regard. The NMS has achieved a closer approximation of exchange price reporting than the previous NASDA system. What it still lacks—and may never have—are the big name, blue-chip issues already listed on the NYSE, such as IBM, GM, Ford, and DuPont.

In late 1984 the NASD introduced the Small Order Execution System (SOES). This allows agency (brokerage) trades for all NMS issues to be made via machine, without requiring the phone call still necessary with regular NMS and other NASDAQ executions. Participants in the SOES may enter orders up to 1,000 shares and have them filled immediately by a market maker at the best price displayed on the NASDAQ screens. Over 33 million shares traded in 1985, SOES's first full year.

A 2-year pilot program was introduced in April 1986 to link 300 NASDAQ issues with a like number of issues traded on the London Stock Exchange. The program is expected to generate more international trading activity than ever before and become yet another link in the globalization of the securities markets. With the London market opening at 4:30 Eastern Standard time, the 600 pilot issues will be available for trading throughout a 12½-hour day.

Sources of Information

Before the advent of the NASDAQ system, traders and investors in the OTC markets had few sources of current information. Some quotations appeared in the daily press but these suffered on two counts: (1) few stocks were listed, and (2) quotations were for the professional "inside" market, not available to customers. The other information source was (and remains) the Pink Sheets, published daily by the National Quotations Bureau. The sheets list market makers and prices of most national issues, but the prices are already suspect by the time they reach the printer, let alone the investor. An apparently attractive price to another dealer may be far from satisfactory to the retail customer when the markup is factored in.

Newspapers, however, now carry information unavailable even to professionals in the pre-NASDAQ era. Over 100 newspapers now carry the entire NMS list featuring high, low, and closing prices as well as net change for the day's trading. Although the prices shown are still "inside" prices, the public gets a much clearer picture of what the actual market is for a stock and how close their order may be to execution. Additionally, some major financial papers like *The Wall Street Journal* and *The New York Times* also carry supplementary listings of shares traded OTC but not in the NMS.

PARTICIPANTS IN THE MARKET

There are over 6,000 member organizations of the NASD. Of these, many are small—some only one- or two-person operations. Many others deal only in products such as tax shelters (reduced by mid-1980s tax changes), mutual funds, variable annuities, and similar packaged investments. These firms have neither the capital nor the desire to make markets in the NASDAQ system. In fact, there are about 500 active market makers in the NASDAQ system, about 8 issues per market maker. As has been the case with the securities industry in general, the NASDAQ participants have been forced to consolidate activities into the hands of larger and larger players. The largest of these in 1986 is probably Shearson Lehman Brothers, with a market-making commitment to about 2,000 different issues. The number two firm is likely to be Merrill Lynch with about 1,250 domestic stocks in its OTC inventory. As institutional investors become increasingly interested in OTC stocks, the number of block trades will doubtless grow, and with such growth, the need for more capital by the industry. In 1985 "block" trading volume accounted for 41.1% of NMS volume, with the average block about 20,000 shares. This type of trading, already common on the NYSE, is sure to make it difficult for small firms to compete with the large houses in providing liquid markets.

The "Third Market"

This expression refers to trades in listed securities executed in the OTC market. With certain exceptions, exchange members are required to execute orders in listed securities on the exchange. The NASD member firms are under no such requirement if they are not also exchange members. There is thus nothing to prevent them from making markets in listed stocks if it appears profitable to do so. Prior to May 1, 1975, NYSE members were bound to a "minimum" commission schedule that was in fact a fixed rate. It was frequently possible for a NASD firm to do an OTC trade in a listed stock at a lower net price (or for greater net proceeds) than an exchange member could do with the commission included. For example, an order to buy 500 shares of a 70 stock would have required a $325 commission on the exchange or total cash due of $35,325. A third market firm might have bought the shares for its own account at 70⅛, marked it up to 70¼, and traded it for $35,250 *net* to a customer. The firm made a $62.50 profit on the trade (the spread from 70⅛ to 70¼) and still saved the customer $75. With institutions frequently in the market with orders for 5 or 10,000 shares, or more, the savings became very substantial. The third market was never as liquid as the NYSE because few participants had sufficient capital to handle really large blocks on an inventory basis, but a large amount of business was siphoned off the exchange floors.

The SEC, at Congress's direction, prohibited fixed-rate schedules in the securities industry after May 1, 1975. Stock exchange member firms were free to negotiate commission rates with customers, and within a short time those customers with strong bargaining positions had whittled down commission rates to minimal figures. Many institutions are now able to trade at rates of 5 cents per share. Because third market firms cannot trade profitably at that rate—the minimum spread for most shares being 12.5 cents—most of them left the market. About 17 firms still make regular trades in this market, but when they do they are required to report all trades on the Consolidated Quotation Service (see Chapter 7) tape just as if the trade took place on the floor. The third market may have seen its zenith in the early 1970s, but as the Intermarket Trading System evolves, the distinction between executions "off board" and "on" will doubtless blur further.

19c-3 Stocks

In its efforts to follow Congress's mandate to establish a National Market System, the SEC approved continued OTC trading by exchange members of stocks that were listed after April 26, 1979. Members of exchanges may now make markets in any new listings they choose. Trading in these stocks, called 19c-3 stocks after the applicable section of the 1934 Act, began in July 1980. Clearly, the rule further weakens any exchange's claim to exclusivity of trading of particular stocks. Thus far NYSE member firms have approached 19c-3 trading in a gingerly fashion. Except in a bear market, trading stocks OTC as principal is considerably more profitable than trading as agent, so it seems logical to expect increased emphasis in this area as it becomes more familiar.

THE NATIONAL ASSOCIATION OF SECURITIES DEALERS

History

The roots of the NASD go back to the New Deal's National Industrial Recovery Act of 1933. In an effort to revive industrial and business activity, and to reduce unemployment, the act created the National Recovery Administration (NRA). The NRA fostered industrial self-regulation through a system of fair competition codes. Investment bankers, along with other industries, developed a code of fair competition. Although the NRA was declared unconstitutional in 1935, investment bankers continued their code of fair practices under the title of the Investment Bankers Conference Committee. In 1938 Congress amended the 1934 Act by adding section 15A, the Maloney Act. The Act sponsored the creation of a self-regulatory body to govern the OTC market in much the same way that the exchanges had been charged with policing their own activities. The NASD has been the only organization so created to date.

The Act gave to a qualified association the power to draw up and enforce rules to prevent fraud and manipulative practices, to prevent unreasonable profits, and to protect investors and the public interest. The association was also empowered to discipline its members by a variety of means including censure, fine, and expulsion. Finally, such an association was also allowed to restrict its membership if this were in the public interest and to draw up rules prohibiting members from offering nonmembers broker–dealers' trade discounts or any other benefits of membership not available to the general public. Membership was opened to all securities firms engaged in investment banking or OTC trading. Banks, however, which underwrite and trade some municipal securities were excluded.

Organization

In 1985 the NASD membership consisted of an all-time high of 6,037 firms. These firms had 15,375 branch offices and a total of 357,133 registered representatives and principals, also a record. The NASD includes firms involved in OTC trading, investment banking, discount brokerage, tax shelters, and mutual funds. In addition, many insurance companies have set up NASD affiliates or subsidiaries to market products such as variable life insurance policies, variable annuities, and mutual funds. It should also be noted that NASD and exchange memberships are not mutually exclusive, but rather so naturally complementary that all of the NYSE firms familiar to both individual and institutional investors are also NASD members. The only NYSE members not likely to benefit much from NASD membership are those which confine their activities to the exchange floor. Typical of these firms, many of which are really sole proprietorships, are $2 brokers, registered competitive market makers, and some of the smaller specialists (most of the larger ones join).

The NASD is directed by a Board of Governors elected from the membership. Twenty-one of the governors are drawn from the membership of the Association's 13 districts and 7 are elected at large. The President of the Association, an employee, rounds out the Board. The Board meets 6 times annually to set policy and handle serious affairs. The day-to-day conduct of the Association's business is handled by the district offices, but the enforcement of ethical conduct rules is in the hands of each district's Business Conduct Committee, composed entirely of representatives of the district membership. Consequently, complaints are heard and judged by an accused member's peers, not by a body of administrative functionaries.

Rules of Fair Practice

The NASD's most important rules are designed to maintain high standards of business conduct. Should a member be found in violation of these rules the penalties may be as mild as a censure, but frequently include fines and suspension. The ultimate penalty is expulsion, because an expelled member would find it virtually impossible to carry on a profitable securities business outside of the Association.

Because of the complex, ever-changing nature of the markets, it is difficult to make arbitrary rules that are rigid in application. Thus, one often finds the word *reasonable* in these rules as opposed to absolute "thou shalt nots." Among the more important rules are those which require that:

Charges for services shall be reasonable and not unfairly discriminatory between customers.

Inventory (dealer) transactions shall be at fair prices, considering all conditions (expenses involved, market conditions, a reasonable profit for the dealer). In other words, markups should be fair.

Dealer quotations be firm unless explicitly stated otherwise.

No deception, manipulative or fraudulent practice be employed to effect a transaction.

Securities taken in trade ("swapped") be fairly valued at the current market price.

A critically important rule restricts the granting of price concessions or discounts to other members of the NASD. In other words, nonmembers must pay the public price for a security offering. No nonmember may participate in the investment banking, OTC, or mutual fund areas at the wholesale prices that members may trade with each other. This provision virtually closes the doors to nonmember firms trying to make a reasonable profit in any of these areas. Some firms do indeed survive without NASD membership, but such firms are invariably small and fit into small, specialized niches, such as "penny stocks," local issues, and direct participation (tax-shelter) programs. Nevertheless, profitable operation in other areas of the corporate securities business is hard to imagine without NASD membership.

Uniform Practice Code

In addition to the Rules of Fair Practice, the NASD has prepared an elaborate code to standardize the means of settling securities transactions. Items covered include receipts and deliveries, confirmations, settlement dates, computation of accrued interest, and transfers and reclamations. By and large, these rules are the same as those used by the exchanges, giving the securities industry a nationwide standard for settling most securities transactions.

Discipline

As mentioned above, the NASD disciplines errant members in a variety of ways. It is sometimes thought that the Association is judge, jury, and executioner, although this is true only to a limited extent. When a complaint against a member is made, it must be in writing to be considered. When the complaint is made, the accused is given the opportunity to respond and may request a hearing at which legal counsel may be retained. The proceedings are held by the local District Business Conduct Committee, that is, by the accused's peers. The member, of course, may be found not guilty. If guilty, the punishment may be censure, fine, suspension, expulsion, or a combination of these. Should the accused be dissatisfied with the findings, they may be appealed to the Board of Governors, then the SEC, and ultimately to the federal courts.

Suspension and expulsion are severe penalties. During the period of suspension, or indefinitely if expelled, the guilty party must be treated as a nonmember, meaning that no participation in the inside or wholesale markets is permitted. This effectively puts the expelled member out of the securities business, and suspended members are frequently removed from the securities business *de facto* for their viability is weakened. Expelled members may return only with the prior approval of the NASD and the SEC. Frequently, a member is already out of the securities business by the time these more extreme penalties are levied.

Note also that the NASD may inspect members' books and records at will. Usually made on a "spot" basis, these audits occasionally turn up violations even when no formal complaint has been lodged. The very possibility of such unexpected audits and inspections means that compliance departments of member firms must be constantly vigilant in monitoring sales and trading practices. Thus the mere threat of such actions tends to keep even the most prudent members zealous in their internal policing activities. Paradoxically in some ways, the largest members with the most representatives and traders are the least likely to be involved in serious complaints, because it is these firms that pursue the most rigorous policies of high ethical standards and adherence to Association rules. The prospective customer should clearly evaluate the firm's reputation before entering into a business relationship. There is no reason to eschew relations with small firms provided such are well capitalized and reputable. Likewise, an account with a major member firm is no guarantee that an individual representative, no matter how well screened and trained, is completely ethical, although the chances would appear relatively good given the resources of major members and their commitment to self-discipline.

The Problem of Markups

The problem of how much profit an OTC broker-dealer should be allowed is a controversial one. Indeed, one faction, citing *caveat emptor,* says this is no one's business, let alone the NASD's. After all, a customer's decision to purchase merchandise from I. Magnin or Bloomingdale's is not dependent on the customer's perception of that firm's profit margins, even if it is apparent that similar (or the very same) merchandise might be available more cheaply at other stores. Nearly 40 years ago the NASD made a questionnaire study, asking members about markups on a variety of typical transactions. Following the survey, the Board of Governors announced that the findings indicated that a markup of 5% seemed adequate to ensure a viable and healthy OTC business. Thus was introduced the NASD's "5% markup policy," which has become the standard in the OTC business. Rigid application of a 5% (or any) maximum markup is, in fact, prohibited by the Maloney Act which permitted the NASD's very existence.

The competitive nature of the negotiated market has made the policy reasonable in practice, and ethical dealers have little difficulty abiding by the rule despite its confining nature. In any event, the policy is flexible enough to consider most exigencies involved in a trade and even permit markups well in excess of 5% in those few circumstances where merited. Ultimately, the basic test is the member's adherence to the first of the Rules of Fair Practice: "A member, in the conduct of his business, shall observe high standards of commercial honor and just and equitable principles of trade.[1]

[1]*NASD Manual,* Para. 2151, sec. 1.

Registered Representatives

Any employee, partner, or officer of a member who deals directly with customers is considered a "registered representative" and must satisfy a number of requirements before being allowed to sell or trade securities. After filing a thorough revelation of past educational and business background, the candidate must pass a 250-question, six-hour examination.[2] Even after such preliminaries, the representative remains under the constant supervision of the employer who is charged with immediately reporting any involvement of the representative with illegal or unethical acts. In actuality, most members will uncover any rules violations well before the NASD and will take the appropriate disciplinary action, which frequently means termination of employment. Once terminated for cause, the ability of a former representative to reenter the securities industry is extremely limited. Customers should understand that passing an examination and the employment by a reputable member in no way guarantee a representative's ability to select or guide successful investments. It does, however, set at least a minimum standard of knowledge that is rather more rigorous than that which applies in such fields as insurance, real estate, or banking.

---

[2]Some who deal only in limited areas such as mutual funds may pass an abbreviated form.

10 The American Stock Exchange and Other U.S. Securities Exchanges

Given its long history and top-heavy predominance in domestic equity trading, the NYSE comes to mind first when most Americans think about the stock market. There is, however, substantial trading on the Amex as well as five "regional" exchanges. In terms of total share volume the NYSE commanded 81.6% of 1985 trading in listed shares on exchanges, while Amex had 5.7%, and the combined regional exchanges figure was 12.7%.[1] The Amex's portion has been slipping for 5 years, although its 1985 share volume of over 2.1 billion shares was an all-time record for the exchange. The reason for the slippage is largely attributable to the unique nature of the Amex, whose shares rarely trade elsewhere. Volume on the regional exchanges, however, is dominated by trading in stocks whose primary market is the NYSE. Trading in exclusive listings is much smaller than that on the Amex.

This chapter will consider these exchanges separately but unequally. The Amex deserves more coverage because of its size and its unique role. The regionals, on the other hand, play a different role and are closer in function to each other than they are either to the Amex, the NYSE, or the NASDAQ (OTC) System. With the conspicuous exception of the struggling Cincinnati Stock Exchange, trading on the regional exchanges is similar to the practices followed on the two New York exchanges.

Because of its special character, the CBOE is not discussed here, but rather in Chapter 22. That chapter also deals with the trading of stock index *futures* on the futures exchanges where securities as such are not traded.

---

[1]*NYSE 1986 Fact Book*, p. 74.

THE AMERICAN STOCK EXCHANGE

The Amex has long been the nation's second most important exchange, although in terms of volume and dollar value of trading it ranks well behind NASDAQ as well as behind NYSE. Unlike the regional exchanges, the Amex serves neither as a market for local issues nor as an alternative execution site for NYSE-listed stocks. Rather, it has come to be regarded as a sort of semipermanent home for corporations that have outgrown the OTC market but as yet do not qualify for NYSE listing. Partisans of NASDAQ will surely take exception to the word "outgrown," as they contend that their market is the superior one. Be that as it may, Amex listing standards are considerably higher than those required by the NASDAQ's premier National Market System.

Exchange listing still carries advantages not enjoyed by the OTC market. The visibility of extensive newspaper coverage of trading helps aid investor recognition and helps develop a national following. As this tends to broaden the shareholder base, the process of future capital raising is made easier. Prospective shareholders and lenders generally feel more comfortable with corporations that have met rigorous listing standards. If a corporation's directors are aiming at an ultimate NYSE listing, the Amex provides a way-station where the shares can acquire some seasoning as traded securities. On the other hand, a number of Amex companies already satisfy NYSE standards but are comfortable with their Amex home. In other cases, the companies may meet the basic financial requisites of the NYSE but have "classified" common stock, which, until recently, precluded NYSE registration. This is the case with such major corporations as the New York Times, Wang Laboratories, and Bergen Brunswig. The Amex also features U.S. listing of many Canadian companies, particularly those engaged in oil and mineral exploration. In recent years, ADR trading has increased here as it has on both the NASDAQ and NYSE markets. In 1985, for example, the most active Amex issue by far were the ADR's of B.A.T. Industries PLC., the giant British tobacco and retailing business once known as British–American Tobacco.

History

The exchange originated as an outdoor market with traders literally standing in the streets or on the curb. The practice was not at all unusual and indeed was common to eighteenth-century markets in Paris, London, and Amsterdam. Although the NYSE dates from either May 17, 1792, or March 5, 1817,[2] depending on the reference, the exact date for the "curb" market cannot

---

[2]The original brokers' (Buttonwood) agreement was signed in 1792. The Constitution and name "New York Stock and Exchange Board" was adopted in 1817.

be pinned down. Historical sources do indicate a lively trade in the growth issues of the 1830s—canal and turnpike shares—carried on by the "curbstone brokers."[3] The Mexican War, the annexation of California, and the subsequent gold strikes not only stimulated the economy, but led to frantic curb trading in companies involved in that area, particularly gold mining, banks, and shipping.

The ever-inventive curbstone brokers recovered from a disastrous crash in 1857 to form several new exchanges, including the famous "Gold Room," during the war-generated boom from 1861–1865. As yet there was still no truly organized association of curbstone brokers, merely a series of markets conducted in floating sites that began at Wall and Hanover Streets, shifted to William Street, and finally located on Broad Street in 1900 until moving indoors to its current location on Trinity Place in 1921.

During this final outdoor phase the market developed its most colorful aspect. Brokers, traders, and clerks were jammed together in a milling swarm in the middle of Broad Street, just a block from the then (and current) headquarters of J. P. Morgan and Company, and the NYSE immediately opposite them. As anyone who has ever visited these locations today knows, the streets are very narrow and under the best of conditions traffic moves at a crawl. With the curb market in operation, Broad Street was virtually impassable. Business was conducted in this mob by brokers sporting distinctively colored derbies and other headgear. This allowed the telephone clerks to spot their firm's men and communicate with them via a system of shouts, whistles, and hand signals, some of which survive to this day. The phone clerks leaned out of office windows to signal brokers in the crowd in what must have been very risky positions, for business was conducted in all kinds of weather including snow and rainstorms.

Under the leadership of E. E. ("Pop") Mendels, a prominent curb broker, the New York Curb Market Agency was organized in 1908. The Agency codified ethical standards that had been practiced and encouraged by Mendels and his associates since the 1870s. The Agency, however, was not yet an exchange. In 1911 it was transformed into the New York Curb Market and finally became an organized exchange.

Flush with cash from the World War I boom the Curb brokers began constructing a permanent home and moved indoors to 86 Trinity Place, about three blocks west of their historic street location and the NYSE. As with all other markets, the Curb of the 1920s experienced a spectacular boom, culminating in 1929. For example, in 1921 a then record 15.5 million shares were traded, $25.5 million worth of bonds changed hands, and a "seat," or membership, sold for $3,750. By 1929 those numbers had increased to 476 million shares, $834.9 million bonds, and a seat sold for $254,000. Also, in 1929 the members changed the name of the market to the New York Curb Exchange.

---

[3]These and succeeding references to Amex history may be found in more detail (and with interesting illustrations) in the *American Stock Exchange 1980 Annual Report*, pp. 5–18.

The market collapse of 1929 and the Great Depression that followed brought hard times to the Curb. Unlike World War I, World War II brought no revival. In fact, by 1942 the average daily volume had slumped to 89,000 shares and a seat was traded for $650. The end of the war brought on tremendous economic expansion and with it a long, dynamic bull market. With prosperity returned, the membership, proud of the exchange's new national reputation, voted to change the market's name to the American Stock Exchange in 1953.

The postwar bull market also culminated in a speculative binge, as such markets are wont to have, in the late 1960s. Amex volume swelled to close to 50% of NYSE volume. For example, in 1968 about 3.3 billion shares traded on the NYSE and 1.57 billion on the Amex, or 47%. Because so much money was being directed toward the smaller companies often seen on the Amex, blue-chip stocks did not fare nearly as well as the less-seasoned junior issues. Veteran traders said that their trading posture was "long the Curb, short the (Big) Board." The bear market that followed was especially hard on the Amex. That fact, coupled with the transformation of the OTC market by NASDAQ, dealt the Amex a blow from which it has never really recovered fully.

Since that time, however, the Amex has constantly experimented with new concepts, some of which have not worked out, such as satellite trading floors in the Midwest and on the Pacific coast, an affiliated commodities exchange, and trading in interest-rate options. The successes, however, have been impressive and profitable. Of these, listed options have been the most impressive. Starting in 1975, and thus 2 years behind the Chicago Board Options Exchange, the Amex has carved out a viable second place with about 25 to 30% of the market. Additionally, the Amex won virtually all of the market in situations where options on the same stock were traded on both exchanges (a lottery system now assigns new listings exclusively to one exchange). This success was duplicated in competition for listed options on NASDAQ stocks introduced in 1985, in which the Amex captured 90% of the total volume.

LISTED SECURITIES

In July 1986 there were 832 different common stock and warrant issues listed on the Amex, roughly half the number of NYSE listings at that time. Also, there were 121 preferred issues, many of which were issued by NYSE listed corporations (Pacific Gas and Electric, to give an example, has 22 preferred issues listed on the Amex). The total market value of all equity issues was $96,118,536,000. Although this is clearly a sizable amount, it is only approximately equal in market value to the IBM shares listed on the NYSE.

In order to list shares on the Amex, corporations are expected to meet certain minimum standards:

$4,000,000 tangible net worth

$400,000 net income (most recent year)

500,000 publicly held shares (exclusive of insider holdings)

150,000 shares held in lots of 100 to 1,000

$3,000,000 market value of listed shares

$5 per share—minimum stock price

Occasionally, an issue falling somewhat short of some of these standards may be listed. Exceptions may be made by the Board of Governors on a case-by-case basis. Listing requirements for Canadian stocks are identical, although consideration is given to outstanding shares in *both* countries. If other than Canadian foreign issuers desire to list shares the exchange provides an alternate set of criteria.

Preferred shares are also listed on a case-by-case basis. Most such listings, however, are those of corporations whose common stock trades either on the Amex or the NYSE, particularly the latter. Convertible preferred shares may *only* be listed if convertible into common shares listed on either of those exchanges.

The Amex has long been a major market for long-term warrants to buy common stock. Warrants ordinarily trade in lots of 100 and typically at relatively low dollar prices, for they usually represent a speculation on later price appreciation of the underlying common. In general, their price behavior is similar to that of listed call options, but they have significantly greater "time value."

Bond trading has never been as important as equity trading on the Amex, but it has grown considerably in recent years. Corporate bond transactions totaled $645 million in 1985 compared with $356 million 5 years earlier. The Amex has also developed an automated market to trade odd lots of U.S. government bonds. After a slow start, the market has become quite active with a record 1985 trading volume of over $2.1 billion (face amount). It is a useful market for small investors who cannot trade in the $100,000 or million-dollar multiples which characterize the OTC market for governments.

Organization and Membership

The Amex is organized as a New York State not-for-profit corporation owned by its members. Any operating profits are thus retained and may not be paid out to the membership. Profits increase the net worth of the organization, but the net worth cannot be distributed unless the exchange is dissolved, an unlikely event. In 1985 the Amex generated net profits of $5,043,000 (the NYSE made $18,160,000 net income in the same period).

There are 661 regular Amex memberships, 95 options principal members, and 108 options trading permit holders. Full members are allowed to trade any item on the floor. As the name implies, options principal members must restrict their activities to that area. The options trading permits were introduced in 1984. Holders are allowed to trade options but do not have the authority to make principal markets, an activity reserved for full members and options principal members. They may, however, elect to purchase a full options principal membership allowing that function.

The price of a full membership, or seat, fluctuates with supply and demand. The 1985 trading range for a seat was between $115,000 and $160,000, well below the $325,000 top price of 1983. The decline in value may represent an opinion that the Amex is losing ground to the NASDAQ system, which has considerably more listings and a much larger trading volume. On the other hand, the value of an options-principal membership, although also considerably below its high, has remained above $100,000, possibly indicating that some members see the long-term course of the exchange as an evolution into an options and specialized product market.

Seats may be leased to persons who meet exchange standards, and some memberships are bought largely for investment purposes. That is, the holder hopes to buy at a time when the membership price is low, lease the seat to another who will actually use the trading privileges that accompany it, and then sell the seat at some subsequent date. The Amex also offers an associate membership, open to those who desire some of the benefits of membership without the expense of actually buying and maintaining the seat. Associate members enter orders through regular members such as $2 brokers. The Amex constitution does not specifically limit the number of associate members. Four new associate member firms joined the exchange in 1985. The typical associate member is likely to be a small- to- medium-sized NYSE member firm that needs access to the Amex for its customers, but does not produce the volume necessary to maintain a full-time presence on the floor. This is especially the case with discount and institutional firms whose customers have an interest in Amex-listed issues. With relatively little third-market and other exchange trading in Amex stocks, the best prices generally prevail on the floor itself.

Floor Trading

Although superficially different from the NYSE floor, Amex trading practices are similar to those used on the Big Board. The PER (post execution reporting) system used by the Amex is similar to the NYSE's SuperDOT. It is operated by computers owned by SIAC which is a joint affiliate of both exchanges. The most conspicuous distinction is that of the options activity. Because of its late start in this area, NYSE options activity remains sparse, whereas Amex options trading averaged almost 193,000 contracts daily in 1985.

The dual agency-principal function of the specialist is essentially the same as that of the NYSE specialist described earlier (Chapter 8). The number of registered specialists on the Amex varies but over the years has hovered around 175. Capital requirements for this function are smaller on the Amex than on the NYSE, but stiff enough so that only a few specialists have the financing to operate as sole proprietors. Most active issues are allocated to specialist units or partnerships that may have several officers or partners at the post handling orders.

Order execution is by the same open-outcry auction system prevalent on most U.S. securities exchanges. Orders away from current market prices are ordinarily left with the specialist who will fill them when and if possible. As on the NYSE, members with large orders, particularly those entered by institutional customers, are reluctant to reveal them to the specialist and may remain in the trading crowd if the market appears likely soon to reach an acceptable price. There is one major difference in acceptable orders when comparing the Amex with the NYSE. Specialists in Amex may not accept stop orders for round-lot transactions. A customer entering an order to buy or sell only after a specified price has been reached must also specify the same price of execution. That is, the order must be entered as a "stop limit" and both stop price and limit price must be the same. This means that an order will not be automatically executed if, for example, the market drops through the stop price and continues down. The position would then be re-evaluated, and the order would either stand or its price would be adjusted to the current situation. The reason for this policy lies in the relatively "thin" supply of many Amex shares.

If prices have risen sharply, many traders will follow the price rise by protecting their positions with "trailing stop" orders to lock in some of the profit. That is, if a trader had purchased shares at 20 and the market had risen to 35, that party might enter an order to sell at 33 stop. If the market dipped to 33 or below, the trader could be reasonably assured of an execution somewhere in the vicinity of 33; but if the price continued to rise to 40, the trader could raise the stop order to 38, and so on. Thus a stock that has had a long price rise would leave in its wake a series of stop orders ready to be touched off on the slightest price decline. The problem then would be that the electing or triggering of one stop order might send the market lower, in turn triggering others, and so forth. This clearly makes for excess market volatility and hence the ban on stop orders. The specialist may, however, accept stop orders for odd lots as they are unlikely to influence round-lot prices.

If the specialist is also registered in options, the functions are quite similar to those in stocks. In this case, however, the specialist's market making activities are aided by "registered options market makers"—options principals who trade for their own accounts and in so doing add liquidity to the market.

At one time a considerable portion of Amex trading was derived from trading in unlisted shares, an old practice permitted to remain after the Securities Exchange Act of 1934. The volume in this area was once as high as 67% of total Amex trading, but went into a steady decline in the 1950s. There is virtually no such trading today, but the electronic linking of exchange markets and NASDAQ makes such distinctions obsolete anyway.

REGIONAL STOCK EXCHANGES

The term "regional stock exchanges" is, at once, slightly demeaning, technically accurate, and a practical way to describe exchange trading away from New York. Regional to some means "parochial," or being concerned more with local matters than with national ones. Although regional stock exchanges do indeed feature listings of some local companies, most of their business is derived from national markets. The SEC makes no such distinction, referring to all registered securities exchanges as "national." There were 14 such exchanges in addition to the NYSE and the Amex in the 1960s. Four of these were very small and not involved in interstate commerce in any meaningful way. These exchanges were thus exempted from registration. Time has taken its toll on the remainder so that in 1986 only five remained significantly active.

With the exception of the Cincinnati Stock Exchange, trading is not very different from that already described. The specialist system and the open-outcry auction market are standard. Each exchange lists some stocks exclusively; usually these have a certain local following. The bulk of the trading volume on all of these exchanges, however, stems from transactions involving stocks whose primary market is the NYSE. The development of the Inter-market Trading System makes it as easy to execute an order for IBM in Chicago or San Francisco as it is in New York. Quotations supplied by specialists in one of the regional markets are competitive with New York quotes, and more than occasionally, the best available prices.

Some of these exchanges have also developed automatic small order execution systems similar to the NYSE's SuperDOT and Amex's PER. Another electronic system discussed in this chapter is the Instinet System. This electronic market isn't an exchange (although the SEC considers it such) and isn't quite OTC.

The Midwest Stock Exchange

This exchange resulted from mergers in 1949 and again in 1960, combining previously separate exchanges in Chicago, St. Louis, Cleveland, Minneapolis–St. Paul, and New Orleans. Invitations to join were also extended to the exchanges in Cincinnati, Detroit, and Pittsburgh but were rejected. The latter two have since closed and the former has considerable problems in remaining a separate entity. The Midwest Stock Exchange is located in the heart of Chicago's financial district, near to the CBOE and the nation's two premier futures exchanges, the Chicago Board of Trade and the Chicago Mercantile Exchange.

Share volume on the Midwest Stock Exchange in 1985 amounted to 2,350,940,000 shares, over three times the reported volume in 1981. This volume makes the Midwest the most active regional exchange by a considerable margin over the Pacific Stock Exchange, its nearest challenger. The Midwest Stock Exchange has exclusive listings of only 31 issues, so it is clear that the bulk of the trading activity features NYSE issues. Of these, 312 have actually listed shares but the exchange has granted "unlisted trading privileges" to 1,499 other issues, mostly NYSE-listed, but some with primary markets on the Amex.

The Midwest Exchange made a belated attempt to establish a market for listed options, but was unable to attract sufficiently attractive contracts or volume to create the necessary liquidity. Options activity was transferred to the CBOE in 1980.

The Pacific Stock Exchange

The Pacific Stock Exchange was likewise the result of a merger (in 1956) between exchanges in Los Angeles and San Francisco. Separate trading floors are still maintained in each of those cities. Most stock trading takes place in Los Angeles, but options activity predominates in San Francisco. Total stock volume for 1985 was 1,361,684,506 shares, or about 57% of the Midwest's stock volume. Also, like the Midwest market, most of the Pacific Exchange's volume derived from NYSE issues traded in California and reported on the Consolidated Tape. Such transactions constituted 1,162,059 of the exchange's reported volume noted previously. The exchange, however, had more executed trades than any other exchange participating in the Intermarket Trading System (save the NYSE) with a market share of 9.51% to the Midwest's 8.16%, indicating that more large block trades are likely to be done in Chicago, producing larger volume with fewer actual executions. The Pacific Exchange also has its own automated execution system called SCOREX (Securities Communication Order System) which allows member firms to route any size order directly to any PSE specialist with whom a prior agreement has been negotiated. Over 700 issues are eligible for this service, which not only reduces execution costs but also gives virtually instantaneous price reporting.

The Philadelphia Stock Exchange

This is the oldest organized stock exchange in the United States, founded in 1790—2 years before the famous Buttonwood Agreement, usually credited with founding the NYSE. Mergers with the Baltimore and Washington, DC exchanges resulted in what was called for a while the Philadelphia–Baltimore–Washington Stock Exchange, later known simply (but officially) as the "PBW Stock Exchange." The name has since been changed back to its original one to reflect the location of the trading floor as well as the real source of the exchange's revenues.

Equity volume was 497,520,114 shares in 1985. Like Amex, the Philadelphia has had great success with options, especially some proprietary products. The best-known of these is the foreign currency option. In the volatile currency markets that have existed since the dollar was unlinked from gold in 1971, these options have provided valuable hedging tools as well as speculative opportunities for traders. Options are offered on the British pound, Canadian dollar, Deutschemark, Swiss franc, French franc, and the Japanese yen. Trading volume in these contracts was 3,701,836 in 1985. In something of a reversal of form, the CBOE has tried to emulate this success by introducing similar, but larger, contracts of its own. Thus far, the attempt seems not to have met with much success and trading consistently lags behind Philadelphia's volume.

The Boston Stock Exchange

Because of its proximity to New York, the Boston Stock Exchange has long had an identity problem much like that of the Philadelphia Stock Exchange. Unlike Philadelphia, however, Boston has always been a center of money management in the United States. It was here that the first American mutual fund, the Massachusetts Investors Trust, was founded, and it remains a major location for money management firms and mutual funds complexes, including the Fidelity Group and Massachusetts Financial Services.

Boston's equity volume was 471,896,726 shares, all but about 8% produced by trades involving NYSE stocks. Only 95 issues are primary listings on this exchange. Its continued viability would seem questionable given the electronic linking of all markets, but its survival to date, without options or unusual new developments, indicates a rather remarkable staying power.

Cincinnati Stock Exchange

The Cincinnati Exchange was founded in 1885 and operated as a typical regional exchange for many years. Squeezed by competition from larger exchanges and the NASDAQ system, as well as the end to fixed commission rates, Cincinnati embarked on a new course in 1978. The Securities Acts Amendments of 1975 had not only mandated an end to fixed commission rates, but also expressed Congress's desire for a National Market System that would provide a single national system in which all orders would be displayed and available to all participants. Congress did not make specific recommendations as to how the system should work. Rather, the SEC was left to oversee its implementation. The SEC in turn simply told the industry to get on with the job.

After the Intermarket Trading System linking the NYSE, Amex, Philadelphia, Boston, Midwest, and Pacific markets was established, the Cincinnati Stock Exchange responded with a computerized system called the Multiple Dealer Trading System. The idea had been developed originally by Weeden and Company, at one time the most prominent "third market firm." The concept was purchased by Control Data Corporation and installed on the Cincinnati Exchange on May 1, 1978.

The system is basically a computer that receives, stores, and displays orders entered into it, matches them for execution, and reports executions immediately. It features an openly displayed limit-order "book" so that all participants may see the size and extent of orders currently entered. The system makes no market judgments or pricing decisions, as a specialist might. This is at once a possible strength and weakness of the system; a strength in that its simple "first come, first served" execution process is open, speedy, and highly efficient and a possible weakness (at least in some eyes) in that it cannot react to critical news developments or price movements with the experience and skill of a knowledgeable specialist.

Despite the enthusiasm of its proponents, the exchange has never caught on. Total volume reported by the Cincinnati Stock Exchange in 1985 was only 52,725,000 shares, by far the lowest of any participating exchange. With the development of the ITS and the "electronic books" now available to most specialists and other market participants, the purported technological advantages of this market have tended to fade. It remains to be seen whether the system will be substantially modified or simply abandoned. Wall Street now views it as something of an obsolete idea; daring in its time, but one whose time has passed.

THE INSTINET SYSTEM

Instinet Corp., originally Institutional Network, is a proprietary computerized execution service that has characteristics of both the NASDAQ system and a stock exchange. It was originally designed to allow institutional investors to display anonymous bids and offers on a videoscreen which would be available to other institutional investors. Although volume is still small, the system appears to have considerable support from some major forces in the securities markets. Equity interests in the company are held by E. F. Hutton, Merrill Lynch, Dean Witter Reynolds, and Shearson Lehman Brothers.

Institutional investors use terminals to display bids and offers of shares they wish to trade. Other subscribers may either accept the displayed quotes or make counter proposals. When bids and offers coincide, a trade is confirmed by touching a key on the machine. The transaction is thus executed without either party knowing who was on the other side of the trade. If a trader wants to find out whether a bid or offer is still "alive" after a trade report, he or she can touch a key to commence one-on-one negotiation not available to other subscribers at that time.

In some cases this anonymity may result in a cost saving because news circulates quickly in the trading community. For example, if a trader at an institution begins "shopping" a large block of stock for sale to the major block-trading houses like Salomon Brothers or Goldman, Sachs, the market is likely to reflect this by less aggressive bids. That is, if it is known that a lot of stock could be for sale, prospective buyers are willing to be a bit more patient and not run after the stock. If, on the other hand, the trader can gauge the depth of the market without making any calls, it is possible that the trader may be able to sell at a slightly higher price as no brokers will be involved.

Of course, there are a number of large ifs in that situation. The system currently has something over 300 subscribers, far fewer than the potential contacts institutional salespersons and traders can reach quickly. Furthermore, on difficult-to-execute trades, few of the subscribers are willing to take the kind of capital risk that the big "block positioners" are willing to take.

The Instinet System produced a volume of 82,345,000 shares in 1985, exceeding only the Cincinnati Stock Exchange among market participants. A proposed merger or joint venture with the big British news organization, Reuters, could help penetrate the burgeoning European equity market. The investment made by the large domestic firms indicates that they feel the system has more promise than it has yet demonstrated.

11 Foreign Stock Markets

Activity in world stock markets increased substantially in the 1980s from previous decades. In 1985 and 1986 trading on most major exchanges set volume and price records. Furthermore, American interest in foreign investments climbed to unprecedented levels. Wall Street now talks seriously about globalization, an abomination to a lexicographer but a word exactly to an investment banker's liking. Today, capital does not stop flowing at the border crossing or the water's edge. It is routine, for example, for an American investment banking firm to underwrite a bond offering denominated in Australian dollars and immediately place the offering in London and on the continent. As a final twist, the issuer may then turn around and swap the proceeds into Japanese yen interest payments. In short, capital markets have become truly international.

Major corporations, or even national governments, have learned to borrow money where it is cheapest or most accessible. In addition, corporations have found they can raise equity capital halfway around the world from their operations. Multinational corporations maintain facilities on several continents, so that a Nissan or Honda car built in the United States is no longer a "foreign" vehicle but rather is accepted as a domestic product. Financing this economic growth has created record activity on the world's financial markets and stock exchanges. Thus far, only the Socialist bloc countries have not participated in this growth.

SIZE OF THE WORLD'S EQUITY MARKETS

Although the NYSE remains the world's largest equity market by far, other exchanges have grown rapidly in both activity and market value of listed shares. Near the end of 1985, the major exchanges ranked by market value of listed shares were:

NYSE	$1,783 billion
Tokyo	731 billion

London	302 billion
Toronto	130 billion
Frankfurt	118 billion
Zurich	63 billion
Paris	58 billion
Milan	45 billion
Amsterdam	42 billion

Exchanges in Hong Kong and Singapore have also grown in value to approximate the market value of the smaller European exchanges and are showing even more dynamic growth as the "Pacific Basin" economies continue to lead world economic development. In December 1985, the six independent Australian stock exchanges agreed to form a single system that will probably be the world's sixth largest.

Put in percentage terms, the U.S. equity markets make up about 48% of total world equity market values, Japan about 22.2%, London 8.3%, other European 15%, and all others about 6.7%. By and large, most smaller exchanges are dominated by the market value of one or two companies. Whereas IBM shares constitute only about 5% of the NYSE's total market value, Royal Dutch Petroleum alone accounts for 43.4% of the entire Amsterdam capitalization. Of course, IBM is hardly a typical example, but its market value alone exceeds the total market value of all shares listed on all other exchanges except those in Toronto, London, Frankfurt, and Tokyo.

This chapter gives a brief overview of major foreign markets, especially those with international significance. Unless otherwise noted, statistical data are derived from the 1985 annual reports of the various exchanges.

TOKYO STOCK EXCHANGE

The growth of this exchange since World War II has been astounding. In that period it has surpassed all other stock exchanges in volume of share trading and is second only to the NYSE in value of shares traded. Despite hectic trading and new price peaks in 1985, the monetary value of the shares traded on the Tokyo Stock Exchange (TSE) was still exceeded by NYSE share values by almost 2½ times.

Stocks traded on a predecessor of the current exchange as early as 1878, but that market was largely dominated by the "Zaibatsu" (giant trading companies like Mitsubishi and Mitsui). American influence became pervasive during the postwar occupation period, and legislation similar to the American securities acts of the 1930s was passed in 1948. Trading resumed in 1949, but did not blossom until the great economic boom of 1955–1961. During those years the Nikkei Dow Jones average soared from 374 to 1,549. That pace slowed for a while, then resumed so that in 1981 the average stood at 7,500 and by 1987 exceeded 20,000.

The TSE is a highly automated market, which is necessary to handle the mammoth trading volume. In 1985, a total of 118,217 *million* shares (representing a value of ¥ 754,603 × 100 million) were traded in the premier First Section. These numbers are impressive by any standards, but they are exaggerated by the relatively low prices of Japanese shares and the number of yen to the dollar—about 155 in mid-1986. If par value of a share is less than 500 yen, about $3.25, the trading unit is normally 1,000 shares; if greater than 500 yen, the customary unit is 100 shares, but typical trades involve many units.

Trading practices differ markedly from either New York or European methods. Major corporations are listed in the First Section and traded at specific locations on the floor designated by industry group—automotive, chemicals, fisheries, and so on. In 1986 there were 1,052 corporate stocks listed on the First Section with a total value of $700 billion. The Second Section had 424 listings, mostly of newer and smaller companies. Trading in this section, also in a specific floor location, dealt a severe blow to the small Japanese OTC market. Some Second Section trading is done through CATS—the Tokyo Exchange's Computer-Assisted Trading System—and in 1983 the TSE opened a Third Section much like NASDAQ trading for such issues.

There are 93 "regular" members of the TSE. These include six foreign members admitted in 1985. The admission of these firms reflects growing awareness in Japan that the status Japanese firms seek in New York and London demands some reciprocity. The six foreign firms are: Merrill Lynch; Morgan Stanley; Goldman, Sachs; S. G. Warburg; Vickers da Costa; and Jardine Fleming, the first three American and the others British (although Vickers is now owned by the biggest U.S. bank, Citicorp). All members are corporations and are generally similar to the U.S. "wire houses," or large full-service firms. They provide a variety of customer services including stock research and handling of individual and institutional accounts. In addition, they may trade large positions for the firm accounts. It is estimated that close to 50% of all Japanese securities transactions are handled by the "Big Four" members—Nomura Securities (the world's largest broker), Yamaichi, Nikko, and Daiwa. It is widely suspected that these firms sometimes tend to move stock prices in the appropriate direction by the use of recommendations and house account trading.

In addition to regular members there are some "saitori" members who function rather like the NYSE's $2 brokers. In a typical transaction, the customer's order is transmitted to a clerk of a regular member on the floor. The clerk then proceeds to the area where that industry group is traded and confirms the trade with a clerk of a saitori member. The market is an auction where high bid and low offer prevail. There is no specialist function, but in some cases the opposite side of a customer order may be an order for a regular member's trading account entered with a saitori broker, thus creating a semiprincipal transaction.

Japanese shares tend to trade at high price/earnings ratios and pay low dividends compared to American shares. Price/earnings ratios in excess of 20 times earnings are common and dividend yields rarely exceed 1 or 2%. Also, Japanese corporations rely much more heavily on debt than do American companies. This produces leveraged capital structures, many with well over 50% debt, considered highly speculative in the United States, but rather routine in Japan.

In addition to the TSE there are several other exchanges in Japan. The next most important is that in Osaka with 1,036 share listings, followed by those in Nagoya, Hiroshima, and Kyoto. The OTC market has not been an important part of Japanese security trading to date.

LONDON STOCK EXCHANGE

The venerable London Stock Exchange ranks third behind New York and Tokyo in trading volume and share values. Unlike either the NYSE or the TSE, however, the bulk of the London Exchange's listings are bonds and debt instruments, about 4,600 of a total of approximately 7,200 listings. By comparison, the NYSE has fewer than 1,600 common stock listings.

There are considerable differences between British and American market terms. For instance, the term "stock" in the United Kingdom generally means a fixed-income security. Thus "gilt-edged stocks" (or simply "gilts") are, in fact, British government debt issues, not common shares. What Americans call "common stock" are termed "ordinary shares" by the British. American "trades" are British "deals"; Americans consider an unlisted company to trade OTC. To Londoners, there is indeed an "unlisted market," but it is actually part of the exchange. These differences are mostly superficial, but the trading mechanism used on the floor is substantially different from the NYSE's auction market.

As with most foreign exchanges, there is no specialist on the London floor. Public orders are transmitted by brokerage firms to their floor brokers who will then proceed to an area where those securities are traded. There the broker will bargain with a "jobber," a market maker who trades only with other members. Because the Exchange allows competition among jobbers, the broker may have to visit several jobbers' "pitches" (something like trading "posts" at the NYSE or Amex) before he or she finds the right price. Exchange rules historically prohibited "dual capacity," that is, the combination broker/dealer function performed by the American specialist.

The London Stock Exchange is undergoing a profound transformation. First, a broad deregulation of the market occurred in October 1986. This so-called Big Bang was far more extensive than the similarly named NYSE experience in 1975, when fixed commission rates were dropped in accordance with Congress's demands. The London version allowed full foreign ownership of exchange memberships. Unlike the NYSE, London memberships are not fixed. In 1985, 86 new members joined the Exchange, raising the total number of members to 5,009. It further allowed the government gilt market to be opened to any firm with the necessary capital to meet the standards set by the Bank of England.

For years, the British securities business had been even more clublike than the NYSE. Almost all business was conducted in the square mile of the City of London and the contractual nature of a verbal promise was sacrosanct, as indicated by the Exchange's motto *Dictum Meam Pactum* ("my word is my bond"). With outsiders largely frozen out, there was little need to develop the techniques, tactics, or capital to compete in the world's markets. This left even the biggest British brokers woefully undercapitalized when confronted with the resources of such international giants as Nomura, Merrill Lynch, Salomon Brothers, or Citibank. This led to a wave of consolidations and acquisitions, snuffing out the independent existence of many of the city's oldest names. Wedd Durlacher and Mordaunt, a large jobbing firm, became part of giant Barclays Bank PLC, as did the brokerage firm of deZoete and Bevan. Union Bank of Switzerland acquired Phillips and Drew, a well-known broker, and Security Pacific Bank from Los Angeles bought another old-line broker, Hoare Govett. These are only a few of the major changes that have hit the London Exchange—many others will doubtless happen in the future.

The transformation of the London Stock Exchange into an international market merely recognizes London's already prominent status as a world financial center. It already dominates the international bank loan business as well as foreign currency trading. In the past decade it has become the center of the vast Eurobond market, an OTC bond market second in size only to the U.S. capital market for the raising of funds through debt issuance. Here, the big players underwrite and trade huge bond offerings denominated in virtually every major free-world currency. As the bonds are sold outside the country where the currency originated and London has let the dealers have a free hand, the underwriters traded largely without any regulation, away from the Exchange floor. The largest factors in the market are mostly international banks and investment banking firms, none of them British: Deutsche Bank, Union Bank of Switzerland, Credit Suisse–First Boston (a joint venture between a major Swiss bank and a high-ranking American investment banker), Morgan Stanley, Salomon Brothers, and Merrill Lynch, to name some of the most prominent. Recently, Japanese firms have made their presence known in this free-for-all market and have established some presence. Given the increased importance of the yen as an international currency, it appears likely that these firms will also become major players in this arena.

The most radical change, however, may be yet to come. In the flurry of activity surrounding the Big Bang, what appeared at first to be *de*regulation has in fact led to *more* regulation. An overall supervisory body called the Securities and Investment Board (SIB) was created with a number of functions and powers similar to those of the American SEC. In addition, several self-regulatory organizations (SROs) came into being to oversee activities previously unregulated. Among these SROs was the International Securities Regulatory Organization, ISRO.

The mission of ISRO was to provide some discipline to the huge ($500 billion capitalization) and otherwise freewheeling Eurobond market. Stock exchange rules precluded members other than jobbers from acting as dealers and also made it difficult, even unnecessary, for them to accumulate the capital needed to participate in the Eurobond market. The two organizations eyed each other with a good deal of suspicion, and some exchange officials publicly questioned the ethics of this sometimes undisciplined market.

It came then as a major surprise when the Exchange and ISRO announced in September 1986 a merger to create a new body, the International Stock Exchange, which would consolidate trading in gilts, options, international securities, both debt and equity, into a single exchange. As the Stock Exchange has already established a link with the NASDAQ system, it appears that the new organization, if approved by the members, could prove to be a potent force in the further internationalization of the securities markets.

The London Exchange began an experiment in November 1980 that has proven most successful. This was the Unlisted Securities Market (USM). Trading takes place alongside shares on the regular list but is designed to encourage the smaller, emerging companies that do not as yet qualify for full listing. For example, a company admitted to the USM need have only 10% of its equity capital in public hands. From 40 issues traded in 1981, the USM has grown until 443 different corporations have had shares traded there since its inception. Of these, 54 were added to full listing and 131 others were taken over by larger entities. The USM has given British venture capital an attractive opportunity to achieve the success of American investors in the same field.

London has no last-sale reporting tape like the NYSE, but a complete newspaper listing of the previous day's trading is available in the *Financial Times,* with shortened listings in many other papers. Share prices tend to be low as a matter of convention, and no lack of quality is implied, as might be the case in North America. Typical per-share prices are in the $2 to $5 range. Daily share volume often exceeds 200 million, but reports include *both* purchases and sales.

SWISS STOCK EXCHANGES

Switzerland's long history of political and economic stability has made it a natural location for an important stock exchange. Swiss companies have an enviable record of efficiency, profitability, and technical prowess, and, of course, the "Swiss bank" is legendary. There are three major Swiss stock exchanges—Zurich, Basel, and Geneva. Of these, Zurich is by far the most active and important to the international investor.

The Zurich Stock Exchange has 395 share listings, of which 190 are foreign issues, largely American and German. The bond list contains 2,182 issues, 776 being foreign. Total market value of listed Swiss shares (31 December 1985) was Sfr174,644.4 million. The combined stock values of the three big banks—Union Bank of Switzerland, Swiss Bank Corporation, and Credit Suisse—constitute about 28% of all share values on the Zurich market. In fact, the 10 largest companies account for about 60% of all Swiss share values. Besides the banks, these world-renowned companies include Nestlé (the largest Swiss company), Ciba-Geigy, Sandoz, and Swiss Reinsurance. "Turnover" volume in 1985 was Sfr451,703,322,678. The Swiss, like the British, record both purchase and sale transactions, thus volume and value figures are doubled when compared to the NYSE, TSE, or Toronto.

The two other major Swiss exchanges are less active but have their niche. The Geneva Stock Exchange is the oldest Swiss exchange, founded in 1850. Although much less active than Zurich, the Geneva market had "turnover" or volume of over Sfr200 million in 1985 (compared to Zurich's Sfr451,703,322,678). The exchange moved into a new trading facility in 1986 and carries listings for 181 Swiss shares and 211 foreign ones.

The Basel Stock Exchange was Switzerland's major market prior to the worldwide 1929 crash. Although superseded by Zurich, it remains a substantial marketplace and a major innovator. For example, it was the first Swiss exchange to offer American shares. Many of the same shares offered in Zurich are also traded here, as they are in Geneva, but Basel is the major market for the shares of Hoffmann-LaRoche, the huge chemical and pharmaceutical concern.

Swiss law restricts ownership of voting shares to Swiss citizens, so the limited number of nonvoting bearer shares available for foreign purchase tend to be bid to high prices. Swiss shares are the most expensive offered on any major exchange. For instance, shares of Hoffman-LaRoche, or just Roche, had a high–low range in 1985–1986 of Sfr89,000 to 146,000. With the Swiss franc at about $0.55, a *single share* could have cost $80,000. It is unusual, in fact, for actively traded Swiss shares to be priced under Sfr1,000 ($550), with prices of Sfr2,500 being much more common.

FRANKFURT STOCK EXCHANGE

The major market of the Bundesrepublik is in Frankfurt-am-Main. Listings include 433 "officially quoted" shares, 246 domestic, and 183 foreign issues. Like many European markets, there are many more bonds than stocks listed, 5,649 versus 433. The two largest stock issues, Siemens and Daimler Benz, make up about 17% of total market value. Frankfurt has also developed an active options market with 461,238 contracts traded in 1985.

In West Germany only banks may trade securities for customers. Banks route orders to the exchange floor where they are executed by the official brokers called *kursmaklers*. For relatively inactive stocks, each designated *kursmakler* posts a "standard quotation" at midday. Active stocks like Daimler Benz or Deutsche Bank are quoted on an ongoing basis as on other major exchanges. German shares trade at rather high prices compared to U.S. shares, but are not nearly as costly as Swiss shares. A sampling of late 1986 prices will illustrate:

Daimler Benz	DM 1,225
Bayer	295
BASF	274
Volkswagen	508

Because the Deutschemark at that time was equal to about $0.45, share prices ranged well over $100, something of a rarity in the U.S. market.

AMSTERDAM STOCK EXCHANGE

Over half of the Amsterdam Stock Exchange's share capitalization of about $36 million is composed of the shares of two companies, Royal Dutch Petroleum and Phillips N.V. Among others actively traded are: KLM, Fokker Aircraft, Heineken, Unilever, and ABN Bank. Here too, bond trading dominates stock trading and accounts for more than half of all volume. At one time, Amsterdam thrived on foreign share trading, but this has become very minor, probably less than 5% of total turnover.

The European Options Exchange (EOE) is also located in Amsterdam. Patterned after the CBOE, it offers standardized exchange-traded options on stocks as well as on gold, silver, currencies, and bonds. Those on precious metals may be offset with trades in Montreal, Vancouver, or Sydney through an electronic network. From its opening in 1978 the open interest has grown from 47,853 contracts to over 600,000.

PARIS

The "Bourse" has declined in importance as an international market, but activity in the past few years has produced record volume and prices. French brokers are called *agents de change* and are awarded a legal monopoly over all share dealings. Their firms are strictly private, but all brokers are grouped into an association loosely similar to the NASD and governed by an annually elected *Chambre Syndicale*. This self-regulatory body manages the exchange and applies its own discipline.

Active share trading usually features such listed companies as Michelin,

Machines Bull, Moët-Hennessey, and Peugeot. Bond turnover exceeds that of stocks by several times.

TORONTO STOCK EXCHANGE

Toronto is Canada's most important stock exchange by a wide margin. Unlike most other non-U.S. exchanges, it concentrates on stocks, not bonds. Listed options were added in 1976. The exchange had 1012 listed stocks in 1986 with a total share value of Cd$44,196,506,129. Most of Canada's blue chips are traded in Toronto. Among these are: Hudson's Bay Company, Molson, Toronto Dominion Bank, and Bank of Nova Scotia. Trading volume in 1985 was 32,984,821,135 shares.

Although Montreal's hold on Canada's finances has slipped through the years, creditable business is still transacted on the Montreal Stock Exchange. Daily volume around 5 million shares is routine compared with about 20 million daily on Toronto. Among Montreal's more popular stocks are: Royal Bank, Bombardier, and Bank of Montreal.

Traders desiring more action than is usually promised by blue-chip issues will find hundreds of oil and mineral exploration stocks on the Toronto list. These highly speculative shares trade in cents, thus a price of 250 is $2.50 per share, not $250. For the really venturesome, the Vancouver Stock Exchange provides a highly speculative market in small companies usually involved in mineral exploration.

AUSTRALIAN STOCK EXCHANGES

For a country of only 16 million inhabitants and companies composing only about 2% of the world's equity capital, Australia would appear to be a poor bet for a major stock exchange. In fact, it has six, one in each of the state capitals. Those six exchanges agreed in December 1985 to form a unified Australian Stock Exchange by 1987. Based on a consolidation of the volumes on the exchanges, the world's sixth or seventh largest exchange would thus be created. The current exchanges are located in Sydney (the largest), Melbourne, Brisbane, Adelaide, Perth, and Hobart. Taken together the exchanges have a composite trading volume of about 60 million shares daily. The Perth Stock Exchange has also started a "Second Board," somewhat like London's USM. Perth has about 50 such listings. The concept has since spread and is now seen in both Melbourne and Adelaide in addition to Perth.

ITALIAN STOCK EXCHANGES

There are Italian stock exchanges of sorts in Florence, Genoa, Naples, Rome, Turin, and Trieste, but Milan's "Borsa" is Italy's primary exchange. It is, however, a small exchange by most measures. Share turnover in 1985 in monetary terms was approximately $17.3 billion, or about one-eighth that of the Zurich Stock Exchange. Milan had unfortunately developed a reputation over the years more fitting a casino than a securities market, and was widely viewed with distaste as a playground for the rich. That reputation is no longer merited. In the past few years trading volume has tripled and prices have advanced sharply, going up about 80% in 1985 alone.

Milan lists only about 181 corporate stocks and has a market capitalization of about $20 billion. Only a few companies such as FIAT, Montedison, Generale (insurance), and Rinascente trade on a regular basis with liquid markets. Institutional buyers have been sparse in Italy, largely because of the government monopoly of pension plans. In July 1984, the sale of mutual funds was legalized after 15 years of debate. Since then, more than $5 billion has been invested in those funds. About 20% of that amount went into Italian stocks. The rejuvenation of this market is one of the most encouraging signs for the Italian economy seen in years.

JOHANNESBURG

The South African Exchange is relatively small but plays a unique role. Despite the sanctions and antiapartheid issue, the "Joburg" Exchange has a history of profitable operations. Shares of 503 different companies are listed. The unique role mentioned previously refers to the production of gold. Because many investors flock to gold in times of perceived economic distress, shares of gold-mining companies often rise when the market is falling. Some of these shares are available in the United States through the ADR mechanism, and active trading of gold shares is also done in London, but the major exchange is still Johannesburg. South African gilts and Krugerrands are traded on the Johannesburg exchange; 1985 volume was R30.3 billion and 88 billion, respectively. The Rand was worth about $0.38 in mid-1986 dollars.

3 Work of the Securities Houses

12 The Customer and the Broker

Over a long period there has developed a vast body of law, customs, and regulations that protect the rights and define the duties of both customers and brokers. The purpose of this chapter is to describe the main business and legal relationships that exist between these parties.

OPENING AN ACCOUNT

Procedure

In general, opening an account with a brokerage firm is not materially different from opening a bank account. A prospective investor will have to provide sufficient information for the member firm opening the account to be sure that the firm "knows its customer." The NYSE Rule 405 charges member firms to obtain "significant facts" about the prospective customer, but is otherwise not very specific.

The minimum information necessary includes full name, address, phone number, employer, social security number, citizenship, an acknowledgment that the customer is of legal age, spouse's name and employer (if any), and investment objective. The remaining information required varies from firm to firm but would generally include bank and personal references, previous or other brokerage accounts, and information on how the account was introduced—referral, advertising response, walk-in, "cold-call" solicitation, and so on.

If the account is to trade in listed options, much more detailed information (including income, net worth, and investment experience) is required. In addition, the customer must acknowledge receipt of a current Options Clearing Corporation prospectus and, within 15 days, return a signed "options agreement" and verify the data on the new account form.

Every new account form should also bear the signature of both the registered representative servicing the account and the branch office manager.

TYPES OF ACCOUNT

Almost all public securities transactions are executed in either of the two major types of brokerage accounts, a cash account or a margin account. In addition, broker/dealers transact significant business with each other through the use of what are called "house accounts" so that Merrill Lynch carries numerous accounts in the name of Goldman, Sachs and vice versa. Customers may also engage in commodities futures trades with many exchange or NASD members, although these require entirely different documentation and usually more detailed financial information on the customer because of the riskier nature of this market.

Cash Accounts

This is by far the most common type of account. The customer may purchase or sell any security on a cash-and-carry basis. That is, if the item can be paid in full, or if it is already fully paid, it can be traded in a cash account. Thus any stock, bond, or comparable security may be bought in a cash account and likewise sold there if already owned. Payment or delivery must, according to Regulation T (Reg T) of the Federal Reserve, be made "promptly," but in no event later than the *seventh* business day following the trade date. One should note that this is 2 days beyond the regular-way settlement that brokers require of each other and of their customers. Consequently, if a customer fails to pay the broker by the seventh business day (usually the ninth calendar day), the broker will be required to take prompt action to liquidate the position—selling-out an unpaid customer long position or buying-in an undelivered short. If the customer, however, does not actually pay by the fifth business day, the broker is in a bind. According to Exchange or NASD rules he must pay the broker representing the other customer although he has not received the appropriate payment from his own customer yet.

Should a customer's position be liquidated because of a Reg T violation it will be "blocked" or "frozen" for 90 days. When an account is so restricted, the customer must precede any order with a deposit of "good funds" (cash, federal funds, or guaranteed check). Furthermore, the customer is liable for any losses suffered in the buy-in or sell-out, and the broker may use any cash balance, or liquidate any securities position already in the account to satisfy this deficiency.

Customers are not allowed to make a practice of "free riding," using the proceeds of the sale of a security to pay for that same security. For example, suppose a customer buys $4,000 of stock on Monday and sells it on the following day for $5,000. While it's clear that the customer has a $1,000 profit, Reg T requires payment in full of all purchases before any sale proceeds may be released. The customer must therefore pay the $4,000 purchase price before the broker is allowed to pay a check for the sale proceeds of $5,000.

The issuance of "difference checks" representing the net profit from a purchase and sale is a violation of Reg T if sufficient funds were not on deposit to cover the original purchase.

Margin Accounts

This type of account can be used when the customer wishes to gain leverage through the use of borrowed funds. The customer must deposit half of the purchase price of any listed or a number of OTC stocks and borrow the remainder, using the securities purchased as collateral. Margin accounts can also be used for short sales and a number of sophisticated strategies prohibited in cash accounts, for example, naked call writing and spreads. As with a cash account, Reg T requires payment within 7 business days although exchange rules may specify shorter periods for some securities such as options.

The margin customer must sign a "hypothecation agreement," also called a "customer's agreement," or, simply, a margin agreement. *Hypothecation* is the act of pledging the securities as loan collateral. Most brokers will also ask that the customer sign a stock-loan consent form. This document allows the broker to lend the client's margined securities to others for the purposes of short sales, arbitrages, and the like. The stock-loan consent is usually a one sentence addendum to the hypothecation agreement, but requires a separate signature. Federal law requires that the customer also be provided with, but does not have to sign, a truth-in-lending agreement showing how the interest on margin debit balances is computed.

Street Name Stock

If securities are purchased in or deposited into a margin account they must be registered in "street name." This means that the customer's name does not actually appear on the certificate or on the transfer agent's records. In effect the shareholder is unknown to the corporation of which he is part owner. Rather, the registered owner of these shares is in fact the brokerage firm acting as the customer's agent. The customer is called the "beneficial owner," whereas the broker is the "record owner." This situation does not disadvantage the customer at all, and, indeed, greatly simplifies the transfer process in the event of a sale. The broker, of course, cannot leave shares in the customer's name if there is a lien on those shares caused by a margin loan. If a price change unsecured the customer's position (made the value of the stock less than the amount of the margin loan, or reduced the value to the margin maintenance level), the broker could not sell those shares to protect his or her loan as the shares would not be transferable without the customer's signature.

As record owner the broker will receive dividends, distributions, proxies, reports, and all corporate communication with the stockholders. These must be promptly transmitted to the customer so that the customer may receive them as promptly as—sometimes more rapidly than—if received directly from the issuer.

Because the broker holds the shares in safekeeping, the customer has no concern about theft or accidental damage. A sale may be made as easily as making a phone call because no signature or certificate delivery must be provided by the customer. Dividend checks are automatically credited to the account so the customer need not be concerned with the loss or theft of a check from his or her mailbox or with the inconvenience of a trip to the bank.

Although leaving securities in street name is not required of cash account customers, it is by far the preferred form of ownership for the typical customer. If the customer wishes, the broker may "transfer and ship" the securities. This process involves sending the certificates to the transfer agent for registration in the customer's name and mailing the newly registered certificates to the customer. The full transfer process normally takes two weeks at a minimum and may occasionally take much longer. If the investor contemplates a quick sale of the securities, he or she may find that they have not even been received before their delivery to the new owner is required. This could create a buy-in possibility and the danger of significant losses. Furthermore, along with the securities the responsibility for their safekeeping is likewise transferred to the investor. Should they be lost, misplaced, stolen, or destroyed, their replacement will be expensive and time-consuming. Unlike a lost credit card or checkbook, missing securities cannot be easily replaced. The transfer agent, for example, will require the owner to post a sizable bond as an indemnity against the reappearance of the certificate at some later date.

Nevertheless, many investors are still enamored of the physical certificate and continue to request delivery. Outside of pure habit, there is some justification for actual delivery. By obtaining the certificates, the investor is not tied to a single broker and may buy and sell through different ones of his or her choice. Substantial investors may direct deliveries to be made to banks or even other brokers versus payment on their account at that location. This method, the standard for institutional investors, is called either COD (collect on delivery) or DVP (deliver versus payment) and allows the customer to use any number of executing brokers. The usual investor, however, does not deal in numbers large enough to make this economical as banks normally require large minimum account balances in order to conduct this type of business without steep service fees.

Finally, one should note that with certain securities the question of location is irrelevant as the physical certificate is not issued. "Book entry" issuance of securities is becoming increasingly popular. Such securities exist *only* as computer entries, and the actual certificate is not even issued. For some obscure reason, Wall Street has taken to calling actual stock certificates the "definitive" form, and, although the choice of words is not very felicitous, it seems to have been widely accepted—probably because it is continually repeated in the rules. Some securities are issued in either book-entry or definitive form. Many current municipal and U.S. government issues (bonds and notes) were so offered.

With other issues, no certificates are *ever* printed. These include Treasury bills, current FNMA debentures, some other government agency securities, and all listed options contracts. Thus far, book entry has not penetrated the American stock markets in a meaningful way, but one might note that the TSE has virtually eliminated the definitive stock certificate and is able to conduct share trading volume far in excess of that on the NYSE.

Joint Accounts

It is possible for two or more individuals to share joint interests in an account. By far the most common of the variations is the account titled "joint tenancy with rights of survivorship," often abbreviated JTWROS or JTROS on brokers' records. This account is most often used by married couples, probably more for psychological reasons than economic ones. The major advantage of such accounts is that property bypasses probate and goes directly to the surviving tenant upon the death of the other. It has thus acquired the name "the poor man's will." Indeed, for married couples it functions well, if—a big "if"—neither divorce nor separation follows. Because of the unlimited allowance for spousal transfers of property, JTWROS normally has no adverse estate tax consequences for married couples. If, on the other hand, the parties were not married and one of them provided all or most of the funds in the account, the assets in the account will be part of the decedent's estate and the surviving tenant may be left with a large estate tax bill.

The second common type of joint account is known as "tenancy in common." Using this method of ownership, the surviving tenant secures no additional interest in the account. That is, each party's interest is clearly defined and independent of the other's. Should one of the tenants die, the deceased tenant's portion goes to his or her estate, and the surviving tenant removes the remaining portion. While this may be used by married couples, it is more likely to appeal to relatives, friends, or business associates. By combining funds, economies of scale (reduced commissions, multiple round-lots, etc.) may be achieved, as well as simplicity of order entry.

Advisory Accounts

Sometimes a customer will not have the knowledge, time, or interest to monitor the securities markets. Although a mutual fund may provide one solution to this problem, some investors prefer to utilize personal management by hiring a professional investment counselor or advisor. The customer may select from a wide variety of possibilities: bank trust departments, large national investment advisory firms, or the investment counseling subsidiaries of most major brokerage firms. The customer signs a trading authorization or "limited power of attorney, which allows the advisor to make transactions in the customer's account without first consulting him or her. The advisor, however, does not have carte blanche and may only effect such trades as are reasonably prudent and necessary to achieve the account's stated investment objective.

Because there are no real nationally recognized criteria to establish an advisor's competence, investors should choose with great caution and carefully review the account status at regular and frequent intervals. The account will be carried with a brokerage firm, either directly or indirectly, through a bank-directed trust account. The customer is thus liable for all regular transaction costs as well as the management fee, not an insignificant expense. Fees vary from advisor to advisor, and depend on the size of the account as well as the amount of service provided. The investor content simply to hold blue-chip positions with infrequent changes can reasonably expect lower fees than one who demands aggressive and complicated options strategies. Most advisors will accept only accounts of certain minimum amounts, $100,000 being typical.

Discretionary Accounts

A customer might, on the other hand, sign a power of attorney in favor of a registered representative. Such an account requires prior approval in writing by an officer or partner of the broker. In addition to the power of attorney some firms have a separate discretionary account agreement or incorporate their trading authorization into a more comprehensive document detailing how the account is to be handled.

The inherent danger in such accounts is a built-in potential for conflict of interest because the broker handling the account derives compensation in one way or another from trading. Thus allegations of "churning" (trading primarily to generate increased commissions) are often made, whether justified or not. Because of the potential legal problems related to such accounts, most member organizations either refuse to handle them or restrict them to the care of experienced officers or partners.

A well-managed discretionary account, however, produces investment results similar to those of advisory accounts without the addition of the investment management fee. The client's only costs are the commissions and those are paid with advisory accounts also, as well as the management fee.

Accounts for Minors

Ordinarily brokers are reluctant to accept an account solely in the name of a minor, no matter how knowledgeable or wealthy that minor may appear. The reason for this is a basic legal precept that minors cannot be compelled to honor binding legal contracts such as brokerage orders. This would leave the broker no defense against the minor who claimed the profit on successful transactions and repudiated all losses, fees, and commissions on losing ones.

There are a number of methods by which a minor may legally participate in the ownership of securities. Various forms of testamentary, revocable, and reversionary trusts can be created, but all require the help of a lawyer or bank trust department specializing in this discipline. By far the most common means of minor security ownership is achieved by simply directing the broker to open a custodial account under the *Uniform Gift to Minors Act* (UGMA). Either securities or cash may be deposited as an *irrevocable* gift to a minor. An adult is chosen to act as the minor's custodian and makes all investment decisions. The account title normally appears as: "John Smith custodian for James Smith UGMA." The custodian may make any investment choice deemed reasonably prudent for the minor's benefit. Margin accounts and transactions like short sales are not permitted, but stocks may be left in street name with the broker. As any gift made to the account becomes the permanent property of the minor, the minor bears all tax liabilities and the minor's social security number must appear on the account documents. Because the typical recipient of such gifts has little other income, the tax consequences of investment income and capital gains are often negligible. This makes UGMA accounts excellent vehicles for building a fund for tuition payments and similar major expenses anticipated in the future. For example, if stocks or bonds are held in the name of an adult, possibly in a 28% tax bracket, almost one third of investment return could be lost through taxes. The same property held by the adult's offspring in a UGMA account may entirely escape taxation.

Upon reaching majority the minor simply presents a copy of his birth certificate to the transfer agent who will reregister the securities in the new adult's name. The broker will generally assist in this process.

Other Special Accounts

Securities industry rules also require special handling for a number of other accounts where the potential for legal or ethical problems is deemed greater than normal. For example, an employee of an NASD or NYSE firm must obtain that firm's prior written authorization to open an account with another member organization. In actuality, most large brokers require their employees to carry their personal accounts with that firm unless special permission is granted. This eases enforcement of internal compliance restrictions which might prohibit certain types of transaction, particularly when a firm might have gained confidential information about a corporate client through an investment banking relationship.

In addition, nonofficer employees of some financial institutions such as banks, trust companies, and insurance companies must obtain the written consent of their employer to open a *margin* account. As some such employees might have access to large amounts of securities, it is thought best to have a sort of check on activities involving such leveraged speculation as margin might involve. This rule exempts officers and directors of these businesses from obtaining written permission—a rather curious proposition if one notes the relative frequency of financial misdeeds attributed to officers compared to those of, say, tellers.

HANDLING THE ACCOUNT

Placing Orders

Once an account has been opened, an order may be placed by a variety of means: telephone, mail, telex, or personal contact. In practice, well over 90% of all orders are placed by telephone.

When an order is received by the registered representative, an order form should be filled out at once. With the advent of computer-switching and other forms of automation, the typical order "ticket" has become quite complex and the representative must be extremely careful to code all entries properly or the computer will reject the order, possibly resulting in the customer "missing the market." A typical order form requires the representative to check off boxes indicating the following:

Buy

Sell long or sell short

Place of execution (NYSE, OTC, Amex, etc.)

Type of account (cash, margin)

Disposition of securities purchased (transfer and ship to customer, retain in street name, deliver against payment to bank or another broker)

Application of sale proceeds (retain or pay out)

Special settlement ("cash," COD, etc.)

Solicited or unsolicited order

In addition, of course, the representative must enter the correct security symbol or description, number of shares, price indication (market, limit, stop, or stop limit), the customer's name and account number, and the representative's name and production number. Also, an indication that "discretion" is being used must be made for all such transactions. As can be readily seen, a hastily completed form omitting a necessary item, or even careless penmanship, could subject the broker to significant loss.

As the securities business has increased in complexity, the typical representative has been asked to handle more and increasingly different types of securities products. Because these investments do not fit the conventions of stock trading, it has become standard practice to utilize a different order form specifically designed for use with a particular product. Many major firms now employ a separate order form for each of the following: bonds, option contracts, mutual funds, commodities, and specialized items like bond unit trusts.

Once the order is executed, the representative should phone the customer as promptly as practical and relay the execution price, approximate net amount of trade (including fees and commissions), and settlement date. An active trader, of course, will want this information immediately. For the more infrequent investor a phone call the following morning will normally suffice because the exact settlement amount is then available from the representative's copy of the trade confirmation. If the investor makes a purchase of an item based on dollars invested or in units where the price is fixed prior to purchase an execution report is unnecessary. This is customary for the purchase of mutual funds, variable annuities, unit trusts, and tax shelter units.

The customer should not await receipt of the confirmation in the mail and, indeed, the broker should ensure that the customer does not develop this expectation. Because Reg T makes no allowances for mail delay, the customer's funds are due in 7 business days, confirmation or no confirmation.

Confirmations

A confirmation ("*con*firm" in Wall Street jargon) is a report by a broker to the customer on how an order was executed. A typical confirmation discloses the following:

1 Trade date
2 Settlement date
3 Security
4 Number of shares/principal amount of bonds
5 Execution price
6 Where executed
7 Principal or agency transaction
8 Commissions or markup
   (a) All commissions must be shown, but the amount of markup need only be shown on trades involving stocks
9 Accrued interest (bond transactions only)
10 Net amount due inclusive of all fees to broker or customer

Brokers usually mail confirmations as soon as processed by their purchase and sales departments, ordinarily the business day following the trade date. As noted previously, however, the customer cannot rely on the receipt of the confirmation before paying. While it may be possible to settle most usual securities trades without major problems, certain trades, like those involving options and U.S. government securities settle on the next business day, making a wait for the mail totally impractical.

Statements

Rules of the NYSE require that a statement of account be sent each customer in any month in which the customer had account activity—trade, dividend credit, deposit, and the like. Where no such entry has been made, the customer must receive at least a quarterly statement. This statement summarizes all account activity within the past period and gives dates for all entries. Because statements only account for funds coming into or going out of accounts, only *settlement* dates are recorded because no money actually changes hands until that time.

   Significant court rulings have grown out of disputes involving statements. Once the customer has received a statement, it becomes binding except for fraud or mistake. A customer should therefore immediately call his or her broker's attention to any mistake, no matter how minor. The law has generally allowed a customer a "reasonable" time after receipt to voice an objection. Given the frequent difficulty investors continue to have in correcting even trivial errors, it certainly behooves all investors to report even small errors as soon as possible. Such errors rarely, if ever, correct themselves, and consequently have a tendency to get worse if not promptly corrected. This is more true than ever as the IRS gets easier access to brokers' records via computer. A customer may thus find himself or herself subject to an IRS inquiry levied against him or her for a transaction that happened in someone else's account.

Cash Balances

Brokers do not require any minimum amount of cash to be carried as a credit balance. Most large retail firms do not pay any interest on credit balances left with them, and there is no requirement that they do so. On the other hand, all large firms and a number of smaller ones offer a combined money-market and brokerage account that automatically "sweeps" idle credit balances into money market mutual fund shares, either weekly or sooner, depending on the amount of the balance. Pioneered by the Merrill Lynch Cash Management Account, this type of account allows the holder to write checks against the balance and even to draw off margin loans by writing checks against the portfolio's loan value. These accounts usually require substantial equity to open, anywhere from $5,000 to $25,000 depending on the broker and the features offered.

Voting Rights

Corporations transmit proxy materials to the broker as record owners when stock is held in street name. The broker in turn sends these materials to the customer. In most situations, the customer simply indicates his or her voting preferences, signs the proxy, and returns it to the broker who will vote the shares as requested. If the customer fails to return a signed proxy, the broker will usually vote the shares according to the corporate management's recommendation. If, however, a proxy *contest* (a significant struggle for control or policy) is under way, the broker may only vote the shares according to a specific written directive from the customer.

Lien on Securities

A broker has a lien on a customer's securities for all commissions, interest, and advances that may be due. In order to enforce the lien, the broker may withhold delivery or, if necessary, may secure payment by selling the securities. The lien applies to all securities, whether owned outright or margined. If brokers are to enforce the lien, they should not surrender the securities to customers until payment for all charges due has been received. If the stock is margined, the broker also has a lien as pledges against dividends paid.

Commissions

Brokers are entitled to commission on all customer agency, that is, exchange-executed transactions. Since its inception, the NYSE specified a *minimum* commission schedule, periodically revised, for all members. In effect this meant a fixed rate for all customer transactions of a given size regardless of which member firm handled the order. A SEC mandate ended this clearly anticompetitive policy as of May 1, 1975, and since then all commission rates have been "negotiable," although the typical investor's ability to negotiate commissions with a broker is quite limited.

Most member firms establish a rate schedule and revise it from time to time. Most revisions have been upwards due to inflation and it is probable that the customer buying 100 shares of a listed stock through an NYSE member is now paying substantially more in commissions than before the imposition of negotiated rates. The smaller members generally wait for the industry giants such as Merrill Lynch to announce their new rates first before making their own revisions. Virtually all such rate schedules favor large transactions at the expense of smaller ones. Also, many firms weigh compensation to representatives in favor of larger orders so that the representative has less incentive to solicit or service smaller investors.

Institutions have been the prime beneficiaries of negotiated rates because of competition among brokers to service their lucrative accounts. A typical institutional (bank, mutual fund, pension fund, etc.) order is likely to be executed at a charge somewhere between 5 cents and 15 cents per share (well below the rate the same firm would charge its average customer) for a smaller transaction in the same securities.

The individual investor, however, has benefited in another way. With the advent of negotiated rates a new branch of the industry, *discount brokers,* sprang up. At first concentrated in New York City, discount operations grew and spread so that there are now several firms with a nationwide branch network and numerous local or regional discounters. Essentially, all discount brokers offer the same services and attractions, the services being quite minimal compared to the full-service firm. The customer ordinarily gets no research, recommendations, or advice on securities or types of order to use. In return for this "no frills" approach, the discounter executes the customer's order at a rate well below that charged by the major brokers—in fact, at a rate quite comparable with the commissions charged institutions. A typical schedule of charges illustrates the differences between firms:

	Shares				Options	
	200 @15	500 @25	1,000 @29	2,000 @29	10 @5	Bonds 20
Discount broker	$ 31	$ 40	$ 55	$ 85	$ 44	$ 65
Discount broker	35	65	102	162	71	77
Discount broker	54	95	144	225	78	100
Discount broker	54	96	138	167	85	108
National "full service" firm	86	235	453	680	165	250

Obviously, the experienced, well-informed investor, especially the active trader, would do well to consider at least some of his or her orders through a discount broker. Many investors still like the personal contact with "their" registered representative at a large or a local firm where they have long done business. Furthermore, relatively few investors, including most novices, are knowledgeable enough to do without the wide variety of products, services, and information provided by the full-service firms at little or no charge. Nevertheless, the growth of the discount industry is ample testimony that many investors do not wish to pay for services they do not require. These investors, at least, have gained substantial benefits through the negotiability of commissions.

Multiple Accounts

There is no reason why a customer may not carry two or more accounts with the same broker. Many have both cash and margin accounts, sometimes in one name and sometimes jointly, usually with a spouse. Also, many active investors carry accounts with several different firms because they find that more different sources of information give them greater opportunities.

Interest on Debit Balances

When a customer carries stock on margin, the difference between the cost of the securities and the customer's deposit (or equity) must be borrowed. The standard method for financing customer debit balances is through "broker" or "call loans"—short-term borrowings that the broker obtains from banks by using the customer's margined securities as collateral.[1] Call money rates, along with all other interest rates, fluctuate considerably. Because the loans are collateralized and brokers are good banking customers, this rate is close to, and often under, the bank's "prime" lending rate. Of course, the customer is unlikely to be afforded a loan as low as the quoted rate that appears in the newspapers. For one thing, the quoted rates are "wholesale" and broker loans are obtained in multiples of $100,000. Few retail customers maintain debit balances of that size. In addition, the broker arranges the loan and does all the detail work on the customer's behalf. Thus, the customer can expect to be charged at least ½% higher than the call money rate. Some firms publish schedules of rates with the lowest rate going to customers with the largest debit balance. Most brokers, however, will be competitive, and a customer who produces statements from another firm indicating active trading and a lower rate of interest can usually negotiate a similar rate with the new firm, even if the size of the debit balance would not qualify for the lower rate.

Interest is computed monthly and reported to the customer on his or her statement. Credits to the account such as dividends or cash deposits reduce the debit balance and consequently the amount of interest charged. If no such credits come into an account, the interest for a month will increase the debit balance by a similar amount, leading to a compounding of debt. With rates around the 20% mark in the late 1970s and early 1980s period, a customer who opened a margin account with a $10,000 debit balance would owe more than $12,000 at the end of the year if no offsetting credits came into the account.

EXECUTION OF ORDERS

Broker as an Agent

A customer must employ a broker as agent before any questions of agency arise. The broker is free to reject this relationship and this occasionally happens. Many brokers consider small accounts unprofitable and set minimum dollar amounts acceptable. Others only want certain types of business, for example, active trading accounts, institutional accounts, and so on. Once

[1]Merrill Lynch now issues its own commercial paper as a source of some of these funds. It is also likely that merger of broker firms with other financial organizations, for example, American Express and Shearson Loeb Rhoades as well as Bache Halsey Stuart Shields and Prudential (both in 1981), will open new financing sources.

the order is placed and accepted, the broker becomes the agent of the customer and must carry out the customer's instructions.

Due Care and Skill

A broker must use due care and skill in executing orders. Failure to do so may result in liability for resulting losses.[2] In the case of *Warwick* v. *Addick,* it was held that due care and skill consisted of that which was typical of good business owners in the same business and community.[3] In other words, the broker is expected to execute orders with the same care and skill that is common in the brokerage business.

Following Instructions

Although the broker must use care and skill in following customer instructions, there is no liability for failure to execute if conditions do not permit filling the order as customer specified. For example, the customer may specify the sale of 500 shares at a price limit of 60. If the stock trades no higher than 59⅞, the order will not be filled. Indeed, the broker would commit a serious violation of NYSE rules (Rule 408) if the price were reduced without the customer's consent in order to achieve execution. Even if this ultimately turned out to benefit the customer, such "unauthorized discretion"—without prior customer consent—could subject the representative to liability for damages as well as discipline from the Exchange.

Partial Executions

Rule 61 of the Exchange states: "All bids and offers for more than one trading unit shall be considered to be for the amount thereof or any lesser number of units." This means that if the customer's order is to buy 1,000 shares @ 12 and the broker is only able to buy 500 at that price, the customer must accept this partial execution. An order for only 100 shares, however, cannot receive a partial "fill" as an odd-lot. There are a relatively small number of securities which trade in round-lot units of 10 shares, and an even smaller number which trade in either 25 or 50 share units. In such cases the execution of the trading unit, 10 for instance, is not an odd-lot execution. To distinguish such securities from more regular stocks on the tape, the symbol *ss* is used. Hence, a tape print of *XYZ 3 ss 109* reports a trade of three 10-share round-lot units @109 (a zero is added to the reported digits to determine total volume; in this case 30 shares).

---

[2]C. H. Meyer, *The Law of Stockbrokers and Stock Exchanges* (New York: Baker, Voorhis & Co., 1931), and *Supplement* (1936), p. 265; W. H. Black, *The Law of Stock Exchanges, Stockbrokers, and Customers* (New York: Edward Thompson Co., 1940), p. 76.
[3]35 Del. 43, 157 Atl. 205.

Cancellation of Orders

A customer may cancel an order at any time, but should understand that entering a cancellation is no guarantee against execution in many cases. A limit or stop order a few points away from the current market price may be usually canceled without problem. If, on the other hand, the order price is within a point or so of the current level, it is quite possible the floor broker may execute it before the cancellation request reaches the floor. In such a case the customer will have to accept the execution. With a few exceptions it is usually virtually impossible to cancel a market order once entered. However, an order may have been entered to sell short at the market, and there may be some lapse of time between the entry and the next "plus tick" needed for executions. There may be some unusual situations such as suspensions of trading in individual or even all stocks which allow time for a cancellation.

Market of Execution

The broker should always attempt to obtain the best available price for the customer. This means the order is usually routed to the principal market for that security because that market customarily has the greatest depth and liquidity. If the shares are NYSE-listed, the best market is normally that exchange. There are frequent instances where the ITS will display better prices on another exchange. When this happens the order should be routed to that exchange, provided the broker is a member. One problem, however, may rise if the best quote showing on the system is a third market quote being supplied by a nonexchange member NASD firm. The NYSE's rule 394 requires its members to execute orders in listed stocks on the NYSE floor or some other exchange where that stock may be listed unless its prior approval has been received.

A number of off-board trades occur regularly. Most major retail firms routinely execute their odd-lot orders internally on a dealer basis. In addition, more recently listed stocks may be executed wherever the broker wishes. These stocks are called 19c-3 stocks after the section of the 1934 Act which permits it.

The primary market for *all* bonds is OTC. A significant number of bonds trade daily on the NYSE, primarily because of the NYSE's 9-Bond rule. Based on the fact that the OTC bond market is a professional's domain where small orders are held in disdain, the NYSE requires that all orders for nine or fewer listed bonds be sent to the floor for an attempt to execute, unless the customer specifically directs otherwise. Although this does not necessarily assure a better price for the customer, at least it exposes the order to the open-outcry auction market and gives an improved chance to obtain the best possible execution.

Crossing Orders

Brokers receive many orders to buy or sell the same stock the same day. The "in-house cross," where the broker simply pairs off its own customers with complementary aims, will likely evolve in the near future. For many years, however, this practice has been prohibited on the grounds that neither customer had the benefit of competing proposals in the open auction market. Thus there was no guarantee that either customer received the best available price. The electronic linking of exchange floors and brokerage firms will ultimately remove this concern.

Under current NYSE rules a broker who receives equal size customer orders to buy and sell at the market (or at a limit price within the current quotation) may act as agent for both sides by publicly bidding *and* offering the same number of shares within the current quotation. The broker's offer must be at least ⅛ higher than its bid to preserve the integrity of the open outcry system because this exposes either order to a counterproposal from another broker. In actuality, the cross is performed with such rapidity that another broker would have little time to react. In a typical situation, the broker who intends to cross 1,000 Polaroid shares goes to the post where the stock is traded and requests a quotation. The specialist might quote Polaroid at 28 bid to 28¼ asked. The broker might then bid 1,000 at 28 (equaling the best bid), rapidly offer 1,000 at 28⅛ (a better offer than the quote), and quickly raise the bid to meet the offer, trading at 28⅛. In this way the stock is traded publicly at a fair price to buyer and seller.

LEGAL RELATIONSHIPS IN GENERAL

Principal and Agent

The law of agency weighs heavily in interpreting the customer–broker relationship. In the typical exchange transaction the customer is the principal and the broker the agent. In this relationship the broker must act in the best interests of the customer and receives a commission for these services. There is no other compensation for the broker, who is taking none of the risks of ownership. The broker's role is that of intermediary.

Debtor and Creditor

The debtor–creditor relationship is important when the customer has a margin account. The customer borrows 50% (or less) of the purchase price from the broker. Whether or not the broker obtains this loan from a bank—a call, or broker loan—or elsewhere is not material. The broker is still the creditor and the customer the debtor. Under such conditions the prevailing laws on debtors and creditors apply.

Pledgor and Pledgee

Another relationship arises when the stock is pledged or "hypothecated" for a margin loan. The customer hypothecates the margined securities as collateral for the broker loan obtained by his firm. The firm in turn rehypothecates the securities, usually to a bank in return for the loan needed to carry the customer position. This relationship will be examined more fully below.

Fiduciary Relationship

A fiduciary relationship exists, at least in part, between the broker and the customer. In this "faith relationship," the customer entrusts money and securities with the broker because of an implicit belief in the broker's honesty, judgment, and responsibility. The broker accepts this responsibility to serve the best interests of the customer. In a sense the broker becomes a quasi-trustee of the customer's affairs. How far the relationship extends is a frequent source of legal problems, but it is widely accepted that the broker should not solicit "unsuitable" orders and may have the obligation to reject an order, even when the customer originates the order and insists on it.

Hypothecation of Securities

Hypothecation was defined previously as an act in which securities are pledged as collateral for a loan. A customer hypothecates stock when it is purchased on margin. The stock serves as a security deposit until the loan is repaid. The broker in turn *re*hypothecates the customer's stock when it is repledged to a bank in order to obtain the *call* (broker) loan that is passed along to the customer, thus financing the debit balance.

Substitution of Collateral

A broker may substitute hypothecated collateral. If a customer were to buy 200 shares of General Motors on margin, the broker would not be required to keep the identical certificate throughout the life of the pledge. Because one stock certificate is identical to any other, it is immaterial whether the broker keeps any particular certificate; certificates are not property, but merely evidences of it. In the case just mentioned, the broker would be legally permitted, if the need arose, to substitute two 100-share certificates for the original 200-share certificates. The broker, however, must at all times keep available for delivery stock of a like kind and amount.

Right to Rehypothecate Securities

The broker is also within legal rights in rehypothecating a customer's securities. Without the ability to use this source of collateral it would virtually be impossible to obtain loans to finance customer debit balances at any reasonable rate. Sometimes a customer may lend fully-paid securities. Of course, there must be some economic interest for the customer to agree to this practice. For example, short sellers may find it difficult to locate a security they wish to borrow and be willing to pay a premium for the right to deliver it against their short sales. A customer must give the broker *written* permission either to lend securities or to rehypothecate an excessive amount.

Rights of the Broker's Pledgee

The next problem concerns the rights of the broker's pledgee, usually the bank that provided the "call loan." Numerous court decisions have established that the bank's rights are strong, generally superior even to those of the customer. Although the situation is infrequent, if the broker became unsecured as a result of price activity and was not able to meet the bank's loan terms, the bank has the legal right to sell the customer's pledged securities to protect its loan. Naturally, the customer in this situation will have a difficult time salvaging much equity.

Sale of Hypothecated Collateral

Initial requirements to margin stock purchases are relatively high—50% currently and as high as 80% in the past 15 years. The NYSE requires a customer to maintain a minimum equity of 25% and many members have a "house" requirement of 30%, or even 35%. Consequently, a customer's equity has to fall substantially before there is danger of his margined securities being sold out by the broker. Usually the process by which a customer's equity is thus depleted takes some time and comes as no surprise to the broker or the customer. Sometimes, however, the customer has all the eggs in one basket—a large position in a single security. A sudden price decline can then force the account below the maintenance level and force the broker to request new funds. The standard margin agreement used by most member firms permits the broker to sell the customer's stock without notice.

Despite the "without notice" wording, brokers rarely insist upon the right and will normally send the customer a telegram advising that a sell-out (or buy-in) will be necessary if funds are not received by a specified time. Unlike initial margin calls, which may be met in as long as seven business days, maintenance calls are to be answered on demand, frequently the day after the telegram has been sent.

CLOSING THE ACCOUNT

Rights in General

The legal relationships in a brokerage account involve the rights of debtor and creditor as well as those of principal and agent, as has been stated previously. The law of agency is that an agency may be terminated at will by either party if it has no fixed terms. Similarly, a pledge may be terminated by either party upon demand and proper performance, that is, repayment of any remaining loan balance by the pledgor and return of the securities by the broker.

Right of the Customer to Close Account

The customer may close a brokerage account on request, provided there are no unfulfilled obligations pending settlement. The broker will forward any credit balances and transfer securities to the customer or to another broker. The transfer of an entire account to another broker is a relatively simple procedure, merely requiring the customer to sign a form designed for this purpose. If the account is margined, the debit balance must be paid in full before securities are released. In the case of an account transfer from one broker to another, the gaining broker pays the debit balance on the customer's behalf and reestablishes the same debit in the new account.

Right of the Broker to Close Account

The typical margin agreement permits the broker to close out customer positions for *any* reason deemed necessary for the broker's protection. The usual reason for this action would be unanswered margin calls, thus leaving the account in violation of either federal or NYSE margin rules. Sometimes, however, a firm will request that the customer close or transfer the account because it feels the trading activity occurring there exposes the broker to considerable financial or regulatory risks. This is especially true of customers who insist on dealing in highly speculative securities and large short sales on a frequent basis.

Death of a Customer

Margin agreements usually allow the broker to liquidate an account upon the death of the customer, but in practice this is rarely done. The usual procedure for the broker upon learning of the death of the customer is to cancel all "open" (good-till-canceled) orders to prevent new positions from being established. In some cases, especially option or commodities futures contracts, the broker may close out the positions because of the limited life span of such instruments. If the account was in an individual name, the broker will require legal documentation before permitting an executor or an administrator to act for the decedent's estate. If joint tenants participated in the account, the broker will usually permit liquidating transactions by the surviving tenant but no new commitments. Any new positions should be made in a new account for that customer.

13 Margin Trading

WHAT IS MARGIN?

The use of borrowed money to acquire capital assets for investment is common in industry and real estate, as well as in securities. The borrower is creating "leverage," an aptly chosen word, to magnify return on investment in much the same way a lever magnifies force applied to it. When leverage is used in the securities business, the term *margin* is employed as it has been for a great many years.

Under current regulations an investor using margin may buy with a given amount of cash twice the number of shares than would have been possible in an outright cash purchase. If the investor's judgment is correct and the stock rises in price, the gross profit would obviously be *twice* what it would have been otherwise.

To illustrate: An investor has $10,000 cash to invest. This would allow for the purchase of 100 shares of XYZ at 100 for cash or 200 shares of XYZ if margined. Should XYZ appreciate to 150 in a year, the cash buyer could liquidate the 100 shares for $15,000, yielding a 50% return on the money invested. The margin buyer, on the other hand, makes 50 points on 200 shares, earning $10,000 and *doubling* the initial commitment. This prospect is precisely what is appealing to the speculative investor, but it is not without risks.

Leverage works every bit as well in reverse, and the investor loses twice as much on an adverse price move. Naturally, interest is charged on the borrowed funds. In the 1970s and early 1980s, these charges for most investors averaged over 10% annually and occasionally exceeded 20%. Likewise, commission charges are usually greater, for the margin trader tends to make more frequent trades and these trades are usually twice as large as would have been possible on outright cash purchases. There is little point in margin for the typical investor; it can be usually assumed that the typical margin investor is an aggressive speculator. Although not necessarily in-and-out traders, they do tend to be more active than other investors and frequently have considerable sophistication. Indeed, many of the more complex strategies may only be pursued in margin accounts for regulatory reasons.

FEDERAL REGULATIONS

Until 1934 there were no national restrictions on the extension of credit for securities purchases, although the NYSE had established a 50% requirement for its own members in 1933. Until those times a lender could finance any amount of a customer purchase. It was common by 1928–1929 for even small investors to control large positions through margin deposits representing as little as 10–20% of the market value of shares purchased. This was reflected in very high share prices as the actual market value bore little relevance to the amounts being invested. Prices in excess of $200 per share were commonplace and price swings of $5–10 daily were precisely what made margin speculation so attractive.

When the market collapsed in the great 1929 break, declining securities values quickly unsecured loans that brokers had obtained from banks to finance customer transactions. The brokers were then forced to sell their customer's holdings in order to protect themselves from bank demands for additional collateral. As this distress selling fed on itself, one sell-out tended to depress prices further, triggering yet another sell-out, and so on in a snowballing fashion. Whatever the ultimate cause of the Great Crash, there can be little doubt that unwise credit extension fueled the speculation that drove the market up and likewise fed the panic that brought it down.

The Securities Exchange Act of 1934 granted regulation of credit extension for securities purchases to the Board of Governors of the Federal Reserve System. The Federal Reserve proceeded to implement several regulations, the terms of which are occasionally altered depending on how the "Fed" perceives the state of the economy and the markets. Regulation T is the one most applicable to the typical securities investor as it establishes the maximum amount of credit that may be extended by a broker/dealer on a securities purchase. Regulations U and G are similar, but apply to credit obtained from banks or other lenders.

All listed stocks may be margined under Reg T. In 1985 OTC stocks included in the NASD's National Market System were extended the same privilege. Other OTC issues must be on the Federal Reserve's OTC Margin Stock List in order to qualify for margin. The list is periodically reviewed and updated. In 1985 about 2,000 such issues met the criteria set by the Fed for inclusion in the list. Stocks not on the list, options, and mutual funds must always be paid in full, although credit may be extended on fully paid mutual fund shares deposited into a margin account.

Except for convertible bonds, debt instruments are generally exempt from Reg T. However, they remain subject to industry *maintenance* requirements, as noted below. In 1985 the Fed extended Reg T lending requirements to certain types of "junk" bonds, often used in the financing of unfriendly corporate takeovers. The intent of this rule is a clear signal that the Board of Governors was becoming concerned about the great increase in low-quality debt and its use to replace equity capital. Indeed, in 1984 and 1985 almost $200 billion of equity capital disappeared to be replaced by debt, much of it of dubious quality. A repeat of 1929 may not have been expressly forecast but was clearly a factor in the decision.

Regulation T

This regulation applies both to margin purchases and to cash (paid-in-full) transactions. In a cash account, an investor may purchase any security as long as payment in full is made within 7 *business* days from the trade date. One should note that this is 2 business days more than is permitted by industry rules for regular-way settlement of corporate securities transactions between broker/dealers. Should an investor fail to pay within the prescribed period, the broker is required by Reg T to promptly cancel the transaction. This means that if a customer has bought, but not paid for, a security, the broker must sell that security and hold the customer liable for any loss suffered through the sell-out. Similarly, if a customer has sold, but not delivered, securities, the broker will buy-in the customer. As a result of this violation of federal rules, the customer's account is blocked or frozen for the next 90 days. This sounds rather more serious than it actually is. A customer is in no way forbidden to trade, but rather must *precede* any order with a deposit of acceptable funds or securities before entering any orders.

In unusual circumstances, the customer may have a valid excuse for being unable to pay or deliver within the 7-business-day period. In such a case, the broker may file an extension request to the exchange where the trade took place or to the NASD. Because each case is weighed individually, customers should not get the idea that the procedure is routinely rubber-stamped. Indeed, many such requests are rejected, and, no matter how good the customer's reason may appear, no individual may be granted a total of more than 5 in any calendar year.

When a margin purchase (or short sale) is made, the customer must deposit at least the current Reg T requirement within 7 business days as with a cash account. The Federal Reserve requires a minimum deposit of 50% of the purchase price in cash, or a deposit of fully paid securities equal in value to the purchase. The same requirements as cited above apply to the prompt payment for purchases.

Regulation T margin calls need be met only once per transaction. That is to say, once the appropriate deposit is made, the investor will not receive another federally mandated request for funds. Any subsequent request for additional funds will stem from a self-regulatory body such as the NYSE. A discussion of such margin calls follows in "Maintenance Requirements." Finally, it should be noted that the Federal Reserve changes the Reg T minimum requirement occasionally, but not frequently. For example, the rate was progressively raised in steps to 80% in the late 1960s in a vain attempt to cool the speculative fever prevailing at that time. Then it was reduced in steps to the current level when it became apparent that the market, through sharp price breaks, had corrected its own speculative excesses.

Margin Purchases

Assume that IBM is trading at $120 per share. An investor with $6,000 cash could buy either 50 shares outright or 100 shares using margin. The investor who feels strongly that the market could rise to perhaps 140 over the next few months might decide to "leverage" position by buying 100 shares in a margin account. If this judgment is correct, the profit achieved will be twice that of a cash purchase as twice as many shares are owned.

In order to pay $12,000 to the seller of the shares the investor deposits the 50% ($6,000) minimum required under Reg T. An investor is free to deposit any larger amount, but maximum leverage is obtained by taking full advantage of the Reg-T minimum. The remaining $6,000 is borrowed from the broker and is collateralized by the 100 IBM shares. At this point the account appears:

$$
\begin{array}{llll}
\text{long 100 IBM @ 120} = & \$12,000 & \text{market value} & \text{(MV)} \\
\text{Less loan} & \underline{6,000} & \text{debit balance} & \text{(DR)} \\
& \$\,6,000 & \text{equity} & \text{(EQ)}
\end{array}
$$

If the market price increases to 140 the investor's equity will increase to $8,000.

$$
\begin{array}{lll}
\text{long 100 IBM @ 140} = & \$14,000 & \text{MV} \\
\text{less loan} & \underline{6,000} & \text{DR} \\
& \$\,8,000 & \text{EQ}
\end{array}
$$

The investor has thus made $2,000 on a $6,000 investment whereas the profit would have been only $1,000 if 50 shares had been bought and paid in full. Of course, the customer's debit balance generates interest charges and the purchase of 100 shares would require significantly higher commissions than the purchase of only 50. Nevertheless, these are minor considerations when compared to the doubled profit—if the investor's judgment proves correct.

Now, suppose the investor does not wish to realize the profit at the moment, but does wish to make use of his or her "paper profits." This may be accomplished through the use of an auxiliary account called the Special Memorandum Account (SMA). Regulation T allows this account as a temporary parking place for equity in excess of current requirements. If an investor has not made full use of the Reg-T credit available, the SMA is automatically employed to preserve this excess. For this reason it is appropriate to think of the SMA as an unused credit line, rather than as a cash credit balance, which it is certainly not.

For instance, the account's current equity of $8,000 exceeds the current Reg-T requirement ($14,000 × 50% = $7,000) by $1,000, and this amount is credited to the SMA. The investor may now withdraw some or all of this amount from the account. In so doing, the debit balance rises and the equity

decreases by the amount of the withdrawal. After withdrawing all $1,000 of
the SMA, the account would now appear:

$$\text{long 100 IBM @ 140} = \$14,000 \quad \text{MV}$$
$$\text{less loan} \qquad \underline{7,000} \quad \text{DR}$$
$$\$7,000 \quad \text{EQ}$$
$$\text{SMA} = 0$$

As an alternative course of action, the investor could use the SMA to buy
more IBM, or any other marginable security. The dollar value of the securities
that may be purchased without adding new funds may be found by dividing
the SMA by the Reg-T requirement, or simply doubling the SMA, as long
as the Reg-T level is 50%. Should this "buying power" be used to its fullest
extent, the market value and debit balance will each rise by twice the SMA
balance. The dollar value of the equity, of course, remains unchanged, although the equity as a percentage of market value declines.

Before Using Buying Power

$$\text{long 100 IBM @ 140} = \$14,000 \quad \text{MV}$$
$$\text{less loan} \qquad \underline{6,000} \quad \text{DR}$$
$$\$8,000 \quad \text{EQ}$$
$$\text{SMA} = \$1,000$$

After Using Buying Power
(Assume IBM is still @ 140 and an additional 14 shares are purchased.)

$$\text{long 114 IBM @ 140} = \$16,000 \quad \text{MV (approx.)}$$
$$\text{less loan} \qquad \underline{8,000} \quad \text{DR}$$
$$\$\,8,000 \quad \text{EQ}$$
$$\text{SMA} = 0$$

It might occur to some speculators that stocks bought on margin occasionally go down, as well as up, in price. Outside of the rather grim realization
that one loses twice as much money when one buys twice as many shares—
and pays interest for the privilege—there lurks the nagging fear of the dreaded
sell-out telegram. Actually, although under-margined accounts may ultimately
be liquidated, the market has to change considerably for this to come about.
Reg-T margin calls are *not* sent out simply because equities fall below 50%.

Continuing the example, assume the investor uses available buying power
to the maximum, now owning 114 shares of IBM @ 140. After the purchase,
however, IBM declines to 130, at which point the account looks like this:

$$\text{long 114 IBM @ 130} = \$14,820 \quad \text{MV}$$
$$\text{Less loan} \qquad \underline{8,000} \quad \text{DR}$$
$$\$\,6,280 \quad \text{EQ}$$
$$\text{SMA} = 0$$

The equity is less than 50% of $14,820 ($7,410) by almost $600. Because the investor has met all of his *original* Reg-T requirements, however, no additional funds need be deposited. In fact, an account can remain at under 50% equity indefinitely and receive no margin calls so long as the equity exceeds the minimum maintenance requirements.

SALES IN MARGIN ACCOUNTS

When a margin trader liquidates or reduces a long position, 50% of the proceeds of the sale are automatically credited to the SMA for the possible uses demonstrated. Following our previous example, suppose IBM retreats to 120, and the now-concerned investor lightens holdings by selling 20 shares at that price. This action will reduce market value by $2,400 and reduce the debit balance by a like amount.

$$
\begin{array}{lll}
\text{long 94 IBM @ 120} = & \$11,280 & \text{MV} \\
\text{less loan} & \underline{5,600} & \text{DR} \\
& \$\ 5,680 & \text{EQ}
\end{array}
$$

The account now shows an equity only $40 more than 50% of $11,280 and yet will now have an SMA balance of $1,200—exactly 50% of the sale proceeds. In other words, the trader could repurchase another $2,400 of marginable stock and reconstitute the account to the condition it was in prior to the sale without depositing new funds. Furthermore, it makes no difference whether this is done the same day as the sale or not, as the SMA balance cannot be adversely affected by market action.

SHORT SALES

The sale of borrowed securities is defined under Reg T as a "short sale." Federal rules require all short sales to be made in margin accounts as a debtor–creditor relationship exists. Unlike a long-margin account, however, the item owed by the customer is stock, not cash.

The securities are borrowed temporarily from other margin customers of the broker, the broker itself, or even from other brokers where necessary. When a short sale is made, the seller must make the same Reg-T deposit as if the stock had been purchased. This deposit plus the proceeds of the short sale establish a *credit* balance in a short-margin account. Thus no interest is charged to the account unless the market goes badly against the customer.

The rationale for the short sale is normally to profit on an anticipated price decline. The speculator is simply reversing the order of the classic "buy cheap–sell dear" idea by selling *first*. If, for example, a price decline from 70 to 60 is foreseen, the short seller borrows shares, sells them at 70, and repurchases them ("covers the short") at 60 and pockets the 10-point difference as the repurchased shares are returned to the lender.

Not all short sales have such a speculative purpose. A fairly common tax-related short sale is the "short against the box," which, far from being speculative, establishes a perfect hedge. In this strategy, an investor borrows shares of a stock already owned and sells the borrowed shares creating a simultaneous long and short position in the same security. It will readily be seen that the current price level is frozen as long as the position is maintained. Any price increase on the long position is offset by a loss on the shares sold short. Conversely, any price decline on the long stock results in an equal price advance on the short stock. The usual aim of the position is to protect a profit while moving the tax consequences of its realization into another year. Once in the new year the investor typically requests the broker deliver the long stock to the lender to close the position and realize the profit.

Short sales can also be employed in various arbitrage techniques. When price disparities appear between the underlying security and either call options or convertible bonds, for instance, nimble traders may sell short the stock and simultaneously purchase the substitute vehicle. The margining of such transactions, as well as the short sale against the box, is a specialized process and need not be described here. Rather, let's observe the more customary speculative short sale and illustrate how the margin computations are done.

Suppose a speculator sees a short-term opportunity for a price decline in the shares of Motorola over the next few weeks. Anticipating that the current market price of $36 per share should decline to about $30 during this period, the trader thus borrows 100 shares of Motorola and sells them @ 36. Under Reg T the speculator is required to deposit $1,800 within 7 business days. When this deposit is made, there will be a cash credit balance in the account consisting of this deposit plus the proceeds of the short sale.

$$
\begin{array}{rll}
\text{cash} \ \$5,400 & \text{credit balance (CR)} \\
\text{less 100 MOT} \ \underline{3,600} & \text{(short) market value (MV)} \\
\$1,800 & \text{equity (EQ)} \\
\text{SMA} = 0 &
\end{array}
$$

If MOT should drop to $30 per share, the speculator's equity will rise by $600 to $2,400.

$$
\begin{array}{rll}
\text{cash} \ \$7,200 & \text{CR} \\
\text{less 160 MOT} \ \underline{4,800} & \text{MV} \\
\$2,400 & \text{EQ}
\end{array}
$$

By taking 50% of the current market value of the short stock position and comparing it to the equity, one finds an excess of $900 ($2,400 vs. 50% × $3,000). This amount is credited to the SMA, and may be used as previously described. Any use of the SMA will affect the credit balance in a manner similar to the way its use affects the debit balance in a long account. A withdrawal of the $900, for example, reduces the credit balance and the equity by that amount.

Similarly, an additional short sale of twice the $900 SMA would be possible. In this case, *both* credit balance and market value rise by $1,800. Assuming the account status *prior* to the cash withdrawal described above, the account would look like this after the purchase.

$$
\begin{array}{rll}
\text{cash} & \$7,200 & \text{CR} \\
\text{less 160 MOT} & \underline{4,800} & \text{MV} \\
& \$2,400 & \text{EQ}
\end{array}
$$

OTHER REQUIREMENTS

The NYSE has long specified that margin customers must demonstrate a certain minimum level of financial ability before being allowed to trade on margin. For a number of years this level has been set at $2,000 in either cash or fully paid securities. Until a customer achieves this level, credit may not be extended nor may securities be sold short. The intent of the rule is to discourage leveraged speculation by those unable to appreciate or afford the attendant risks.

Besides this initial criterion, the exchanges and the NASD have also prescribed various margin *maintenance requirements*. These requirements are designed more to protect the broker who has extended the credit than the customer who has received it. Under circumstances where an adverse price move has reduced the customer's equity to a level where the broker's loan of cash or securities is jeopardized, the rules demand the customer deposit additional equity or face a forcible closing out of the position.

For long stock positions the minimum equity requirement is 25% of the market value. With Reg T set at 50%, it is apparent that the investor must be very wrong indeed to incur a maintenance margin call. In fact, the great speculator Jesse Livermore considered a margin call "the only sure tip" a customer would ever receive from his broker. That is, it is the final signal to a stubborn speculator that the market has gone against him.

To illustrate, assume an investor opens an account with a broker, buys 200 McDonald's Corp. @ $60 per share and promptly deposits the Reg-T requirement of $6.000. The account now appears:

$$
\begin{array}{rll}
\text{long 200 MCD @ 60 =} & \$12,000 & \text{MV} \\
\text{less loan} & \underline{6,000} & \text{DR} \\
\text{SMA = 0} & \$\ 6,000 & \text{EQ}
\end{array}
$$

If the investor is concerned about what danger level he must be prepared for, he can find it by dividing the debit balance by the complement to the maintenance requirement. Thus .75 divided into $6,000 yields a market value of $8,000. If MCD's market value drops to this level, that is, $40 per share on 200 shares, the investor's account is in jeopardy of a margin call.

$$\begin{array}{rl}
\text{long 200 MCD @ 40} = \$8,000 & \text{MV} \\
\text{less loan} \quad \underline{6,000} & \text{DR} \\
\$2,000 & \text{EQ}
\end{array}$$

The investor's $2,000 equity is now exactly 25% of the market value of $8,000. Any further price decline would result in the issuance of a maintenance call requesting a new deposit, and resulting in the sale of some of the stock if the deposit is not made. It is standard Wall Street practice for brokerage firms to have higher "house" requirements, 30 or 35% figures being the most common. The higher requirement gives the broker a somewhat greater cushion and also allows the flexibility to waive a house rule in certain circumstances. For example, a good customer hits an unlucky streak and the equity in the account dips below the house requirement of 35% to about 32%. The firm could waive the house policy at its discretion and not send a margin call because the account's equity is still above the NYSE's 25% level.

Maintenance calls must be met on demand. Brokers generally give customers one or two days to provide the necessary funds but rarely much longer. If the customer is unwilling or unable to make the additional deposit, the broker will have no alternative but to sell out sufficient securities to answer the call. With a 25% maintenance requirement, it follows that selling $1 of stock cancels only 25¢ of the call. Hence, the broker will be forced to sell stock worth 4 times the cash value of the call. Such forced liquidation often occurs in waves in the climactic phase of a bear market because many margin accounts will have deteriorated to similar, dangerous levels. Forced selling in a number of such accounts tends to depress prices, in turn triggering new margin calls and so on.

To demonstrate how sellouts force large amounts of stocks to be sold, assume an account in the following status:

$$\begin{array}{rl}
\text{long stock} \quad \$100,000 & \text{MV} \\
\text{less loan} \quad \underline{78,000} & \text{DR} \\
\$\ 22,000 & \text{EQ}
\end{array}$$

The trader's position is now $3,000 short of the required $25,000 or 25% equity required by the NYSE. If the deposit is not made, the broker will have to sell $12,000 ($3,000 × 4) worth of stock to restore the equity to 25%. Selling this amount will reduce both market value and debit balance by the same amounts, thus raising the percentage of equity:

$$\begin{array}{rl}
\text{long stock} \quad \$88,000 & \text{MV} \\
\text{less loan} \quad \underline{66,000} & \text{DR} \\
\$22,000 & \text{EQ}
\end{array}$$

At this point the trader's equity of $22,000 is exactly 25% of the current market value of $88,000.

SHORT STOCK MAINTENANCE

Short stock positions carry inherently greater risks than long ones. Because the extent of the risk is not limited by the original margin deposit as in a long position, the NYSE demands a greater protective margin of 30% of the market value. In fact, because of the disproportionate risks in low-priced short sales—where small dollar price changes may mean huge percentage changes—stocks selling at under $5 per share have maintenance requirements equal to or actually higher than their market prices.

To find the price level where the NYSE 30% level is touched, one divides the credit balance by 130%. Suppose a customer is currently short 100 Atlantic Richfield @ 50. The account appears as follows:

$$\begin{array}{rrl}
\text{cash} & \$10,000 & \text{CR} \\
\text{less 100 ARC} & \underline{7,687} & \text{MV} \\
& \$\ 2,313 & \text{EQ}
\end{array}$$

If ARC were to rise from its current market price of 50 to about $76⅞ ($10,000 CR ÷ 130% = $7,692), the equity would be reduced to 30% of the current value of the short position. Any further price increase would generate an immediate margin call.

$$\begin{array}{rrl}
\text{cash} & \$10,000 & \text{CR} \\
\text{less 100 ARC} & \underline{7,687} & \text{MV} \\
& \$\ 2,313 & \text{EQ}
\end{array}$$

MARGIN ON DEBT SECURITIES

Sophisticated speculators are sometimes interested in margining the purchase of bonds. In general, nonconvertible corporate bonds, U.S. government and agency securities, and municipal bonds have no Reg-T initial requirement. They are, however, still subject to the industry maintenance requirements, which are substantially lower. This gives the aggressive speculator much greater leverage, but naturally much greater risk than in the margining of stock purchases. While house requirements are usually higher, the NYSE minimum maintenance levels are:

Corporate bonds	25% of market value
U.S. government securities	5% of principal amount
Municipal bonds	25% of market value or 15% of principal, whichever is less

Municipal bonds are rarely margined as the margin interest used to carry them is not tax deductible, as margin interest normally is. Margining of convertible corporate bonds is essentially similar to the stock examples already given.

If a speculator anticipates a significant decline in interest rates he or she is also anticipating a price rise in bonds. In October 1984, U.S. Treasury 9⅛%s of 2004–09 were trading at 76.24 or $767.50 per $1,000 principal. A purchase of $100,000 principal amount requires a minimum deposit of the 5% maintenance requirement, $5,000 in this case. The remainder is of course borrowed, so that the account appears this way:

long 100M Treasury Bonds $76,750 MV

71,750 DR

$ 5,000 EQ

With the bonds paying $9,125 annually in income, the investor can carry the position with net interest income (a "positive carry" to traders) if the debit balance can be financed for less than 12.7%. A 3-point rise in the bond price would produce a $3,000 profit on a $5,000 investment, a 60% return. On the other hand, a 5-point drop in bond prices would wipe out the investor's equity.

Margin Interest

The interest brokers charge on margin accounts has long been a significant source of revenues for them. The standard borrowing arrangement is for the broker to pledge ("rehypothecate") customer's margined stock to a bank as collateral and receive a call, or broker loan. In turn, the broker marks the loan rate up and passes it along to the customer. The loans can be terminated, or called on demand (hence the name), although they rarely are. Because they are collateralized by readily marketable securities these loans are considered safe and normally carry interest rates below the bank's prime rate.

Brokers typically add on at least 1/2% above the call loan rate and usually considerably more. The lowest rates ordinarily go to the customers with the largest debit balances, so that relatively small accounts, for example, debit balances below $10,000, may well pay 2% or more above the minimum rate. Even at that, however, rates are less than those otherwise available to non-corporate borrowers.

Large retail firms tend to be rather inflexible about their rate schedules. Smaller firms, on the other hand, are more likely to negotiate, so that a customer with a relatively small but active account may be able to achieve a lower rate based more on commission revenues generated than net interest income to the broker.

The call money rate changes regularly, as do other money market rates. Investors must therefore realize that a current rate may change next month.

Indeed, during the extreme interest rate environment in the late 1970s many margin customers were paying an annual rate of over 20%. In such circumstances, one must be extraordinarily successful in trading stocks to overcome the transaction costs and interest charges.

14 Investment Banking

The term *investment banking* has always been regarded as something of a misnomer, but developments in finance have made it rather an accurate name for the function. Commercial banking consists largely of taking deposits and making loans at higher rates than are paid on the deposits. Profits in the banking industry come from an interest rate "spread" between the cost of money (paid on deposits) and the return on assets (interest charged on loans). Investment banking, on the other hand, is less widely known to the general public. For many years it was a specialty that was the preserve of a few prestigious and highly profitable partnerships. Investment banking meant underwriting new securities offerings, the ancillary function of advising clients which type of security to issue, and advice about when and how to make the offering.

Through the 1920s the functions were often combined. The Great Crash changed this radically. Many banks had in effect speculated with depositors' money, both in trading on the market and with underwriting the speculative favorites of the day. When the market broke in 1929, a number of these banks foundered, largely because of these practices. Depositors who banked in what they thought were safe institutions found savings, sometimes those of a lifetime, wiped out. There was no federal protection offered depositors at the time.

Congress acted with the decisiveness characteristic of the early years of the New Deal. The Glass–Steagall Act was passed in 1933 and was directed against these very problems. The Federal Deposit Insurance Corporation was established to provide all commercial bank depositors some protection against a bank failure. In addition, the Act separated commercial banks from their investment banking affiliates, so that depositors' money should not again be used in speculative endeavors like the stock market. Today, one might take a certain wry amusement in the use by banks of depositors' funds in making loans to such "safe" borrowers as the sovereign nations of Brazil, Argentina, and Mexico.

Glass–Steagall broke up the "House of Morgan," the greatest of all American financial institutions. The commercial banking operation evolved into the current Morgan Guaranty Trust, one of the premier wholesale banks. The securities underwriters, on the other hand, formed a new partnership, Morgan Stanley and Company. Another separation split the First National Bank of Boston from its investment bankers who established what is today's First Boston Corporation. Indeed, it is still common on Wall Street to refer to the latter firm as "First *of* Boston" or "FOB," harking back to its banking beginnings.

The Act permitted commercial banks to remain active in the underwriting and trading of municipal general obligation bonds and some money market instruments. Investment banking activities involving corporate securities and most municipal revenue bonds, however, were removed from banks' permissible activities. The "new" investment banking firms joined some of the old-line firms which had never aligned with commercial banking, partnerships like Goldman, Sachs; Lehman Brothers; and Kuhn, Loeb; to dominate this branch of the business for nearly 30 years.

Well into the 1960s the investment banking community was very nearly a club, a small inbred group of partnerships relying heavily on the old school tie and traditional relationships that often went back for generations. The business was prestigious, lucrative, and exclusive. It was, however, vulnerable to aggressive and innovative competition. Gradually, nontraditional firms began to challenge the established ones, and, ultimately, they too joined the club. In some cases, the ability to make nationwide distribution of large amounts of new issues provided the entry key. First, Merrill Lynch forced its way into the top underwriting ranks because its retail distribution system allowed it to place new issues in virtually every major city in the country, as well as numerous smaller ones. Issuers are usually delighted to have share ownership spread in such a manner because it becomes difficult for dissidents to assemble large blocks of shares. Following Merrill Lynch's lead, other basically retail-oriented firms likewise moved into the ranks of investment banking, such firms as E. F. Hutton, Dean Witter Reynolds, and Paine Webber Jackson and Curtis.

Other firms made their mark by aggressive pricing (risk taking) and the development of new securities and investment techniques. Salomon Brothers is probably the premier example of this type of organization. The traditional investment bankers soon responded to these challenges. In some cases the response was merger with stronger, better-capitalized firms. Sometimes multiple mergers took place with an initial linking of two firms followed by subsequent mergers with even larger firms. This was the route chosen by Blyth and Company (Paine Webber), Halsey Stuart (Bache), and ultimately one of the classic old-line investment bankers, Lehman Brothers (Shearson American Express). In others, it was the decision to stay competitive by buying or developing the talent necessary to meet the challenge of the newer powers. Morgan Stanley and First Boston are the best examples of such firms. Even though their stranglehold on certain aspects of this business has been broken and they seem unlikely ever to regain the dominance they once possessed, they nevertheless remain major powers in the field.

UNDERWRITING

In the securities business, underwriting represents a guarantee to an issuer that a certain minimum amount of money will be derived from a particular sale of securities. In this way the issuer may make plans to deploy the capital realized without fear that the entire offering will not be sold. Small issuers may try this themselves through such devices as "tombstone" advertisements or more aggressive techniques like direct mail, newspaper supplements, or even radio and television ads. Larger issuers, however, turn to investment bankers who will form syndicates to distribute the issue on a national basis.

The underwriting business has become a global endeavor. Tables 14-1 and 14-2 give some idea of the size and extent of this function. The preponderance of banks in the Eurobond rankings indicate the freedom from Glass–Steagall restrictions abroad. Thus the European arm of the Morgan Bank is a ranking investment banker abroad, but, at least to date, not in the U.S.

The underwriters contract with the issuer to purchase an issue directly from the corporation at a specific price. This assures the issuer of the requisite funds. Immediately thereafter, the underwriters and their affiliates begin a public distribution of these securities at a slightly higher price than the purchase agreement with the issuer. If successful, the underwriters can make substantial profits. If unsuccessful, severe losses may result. This may happen because the public finds the offering price too high, usually indicating unrealistic demands by the issuer or a pricing error by the underwriters, or both. It may also occur because of a sharp price break in the market occurring simultaneously with the offering. No matter how attractive the offering may have appeared previously, investors become wary of new commitments and demand dries up. Prospective buyers then feel that they may buy the same merchandise at a discount in the secondary (postoffering) market.

Regulation

Before the underwriting process may be completed the issuer and the investment bankers must comply with the provisions of the Securities Act of 1933. The Act, a companion piece to the Securities and Exchange Act of 1934 (Chapter 17), was designed to afford the buyers of new offerings of securities protection in the form of "full disclosure" of relevant financial information. This is provided by requiring the issuer to file a registration statement with the SEC prior to the sale. In addition, a prospective buyer of the security undergoing the registration process must be provided with a "red herring," or preliminary prospectus which is prepared from the information in the registration statement. The term "red herring" is at least partly derived from a warning printed in red type in the left-hand margin of the document, cautioning that a registration statement has been filed and is currently being examined by the SEC.

For the first public offering of any company's securities, an IPO (initial public offering), the period between the filing of the registration statement

Table 14-1 U.S. Domestic Markets

Book Manager	1985				1984			
	Amount ($ Millions)	Rank	%	Issues	Amount ($ Millions)	Rank	%	Issues
Salomon Brothers	30,899.4	(1)	22.3	293	21,237.3	(1)	25.8	187
First Boston	21,573.3	(2)	15.6	274	10,020.6	(3)	12.2	129
Goldman, Sachs	16,365.1	(3)	11.8	145	7,908.8	(5)	9.6	97
Merrill Lynch Capital Markets	15,375.9	(4)	11.1	188	8,712.2	(4)	10.6	126
Drexel Burnham Lambert	13,336.7	(5)	9.6	171	10,484.8	(2)	12.7	102
Morgan Stanley	10,050.1	(6)	7.3	104	4,896.6	(7)	5.9	58
Shearson Lehman Brothers	9,609.5	(7)	6.9	164	6,688.9	(6)	8.1	94
Kidder, Peabody	3,829.1	(8)	2.8	83	1,932.3	(8)	2.3	45
Paine Webber	2,920.5	(9)	2.1	74	1,677.3	(10)	2.0	33
Smith Barney, Harris Upham	1,639.0	(10)	1.2	37	839.3	(13)	1.0	25
Dean Witter Reynolds	1,422.8	(11)	1.0	33	989.6	(11)	1.2	25
Dillon, Read	1,352.8	(12)	1.0	12	459.7	(15)	0.6	6
Prudential-Bache	1,346.8	(13)	1.0	41	1,776.9	(9)	2.2	34
Bear, Stearns	1,320.4	(14)	1.0	30	847.8	(12)	1.0	24
E.F. Hutton	955.6	(15)	0.7	24	569.2	(14)	0.7	18
Industry Totals	138,301.7			2,223	82,434.9			1,419

SOURCE: *Investment Dealers Digest*, January 13, 1986

Table 14-2 Eurobonds and Other Foreign Offerings

1984	1985		$ Volume (millions)	No. of Issues
2	1	Swiss Bank Corp.	$5,919.1	885
3	2	Union Bank of Switzerland	5,349.0	794
5	3	Credit Suisse First Boston	5,235.6	755
1	4	Salomon Brothers	5,100.2	516
6	5	Nomura Securities	5,082.3	701
4	6	Deutsche Bank	4,793.5	611
9	7	Merrill Lynch	4,636.9	644
11	8	Morgan Stanley	4,278.7	656
7	9	Morgan Guaranty	4,246.0	621
8	10	Daiwa Securities	4,042.1	649
10	11	S.G. Warburg	3,366.2	584
12	12	Orion Royal Bank	3,266.9	614
18	13	Banque Nationale de Paris	3,205.5	582
22	14	Banque Bruxelles Lambert	2,968.7	717
13	15	Dresdner Bank	2,910.0	554
14	16	Banque Paribas	2,903.9	603
16	17	Yamaichi Securities	2,872.7	428
15	18	Nikko Securities	2,848.3	418
17	19	Goldman Sachs	2,826.2	403
19	20	Commerzbank	2,681.7	478
27	21	Credit Lyonnals	2,454.5	526
30	22	Shearson Lehman Brothers	2,162.7	274
20	23	Algemene Bank Nederland	2,100.7	470
33	24	IBJ Int'l	1,977.9	399
38	25	LTCB Int'l	1,854.8	347

SOURCE: *Institutional Investor*, March 1986

and the actual sale date may be as long as 20 days, or sometimes even longer if the SEC has been flooded with many other IPOs at the same time. For established issuers the period may be much shorter, often only a day or two.

The registration statement must contain significant financial information about the issue. It is important to understand that the SEC makes no judgment about the investment merits of a registered offering. Indeed, it is a violation of federal law to imply in any way that because an offering is registered, it is therefore approved or endorsed by the SEC. The registration of the offering, however, means that investors have been provided with significant information about the issue and may make up their own minds based on this information. Should any data in the registration statement prove false, those who provided it stand liable for both criminal and civil charges if investors lose money through a purchase based on such misleading information.

The information in the registration statement is provided to the investor in an abbreviated format called a "prospectus," similar to the red herring mentioned previously, but more complete, including the final offering terms, such as price, coupon rate, or various other terms not set at the time of filing. The prospectus must be sent to every buyer of a new offering and failure to send one may invalidate the sale. Most underwriters enclose a copy with the sale confirmation.

EXEMPTIONS

Typical of most federal securities regulation, a number of issues are not subject to the full disclosure requirements of the Act. Securities issued by the U.S. government or its agencies are exempt from the provisions of the Act, and thus offerings of new issues need not be registered. Also, municipal securities are not subject to the law, although many states and other municipal issuers have a rule requiring the provision of a prospectuslike document called an "official statement" to buyers of new offerings.

Other offerings exempted from the Act are: private placements (sales not involving a public distribution), intrastate offerings, commercial paper with maturities of less than 270 days, and some securities offered by common-carriers (usually equipment trust certificates).

Because buyers of these securities do not receive the legal protection of the full disclosure features of the Act, they may not seek redress in federal court over information contained in the official statement or other offering circular, if, indeed, one was provided. On the other hand, it must be re-membered that the prospectus itself in a registered offering is no guarantee of quality and does not represent SEC approval of the sale or the security. Although the Act clearly goes beyond the caveat emptor doctrine, it provides no defense against foolishness on the part of an investor who persists in buying a new issue, the investment merits of which would have been shown to be negligible upon reading the prospectus.

SEC RULE 415 (SHELF REGISTRATION)

The SEC now permits experienced issuers who meet certain criteria to pre-register offerings through the provisions of Rule 415. This rule was adopted on a permanent basis in November 1983. It allows the issuer to file a registration statement well in advance of an intended distribution and await the proper market conditions for the offering. Volatile interest rate and stock markets in the early 1980s made it difficult to judge when best to sell an issue. Just when interest rates seemed right, an issuer might file a statement only to find that by the time the SEC gave permission to go ahead with the offering, rates had again changed to an unsatisfactory level.

Rule 415 allows the issuer to strike quickly when a window opens in the market by immediately offering these preregistered securities to any investment bankers prepared to make an immediate distribution. The decisiveness and capital required to make such commitments were not characteristics of more conventional investment bankers, and the ascendancy of the more aggressive and better capitalized bankers shown at the top of the rankings in Table 14-1 is in no small measure due to the "shelf registrations" available under Rule 415. In effect, the rule allowed such firms the ability to demonstrate performance much more rapidly than would have been the case under more traditional circumstances. With the rule now a permanent part of the underwriting scene, the historic underwriting syndicate has diminished in importance as many 415 sales are done by one or two investment bankers in a single large transaction with the issuer.

A PUBLIC DISTRIBUTION

Following is a brief description of a typical corporate underwriting done through the conventional method of filing the registration statement before an anticipated offering date, even though this date may be changed before the actual sale occurs. Offerings of this type are said to be "negotiated," as the investment bankers arrange the distribution privately with the issuer. Few corporate underwritings (other than Rule 415 deals) are subject to public competitive bids in which underwriters vie with each other to provide the most attractive terms to the issuer. Common stock offerings of some public utility holding companies and some railroad equipment trust certificates are sold through such methods. The sale of almost all major municipal general obligation, on the other hand, is done through competitive bid.

Origination

The first step involves a series of discussions between the corporation's management and the investment bankers. Although a particular offering may well be "negotiated," this does not mean it is accomplished without competition. It is typical for an issuer to hear presentations by several teams of competing investment bankers before selecting the firm to manage the offering. A firm which fails the selection process on a specific issue may well participate as a co-manager or as an underwriter in the offering.

There are two key issues to be resolved: (1) How much money must be raised? and (2) Which type of security is the best choice given current market conditions? For instance, it is clearly easier to sell stock when prices are in a well-defined bull market. Bonds, alternately, tend to be more popular when equity investments are out of favor. If the decision is for bonds, other questions arise: Should the financing be long term (20–30 years) or intermediate term, fixed rate, or floating rate, callable or noncallable, convertible or "straight"? The features developed to enhance the attractiveness of offerings to both the buyers and the issuers have become extraordinarily complex. It has almost reached the point where an old-fashioned 20-year bond with no unusual features has itself become something of a rarity.

Once the decision has been reached, counsel for both the investment bankers and the issuer will proceed to prepare the documents necessary to satisfy the various laws and regulations governing the sale. Naturally, these include the registration statement filed with the SEC, but in addition must include the "blue-sky" filings in every state where the offering is to be made, and also disclosure documents to the NASD's Committee on Corporate Financing, which will scrutinize the investment banker's offering plan and pay special attention to any unusual compensation arrangements that might be unfair to the buyer.

Syndicate Formation

With the filing procedure underway, the managing underwriter starts to form a syndicate to distribute the issue. A *syndicate* is a temporary business organization designed to spread the risk in an offering so that an adverse market turn does not have to be borne by only a few firms. As the size of offerings has increased, somewhat paradoxically, the size of syndicates has declined rather sharply. For example, prior to 1980 syndicates for large offerings, say $300 to $400 million, often had 200 or so members. Today, the average size for such a transaction might typically be 60, and frequently, fewer.

For example, the "tombstone" shown in Figure 14-1 illustrates an offering that would have been exceptionally large at one time, but is now rather commonplace. Part of this, of course, is due to the inflationary erosion in the value of the dollar, making deals appear larger when, in fact, they are often comparable to smaller offerings of a decade ago.

This syndicate illustrates several points. First, there are only 27 participants compared to over 100 which would have been required in the 1970s or earlier. Second, there are three co-managers, indicated by the staggered listing at the top. The lead-manager (the one who really controls the offering) is at the upper left.

New Issue / December 11, 1986

$200,000,000

Private Export Funding Corporation
PEFCO

7.70% Secured Notes, Series X, Due January 31, 1997

The due and punctual payment of interest on the Notes is directly guaranteed by the Export-Import Bank of the United States, such guarantee being backed by the full faith and credit of the United States. Repayment of principal of the Notes is secured by the pledge with the Trustee under the Indenture of an equivalent principal amount of obligations backed by the full faith and credit of the United States, all of which obligations mature prior to the due date of the Notes.

Price 100% and accrued interest, if any, from December 18, 1986

Copies of the Prospectus may be obtained in any State in which this announcement is circulated only from such of the undersigned as may legally offer these securities in such State.

Salomon Brothers Inc

Dillon, Read & Co. Inc.

Merrill Lynch Capital Markets

The First Boston Corporation	**Goldman, Sachs & Co.**
Morgan Stanley & Co. Incorporated	**Shearson Lehman Brothers Inc.**

Bear, Stearns & Co. Inc.   **Alex. Brown & Sons** Incorporated   **Daiwa Securities America Inc.**

Deutsche Bank Capital Corporation   **Donaldson, Lufkin & Jenrette** Securities Corporation   **Drexel Burnham Lambert** Incorporated

E. F. Hutton & Company Inc.   **Kidder, Peabody & Co.** Incorporated   **Lazard Frères & Co.**

The Nikko Securities Co. International, Inc.   **Nomura Securities International, Inc.**   **PaineWebber** Incorporated

Prudential-Bache Securities   **L. F. Rothschild, Unterberg, Towbin, Inc.**

Smith Barney, Harris Upham & Co. Incorporated   **Swiss Bank Corporation International** Securities Inc.

UBS Securities Inc.   **Wertheim & Co., Inc.**

Dean Witter Reynolds Inc.   **Yamaichi International (America), Inc.**

Fig. 14-3. Tombstone ad. (*Source: The Wall Street Journal,* December 11, 1986). Reprinted by permission of The Wall Street Journal, © 1986. Dow Jones and Company, Inc. All rights reserved.

There are no small or regional underwriters in this particular sale, but the preeminent status of Goldman, Sachs and First Boston can be derived from their separate location at the top of the nonmanagers. Had one of them been the lead manager, firms such as those at the top would normally be extended a similar favored place. Location is more than a simple matter of prestige, although that, too, is important. The higher a firm's "bracket," the more of the offering it may expect to receive and the more profit will be produced.

A more subtle point is the appearance of U.S. affiliates of foreign banking and brokerage firms, each on a par with domestic underwriters. Daiwa, Nikko, Nomura, and Yamaichi represent the names of the Big Four of the Japanese securities industry. Deutsche Bank Capital and UBS Securities (Union Bank of Switzerland) give further indication of the globalization of securities markets. In June 1986, for example, UBS lead-managed a large offering by Allied Signal, a major U.S. corporation, in the domestic market, a first but not very likely the last such syndicate so managed.

Most large syndicates are managed or co-managed by a small number of underwriters, in fact, the same firms already indicated. The manager's job is to assemble a syndicate that will successfully distribute the issue in a manner satisfactory to the issuer. Although no two syndicates are exactly alike, the "syndicate desks" of the underwriting firms have close rapport and generally know what type of performance and capital commitment are expected from each member. The managers take the largest share of each offering, with progressively decreasing amounts allocated to other members; the amount is determined by successful past performance in similar situations. Because a successful sale can be lucrative, every participant desires the maximum possible allocation, but this is simply not possible. In fact, underwriting participations are structured into "brackets" as mentioned previously, and working its way up to a higher bracket is an arduous task for an investment banking firm. Needless to say, top-bracket firms are not particularly anxious to permit new entrants to share their slice of the pie.

Syndicates are rarely able to finance the purchase from the issuer solely from the members' own capital. Consequently, they rely heavily on short-term financing, often to the extent of 80 to 90% of the cost of the offering. The risk and reward are thus substantially increased. A failure to sell the securities at the agreed price may ultimately compel the syndicate to sell at prices less than those paid to the issuer—and to pay financing costs as well. In a typical corporate underwriting, the liability for unsold securities rests with each member individually, not with the syndicate as a whole (the reverse is true for most municipal bond offerings). Obviously, the faster a new issue sells out, the better. In some cases, this may involve help from some nonmembers.

The Selling Group

Although virtually all underwriters will attempt to sell the issue also, there are occasions when additional help may be needed. The manager will assemble, if necessary, a "selling group," affiliated with the syndicate but not legally part of it. The selling group members help distribute the securities but have no responsibility for any unsold merchandise. They may simply turn back unsold securities to the manager without incurring a legal liability. Failure to perform satisfactorily, however, while not a legal matter, may well prejudice the manager in filling out future groups. With no liability, selling group members cannot expect much compensation for their efforts and are usually rewarded with a "concession," which is only a fraction of the overall spread earned by syndicate participants. Selling groups are most often seen with large, slow-moving deals. Syndicate members prefer to give up a portion of their profit in order to allow selling group members to take hard-to-sell goods off their hands.

Pricing

Fixing the offering price of a new issue is surely as much art as science. The actual price, or coupon rate of a bond, is not set until the "effective date," when the security may be legally offered for the first time. Because market prices are notoriously whimsical, what may seem an attractive price on the morning of the effective date, or the previous evening when price meetings are sometimes held, may not be so by the time representatives call their customers asking for firm orders based on the customers' previous indications of interest.

The pricing of most bond offerings is possibly a little more structured. That is, there are ready market quotations from dealers at all times for bonds of similar quality rating and maturity. There is surely less distinction between two AA-rated 15-year bonds than there would be between new common stock offerings of different corporations. Nevertheless, pricing a new bond to be precisely in line with supply and demand forces is not at all easy.

Pricing a first-time stock issue poses considerably different problems. Here the managing underwriter faces a dilemma: On the one hand, the issuer wants to receive the maximum possible proceeds from the sale; on the other, the manager wishes to price it at a salable level. If too high, the price will cool off public desire to purchase. If too low, the issue may turn "hot" and zoom to a premium in the secondary, or after-market. Generally, the pricing is derived from an evaluation of many factors: the company's record of earnings, anticipated dividend payments, number of shares being offered, price-earnings ratio compared to similar companies, and overall tone of the equity market at the moment of offering. If the issue is in fact underpriced and public demand spills over into the secondary market, the higher prices paid by those unable to obtain the primary-offering yield proceed not to the corporation but to the previous holders. Ordinarily one might think this would make a corporation unhappy. Corporations, though, may be "legal persons" but are not real ones. It is usually the case that corporate officers and families still hold substantial quantities of the stock and are not at all distressed by seeing their personal net worths appreciate sharply.

More commonly, the price does not jump, but rather begins to give signs of dropping as disappointed buyers begin to sell stock back into the market. When this happens, the entire offering may be jeopardized and the managing underwriter will take steps to prop up the price.

Stabilization

This quite legal method of price fixing may be utilized by the managing underwriter as long as the issue is not "hot." The basic idea is for the managing underwriter to buy stock being offered for sale by those who have just purchased it. If the manager bids at or just under the public offering price, the shares will not become available at cheaper prices in the secondary market, at least until the distribution is completed. In the usual underwriting, any losses suffered in the process are prorated to each syndicate member. The method and amount of stabilization must be shown in the prospectus.

Fees

The compensation to investment bankers in an underwriting varies a great deal. Some sales are clearly riskier than others. Some are unfortunately brought to market at an inopportune time. In such offerings the underwriters will normally demand greater compensation for the increased risk. An idea of typical fees might be found by glancing through the *Investment Dealers Digest,* a weekly magazine carrying news of new and recent offerings. A typical stock offering described listed the price at "$16.25, less 68 cents, underwriting 23 cents, manager 23 cents, reallowance 25 cents." The offering involved 774,000 shares and was thus not particularly large.

The issuer receives $15.57 per share, the remaining 68 cents being retained in various proportions by the participants. The manager's compensation is the entire 68 cents ("the gross spread") on every share sold to one of its customers. On every other share sold, the manager receives 23 cents. Underwriters who underwrite only make the indicated 23 cents underwriting fee, whereas underwriters who also sell the shares make the "spread" less the manager's fee, or 45 cents per share. Other dealers not in the underwriting group would receive the reallowance of 25 cents for each share sold. It should be apparent that managing an underwriting is very profitable business, presuming one has both the skill and the capital necessary.

The Secondary, or After-Market

When a new issue is released from syndicate it will begin trading at once in the secondary market, where firms need not have been in the syndicate in order to make an offering. If the security was a corporate bond such trading is likely to be largely conducted OTC, even if a listing application has been filed. Most new stock offerings will also trade OTC, at least for some time.

Although the investment bankers are not legally required to do so, to show good faith to the issuer they will almost always "make a market" for the shares.

Occasionally, exceptional new issues will start trading on the NYSE immediately on release from syndicate. Such issuers already meet the NYSE's listing requirements except for public ownership, and a listing application is filed simultaneously with the registration statement. Two such examples of immediate listing were The Tribune Company (the owner of the *Chicago Tribune,* the *New York Daily News,* and a number of other communications facilities) and British Telecommunications, the huge British telephone network "privatised" in 1985.

Secondary Distributions

A *secondary distribution* results in the proceeds of the sale being paid to the previous shareholders, as opposed to the *primary,* where the proceeds accrue to the issuing corporation. Occasionally, a large block is offered for sale by corporate insiders, or sometimes by a trust or charitable foundation created by the founder or the families of those who started the enterprise. These sales usually require registration similar to new issues, as the particular shares being offered have never been registered before. Smaller amounts, up to 1% of the outstanding shares, may be offered through a simplified procedure specified in SEC Rule 144. Larger sales are often done through syndication similar to the new issue sales already discussed. As has become true with syndications in general, however, many of these are effected by one or two firms acting independently of any syndicate.

On occasion, large blocks become available from those whose connection with the issuer is not as founder or insider. For example, Shearson Lehman Brothers and Salomon Brothers traded a single block of Navistar International (formerly International Harvester) totaling 48.7 million shares and worth $487 million in April 1986. This has been the largest single transaction done on the NYSE floor to date. Of the 48.7 million shares, 43.5 were sold in a secondary distribution by banks which had obtained the shares through a "debt for equity swap," a device popular with corporations in the time immediately prior to the great 1982 bull market.

PRIVATE PLACEMENTS

Besides public offerings, investment bankers also arrange many private placements. As the name indicates, no public market is involved and, consequently, no full disclosure via registration with the SEC. The usual buyers of private placements are life insurance companies, although other financial institutions and even wealthy individual investors have participated, the last-named have been particularly prominent in a number of the large junk bond financings done by Drexel Burnham. The reason for the private placement is not only confidentiality, but also the fact that the buyer may demand a tailormade obligation having exactly the terms specified. The most typical borrowers in the private placement market are issuers with a medium (Baa) quality rating, but the method is by no means restricted to their use. The same firms at the top of the regular underwriting rankings are likely to be at the top of the private placement list also, although by its very nature, the market is not open to complete public scrutiny. With no public distributions involved, banks are allowed to participate in this field, and several gained ranking in the twenty largest for 1985. These included Citicorp, Morgan Guarantee, Bankers Trust, and Bank of America, although the leading bank (Citicorp) placed less than a third of the leading investment banker's (Salomon) sum, $2.97 billion to $10.5 billion, respectively.

MERGERS AND ACQUISITIONS

The M&A business is probably the most glamorous phase of the investment banking business. It puts investment bankers in the public eye, and actually creates a type of superstar who is frequently recognizable in the regular media, not to mention the financial press. Mergers and acquisitions reached a fever pitch in 1985 with a total of 3,001 deals, valued at $179.6 billion. Although some of these transactions were friendly, many others were hostile with the target companies resisting the offer by the would-be acquisitors. Indeed, many of the friendly deals were precipitated by a hostile offer which forced the target company's management to seek a friendly partner rather than be swallowed up by a raider.

There is some reason to believe that the acquisition wave may have crested, although large deals may still come at any time. Part of the rationale for this view stems from the rapid increases in share prices in the 1980s, sharply reducing the number of companies "undervalued" by the stock market. The other reason is a heightened awareness in Washington that such deals may be counterproductive to the economy. For example, healthy companies such as Phillips Petroleum or Unocal (formerly Union Oil of California) were forced to assume enormous debt burdens to fend off the unwanted advances of certain corporate raiders who appeared more interested in a financial transaction than in operating a going concern. Academics often argue that these transactions merely juggle the assets of American industry without causing any real loss of productive capacity. In addition, the raiders claim to be assisting the shareholders of the target company by allowing them to realize higher share values through tender offers at higher prices than the current management is able to produce. This protestation is not very convincing so far as intent is concerned, albeit quite convincing in the actual end result which often sees company's shares bid to prices not seen in several years, or ever.

Besides acquisitions, however, M&A specialists are also active in corporate restructurings which often involve selling a division to a competitor, for example, General Electric's sale of its small appliance business to Black and Decker, or sometimes to the management through a "leveraged buyout." In the latter strategy, a management group borrows enough money to buy majority control of the outstanding shares, and then returns the company to private ownership. Sometimes only divisions are involved; at other times, entire corporations "go private." In some cases, corporations realize that they are in too many varying businesses to achieve consistent profitability. In fact, what happens often in these "divestiture" moves is the undoing of some of the unwieldy conglomerate mergers of the late 1960s. A particular case in point is ITT which has spun off almost all of its major acquisitions except the highly profitable Hartford Insurance Group.

Finally, the internationalization of business has made the M&A business worldwide. Acquisitions across national boundaries encounter various cultural and legal problems not encountered in the domestic markets. Certainly, a hostile tender offer made for a Japanese company would be difficult to effect because of the closed nature of many Japanese business practices. On the other hand, General Motors succeeded in a friendly takeover of the British racing car and research combine, Lotus; and Beecham Group, one of the U.K.'s largest health-service corporations, spent $360 million to acquire some business lines of Revlon Inc., an American firm that was itself overwhelmed by a hostile takeover by another domestic company.

BEST-EFFORTS

In this type of financing the investment banker is not truly an underwriter because the securities are taken down from the issuer only as sold. The dealer is actually performing in a near-agency capacity, disclaiming responsibility for the unsold shares. Major investment bankers rarely, if ever, participate in such offerings for they are invariably small and not remunerative enough. The best-efforts deal is ideally suited to the fledgling company with perhaps an interesting concept or product to sell, but little track record.

Like the "firm commitment" underwritings already described, best-efforts sales are registered with the SEC. Unlike them, however, they do not have a single offering date. Rather, there is a selling or subscription period lasting between 30 and 90 days. Buyers' checks are deposited into a noninterest-bearing escrow account. When sufficient shares are sold, the escrow account is closed, the shares issued to the buyers, and a check sent to the issuer. If the selling period ends before enough shares have been sold, the period may be extended. Many best-efforts offerings are done on a "min-max" basis, which means that no shares are issued unless a certain minimum number are sold and selling continues until either a specified maximum is sold or the subscription period ends, whichever comes first. If not even the minimum number of shares are sold after an extension, the offering may either be canceled or deferred to a later date. In such a case the buyers' checks must be returned from the escrow account.

Most best-efforts underwriters are small NASD member firms which can participate in this type of underwriting with a minimum capital of only $30,000. Although the method may seem fitting only for questionable ventures, such is not always the case. Start-up companies must receive capital from somewhere, and the best-efforts provides a means for that capital to be raised. In 1984, 224 firms made an initial public offering on a best-efforts basis and raised about $700 million in the process. Major investment bankers, of course, do single deals larger than that amount, but somewhere in those 224 companies may lie the germ of what could become one of their blue-chip clients in the future.

REGULATION-A OFFERINGS

These offerings are something of a halfway house between a best-efforts and a firm-commitment deal. The SEC allows smaller registered offerings to be completed using an abbreviated full disclosure document called an "offering circular" instead of a prospectus. Unlike the prospectus which must be printed, the circular may be either typewritten or mimeographed. These offerings are limited to a maximum size of $1.5 million, although affiliates of the company, for example, officers and directors, may sell an additional $100,000 each.

Stand-by

As rights offerings have become rarer in the United States, so too has become this type of underwriting that is used to assure their success. When a corporation attempts to raise capital through a rights offering, it is a virtual certainty that not all the rights will be exercised by current holders. Some will not have the money to subscribe; others will simply choose not to do so. The corporation will engage an underwriting syndicate to purchase the unexercised rights when holders sell them and, in turn, to subscribe to new shares by exercising the rights. The syndicate members then attempt to reoffer the new shares (net of commissions) to their customers. A generous fee is paid to the syndicate members for their efforts, for the corporation feels the expense is justified by the guarantee that all shares offered will be sold and the necessary capital raised.

15 Securities Delivery, Transfer, and Clearing

The sale of a registered security is completed by the transfer of title to the buyer at the time payment is made. Although the customer may well pay the broker earlier, the actual transfer takes place on a "settlement date" prescribed by industry rules. Delivery of the securities from the seller's broker to the buyer's broker is required, but automation has considerably reduced the number of actual deliveries of physical certificates. Through the facilities of the Securities Industry Automation Corporation (SIAC) and the National Securities Clearing Corporation (NSCC) enormous trading volume is routinely processed. For example, the bull market of the late 1960s produced then-record volumes that clogged the transfer process so badly the market was forced to close at 2:00 P.M. for an extended period, and even to close all day Wednesdays to catch up on the accumulated paper glut. In 1968 average daily volume reached an all time record of 12,971,000 shares with a high day of 21,351,000 shares. By 1985 the *average* daily volume was 109,169,000 shares, and the high volume day was 181,027,000 shares.[1] All this could now be handled without undue disruption of the trading process and no reduction of trading hours. Indeed, in 1987 a record trading day of more than 300,000,000 shares was handled with little more than ordinary effort by the operations personnel on Wall Street.

Such performance is, of course, largely due to the vastly improved data processing systems now available, but is also attributable to the standardization of receipt and delivery terms codified in the NASD's Uniform Practice Code and the rules and regulations of the NYSE and the other exchanges whose rules are similar. A brief description of the main contract types as prescribed by these rules follows.

---

[1]*NYSE 1986 Fact Book*, p. 70.

CONTRACTS

Regular-Way Contracts

Unless otherwise specified, contracts entered into on an exchange floor or OTC are "regular way." Trades in corporate stocks, bonds, and municipal bonds call for settlement five business days after the trade date. This means that a trade entered into on Monday, January 4, will "settle" on Monday, January 11. Although a customer's securities may already be in the broker's possession, or be delivered by the customer within a day or two, actual receipt and payment with the broker for the other side of the trade will not occur for one calendar week. If the exchanges or banks are closed for a holiday at any time during this week, settlement is postponed for one additional day. Thus, a trade made on the Thursday before Thanksgiving will settle on the Friday immediately following the Thanksgiving holiday. Regular way settlement for U.S. government securities trades in "round lots" (usually $100,000 principal amount) is the business day following the trade date. If an odd lot is involved, the brokers involved may settle as mutually agreed, but the common practice is the same five business days used for other regular way trades. On all regular way trades NYSE Rule 176 specifies 11:30 A.M. on the appropriate day as the latest acceptable time.

Extensions and Prepayments

These are not actually contracts but rather methods of settling regular-way contracts at times other than those called for under normal procedures. As noted in Chapter 13, if a customer fails to pay or deliver promptly, the resultant Reg T violation will normally lead to liquidation of the position and a 90-day block being applied to the account. The exchanges and the NASD are permitted to grant extensions of time to the customer on rare occasions, provided the customer has a serious bona fide problem in meeting the settlement on the appropriate date. In any event, the broker must still settle with the broker representing the other party on settlement date. This means, for example, that Merrill Lynch must still pay E. F. Hutton on the settlement date although its own customer may not have paid yet. This is obviously costly and becomes more so the longer it takes for the customer to honor the commitment. It is thus not surprising that some brokerage firms (or individual branch offices) have adopted a no extension policy as an internal rule. Because government and municipal securities are exempt from Reg T, dealers may arrange any type of extended settlement they please without the NYSE's approval.

Sometimes a customer may sell a security for regular-way settlement and then discover a need for the funds prior to settlement date. A branch office manager may authorize a "prepayment" provided the customer is an established one and has not abused the privilege in the past. A prepayment need not be approved by an exchange or the NASD. As prepayments involve the extension of the broker's own funds to the customer (the other broker having 5 business days to pay), brokers reserve the right to charge a customer interest on the cash payment for the days between prepayment and the receipt of the funds from the other broker on settlement day. Brokers will occasionally waive this charge for a good customer who makes infrequent requests for service.

Cash Contracts

Although the overwhelming majority of trades settle regular way, a number of other methods may be used. Of these the next most common is the cash contract, which calls for delivery and payment on the same day the trade is made. In order to make such a transaction the initiator must clearly bid or offer for cash, and occasionally one will note on the tape a stock symbol followed by the expression "offered for cash," indicating a seller is trying to locate a buyer willing to settle that day. As it requires an accommodation by the other party, it is not uncommon for the buyer to demand a concession from the seller—sometimes ⅛ point below the current market level.

The NASD Uniform Practice Code does not specify any particular time for settlement during that day. On the other hand, if a cash trade is done on the NYSE before 2:00 P.M. it must settle by 2:30 that day. If the execution occurs after 2:00 P.M. the settlement must be completed within 30 minutes. Because stock must be exchanged for cash on such short notice, brokers will only accept such orders from established customers who have already delivered (or left in the broker's possession) the requisite securities in good negotiable form or the funds necessary to settle. Requests for cash trades generally originate from the seller who needs the funds more promptly than is possible in regular-way settlement, but there are occasional orders on the buy side.

Cash trades may also be useful in certain other situations in which time becomes an overriding factor. For example, if the last day to take advantage of a rights offering were on a Friday, all rights trading that day would be for cash, whereas trading on the prior day would have called for "next day" settlement. Cash trades are also widely used by arbitragers, especially during tender offers that usually have specific cutoff and delivery times.

Sellers Option Contracts

This type of contract is much less frequently seen than even cash contracts. It is a method of delaying delivery until some stated date, as much as 60 calendar days in the future if done on the NYSE. A typical reason for requesting this type of settlement is the unavailability of the securities for delivery in time for regular-way handling. Once entered into the contract, it is then necessary for the seller to deliver the security on a specified date and the buyer to receive and pay on that date. Such contracts always call for a specific number of calendar days, for example, a "seller's-20" settles on the twentieth calendar day following the trade date. Should the seller choose an earlier date than specified, one day's prior written notice must be extended to the buyer who must then honor the delivery. This request, however, may not be made prior to a regular-way settlement, thus setting a minimum settlement of six business days (two for U.S. government securities) and a maximum of 60 calendar days. If the trade was done OTC, no maximum duration is specified by the NASD's Uniform Practice Code.

THE NATURE OF THE CLEARING PROCESS

The "P and S" Department

Once a transaction has been completed on the floor, the details are reported to the Purchase and Sales (P and S) Departments of the respective firms. The P and S personnel will then match or compare their details with the firm that is identified as the other side of the transaction. Also, the P and S Department will run these data through the firm's computers and produce a confirmation, or "confirm," detailing this information to the customer and specifying funds due the broker or the customer. The confirmation is ordinarily in the mail to the customer on the business day following the trade date. Failure of the U.S. Postal Service to deliver the confirmation promptly is not considered a sufficient excuse for late payment or delivery on the customer's part.

The comparison data from each broker party to the trade are then submitted to the SIAC. The data are then fed into SIAC's computer, which prints out a "contract sheet" summarizing these details and noting any discrepancies in trade reports; for example, a firm reports the same trade but specifies a different execution price or number of shares. Such discrepancies, or "breaks," must be promptly reconciled by the firms involved. At this point, we turn our discussion to the clearing process itself.

The Meaning of Clearing

In the clearing process, sales of securities are offset by purchases so that only net balances of shares are either received or delivered. Similarly, money balances of funds due are netted out. If there were no clearing process, all transactions would have to be settled by individual share certificate delivery and payment. The handling of such activities on a daily basis for even a small broker would be absolutely staggering. Hundreds, possibly thousands of transactions occur daily between customers of major firms like E. F. Hutton and Paine Webber Jackson and Curtis. The amount of paper, negotiable securities, and cash necessary to settle such trades directly would run an army of messengers ragged in short order, even presuming the two firms were within close proximity, let alone a continent apart. Fortunately, there is a central body that eliminates the need for well over 90% of this activity. The route to establishing this body has been long and circuitous.

HISTORY OF STOCK CLEARANCE

Early Attempts at Clearance

The first attempt at stock clearance, anywhere in the world, was apparently at Frankfurt-am-Main, Germany, in 1867.[2] This experiment was followed by similar plans in most of the leading exchanges of the Continent. In the United States the first successful system was that of the Philadelphia Stock Exchange, which began clearing in 1870. The New York Stock Exchange was not able to introduce a successful clearing plan until 1892. It is interesting to note that the clearing operation for banks was introduced in New York 39 years before that for the stock market.

Repeated attempts were made in New York to establish an informal clearing system before any measure of success was obtained. In 1868 some members of the Exchange organized a voluntary system on a fee basis. It soon collapsed for want of support. Another attempt was made five years later, only to suffer the same fate; these were followed by equally futile plans in 1877, 1879, and 1880.

The delay in establishing a sound clearing system was due to two causes. The early plans were voluntary, and many members were reluctant to enter them because their merits were as yet unproved. Also, it was sheer horror for brokers to consider the effects of the plan upon the secrecy that shrouded transactions in the market at that time. It was feared that the system would reveal business secrets to the clerks in the clearing house to the detriment of the clearing firms. The horror just mentioned was, of course, no monopoly of brokers. A love of secrecy was characteristic of all business operations. Corporations would not reveal their financial status to banks, the public, their customers, the press, their stockholders, or to the Exchange. The stock market, however, paid a heavy price for this gospel of business secrecy.

Since there was no clearing system, it was necessary for each firm, before 1892, to handle all transactions on a cash basis, settling each transaction with a separate payment. This posed a perplexing problem. When a firm delivered 100 shares of stock, it expected payment at the time of delivery by messenger. In many cases the buying firm had insufficient funds to meet all such payments. Of course, once the buying firm secured title to the stock, it could pledge the stock at the bank for enough money to meet the entire amount due; but it could not pledge the stock until it secured title, and it could not secure title until it paid for the stock.

This seeming impasse was broken by two expedients, neither of which

[2]B. E. Shultz, *The Securities Market* (New York: Harper & Row, 1946), p. 281.

pleased the bankers of that day.[3] First, the purchasing broker could secure temporary funds by overcertification of a check. In this process the bank certified the check for more than the broker's balance. The check became, in effect, an unsecured loan, which neither the bank nor the government looked upon with approval. Another method was for the bank to give the broker a "morning loan." This was a loan for a few hours, which was to be secured as soon as the broker received possession of the collateral. In both cases the banks were extending vast amounts of credit to brokers, often without sufficient credit standing. In the end, the bankers threatened to curtail this excessive credit and a clearing system became imperative.

The Clearing House of 1892

The New York Stock Exchange put into operation its first successful clearing system in May 1892, exactly 100 years after its first formal organization with the famous "Buttonwood Tree Agreement." The system was, at first, strongly opposed by the most conservative members of the Exchange, but its value was soon apparent to all. The new system was compulsory, but involved only four railroad stocks. On the first day's clearing, the system obviated $7 million in certified checks and operated with only one error. Opposition, because of the secrecy factor and the possible extra clerical expense, died down as the system revealed its inherent advantages.

The Clearing House was not a corporation but an informal organization, managed by a committee of five members of the Exchange appointed by the Board of Governors. In 1920 this informal plan was superseded by the Stock Clearing Corporation (SCC).

The Stock Clearing Corporation functioned as the clearing arm of the New York Stock Exchange. Because of the rudimentary nature of automation, there were still numerous physical deliveries, albeit far fewer than there would have been without the SCC. A Central Certificate Service was created in the 1960s to act as a depository for shares and further reduce physical movement of securities.

The National Securities Clearing Corporation

The National Securities Clearing Corporation (NSCC) began operations in 1977, succeeding to tasks previously performed independently by its predecessors. Until that time, clearance functions were the responsibilities of the SCC (most NYSE trades), the National Clearing Corporation (a large number of OTC stock trades), and the American Stock Exchange Clearing Corporation. Shares in the NSCC are owned equally by the NYSE, Amex, and NASD.

With the Securities Industry Automation Corporation as its processing

[3]S. S. Huebner, *The Stock Market* (New York: Appleton-Century-Crofts, 1934), p. 236.

agent, the NSCC nets all trades submitted to it and then determines securities positions and monies to be settled. Then the NSCC transfers securities held in participants' accounts at the Depository Trust Company (DTC) or produces "balance orders" that will direct the physical delivery of securities to firms as required. The DTC is an exchange subsidiary that performs securities certificate safekeeping duties. It maintains accounts for members and holds on deposit certificates for the most frequently traded issues. Thus, for example, a directive by the NSCC to the DTC to transfer 500 shares of IBM from the account of A. G. Edwards and Company to the account of Advest Company does not require any physical handling by either firm.

Examining a simplified series of transactions will demonstrate the process. On a certain day, a customer of Shearson Lehman submits an order to sell 1,000 shares of DuPont on the NYSE. Shearson's floor broker sells 600 shares to a broker from Smith Barney, Harris Upham and 400 to one representing E. F. Hutton. On the same day, two other Shearson customers enter purchase orders for DuPont. One order for 700 shares is bought from the specialist and the other for 600 is purchased from Bear, Stearns. In sum, Shearson's customers traded a total of 2,300 shares of DuPont that day and involved four other firms besides their own. Because every buyer must have a corresponding seller, the number of DuPont shares bought and sold that day must be even. Because Shearson's customers bought 300 shares more than they sold, some other firm (or firms) must have a sale imbalance of that amount. Once the trade details have been compared and resolved, the NSCC on settlement date will transfer 300 shares of DuPont to Shearson's account at the DTC. The firm from whose account the shares will come may not have even been one of those which Shearson dealt with on the trade date. Rather, it could have been any other NSCC participant that happened to be a net seller of 300 or more DuPont shares on that particular day. One internal transfer, therefore, eliminates the need for any of the firms actually involved in the transactions to make or receive delivery of any physical stock certificates on their premises. This process is referred to as "continuous net settlement." If a security is not eligible for this process, some thinly traded OTC issues for example, the NSCC will produce a "balance order" which will direct one broker to make physical delivery to another.

Money settlements are a bit more complicated, but are ultimately netted out in a similar manner. In the example cited, the firm that eventually delivered the DuPont shares to Shearson via DTC may in fact have done no business at all with that broker and not be owed a cent by Shearson. As a net seller, however, it is obviously owed money by someone. The NSCC will then pay out funds from its own account to that firm's, simultaneously debiting the account of another firm that had been a net buyer the same day.

The foregoing naturally presumes that all goes smoothly and that all commitments are met. Indeed, they usually are. Given combined NASDAQ and NYSE daily trading volume averaging close to 300 million shares daily in 1986, errors and problems are small in proportion. Nevertheless, they do occur daily and must be resolved. When a member organization's account does not have sufficient shares to deliver on settlement day, the firm is said to "fail to deliver," or simply "fail." Naturally, one firm's fail to deliver immediately becomes another's "fail to receive." Such problems must be quickly resolved or the broker's "net capital" (liquidity) will be impaired. The Securities Exchange Act, as amended, requires strict adherence to net capital requirements, and the SEC may close brokers who violate the provisions.

The failure of several major brokerage firms in the late 1960s and early 1970s can be largely laid to their inability to process the volume of transactions their sales forces were generating. Often the problem was caused by neglect of the critical functions described in this chapter. In the opinion of many Wall Street observers, the real problem was greed. Those bringing in the record volume of business were handsomely compensated, but little was spent on automation and trade-processing. Instead, these firms attempted to handle the increased processing needs by simply hiring more clerks, usually inexperienced, to handle problems in the same inefficient ways that had already created the problems. This simply compounded existing problems and left the brokers with even more fails than previously, until ultimately they had to pay the piper.

Fortunately, the financial community learned its lesson well. Trading on the NYSE increased from a daily average of slightly less than 13 million shares daily in 1968 to over 109 million shares in 1985.[4] Volume in major markets in 1985 grew to about 50.2 *billion* shares in 1985, up from 39.6 billion in just the previous year.[5] In addition, the NSCC also clears a substantial amount of corporate and municipal bond transactions. For all securities, the NSCC processed an average of 290,000 separate transactions daily in 1985 for a value of approximately $7.6 billion. The continuous-net-settlement process reduced the need for actual deliveries to fewer than 63,000 daily.[6]

The Clearing Fund

All participants must contribute to the NSCC's clearing fund. The purpose of the fund is to secure the corporation's obligations and spread the risk of loss should one or more of the participants default to an extent exceeding their required contribution. Each participant's requirement is based on its processing activity. Fund contributions may be in cash, U.S. government issued or guaranteed securities, municipal securities, or letters of credit. Title to the deposits and any interest earned on them belongs to the participant, subject to the need for their use by the NSCC in case of default. The size of the clearing fund has grown substantially in recent years, reflecting increased processing assessments from existing members as well as deposits

[4]*NYSE 1986 Fact Book*, p. 70.
[5]*National Securities Clearing Corporation Annual Report*, 1985, p. 10.
[6]*Ibid.*, p. 10.

from new ones, both broker/dealers and banks. Bank participation has grown rapidly since the addition of municipal bond clearing capability, which was phased in gradually in 1980 and 1981. By the end of 1985 the clearing fund had reached $245,781,000, more than 230% greater than its size only 5 years earlier.[7]

Stock Transfer

Stock (or bond) transfer is the process by which the title of ownership to a security is changed and recorded on sale, gift, or for various other reasons. In the delivery and clearance method employed internally within the industry, as just discussed, physical transfer of securities is kept to a minimum, and the long-range goal is to have such eliminated entirely. In some markets, notably for listed options, no physical certificates are ever issued. Americans, however, seem particularly attached to their stock certificates, and efforts to record ownership and transfer solely by "book entry" have not made much headway with stocks and corporate bonds. In June 1986, the Treasury Department stopped issuing any physical certificates for Treasury notes and bonds (T-bill certificates have not been issued for many years). Also, an increasing number of government agency and municipal securities are being issued in book-entry form, either exclusively or as an optional format.

Street Name Stock

This is stock which has been purchased by the customer but left in the broker's name, hence (Wall) "street name." The customer is said to be the "beneficial owner" although the broker is the "record owner," that is, the broker's name is on the transfer agent's record as the owner. The customer is not known to the transfer agent. Thus all communications such as proxy (voting) material, quarterly and annual reports, and, of course, dividends will be sent to the broker who in turn must promptly forward them to the customer, or credit the customer's account with any cash or property received. This format greatly simplifies the transfer process as the shares do not have to be shipped back and forth between customer, broker, and transfer agent. Not being in the customer's name to begin with, they do not have to signed by the customer and delivered to the broker to complete delivery. The value of this form of security ownership is discussed in more detail in Chapter 12.

Techniques of Stock Transfer

There are two aspects to the transfer of title to stock: (1) the transfer is accomplished by the delivery of properly endorsed certificates, and (2) the transfer is recorded on the books of the issuer. In most cases the broker

[7]Ibid., pp. 23–24.

acts as the customer's intermediary and handles the details necessary to complete the transfer from the previous owner and shipment to the new owner. More rarely, some customers may request that the broker transfer ownership to them but retain the certificates in safekeeping. In this case, the customer receives payments directly from the issuer but must still sign the certificates to make them negotiable when sold. The service is a costly inconvenience to brokers and is not offered by some. Where offered, the broker usually charges a substantial fee for the service.

On the back of every registered security certificate is a printed form known as an "assignment and power of substitution." When a stock certificate with a properly executed assignment is delivered with intent to pass title, the title passes from the previously registered owner to the new owner. This is true even if the transfer has not yet been recorded on the books of the issuer or its transfer agent. From this point the new owner is entitled to all rights of ownership.

The assignment has spaces for the name of the new owner, the number of shares, and the broker who will be the customer's "attorney" in the transfer process. Hence, the phrase "power of substitution" in which the broker is authorized to substitute his name for that of the seller in the transfer. This wording is duplicated on a separate form called a "stock (or bond) power" which is readily available in all brokerage offices. Instead of signing the actual certificate, the seller may instead sign a stock power for each separate certificate being delivered. The broker then attaches a signed power to each certificate to complete transfer. Because endorsed certificates are negotiable, many investors are reluctant to mail them to brokers when they are sold. This concern may be alleviated by mailing an unsigned, and thus nonnegotiable certificate in one envelope and a signed stock power in another. Upon receipt of both, the broker reattaches them and proceeds with the transfer process. Thus, if the certificate goes astray in the mail, no irreparable harm is done.

Name of Owner

Each stock certificate should carry on its face the exact name of the rightful owner. Accuracy is paramount and an owner who receives a stock certificate with a misspelled name should immediately return it to the transfer agent for correction. Under no circumstances should one erase or in any way alter the name on the certificate. To do so would almost assuredly render the certificate untransferable until the transfer agent received supporting documentation to verify ownership. This could be quite time consuming. Joint names may appear on a stock certificate. Of these the most common are three types of tenancy:

Joint tenancy with rights of survivorship
Tenancy by the entireties
Tenancy in common

Some states restrict the use of either of the first two types. Joint tenancy with right of survivorship (JTWROS, or some similar abbreviation) is used largely by married couples. The typical account title might be "John A. Smith and Mary T. Smith JTWROS." The death of any one tenant automatically transfers full ownership to the survivor, thus avoiding probate delays. At one time this advantage was offset by potential tax liabilities for the decedent's estate, but at least in the case of husband-wife joint tenancies, the tax reforms passed in 1981 have largely eliminated this drawback. All joint tenants must sign a certificate exactly as registered to transfer the property. Indeed, this is true of all tenancy accounts.

Tenancy by the entireties is similar to JTWROS and right of survivorship is implied. It is used in some "community property" states and has certain provisions in the case of death or divorce different from those in JTWROS.

Tenancy in common differs markedly from the other two, because each tenant has an individual interest in the account with no right of survivorship. The fractional interest of a deceased tenant becomes part of the tenant's estate.

Dividend checks, proxies, and any other documentation such as the acceptance of a tender offer must be endorsed by all joint tenants, as with stock certificates. If certificates are registered in the name of a custodian, guardian, trustee, or administrator, or any person legally responsible for another, that person must sign. In the case of a deceased shareholder additional documents may be required before transfer may be effected to others. These ordinarily include a copy of the death certificate, estate tax waivers, a copy of a will, a copy of the court appointment of an administrator if the decedent died intestate (without a will).

Signature Guarantees

To guard against the possibility of forgery, NYSE Rule 209 requires that all signatures on certificates presented for registration be guaranteed by an NYSE member or member organization, a commercial bank or trust company, or some other entity whose signature is on file with and is acceptable to the transfer agent. Exceptions are made for registered U.S. government securities and securities in broker names (or their nominees).

A space is provided on all stock powers for witnesses to the signature, but it has long been the practice not to require such. Because all stock transfers are made only on the guaranty of an authorized person or organization, the use of a witness has become superfluous.

OTHER TRANSFER REGULATIONS

Transfer Agents

Most companies utilize a bank or trust company as a transfer agent, although some companies prefer to act as their own. If a company is listed on the NYSE, it must have a transfer agent with an office in the New York financial district. Upon presentation of a properly endorsed certificate, the transfer agent will cancel the old one, usually by perforation, and issue another one in the name of the new owner. If the transfer agent is presented with a certificate that requires legal documentation to complete transfer, the documentation must be complete and in perfect order.

Transfer agents may also act as paying agents for corporate cash dividends and the distribution of new shares in the event of a stock dividend or split. With mutual funds the transfer agent has in addition the responsibility for redeeming (liquidating) shares upon receipt of customer's written or wired request and a signed stock power. The transfer agent also maintains the record of names and addresses of current shareholders, although it should be remembered that many of these are unknown to the transfer agent because they are beneficial holders of "street name" stock. Only the names of the brokers holding this stock would actually appear on the record.

Registrar

Despite its somewhat imposing title, the job of a registrar is mostly routine. Upon notice from the transfer agent that a certain certificate has been canceled and replaced with another, the registrar checks its records to ensure that the number of shares represented by the new certificate corresponds to the number of shares on the canceled one. This prevents a possible dilution of equity through overissuance of stock. If the transfer agent performs the original job carefully, the registrar's job is purely nominal. There were cases, however, many years ago when this job was not performed accurately and the interest of shareholders was indeed watered down; this resulted in the current regulations requiring the registrar function to be separate from that of the transfer agent.

Transfer of Bonds

The transfer of registered bonds is basically the same as described for registered stocks, except that the trustee for the bond ordinarily acts as transfer agent. If the bonds are bearer certificates, however, title passes by delivery and there is no formal record of transfer, or indeed, even of ownership. Such bonds are merely signed by the owner with no transferee named, a condition referred to as "endorsement in blank." In effect, they belong to whoever has physical possession, making extreme caution necessary in their storage and handling. If lost or stolen, replacement is a costly, difficult, and time-consuming process, even more so than for a lost or stolen registered security.

Stolen, Lost or Destroyed Certificates

Each year many certificates disappear—in the mails, in fires, through burglary, or simply by being misplaced. Even if a house burns down, the transfer agent and the issuer have no guarantee that the securities may not fall into the hands of a dishonest person and make their reappearance at some future date, requiring payment of interest, principal, or dividends.

Upon discovery that the certificates are missing, the owner should at once contact the issuer and transfer agent. The transfer agent will place a "stop transfer" order against this certificate should someone else attempt to place it in transfer. Of course, there is no guarantee that this will be effective, for the certificate may never be presented. Next, the owner will have to file an affidavit setting forth all the details of the loss. Finally, the owner will have to file an expensive surety bond. The bond's cost is high because the surety company issuing it may be required to buy in the security at some future date regardless of price should the missing item reappear in someone else's possession. All of this forms a strong argument in favor of street name securities whenever possible.

UNIFORM COMMERCIAL CODE, ARTICLE 8

This effort to codify various laws deals primarily with the sale of goods, both tangible and intangible, and with secured transactions. The basic provisions have been adopted in most states.

Article 8 of the Code applies to transactions in investment securities.[8] A basic consideration is protection of the rights to title of bona fide purchasers of securities for value without notice of any adverse claim at the time of purchase or before. The notion of negotiability is adapted to problems of securities transactions, including the formal problems of transfer and registration. A purchaser is afforded protections against claims by the issuer or by third parties.

If a purchaser acquires a security for value, without any notice of adverse claims, and it is properly endorsed by the appropriate persons (if the security is registered as stock is), the purchaser can have title and can have a certificate registered in his or her name. This right obtains even if the issuer may subsequently claim that there were faults in transactions prior to delivery unless (1) the security is counterfeit; (2) the signature of the issuer is forged; or (3) the issue was illegal or unconstitutional. The purchaser also has clear title even though another person may show that the delivery was wrongful, provided the certificate was properly endorsed and no notice of adverse claim was given at or before the time of the purchase transaction. The effect is to

---

[8] Prior to passage of the Uniform Commercial Code, two statutes, the Uniform Negotiable Instruments Act and the Uniform Stock Transfer Act, together with the body of common law, were significant for transfer of title to stock in the states that did adopt the Code. They remain significant in other states. The fundamental characteristics of the law under them, however, is not greatly different from that to be described here.

The comments in this section are based primarily on a *Summary of the Uniform Commercial Code for Illinois*, published by the Continental Illinois National Bank and Trust Company, November 1961.

protect buyers against loss of their rights because of faults in relationship between or among persons of which they had no knowledge and that were not present in the transaction to which they were a party.

The Code makes clear that a person transferring a security warrants that the transfer is effective and right, the security is genuine, and that there is no impairment of the validity of the security as a claim of the issuer. It also makes clear that a signature guarantor warrants that the signature is genuine, that the signer is an appropriate person to endorse the certificate, and that the signer had the legal capacity to sign. The issuer, or a transfer agent, in issuing a new certificate to the purchaser warrants that the security is genuine and in proper form, it is issued under proper authorization, and that it is within the limits authorized for the issue. In presenting a certificate for cancellation and for issue of a new certificate, the transferee warrants that there is no unauthorized signature in the necessary endorsement. Obviously, if the persons in this sequence act to make each one's warranty good, stock transfer is effectively accomplished.

4 Regulations

16 Manipulation in the Old Market

One of the most colorful and most criticized aspects of the old stock market was the flagrant manipulation of security prices. Much of the criticism of the stock exchanges and brokerage firms during the Senate investigation of 1933–1934 was based on documented cases of massive manipulation. The passage of the Securities Exchange Act of 1934 was due in no small part to such activities.

The passage of a law does not mean that people will not try to find some way to break it without getting caught. Regulatory bodies, arbitration panels, and courts still deal regularly with manipulative practices, some real and some imagined. Some rival the old manipulative practices in scale if not in brazenness; hence, this chapter provides something more than an insight into a historical curiosity. An understanding of the reasons for many of the regulations of the Exchange Act, the SEC, various states, and the exchanges requires a rather broad knowledge of conditions that prevailed in the market as it operated in earlier years.

It is not intended to justify here the actions of those who manipulated markets, or those who profited by manipulation, or the attitude of the public and officials who tolerated or participated in such activity.

Lest one be too hasty in condemning the securities business and blaming abuse in that business for all economic and social ills of the time, it is important to note that ethics in a variety of social activities during the same period of about 75 years were of an equally low state. There were insurance scandals, bootlegging, land grabbing, timber thieving, the baseball scandals, the political spoils system, the Teapot Dome scandal, war profiteering, draft dodging, patent medicine frauds, sales of impure foods, corrupt political machines, misleading advertising, child labor exploitation, sweat shop manufacturing, unfair trade practices of the trusts, and bribery of legislators—to mention only a few examples that may come to mind.

Before one becomes too sanctimonious about condemning all the evil that was done or dismisses this chapter as an unnecessary negative exposition of bygones, it should be noted that many goods are still sold today that do not deliver what is promised or even harm their buyers; whole new industries of computer crime, drugs, and credit card fraud have appeared; people still try to get something for nothing; all brokerage employees do not always tell the truth or disclose all that should be disclosed; and government officials apparently still take bribes now and then. Furthermore, some of the practices described herein which are now regarded as heinous crimes against the public were not illegal when perpetrated.

Some kinds of manipulation discussed in this chapter are now almost nonexistent because of regulations. It is not intended to condemn the brokerage industry because some of its past activities are now considered to be unethical, illegal, or both. It is important to note that the industry now functions well, although not perfectly, in the public interest. Some of the credit belongs to the safety provided by regulations. The same is true of many other industries such as foods and transportation.

CHARACTERISTICS OF MANIPULATION

Its Nature

Manipulation is an artificial control of security prices; it is an attempt to force securities to sell at prices either above or below those that would exist as a result of the normal operations of supply and demand. The manipulator hopes to make a profit or avoid a loss by creating fictitious prices that might be at the expense of the trading public. It should be noted that some manipulation even today is legal. The characteristic of an activity that makes it manipulative is the artificial control of price, not its illegality.

Purposes

Manipulation has three possible objectives. The first is to raise the price; the manipulator then unloads on the buyer. This is the most common type. The second purpose may be to stabilize the price. The net result is usually that the security sells at a better price than it would if it were allowed to seek its own level. This is often done in the underwriting of new securities; it is a condoned practice permitted by the SEC provided the public is fully informed that such operations are contemplated. It is a seldom condemned manipulative practice. The third objective is to force prices down; this type of manipulation is rarely found except in the activities of the so-called bear raiders who hope to obtain short selling profits in this way.

Classification

Manipulative activities are difficult to classify in that there are so many different forms and so many diverse devices by which they can be carried on.

For purposes of simplicity, the discussion which follows will consider the subject under three main heads: wash sales, corners, and pool operations. The first is least important; the second was largely a nineteenth-century activity; the third was typical of the market of the 1920s and included almost every device used in the manipulator's handbook.

WASH SALES

Little need be said of the wash sale, which was one of the earliest forms of manipulation. It was a fake sale; no real change in ownership took place. There was no one meaning of the term, because several methods could be used to obtain the same result. One of the earliest devices was for two brokers to simulate a sale on an exchange; a price was agreed upon, an offer or bid was accepted, yet no stock or money changed hands. Another device was for a speculator to place a matched order with two brokers; he sold a given amount of stock through one broker and bought it through another. Although more subtle and secretive than the first method, no real change in ownership took place. A third method was for a trader to sell a given block of stock and have a friend or accomplice purchase it. The accomplice was then indemnified for his expenses and the stock was retrieved. A fourth method was for a man to execute a wash sale to his wife, often to establish a tax loss. Some highly placed individuals did this in the past. Income tax officials, however, took a dim view of this evasion procedure.

Wash sales have as their primary purpose the establishment of a fictitious price, either to create a profit opportunity or to establish a loss, generally for tax purposes. They have been illegal for many years; the stock exchanges have long barred them. In later years manipulators were able to obtain essentially the same results in some cases by matched orders placed by different individuals so as to conceal the identity of the operation.

A complete discussion of manipulative practices covered by the 1934 Act and its amendments, particularly those of 1975, would fill a book in itself, but examples of some of the more important types of manipulative practices that were formerly prevalent will indicate the nature of the game as it once was played.

CORNERS

Nature

A corner is a speculative situation in which the ownership of outstanding shares becomes so concentrated that short sellers are unable to secure stock except from this owner group. It grows out of a price rise in a stock, whether natural or manipulated. As the stock rises in value, it is sold short by speculators who feel that it is too high and is certain to decline. They borrow the stock to short sell; it is often loaned by the controlling group. Eventually, they attempt to cover by buying back the stock that they have sold short. Because the controlling group is the only one that has any stock to sell, the short sellers are forced to settle with them at whatever price the group dictates. At this point the short sellers are "cornered."

Corners were frequent in the early years of the New York Stock Exchange. In fact, they were so common and so profitable in the nineteenth century that Henry Clews, a noted financier and chronicler of Wall Street, observed in the post-Civil War period that "all large fortunes are made by corners."[1]

In many cases they were deliberately engineered as "traps" for unsuspecting speculators, who were often great operators. Such situations have been labeled as manipulative corners. Examples have been the Harlem Railroad corner of 1863, the "Erie raids," the Stutz corner of 1920, and the Piggly Wiggly corner of 1923. In these instances the manipulators freely loaned stock to the short sellers. As the price rose, short sellers continued to sell while the manipulators purchased all stock offered on the market. The stock was reloaned for more short selling. Eventually more stock would often be on loan than was actually outstanding. When this situation had continued to a point where the short sellers sought to cover either as a precautionary measure or in desperation, the manipulators called the stock loans. The corner was complete and the short sellers had no recourse but to settle.

Other corners have sometimes been called natural corners in that they were a result of speculative activities not connected with manipulation. In such cases several controlling groups may have attempted to purchase control of a given company. As the stock was bid up for control, short sellers, without realizing the background of the situation, would sell. In the end they were cornered as before, since only the controlling group had stock to sell. The classic example of this situation was the famous Northern Pacific corner of 1901.

Some of the most colorful episodes of Wall Street history are those of the corners executed by the great stock market operators of an earlier day. A few examples will be cited.

The First Harlem Railroad Corner

The two Harlem Railroad corners involved principally two men. The first was Commodore Cornelius Vanderbilt, whose early fortune was made in the steamship business; he turned to railroads in the early 1860s as a greater opportunity. The second was Daniel Drew, a deeply religious man on Sunday and as ruthless a businessman as ever operated in Wall Street.

In 1862 Vanderbilt purchased stock in the Harlem Railroad in New York City for $8 a share.[2] By the time he had control, it had reached 50. He then

---

[1]Henry Clews, *Fifty Years in Wall Street* (New York: Irving, 1908), p. 101.
[2]R. I. Warshow, *The Story of Wall Street* (New York: Greenberg, 1929), p. 91.

proceeded to extend the road to lower Manhattan. Drew also bought some shares, but was not content with his modest profit. The stock had now reached 100. At this point Drew conspired with Boss Tweed and the members of the Common Council to repeal the Harlem Railroad franchise; at the same time all heavily short sold the railroad stock. It was driven down to 72, but refused to go further as Vanderbilt purchased every possible share at that point. The short sellers then realized that something had gone wrong. It had indeed, because they had short sold 137,000 shares, or 27,000 shares more than were outstanding. Vanderbilt then jumped the price back to 179, at which price Drew, Tweed, and the members of the Common Council were forced to settle.

The Second Harlem Railroad Corner

The second corner involved Vanderbilt, Drew, and the members of the New York State Legislature. Vanderbilt, now determined to get a charter from the state government, went directly to the legislature. Drew, by instigating a favorable report by the legislature, forced the price up to 150 from 75 in a few days. At this point Drew and the chief members of the legislature heavily short sold the road's stock. The legislature now defeated the petition for a charter by a heavy vote. In two days the stock fell 50 points and then began to rise rapidly. There was no stock to be obtained for short covering. Once again, more stock had been short sold than could be covered. Up and up went the price, and Vanderbilt began to corner the speculators. At 285 he finally settled with the short sellers. Drew paid Vanderbilt $500,000 in a private settlement.

The Erie Raids

In its early years the Erie Railroad was one of the great roads of the nation. It was also the victim of some of the worst stock manipulations in the history of American railroading.[3] These manipulations are commonly known as the "Erie raids."There were a number of them; two are typical. The market operators who engaged in these raids were principally Vanderbilt, Drew, Fisk, and Gould.

Jim Fisk began his business career as a dry goods peddler in Vermont. Later he became a partner in a large dry goods firm in Boston. During the Civil War his highly unorthodox methods of securing army blanket orders were so unsavory to his partners that he was given some $60,000 in cash to withdraw from the firm. He next joined forces with Drew and Gould.

Jay Gould was one of the shrewdest market operators who ever speculated in Wall Street. He married a wholesale grocer's daughter in his early twenties and was given control of a small, bankrupt railroad—its stocks were worth-

---

[3]Warshow, *op. cit.*, p. 109; Clews, *op. cit.*, p. 137.

less. In a short time he reorganized the road and sold it at a handsome profit. His next venture was the purchase and sale of a road connecting Pittsburgh and Cleveland at another high return. He was still only 25 years of age.

After the Erie Railroad passed into receivership in 1859, it received a loan of $1 million from Drew on the condition that he be made a director. By 1868 it had accumulated a surplus of $16 million and had become a valuable piece of property. At that time Vanderbilt, flushed with his successes with the consolidated New York Central, determined to wrest control of the Erie Railroad from Drew and his two associates, Gould and Fisk. He bought heavily of the stock as Drew and his associates sold at steadily advancing prices. Not only did he buy all of the outstanding stock, but he also bought an additional 50,000 shares; he felt certain that, again, Drew was cornered.

This time Drew avoided a repetition of the disastrous Harlem Railroad corners. At a secret midnight meeting, the board of directors issued $10 million in convertible bonds. Through a wash sale to Drew, these were converted into 100,000 shares of common stock. Vanderbilt was now confronted with 100,000 new shares thrown on the market in a few days. He bought every share at a cost of $7 million. Now he had 100,000 shares he dared not sell and which no one would buy; his money was tied up completely. In desperation he turned to a friendly judge who vowed to have the triumvirate in jail by nightfall. In order to avoid arrest, the three members of the executive committee of the Erie Railroad now rushed with their money and account books to the shores of New Jersey; with them they carried $4 million in greenbacks.

The situation was now a stalemate. Drew, Fisk, and Gould were safe in New Jersey with their money, but they could not return to their homes. Vanderbilt had lost his $7 million; he was unable to borrow at the banks; his resources were badly strained. A compromise was agreed upon: Drew and his two associates were to keep their $7 million, but were to repay Vanderbilt that sum out of the Erie Railroad treasury. This was done and that ill-fated railway was left a weakened hulk.

Drew was required by the agreement to leave the management of the Erie Railroad to Gould. He was now a wealthy man with a fortune of $13 million. His retirement, however, left him an unhappy man. Eventually he came back into the market like the proverbial moth attracted to the scorching light.

Again, Drew became associated with Gould and Fisk in another "Erie raid." It was decided that the scene would be set with a created panic. The men suddenly withdrew $14 million in cash from their banks, which severely restricted the credit situation; call money rose to 160%. All three men were to short sell Erie stock. For a while the pool was a success and Erie stock fell 30 points. Drew now became timid and withdrew from the joint operation as Gould and Fisk planned to continue the raid with a new campaign. In a short time Drew regretted his timidity as the market weakened; he began to short sell on his own account. Since they knew of his operations, Gould and Fisk now determined to break Drew. As he short sold, they reversed their operations and bought every share thrown on the market. Soon Drew found himself 70,000 shares short; he could not cover because Gould and Fisk controlled the entire floating supply of the stock. Drew was cornered by his erstwhile associates; he had no legal recourse; he had not a friend in Wall Street; his losses were staggering.

From then on Drew was a beaten man. In several successive operations his entire fortune melted away. In a few years, he died a poor man; his total assets were less than $1,000. Wall Street smiled with relief; "Uncle Daniel" was gone. A fitting epitaph on his tombstone would have been a jingle, which he once composed:

> He who sells what isn't his'n,
> Must buy it back or go to prison.

From the Erie raids Jay Gould emerged stronger than ever. His most publicized corner was not in stocks but in gold. On October 4, 1869, he attempted the audacious feat of cornering the gold market. On that "Black Friday" he met his worst defeat. Always wily to the last, he made Jim Fisk bear the brunt of the losses; Fisk's firm went down in complete ruin.

The Northern Pacific Corner

The great Northern Pacific corner took place in 1901; it was perhaps the most remarkable corner ever to occur in Wall Street.[4] It grew out of an attempt of two financial giants to acquire control of one small railroad, the Chicago, Burlington and Quincy, commonly known as the Burlington. The two opposing contestants were James J. Hill of the Northern Pacific and Edward H. Harriman of the Union Pacific. Behind Hill was J. P. Morgan and Company; behind Harriman was Kuhn, Loeb and Company. Hill wanted the Burlington to prevent the encroachment of the Union Pacific in his territory; the road would also provide him with a much-needed Chicago terminus. Harriman wanted the road because it paralleled his own Union Pacific and, as such, was a potential competitor.

Both parties started to buy up the Burlington stock at about the same time. At first the Harriman syndicate attempted to buy the stock in the open market. This resulted in failure when the Hill group negotiated with the majority stockholders of the road and bought control at $200 per share. The Harriman interests now took a very bold step. As someone described it, they "bought the cow to get the calf." Their operation was to secure control of the Burlington by buying the Northern Pacific. Without a single share to start with, Kuhn, Loeb and Company bought a clear majority of all the stock in two months. Although they had a majority of all the stock, they did not have a majority of the common stock alone.

Morgan, however, was not disposed to accept defeat. On his orders 150,000 shares of common stock were purchased on the Exchange; as they were bought, the stock rose from 112 to 150. Morgan was now in a position to exercise a very unusual clause in the charter of the Northern Pacific. This clause permitted the board of directors, at its option, to retire, on any January 1, the preferred stock. Controlled by Morgan, the board immediately made this decision in order to eliminate the influence of the other group.

In the meantime the great struggle had created a very large volume of short selling. In a brief period more shares had been sold short than the total number issued by the company. The shorts, in desperation, found that no stock could be borrowed and were forced to enter buy orders in a seller's paradise. An unintentional corner had been created. The stock soared to 170, 225, 280, 300, 650, 700, and then one sale was reported at 1,000. Call money went to 70%. The market crashed as speculators dumped conservative issues on the market to raise cash. Near the close of the market on May 9, the two great banking interests made a truce; they announced that they would lend their stock to the short sellers. The market quickly subsided and call money fell to 3%; the greatest volume on record up to that day was reported by the Exchange, a total of 3.2 million shares. On the following day the shorts were allowed to settle at $150 per share and the corner was ended.

The struggle between the two financial interests was terminated with a compromise. Morgan did not retire the Northern Pacific's preferred stock; Harriman did not attempt to control the Burlington. Instead, the stock of all the roads was taken over by a new holding company known as the Northern Securities Company, and each interest was given equal representation. The greatest financial battle in Wall Street was over.

The Stutz Corner

Only two important corners took place on the New York Stock Exchange after World War I: the Stutz corner in 1920 and Piggly Wiggly Stores corner of 1923.[5] In the Stutz corner the operation involved the stock of Stutz Motors, producer of that popular young man's medium of fast transportation, the Stutz Bearcat. The company had 100,000 shares of capital stock. Allan A. Ryan, of the Stock Exchange firm of Allan A. Ryan and Company, engineered a manipulative corner in the stock. As it rose to great heights, much short selling took place. Ryan and his associates accumulated contracts which totaled 110,000 shares, or 10,000 more than were outstanding. Seeking to take advantage of his fortunate position, Ryan agreed to settle with the shorts at prices varying from $500 to $1,000. The Exchange, alarmed at the situation, suspended dealings in the stock. The contracts immediately became the subject of extensive litigation; the short sellers declared that the whole operation was illegal. Subsequently the stock fell to 20. Allan Ryan and his firm were

[5]J. E. Meeker, *The Work of the Stock Exchange* (New York: Ronald Press, 1930), p. 604.

ruined; heavy losses were accepted by several banks that had backed the venture.

The Piggly Wiggly Corner

In 1923 Clarence Saunders, president of Piggly Wiggly Stores, attempted to corner the market in his own company.[6] For a time he was able to corner the entire floating supply of the stock. He offered to settle with the short sellers at prices varying from $100 to $1,000. The Exchange, however, suspended delivery requirements on the stock. As soon as stock held out of town could be rushed to New York, the corner was broken rapidly and Saunders received all of the stock due him. In the meantime the stock was stricken from the list.

POOL OPERATIONS

Nature of the Pool

A pool is a temporary association of two or more individuals to act jointly in a security operation of a manipulative character. There is no inherent reason why manipulation should be carried on through the use of pools; many such manipulations have been carried on with great financial success by single operators; such as Drew, Little, Vanderbilt, Gould, and Keene. During the 1920s, however, the pool developed a high degree of popularity. The possibility of combining capital, trading skill, experience, and corporate connections into one cooperative venture appeared so attractive that it became the typical organization procedure of the manipulators of that era.

There was no particular size of the pool of the 1920s and early 1930s. The Radio pool, one of the largest, had about 70 members; the first Fox pool had 32, and the second, 42. The profitable alcohol pool of 1933 had only eight participants.

Pool Contracts

A pool contract was typically used in pool operation. It may have ranged from a simple, verbal agreement of several men to trade actively in one security through a joint account to a very long and complex contract which described every aspect of the rights and liabilities of the members. In the more formal contracts, the pool was usually known as a syndicate. The contract named the manager and his compensation; it indicated the capital contribution of each member; it stated the time limit and the manner in which profits and losses were to be divided; it noted any option agreements. Letters were usually sent to participants; these were countersigned and returned to the pool organizers.

[6]*Ibid.*, p. 605.

Management

Successful pool operations necessitated skillful, experienced managers. These may have been traders with a past record of deft handling of such operations; they may have been corporate executives; often they were brokers and dealers. Members of exchanges were frequently asked to be managers; their knowledge of the market and their skill in executing orders were invaluable. Through them discretionary orders could be placed for execution at the best possible time.

Managers shared in the profits of the pool, both as participants and as paid managers. A compensation of 10% of the net profits was often a manager's compensation; no losses were shared. The manager if a broker also received the regular commissions for execution of orders.

Stocks

Many of the most prominent stocks on the New York Stock Exchange and the New York Curb (now American) Exchange were subjected to syndicate, pool, or joint account operations. In 1929, 107 stock issues of the larger Exchange were manipulated one or more times by pools in which members of the Exchange were interested.[7] Although no attempt was made in that year to manipulate General Motors or U.S. Steel, such illustrious names as American Tobacco, Chrysler, Curtiss-Wright, Goodrich, Montgomery Ward, National Cash Register, Packard, Radio Corporation of America, Standard Oil of California, Studebaker, and Union Carbide appeared on the list of manipulated issues. After 1929 the number of manipulated stocks declined rapidly; in 1930 it was only 35 issues; in 1931, 6; in 1932, 2; in 1933, 23. These figures include only operations in which Exchange members participated. There are no definite figures on the total number of stocks manipulated. Less activity took place on the New York Curb Exchange in these years. For example, in 1929 there were 27 on that Exchange that were manipulated by pools in which members participated.

Pool Profits

Successful manipulation was not without compensation. In a few cases the profits of pools have been publicized. One of the most profitable was the Sinclair Consolidated Oil pool in 1929; its profit from purchasing and trading syndicate operations was $12,618,000.[8] The spectacular operations of the Radio pool of 1929 netted the participants $4,900,000. Those of the American Commercial Alcohol pool yielded $210,000. The first Fox pool made a profit of $433,000; the second netted $1,938,000. Four participants of the Kolster Radio Pool divided $1,341,000 among them.

[7]*Stock Exchange Practices*, Senate Report No. 1455, 73d Cong., 2d sess., p. 32.
[8]*Ibid.*, p. 63.

Insider Collusion

It was a rather common practice during the 1920s to invite important directors and executive officers of corporations into the pools. As a matter of fact, many of such so-called insiders often were instrumental in getting the pools organized in the first place. This collusion worked to the mutual benefit of the pool and the insiders. It was collusion of the most obvious sort; the pool and the insiders profited at the expense of the public stockholders.

Collusion benefited the pool in three ways: (1) it enabled the pool to secure options from the company; (2) it guaranteed a friendly attitude toward the pool by the company's management; and (3) it yielded invaluable information to the pool managers. The use of options will be discussed fully later; the other two advantages will be mentioned briefly.

By collusion the pool was assured of a friendly attitude. The insiders, since they profited by the pool operations, cooperated in every way. They did not release unfavorable information about the company or the pool operations; they did not attack the pool nor give anyone else any opportunity to do so.

The pool also had the advantage of inside information. This could be obtained at will but withheld from the public and the stockholders. It could be properly interpreted; it was entirely adequate. In addition, the pool could release the information on corporate affairs at times when the most benefit to the pool activities would result. Such advantages were exploited to the full. There were many ways to disseminate information favorable to the stock; the pools neglected none of them, as will be pointed out later.

Insider collusion was not uncommon in pool operations of the 1920s. In one pool the wife of the top executive of the company received a substantial share of the profits with no personal capital commitment. In another, substantial participation was reported for the chairman of the board, the president, the chairman of the executive committee, and several directors and principal stockholders. In another operation among the participants were the president, the chairman of the executive committee, the treasurer, the counsel, several directors and vice presidents. In another the president of the company received 25% of the net profits.

That such collusion was the grossest breach of the fiduciary relationship is beyond dispute. It did, however, exist; and in certain circles it was considered a strictly legitimate activity.

Specialist Collusion

Another form of collusion involved specialists. The services of such members often proved valuable to the managers of the pools. Their knowledge of the market was firsthand; this could be used to great advantage in timing pool operations. In numerous cases the manager of the syndicate would give discretionary orders to the specialist who was handling the account on the floor.

By using his best judgment, he could conduct the pool's buying and selling operations so as to make the greatest possible profit for the pool.

That specialists benefited from such operations was clearly indicated by the Senate investigation of stock exchange practices. For example, in one of the Fox pools, two specialists, who were vested with discretionary orders to execute on the Exchange floor, received $42,000 as participants plus a check of $10,000 from the manager in "appreciation for the work done in running an orderly market."[9]

Trading Pools

Two types of pools were present in the 1920s. One was known as a trading pool. It did not acquire its stock through options but bought it in the open market. The managers of these pools had to buy the stock in the open market at the most favorable price possible. There would, of course, be no purpose in running up the price of the stock unless the pool was able to unload it on the market at the new high price. Several methods were used to purchase the stock. The first was to depress the price of the stock by short selling or dissemination of unfavorable publicity about the issue, thus forcing it down to prices advantageous to the pool. A second method was to stabilize the price; its failure to rise with the rest of the market made the stock unpopular. As owners shifted to other issues, the pool quietly acquired substantial blocks of it. The third method was to buy it at advancing prices, an expensive method at best. In trading pools the managers employed various devices, such as "shake-outs," to discourage public ownership until the pool had accumulated a sufficient supply of stock to justify price increases or "markups."

The famous Radio pool of 1929 was an example of a trading pool in which the manager used no options. Its operations will be described in more detail later.

Option Pools

The option pool was one that acquired much, if not all, of its stock at fixed prices agreed upon before the pool started operations. These options were acquired from the corporation itself, large stockholders, directors, officers, banks, and speculators. The use of calls was often a device for acquiring stock. Once the option was acquired, the manager could exercise it at the stated price at any time during its life.

These options had various maturities. Some ran only three or four weeks; nearly half ran as long as one year. In one reported instance an option ran for 25 years.

The options did not have to be exercised unless the price was favorable. In other words, if the option permitted the manager to acquire the stock at

$50, it would not be exercised unless the price could be forced above this $50 limit. In a successful pool it was often raised substantially above the option price.

Option pools were very common in the 1920s; a majority of them seem to have been conducted in that way. The Senate Committee found a record of 286 options involving 17,380,000 shares over the period 1929–1933.[10]

The reasons for the popularity of the option pool were not hard to discover. The managers were assured a definite supply of stock at no financial risk; the makers of the options were often able to unload large amounts of undigested stock at attractive prices, and if calls were written, they received the usual premiums of $137.50 per 100 shares for 30-day options. There were many option pools on record; for example, Sinclair Consolidated Oil, American Commercial Alcohol, Goodyear Tire, Fox Theaters, Remington Rand, Curtiss-Wright, National Cash Register, Park and Tilford, National Steel, Crosley Radio, Canada Dry, Colgate-Palmolive-Peet, North American Aviation, Standard Brands, Republic Iron and Steel.

In many cases pool managers were able to secure, at no cost to the syndicates, options given by the corporation. These options involved authorized, but unissued, stock. Sometimes the options involved as much as 20–25% of the outstanding stock. The reason the pool could obtain this option without expense was that many insiders profited from the pool operation; these directors and top executive officers were participants in the pool.

Several examples will indicate how an option pool operated. In the Sinclair Consolidated Oil pool, the managers received from the company an option to buy 1,130,000 shares at 30; this was about 20% of all authorized stock.[11] At the time the negotiations over the option began, the stock was selling at 28. However, on the day the agreement was actually signed, the stock opened at 32 and closed at 35¾. On the next day it sold as high as 37¼ and closed at 36¾. The syndicate acquired the entire 1,130,000 shares at no risk to itself; these were disposed of at substantial profits in the market. In addition, the syndicate acquired 634,000 shares in the market and disposed of them at a gross profit of $465,000. It also sold short an additional 200,000 shares at a profit of $2 million.

In early 1933 there was great speculation in the so-called repeal stocks. To take advantage of this situation, the American Commercial Alcohol pool was formed. It was given an option to buy 25,000 shares of that company's stock at $18 per share.[12] On the day that the directors actually authorized the issuance of the new stock, the price range of the stock was 30⅞ to 33½. The stock sold as high as 89⅞ within two months after the option was given. Officers, directors, and principal stockholders made heavy profits from the pool's operations.

[10]*Ibid.*, p. 45.
[11]*Ibid.*, p. 63.
[12]*Ibid.*, p. 55.

Publicity

Adequate publicity was an invaluable tool in the operations of a pool. Its purpose was to attract the general public into the stock and to keep it there until the pool had unloaded its holdings. Operations of the pool were carefully timed with news releases about earnings, dividends, new orders, stock splits, and favorable company developments. Even reports right at the time that the pool was operating were found beneficial to the price of the stock being manipulated. There were many ways to obtain publicity.

Tips and rumors were a profitable field of publicity. Such rumors, planted in receptive ears, found wide circulation. They flew from board room to board room, from trader to trader. Many eventually found their way over the ticker service and into financial news columns. Often there was no way to confirm or refute them. Why were they so often believed? Part of the answer, no doubt, was in the large extent of gullibility of the market in that period. On the other hand, many correct facts about corporate affairs first appeared as rumors and ''news leaks.'' Not many persons were able to distinguish between actual fact and fabricated rumor.

Many brokerage firms were not above the practice of sponsoring stocks in which they were interested as pool participants or managers. These subtle references were often used to encourage speculators to purchase the pool stock. The method was the market letter issued by the firm. Seemingly objective analyses of the particular stock were used to attract outsiders.

Paid publicity experts were also highly effective in establishing public interest in the stock. One of these gentlemen made no less than $500,000 in three years; his compensation came from cash payments, stock options, and calls. One of his most effective devices was a short radio program entitled ''The Friendly Economist.'' Presented each night at 10 o'clock, it reviewed the day's market and was judiciously interlaced with subtle comments about the profit possibilities of the pool stocks being sponsored. This particular expert was said to have conducted publicity for as many as 250 pools in three years, often as many as 30 at a time.[13] There were many instances of such paid publicity revealed by the Senate investigation of 1933–1934.

Much of the pool publicity eventually found its way into newspapers. Glowing stories about company prospects often found ready acceptance in financial columns. These stories contained not only statements of fact, but also forecasts of brilliant prospects. During the peak of activities in the Radio pool, a New York paper played up a story about how the company was planning to extend activity abroad, how its business was expanding, how many developments were pending, and so on. In another paper a subsidized columnist reported that Radio was a wonder stock and making history every day; he stated that those who had sold it at 100 were buying it back, and the latest rumor was that it was going to 200 very soon. It did go to 109 and then the pool unloaded. It fell back to 80 within a month. This particular

[13]*Ibid.*, p. 44.

writer was found to have been given a guaranteed account at a brokerage firm; his profit in eight months was $20,000.

"Ticker support" or "painting the tape" was another publicity device. This consisted of generating trades for the stock exchange tape and providing the news ticker a constant stream of publicity. On the stock ticker this was done by repeated transactions designed to attract attention; on the news ticker it was achieved by a succession of news stories about the corporation. The method was subtle but effective, because a great many traders then as now were "tape readers" and speculated almost entirely on the basis of the ticker tape action and news reports. Public traders watching for "chart signals" or news items as a basis for acting were obliged with both.

Artificial Market Activity

A final device of the pool was artificial market activity. This consisted of a heavy "churning" of the stock in the market; it was bought and sold by the pool in heavy volume. If the public participated, the operation was easy; if not, the pool members bought and sold to each other. This device is sometimes called a daisy chain.

Its purpose was obvious to all familiar with pool operations. The public must be attracted to the stock; few things attract speculators more quickly than a rising volume. The public's attitude became whetted in anticipation of "something big going on." It rushed in to buy before it was "too late." As the stock rose under increased activity, the public entered the market in ever-increasing numbers; this was exactly the purpose of the operation.

Artificial market activity was accomplished in two different ways: (1) through matched orders and (2) without matched orders. In the former method the pool placed identical orders with two different brokers; for example, one to buy 10,000 shares at 60 and one to sell 10,000 shares at 60. It was not a wash sale in the technical sense of the term because the 10,000 shares actually did change hands and two parties were involved. It had, however, the same net effect because both parties were members of the same pool. Such activities were hard to detect because orders were placed with different brokers and identification of the orders with pool memberships was carefully concealed. Matched orders were in violation of state law and the rules of the NYSE; hence, they were only infrequently used.

In some cases, a buyer agreed to hold securities for a time and then resell them to the original buyer at a preset price. This is a repurchase agreement sometimes called warehousing. Like daisy chains, warehousing is forbidden under Section 10 of the Securities Exchange Act of 1934.

The same effect as the matched order could be obtained without its actual use. The pool would buy and sell many thousands of shares in different orders of varying sizes. For a while it would sell on balance; then it would reverse its operations and buy on balance. Orders would vary in size from 5,000 to 25,000; they were placed with different brokers by different individuals. Such actions made detection difficult. As a matter of fact, there were no rules against such activities by the NYSE. It was considered a perfectly legitimate activity.

The immense amount of artificial market activity which often accompanied the activity of large pools was often difficult for those outside the market to believe. Perhaps the classic example of this was the Radio pool of 1929. This pool began on March 12. In five days it bought 988,400 and sold 1,176,300 shares; during that time the stock rose from 93 to 109.[14] At the end of these five days, the pool was short 187,900 shares; this proved highly profitable because the stock dropped to 80 by the end of the month. As already indicated, the operations of the pool were very successful; the syndicate netted $4,900,000.

During the peak activity of the Sinclair Consolidated Oil pool of 1928, it was operated through a purchase and a trading syndicate. On one day alone, November 5, the two syndicates sold 101,000 shares and purchased 62,000 shares.[15] Similar activity was found in the operations of many other pools of the late 1920s.

Steps in a Pool Operation

Now that all of the devices of pool activity have been examined, it would be well to trace through the steps of a typical pool operation as it was practiced in the heyday of such activities.

The first step was to select an auspicious time for the operation. This would be one in which the market was in a position to make a substantial advance. The company's position would be suitable for good publicity because of the fine earnings, attractive trade reports, increased dividends, or new developments.

The second was the accumulation of a supply of stock. As already indicated, this was obtained either by trading in the market or by options. Once this was assured, the pool was ready to begin extensive operations.

The next step was to create activity in the stock. This was done through artificial market activity; the pool was always careful to effect a change in beneficial ownership on each transaction. As this activity increased, the public became attracted to the stock.

The next operation was to create favorable interest in the stock through a steady flow of glowing publicity. Increased activity plus favorable reports made the stock a speculative favorite. Its price would then rise steadily, often precipitously.

The final step was distribution. The pool with its heavy accumulation of stock would seek to unload at advantageous prices. This required the highest skill that the manager could command. The problem was to distribute the

---

[14]*The Security Markets* (New York: Twentieth Century Fund, 1935), p. 479.
[15]*Stock Exchange Practices*, p. 65.

stock without breaking the market. Stock would be sold on days when the market was strong and purchased when it was weak. Finally, the manager would find a day on which the market was especially strong; all of the remaining stock would be dumped on the market; in addition, he would short sell the issue heavily. Not long afterward, the market, shorn of its artificial pool support, would collapse. The pool was a success for the participants; a disaster for the outsiders.

Present Regulations

Restrictive rules now make difficult, if not impossible, the pool operations of the 1920s. These rules have been formulated both by the exchanges and the SEC. The Securities Exchange Act of 1934 forbids manipulations in any form on national securities exchanges. Pool operations must be reported. No member of an exchange may participate in pool operations; he may not manage a pool; he cannot advance credit to one. Members may not execute orders for the purpose of creating an artificial appearance of activity in a security. Specialists may not execute discretionary orders. The market activities of corporate directors, executive officers, and principal stockholders are sharply curtailed. These and numerous other regulations are designed to curtail manipulative operations, which formed so much a part of the old market.

Additional Safeguards

In addition to the SEC and the exchanges, the NASD and various state corporation departments have been increasingly vigilant in their efforts to assure fair practices. Increasingly sophisticated electronic communications and surveillance devices have made their efforts increasingly effective.

Ever more sophisticated customers and attorneys are quicker to sue or demand arbitration if wrongs are suspected than they once were. The high cost of such proceedings and the frequency with which customers have tended to prevail have caused most firms to form internal compliance departments. Vigilant personnel in such departments, utilizing computerized control devices, have done much to preclude brokerage house personnel from conspiring with customers, customers from using the broker's facilities for illegal practices, or sales personnel from engaging in abusive practices. There are, of course, still unethical brokerage house personnel, lawyers, accountants, favored customers, and insiders who succeed in breaking or bending the rules, but the incidence of such practices has been sharply reduced, and the attitude toward unsavory practices is far less tolerant than it was in the bad old days.

17 Regulation, Self-regulation, and Compliance

This chapter deals with the legal and quasi-legal regulation of American securities markets. These markets are at the same time both the freest, in the sense of innovation, and yet the most heavily regulated in the world. It is in the domestic market that the really new security variations are most likely to be developed. The zero coupon bond, the floating rate note, the money market preferred, the listed option, and numerous others all came out of the investment banking and trading departments of U.S. firms. These innovations may have spread overseas virtually instantaneously, but revolutionary ideas in the European and Japanese markets are few and far between. Of course, there are cultural reasons for this; one does not expect conservative societies to produce or accept new ideas regularly. The "globalization" of the markets mentioned earlier (Chapters 9 and 14) indicates that new ideas are spreading rapidly, and the country of origin of a useful investment idea will become increasingly less relevant, in much the same manner that it no longer makes any real difference in what country the cure for a disease will ultimately be found.

The other aspect is that of regulation. Although the British markets are moving toward much the same kind of regulation that Americans have had in place for over 50 years, no other country has markets so closely regulated. There are doubtless those who would prefer much less regulation, but the American securities industry has learned to live with the regulators and, indeed, prosper in the regulatory environment.

In the United States there are three levels of regulation—federal, state, and by the industry itself. Most federal legislation is in one way or another derived from the two great national securities acts, those of 1933 and 1934. The Securities Act of 1933 has already been considered in Chapter 14. The emphasis in this chapter will be on the 1934 Act and the various self-regulatory features derived from it.

BACKGROUND TO FEDERAL REGULATION

Federal Regulation Before 1933

The U.S. government did little in the way of regulating the stock market prior to 1933. Security dealers, of course, could not use the mails to defraud. This section of the postal laws applied to all types of business. Little use seems to have been made of postal laws in regulating the stock exchange.

It might be said, therefore, that the stock exchanges before 1933 were regulated by their own rules and by state criminal and civil law. The statutes of New York and the court decisions of that state that related to the stock market were particularly important, because the two leading stock exchanges of the nation were located there. Control of such markets was not considered as being within the jurisdiction of the U.S. government.

Gold Speculation Act of 1864

A brief venture in federal regulation of speculation took place in 1864. At that time the nation was off the gold standard and the United States notes or "greenbacks" were fluctuating at various fractions of face value; as a result, gold was selling at substantial premiums in terms of paper currency. Much speculation took place in currency, and gold was bought and sold on the Exchange by brokers and dealers. Considerable bitterness developed in Congress over this situation; it was popularly believed that the federal currency was selling at a discount because of the speculation that was being carried on. The Gold Speculation Act of 1864 was passed, therefore, to forbid this practice; this promptly stopped speculation in the "Gold Room." To the amazement of Congress, however, the price of $100 in gold bullion in terms of paper currency immediately jumped from $200 to $300.[1] The law was repealed in 15 days; it was something less than a complete success. An investigation of the stock market that received wide attention at the time took place in 1909. Charles Evans Hughes, then Governor of New York and later Chief Justice of the United States, appointed a commission to investigate security and commodity speculation. The commission was headed by Horace White, a noted authority on money and banking. Its report dealt extensively with the operation of the New York Stock Exchange.[2] The commission, although critical of a number of practices of the Exchange, believed that correction could be attained better by self-regulation than by any other method. It did not favor incorporation of the Exchange as a satisfactory solution of its criticisms. There was no suggestion in the report that federal

[1]W. C. Antwerp, *The Stock Exchange from Within* (Garden City, NY: Doubleday, 1914), p. 251.
[2]New York State, *Report of Governor Hughes' Committee on Speculation in Securities and Commodities*, June 7, 1909.

control was either desirable or necessary. No investigation of equal importance by a public body was made of the stock market for another 20 years.

The Pujo Money Trust Inquiry of 1912

Although the 62d Congress authorized a committee to investigate Wall Street, the investigation centered largely on the concentration of economic control by a system of interlocking directorates of banks and corporations. Any investigation of the stock exchanges that may have been made received little or no public attention.

The Market Decline of 1929–1933

Two events of great importance serve as a background for the Securities Exchange Act of 1934. The first was the public clamor which developed from the precipitous drop in stock prices from 1929 to 1933. In that period, declines in industrial stock prices of 89% were registered by the Dow Jones average and 87% by that of *The New York Times*. The sharp declines, with resultant losses to thousands of small speculators and investors, brought about a great outcry for investigation and control of the securities markets. The pleas fell upon receptive political ears. Such a program of investigation and control would have been "good politics" in 1933 without regard to its economic merits.

The Senate Investigation of 1933–1934

During the 72d and 73d sessions of Congress, the Senate Committee on Banking and Currency made a very thorough investigation of manipulation in the securities markets, as already indicated in Chapter 5. Out of this investigation came the Securities Exchange Act of 1934.

SECURITIES EXCHANGE ACT OF 1934

Purposes and Objectives

The Securities Exchange Act was passed for the broad purposes of regulating the securities exchanges and the over-the-counter market and preventing inequitable and unfair practices in such markets.[3] Specifically, it may be said to have these objectives: (1) to set up machinery to regulate these markets; (2) to limit the amount of speculative credit; (3) to regulate unfair practices of dealers and brokers in both the organized and unorganized securities markets; and (4) to ensure that the general public receives adequate information

[3]Sec. 2.

about securities traded in such markets and that so-called insiders, that is, directors, officers, and large stockholders, do not benefit from an unfair use of such information. It was hoped that the attainment of these objectives would enable the markets to perform their expected functions more satisfactorily.

The Act created a new federal agency, the Securities and Exchange Commission. The SEC has five members, no more than three from the same political party. Appointed by the President and confirmed by the Senate, commission members serve 5-year terms. The SEC was given wide-ranging powers, as was typical of the New Deal bureaucracies set up by the Roosevelt administration. The first chairman was Joseph P. Kennedy, who besides being a loyal Democrat and supporter of the President had also been an extremely successful Wall Street "operator" in the great bull market whose collapse precipitated the Act. In fact, it is probable that he had employed many of the devices the Act was designed to counter, but, of course, there had been no federal law restricting those practices in the 1920s when he was active in the market. Mr. Kennedy served in 1934 and 1935, and was replaced by another New Deal stalwart, James M. Landis. The latter was succeeded in 1937 by William O. Douglas, later to become a Supreme Court Justice.

The SEC has a number of departments and divisions. Many of these deal with statistics, and the SEC regularly publishes comprehensive data on securities trading in the United States. The division with which most of the public is familiar is the Enforcement Division, as this is the arm of the SEC that pursues those accused of violating the Act.

In order to provide close surveillance of securities activities, the SEC has set up regional offices. A major problem which the SEC has had for many years, and indeed one likely to continue without much relief, has been the loss of talented personnel to private industry. There are great disparities between salaries paid by the Commission and those paid by private industry, particularly Wall Street. Wall Street financial and law firms are heavily populated with persons who got their start at the SEC. Congress must ultimately address this problem, as further losses of talented staffers will greatly hinder the Commission's efforts. Although long a problem, as is true for government service in general, this turnover is crippling to an agency trying to stay abreast of the rapidly changing financial services industry.

Exempted Securities

A number of securities were exempted from most provisions of the Act. They are U.S. government and agency obligations, municipal securities, those of intrastate character, and other securities that the SEC may deem necessary to exempt. An important facet of the law, however, is that *all* securities are subject to the antifraud provisions of the Act, so that misrepresentation of the features of a government or municipal bond by a salesperson is a violation of the law, not merely a violation of exchange rules.

Unregistered Exchanges

The SEC is permitted to exempt some organized exchanges from registration if, in its view, the public interest is thereby served. This exemption was extended to a few small exchanges whose trading volume was not considered enough to warrant the protection of the Act. These exchanges were located in Colorado Springs, Honolulu, Richmond, and Wheeling. All are either defunct or nearly so, and no significant trading occurs on any. It is thus fair to say that all exchange trading in the United States takes place on an exchange registered with the SEC.

Registered Exchanges

Any exchange that operates in interstate or foreign commerce or through the mails must register with the SEC. Under the procedure of registration, an exchange must file a registration statement as well as data on its organization, constitution, bylaws, rules of procedure, and membership. Registration is not granted unless that exchange has adequate rules for disciplining its members. Under the Act, exchanges are permitted to make and enforce their own rules so long as such are not inconsistent with the law. Exchanges currently registered with the SEC are those in Cincinnati, Boston, San Francisco and Los Angeles (Pacific Stock Exchange), Chicago (Midwest Stock Exchange), Philadelphia, and the two New York City exchanges, the NYSE and the Amex. In addition, the CBOE and the Instinet System are registered. It is worthwhile to note that futures exchanges are not registered with the SEC, although several trade equity index contracts are traded on them which are closely linked with stock exchange share trading.

A registered exchange pays an annual registration fee to the SEC. This fee (currently .003 of 1% of the trade value—3 cents per $1,000) is levied on the sell side of all equity transactions. The fee is also charged when a listed stock is traded OTC in the "third market." The fee is passed along to the seller of the shares and is subtracted from the sale proceeds.

Margin Requirements

The power to determine minimum margin requirements is given to the Board of Governors of the Federal Reserve System under sections 7 and 8 of the Act. The Board periodically changes the initial margin requirement according to its view of trading activity, raising it to cool speculation and lowering it to encourage equity investment. The application of these rules is discussed in Chapter 13. Regulation T regulates the extension of credit by broker/dealers, Reg U regulates the same activity by banks, and Reg G covers all other lenders, primarily insurance companies and credit unions. The regulations do not apply to securities exempted from the Act, such as government or municipal bonds, but exchanges and the NASD have set minimum maintenance margins for these.

Manipulation

A very important part of the Act deals with manipulation, which Congress found to be a real evil in the markets prior to the passage of the Act.[4] The prohibition against manipulation applies not only to brokers and dealers, but to any person who uses the mails or the facilities of any national securities exchange.

Certain types of manipulation are definitely barred: (1) wash sales; (2) matched orders; (3) artificial market activity; (4) circulation of manipulative information for a remuneration; and (5) making false and misleading statements about securities.

In addition, the Act lists certain practices that, although not forbidden, are brought under control by the Act. They include (1) pegging or price stabilization; (2) puts, calls, spreads, and straddles; (3) short sales; and (4) stop orders. In addition, the SEC is given power to make rules about any other manipulative or deceptive device in the public interest.

In summary, therefore, the Act defines and prohibits certain practices; it provides regulation for others, which are specifically identified; finally, it gives the SEC power to make other regulations in the public interest.

Segregation

A member of an exchange may operate in a transaction in either one of two capacities: as a broker or as a dealer. In the former he acts as an agent for a principal; in the latter he acts on his own behalf and for his own risk. On no occasion may a member act in both capacities in the same transaction; this has been a rule of law and the exchanges for years. Segregation would confine each member in all transactions made to one or the other of the two activities; one cannot engage alternately in one and then the other.

The Act does not require segregation nor does it demand that the SEC effect segregation. The SEC may make such rules as it believes in the public interest. For example, it may regulate or prohibit floor trading; it may make rules to prevent excessive trading by members of an exchange either on or off the floor. In addition, it may require the registration of odd-lot dealers and specialists and make rules to govern their activities. The section that deals with specialists is specific in stating a number of regulations about these members: (1) they should restrict activities to making a fair and orderly market; (2) they must disclose their books only under certain conditions; (3) they may accept only limited price and market orders when acting as brokers.

The Commission was also charged with the responsibility of studying the feasibility and advisability of complete segregation of the functions of dealer and broker. This report was made and duly presented to Congress. The SEC has not seen fit to take any segregation measures.

[4]Secs. 9 and 10.

Registration

No member of a registered exchange may effect a transaction on such an exchange except in registered securities; the only exceptions are exempt securities and those given unlisted trading privileges.

To register a security on a national securities exchange, the issuing company must file an extensive application with the exchange and with the SEC. This application contains a great amount of information about the company and its financial affairs. These are the principal items required.

1 Organization, financial structure, and nature of the business.
2 Terms, position, rights, and privileges of the different classes of securities outstanding.
3 The terms on which their securities are to be, and during the preceding three years have been, offered to the public or otherwise.
4 The directors, officers, and underwriters, and each security holder of the issuer; their remuneration and their interests in the securities of, and their material contracts with, the issuer.
5 Remuneration to other than directors and officers exceeding $20,000 per year.
6 Bonus and profit-sharing arrangements.
7 Management and service contracts.
8 Options existing or to be created in respect of their securities.
9 Balance sheets for not more than three preceding fiscal years, certified, if required by the rules of the Commission, by independent public accountants.
10 Profit and loss statements for not more than the three preceding fiscal years, certified, if required by the rules of the Commission, by independent public accountants.
11 Any further financial statements required by the Commission.
12 Copies of articles of incorporation, bylaws, trust indentures, underwriting agreements, and so on, as the Commission may require.

Issuers of registered securities must file periodic reports each year to keep the information in the registration statements reasonably up to date. Of particular interest to investors is the requirement about annual financial statements. The periodic reports, as well as the original registration statements submitted by issuers, are available for public inspection at the offices of the Commission and the regional offices and are widely used by financial services, publishers of securities manuals, and advisory services; thus their information is widely disseminated.

"Insider" Holdings of Stock

An important section of the Act pertains to the reporting of holdings in equity securities by so-called insiders. An insider is a director, executive officer, or a stockholder who owns 10% or more of any class of stock. The names of these parties are filed with the Commission at the time of registration, as already noted. In addition, anyone who attains this status after registration of the security must file his holdings of stock within 10 days. If there is any change in such ownership in a given month, the insider must file a report within 10 days after the close of the calendar month; this report indicates this ownership at the close of the month and such changes as have occurred during the month.

The purpose of this regulation is to enable the SEC and stockholders of the company to watch the actions of such holders, who may speculate in their own stocks to make profits on the basis of insider information. Such information is given out through public releases of the SEC.

Short-Term Profits of Insiders

A further provision of the Act limits the right of insiders to speculate in the stock of their own companies. Any profit from the purchase or sale of the stock realized within a period of six months can be recaptured for the company. A suit to recover this profit may be brought either by the issuing corporation or by a stockholder on behalf of the company.

The purpose of this provision is to prevent such individuals from speculating in the stocks of their companies on the basis of an unfair use of confidential information. It does not, however, prevent speculation for a period longer than six months. For example, a top executive in an important automobile company in 1935 purchased 6,000 shares of his company's stock at 44 and sold it a year later at 77; he thus realized a gross profit of about $200,000.

Some criticism is made of this section of the Act in that it may discourage the ownership of stocks by the top management. It is possible that some evasion of the Act is possible in that there would be nothing to prevent an executive of one steel company, who felt optimistic about the prospects of the entire steel industry, from buying the stock of another steel company. This is true, of course, but the profit opportunities are not so certain and the abuses of confidential information are not so flagrant as they formerly were. Certainly, the provision is an advance in business ethics over conditions prevailing before World War I, when it was a common practice of corporate boards of directors to declare or pass dividends at board meetings and then run to the nearest telephone to order brokers to buy or sell the stock before the information was released to the general public.

In probably its best known case, *SEC* v. *Texas Gulf Sulfur* (1965–1966), the SEC went to court to force the repayment of insider profits not only by those within the company but also by some who had heard the information from insiders and bought the stock ahead of the public release of information about a huge ore find in the company's Kidd Creek, Ontario, property. The SEC had thus extended the doctrine to the "tippee" as well as the "tipper." Further extensions of this policy have not been so successful for the SEC.

In the *Chiarella* case, the SEC attempted to prosecute some employees of a financial printing concern who were able to piece together inside information from take-over prospectuses. The court, however, held that the 1934 Act did not cover such circumstances.

In another case the Commission prosecuted Raymond Dirks, a securities analyst who uncovered a massive fraud in the accounting of the Equity Funding Corporation, a fast-growing insurer. Dirks claimed that he simply did what any good analyst is paid to do; that is, uncover the truth and tell his customers. The SEC held that by telling his customers first, he was using inside information. After extended court appeals Dirks finally prevailed, and the SEC has since been more cautious in trying to stretch the meaning of "insider."

Nevertheless, there are still cases of apparently clear violations of the Act. Several major ones surfaced in 1986 when the SEC prosecuted a managing director of the investment banking firm of Drexel Burnham for trading on the basis of information received in confidence from his investment banking clients. Also involved in similar situations were an attorney for a New York law firm and two arbitrage traders. Given the amount of money at stake and human nature, it seems likely that others will sooner or later fall victim to the temptation, and that the SEC will be prosecuting insider trading violations for some time to come.

Short Selling by Insiders

A provision similar to that on short-term profits is the one on short selling by insiders. These individuals may not sell a stock of the issuer (1) that they do not own or (2) if owning the security they do not deliver it against such a sale within 20 days thereafter, or do not deposit it in the mails within five days. It will be seen that this provision covers not only the speculative short sale in which the seller must borrow the stocks; it also covers the sale "against the box" in which the seller owns the stock but is making a short sale as a hedge against a drop in the price of securities owned.

The purpose of this section is also to prevent the insider from taking an unfair advantage of confidential information. The practice at one time was very common, particularly during periods of severe market declines.

Proxy Regulations

The Act also provides that the SEC shall make regulations about the issue of proxies by registered issuers. When solicitations for proxies, consents, or other authorizations from holders of registered securities are made, the security holder must be supplied with a reasonable amount of information so that he may make an informed judgment on the merits of the proposal when he votes. The information must be complete and accurate. A copy of the proxy, consent, and authorization must be filed with the Commission for review before solicitation is possible.

Termination of Registration

The SEC is given the power to deny registration to a security, to suspend the effective date, to suspend registration, or to withdraw it from registration if it finds that the issuer has failed to comply with the Act or any regulations made under it. The Commission would prefer that the exchange take this action itself, but it holds this weapon in reserve in case action is not taken to protect the interests of the public. The power has been used sparingly.

Registration and Listing

Now that the chief aspects of registration under the Act have been stated, it may be well to make some comparisons between registration and listing. It may be supposed that listing and registration represent a duplication of the activities of the work of the stock list department and the SEC. In some cases this is true, since much of the information required at the time of listing is also required at registration and, as a matter of fact, the same information is used for both operations.

The listing standards of an exchange, such as the New York Stock Exchange, however, still play an important part in determining the desirability of securities for listing. The Exchange must decide whether there is a listed market for a given stock. It is free to make, and has initiated, a number of excellent listing policies in recent years, such as those on depreciation, accounting standards, and voting rights of stock. Although listing standards are not so vital to public protection as they once were because of registration requirements, they still have a real function in protecting the public and making a free market. This is particularly true when additional shares of a registered issue are sold. No new registration statements are required, but new listing information must be filed and thus becomes available.

Investors in listed securities have more information about these issues than ever before. Such a condition is highly desirable; it is up to the public to use the information wisely. Neither the exchanges nor the SEC can or does guarantee any security. The buyer must take the responsibility for purchase and ownership. The public would seem to have been given reasonable protection.

Over-the-Counter Markets

The Act as originally passed in 1934 did not make specific regulations for the OTC market; it merely gave the SEC authority to make such rules and regulations as it saw fit. In 1936 the Act was amended to provide for registration of all brokers and dealers dealing in corporate securities in this market. In 1938 the Act was further amended by the addition of Section 15A, usually called the Maloney Act. It provided for the formation of a self-regulatory body to govern the OTC market with powers similar to those the exchanges were allowed in the listed markets. To date, only one such organization, the NASD, has been organized under provisions of this act. The creation of the Municipal Securities Rule Making Board in 1975 was accomplished under separate legislation.

Enforcement of the Act

Enforcement of the Exchange Act and its rules is obtainable in a number of ways. Criminal penalties include fines up to $10,000 and imprisonment up to two years for individuals and fines up to $500,000 for exchanges.

Civil suits by injured parties are permitted under the Act; these suits may be brought only in federal courts. Thus, injured individuals become part of the enforcement machinery of the law.

The Commission itself has many actions which it may take to enforce the Act and the rules under it. This is a list of methods available:

1 Withdrawal or suspension of an exchange from registration.
2 Expulsion or suspension of a member or officer of an exchange, or an allied member.
3 Suspension of trading in a particular security.
4 Request exchanges to make changes in organization or to prescribe rules for trading. In the event an exchange refuses, the SEC has broad powers to make such changes and rules in its own right.
5 Require exchanges and their members to keep such books and records as may be necessary; to examine such books and records; and to require reports when necessary.
6 Make investigations and conduct hearings to assist in the enforcement of the Act.
7 Prevent violations of the Act by injunctions.
8 Compel compliance with the Act by writs of mandamus.

In summary, the Act permits an extensive amount of self-regulation in securities markets; the markets and exchanges may make their own rules and regulations so long as they are not inconsistent with the Act and the regulations of the SEC. In the last analysis, the SEC possesses the well-known "iron hand within the velvet glove" which it can use as a last resort.

It is worth noting that civil injunctions and criminal prosecutions may be used against anyone who engages in securities transactions, whether or not the person is in the securities business. Administrative measures by the SEC, however, may be directed only against exchanges, registered associations, and registered brokers and dealers.

INVESTOR RESPONSIBILITY

In a statement of its work, the SEC points to the need for investor responsibility in the stock market. The comment reads: "It should be understood that the securities laws were designed to facilitate informed investment analyses and prudent and discriminating investment decisions *by the investing public,* and that it is the investor and *not* the Commission who must make the ultimate judgment of the worth of securities offered for sale.''[5]

THE SECURITIES INVESTORS PROTECTION ACT OF 1970

Although separate from the 1934 Act, the Securities Investors Protection Act of 1970 is in keeping with customer protection features of Section 15 of that Act. Just as bank failures in the Depression sparked the legislation that led to the FDIC and the FSLIC, brokerage firm bankruptcies (and near misses) in the 1969–1971 period caught Congress's attention. In theory, strict adherence to the net capital rules and other safety features embodied in the 1934 Act should have resulted in all customer claims being met, even if a firm went under. Reality, however, was quite different. Chaotic market conditions and even more chaotic record keeping at some firms make it virtually impossible to compute accurately a net capital position. Fidelity bonds offered protection against dishonesty, but, unfortunately, little was offered as protection against incompetence.

Earlier Protective Measures

If an NYSE member firm was involved in serious financial difficulty, it was usually considered a problem for the exchange community itself to solve. Between 1963 and 1974, the NYSE directly intervened into the affairs of roughly 200 member organizations. In some cases, the result was transferring customer accounts and positions to stronger members and then liquidating the failing member. In other cases, mergers with healthier firms were consummated.

In 1963 the Exchange assisted in the liquidation of Ira Haupt and Company, a substantial and respected member firm that was brought down largely because of a huge default on commodity contracts held by a customer, later convicted of various fraudulent acts involving the soybean oil market. The NYSE provided $9 million of customer assistance funds to oversee the liquidation of the firm and successful transfer of most customer accounts.

The volume generated by the 1960s bull market swamped the operational capacity of a number of members and led them to the brink of disaster. In all, about $61 million was expended from the NYSE Special Trust Fund between 1968 and 1980 to complete the liquidation or merger of firms suffering financial and operational problems. Among the once large and well-known firms that disappeared through one of these methods were DuPont, Glore Forgan, Walston and Company, Dempsey-Tegeler and Company, and Hayden Stone and Company. These firms were nationally known and some had a coast-to-coast branch office network. The Exchange's action caused min-

---

[5]*The Work of the Securities and Exchange Commission,* April 1, 1958, p. v.

imal customer loss and inconvenience considering the size of the funds involved. It also virtually depleted the NYSE Special Trust Fund set up for this purpose. Clearly, another major firm collapse would have been the last straw for many investors, raising the specter of a "run" on the remaining firms and the complete demoralization of the markets.

Congress, acting with exceptional speed, passed the Securities Investors Protection Act in 1970. Just at that time another major member firm was undergoing difficulties. In early 1971 the large retail partnership of Goodbody and Company teetered on the brink of insolvency. Goodbody was widely known, having over 90 branch offices. Fearing the crisis of confidence already noted, the NYSE approached Merrill Lynch to urge an acquisition of Goodbody. Certainly, Merrill Lynch was the only firm large enough and strong enough to acquire Goodbody. Merrill Lynch reluctantly agreed to the takeover, but demanded a stiff price. Merrill Lynch was to be compensated for all losses suffered up to $15 million in the acquisition. As it turned out, the losses ran far greater than those and hurt Merrill Lynch's earnings for several quarters. Although disaster was averted, it became clear that if ever another major NYSE member collapsed, the new Securities Investors Protection Corporation would be involved.

SECURITIES INVESTORS PROTECTION CORPORATION

As a result of the act the Securities Investors Protection Corporation (SIPC) was formed in December 1970. It is government-sponsored, but is funded purely by the securities industry. Under provisions of the act all members of national securities exchanges are required to be members as well as most NASD members. If an NASD member firm deals exclusively in mutual funds and variable annuities, membership is not mandatory because these firms do not hold customer funds or securities, being legally required to transmit them to the fund sponsor or insurance company promptly. Other firms may join if they wish.

Initially, members were assessed a fee based on their gross securities related business. The fund has now grown to over $300 million from both member assessments and earnings on the fund. For a while in the early 1980s the fund had grown to a size considered adequate, and assessments were replaced with a flat $25 annual fee. Troublesome conditions, including the failure of some unregulated government securities firms, led to the return of the annual assessment in order to build a more secure fund.

The SIPC coverage originally protected customer accounts up to a maximum of $50,000 for both cash and securities, but only $20,000 of that could be for cash. If the assets of a failed member are insufficient to satisfy customer claims, SIPC's trust fund is employed. Once all of a customer's "specifically identifiable property" (fully registered or segregated street name stock, for the most part) has been returned, if the customer still has claims, the SIPC coverage is then applicable. If the customer has claims beyond SIPC's coverage, the customer becomes a general creditor of the failed broker. The probability of receiving further satisfaction from this point seems small.

The SIPC coverage has been increased twice, first to $100,000 cash and securities with a $40,000 maximum cash coverage and finally in 1980 to its current level of $500,000 cash and securities with a $100,000 cash maximum. Through 1980 only one NYSE member firm, Weiss Securities, was liquidated by a SIPC-appointed trustee. The firm was medium sized and SIPC trustees received $8.1 million in advances from the SIPC fund. It was the largest liquidation undertaken by the corporation, and the general Wall Street consensus is that it was not well done. Unfortunately, the problem coincided with a severe market drop that aggravated already serious problems. Also, the corporation was new and relatively inexperienced, although it had successfully liquidated a number of small over-the-counter firms previously. In 1981 SIPC commenced liquidation of John Muir and Company, only the second NYSE member to be thus affected. By mid-1984 SIPC had liquidated 168 firms.

A major question is still to be asked. No one knows for sure how SIPC would handle the failure of a major firm. A former SEC commissioner, Bevis Longstreth, pointed out in an article that the corporation's staff numbered only 36 in 1984, one-hundredth the size of the Federal Deposit Insurance Corporation (FDIC), its most closely comparable organization.[6] Furthermore, trading volume, securities values, and numbers of shareholders have increased significantly since its founding. For example, the top 10 retail brokerage firms each carry more than 250,000 accounts. The largest failure ever handled by SIPC involved fewer than 33,000 accounts.

Although the SIPC fund has grown to over $300 million and emergency borrowing lines to the Federal Reserve total $1 billion, one can hardly be sanguine about the prospect of a major firm failure. It is to be hoped that increased scrutiny by the SEC and the self-regulatory bodies will prevent a repetition of the worst aspects of the 1969–1970 period and make such problems less likely. The diversification of brokerage firms into many different financial areas also lends an element of stability, as these firms are no longer so heavily dependent for earnings on the vagaries of share prices. Most major brokers are now involved in such areas as insurance, real estate, and even banking, in a limited sense. Also, a number of brokers have taken the precaution to obtain additional coverage from commercial insurers, so that many advertise insurance up to $2.5 million.

The jury is still out. In view of the bail-outs of Lockheed, Chrysler, and more recently the Continental Illinois Bank, there is a strong feeling that the federal government has established a precedent that "the big shall not fail." The securities industry is ill-advised to rest on that assumption. The major

[6]Bevis Longstreth, *Why SIPC Can't Support a Big Failure*, The New York Times, August 26, 1984, Business Section, p. 2.

task ahead is to strengthen SIPC, give it inspection powers similar to those of the FDIC, and most of all, make certain brokers are closely monitored to stay in compliance with rules and regulations guaranteeing their financial health.

State Regulation

In addition to federal law, the securities industry must be in compliance with the laws of the various states. Although there are a number of similarities in state law, each state has its own particular interpretations. Filing a registration statement with the SEC covers only federal requirements. In order to sell securities legally in any of the 50 states, securities must in addition be registered in those states. Fortunately, many states allow "registration by coordination," which permits the issuer to qualify an offering by submitting a copy of the prospectus sent to the SEC to the state securities commissioner. Other states, however, have more restrictive laws, and it is not unusual to find that certain securities offered by national syndicates of investment bankers cannot be legally sold in some states.

States also require sales personnel to be registered in order to conduct any business, even for "unsolicited" orders. At one time, this meant that a registered representative might have to sit for several different state securities examinations even though the NYSE and NASD exams had already been successfully completed. A uniform state licensing exam now prevails, so that a single test satisfies all state testing requirements. The registered representative as well as the employer must still register in any state where they intend to do business.

State securities regulations and laws are often referred to as "blue sky" laws, and "blue skying" an issue means the underwriters are filing a state registration form. Where the term originated no one seems to know for sure. It's a bit like the origin of such terms as bull, bear, and over-the-counter. Many likely explanations are offered, but none seems to be universally accepted. In the case of "blue sky," the most widely accepted version is that it stems from a Kansas court ruling that an investor who bought what later turned out to be worthless securities had been sold nothing more than a patch of blue sky.

Self-Regulation

As Congress intended, the domestic securities markets are largely self-regulating. This means that, within the limits defined by various federal and state statutes, the participants in the markets draw up their own rules for fair and ethical conduct in much the same manner that professional organizations like medical societies and bar associations do. This regulation is far more extensive than prevails in either the banking or insurance industries, or in the sale of real estate—to give the nearest analogies.

The typical investor has little direct contact with securities law. Despite the fact that lawyers specializing in securities-related cases never seem to lack for work, most investors pursue grievances, real or imagined, through the industry's self-regulatory mechanism. By and large, member firms go to considerable expense to implement compliance policies whereby the firm's internal rules normally exceed the minimum level stipulated by federal law or by the SROs (self-regulatory organizations) to which they belong.

Complaints only rarely reach the SEC for action, despite the fact that customers will often write to the Commission for redress. Normally, the SEC will forward the complaint to either the broker or the SRO which has jurisdiction in the matter. The SEC itself becomes involved only in major cases where a violation of a federal statute is alleged, particularly in cases involving fraud, insider trading, take-over attempts, and the sale of unregistered securities.

The large national brokerage firms are members of the New York Stock Exchange, the National Association of Securities Dealers, the American and various regional stock exchanges, and also a number of futures exchanges like the Chicago Board of Trade. Additionally, they are subject to the rules of the Municipal Securities Rule Making Board and the Commodities Futures Trading Commission. Thus, depending on what is alleged by the complainant, any of these self-regulatory bodies might be involved in the investigation. Each of them has the authority to censure, fine, suspend, or expel a member organization or one of its employees. Each also has a method of settling disputes internally, that is, without going into litigation, although the use of this procedure (arbitration; see the discussion later in this chapter) is voluntary for the customer.

Registration of Personnel

The most basic self-regulatory step in the industry is barring unqualified people from entering it. All sales personnel, whether called account executives, investment brokers, financial consultants, or whatever, must be registered with the appropriate bodies. In addition, they must also be registered in any state where they handle business.

To be registered one must first be sponsored by a member organization. Thus one cannot become a registered representative independent of a member firm responsible for one's activities and adherence to industry standards. To start this process the applicant submits a U-4 form on which all employment and periods of unemployment for the past 10 years are recounted. Also required on this application is a complete accounting for all formal education from high school onward, as well as all arrests or involvement in major litigation. The applicant is also fingerprinted and made subject to a fidelity-bonding investigation.

Once this process is complete, the would-be salesperson starts a minimum 4-month training period leading to the basic industry qualifier, the Series 7 examination. There are several other exam series covering specific products and various supervisory responsibilities.

The Series 7 exam is a 6-hour, 250-question multiple choice test, jointly administered by the NYSE and the NASD. Candidates must score 70% or better to pass. The test, given once monthly, is defined as a "minimum competency" examination, meaning that the successful candidate has demonstrated at least the most basic level of knowledge necessary to practice the trade. Most candidates find the exam difficult, and the failure rate tends to hover around the 30% mark of all candidates on any given test, although the rate has occasionally reached 40%.

Needless to say, filing a job history and passing an examination are no guarantees that the candidate will become an ethical and competent registered representative. They do, however, eliminate those who cannot measure up to at least the industry's minimum standards. Certainly these standards, basic as they may be, are far higher than those required for analogous functions in banking, insurance, or real estate.

In addition, a securities broker may have to take several other exams depending on the services he or she intends to provide. Passing the Series 7 hurdle satisfies only the various securities exchanges and the NASD, but does not satisfy the individual states wherein the broker might do business.

There are also separate tests to qualify a registered representative for commodity futures trading and various supervisory functions. Among the latter are branch office manager, general securities principal, options principal, and municipal securities principal. In 1986 separate exams for qualification to trade interest rate options and foreign currency options were eliminated and questions covering these areas were blended into the Series 7 exam.

Registered representatives may dispense investment advice in accordance with their firms' standards and industry norms. In general, most firms prohibit the solicitation of transactions in securities not recommended or approved by their research departments. Occasionally, exceptions may be made at some firms for experienced brokers with a sophisticated clientele, especially with shares of companies too small for a research analyst to follow closely. In these situations, however, the broker is operating at his or her own risk, and if the investment turns sour, the broker will have to answer to the customer without the firm's backing. As major brokerage firms move more and more into the realm of prepackaged goods (mutual funds, unit trusts, tax partnerships, etc.), there will be less and less incentive for brokers to try to be their own securities analysts. Ultimately, of course, brokers are salespersons and are paid to move merchandise, not to pontificate on the direction of the market or individual stocks.

While brokers may give investment advice, they may not call themselves "investment advisors" unless they are registered with that title under the provisions of the Investment Advisors Act of 1940. A broker acting in his or her customary fashion is specifically exempted from the Act. On the other hand, some brokerage firms do register under the act so that they may directly handle customer investments on an advisory, usually "discretionary," basis. Among such firms are David J. Greene and Company, J. and W. Seligman and Company, and Sanford C. Bernstein and Company. Large national brokers like Merrill Lynch have set up an investment management subsidiary not directly affiliated with the broker/dealer entity.

In fact, one can become a registered investment advisor simply by paying a fee and filing the appropriate documents with the SEC. There are no testing requirements or other employment qualifications at the national level, although some states require a simple exam. Investment experience, knowledge, or expertise do not have to be evidenced, as even a casual scan of published market letters by such writers will quickly reveal.

The typical stockbroker is essentially an interpreter of research reports written by his or her firm's analysts, and acts as an information conduit to his or her customer. Because the broker is clearly a salesperson, not an analyst, industry rules place upon him or her the responsibility for making "suitable" recommendations to customers. The concept of suitability is embodied in Rule 405 of the NYSE, the "know your customer" rule.

Rule 405. Every member organization is required through a general partner, a principal executive officer or a person or persons designated under the provisions of Rule 342(b)(1) [¶2342] to

(1) Use due diligence to learn the essential facts relative to every customer, every order, every cash or margin account accepted or carried by such organization and every person holding power of attorney over any account accepted or carried by such organization.

Supervision of Accounts

(2) Supervise diligently all accounts handled by registered representatives of the organization.

Approval of Accounts

(3) Specifically approve the opening of an account prior to or promptly after the completion of any transaction for the account of or with a customer, provided, however, that in the case of branch offices, the opening of an account for a customer may be approved by the manager of such branch office but the action of such branch office manager shall within a reasonable time be approved by a general partner, a principal of Rule 342(b)(1) [¶2342]. The member, general partner, officer or designated person approving the opening of the account shall, prior to giving his approval, be personally informed as to the essential facts relative to the customer and to the nature of the proposed account and shall indicate his approval in writing on a document which is a part of the permanent records of his office or organization.

Thus, merely saying that one's firm recommends a particular security is not nearly enough. An analyst might develop a recommendation on a company with high growth potential and commensurately high risk. Paying no dividends but with the potential to triple in price in 2 to 3 years, it might well be an ideal choice for the high tax bracket, "businessperson's risk" investor. It would also be totally unsuitable for the modest investor seeking preservation of capital and income. Should an investor lose money on an unsuitable recommendation, the broker would have a difficult defense. Most courts have clearly held that the broker has a fiduciary relationship of trust with the inexperienced investor.

Brokerage office managers must be alert to abuses of this relationship. Among the practices barred by industry rules are:

"Blanket recommendations": broad-scale solicitations to purchase an issue without regard to suitability

"Churning": recommending excessive transactions for customer in order to generate high commissions

"Boiler-room sales": use of high-pressure telephone sales techniques

Unauthorized discretion: trades entered in the customer's account without first adequate receipt of the customer's written or verbal approval, as the situation requires.

A registered representative found in violation of industry rules governing these and similar unethical practices is subject to discipline which takes such forms as censure, fines, and/or suspension or revocation of licenses.

The growth of the discount brokerage business has created new problems and reduced some existing ones. Essentially these "no-frills" firms offer execution and safe-keeping services but little else. With most discount firms, no investment advice of any kind is provided, although some will pass along the familiar Standard & Poor's research sheets readily available through any broker. A discount brokerage registered representative is not legally distinguishable from one doing business for a full-service firm because both have passed the same examination. They are, however, order takers rather than solicitors and have a function more nearly clerical than advisory; thus they are relatively immune from complaints involving suitability or churning. On the other hand, they must confront a number of problems which are identical to those faced by full-service brokers.

Primary among such problems are order entry and execution. Even though the discount broker's role may seem comparatively simple, even mechanical, it banks heavily on the assumption that the customer knows what he or she is doing—more than occasionally a dubious proposition. Indeed, it is a rare investor who knows (or cares) about the nuances of such industry terms as the stop-limit order, fill-or-kill execution, or ex-dividend procedure. As long as the investor stays with straight market or limit orders, few problems should arise. A new element enters when a customer asks to execute such exotic items as option spreads or "scale" orders.

Not only may the representative be unfamiliar with relatively unusual orders, but the customer may be only a disembodied voice at the other end of the phone line. Does the customer understand the risks? What does the customer do, and who advises the customer, if the order is only partially filled? Are the implications of margin rules understood?

Certainly some discount representatives could give sound answers to such problems, but given the bare-bones training usually provided by discounters, there is little wonder that some investors feel that what has been gained in commission savings has been lost through unsatisfactory executions.

If an error occurs because a representative accepted an invalid order or entered a valid one improperly, the discount broker's problem is no different from that of a full-service broker in the same circumstances. If, on the other hand, the error occurs because the customer did not understand the risks involved—for example, short selling—what share of the blame belongs to the representative for failing to know the customer? In the discount context the answer is not so clear as it would be with the full-service broker. In any event, it appears that conventional compliance assumptions may have to be modified when dealing with discount firms and their customers.

If a customer feels aggrieved and receives no satisfaction from his or her representative, the next logical step is to contact the branch office manager. Generally this course of action is likewise unrewarding because the firm can be expected to back its broker unless a clear violation of firm policies or industry rules is apparent. Naturally, new investors are sometimes distressed for reasons the broker cannot control, namely the course of the market. Feeling aggrieved is not the same as being correct. However, managers may often be helpful in ironing out minor but irritating problems often caused by the broker's lack of concern for, or knowledge of, certain operational problems. As often noted, brokers are salespeople and sometimes "above" mundane problems such as why a customer's dividend check was not received, or why the account was charged interest at a certain rate. All too often the broker tends to shrug off this type of complaint by blaming operations personnel, often in unflattering terms. Managers are usually sensitive to customer frustration and can quickly resolve many minor problems. In matters of real substance, the manager, as noted earlier, is likely to back the broker.

The customer, of course, retains the right to sue (barring an enforceable arbitration agreement), but this can be an expensive proposition. Sometimes the *threat* to sue may provide the catalyst for action. A phone call or letter from an attorney doubtless carries more weight than a customer's verbal complaint. Many customers, however, may not wish to pursue this course or, having pursued it, found it too costly or protracted to make economic sense. There seems little point in suing for something like $5,000 damages when the litigation takes months and the suit costs more than the money recovered. Naturally, if a more substantial amount is involved, a suit may be the only realistic course of action. In some circumstances the brokerage firm may make an offer to settle, as it too would normally like to avoid the courts. In such cases the customer would be well advised to retain counsel before agreeing to any restitution agreement.

There remain two other means of possible redress. One is to complain in writing to the self-regulatory body governing the transaction; that is, an execution complaint involving an OTC stock should be addressed to the NASD, even if the firm were also an NYSE member. In all cases the letter should be as specific as possible, citing exact dates, times, and prices. Copies of any relevant confirmations and statements should be included.

The greatest number of complaints is likely to be directed to the largest of these bodies:

The National Association of Securities Dealers
1735 K Street, N.W.
Washington, DC 20006
The New York Stock Exchange
20 Broad Street
New York, NY 10005

This method often produces a prompt investigation and action if such are warranted. Consumers used to getting the run-around from manufacturers or public utilities are often pleasantly surprised at how quickly such complaints produce results. Once again, however, the customer should be prepared to face the fact that not everyone will see the "justice" of his case or even consider it a valid one.

ARBITRATION

For those disputes falling somewhere between the Scopes Trial and a complaint to the Exchange, the industry has adopted a Simplified Arbitration procedure. When $2,500 or less is involved, a customer may initiate arbitration by filing a typewritten letter stating the claim, a signed and notarized copy of a Uniform Submission Agreement, and a check for $15. The Submission Agreement binds the customer to abide by the arbitrator's decision, thus nullifying the threat of a suit should the decision prove unfavorable.

On receipt of these documents the Director of Arbitration forwards copies to the broker, who has 20 days to respond in writing. When the arbitrator receives the broker's response (or counterclaim), the claims are examined and a judgment rendered, usually without a hearing. If the arbitrator thinks a more detailed examination is merited, the case may be referred to a three- or five-member panel. In any event, the maximum cost remains small.

Arbitration is also available for larger disputes and, indeed, is mandatory for disputes between exchange or NASD members. For the public customer arbitration is voluntary, but it is required of industry members. That is, a customer (or another member) may compel any member to arbitrate, but a member cannot compel a customer to do so unless the customer has voluntarily agreed to the procedure.

The major advantages of arbitration over a court procedure, beyond a small-claim level, are speed, low cost, and finality of the decision. Arbitrators' decisions are rarely appealed successfully. The major drawbacks are that the findings of some arbitrators are all too arbitrary and the chance of recovering punitive damage is poor. Because of this last fact, brokers are much less likely to settle in advance of an arbitration than they are before a court hearing.

5 Investing Practices and Special Instruments

18 Stock Price Averages and Indexes

This and the next several chapters are concerned with factors which many investors believe affect their investment opportunities and their results. Many believe that price increases and declines provide a major forecasting tool as well as an obvious indication of short-term market direction. This chapter discusses some ways in which price movements for the market as a whole are measured. Subsequent chapters in this part are concerned with relationships between stock prices and changes in economic activity, and selection of investments for a portfolio. Other subjects discussed include different plans and techniques that some investors have used to aid their decisions on timing of purchases and sales and of different special instruments that may be helpful under certain conditions for investment operations.

Although the market has shown an upward trend over the long term, price movements have sometimes been quite wide, as indicated in Figure 18-1. In order to indicate graphically where the market is as well, perhaps, as where it might be going, the daily newspapers, financial publications, and investment services publish a number of stock price averages and indexes. Some of these have received wide acceptance over long periods. (See Table 18-1.) Others have been abandoned as other indicators have become more popular with investors.

STOCK PRICE AVERAGES

There are a number of well-known stock price averages. Certain characteristics are common to all.

Common Characteristics

These averages are all based on what is considered to be a representative list of issues. The list may number from 15 or 20 upward. Usually, the full

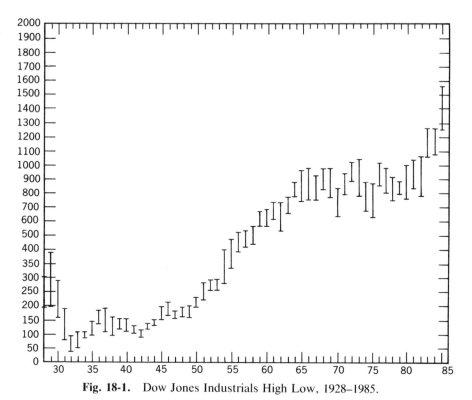

Fig. 18-1. Dow Jones Industrials High Low, 1928–1985.

list is divided into at least two subdivisions: the industrials and the transportations. Separate averages of the prices of stock in these subdivisions are computed and published. A third group, public utilities, is added to some of the averages. In other cases, one or more utility issues may be added to the industrial classification. The usual method of computation is to add the daily prices of the issues and divide by some sort of divisor. The typical average is unweighted in the sense that the importance of the company in the market or in the economy is not considered. In another sense, however, the averages are weighted in that the higher-priced stocks have more effect than the lower-priced ones. Stock price averages always show at least daily closing prices. Most also indicate the high and low for each trading day. The Dow Jones averages, formerly computed hourly, are now computed every minute that the market is open. Many of the services publishing stock averages have booklets that show the averages in detail as far back as they have been computed.

Problems after Original Computation

Unfortunately for the editors of the averages, these devices constantly present problems of compilation. There are three main problems, and each service has developed routine methods of dealing with them. The first is making substitutions; the second, changing the size of the list; and the third, adjusting for stock splits.

Making Substitutions

It is occasionally necessary for a service to drop one stock and add another. The dropped issue may have declined in importance. Again, it may have disappeared in a merger or consolidation. Sometimes it may become subject to such unusual influences that it is no longer considered a representative issue. Two possibilities present themselves to the editor of the average. One method would be to select another stock in the same industry that sells at about the same price. If one selling at the exact price is not obtainable (the usual situation), the difference between the prices of the old and the new issues could be adjusted for by adding to, or subtracting from, the average a certain number of dollars. This is not a very sound statistical procedure, but works satisfactorily for rough accuracy. A second method would be to adjust the divisor as described shortly.

It is not usually necessary to make many substitutions. From 1950 to 1955 inclusive, there was no change in the Dow Jones industrial average and only two changes in the rail average. From 1956 to 1961 five substitutions were made in the industrial and one more in the rail average. The dropping of Northern Pacific from the rail average in 1952 is illustrative of such substitutions. In that year oil was discovered in the Williston basin in which the road had substantial land holdings. The stock became so erratic in behavior that it was dropped and a more stable issue was added to the list. When General Foods was absorbed by Philip Morris, the former was replaced in the averages by the latter. Within the last few years, American Brands and Johns Manville were dropped from the averages and American Express and McDonald's were added. From 1962 to 1986 all but eight of the industrial issues remained the same, although there were some name changes. There were, however, major changes made in the former rail average when it was broadened in 1970 to include stocks representing other types of transportation.

Changing the Size of the List

This situation would arise if it were desired to increase an average from, say, 25 to 30 stocks, or the reverse. The average for the new list must be made equal to the average of the old list at some point if a continuing series is to be published. This could be done either by recomputing the old average over its entire period to conform to the average of the new list or by using a divisor that makes the new average identical to the old one at the moment of change in the list. This situation seldom arises. For example, the Dow Jones industrial and rail averages have remained constant in number since 1928 and the public utility average since 1938.

Adjusting for Stock Splits

An ever-recurring problem is that of adjusting the average for stock splits. These occur with great frequency in periods of bull markets. For example, the period 1968–1970 experienced many stock splits. The splitting of a stock presents a serious problem. Let us suppose that a stock selling at $250 is split five for one. In this case $200 would be immediately subtracted from the total if no adjustment were to be made. If the average included 25 stocks, there would be a drop of $8 per stock. The resultant sharp decline in the average would indicate a drop in the market that would not be illustrative of what had really taken place. Accordingly, an adjustment must be made that is typically one of three types.

First, another stock could be substituted. This was formerly done in some averages but was difficult to do, because stocks in the same industry and at the same price level are hard to find. If the stock were an important one, this method would be severely criticized.

A second method would be to use a multiplier. If the stock were split five for one, the new price would be multiplied by five. If it were split two for one, the new price would be multiplied by two. This is an acceptable method of operation.

A third possibility is to change the divisor so that the level of the average remains unchanged. This method is used by the editor of the Dow Jones averages. The divisor is merely a figure that, when divided into the new aggregate of prices, will give the same level on the new basis as that reported on the old basis on the day before the new divisor was put into use. A simple example will illustrate this method. Let us suppose that we have an average of only three stocks:

Stock	Price
A	20
B	25
C	45
	90 ÷ 3
	30

Stock C is now split three for one; its price falls to 15. The aggregate of the three stocks is now 60, which divided by 3 would give 20. Obviously, no editor could allow this average to fall from 30 to 20. At this point the divisor is changed. Its formula is

$$\text{Divisor} = \frac{\text{New price aggregate}}{\text{Old average price}}$$

$$\text{Divisor} = \frac{60}{30} = 2$$

$$\frac{60}{2} = 30$$

The average is now restored to 30, and the level is unaffected by the three-for-one split.

In May 1986 the Dow Jones industrial average was employing a divisor of 1.008, the transportation average was using a divisor of 1.019, and the utility average one of 2.437. The entire 65-stock average had a divisor of 4.387. If the prices of the stocks used in the averages are totaled and the sum divided by the divisor, the result is the average. For example, if the 30 stocks in the industrial average each sold for $50 per share, the $1,500 total value would be divided by the current divisor of 1.008 to yield an average of 1,488.10. Like most averages and indexes, the figure of 1488.10 is correctly described as a number of points, not dollars and cents.

The theory behind changes of divisors as used by this service is that no one stock should be counted more than once. This theory necessitates the use of the divisor changes and rejects the alternative theory that multiplication by the amount of the split is a suitable adjustment.

The Dow Jones Averages

These are probably the best known of all of the averages. For this reason, and because their characteristics are for the most part common to other popular averages, they will be discussed here in somewhat more detail. These averages were developed by Charles Dow, founder of the Dow Jones Company, publisher of *The Wall Street Journal*. He developed the theory of the average. His first list went back as far as 1884 and consisted of only 11 stocks. As will be observed, it was almost entirely a rail average, railroad shares being the leading stocks at that time.

Chicago & North Western	New York Central
Delaware, Lackawanna & Western	Northern Pacific Preferred
	Pacific Mail
Lake Shore	St. Paul
Louisville & Nashville	Union Pacific
Missouri Pacific	Western Union

The original average of 11 stocks was converted into a 20-stock rail average in 1897. This number has been retained to the present, although the rail average was changed to the transportation average on January 2, 1970. The use of the constant divisor was introduced in 1928. The transportation averages in May 1986 consisted of these stocks:

AMR Corp.	Leaseway Transportation
American President	Norfolk Southern

Burlington Northern	NWA Inc.
Canadian Pacific	Overnite Transportation
Carolina Freight	Pan Am Corp.
Consolidated Freight	Santa Fe Southern Pacific
CSX Corp.	TWA
Delta Air Lines	UAL Inc.
Eastern Air Lines	Union Pacific Corp.
Federal Express	USAir Group

The first Dow Jones list of industrials consisted of 12 stocks and goes back as far as 1897. The averages were computed by simply adding the prices of the 12 stocks and dividing by 12. In 1916 a number of changes were made and the list was increased to 20. Before 1928 the company used the policy of frequent substitutions and also the multiplication method to adjust for stock splits. In that year it was decided to adopt the constant divisor method, which has been used ever since. In the same year the list was increased to 30 stocks. A number of changes in the stocks have been made since 1928, but the size of the list has remained the same. The list in May 1986 included the following stocks:

Allied Signal	International Paper
Aluminum Co.	McDonald's
American Can	Merck & Co.
American Express	Minnesota M&M
American T&T	Navistar International
Bethlehem Steel	Owens-Illinois
Chevron	Philip Morris
DuPont	Procter & Gamble
Eastman Kodak	Sears Roebuck
Exxon	Texaco
General Electric	Union Carbide
General Motors	United Technologies
Goodyear	U.S. Steel
Inco	Westinghouse Electric
IBM	Woolworth

The first utility average was introduced in 1929 when a list of 18 stocks was compiled. This was increased to 20, but in 1938 it was reduced to the present level of 15:

| American Elec. Power | Niagara Mohawk Power |
| Centerior Energy Corp. | Pacific Gas & Electric |

Columbia Gas Systems	Panhandle E.P.L.
Commonwealth Edison	Peoples Energy
Consolidated Edison	Philadelphia Electric
Consolidated Natural Gas	Public Services Energy & Gas
Detroit Edison	Southern California Edison
Houston Ind.	

The Dow Jones averages are quite popular among investors. Several reasons account for this popularity: (1) they are the oldest of the averages, running back more than half a century and (2) they are best known and enjoy a wide press distribution. Historically, they also enjoyed a special advantage not possessed by other averages. That special advantage gave them a certain respect which greatly contributed to their use and reputation. The advantage consisted of their use as the basis for interpretation of the Dow theory. The theory is no longer widely utilized and its basic soundness has always been a matter of personal judgment, but devoted followers of the theory felt that no other averages, however good, could be used in the interpretation of their theory. It might be noted that the Dow Jones industrial average is used extensively in the construction of formula trading plans.

Despite their popularity, the Dow Jones averages have had their share of detractors. Some criticisms are based on statistical and sampling weaknesses and others upon what is alleged to be sheer lack of logic. Some of the more frequent adverse criticisms are mentioned here.

Many critics have pointed out the use of AT&T stock in the industrial average. Historically this company was usually classified as a utility, and it was part of the utility average until 1931, when it was transferred to the industrial average. Its typically high price before the company was broken into several parts tended to give it substantial weight in the average. Furthermore, its relative price stability has at times made the average itself seem to be more stable than it should have been. Although the price of AT&T today is much lower than other, far more dominant stocks such as IBM, its past reputation still influences those who rely on past performance of the averages as a guide to the future.

A second criticism is that the Dow Jones averages do not include large enough samples of stocks. This is particularly true of the industrial average, where only 30 issues are purported to be representative of the vast list of stocks in that classification. Others have countered that these 30 stocks account for about 25% of all shares listed on the New York Exchange and about 20% of the value of all stock in the United States.

There is some concern that warping is caused by a tendency toward concentrating in the averages stocks considered to be of high-grade or "blue-chip" companies. Because these stocks tend to be high priced, the list is not really representative. It is unusual for low-priced issues of less than top grade to be used. When a stock formerly considered to be a blue chip begins to lose its luster, it is frequently replaced in the averages. This is a clear weakness when it is recognized that low-priced issues might well show a distinctly different trend at times from that of the blue chips.

Until the mid-1960s the Dow Jones industrial average served reasonably well as an indicator of the market's level and direction, but then an obvious change appeared. The average began to show less rise in bull markets and less decline in bear markets. One reason for this was probably the fact that some companies in the industrial average were not as representative of American industry as they once were. Changes occurred both within companies and in the economy as technology became more complex. Chrysler and Esmark, for example, were included in the average long after most analysts had stopped regarding them as blue-chip companies. In June 1979 the stocks of these two companies were replaced in the industrial average by those of Merck & Co. and IBM. The troubled Johns Manville Company was replaced in 1982 by American Express. General Foods, which had caused great gyrations in the averages because of take-over rumors, was taken over in 1985 by Philip Morris, which itself became part of the averages.

A further problem with most of the companies whose stocks make up the averages involves their size. Many are among the nation's largest. In such companies the development of new products or changes in production methods may take a long time to affect sales and profits. The averages, furthermore, do not reflect the increasing importance of service companies.

The volatility of averages is greatly affected by stock splits. Every time a stock is split, its influence drops in direct proportion to the split. This tends to reduce the effect of gains by companies whose stocks are split. Such companies are often perceived as among the most successful. This has given the industrial average a distinct downward bias. Over time, therefore, the average may not have risen as rapidly or as far as it might have otherwise. *Barron's,* also a Dow Jones publication, prepares an unweighted average of 50 leading stocks based on Thursday closing prices. It also prepares an unweighted average of stocks in 32 industry groups.

Like the much more widely followed Dow Jones averages, the various *Barron's* averages attempt to compensate for the effect of stock splits, stock dividends, and substitutions. This is accomplished by assigning individual multipliers to each stock and a divisor to each group. Changes in components, multipliers, and divisors are indicated in the Market Laboratory section of *Barron's.*

Some analysts find the group averages of particular interest. In bull or bear markets it is not unusual for a limited number of industries to have a disproportionate effect on the movement of the market. The group averages allow such industries to be identified easily.

The Value Line Composite Average

The Value Line Composite Average measures the value of about 1,700 common stocks, most of which are on the major New York exchanges. More than 80% are on the NYSE. Although this stock average is presented as an unweighted average, its computation gives it some characteristics of weighted average and its expression as a percentage of 100 could well qualify it as an index rather than an average, or at least as a hybrid. The equally weighted geometric average of stock prices is expressed in index form with June 30, 1961, set at 100. Adjustments incorporate daily net percentage price changes for each stock as well as for stock dividends and splits. The composite consists of over 1,500 industrial issues, about 160 utilities, and about 11 rails.

The Value Line Composite Index, based on the movement of 1,700 stock prices, was adopted by the Kansas City Board of Trade in 1982 as the basis for its pioneering stock index futures contract. Those who favor this index over others point to its wide base and tendency to somewhat wider volatility than the other indexes. Its component issues make up more than 96% of all dollar trading volume in U.S. equity markets. Nevertheless, the great number of second-tier stocks overcome the somewhat more staid performance of the blue-chip issues to give it a beta of about 1.2, which is the highest of all broad-based indexes.

Choice of an Average

The investor who chooses to rely on the averages discussed previously or others which are available has not historically been faced with any great problem in determining which of available averages is most useful. In their daily fluctuations, extant averages have tended to go up and down together more than 90% of the time, although they do vary somewhat in the extent of their fluctuations. Major changes in market direction have almost invariably begun on the same day in all of them. So far as forecasting rather than describing is concerned, no regularly published average has shown any particular superiority over any other in indicating turning points in market cycles.

STOCK PRICE INDEXES

Common Characteristics

Although the terms *average* and *index* are sometimes treated as synonymous terms, technically stock price indexes are more refined methods of measuring changes in the level of stock prices than are the averages. This is especially true when exchanges are being observed over long periods. All use base periods that vary from index to index, whereas averages are merely a weighted or unweighted arithmetic mean of a group of stocks. Indexes are usually weighted by one of various methods; a common one is by multiplying the number of shares outstanding for each stock by the price of the stock. The number of stocks used is invariably large. Precise statistical formulas are used to eliminate the statistical weakness present in averages. As a result, the indexes are extremely useful in measuring changes in the entire market. Often, the indexes are broken down into a large number of stock groups, which give a more representative picture of what various industries are doing.

Despite their advantages, traders find certain objections to indexes. There is a popular belief that certain averages, even admitting their limitations, are more sensitive than the indexes with their larger stock lists. As a rule, the indexes receive less publicity than do the averages.

Standard & Poor's

Prior to 1957, this service used two indexes, one daily and the other weekly. In 1957 the service scrapped these indexes for a modern composite index, the S&P 500, which is a combination of the other Standard & Poor's indexes. This consists of an industrial index of 400 stocks, a transportation index of 20 stocks, and financial and public utility indexes consisting of 40 stocks each. All together, stocks represent 88 industry groups. The index is based on a value base of 10 established in the period 1941–1943. It is weighted by the number of outstanding shares of each issue included. Like the Dow Jones averages, it is properly expressed in points and not in dollars and cents.

Because it includes such a broad base of leading listed and OTC stocks, the S&P 500 is held in high regard by many technicians, especially institutional investors. The index includes stocks representing about 80% of the market value of those listed on the NYSE.

The CBOE began trading puts and calls on its proprietary index, the CBOE 100, on March 11, 1983. Within a matter of weeks the enormously successful new contract began setting volume records. In July of that same year, its name was changed to the S&P 100, although it is widely referred to by its ticker symbol, OEX. Its value is set to a base of 100 as of January 2, 1976.

The 100 stocks which make up the index are all included among those in the S&P 500. The 100 stocks include 92 industrials, 1 utility, 2 transportation companies, and 5 financial institutions. Although there are one-fifth as many stocks in the S&P 100 as in the S&P 500, it should not be considered to be one-fifth of the size. In terms of market value, it is actually about one-half the size.

Both of the S&P indexes are weighted by capitalization. Such weighting eliminates the necessity for adjustments to compensate for stock dividends and splits, but mergers or bankruptcies sometimes necessitate substitutions. Both indexes are recalculated every few seconds and are immediately widely disseminated through market quotation systems.

New York Stock Exchange Index

This composite index, published since July 14, 1966, includes all the common stocks listed on the NYSE. When the index began, the number of stocks was about 1,250; it now exceeds 1,500. It divides stocks into four groups: industrial, utility, finance, and transportation issues. The New York Stock Exchange Index is a composite of these four groups, although each group index is also published separately. All of the indexes are weighted by multiplying the price of each stock by the number of shares listed. The four component indexes are stated in points, but the composite index is expressed in dollars and cents. The base of all five indexes is 50, which was the approximate weighted average price of stocks listed on the Exchange when the indexes were originally computed. The base date is December 31, 1965.

Stock splits and stock dividends do not require an adjustment in the index because they do not affect aggregate market value. Sometimes, however, adjustments are necessary. New listings and delistings require an addition or deduction from the base. Mergers of two listed companies usually do not change aggregate market value, but merger of a listed company with an unlisted company or one formerly listed elsewhere will require an addition to the base because of the value added by the outside company. Rights offerings also will add value to the base equivalent to the value of the new shares.

The NYSE composite has only been published since 1966. Some historians, however, want older data to study in their never-ending quest for forecasting signals. Accordingly, the index was computed on a daily close basis from May 28, 1964. The SEC index, which had been discontinued in 1964, was then converted to the NYSE composite base for the period of January 7, 1939, to May 28, 1964. The frequency of calculation increased as computerization progressed until the point where this index, like most others, is updated virtually continuously.

The NYSE composite index is traded as a futures contract on the New York Futures Exchange (NYFE). An option on the futures contract is also traded on the same exchange. Although both the futures contract and the option on the contract have attracted enough following to survive, efforts to establish similar markets based upon the four subsector indexes have been less successful.

American Stock Exchange Index

The Amex replaced its Price Change Index, used since 1966, with its Market Value Index and 16 subindexes on September 4, 1973. The original base level was 100 as of the close of trading on August 31, 1973, but on July 5, 1983, the index was adjusted to one-half of its previous level. The base levels of the index and the 16 subindexes were all changed to 50.

The index measures the change in the aggregate market value of issued common shares, American depository receipts, and warrants listed on the Amex, numbering about 800. Half of the subindexes consist of eight industrial groups which include among them over 90% of the stocks listed on the exchange. The remainder of the subindexes consist of eight geographic groups which include among them all companies listed on the exchange.

A somewhat unusual practice is the inclusion of dividends paid as additions to the index; these are treated as if reinvested and thereby enable the index to reflect the total return of its components. Changes in listings, stock splits, and stock dividends are not included.

More recently the Amex has developed several specialized price-weighted indexes which serve as the basis for options traded on that exchange. The airline index is based on about five major airline stocks. The oil index is based on the prices of about 15 large petroleum companies. The Computer Technology Index is based on about 30 high technology stocks, with most of its weight coming from IBM. Although the indexes were all developed by the Amex in the early 1980s, all of the stocks that made up some of the indexes and most of those on the remainder trade on the NYSE.

In 1980 when most exchanges were developing indexes to serve as the basis for futures contracts, options, or both, one of the more successful entries was the Major Market Index of the Amex. It is traded as a futures contract by the Chicago Board of Trade and as an option by the Amex.

The Major Market Index is a price-weighted index based on the prices of only 20 stocks. The tendency of the index to approximate closely the direction of larger indexes makes it popular with traders who trade "baskets" of securities against indexes. The calculation of the index and its dissemination are virtually continuous.

The stocks making up the index in 1986 all traded on the NYSE; the 20 well-known stocks represented a broad range of industries. The list included:

American Express	IBM
AT&T	International Paper
Chevron	Johnson & Johnson
Coca-Cola	Merck
Dow Chemical	Minnesota M&M
DuPont	Mobil
Eastman Kodak	Philip Morris
Exxon	Procter & Gamble
General Electric	Sears Roebuck
General Motors	U.S. Steel

Generally a one-point change on the Major Market Index will take place when the Dow Jones industrial average changes five points. The correlation between the two indicators varies somewhat but to date is well over 90%. This should not be too surprising, because the Major Market Index in its construction is actually more like an average than an index and the stocks which it has in common with the Dow Jones industrials were chosen to provide a good cross section. Sixteen of the 20 stocks in the Major Market Index were also included in the Dow Jones industrial average.

Wilshire 5000 Equity Index

The Wilshire 5000 includes more common stocks than any other well-known index. It represents a value of well over $1 trillion consisting of all actively traded common stocks in the United States. It was created in 1974 and has been well publicized because of its regular appearances in, among others, *Forbes* and *Barron's*.

It is a capital-weighted price index with a base of December 31, 1970. It is calculated in about the same manner as the NYSE and S&P 500 indexes. Over 87% of its value is represented by stocks trading on the NYSE, with the remainder consisting about equally of stocks traded on the Amex and OTC. The inclusion of many stocks tends to reduce the influence of the more staid blue chips. Accordingly this index tends, like the Value Line Index, to be somewhat more volatile than the smaller indicators.

NASDAQ OTC Index

During the past few years ever-improving communications, increased publicity, more sophisticated and reliable order–execution procedures, increased number of companies listed, and wider availability of margin have helped NASDAQ improve its volume considerably. By 1986 it had developed nine indexes. Like many others, these were devised not only as measures of this market and its subdivisions but also to serve as the basis for trading on futures and options markets.

In 1986 NASDAQ volume for the year approached 30 billion shares. This equaled over 80% of NYSE volume, and on some days actually surpassed it. There was a substantial growth in institutional participation.

The NASDAQ OTC Composite Index with a base year of 1970 has been compiled since 1971 by the NASD using their automated communication system, NASDAQ. The composite system combines stocks in six categories: industrial, bank, insurance, other finance, transportation, and utilities. All domestic stocks traded through NASDAQ are included.

In 1984 the NASDAQ National Market System introduced two indexes of its own. One is the NASDAQ/NMS Composite Index and the other is the NASDAQ/NMS Industrial Index. Both are market weighted and have a base of 100. These two newer indexes are published regularly by many financial publications along with the older NASDAQ Composite and some or all of the various subindexes.

Bond Averages

Bond traders and institutions have available a number of bond indexes and subindexes. Some believe that these are useful not only as indicators of bond levels and trends, but also as indicators of stock trends. Some believe they are predictive, and others believe that they confirm perceived stock trends.

Among the most widely followed bond indexes are four indexes published by Dow Jones in *The Wall Street Journal* and *Barron's*. A 20-bond average is a composite of two subindexes, 10 utility bonds and 10 industrial bonds. The components of these indexes in May of 1986 consisted of:

Public Utilities

Alabama Pwr	9¾%	2004
Amer T&T	8.8%	2005
Comwlth Ed	8¾%	2005
Cons Ed	7.9%	2001
Cons Pwr	9¾%	2006
Detroit Edison	9%	1999
N.Y. Tel	4½%	1991
Pac G&E	7¾%	2005
Phil Elec	7⅜%	2001
Pub Svc Ind	9.6%	2005

Industrials

BankAm	7⅞%	2003
Beth Steel	6⅞%	1999
Dow Chem	4.35%	1988
Exxon	6%	1997
Ford Mtr	8⅛%	1990
GM Accept	12%	2005
NCR	4⅜%	1987
Pfizer	9⅛%	2000
Socony	4⅛%	1993
Weyerhaeusr	5.20%	1991

Dow Jones also publishes an index of 10 government bond issues. Historians might also be interested in the railroad bond subindex which was published for many years until it was abandoned in 1976.

Many other bond averages and indexes covering a wide-ranging group of classifications are issued frequently by some of the bond-rating services, the Federal Reserve, financial publications, and brokerage firms. Merrill Lynch, Pierce, Fenner & Smith, for example, publishes its municipal bond index, the Merrill Lynch 500, based on the yields of 500 issuers. These are broken down into two basic components, revenue bonds and general obligations, each of which is further subdivided by type of issuer.

Other Averages and Indexes

There are a tremendous number of stock and bond averages and indexes issued by various exchanges, financial firms, government agencies, and pub-

```
┌─────────────────────────────────────────────────────────────────────────────┐
│ STOCK MARKET DATA BANK              July 15, 1985                             │
```

Major Indexes

HIGH	LOW	(12 MOS)	CLOSE	NET CH	% CH	12 MO CH	%	FROM 12/31	%
DOW JONES AVERAGES									
1338.60	1086.57	30 Industrials	x1335.46	− 3.14	− 0.23	+ 218.63	+19.58	+ 123.89	+10.23
689.26	444.03	20 Transportations	x689.26	+ 1.29	+ 0.19	+ 228.66	+49.64	+ 131.13	+23.49
168.91	123.03	15 Utilities	168.65	− 0.26	− 0.15	+ 41.66	+32.92	+ 19.13	+12.79
559.61	421.36	65 Composite	x559.03	− 0.58	− 0.10	+ 125.28	+28.88	+ 69.17	+14.12
NEW YORK STOCK EXCHANGE									
112.13	85.13	Composite	111.93	− 0.20	− 0.18	+ 24.59	+28.15	+ 15.55	+16.13
126.63	99.73	Industrials	126.43	− 0.20	− 0.16	+ 23.75	+23.13	+ 15.85	+14.33
61.43	44.15	Utilities	61.24	− 0.19	− 0.31	+ 17.06	+38.61	+ 9.67	+18.75
112.63	73.11	Transportation	112.63	+ 0.42	+ 0.37	+ 36.47	+47.92	+ 22.02	+24.30
121.93	76.74	Finance	121.60	− 0.29	− 0.24	+ 42.26	+53.26	+ 23.97	+24.55
STANDARD & POOR'S INDEXES									
193.29	147.82	500 Index	192.72	− 0.57	− 0.29	+ 41.12	+27.12	+ 25.48	+15.24
212.48	167.75	400 Industrials	211.78	− 0.70	− 0.33	+ 39.51	+22.93	+ 25.42	+13.64
179.10	117.21	20 Transportations	179.10	+ 0.12	+ 0.07	+ 57.47	+47.25	+ 35.19	+24.45
90.24	64.73	40 Utilities	90.18	− 0.06	− 0.07	+ 25.22	+38.82	+ 14.29	+18.82
23.69	14.09	40 Financials	23.54	− 0.11	− 0.47	+ 8.78	+59.49	+ 4.74	+25.21
NASDAQ									
303.04	225.30	OTC Composite	303.04	+ 0.65	+ 0.21	+ 69.35	+29.68	+ 55.69	+22.51
312.43	250.18	Industrials	308.10	+ 0.49	+ 0.16	+ 46.30	+17.69	+ 47.37	+18.17
363.28	226.87	Insurance	363.28	+ 2.97	+ 0.82	+ 126.98	+53.74	+ 80.17	+28.32
299.61	195.18	Banks	299.61	+ 2.13	+ 0.72	+ 103.35	+52.66	+ 69.84	+30.40
128.48	93.94	Nat. Mkt. Comp.	128.48	+ 0.30	+ 0.23	+ 30.30	+30.86	+ 23.76	+22.69
118.23	92.55	Nat. Mkt. Indus.	115.09	+ 0.23	+ 0.20	+ 17.62	+18.08	+ 17.06	+17.40
OTHERS									
233.72	187.16	AMEX	233.72	+ 0.53	+ 0.23	+ 40.66	+21.06	+ 29.46	+14.42
1024.5	755.3	Fin. Times Indus.	937.2	+ 11.2	+ 1.21	+ 162.2	+20.93	+ 15.1	+ 1.59
13040.10	9703.35	Nikkei Stock Avg.	12598.77	−240.7	− 1.87	+2421.19	+23.79	+1056.17	+ 9.15
204.19	162.46	Value-Line	204.19	+ 0.40	+ 0.20	+ 35.95	+21.37	+ 26.21	+14.73
1998.10	1508.83	Wilshire 5000	996.18	− 1.92	− 0.10	+ 445.85	+28.76	+ 294.17	+17.28

Fig. 18-2. Stock market data bank. (*Source: The Wall Street Journal*, July 15, 1986.) Reprinted by permission of *The Wall Street Journal*, © 1986. Dow Jones and Company, Inc. All rights reserved.

lications. They cover almost every imaginable classification of stocks, bonds, and investment companies.

Many of the indicators discussed above, as well as others, are listed daily in the Stock Market Data Bank of *The Wall Street Journal* (see Figure 18-2).

In recent years there has been introduced a bewildering array of indexes, subindexes, averages, and hybrids. Some are organized by product, such as stocks, bonds, money market instruments, or investment companies. Others are based on instruments which trade in a particular market such as OTC or on a single exchange. Subindexes may indicate the performances of any of a long list of financial products organized by industry, geographical location of the issuer, risk, type, or almost any other subdivision that may interest investors.

Most of the indexes have been developed primarily as a base for trading in futures, options, or options on futures. There has even been a beginning to a market in options on options. Some of these indexes have proved to be outstandingly successful for these purposes. Some are widely used by institutional investors for bona fide hedging purposes. Others are used primarily as speculative vehicles by small and large traders alike. Large traders utilize complex arbitrages in securities against futures contracts or options on indexes.

It can be argued that the proliferation of indexes and the trading that they support warps the securities markets and reduces the value of one of their most important functions; namely, liquidity. Others may argue that the introduction of the trading against indexes may have had much to do with the great increase of trading volume in recent years and that serious technical market disruptions occur only on a few days each year and are quickly corrected.

In any event, it would appear that most of those who use averages or indexes to follow market direction use only a few of the myriad available, such as the venerable Dow Jones industrials and the S&P 500. For indicating tops and bottoms after the fact, volatility, or for judging the extent of moves on a daily basis, one indicator seems to be just about as good as another.

THE DOW THEORY

The Dow theory seeks to forecast stock prices by interpretations of the interaction of the Dow Jones industrial and transportation (formerly rail) averages. Its principles were formulated by Charles Dow and S.A. Nelson at the turn of the century and popularized by William P. Hamilton. Both Dow and Hamilton were editors of *The Wall Street Journal*. The theory once had a considerable following, but has declined greatly in popularity and prestige in recent years. It was once the best known of all trading plans, and has some followers to this day.

Although the theory was always extensively defended and criticized, the criticism eventually overwhelmed the defense. It was never a system for "beating the market" and was not considered so either by Dow or Hamilton. Because it was the first widely known trading plan, an understanding of its features might be a useful introduction to a study of more modern trading plans.

Much has been written about the theory. Later writers on the theory have attempted to amplify, extend, or modify the original theory as their individual contributions. The following discussion, however, will be confined as far as possible to the original theory as first presented by Dow and Nelson, and later developed by Hamilton.

Today there is no longer an authoritative voice to discuss the theory. *The Wall Street Journal* no longer carries editorials at frequent intervals to interpret it. No well-known Dow service operates in New York, although there are still a few located in various other cities. Robert Rhea, perhaps the best-known writer on the subject since Hamilton, has been dead for a number of years.[1]

ORIGIN

Charles Dow

Charles Dow was a New Englander, born in 1851.[2] His early newspaper experience was on a Massachusetts paper, *The Springfield Republican*. From this stepping stone he went on to New York in search of greater opportunities. For a time he owned a seat on the NYSE. Eventually he left the Exchange and in 1882, with Edward Jones, founded the Dow Jones Company, a financial service. This organization is well known today as the publisher of *The Wall Street Journal*.

During 1900 to early 1902, Dow was editor of the *Journal* and wrote a number of editorials that dealt with the movement of security prices. It is interesting to note that he never wrote a single editorial devoted exclusively to the Dow theory, nor did he at any time outline it in precise terms or label it as such. The only material he ever wrote on the theory is contained in his editorials.

Nelson and Hamilton

The theory became crystallized in the writings of Nelson and Hamilton. Dow died in early 1902. In the same year a reporter on the *Journal*, S. A. Nelson, prepared and published a modest little volume entitled *The A B C of Speculation*.[3] It was based partly on Dow's editorials and partly upon his experience as a financial reporter in Wall Street. Nelson was the first person to state the principle of the theory in definite form; he also named it "Dow's theory." Later the phrase "the Dow theory" replaced Nelson's nomenclature.

Dow was succeeded as editor of *The Wall Street Journal* by T. F. Woodlock, S. S. Pratt, and, in 1908, by William P. Hamilton. Hamilton held the editorial post until his death in 1929. His editorials continued and refined the development of Dow theory.

Although the original purpose seems simply to have been measurement of change in stock prices, both Dow and Hamilton believed that changes in the averages anticipated changes in business activity. The belief that the

[1]His exhaustive study of the theory was published in *The Dow Theory* (New York: Barron's, 1932).
[2]For a definitive study of Dow's life and work, see George W. Bishop, Jr., *Charles H. Dow and the Dow Theory* (New York: Appleton-Century-Crofts, 1960).
[3]S. A. Nelson, *The A B C of Speculation* (New York: Stock Market Publications, 1934). This is a facsimile reproduction of the original work, now out of print.

theory could anticipate business conditions eventually evolved into the belief that it could forecast trends in the stock market, and the theory became widely popular. Finally Hamilton became convinced of the forecasting ability of the theory.

Basic Features

The theory is based on the fundamental premise that at all times there are three movements in the stock market: (1) the primary, (2) the secondary, and (3) the daily movement. These operate simultaneously.

The first or primary movement is also called the major or primary trend; it is the long-term trend, the major bull or bear market. Coincident with it is the secondary movement, or secondary reaction. This is a sharp and discernible rally in a primary bear market or a steep reaction in a primary bull market. Usually two or three of these will take place in each bull or bear market. The third movement is the day-to-day fluctuation of stock prices. Of the three movements, the first is the most important; the second aids in forecasting the first; the third is unimportant.

Dow conceived of the stock market as having movements very much in the way that the tides of the ocean ebb and flow. The primary movement was the tide; the secondary movements were the waves; the daily movements were the ripples.

His followers have often followed the analogy, which is imaginative but entirely misleading. Few things are as regular and periodic as the tides; few are as uncertain as the movements of the stock market. Various governments have developed the principles of tidal movements so accurately that the tide for any given harbor for any desired period can be predicted far in advance. These predictions are so accurate that variations from actual tide records are so minor as to be without significance. On the other hand, the stock market has no such regularity of movement, and any attempt to forecast it upon the basis of a purely mathematical formula is doomed to failure in advance.

Hamilton in his editorials at no time stated his belief in any regular stock cycle. Its duration he felt to be incalculable. The Dow theory is based on the assumption that the cycle will be irregular; its only objective is to tell when either a bull or a bear market has terminated; it does not predict how long that market will last.

Forecasting Movements

Dow wrote editorials, as already indicated, from 1900 to early 1902. At that time his first average, largely a rail one, had been compiled for 16 years, but his industrial average had been in existence only 3 years. On this evidence he made certain observations. It was his belief that no one could forecast the length of a major bull or bear market. He did not believe it was possible to tell the length of any primary movement. Dow, Hamilton, Rhea, and other advocates of the theory adjusted their views of the significance of major, secondary, and day-to-day movements as time passed. Many kinds of signals were developed, but most were later adjusted or abandoned.

Hamilton used both the Dow Jones rail and industrial averages as the key to stock market movements. These two averages must corroborate each other to give a positive indication of trend; without such corroboration nothing is indicated by the market's action.

A reasonable justification could be made for the use of the two averages. The rail average was based upon 20 leading rail stocks. Their prices were believed to reflect the present and future business of their respective roads; this traffic affected their earnings, which were discounted by market action. The railroads were believed to be the best indicator of the movement of goods in commercial and industrial channels. In recent years, railroads became much less important as traffic carriers than they were years ago. The rail stocks, once the most popular of all stock issues, accounted for less than 10% of the trading activity on the NYSE by the middle of the twentieth century. Most Dow theorists were advocating the elimination of the rail average in interpreting the theory even before that average was replaced by the wider transportation average.

The industrial average, which is now based on 30 leading stocks, is used as an indicator of the volume of production of the country. Industries in manufacturing and mining operate upon both present orders and anticipated business. Industrial stocks should therefore reflect the production level of the country; their prices should discount the earnings of such companies. Hence, the two averages, in theory, will discount changes in corporate earnings, dividends, production, and the movement of goods. The theory is based on this premise.

There was no Dow Jones public utility average, of course, until 1929, the year of Hamilton's death. Dow theorists have never considered the average as necessary to interpreting the theory because utility stocks are not subject to the same influences as the transportations and industrials.

Because both men were editors of *The Wall Street Journal,* they wrote about the Dow Jones averages in the interpretation of their theory. Hamilton stated in his writings that, although these averages had been widely imitated, they were still standard, and no other series had proved to be as satisfactory.

Summary and Evaluation of the Dow Theory

The essential features of the Dow theory, as first presented by Dow, Nelson, and Hamilton, were these:

1   There are three movements in the stock market: (a) the primary movement, (b) the secondary reaction, and (c) the daily fluctuations.

2   The primary movement may be either a long-term bull market or a long-term bear market. These markets are forecast by the action of the Dow Jones industrial and rail averages.

3   The averages forecast bull and bear markets only when one average confirms the signals of the other. This confirmation may take place either by both averages making lines and then showing a break-out in the same direction or by both averages showing new highs or new lows through secondary reactions.

4   The averages do not forecast how long a primary movement will last, but only indicate when a new bull or bear market is under way.

5   The market is forecast solely by the movements of the averages, which discount everything. The importance of volume of trading is not clear from the writings of Hamilton, but is stressed by later students of the theory. No use is made of series other than the averages nor is use made of extensive charts and records. The study of chart formations, such as double tops and double bottoms, is not a part of the theory.

6   The purpose of the theory is to indicate the reversal of primary trends.

7   Primary trends will continue as long as the averages confirm each other as to the direction of the trend.

8   The theory is not a system for "beating the market," but rather one that can benefit the intelligent speculator who wishes to protect himself against changes in primary bull and bear markets.

Those who have indicted the theory have pointed to the overrating of its perceived successes, superficiality, lack of precision, failure to forecast tops and bottoms, uncertainty of confirmation, slowness of confirmation, and reliance on rail averages. Above all, they have with time become concerned that the forecasting value of the theory after its apparent prediction of the 1929 crash has been overcome by so many failures since. Some have cynically concluded that the theory's record of prediction could be roughly duplicated by flipping a coin.

The mixed results and varying opinions concerning the Dow theory trading results indicate the difficulty of evaluating trading systems and formula plans. Perhaps the greatest value of the theory has been its clear indication of the danger of accepting track records over short periods. The Dow theory, which was so widely accepted over such a long period, became largely discredited or, at best, greatly suspect when its performance was poor over a period of years. Most systems and plans are similarly found wanting when subjected to critical analysis over time. All have shown some weaknesses—at least all that anyone has chosen to make public.

19 Investing and Trading in Common Stocks

This and the following chapters deal with the basic procedures for investing and trading in common stocks. There is no easy road to riches in the stock market any more than in any other type of investment, so none will be described here. The following material deals with procedures, policies, and principles that many investors have found useful in the purchase and sale of common stocks, both directly and indirectly. More comprehensive discussions of investment analysis and portfolio management can be found in the many excellent texts dealing in considerable detail with these important subjects.

BASIC CONSIDERATIONS

The problems connected with investing and trading in common stocks are so numerous and complex that it would be hopeless to attempt to discuss all of them here. Rather, emphasis will be placed upon introducing them briefly in the hope that readers will pursue them further and in greater detail. Subjects discussed will include some of the problems involved in choosing and managing an investor's portfolio. Attention will be directed to both formula and nonformula plan buying. Indirect ownership will also be outlined.

Problems in Buying Stocks

The basic problems connected with carrying out personal investment objectives through purchase of common stocks can be largely summarized with five questions:

1 Should stocks be bought at all?
2 How many stocks should be purchased?
3 What stocks should be purchased?

4 By what plan should stocks be purchased?

5 When should stocks be purchased?

The first question has to do with the investor's attitude toward his or her capital and opinion about the stock market. Common stocks are speculative financial instruments and are not suitable for those concerned above all with conservation of capital. The common stocks of the highest quality companies have a history of price variability far too great to qualify as low risk in the same sense as money market instruments or savings and loan accounts. Dividend yields are rarely enough to justify incurring the risk of intentionally entering a market that is expected to remain in a narrow range. Those who anticipate a falling market and buy stocks which they expect to go up probably are relying more on hope than on wisdom. Buying so-called "defensive stocks" that will go down less than the market is hardly calculated to provide returns adequate for the risks incurred.

The second and third questions have to do with planning investment portfolios and investment analysis. An extensive discussion of these problems must be left to the standard texts on investment. The questions involving planning and timing will be treated extensively in this chapter and those following.

THE EFFICIENT MARKET

Some investors believe that the efficient markets hypothesis and its mathematical model, the random walk, is the best explanation of market behavior. Some accept the hypothesis to some degree. Some do not believe it at all. Individual investors who hope to make intelligent market decisions would do well to be aware of the implications of the hypothesis, make up their minds whether to accept it in whole or part, and then act accordingly.

Entire books have been written about this interesting and disturbing subject; but reduced to essentials, the theory maintains that the prices of stocks reflect all or most of what information is obtainable and also the reactions to that information. This is true because of the competition by large numbers of stock traders and analysts who are interested in maximizing returns and are actively and effectively competing with one another. The increasing availability of sophisticated communications and information systems makes the market even more efficient.

What this means is that, at a minimum, the average investor is faced with stock prices that reflect all available information, so that any amount of technical analysis or research cannot yield extra returns. At a maximum, it means that even those with superior sources of information or the ability to act with greater speed cannot obtain extra returns. After the fact, of course, there are those who will achieve spectacular returns, but this is not inconsistent with the efficient markets hypothesis, which merely maintains that such results are not to be *expected* before the fact.

There are those who maintain that the efficient markets theory is invalid, but they find small comfort in any formal research or financial publications. Cynics have always held that those who achieve superior results do so while maintaining a low profile. It seems doubtful, however, that the small investor has the knowledge or facilities to beat the market consistently—if, indeed, anyone does. The disturbing conclusion may be that stocks are worth precisely what they are selling for. This does not mean that the market will not go up or down. It merely means that it will get there in a random fashion as people react in unknown ways to events that have not yet transpired.

The efficient markets hypothesis does not mean that investors in the stock market are without hope. It only means that the best approach is the development of a good portfolio to be held as long as a rising market is anticipated and sold when a significant decline is expected. Any other approach is destined to yield lower returns. Those who are aggressive still cannot justify concentration of holdings or in-and-out trading. All such investors need do is satisfy their aggressiveness by buying a portfolio that is designed to vary more widely than the market.[1]

PORTFOLIO OF AN INVESTOR

Characteristics

The term *portfolio* has a technical meaning in the field of investments. It is the investor's program and refers to his holdings of securities. For example, a given investor owns five different bonds and shares of stock in 10 corporations with a total valuation of $25,000. That is his portfolio. However, the two major problems connected with the portfolio are its planning or construction and its management. Decisions must be made on the initial purchases, and the securities must be managed as long as they remain in the portfolio.

The size of a portfolio necessitates a basic decision of policy for investors. They have at their disposal only limited funds over and above living expenses, although they may have accumulated wealth that can be invested in securities. Surplus income can be invested in any one or a number of outlets or media, such as a home, other real estate, life insurance, savings accounts and deposits, money markets, shares of building and loan associations, issues of investment companies, and stocks and bonds of business corporations.

This basic question of how much money to put into the securities portfolio can be decided only by the investor himself, regardless of how much advice

[1]See Chapter 20 for further discussion of market efficiency.

he may obtain from others or from reading publications on the subject. For a given individual, it may be nothing or a very large sum; this depends on circumstances.

Certain criteria are useful in making a decision upon the size of the securities portfolio:

1   Income
    (a)   Size
    (b)   Sources
    (c)   Stability
    (d)   Expectations
2   Number of dependents, degree, and expected length of dependency
3   Age and health of the investor and members of family
4   Insurance status
5   Tax bracket
6   Ownership of home
7   Retirement or pension plan
8   Accumulated wealth available for investment
9   Unusual expenses expected in the future
10 Temperament of the investor—willingness to assume risk
11 Knowledge of and skill in handling investments
12 Time available for management of investments
13 Need for preservation of principal
14 Dependence upon investment income
15 Occupation, business, or profession of the investor

Ideally, an investor's portfolio should be "tailor-made" to fit one's individual needs. The 15 criteria just mentioned could be augmented. The combinations of criteria for any particular portfolio are as numerous as contract bridge hands. Generally speaking, few investors compute with any degree of precision the amount of surplus family funds that can be put into securities investments. But a decision must be made if there is to be a portfolio. Whether it be $500, $5,000, or $50,000 per year, only the investor can make that decision. Once this decision is made, certain broad generalizations are possible concerning what securities should be purchased and when such purchases should be timed, although even here there is more uncertainty than many laypeople realize.

Tests of a Good Investment

There is no such thing as an ideal investment any more than there is anything else in life that is ideal. The reason is that the ideal investment would have to meet a number of tests which are incompatible, even if attainable. All of the qualities of a good investment cannot be combined in any one security. Individual investors must decide on what tests or combinations of tests are most desirable to them and settle for that.

There are a number of possible tests of an ideal investment:

1 *Safety of principal*   This would mean two things. First, the principal would be safe in dollar values. No one would ever lose the dollar amount of the original investment. In addition, the value of the principal would never lose its purchasing power, regardless of changes in the price level. It should be invulnerable to the twin dangers of inflation and deflation.

2 *Safety of income*   The investor would always receive an income invulnerable to economic changes.

3 *Stability of income*   The income would be safe in two ways. It would never fluctuate. In addition, it would have constant purchasing power, regardless of changes in the price level.

4 *Maximum income*   The income should be as large as possible.

5 *Acceptable maturity*   The security should not mature as long as the investor desires to hold it in the portfolio.

6 *Acceptable denomination*   It should not be too expensive to buy or to prevent proper diversification in the portfolio.

7 *Potential appreciation*   The security should have potentialities for future growth.

8 *Freedom from management cares and worry*   The investor should be able to buy it, lay it away in the safety deposit box, and forget it with no other responsibilities than the deposit of the always regular and always generous interest or dividend checks.

9 *Freedom from taxation*   It should be tax free: no federal, state, or local taxes; no income, inheritance, transfer, or property taxes; no tax reports and no inquisitive tax officials.

10 *Marketability or liquidity*   It can always be sold at once at the going market price (which, incidentally, would always be above the original cost).

11 *Noncallable*   The issuer should never have the right to deprive the investor of his ideal investment against his will.

12 *Convertible*   If it is a preferred stock or bond, the investor should always be permitted to convert it into common stock whenever it is profitable to do so.

13 *Low commissions*   Commissions on the purchase or sale should be as low as possible.

14 *Strong issuer*   The issuer should be a growth company; a leader in its field; long established; invulnerable to depression; with strong finances, able management, an enviable and unbroken earnings and dividend record; an excellent sales program; valuable patents; and a research program

of high quality, which continuously develops new and better products with a high and continuing demand and better-than-average profit margins.

The above tests were, of course, somewhat exaggerated for purposes of emphasis. Needless to say, however, no one investment can meet all tests of the ideal security. For example, no security is free of all taxes. Again, no security is immune to both inflation and deflation, not even government bonds. The best that the investor can hope for is to combine as many good qualities as possible in the portfolio.

Selection of Investments

Once the investor determines the size of the securities portfolio, he must decide what part should be placed in common stocks. Again, a review of the criteria for making a decision on the size of the portfolio will be useful. Common stocks have decided advantages and definite limitations. These should be carefully weighed as they concern the investor.

Once the investor has decided upon the amount of money to be put into common stocks, either at regular intervals or in a lump sum, he must determine what securities to purchase. Here, the whole field of investment analysis is opened up. It would be well for him to study this field carefully or to consult with a qualified advisor at this point, if he has not already done so, unless he has experience in the field. There are few ways to lose money more quickly than in the purchase of bad common stocks.

The following is a general and by no means complete outline of some of the decisions, problems, and lines of investigation involved in the selection of common stocks:

1 General decisions in advance of stock selection
   (a) Degree of risk to be assumed
   (b) Priority given to the tests of a good investment
2 Selection of industrial fields
   (a) Chemicals
   (b) Electronics
   (c) Motors
   (d) Oils, and so on
3 Analysis of the industrial field
   (a) Nature of the industry
   (b) Current and potential demand for products
   (c) Growth factor
   (d) Competition within and from outside the industry
   (e) Cyclical influences

4 Selection of the individual company within the industry
5 Analysis of the company
   (a) Financial statement analysis
   (b) Earnings, dividends, and dividend policy
   (c) Capital requirements
   (d) Capitalization and senior securities
   (e) Company control and financial backing
   (f) Financial valuation of the common stock
   (g) Position of the company within the industry
   (h) Management and management policies
   (i) Location, transportation, labor supply, and raw materials
   (j) Patent position
   (k) Other relevant factors

A thorough analysis of an industrial common stock dictates an investigation of the numerous factors listed above. An examination of stock ratings issued by Standard & Poor's, Value Line, and others might aid some stock buyers in arriving at their decisions. Brokerage firms will supply much factual information which can help in making analyses, and even make recommendations on particular stocks. They are justifiably wary of making short-term price predictions and are especially reluctant to recommend selling, preferring to take the more cautious approach of recommending holding when they are unwilling to suggest buying. Financial magazines and newspapers are sometimes helpful. Some investors prefer to make selections from lists of stocks currently popular with financial institutions.

Diversification

Investment experts stress the value of diversification in building a good securities portfolio. In simple terms, this means to spread out one's investments as a protection against risk. It is based on the age-old axiom: "Don't put all your eggs in one basket." Diversification gives protection against (1) cyclical movements of business; (2) long-term or secular changes in industry; and (3) losses in the position of individual companies (unique risk).
   Diversification is possible in many ways:

1 Buying issues in different industries
2 Buying issues in different companies
3 Spreading investments over a wide geographical area
4 Buying different kinds of securities, such as bonds, preferred stocks, and common stocks
5 Buying investment company issues with well-diversified portfolios

6 Buying issues of companies with diversified product lines

7 Timing purchases over different periods of the stock cycle

8 Balancing the portfolio as between defensive and aggressive securities, that is, high quality income stocks which do well during a business recession as opposed to cyclical stocks which may bring higher speculative returns when business is expanding

Diversification can be overdone and has its limitations. These include:

1 Increased management problems

2 Increased work of investigation and analysis

3 Increased buying and selling costs

4 Reduced opportunity for better-than-average profits

Within reasonable limits proper diversification is a sound way of reducing or eliminating all but market (systematic) risk.

NONFORMULA STOCK BUYING AND SELLING

Nature

In the following section of this chapter there will be a discussion of a number of leading plans and systems now in vogue for buying and selling common stocks. Some of these are good and some are inferior. Nearly all have their limitations. Intelligent investors will select those that seem to fit their needs. A critical examination of all is recommended.

Trading by Market Axioms

There is a universal love for the simple axiom which seems to condense the wisdom of the ages into a few precise words. The axiom is simplicity itself; it relieves the mind of the painful mental processes of inductive and deductive reasoning. These digested capsules of wisdom find their place into all branches of human knowledge and into all vocational activities; they honeycomb literature, religion, ethics, marriage, agriculture, philosophy, photography, child-rearing, the arts, and business. It is therefore not illogical that the follower of the stock market is so often an easy victim of the plausible maxim.

The list of market axioms is endless. Many of them appear in books on the stock market written 50 to 75 years ago; even at that time they were well established in the lore of profit-making in the market. Perhaps the oldest is one ascribed to Meyer Rothschild, founder of the fortune bearing his name. In explaining how he was able to make so much money in securities, he stated in his broken accent, "I buys 'sheep' and sells 'deer.' " He spoke with authority. The Rothschild family acquired vast wealth after the Battle of Waterloo; his remarkable carrier service permitted him to buy vast blocks of securities very cheaply in the London market, when that exchange still believed that Napoleon had won the battle. When the regular carrier service reached London with news of Napoleon's defeat, securities soared in value and the Rothschild fortune was firmly established.

Space permits a listing of only a few of the many market axioms which have long been popular in Wall Street. Some are of unquestioned merit; others are superficial as well as trite. Some of them are directly contradictory to others. A few are entirely sound under certain conditions but entirely misleading under others.

When to buy and sell is more important than what to buy and sell.

Don't rely on the advice of "insiders."

Cut losses and let profits run.

Sell when the good news is out.

Never quarrel with the tape.

There is no need to be always in the market.

Never put a halo around a stock.

Avoid too-frequent switching.

The stock market has no past.

Never speculate for a specific need.

Don't try to get the last eighth.

No one ever went broke taking profits.

A bull can make money in Wall Street; a bear can make money in Wall Street; but a hog never can.

Opinions are worthless; facts are priceless.

Buy when others sell; sell when others buy.

Sell on the first margin call.

A margin call is the only sure tip from a broker.

Put half your profits in a safety deposit box.

Never buy a stock after a long decline.

Never answer a margin call.

Many a healthy reaction has proven fatal.

Never sell on strike news.

Stocks look best at the top of a bull market and worst at the bottom of a bear market.

It is not the price you pay for a stock, but the time you buy it that counts.

When in doubt, do nothing.

Learn to take a loss quickly.

Don't buy an egg until it is laid.

When prices close strong, after an all-day advance, the next move is generally downward.

Stocks that have the longest preceding advances have the largest declines.

All stocks move more or less with the general market, but value will tell in the long run.

Value has little to do with temporary fluctuations in stock prices.

Beware of one who has nothing to lose.

The public is always wrong.

If you would not buy a stock, sell it.

Cut back your stocks to the sleeping point.

The market will continue to fluctuate.

An investor is just a disappointed speculator.

Investment Club Buying

A surprising number of stocks were formerly purchased through investment clubs. The New York Stock Exchange at one time estimated that their purchases averaged as much as 2% of the volume on the Exchange. The members of typical clubs operate under articles of agreement as an unincorporated association. An investment club account is opened with a brokerage firm and the articles filed with it. The association has a regular set of officers. New members are voted in after the initial group has organized. The group meets regularly to discuss the club's investment program. Periodic dollar contributions are made to the club investment fund. Purchases generally are on a cash basis.

The purposes of such clubs are to educate members on the fundamental principles and practices of sound investing, to enable members to invest surplus funds mutually, and to permit them to engage in a regular investment program. Investments are received from members in various units such as $5, $10, or $25. The liquidating values of these units or shares are computed regularly, such as once a month or before each regular meeting. The club designates one member to act as agent for the group. A member may withdraw from the club upon notice and receive the liquidating value of one's shares.

Although many such clubs were successful and performed a useful service to their members, they are no longer an important device for investment. Increasing interest rates and the failure of the market to provide a refuge for those seeking protection against inflation have considerably reduced the small investor's participation in the market. This has been accompanied by the tendency of brokerage firms to expand into areas of financial merchandise more profitable than small stock accounts.

A similar fate has befallen the Monthly Investment Plan of the NYSE that was launched in 1954 to stimulate investments in small periodic purchases of listed stocks. Although this plan has been abandoned, some stock exchange firms have offered similar plans of their own in an effort to attract small customers who might one day develop into large customers.

Special Situations

This plan contemplates the purchase of common stocks in companies in which the profit opportunities are exceptionally high. These unusual opportunities are called *special situations* by Wall Street. Such stocks are those of companies that are presently undervalued but destined for sharp gains in the future. These are not growth stocks, but they have many similar characteristics.

These special situations develop for many reasons. The company may be experiencing a rapid recovery from a successful reorganization. A new management may be making radical changes in policy and operations that are destined to be unusually profitable. A heavy volume of new orders may have been received. New products with wide public acceptance may have been introduced. The company may have developed some natural resource for new uses at a great profit such as occurred with uranium. Proposed mergers may cause considerable price increases in the stocks of one or more of the companies involved. Perhaps one company was selling well below book value or there might be great synergistic advantages anticipated.

The advantage, of course, of purchases in special situations before they develop is the immense profits obtainable. Unfortunately, they are not for the average investor or trader. No one on the outside has the knowledge—and probably the luck—to pick these stocks in advance. Only the most skilled analysts can do so. A few investment funds specialize in this type of investing. The management aspect of the special situation is often highly important. The financial group interested in the situation takes over control, installs its own management, and invests new capital which may be required. In effect, the financial group often makes the special situation. It is in the best position to capitalize upon its efforts and it frequently does.

Industry Selection

This term is chosen because there seems to be no better one available. In fact, this method of stock trading is given no name at all by the financial community, although it has been used for years. Traders who follow the industry selection plan base their operations on the expected actions of stocks of particular industries. Certain industries, in their opinion, appear promising in their market outlook in the coming months because of special conditions. A given industry may be experiencing a sharp revival as new orders pour into it. New models may be meeting unusually good public reception. Defense spending may have been creating a heavy volume of new contracts. Business recovery may have resulted in a large gain in freight traffic.

As such situations develop, traders rush into the industry that shows such promise over the short run. In a few months, or a year, profit opportunities are past and traders seek other industries with greater promise. Thus, there is a constant shift of trading from oils to steels, to motors, to chemicals, to building materials, to railroads, to road building equipment, to electronics, to aircrafts.

The rewards of this type of trading are substantial for those who can accurately "pick a winner." Gains of 50% or more in a year are often possible. The trader who could successfully pick these industries over a long period would reap immense, if not fantastic, profits. In an interesting hypothetical study made by Hugh W. Long and Company, an investment firm, for the period 1915–1944, a sum of $100 was turned into one of $70 million by successfully shifting funds from stocks of one industry to another as profit opportunities developed.[2] Hindsight is a wonderful thing.

Trading by industry selection requires the most accurate forecasting possible, as well as perfect timing. A further limitation is that it works against the principle of portfolio diversification; it creates a risk few can assume.

GROWTH STOCKS

Characteristics

These are the glamor stocks of Wall Street. No group of stocks can compare with them in attraction. They are stocks that have shown a much better than average appreciation over a period of time. Often they double in value from the crest of one stock cycle to another. Their growth in sales and earnings is much larger than that of common stocks as a whole.

A growth stock is usually considered to be one issued by an expanding company. Generally the company is in an expanding industry. Such companies may be in old, established industries like chemicals and electrical equipment, but many examples are found in younger industries, such as electronics. A growth stock can be looked upon in two ways. First, it can be identified as a stock that has shown very high appreciation in the past. It has now become a strong, well-known blue-chip stock, such as DuPont, General Motors, General Electric, or Coca-Cola. Second, it can be identified as a stock that has great potentialities for growth in the future. The two are not the same. Some companies have been growth companies in the past. For others growth is in the future. For still others the growth of the past seems destined to continue into the distant future. A danger to the investor is that one might buy into a company whose period of growth is past.

Many companies have qualified as issuers of growth stocks in the past. These include such outstanding examples as General Electric, Westinghouse, IBM, DuPont, Dow, Monsanto, Union Carbide, Sears, Minnesota Mining and Manufacturing, Exxon, Coca-Cola, General Motors, Ford, Eastman Kodak, and International Paper, to mention only a few. Some of these will doubtless continue in this category.

The type of industries in the growth field changes over a period. Years ago, in the 1920s, automobiles, chemicals, radios, and motion pictures were in this classification. Predictions of growth stocks for the future are limitless.

[2]*The Thirty Year Bull Market,* (New York: Hugh W. Long).

Some of the industries listed in this category for coming years include electronics (particularly home computers, automatic controls, and business machinery), chemicals, pharmaceuticals, certain synthetic fibers, petrochemicals, plastics, light metals, oceanography, silicone plastics and products, biochemistry, solar energy devices, high temperature alloys, and fast foods.

When looking back over time, outstanding companies in the growth category have been noted for certain rather definite characteristics. Anderson, in an outstanding study of them, found that as a group they were noted for producing goods and services enjoying high and continuous demand; for continuously developing new products with wide appeal and better than average profit margins; for large and continuous expenditures in new plant and equipment; for possessing excellent sales programs; for enjoying highly competent management; for having large and high quality research programs; for possessing the ability to secure adequate amounts of new capital easily; and for flourishing in mass production industries with relatively low labor costs.[3]

Performance

Examples of highly profitable growth stocks are well publicized. A few will suffice here. An investment of $13,000 in 100 shares of DuPont common in 1922 would have grown to $1.5 million by 1961, disregarding more than one-quarter million dollars in dividends received. An investment of $4,320 in 100 shares of Minnesota Mining and Manufacturing stock in 1946 would have been worth $210,000 plus dividends by 1961. A large firm made a study of 25 typical growth stocks for the period from January 1939 to September 1955. A total of $1,000 was placed in each stock. The hypothetical fund of $25,000 increased in the 16 years to $235,000.[4]

One of the most careful studies of growth stocks ever made was that of Anderson.[5] Twenty-five such stocks were selected to eliminate any advantage due to hindsight. The period was from 1936 to 1954, a period of 18 years. Yields were found to be only 3.8% or distinctly inferior to the 5.3% rate of the Dow Jones industrial average. However, when dividends were reinvested and appreciation considered, the portfolio increased 514% for the period in contrast with 400% for the average. In other words, the growth stock portfolio increased 28% faster than the blue-chip average. The gain over typical income stocks for the same period was nearly 70%.

The 1970s and 1980s have provided countless examples of growth stocks yielding extraordinary profits. Given the emergence of many new products, especially in electronics, and the great bull market of the mid-1980s, it would have been surprising not to find so many examples.

[3]Robert W. Anderson, "Unrealized Potentials in Growth Stocks," *Harvard Business Review* 33 (March-April, 1955), 61.
[4]*111 Growth Stocks* (New York: Merrill Lynch, Pierce, Fenner & Smith, 1956), p. 50.
[5]Anderson, *op. cit.*

Advantages

There are three advantages to buying growth stocks. First, they produce a faster growth in the investment portfolio than the purchase of income stocks or blue-chip stocks which characterize the averages. Second, they have a tax advantage to investors in the higher brackets. Dividends are smaller than those on income stocks; hence, there are lower taxes on current income. Appreciation is not taxable until the stock is sold. Third, the continuous appreciation tends to offset errors in timing of purchases, because they are believed to recover faster from a market decline.

Criticisms

A number of criticisms have been directed at the purchase of growth stocks. The most important is the difficulty of selection in advance. To secure the largest gains requires that they be purchased when they are undervalued. This means selection before they are recognized as such, when the companies are small and perhaps struggling to get established. It is then difficult to estimate future growth. Even if the industry appears to have growth possibilities, it is not easy to pick the companies that will become leaders in the industry. This selection before growth appears or is well recognized requires the highest possible investment skill.

Second, growth stocks characteristically pay low dividends and give low current yields. Hence, an investor interested in high current income finds these stocks unattractive. Eventually, a good growth stock will pay substantial dividends on the original investment, but it may take many years to reach this stage.

Third, these stocks sell at very high price–earnings ratios. When fully recognized as growth stocks, they are bid up to high prices and sell at such high price–earnings ratios that they represent unusual investment hazards. The market may have discounted future growth and earning power so much and so far in advance that no real profit is obtainable at current prices.

Fourth, growth industries eventually reach a plateau of stability or maturity. Without realizing this, the investor is apt to pay too high a price for the stock and buy a quality which has ceased to exist.

Fifth, there is a danger of competition. Because growth industries make larger than average profits, many competitors come into the industry. In the early stages most of the weak units are eliminated until only a handful of major producers remain. The investor runs a big chance of buying into a company which fails to come out on top. The automobile industry is a classic example. More recently computer manufacturers followed this pattern.

Sixth, purchase of growth stocks creates a danger of concentration of financial risk as opposed to sound diversification. Growth stocks at their inception are usually highly speculative.

Seventh, investment in growth stocks requires patience. If they are purchased at the period that gives maximum profit, the investor must wait years to realize the full potential growth. In the meantime there are uncertainty and low return, which many buyers are unwilling to assume. If they are sold too quickly, the return will be less than if income stocks had been purchased.

FORMULA STOCK BUYING AND SELLING

Untold numbers of people have spent untold numbers of hours to reduce the art and science of investing and trading to a plan or formula that would be sound in theory and profitable in practice. Some of these formula plans are still used by some individuals and institutions. Most, however, have been overshadowed by plans incorporating some aspects of Modern Portfolio Theory and the ready availability of computerized programs which permit the quick and accurate digestion of large amounts of data. A brief discussion of some of the efforts to develop formula plans follows, along with an evaluation of their results.

Characteristics of Formula Plans

Formula plans have grown out of a desire by investors and traders to obtain protection against purchases and sales at unfavorable price levels. Stated in another way, the plans were created to obtain better timing, thus avoiding the heavy losses such as were suffered in 1929, 1946, and 1974.

It was hoped, and for a time confidently expected, that a successful formula plan would avoid mistakes in judgment. In fact, it was hoped that judgment could be eliminated and that a mechanical set of rules could dictate purchases and sales to assure reasonable profits at all times. In this way the emotional aspect of investing and trading would be eliminated. Buyers would no longer have to trust their own judgment or consult their fears and hopes; the set of rules would take over decision making.

Spurred on by this philosophy, a number of plans were developed. Two general types emerged. The first type consisted of a group of plans that operated without the computation of normal values. The second group operated on the basis of normal values, computed by a number of methods. Selected examples of each classification will be examined later in the chapter.

Before doing so, however, an objection against all such systems should be pointed out. It is the criticism that there are many investors who should not purchase stocks under any of the plans, because all involve dangers that they ought not to assume. Such investors include those who are uninformed about stocks and those who should not assume the risks of stock ownership. Many economists feel that this group should either stick to more conservative investments, such as savings accounts and savings bonds, or restrict stock purchases to investment companies.

Classification

No classification of formula plans is entirely satisfactory. The following classification, although not all inclusive, is believed to cover enough plans to be representative and reasonably satisfactory:

1 Non-normal value formula plans
   (a) Dollar cost averaging
   (b) Constant dollar plan
   (c) Constant ratio plan
2 Normal value formula plans with variable ratios
   (a) Plans based on price
        (i)   Moving average plans
        (ii)   Trend plans
   (b) Plans based on intrinsic values
        (i)   Yield plans
        (ii)   Price–earnings plans
        (iii) Quality plans
        (iv)   Growth stock plans
        (v)   Book value plans

DOLLAR COST AVERAGING

Characteristics

This is among the simplest and oldest of all formula plans, but there are some who still consider it to be the best. Some are so enthusiastic as to characterize it as unbeatable.

The plan consists of investing a constant amount of money in common stocks over a long period, regardless of the level of stock prices. This steady accumulation of stocks proceeds at regular intervals, such as monthly, quarterly, or annually. For example, an investor with $6,000 per year would invest $1,500 each quarter over a period of years.

It is not an in-and-out trading system, but a long-term investment program. It is also not a method for investing a large sum at any one time but, rather, one for investing regular amounts out of current income. When the program begins is of no importance, but when it ends is of great importance.

There are two requirements for success. First, the investor must take a long-term point of view. Second, the investor should have a steady flow of income to invest, the steadier the better. Given these requirements, the results can be highly gratifying.

An Example

There are a number of advantages to the formula. One advantage is that the average cost of stocks should be less than the average market price of the stocks held in the portfolio. This happens because a constant amount of money buys only a few shares at high prices but many at low prices. This is best illustrated by a simple example. Only two years are necessary. In each year the investor places $6,000 in the shares of a given company. In the first year he buys 200 shares at $30. In the following year he buys 100 shares at $60. His average cost is $12,000 divided by 300 shares, or $40. The market price, however, was $60 in the latter year. The theory is that stocks always can be sold on the average for more than they cost.

Technical Problems

Stocks that fluctuate greatly give better profits under this formula than those that do not. However, this entails considerable risk and should be avoided by conservative investors. A well-diversified portfolio is best. Shares of investment companies give excellent diversification and can be used to advantage in dollar cost averaging. It is not necessary to use the same stocks throughout the investment period. The portfolio should be managed just as though no plan were in effect, with elimination of undesirable issues when justified. An important consideration is that stocks chosen eventually go up. Money certainly cannot be made on stocks showing a continuous downward movement. This is the danger of attempting to average on one stock. It may go down and not come back up. This danger is greatly reduced by proper diversification.

The problem of purchases at high stock price levels presents itself. Strict adherence to the program dictates that regular purchasing policies be continued. Some suggest that purchases be discontinued when stocks get very high. Such a policy seems reasonable, but has three objections: (1) it is difficult to tell when they are "too high"; (2) money not invested is likely to be spent elsewhere; and (3) there is a danger of abandoning the program. If stocks are believed to be very high, the money can be put into "defensive stocks," or those that perform well in a declining market, such as utilities. An opposite situation develops during a period of falling prices. Investors, anticipating still lower prices, withhold purchases. If they are in error, they lose an opportunity to pick up a large number of shares at low prices. However, one suggestion would be that in periods of low prices investors concentrate on volatile issues or those with a wide cyclical range. The danger of departing from regular purchases at any time is that investors will turn into speculators and never buy except when prices look low to them. If this happens, their dollar cost averaging program is lost.

The termination date of a given program is important. The program should terminate a few years before the total fund is needed, such as for retirement. In this way investors can wait for a year or two for liquidation in case the stock cycle should be in a trough. There is always, of course, some danger that a plan will terminate at a time when stock prices are low.

Advantages

The first advantage is that the average cost of shares purchased is always less than the average market price. Another advantage is that it is a simple plan, involving no computations of normal periods, trend lines, or trading zones. A third advantage is that the investor avoids the danger of buying too many shares when prices are too high. For many years, the greatest advantage of dollar averaging was purported to be the benefit of the long-run appreciation in stock prices and the high yields possible from common stock. With annual returns from stock generally assumed to exceed 10% per year, compound interest would permit one's investment to double in about seven years. During periods when the stock market trades in a relatively narrow range and when stock yields are greatly overshadowed by yields on more conservative money market instruments, this advantage may prove to be elusive. the purported advantage offered by the opportunity to invest dividends continuously may also be reduced during periods when dividend yields are low. A final advantage is that declines in market price not only do not injure the portfolio, but also benefit it, because they provide an opportunity to buy additional shares at low average costs.

Limitations

The first limitation is the danger of liquidation of the fund during a period of low stock prices, thus causing a portfolio loss. Protection against this danger is much reduced by planning to liquidate the fund several years before it is needed. In this way the investor can defer final liquidation if the level of stock prices is not satisfactory. During this waiting period stock prices may rise, permitting liquidation at a satisfactory level. A second criticism is the difficulty of stock selection, a criticism directed against all stock buying plans. Some stocks develop a downward trend and never show satisfactory results. This may even be true of entire industries. In answer to this criticism, it is suggested that investors need only diversify their portfolios. Those who have only small amounts to invest can utilize shares of investment companies.

A third limitation is the financial danger of missing purchases. Many investors do not have the stability of income which assures a continuous investment program. In a depression, when salaries are cut and professional income drops off, payments are likely to be reduced or terminated at the very time when stock prices are at their most attractive levels. A fourth limitation is the psychological danger of stopping purchases when stock prices appear too high. Hoping for better prices, investors stop their buying. They become speculators. If their judgment is faulty, the results of their programs are badly damaged. A fifth danger is that of diverting investment installments into more attractive or urgent channels, such as vacations, new cars, or family weddings. This danger can be lessened by starting a program that can be sustained under adverse conditions or by keeping a liquid reserve, such as a savings account, which can be drawn upon during periods of reduced income.

CONSTANT DOLLAR PLAN

Basic Features

The principle of the constant dollar plan is to keep a constant number of dollars, say $50,000, invested in stocks regardless of the stock price level. The rest of the investor's portfolio should be in bonds or preferred stocks. If stock prices rise, stock should be sold to reduce the stock fund to $50,000. If stock prices fall, so that the stock portfolio is reduced below $50,000, funds should be invested in common stocks to bring it back to the $50,000 level.

Diversification of the stock portfolio would be not only possible but also sound management. However, the plan can be operated for individual stocks, and diversification achieved by having a number of plans in simultaneous operation.

Three basic problems present themselves: (1) the ratio between stocks and bonds; (2) the basis for timing purchases and sales; and (3) the stocks to be used. The last problem, of course, is characteristic of all formula plans and will be discussed no further.

The stock–bond ratio is a question of individual judgment. The usual assumption is that the ratio should be 50–50 at the inception of the plan, which should be started during a period of apparently normal prices. The problem of timing can be settled in several ways. First, purchases and sales can be made at set intervals, one year being a general recommendation. Second, they can be made after stock prices go up or down by a certain percentage, such as 20 or 25%.

Advantages

There are two advantages. The first is the great simplicity of the plan. Stocks are sold as they rise and purchased as they fall on the basis of arbitrary, prearranged signals. There are no calculations of any significant difficulty. The second advantage is that the plan provides for an automatic sale of stocks as they rise in price, thus restraining enthusiasm for stock purchasing at high price levels.

Limitations

The first objection is that the original fund must be started during a period of normal prices, the determination of which is no mean achievement. Otherwise, there is the danger of having too large or too small a stock fund. The second limitation is that for best results a period of substantial fluctuations above and below the original price level is essential. The plan does not work well in a period of continuously rising or falling prices.

CONSTANT RATIO PLAN

Basic Features

This plan is based on the principle of maintaining at all times a constant ratio, such as 50–50, between the value of stocks and the value of bonds held in the portfolio. As stock prices go up, stocks are sold to bring the portfolio back to the original ratio; as they go down, stocks are purchased to achieve the same result. The result is that stocks are sold as prices rise and the profits are converted into additional bonds. As stocks fall, bonds are sold to take advantage of lower stock prices. Modest profits are therefore possible as prices fluctuate above and below the original purchase level.

Our problem involves deciding the basic ratio between stocks and bonds, such as 50–50, 35–65, or 60–40. A second problem is that of a suitable buying and selling schedule. In other words, when should the original ratio, for example, 50–50, be reestablished? Three possible options present themselves: (1) whenever the stock part of the portfolio rises or falls by a certain percentage or amount; (2) whenever a certain change takes place in a selected stock index; and (3) at established time intervals. A third problem is that of timing the start of any given plan. This involves forecasting, because the investor must avoid the danger of starting a plan during a period of very high stock prices. Hence, judgment is required when starting the plan.

Some consider that delaying action is desirable, notably when stock prices are declining. Under such a plan stock purchases would be delayed beyond the normal buying schedule as long as stock prices continued to fall. Suggested methods of delaying action include (1) a requirement that there must be a definite time lapse between successive stock purchases and (2) a requirement that the amount of stock at any one time be limited to a certain percentage of the total fund.

Advantages

The first advantage is that the plan is a simple one. It is easy to understand and to administer. A second advantage is that small profits seem obtainable when stock prices fluctuate over and under a normal level. A third advantage is that the investor reduces stock holdings when stock prices rise and increases them as they decline, a characteristic of all formula plans except dollar cost averaging. Fourth, it is relatively easy to increase the size of the fund when additional funds are available for investment.

Limitations

First, for best results the plan should be started during a period of normal prices or an adjustment should be made in the initial ratio if prices appear too high or below normal; this involves judgment and forecasting. There is nothing in the plan that defines a normal level of stock prices. Second, the evidence is not conclusive that the plan is superior to other plans, such as "buy-and-hold" or dollar cost averaging.

NORMAL VALUE PLANS WITH VARIABLE RATIOS

History

Normal value formula plans with variable ratios developed in the investment field in the latter part of the 1930s because of dissatisfaction with the results of portfolio management after the 1937–1938 market break. Considerable interest developed among colleges, insurance companies, trust companies, and some mutual funds. Many individuals adopted the idea in the management of their portfolios, particularly wealthy investors. Interest was high in the early 1950s before the 1949–1960 bull market reached an advanced stage. After 1953 enthusiasm declined because many plans proved unrealistic as stock prices soared to unprecedented levels. Many plans were abandoned after they caused investors to sell out of common stocks, leaving them with substantial funds to invest but without an attractive place to invest them. As time passed, price levels which had appeared too high began to seem increasingly normal to enough investors to create some new interest in normal value formula plans.

Classification

These plans may be divided into two types. The first type consists of those plans that use price as the central or normal value. In this type two main methods are used in arriving at that value: (1) the moving average and (2) the trend line. The second type consists of those plans that use some intrinsic value in arriving at the median value, such as earnings, dividends, or yields.

Basic Theory

All these plans are aimed at avoiding the worst mistakes of timing. Purchasing takes place when stocks appear low by the formula. They are sold when they appear high. In all cases a central or median value is determined. When stocks are selling below this median value, they are purchased; when above, they are sold. Purchasing and selling are done through mechanical rules, rather than judgment. Although these operations do not give the maximum profits possible from buying at the bottom and selling at the top of the market, such plans are defended on the ground that smaller but more assured profits are obtainable with less risk.

The Portfolio

All plans with variable ratios operate through a portfolio divided into two parts. The first part is known as the "defensive" part and consists of bonds and high-grade preferred stocks. The second part is the "aggressive" section and consists of common stocks which move with the general level of stock prices. The first part provides protection against a decline in stock prices, whereas the second part provides profits during a rising stock cycle.

The various plans differ in the ratio of defensive to aggressive securities, when stock prices are at a normal level. Usually the ratio is 50–50. In some cases, however, the ratio may be as much as 60–40 or 65–35. The ratio is determined by the degree of risk which the investor is willing to assume and the need for current income.

These ratios change as stock prices rise and fall. In some funds the ratio of bonds to total portfolio holdings may range from 100 to 0%. In others it may never be more than 65% or less than 35%.

At this point it seems desirable to divide the discussion into two parts: (1) plans based on price and (2) plans based on intrinsic values.

NORMAL VALUE PLANS BASED ON PRICE

Computation of Normal or Central Value

All formula plans provide for some method of computing the normal or central value for stock prices. In some cases this normal value is called the median value. One of the well-known indexes or averages is usually used as the yardstick for measuring the level of stock prices. The first problem is how to find the normal or median value for the index or average which is chosen. Two basic approaches are used: (1) the moving average and (2) the trend line.

Let us first consider the moving average. Although various periods are used for the computation of moving averages, 10 years or 120 months are considered the most satisfactory. The average for these 120 months becomes the central value. The trouble with using this unadjusted 120-month average is that stock prices over a long period show an upward secular trend.

The other method of computing normal value is by the use of trend lines. These can be either arithmetic or geometric trend lines. Some plans use one and some the other. There is no general agreement as to which is better, because no analysis of stock prices has ever clearly indicated whether stock prices over a long period increase at an arithmetic or a geometric rate. Once the trend line is calculated, it is necessary to determine certain action points above and below the trend line or normal value, so that sales and purchases may be made. The usual method is to draw several zones above and below the trend line or normal value. These zones are based on scales, which may be so many points apart, such as 15 or 20 points, or a certain percentage of the normal value, such as 10 or 15%. These zones then become action points and indicate when buying and selling are in order.

Typically, stocks are never sold until they rise to or above the normal value or trend line and are then sold as they go through each zone or action point. On the way down they are not purchased until they fall to or below the central value and are then purchased as they drop through each zone or action point.

The theory is that during a typical stock cycle stock prices will fluctuate between the top and bottom zones of the formula chart, as they have done historically. The assumption is that stock price behavior in the future can be forecast by the projection of historical trends, an assumption seriously questioned by many students of the market.

Frequency of Trading

There is some difference between the various plans as to the frequency of trading. In some, buying and selling takes place at the exact moment when stock prices pass through a zone or action point. In others, there may be a delay, with buying and selling taking place only at certain intervals, such as at the monthly meeting of the investment committee or at three-month intervals. This delaying action is based on the assumption that stock prices, once they have established a given trend, will continue in that direction for some time.

Advantages

The first advantage is that such plans permit orderly purchasing and selling without forecasting stock prices. A mechanical set of rules determines buying and selling points in the stock cycle. Thus the element of judgment can be dispensed with and the danger of faulty, emotional decisions is eliminated. Hence, the worry about future price movements is decreased because there is no need for making numerous decisions of when to buy and sell; the formula takes care of that.

The second advantage is that plans provide for small but fairly certain profits over a period of time. Conceptually, plans are designed to cause stocks to be bought when they are low and sold when they are high judged by some historical standard. Although maximum profits cannot be obtained, the investor aims at smaller but more certain profits. Such investors are willing to forgo maximizing profits in return for reducing risk.

Limitations

Miscalculation of the normal value is a great problem. In retrospect it can be too high or too low. Trend lines that terminated in the late 1920s proved far too high considering the events of 1929. The carnage suffered by those who followed plans at that time is still remembered. The high levels of stock prices in the mid-1980s have convinced even many diehard followers of formula plans that historical trend lines are not realistic and that the normal level of stock prices, if there is one, might be considerably higher than was previously thought. Most students of the stock market believe that it is extremely hazardous or entirely useless to attempt to forecast prices by the projection of trend lines based on prices of years ago.

The highly mechanistic calculation of future stock prices ignores rational analysis and disregards changes in economic conditions. Events of recent years such as tremendous fluctuations in interest rates, metals prices, and petroleum production have caused movements in stock prices without precedent. As a result, stock prices can hardly be related to previous levels arbitrarily designated as "normal."

A second and important weakness in such plans is that they ignore earnings and dividends. They assume that a stock that was selling at $50 10 years ago is now overpriced because it is selling at $100. High stock prices can be justified if they are accompanied by high earnings and dividends. A $100 stock earning $8 and paying $5 is just as good an investment as a $50 stock earning $4 and paying $2.50. Yet the only factor considered by the formula is the stock price level.

A third criticism is that such plans make it difficult to reenter the market after extended rises. At such points many portfolios are entirely without stocks. A literal adherence to some formula policies would have precluded owning stocks since the rise of 1953, thereby missing the greatest bull market in history.

A fourth limitation is that the plans provide less profit than is gained by those who forecast stock prices based on judgment, experience, and intuition. Granted that consistent success in forecasting by such a method is difficult, many question whether the reduced profits of formula plans are not too high a price to pay for greater latitude in investment policy.

Another criticism by those who believe stocks offer protection against inflation is that such plans prevent investors from securing such protection by causing them to sell stocks just when inflation gets under way or, at least, increases in intensity.

A sixth criticism is that such plans are usually complex and require rather formidable statistical calculations. While these may be no great problem to the investment institution, they are a handicap to most investors.

A final criticism is that they are not practical for small investors with a limited portfolio. It is not very realistic to expect them to shift their funds from stocks to bonds and back at frequent intervals, as indicated by a formula chart. They will be much more inclined to "buy-and-hold" or to turn their troubles over to a mutual fund.

As in all stock buying plans, there is the inevitable problem of stock selection. It is a weakness of all formula plans.

NORMAL VALUE PLANS BASED ON INTRINSIC VALUES

Basic Theory

These plans are based on the premise that the normal or real values of stocks are not based on price alone but upon other factors. The important thing is not what a stock sold for five, ten, or fifteen years ago—or even yesterday—but what it is worth in terms of book value, earning power, dividends, and yield. An increase in price will not diminish the value of a given stock in investment quality if its intrinsic value increases as much as or more than its price.

There is considerable disagreement as to exactly what constitutes the intrinsic value of a stock. There is not even any agreement on the meaning of the term. It can well be argued that the real value of a stock is the price at which it is selling at a given time. If this is true, a stock will prove to have been "overvalued" or "undervalued" only after the fact, and such opportunities cannot be consistently forecast successfully. Given this scenario, those who rely on normal value plans based on intrinsic values to identify stocks which are too high or too low will find their efforts doomed to failure.

Stock Yields

There are not many publicized formula plans based on stock yields, but there are some investors who believe that this important intrinsic value provides a valid base for a plan. Some consider stock yields to be one of the best simple measures of the level of stock prices available to the ordinary investor. A simple plan might be based on the Dow Jones industrial average. A long period, say 25 years, might indicate an average dividend yield on the stocks making up the average of about 5% that could be taken to be the norm. When the average is yielding 5%, a fund would be half in stocks and half in defensive investments. At 6%, stocks might be considered cheap and all the portfolio be invested in stocks. On the other hand, stocks might be purchased only selectively when yields are below 4%.

There have been too many exceptions to the observed general correlation between low yields and bull markets and high yields and bear markets to suggest that this method be followed in a naïve manner. Some use the ratio between high yielding and low yielding stocks only along with other indicators as a guide to general market strength rather than using yield alone to make investment decisions.

Price–Earnings Ratios

Another possible formula for intrinsic values would be to use price–earnings ratios. For example, over a 25-year period the average price–earnings ratio of the Dow Jones industrials might be calculated as, say, 12 to 1. This figure could be used as normal for an intrinsic value formula. At this level half a portfolio could be invested in stocks and half in defensive securities. At 18 to 1 the entire portfolio, or most of it at least, could be placed in defensive securities. At 9 to 1 all, or nearly all, of the portfolio would be placed into common stocks. The indicator sought would be the high ratio that would characterize a bull market top and a low ratio which would characterize a bear market low.

More likely, price–earnings ratios find value as an adjunct to other methods in making investment decisions. Investors might devise plans, for example, which buy portfolios of stocks with low price–earnings ratios. Others might compare the performance of stocks with low price–earnings ratios with those of high price–earnings ratios as a guide to anticipated market action.

THE STOCK CYCLE

Closely related to formula trading is the possible reliance of a stock cycle. For many years after the Civil War, a typical stock cycle averaged about 4 years.

The purchaser of common stocks would seem well advised not to rely too heavily upon cycles as a guide. Individual cycles have run from less than 2 years to more than 10. The length of a particular cycle offers little clue to the length of the succeeding cycle. A 5-year cycle can be followed by a 2-year cycle, which in turn can be followed by a 6-year cycle.

The amplitude of the cycle is its upward and downward swing—the distance between the peak and the trough. Stock cycles vary greatly in amplitude, and to make things more difficult, there appears to be no way in which the amplitude of any given cycle can be forecast. In some cycles the amplitude is small, whereas in others it is large. To complicate matters more, stock cycles in the past half-century appear to be changing their character, apparently getting longer in duration and displaying greater amplitude. It is evident, therefore, from this modest discussion of the cycle that the investor must guard against any superficial rules designed to aid him in getting into and out of the market at the right time.

Barometers of Stock Prices

Every market analyst would be delighted to discover a reliable barometer of stock prices, particularly if the barometer were not known to other analysts. Such a barometer would be a single economic series such as building contracts, money supply figures, consumer price index, employment, retail sales, inventories, or industrial production that would move in advance of the stock cycle and thus forecast changes in the stock cycle. Even if the stock cycle concept itself has any long-term value, there is no evidence that there is any reliable barometer that predicts it.

Practically all economic series lag behind the movement of stock prices on the average; hence, they cannot be used to forecast changes in the market. Even such apparent exceptions as dollar liabilities of industrial and commercial failures depart sharply from the averages in individual cycles. There is a rather general and apparently well-founded opinion that no reliable barometer of the business cycle exists, much less a barometer of stock prices. The formula trader had best assume that there is no single barometer that provides a satisfactory mechanical guide to stock purchases.

Proprietary Formula Plans

Many plans have been developed by investment companies, universities, investment advisers, brokerage houses, and scholars in the investment field. Some of these plans are used regularly whereas others have been tested and abandoned. Some of these plans have been described in the financial literature. Some have had records of success for a time.

There are doubtless many plans being used by individuals or institutions which are not discussed publicly for fear that if successful, widespread use would ultimately destroy their value. It appears doubtful that any simplistic system will ever replace good information, wise diversification, care, and common sense as the requisite qualities in investment operations. In the short run, at least, a little luck does no harm either.

Modern Portfolio Theory

The enormous amounts of available data concerning the financial markets and the ability of computers to digest the data have resulted in much attention being paid to Modern Portfolio Theory (MPT). Students of this subject have become vitally interested in such primary concepts as the Capital Asset Pricing Model and optimal portfolio construction. Risk of assets in portfolios has become widely measured by the beta of each asset. This is the risk of an asset held in a portfolio relative to the risk of the market taken as a whole for that type of asset.

The details of MPT must be left for specialized investment books, but some widely held basic conclusions should at least be considered by the reader. If the theory is correct, it would appear that there probably is no viable wise alternative to the holding of a well-constructed portfolio. Risk and return are dependent, as always, upon subsequent market direction, but if the direction is correctly anticipated, risk and return can be built into a wisely constructed portfolio. Concentration in only one or two stocks is not only unwise, it is downright irrational. Unique and industry risks that are taken when the portfolio is too small need not be taken. Aggressive portfolio managers can best satisfy their needs for aggression by buying high beta portfolios without unduly high correlation of the securities therein, by using financial leverage, or by both.

MANAGEMENT INVESTMENT COMPANIES

Investment companies provide a method by which the investor can purchase common stocks and other securities indirectly. He purchases the shares of the investment company, which in turn invests his funds in the securities of many issuers, often 100 or more.

Although investment companies trace their origins back to at least nineteenth-century Europe, the growth of such companies in the United States since World War II has amounted almost to a phenomenon. The number of such funds from the 1940s to the 1980s grew from under 100 to more than 2,000.

There are three basic types of investment company. These include the face-amount certificate company, the unit investment trust, and the management company. Little need be said about the first of these, which is infrequently seen today. It is essentially a fixed-income vehicle sold to conservative investors and is rather more like a savings bond than a true security investment. The investor buys a certificate with a certain face amount, say $5,000, and puts up a payment of something less than half that amount depending on maturity and interest rates. The face amount is received at maturity, but an early redemption will yield less.

Unit trusts have become enormously popular since the 1960s. They are primarily used to offer low-cost entry to the municipal bond market, but have been used to package such diverse items as corporate bonds, government bonds and notes, certificates of deposit, and even common stocks. A dealer assembles a portfolio of securities such as $25 million of municipal bonds, places them in a trust, and offers units of participation in the trust at about $1,000 each.

Because the trust itself bears no tax liability, it passes investment returns directly to the investor. In the case of municipal bonds, therefore, tax-free income flows through to the holders. The unit trust offers the smaller investor both entry to a market characterized by $100,000 round lots and diversification which would be difficult to obtain in the municipal market with capital of much less than $250,000. Although the units bear a sales charge of 3½ to 4½%, they are usually redeemed or repurchased by the dealer for the net asset value prevailing at the time with no further charge. The trusts usually have finite lives, after which time the par value is returned to the investors (assuming no defaults).

Although the trust units are redeemable—that is, they may be cashed in at the net asset value—they should not be confused with mutual funds. The trust is not managed; what you see is what you get. There may be some drawbacks to this if one of the securities defaults, but the offsetting advantage is that there is no management fee.

By far the greatest number of investment companies are management companies which can be classified in many ways. The most usual classification is closed end and open end, the bulk being open end. Open-end management companies are popularly known as mutual funds. These in turn can be classified in many ways including sales cost, if any, and the types of securities in which the funds specialize.

A detailed description of investment companies would constitute a book in itself, thus only a brief summary is possible here. Given the constant change in this explosive industry and the varieties of choice, the reader is urged to make a full and careful investigation of them before investing in one or more. Information is readily available in prospectuses, annual reports, information statements, and various publications.

Closed-End Companies

There are about 60 closed-end investment companies in operation. Shares of a few of them are traded over the counter, but most are traded on the exchanges, particularly the New York Stock Exchange. Leading closed-end companies listed on this Exchange include Adams Express, Lehman Corporation, and Tri-Continental Corporation. Although sometimes mistakenly designated as mutual funds, closed-end funds are significantly different. Like operating companies, the floating supply of stock is relatively fixed and prices vary with demand and supply pressures like those of other stocks. They may sell at prices above or below their net asset values. They are purchased on a commission basis rather than on a markup from their asset value. They are seldom marketed aggressively by commission houses, perhaps because the incentive to the salesperson is usually less attractive than from the sale of mutual funds, but the performance of closed-end funds has often been creditable. The buyer is sometimes rewarded by not only an increasing net asset value of such stocks, but also the tendency for them to trade at decreasing discounts or even at premiums relative to their net asset value in rising markets.

Open-End Companies

These companies have always been the most popular type of investment company. There are currently about 1,300 such companies which manage well over 90% of the asset value of securities under management. Each fund is operated by a management group, which is compensated for its services. Investments usually show wide diversity. Portfolios consist mostly of common stocks, although "balanced funds" may also purchase bonds and preferred stocks. Stocks may be concentrated in a single industry or in companies operating in a concentrated geographic location, but broad diversification is more typical. Management companies make clear policies concerning diversification or concentration.

Objectives may be income, good quality or speculative growth, capital gains, tax-free income, or preservation of capital. Managers, in an effort to compete with the performance of their competitors, are under considerable pressure to show good short-term performance records so a considerable turnover of investments may take place in any given fund portfolio over even brief periods. They must also invest money constantly if capital generated from the sale of new shares exceeds the money lost because of adverse market or redemptions. The skill of management, performance, and return to stockholders varies widely among funds and often in the same fund from one period to another. Great stress today is put on management, in part induced by competition and in part because of still-lingering memories of 1929, when investment trusts showed a record of incompetent management verging on the incredible.

The Portfolio

Most funds widely diversify their portfolios, often owning securities of over 100 issuers. The total value of a fund's securities is often hundreds of millions or over a billion dollars. Portfolios are usually published quarterly by the companies and by various financial services. They can thus be examined by shareholders, potential buyers, and those who use such holdings as a guide to personal market investments.

The high degree of diversification provides a protection against all but systematic risk, but it also prevents many funds from showing an average performance as compared with the market averages. A policy of keeping significant amounts of cash on hand also causes performance to lag in rising markets. The inability to liquidate quickly in falling markets may add to losses or cause profits to deteriorate more than would be the case in more flexible smaller portfolios.

Management Cost

Funds are managed by a relatively small group of trustees, directors, investment counselors, or an advisory board, assisted by a staff of analysts. The sponsor of the fund usually is responsible for its management. Compensation comes in two ways. First, the sponsor receives part of the selling commission or "loading charge" unless there is a separate selling organization. This is typically one-fourth to one-third of the total loading charge, which runs from 6 to 8½% but is usually near the top of this range. The sponsor therefore receives about 2–3% when the shares are sold to the investor. The fund itself receives only net asset value.

Second, the management retains an annual management fee. This varies from ¼ of 1% to over 1%, but averages about ½ of 1% of the assets. This would mean about 10% of the annual income. In addition, the fund charges off certain expenses from gross income before arriving at the total available for dividends, such as taxes, fees, cost of reports, and expenses of paying dividends. No-load funds may write off sales, advertising, and other marketing costs against their net assets. Such costs may exceed 1%. Closed-end funds, of course, deduct operating expenses before payment of dividends.

Selling Costs

The purchase of most mutual funds involves payment of a markup or load. A "full load" tends to be about 9% of the amount invested, although reductions are usually offered when large investments are made. Other funds charge a "low load" of 2 or 3%. Most of these were formerly no-load funds which had marketing problems.

In the case of full-load funds charging 8½%, the sales organization would retain about 6% with about one-half of this amount going to the salesperson. The relatively high take-home pay, as compared with the compensation for listed security business, might well explain some of the enthusiasm by salespeople for mutual funds, as well as some of the rapid growth of these issues in recent years. Not only does the customer pay more dollars for the cost of purchasing, but the salesperson typically receives a larger percentage of the markup than he or she does of listed commissions.

Although some mutual funds charge up to 2% to redeem their own shares, most do so without charge, so there is usually no cost of liquidation as there would be when listed shares are sold. The high-load charge materially cuts down on the return to the buyer, particularly when shares are redeemed after only a short period.

Open-end companies which sell their shares at net asset value, known as no-load funds, are becoming increasingly popular. Despite the obvious lack of enthusiasm for such funds by salespeople, their numbers have increased to the point where they now constitute over one-third of all open-end funds. Because they offer no compensation to salespeople, shares must be bought directly, usually by mail, by buyers who respond to advertising or word-of-mouth recommendations. The performance of no-load funds seems to be generally about the same as that of load funds despite protestations to the contrary of those who sell the latter.

Price Computations

The values of mutual fund shares are computed at least once daily by each fund. The investor can always redeem his shares by selling them back to the fund at the bid price. The offering price quoted in the papers represents the net asset value per share. In other words, it is computed by dividing the total market value of the portfolio by the number of shares outstanding.

Tax and Income Aspects

Registered investment companies are required by law to pay out 90% of their dividends and interest. In addition, they are taxed on any income or capital gains retained. Hence, the general policy is to pay out nearly all of their earnings. They receive two kinds of income or earnings: (1) the ordinary dividends and interest, or net investment income, and (2) the profits from buying and selling securities, or capital gains.

Payments from both sources of income are made to stockholders. The funds must distinguish between the two in their distribution. The stockholder pays the ordinary income tax rate on the net investment income and the capital gains share of the distribution. In figuring the yield on earnings received, the stockholder is often confused. The yield is based on the net investment income. The capital gains return is really a return of the capital invested in the fund and should not be regarded as a yield. These capital gains are really not spendable income, but a repayment of part of the original investment by the stockholder. It is the same as though an ordinary stockholder in a listed corporation were to sell part of his shares each year and count the capital gains so obtained as dividends on his stock.

Selection of a Fund

The selection of a suitable investment company is no easy matter. Often the danger is that one will buy the shares of the first salesperson to approach him. Companies vary greatly in their objectives, diversification policies, type of securities issued, reputations, size, and management records. It is possible to check their portfolios, which are reported quarterly. Their performances are a matter of record. Brokers can supply this information. Certain magazines, such as *Barron's* and *Forbes*, report quarterly on performances. There are also a large number of services which report on all investment companies or on certain types of funds such as the no-load variety.

Performances

Salespeople for mutual funds can usually show excellent performance records for these organizations. This is sometimes accomplished by picking time periods long enough or short enough to show the fund in its best light. In that the market generally tends to rise on balance, a well-diversified fund can show an impressive increase in asset values, sometimes despite its management rather than because of it. The question then is: Have funds shown a good performance in reaching investment objectives?

A number of studies have been made of the performance of mutual funds.

In general, mutual funds show a net performance over time somewhat poorer than that of the market averages. It should also be noted that past performance is not a valid indicator of the future, and fund salespeople do not properly maintain that it is a good indicator. Excellent results attributable to the work of analysts who might have left the organization or to a spectacular rise in a single security which unexpectedly proved to be a take-over target are unlikely to occur. Excellent results in a small fund attributable partly to flexibility may well be lost if the results themselves attract too much capital to retain the flexibility.

Special Purpose Funds

The variety of funds available is restricted only by the tastes of the investment public and the imagination of sales organizations. There have long been funds stressing particular industries, such as chemicals or electronics, stocks issued by a particular country, and various types of security such as bonds, preferred stocks, or options. There are dual funds offering shareholders their choice of dividend and interest income or capital gains depending on their objectives. Increasing interest rates have encouraged a tremendous growth since 1972 in money market funds. Although they offer brokerage companies little or no sales revenue, they at least have prevented many billions of dollars from being diverted directly into savings accounts or such money market instruments as Treasury bills, certificates of deposit, bankers acceptances, or commercial paper. High interest rates have also encouraged the growth of diversified and interest-free bond funds.

Some closed-end funds have directed funds into instruments outside the securities markets altogether. A Real Estate Investment Trust (REIT) raises money by selling securities or by borrowing, and it places the funds it accumulates directly into real estate or into loans secured by real estate. The stocks of such trusts may be listed on exchanges or trade over-the-counter. Specialized and diversified commodity funds have also become popular in recent years. Such funds may invest in cash commodities, commodity futures, commodity options, or all three. Because of their concentration in high risk vehicles, their need for attractive short-term performance, and lack of flexibility in thin markets, commodity funds are highly aggressive vehicles and are not designed for the fainthearted.

Advantages

Diversification is one of the main advantages of purchasing shares of an investment company. All funds have diversification, even those of the special industry type. Generally, the fund has a high degree of diversification by industries and companies, often numbering well over 100 situations. No small investor can hope to match this unquestionable characteristic of the investment company. The only objection comes from those who can or hope to obtain better than average returns. Diversification is obtained more cheaply through investment company shares than through the purchase of individual stocks.

A second advantage is professional management of one's investments. The companies are managed by skilled and experienced investment experts, aided by trained research staffs. Few small investors have the time, skill, and experience to manage their own investments as well as can the board of managers of a fund. Professional skill is therefore substituted for amateur skill. For many this is a real gain and well worth the cost involved. It was pointed out earlier that the average fund does no better, and often not as well, as the averages. In justice to the management of the funds, it should be pointed out that high diversification tends to bring average returns. Also conservatism and the purchase of senior securities reduce returns. Some funds, of course, are not well managed. On the other hand, many small investors cannot do as well in their investing as the averages perform, when commissions and taxes are considered.

A third advantage is that the small investor can invest small sums of money regularly and systematically with a minimum of worry, inconvenience, record keeping, security analysis, and time consumption. To many this is worth paying for.

Investment companies have become popular with some who have small retirement plans such as Keogh plans and individual retirement accounts (IRAs). There are hundreds of thousands of individual Keogh accounts invested in mutual funds and about an equal number of IRA accounts. As the funds invested in the IRA program have expanded, the interest of investment salespersons in this area has expanded accordingly. The market value of securities in such accounts is about $5 billion.

Criticisms

The first criticism is the high selling cost, which may exceed 8%. This is very much higher than for buying stocks in round lots, which comes to about 1%. It is also higher than for odd lots, except when very small purchases are made. These high loading charges are especially costly in the event the investor redeems his shares within a few years after purchase, because returns are thus greatly reduced.

Another criticism is that successes are overrated by many funds. The average performance, as indicated, is no better than that of the stock averages, in spite of the well-advertised professional management aspect of the investment. Although many amateur investors cannot do as well as the averages, many experienced ones can.

A third criticism is the handling of capital gains. These are paid out to the investor, who must pay taxes on them whether he reinvests them or spends them. If he purchased ordinary corporate shares, he would pay no capital gains tax until his stock was sold. The effect of this investment company policy is that the shareholder's capital is often spent rather than kept in the capital fund.

A fourth criticism is that there is cause for doubting that past performances can continue. There was a very strong bull market in stocks for a number of years. This aided funds in making very creditable performances. The question may well be asked: Can the funds justify their costs and risks in a period of stable or falling markets?

A fifth criticism is that years ago investment trusts rose to prominence by the same arguments of merit, skilled management, and diversification as are heard today, yet their records after 1929 were dismal. Will history be repeated? It is probable, however, that the lessons of 1929 have been well learned. In addition, there is a considerable degree of regulation today that was nonexistent many years ago.

A final criticism can be made. Investors in such companies have less control over their investments than if they were to purchase ordinary corporate shares. Their investments become inflexible and they become locked in with the fortunes of the fund in which they have invested.

A Final Comment

For many small investors the investment company offers several real advantages, although the cost may be high and the return only average. Such investors could do far worse on their own. For larger investors, particularly those with experience, a policy of going it alone has much to be said for it. However, for large investors, two points are significant: (1) they may be able to acquire a complete portfolio and management relatively inexpensively and (2) they can liquidate quickly without cost and without individual impact on the market.

20 Fundamentals of Stock Prices

This book will not attempt to present a complete discussion of investment analysis and portfolio selection such as can be found in most of the excellent works published in the broad field of investments. One concept covered in detail in such books, however, must be dealt with here because of its important implication to the reader. This concerns the problem introduced in Chapter 19; namely, the apparent efficiency of financial markets often described as the "random walk." Readers of Chapter 21 should particularly consider this discussion. Efficiency means that prices of investment instruments reflect a minimum of all information that is publicly available and possibly even all information that is discoverable by the most sophisticated analysts.

An efficient market is populated by large numbers of well and equally informed profit maximizers. Intrinsic investment values may change and may even be anticipated in some instances by extremely well-informed and agile analysis, but prices can be expected to adjust quickly to their new levels and to move there in a random manner. The random walk does not imply that price levels cannot change or that direction cannot be anticipated, but does maintain that successive price changes are independent.

A RANDOM WALK IN AN EFFICIENT MARKET

There is some argument as to the strength of market efficiency, but there is virtually unanimous agreement that efficiency is the best explanation of why markets act as they do. Furthermore, most analysts believe that the stronger versions of market efficiency probably provide the more accurate description of market behavior. Although the efficient market theory cannot be said to have been proved, there is no widely accepted body of published research indicating that any other explanation is better. The unpopularity of this conclusion among brokers and clients of brokerage houses is easily understandable. If markets are efficient, research intended to forecast short-term price movements is, at best, extremely difficult. Such research intended to guide large numbers of people to worthwhile profits can hardly be expected to be successful.

The more research that is done and the more areas that are researched, the more efficient the market becomes and the less useful the research. Those who accept this would be best advised to develop a portfolio of assets large enough to filter out most of the risk attributable to individual stocks (unique risk), but small enough to keep commission costs reasonable. The portfolio need be devised only to reflect the degree of risk a buyer wishes to accept which will reflect primarily the undiversifiable (systematic) risk of the market and which would then need only periodic review and culling. Such a policy, followed by many security buyers, would not create much income for brokerage houses. The latter rely upon frequent trading in accounts, rather than making profits for their customers by being correct in forecasting significant market movements.

Many brokerage house customers themselves are unwilling to accept the efficient market hypothesis and its mathematical model, the random walk, despite the fact that few of them have especially good sources of information or technical devices that yield validated results. We emphasize again, however, that there is no evidence whatever to indicate that there is any better approach to trading than to assume that the market acts efficiently and that the best trading approach is to buy a well-diversified portfolio and hold it. The die-hard analyst, of course, could maintain that if anyone had a way of trading that would yield consistently impressive results one would be foolish to publish it and thereby attract a crowd that would use the method and destroy its usefulness.

Both fundamentalists and technicians find the efficient market concept uncomfortable. If all or most significant information is quickly reflected in prices, the fundamentalist who relies on such information could hardly be expected to learn anything of value not available to anyone else who could readily discover the same news and act upon it just as quickly. The technician fares no better except that he wastes less time reading news. If all news is reflected quickly in prices and prices have no memory, then charts, tables, and computerized data banks might just as well be replaced by ouija boards.

Given all the people who spent generations searching for ways to turn base metals into gold, trying to locate a fountain of youth, or burning witches, it is not surprising that many will go on looking for trading ideas or systems that will lead to quick and easy riches. The fact that there are people like stock exchange specialists and arbitragers who make large amounts of money over long periods helps provide hope. Of course, specialists make most of their profits from market making, and so most of their profits are attributable to their advantages of position and capital rather than to any extraordinary market judgment. Arbitragers have substantial capital, the ability to devise and communicate orders quickly and accurately, and excellent sources of good (sometimes too good) information. An important part of their profits may result from lower trading costs or other financial benefits from brokers not available to smaller traders less well connected.

Nonrandom Opportunities

It may well be argued that there are some nonrandom inefficiencies. The complicated accounting, tax, regulatory, and political climate may give a real advantage to those who have time to interpret or even anticipate the significance of factors such as these. A blessed few might even have isolated some complex but consistent market aberrations that might yield consistent profits. Such aberrations to be worthwhile must occur often enough to provide profits sufficient to justify the costs and risks of trading. Valuable discoveries are not likely to involve simplistic approaches such as selling on Mondays and buying on Thursdays, always selling rights early or late, or basing decisions upon two lines drawn in different colors on a piece of graph paper. Such observations can be assumed to be erroneous, based upon too small a sample, or to be quickly self-defeating. Furthermore, it is likely that such profits achieved by the few are attributable in part or even primarily to the judgment and sensitivity of the trader rather than to the device that he has discovered. In other instances, an inside source may be of real value, but if so, it is probably illegal so that the total risk that includes possible incarceration still equals or exceeds the value of accepting it. None of this is to suggest that research is useless, but rather that it is a far more difficult endeavor than is widely suggested.

Probably the most difficult aspect of the stock market is understanding the many factors and conditions that affect prices. There is no easy road to fathoming how and why they move, nor is there any set of rules that can be used to obtain quick and certain profits in the market. The movements of prices, however, are often more significant to investors than the dividend income received from their stocks.

The multiplicity of factors or conditions that affect the market may be classified in two categories. First, there are fundamental conditions that develop outside the market. These are the underlying or basic causes of price changes that in the long run dominate the market. Second, there are the so-called technical factors or conditions that operate entirely within the market over short periods. They also affect stock prices, no matter what the long-run or fundamental conditions may be.

These two sets of conditions sometimes work together and sometimes in opposition. Thus, a given market may be fundamentally strong but technically weak, or the reverse. Again, both sets of conditions may be strong or weak at the same time. The student of the market will do well to distinguish between the two elements of market determination at all times.

This chapter will examine so-called fundamental factors and conditions outside the stock market that many consider important in influencing stock price movements. As will be seen later, many of these fundamental factors have much less direct influence on the market than is generally supposed.

Chapter 21 will deal with a technical analysis of the market, which means a study of the internal factors or conditions of the market that are believed to influence stock price movements. Both fundamental and technical analyses are difficult and each has its limitations.

TWO THEORIES OF STOCK PRICES

The Conventional Theory of Stock Prices

For many years there has been a fundamental, orthodox, and conventional theory to explain the movement of stock prices. Reduced to the simplest phraseology, it can be stated in this way: *The basic cause of stock price movement is the anticipation of change in corporate earnings.*

The expected result, according to conventional theory, of all changes in fundamental conditions is that they will affect the earnings of corporations, either individually or as a group. These changes in earnings will, in turn, affect dividends. The belief is that earnings constitute the most important single factor in determining stock prices. The shrewd trader or investor, therefore, must properly evaluate all fundamental conditions as they affect future earnings. By buying and selling in advance of changes in fundamental conditions, traders and investors are said to "discount" changes in earnings before they occur. To wait until actual changes in earnings take place is too slow for maximum profits.

Subscribers to this theory recognize that the price of a stock is the present value of all anticipated future dividends. They are further aware, however, that dividends can only come from earnings (except for liquidating dividends). Changes in earnings will change the outlook for dividends and therefore justifiably affect the prices of stocks. Any condition that indicates a change in earnings of a particular company, an industry, or the entire economy will affect stock prices, which will usually move in advance of actual changes in earnings and dividends.

This is the classic theory or explanation of stock price movements. There are exceptions, of course, but in general stock prices will move in advance of changes in business and in advance of changes in earning power.

The theory considers dividends as an important factor, but gives them secondary consideration. It is the belief that dividends must follow earnings and will change as earnings change.

In summary, any condition or situation that indicates a change in earnings of a particular company or of a specific industry, or of many companies, or of the entire economy will affect stock prices, which will move in advance of actual changes in earnings and dividends.

This is the classic theory or explanation of stock price movements. They move in advance of changes in business and in advance of changes in earning power.

The Confidence Theory of Stock Prices

This theory of stock price movements is even less formalized than the conventional theory. In fact, a formal statement of the theory is not a part of the literature of the stock market. In some people's opinion, however, the theory justifies at least equal emphasis with the conventional, or orthodox, theory. In view of many recent developments in the market, a good case can be built up to give it precedence as the dominant explanation of stock price movements.

The theory may be formalized in these terms: *The basic factor in the movement of stock prices is the rise and fall of trader and investor confidence in the future of stock prices, earnings, and dividends.*

This theory would seem to be but a variation of the theme of the conventional theory; namely, that stock prices depend upon earnings. Actually, it is fundamentally different in that it explains stock prices on the basis of market psychology rather than on statistical fundamentals. Its value is that it can be used to explain many vagaries of stock price movements not explained through conventional theory.

The confidence theory does not accept the precise principles of the conventional theory. The latter theory assumes that fundamental conditions are cold, objective facts about earnings, dividends, levels of interest rates, price changes, production, sales, gross national product, political developments, and similar factors. The theory is based on the premise that decisions on buying and selling are made on the basis of well-developed rules and standards, such as that stocks should sell at certain price–earnings ratios or that stocks should carry certain yields as compared to bond yields. The trained statistician and investment expert would therefore be ideally situated to forecast the market because of their skilled knowledge of, and handling of, economic data. When fundamental conditions were favorable, stock prices should move upward in accordance with well-discounted changes in earnings and dividends. When conditions turned unfavorable, stock prices would move downward in accordance with scientific discounting of these changes.

To this mechanistic theory of the market, the followers of the confidence theory cannot subscribe. They believe that the market does not respond to statistics and economic data with any high degree of exactness. They believe that the market's indifference to both good and bad news is often incredible. They are aware that measurements of stock price levels, such as price–earnings ratios and yields, change constantly; sometimes they are very high, sometimes very low, but seldom unchanging. Finally, they know that a very old axiom is still very true: "The market can do anything."

According to the confidence theory, if a sufficient number of traders and investors become optimistic about fundamental conditions, or about prospects for an individual company, they will buy stocks. If they become overoptimistic, they will buy stocks until prices reach unwarranted levels, as measured by normal levels of prices, earnings, and dividends. On the opposite side, when they become pessimistic they will sell, regardless of basic, fundamental conditions. If their pessimism becomes excessive, they will dump stocks on the market until they fall to entirely unrealistic levels as measured by normal standards. In this theory the buyers and sellers are extremists, whose moods range from extreme optimism to exaggerated pessimism. Like the fabled southern judge, they are often in error but never in doubt.

The confidence theory can be used to explain many bull and bear markets that appear inexplicable by the conventional theory. It can explain a bear market in the face of pronounced strength in economic conditions. It can explain a bull market in the face of unfavorable economic developments. It can explain falling stock prices during a period of rising earnings, or the reverse.

Although many examples can be used to illustrate the movement of stock prices according to the confidence theory, few are better than the bear market of 1946. At that time fundamental conditions were strong. The Gross National Product was rising; price controls had been abandoned and both retail and wholesale prices were increasing; corporate dividends and earnings were improving. Then the speculative public became pessimistic. It was convinced that a postwar depression was in order as it had been so many times in the past. Stocks were sold and the market broke badly in August and September. It did not recover its 1946 level until 1950. The year 1947, it turned out later, was "the year of the depression which never came." Business conditions continued to improve almost without interruption until late 1948. Confidence in the market in 1946 disappeared. Traders and investors were in error as to the facts, but the market broke anyway.

The confidence theory was again vindicated by the bull market of 1985–1986. Foreign competition was severe; interest rates, although below recent highs, were still historically high; the dollar was strong, helping create a record unfavorable trade balance; the huge federal deficit was becoming ever higher; commodity prices were low; and the growth of American businesses was unimpressive. The stock market, however, rose almost vertically on huge volume.

The difficulty of measuring public confidence in the market increases the complexity of stock market analysis. Many traders on technical conditions who attempt to measure confidence by various methods often achieve less than perfect results. Many investors still follow faithfully the conventional theory. Its apparent concreteness and its limitless statistical raw material give it an air of realism that carries great weight. Yet followers of the conventional theory are often perplexed and not a little dazed because their precise calculations often fail to yield the plausible results they anticipate so confidently.

BUSINESS FUNDAMENTALS

Nature of Fundamentals

Fundamental conditions are those economic and political factors outside the market itself that many consider as dictating market trends either for individual stocks, for groups of stocks, or for the market as a whole. They can be divided into two groups: (1) business or economic fundamentals and (2) political fundamentals. There are many thousands of traders and investors in the market at all times, and each is seeking to forecast the trend of prices. Their verdict as to this trend is based mainly on their estimate of fundamental conditions as they affect prices. If a majority believes that fundamental conditions are bullish, stocks will be bought and they will rise; if the reverse, stocks will be sold and price declines will take place.

It should come as no great surprise that historical comparisons of stock indexes with measures of economic activity such as the Gross National Product (GNP) or the Index of Industrial Production indicate a correlation between the direction of stock prices and the observed state of the economy. Stock prices tend to be strong when the economy is strong and weak when the economy is weak; however, there are significant differences among groups of stocks and in the performance of individual stocks that reflect special circumstances in the fortunes of particular companies.

Efforts to correlate stock prices with various specific economic indicators have not proved too useful. Stock prices sometimes lead some business series and sometimes lag. The length of time involved and the degree of leads and lags can vary considerably. Over a long period, about the best that can be concluded is that stock prices usually lead other series. This offers little solace to the fundamentalist attempting to use business conditions to forecast stock prices. He might be better advised to use stock prices to forecast business conditions.

Earnings

Under the conventional theory of stock prices, earnings or corporate profits are considered the most important single fundamental influencing stock prices. Traders and investors buy and sell stock largely on the basis of anticipated earnings. As a result, stock prices are believed to discount or anticipate changes in earnings.

A good theoretical defense can be built up for this premise. Stocks are bought for two purposes: (1) appreciation and (2) yield. A rise in earnings over a period of time causes appreciation in the value of the stock. The yield of stock is determined by the relationship between dividends and the market price. A stock can yield a return to a stockholder only because the company pays out part of the earnings as dividends. Thus, both appreciation and yield are determined by the volume of earnings.

Under this theory it is not too important whether earnings be retained in the company or paid out in dividends. In either case the stockholder gains. If a large proportion is retained as reinvested capital, the company expands. This expansion increases future earnings and hence both future dividends and stock price. A large retention of earnings may be a sign that the company can employ the funds profitably; otherwise they would not have been reinvested. Although a heavy reinvestment of profits may mean a small payout in dividends, the stockholder is satisfied because he feels that he owns a "growth stock," and this policy is considered a good indication of growth.

Although it may be argued against this theory that reinvested profits may be lost or wasted or produce only low return, advocates of this theory are not impressed by the argument. They believe that the past performance of management can be used to test the company's performance. By employing certain ratios, such as the ratios of profit to net worth, invested capital, and sales, they can continually measure the skill of management. As long as profit ratios remain favorable, they believe that their reinvested profits are being put to profitable use.

Sound as this theory appears, stocks are not always highly correlative with earnings. At times stocks move much faster than earnings; at other times they lag behind earnings. Sometimes they actually move in an opposite direction. Hence, even though a skilled follower of the market were to forecast correctly the trend of earnings, there is no assurance that he would be able to forecast correctly the movements of stock prices.

Even a casual observation of the Dow Jones industrial average compared with earnings on the stocks utilized in the averages demonstrates that stock prices and earnings often show a poor correlation and have frequently moved in opposite directions for extended periods. Although it seems reasonable to conclude that earnings are probably the most important long-term fundamental factor determining stock prices, one must not rely upon the relationship too much in making short-term decisions. If the confidence theory explains stock prices, it should be realized that stock prices may well over- or underdiscount earnings in a random manner and may well move in the opposite direction for periods of varying lengths.

That there is not a closer relationship between stock prices and earnings is easily explainable. Stock prices over a long period have tended to move ahead of earnings. Hence, announced changes of earnings come too late to affect stock price movements. In an exhaustive study of statistical indicators in the business cycle, the National Bureau of Economic Research found that common stock prices tended to lead business cycle turns by 4½ months.[1]

The Price–Earnings Ratio

The most frequently used measurement of the relationship of stock prices and earnings is the price–earnings ratio, which is the current market price divided by annual earnings. For example, a given stock is selling at $60 and earnings per share are $5. It is then said to be selling at a price–earnings ratio of 12 to 1. If earnings were to remain level but the price were to rise to $70, it would then be selling at 14 to 1.

The price–earnings ratio has long been used to measure the value of stock prices. Many years ago a ratio of 10 to 1 was considered standard, and a purchase of a given stock at that ratio or lower was considered a sound

---

[1]G. H. Moore (ed.), *Business Cycle Indicators* (2 vols.; Princeton: Princeton University Press, 1961), vol. 1, e.g. p. 56.

investment. Today, standards have changed and less reliance is placed upon price–earnings ratios. The volatility of such ratios has caused increasing numbers of analysts to conclude that they are based upon little or no intellectual foundation.

One might assume that a given stock or a given group of stocks would always sell at approximately the same price–earnings ratio. In this way one could determine the true intrinsic value of this stock or group of stocks. If earnings rise, the stock prices should rise accordingly to maintain approximately the same ratio; as they fall, stock prices should drop in sympathy.

Actually, the price–earnings ratio fluctuates with amazing frequency and over a wide range. The ratio over the short period of a stock cycle may range from 9 to 1 to more than 15 to 1. Let us take the 30-stock Dow Jones industrial average as typical for a group of high-grade, blue-chip stocks. In the 25-year period from 1935 to 1960, the price–earnings ratio ranged from as high as over 25 to 1 to as low as almost 7 to 1. For the entire period the ratio was over 14 to 1.

An indication, after the fact, of the peak of a bull market or the trough of a bear market is the price–earnings ratio. For example, in the bull market of 1929 the Dow Jones industrial average reached about 19 to 1. In 1938 it rose to over 25 to 1. Early in 1946 it was up to about 20 to 1. In 1961 it reached 23 to 1, and this level was not surpassed until the spectacular rise to over 100 attained in 1982. At one point during that year, the figure surpassed 130. This was caused by extremely unfavorable earnings, including some deficits, for several stocks in the industrials which warped the figures considerably. During the years immediately following, the ratio returned to its more usual range of 10 to 20.

The bear market of 1941–1942 showed a 9 to 1 ratio; the low of 1949 was 7 to 1, and the low of the moderate decline of 1953 was 10 to 1. The low during the sharp 1974 decline was 6 to 1. After the ratio rallied to levels of over 11 to 1 during 1975 and 1976, it fell below 10 to 1 in 1977, where it remained during the flat markets of the ensuing highly inflationary years until the spectacular rise in the ratio (not the market) in 1982. Under the confidence theory of stock prices, such an amplitude in ratios is entirely logical. During bull markets stock buyers become overly optimistic and bid up stock until the price–earnings ratios are very high, always in excess of 15 to 1. In bear markets they become pessimistic and sell, driving stocks down to very low ratios, always under 10 to 1 for the Dow Jones industrials.

Stocks should be separated when examining their price–earnings ratios. As indicated, the average ratio for the 30 stocks in the Dow Jones industrial average has been about 14 to 1 over a considerable period. For strictly growth stocks, such as the drugs, ratios will normally be substantially higher. These frequently sell at ratios of 20 to 1 and 25 to 1. A conservative rule of thumb would be that growth stocks should generally not be bought if they sell at more than 20 to 1 and that 25 to 1 should be the upper limit in all cases. On occasion investors will buy stocks at ratios much higher than these mentioned.

For example, in 1961 IBM at its high of 607 was selling at 80 times its indicated annual earnings of $7.60.

High price–earnings ratios also seem justified for moderate-growth companies with great stability in earning power, such as food companies, although their ratios are typically lower than for the more spectacular growth stocks. Ratios of 15 to 1 might be considered satisfactory in such companies. On the other hand, companies subject to large cyclical fluctuations, such as the automobile and steel companies, should sell normally at 10 to 1, the traditional ratio of the sound investment stock of years ago.

Price–earnings ratios show wide fluctuations between high and low points of the stock cycle. They also show marked differences between stocks because of the growth factor, size of company, management, trend of earnings, financial strength, and current popularity.

Dividends

In the conventional theory of stock prices, dividends come next to earnings as the basic, fundamental factor in the determination of stock prices. Indeed, many traders and investors are inclined today to attach to this factor just as great importance as to earnings in determining the intrinsic value of stocks. Some give even greater stress to dividends. Various reasons are presented in defense of this attitude. One is that dividends are tangible and concrete. They are here today and represent real assets to the stockholders. There is no danger that earnings reinvested in the company will be lost, wasted, or poorly used, because the stockholder receives them today in the form of cash. This is but a variation of the old axiom, "A bird in the hand is worth two in the bush." The second reason for favoring dividends more highly than retained earnings is that the present value of dividends is greater to the stockholder than future earnings paid out in dividends, even when he or she may be reasonably certain of receiving them.

The importance of dividends is least in growth stocks, where appreciation is highly important, often bringing in a greater ultimate return than current dividends. The growth company can utilize the money more productively than the stockholder, who would have to seek an alternative investment for the dividends. The stockholder would also have less to invest because he or she would have to pay taxes on any dividends received whereas the company, if it is growing, would have to acquire funds elsewhere at a cost to maintain its growth. Growth companies cannot rely on reinvestment of earnings to support the increase in their assets even if they pay out little or nothing in current dividends.

Dividends per share have varied tremendously over time and hence are questionable as a sound analytical device. Furthermore, dividends have shown an imprecise and inconsistent relationship to corporate profits. During some historical periods, profits rose far faster than dividends, and during other periods, dividends went up much faster than profits.

Of all the factors used by newspaper editors to explain day-to-day fluctuations in the prices of individual stocks, news about dividends has always
ranked near the top in importance.

Stock Yields

One way to examine changes in dividends is to study stock yields. Stock
yields are derived by dividing the annual dividend by the current market
price. One way to indicate the annual dividend is to add up the last four
quarterly dividends.

Stock yields, like price–earnings ratios, provide one of the simplest tests
for measuring the peak of a bull market or the trough of a bear market. At
the peak of every bull market from 1929 to 1986, they were close to 3%. At
the trough of every bear market during the same period they ranged from 7
to 10%. For the entire period the Dow Jones industrial average showed an
average yield of about 5%.

Stock yields show a wide variation among individual stocks. Some growth
stocks, such as DuPont and Allied Signal, have shown yields as low as 3%
over long periods, whereas others have yielded over 6% consistently. Many
factors—such as growth, status of the company in its industry, size, management, stability and trend of earnings, dividend policies, source of new
capital, age of company, popularity with investors, and risk—explain these
variations. An additional factor should be mentioned. Uncertainty about a
company's ability to continue dividends at the current rate of payment is
frequently a cause of high yield, even in the case of strong, high-grade companies.

In conclusion, stock yields are another useful tool for working with stock
valuations. It must be remembered, however, that they show marked changes
during the stock cycle and that they vary greatly between stocks. Examined
over a period of time, they are valuable in determining whether stocks are
selling at too high a price or at an attractive level. The investor should not
confuse dividend yield with the total return on a stock.

Stock Splits and Dividends

Stock splits and stock dividends frequently act as stimulants to the market
price of the stock. Despite the fact that the stockholder has received nothing
toward increasing his wealth, there are those who believe that an increase
in price is justified. Some attribute a benefit to the maintenance of per share
cash dividends at a level equal to or greater than the previous amount, but
paid on an increased number of shares. Those who would rebut this point
out that more is being paid out in dividends, and increased value is received
from the increased cash received, not the increase in the number of shares
held. Others maintain that splits and stock dividends reduce the price of the
stock to a point at which it is more in demand and that this has the effect
of raising its price. Others indicate that the lower price results in greater

spreads and other transaction costs so there is no real net benefit. A stock split may result in higher prices because it is believed that it is followed by good earnings or dividend news. If this is true, the increased prices, of course, are really justified by the expectation of increased earnings and not by the split.

Interest Rates

Endless hours of research have gone into the study of the relationship between stock prices and interest rates. Do changes in interest rates bring about changes in stock prices? Do interest rates precede changes in the latter series, or does the market perform well its usual discounting function and anticipate changes in interest rates? If the latter is true, the investor would do better to watch the stock market and trade interest rates rather than use changes in federal funds, the discount rate, and Treasury bill yields in an effort to anticipate stock market direction. The results of investigations have been consistently discouraging to the student of the stock market. Some have attempted, on one theoretical basis or another, to justify a relationship. One theory is that cheap money makes funds available for stock speculation at favorable rates. Speculators can borrow plentiful funds at low rates and make high returns on stock ownership because of the differential between stock yields and the cost of call money; hence, stocks will rise. Conversely, when interest rates become high and call money scarce, speculators will reduce loans because of tight credit conditions and lack of profit in carrying stocks on margins; stocks will therefore fall in price.

More common is the theory that high rates make it more difficult for companies to earn enough to overcome their high costs of capital, thereby reducing their attraction to investors who would prefer to place their funds in high-yielding debt instruments which are basically less risky anyhow.

A few students of the problem have concluded that changes in interest rates do precede changes in stock prices. Thus, Leonard M. Ayres, who examined 25 business cycles over a 100-year period, concluded that on the upswing of the business cycle, the low point of interest rates was 12 months in advance of the top level of stock prices; on the downswing the top level of interest rates was 4 months in advance of the low point of stock prices.[2] Ayres' findings, however, were not accepted by later writers.

Owens and Hardy made an early thorough study of the accepted theory that cyclical variations in speculative activity are caused by fluctuations in interest rates. They stated: "The conclusion reached is that neither economic analysis nor historical approach reveals any foundation for the accepted theory."[3] They also noted: "In summary, the data for both periods show clearly that there is a pronounced tendency for the interest rate to lag behind stock

[2]L. M. Ayres, *Turning Points in Business Cycles* (New York: Macmillan, 1940), p. 67.
[3]R. N. Owens and C. O. Hardy, *Interest Rates and Stock Speculation* (Washington, DC: The Brookings Institution, 1930), p. vii.

prices in their upward and downward movements, with an interval of about twelve months.''[4] Moore, in later years, found that industrial stock prices led bank rates on business loans by 9½ months, an estimate close to that of Owens and Hardy.[5] Another well-known authority on the stock market, Joseph Mindell, concluded: "There is no direct correlation between the interest rate and stock prices."[6]

High interest rates do not necessarily discourage speculation. They were high in 1928 and in early 1929—the highest since 1920—and yet a bull market was nearing its crest. Again they increased during 1954 and 1955, and yet the stock market enjoyed one of its best gains on record. High price levels were reached in the early 1960s, the late 1970s, and the mid-1980s when interest rates were also at historically high levels.

Stock Yields and Bond Yields

Many students of the market give close attention to the ratio between stock yields and bond yields. This attention stems from a belief that the spread between them has a significant influence upon stock prices. When stock yields are high as compared with bond yields, some investors will keep money invested in stock and place additional funds in stocks as they become available for investment. This acts as a bullish influence on stock prices. On the other hand, when there is a narrow spread, the investors will hesitate to place money in stocks and will turn to bonds because the difference in yield does not compensate for the additional risk. A narrow or negative spread is interpreted as bearish.

For most of the early twentieth century, the two yields were reasonably close, with stock yields generally slightly above bond yields. In 1928 they were about the same, and in 1929 stock yields were actually lower until after the crash. Since that time, the value of relative yields as a predictive device has been questionable, perhaps because this factor is overwhelmed by so many other considerations. Between 1938 and 1959 stock yields remained above bond yields by varying amounts, and since 1959 bond yields have been consistently above stock yields. Both of these long periods witnessed numerous bull and bear markets.

Commodity Prices

A fair theoretical case can be made to the effect that commodity prices, as indicators of inflation and deflation, influence stock prices. In many mercantile and manufacturing companies, inventories play an important part in the determination of profits. Rising prices mean that inventories can be sold

[4]*Ibid.*, p. 98.
[5]Moore, *op. cit.*, p. 57.
[6]Joseph Mindell, *The Stock Market* (New York: B. C. Forbes, 1948), p. 130.

at higher prices than those that prevailed when they were purchased, especially when there is a substantial time lapse. On the other hand, falling prices mean that inventory losses must be assumed. During the depression of the 1930s many considered stocks as good investments because of the possibility of an inflation in commodity prices. Many accepted the same theory in the post–World War II period of rising prices. Inflation again received much attention in the early months of the Korean War.

Common stocks have been considered by some as hedges against inflation. Not only were they considered to rise as the price level increased, but earnings and dividends would improve at the same or at a greater rate; hence, stockholders would be protected against the depreciating value of their income dollar. Many corporations have heavy fixed obligations, such as rentals, interest charges, and preferred stock dividends. Because these charges are constant, any gains in net income before these charges would go to the common stockholders.

Whether inflation will benefit the stockholder is dependent upon many conditions. In the industrial corporation the benefit is more probable than it is in the public utility corporation, whose charges are fixed by public regulatory bodies. The traction companies were ruined by the "nickel fare" of World War I. Railroad stocks did poorly during the inflationary period from 1913 to 1920 as rising costs outstripped the gains in revenue.

One difficulty about purchasing stocks in anticipation of inflation is that inflation itself is extremely difficult to forecast. During the depression of the 1930s wide fears were harbored that the government, through deficit spending and numerous deliberately inflationary policies, would bring on a sharp price rise; many bought stocks on this theory. No great inflation occurred, however, in spite of governmental policies because of the high productive capacity of the country and a large labor force, much of which was unemployed. The efforts to induce inflation, which included a substantial expansion in the monetary supply, simply did not work.

In World War II extreme inflationary forces were present in this country; yet there was no such rise in prices as would seem to have been indicated on the basis of the increase in bank credit and money in circulation, as well as the high level of deficit spending. Investors who would have purchased stocks in 1941 in anticipation of the beneficial effects of commodity inflation on stock prices would have been gravely misled. Commodity prices did rise during the war and particularly after price controls were lifted, but this inflation had no pronounced effect on stock prices.

Stock exchange history is replete with examples of the failure of stock prices to correlate with commodity prices. From 1923 to 1929 a remarkable period of wholesale price stability was present, showing only a slight downward tendency. Yet, in that period, stocks boomed in probably the most publicized bull market on record. Commodity prices rose in 1940, 1941, and 1942, but stock prices receded. In the spring of 1946, commodity price controls were scrapped, and a sharp inflation in prices took place for the rest of the year and continued upward until mid-1948, a steady two-year advance. On the other hand, stock prices began to waver at almost the same date in 1946 that commodity prices began to increase; they fell badly in August and were down substantially for the year. In other words, stock prices collapsed in 1946 at the exact time that the inflationary forces growing out of World War II became greatest.

By January 1951, the inflationary effects of the Korean War were past. Commodity prices then declined slightly and leveled off until mid-1955. During this period industrial stocks doubled in price. Record inflation rates in the 1970s convinced many analysts that rising prices might well be a cause of falling stock prices, because increasing production costs resulted in a decline in earnings because prices of finished products lagged behind some of the costs, particularly labor. Rising costs of new equipment outrunning depreciation allowances caused great problems in some industries.

The spectacular rise of the market in 1985–1986 was accompanied by a commodities market generally in the doldrums. Grains, soybeans, livestock, sugar, cocoa, and most other commodities sold at levels far below historical highs, and the formerly high-flying metals were downright lethargic.

The inconsistency of the response of stock prices to that of commodity prices is rendered even more frustrating to the analyst because historically stock prices have tended to move ahead of commodity prices by several months. It would seem, therefore, that commodity prices as an indicator of stock prices are unreliable and perhaps worthless.

Gross National Product

For some years, particularly in those immediately following World War II, the statistical concept of the Gross National Product (GNP) loomed large in the study of business conditions. The GNP expresses in dollars the sum total of final goods and services produced in the economy during a stated period. It also indicates the sum total of expenditures in that the income of an economy equals its expenditures. Stock traders attempting to correlate stock prices with GNP in order to create a predictive device did not have much success. Increases in GNP have often been accompanied by drops in stock prices, and declines in the former have been accompanied by increases in the latter. Sharp changes in one series have been accompanied by flat periods in the other. Attempts to use such elements as GNP as national income, personal income, or personal disposable income have proved no more useful over long periods.

Other Business Indicators

The student of business fundamentals can find elaborate discussions of many indicators in investment literature. Many students of the market have long searched for isolated economic series that could predict the market. Their task has been made more difficult because of the probability that the market is itself a leading indicator. It would appear that those who believe that pursuit of this subject is fruitful would be advised to begin with indicators designated by the U.S. Department of Commerce as leading indicators in its monthly *Business Conditions Digest*.

In recent years, the leading indicators most often noted by securities forecasters are employment figures, changes in inventories, and changes in the money supply. The prime rate in recent years has attracted considerable attention despite the fact that it has long been considered to be a lagging rather than a leading indicator. In that security prices themselves are one of the most respected of the 12 leading indicators, forecasters might be better advised to predict the prime rate from security prices rather than the more popular endeavor of trying to predict security prices from the changes in the prime rate.

Other indicators frequently considered important by some are federal funds, commercial and industrial loans, money market funds, and mutual fund activity and liquidity figures.

Strikes

A time-honored axiom in Wall Street is: "Never sell on strike news." The theory stands up well under historical analysis, although there are some exceptions. The belief is that any temporary decline in stock prices should be ignored. Prices will promptly return to previous levels after the strike is over. In many cases the market will refuse to break because of the strike. In either case selling is not justified. The theory is based on two arguments. First, losses in production, sales, and profits during the strike will be made up when the industry gets back into full production. Thus, the steel industry may be operating at only 80% of capacity before the strike; after the strike the plants are speeded up to near capacity operations, and within a few months the loss in production is entirely wiped out. At that time the plants drop back to the prestrike production level. The second reason that justifies the strike axiom is that manufacturers, wholesalers, and retailers usually have adequate inventories when the strike begins. These may last for one or two months and are sold at the usual profit with no loss in sales. After the strike inventories are replenished.

Business has been able to weather strikes in recent years in such industries as steel, coal, and automobiles with marked equanimity. These industries have very high productive capacities when in full operation and can usually meet pent-up demands after strike settlements within a reasonable time. In fact, these industries often face seasonal declines in production. The strike merely reduces the amount of the seasonal decline. The press gives much attention during a strike to losses in wages and production. Actually, seasonal and cyclical declines have the same effect. This explains why management and labor often take their time in settling new wage contracts.

POLITICAL FUNDAMENTALS

Importance

Political fundamentals are those developments in the field of government and politics that affect security prices. In the last half-century, they have assumed an immense importance in the economic life of the country. There has been a great increase in government regulations and controls. In addition, the policies of government spending and taxation have had an immeasurable influence over business conditions. The control of the credit system has been far more widespread than at any time in the nation's history. The federal government has become the largest business in the country, the biggest employer, and the greatest consumer.

War

The importance of war as a political fundamental since 1939 would be difficult to exaggerate. From 1939 to 1945 it was the dominant influence in the world. This dominance, extended to the entire economy, naturally had great repercussions in the stock market. This influence has already been examined in Chapter 5. Following the close of World War II, the country suffered a postwar inflation and boom. This began to diminish in 1948 and 1949. A setback to the economy, however, was prevented by the opening of the Korean War, the immediate effects of which were highly stimulating to the economy. After that conflict terminated, the federal government continued a high level of spending, compounded by the Vietnam conflict.

War is usually an event that cannot be forecast, but once declared, its effects on the stock market are often pronounced and unpredictable. They increase the difficulties of the market follower who seeks to predict stock price changes based on a normally functioning economic system.

Other Political Fundamentals

The President of the United States has become a political factor of tremendous significance in affecting the stock market. His messages to the Congress, unless well discounted in advance, often influence the market, as in his recommendations on new taxes, recovery measures, foreign aid, the budget, farm program, public power policies, road program, defense spending, and similar measures. Many industries are affected by government spending programs, an outstanding example being the airplane industry. Even calling Congress into special session has had substantial repercussions in the market. Elections are watched closely to see their effects upon the market. Although presidential elections are supposed to create uncertainty in the market, and uncertainty is supposed to be bearish, most elections in the twentieth century have been followed by rising stock markets. Assassinations, attempted assassinations, and serious presidential health problems have generally proved to have severe bearish effects on the stock market.

Congressional actions often influence the stock market strongly. Because Congress controls the purse strings of the federal government, its acts concerning taxes, recovery programs, foreign aid, defense spending, and similar legislation are watched with great care by followers of the markets.

Various government agencies influence the market with their actions. Rate decisions affect the earnings of railroads and public utilities. Antitrust actions often depress the stocks of companies affected. Corporate mergers may be approved or disapproved by the government. Particularly important in recent years have been the actions of the Federal Reserve Board. Its control over margins often depresses or stimulates the market. Of even greater importance is its control of the banking and credit system, which affects not only the lending and investment policies of all the commercial banks of the country, but all business that uses bank credit. The attempts by the Board to stabilize and control the national economy are certain to affect the economic life of the country. The market will evaluate these attempts. Regardless of the success of these attempts and evaluations, there will be market repercussions and effects.

On many occasions the decisions of the Supreme Court and the lower courts affect the market when these decisions have a direct bearing on the welfare of a given company or industry.

For these reasons the careful investor and trader in the market must be constantly on the alert for new political developments and must be able to evaluate them in terms of market reaction. He can no more afford to ignore them than he can afford to ignore the latest corporate reports on earnings.[7]

[7]The serious market analyst has available a vast amount of information about individual companies, industries, financial markets, and government fiscal, monetary, and other activities which affect investments. An excellent summary of such sources may be found in John D. Finnerty, *Corporate Financial Analysis* (New York: McGraw-Hill, 1986), pp. 527–538.

21 Technical Analysis of Stock Prices

Although technical analysis is sometimes used by those who are basically fundamentalists in their efforts to fine tune their timing, it is used primarily by those interested in the interpretation of stock price movements over short periods. Few forms of speculation are more illusive in their rationale or more frustrating for public investors than trading to obtain short-term profits.

NATURE OF TECHNICAL ANALYSIS

Technical analysis of markets is often discussed as if it were utilized entirely apart from fundamental analysis. Actually it is difficult to isolate one approach entirely from the other. Technicians are usually aware of and consider fundamental forces. Fundamentalists likewise are aware of market levels, recent direction, and volume, and most take these and other technical forces into consideration.

In essence the fundamentalist seeks first to ascertain the action of the market as a whole as determined by fundamental economic and political conditions—by forces outside the market. Some go no further but merely buy a diversified portfolio of stocks with a satisfactory risk level when the market is expected to go up, and later get out of the market if it is expected to go down far enough and long enough to justify the costs of liquidation and possible later reinstatement of positions. Other fundamentalists attempt to improve their returns by attempting to determine the relative investment merits of individual industries and individual stocks. They seek to find the intrinsic values of stocks, or what they consider the real worth. They are generally interested in the total return in stocks over relatively long periods, and thus they carefully consider dividend return as well as expected price appreciation.

Technical analysts, to the contrary, are usually short-run traders. The chief or entire interest of a technician is in capital gains, whether they be attained in a day, a week, a month, or over longer periods. Technical considerations are of primary or sole importance. These are factors or conditions that may be observed in the market itself as contrasted with fundamental conditions that exist primarily or entirely outside the market. Technical conditions result from the activities of both professional and amateur interests.

Technicians study the stock market as a whole or the markets for individual stocks rather than external factors such as those that affect the supply of and demand for products produced by companies. They believe that because people make markets, and people do not change all that much, they will repeat their previous actions under similar conditions. They believe that the study of statistics involving transactions can forecast the direction of future prices and that the market has enough nonrandom and predictable elements in it to make such studies profitable over time.

Fundamentalists believe that it is possible to isolate and quantify information about the market, industries, or individual companies' operations in sufficient amount that has not yet been discovered and utilized by others to create profitable opportunities. In a word, they believe that stocks may be selling at levels significantly above or below fair levels because the market has not yet correctly evaluated some information which can be discovered and utilized by the fundamentalists.

Technicians believe that fundamental analysis at best is inefficient and at worst futile. There are so many factors affecting the value of a company that the fundamentalist can deal only with a small sampling in the time they have available. Not only may they deal with the wrong facts or place improper emphasis upon them, but they are forced to deal with a fluid body of information because new facts appear and old ones change. Even if fundamentalists succeed in identifying all of the correct data and appraise them properly, their task is only half completed. They must still deal with people's reactions to these facts when they in turn learn about them, and they may well misinterpret their reactions. People do not always buy on good earnings reports or favorable dividend news or always sell on strike news. They may take opposite actions or no action at all.

Despite high margins and the costs of trading, it is not difficult to explain why the technical approach is popular with many security traders. Most use limited data, in some cases either only price or price and volume. These data are easily and quickly acquired, stored, and utilized. The availability of sophisticated calculators and low-priced computers has made technical analysis even easier, at least mechanically. A cynic, of course, would be quick to point out (probably correctly) that the wide use of such equipment really tends to make a basically efficient market efficient in even more ways and therefore tends to make useful analysis more difficult or even impossible. In that the technician believes that he or she is dealing with the attitudes of people toward markets, his or her statistical models can be applied to whatever is traded. What applied to stocks 50 years ago can be usefully applied to listed stock options or indexes today. Moreover, many technicians find their analyses provide them with an interesting and stimulating way to spend their time. Some who eventually break even still might well consider their time well spent.

Although a complete description of all technical devices would fill many volumes, it is possible to present here an overview of the approach. All methods, whether described here or not, attempt to anticipate prices from past market statistics in a rapid and reasonably easy manner. Technical approaches may be classified in various ways. The broadest classification would be that which groups together devices designed to succeed in trending markets and places the remainder in a group designed to succeed in trading markets. The technician, of course, would have to determine what kind of market was anticipated or have another technical device for making such a decision.

Technical devices may also be placed into one of four broad areas: (1) patterns on price charts; (2) trend-following methods; (3) character-of-market analysis; (4) structural theories. Popular examples of each are presented for those readers who either do not believe the efficient market theory or choose to ignore it.

PATTERNS ON PRICE CHARTS

This approach to technical analysis is among the oldest and is the most popularly known. It rests on the assumption that repetitive patterns will forecast significant price movements. At the turn of the century, the value of charts was thought to be proven by the successful identification of trading pools engaged in attempted secret manipulations. When pools became illegal, chartists who were loath to abandon their craft claimed that they were able to identify changes in psychology and thus anticipate price change.

Bar Charts

Bar chartists typically indicate time on the horizontal axis of their chart paper and price on the vertical. Price is indicated by a vertical line drawn on the chart for a specified period that may be a day, week, month, or any length time period deemed significant by the chartists. The bar drawn indicates the price range from high to low. Tick marks may be added to indicate the opening and the close of the market if the chartists believe these to be of value. Each period is plotted to the right of the previous plot. Some chartists indicate other data on their charts such as volume or brief comments on important news events that may have caused unusual changes.

Many variations are possible. Some chartists might graph only closes rather than ranges. Some may indicate mid-ranges on the price range bars or may plot only the mid-ranges.

Some chartists consider it desirable to construct ratio charts, technically known as a chart with a "semilogarithmic scale." These are difficult to construct unless one is trained in statistics. The great advantage of these charts is that they show rates of changes instead of differences in amount. On a ratio chart, if a stock is rising at a rate of change of 10% per year, the chart will show a straight trend line. If two stocks are plotted, the one showing a greater percentage gain will show a steeper line than the other. Once the principle of the ratio chart is grasped, its advantages for skilled analysis are readily apparent. It does not require any knowledge of higher mathematics or logarithms to understand these charts.

When the trader has enough recorded data, he will begin to search for patterns that chartists generally believe to be significant or those that follow patterns that he himself has identified and believes significant.

Point and Figure Charts

Point and figure charts are designed to indicate price change and nothing else. The passage of time from one price to the next is not considered. Unlike some bar chartists, the point and figure chartists give no consideration to volume. The chartist decides what fluctuation he considers to be significant, which may be as little as $\frac{1}{8}$ to as much as $2 or $3 per share. Each box on the graph may represent this chosen amount. Each time the stock rises by the selected amount, an X is entered to indicate the change. As long as the stock continues to rise, additional Xs will be entered on top of those previously marked. If the price drops by the selected amount, the chartist moves to the next column of the chart and places an X lower by the minimum amount selected. At this point the market is said to have reversed, which is why point and figure charts are sometimes called reversal charts. In order to increase legibility, many point and figure chartists indicate rising columns with Xs and falling columns with Os. As an added effort to make reading easier, the closing price for each day, week, or month may be blacked in.

A chartist interested in extremely short-run changes might indicate changes of only $\frac{1}{8}$. An active day in an active stock might well use up many columns on the chart. A trader interested in longer periods might plot only reversals of $3, which would result in a long history of price movement on a small chart.

Really dedicated point and figure chartists believe that they can predict not only potential changes of price direction, but also how long the new direction will prevail. They do this by using what is frequently called *the count*. They believe, briefly, that the length of a lateral movement on the chart indicates the magnitude of the rise or fall that will follow. Lateral movements also become support zones if the market later moves up or resistance zones if the market moves down. A comparison of a bar chart and a point and figure chart for the same price fluctuations and same time period is illustrated in Figure 21-1.

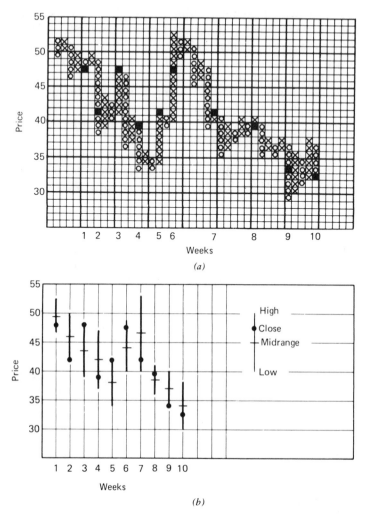

Fig. 21-1. Point and figure chart versus bar chart. (*a*) Point and figure chart for a 10-week period: each X or O represents a change of one point; (*b*) bar chart covering the same 10 weeks.

Chart Formations

There sometimes appear to be as many possible chart formations as there are chartists. Some formations apply only to bar charts, others only to point and figure charts, and some to both. To give an idea of the elaborations developed by chartists, the following list shows some types:

Head-and-shoulders top	Broadening top
Head-and-shoulders bottom	Broadening bottom

Double top	Dormant bottom
Triple top	Right angle triangle
Double bottom	Ascending triangle
Triple bottom	Descending triangle
Rectangle	Exhaustion gap
Diamond	Island reversal
Rising wedge	Double trend line
Falling wedge	Trend channel
Flag	Intermediate down trend
Pennant	Major down trend
Scallop and saucer	Major trend channel
Common or area gap	Spiral or coil
Continuation or runaway gap	Complex top
Fulcrum	Delayed ending
Compound fulcrum	Inverse head and shoulders
V base	Duplex horizontal
V extended	Inverse fulcrum
Inverted V	Inverse compound fulcrum
Inverted V extended	Inverse saucer

For additional formations, illustrations of the above, and interpretations, the reader is best advised to turn to one of the many excellent books available on the construction, use, and interpretation of charts.[1]

Value of Patterns

Traders who rely upon charts or their equivalent need not work nearly so hard as the fundamentalists. They do not even have to prepare their own charts, but may buy them from services or even get them from a broker at low or no cost, particularly if they trade with the broker. There are many examples of traders who use charts and make money too often to attribute their success to sheer luck.

Others believe that chart reading is no more than a cult that tells its fol-

---

[1]Representative books on various aspects of charts include R. D. Edwards and John Magee, Jr., *Technical Analysis of Stock Trends* (5th ed., Springfield, MA: John Magee, 1966); William Jiler, *How Charts Can Help You in the Stock Market* (New York: Commodity Research Publications, 1961); Martin J. Pring, *Technical Analysis Explained* (2d ed., New York: McGraw-Hill, 1985); Alexander Wheelan, *Study Helps in Point and Figure Technique* (New York: Morgan, Roberts and Roberts, 1962); and A. W. Cohen, *The Chartcraft Method of Point and Figure Trading* (New York: Chartcraft, 1960). The student interested in charts as applied to commodities as well as a long list of references to charts, can turn to Richard J. Teweles and Frank Jones, *The Futures Game: Who Wins? Who Loses? Why?* (New York: McGraw-Hill, 1987), chap. 7.

lowers where the market has been but not where it is going. They attribute
the success of such chartists who are successful to the chartists' judgment
and not to their charts. Successful chart patterns would soon be discovered
and followed by so many chartists that they would initially create self-fulfilling
prophecies and would eventually create chart traps as chartists stumbled
over each other creating their own market strength and weakness.

Although many statistics books indicate how to construct charts, none
presents any statistics indicating that charts will probably lead to significant
profits over time for the chartist. In fact, some studies indicate that charts
in and of themselves are quite useless.[2]

TREND-FOLLOWING METHODS

The trend follower believes that a trend once established is more likely to
continue than to reverse. It is therefore necessary only to identify the existence of the trend and determine how to identify the end of the trend. In
effect, the trend follower buys strength and sells weakness. He is quite fond
of advising traders to "go with the market" or "not fight the trend." He is
somewhat less fond of defining trends precisely or offering validated figures
to prove that his advice is worth anything. Aside from a few obscure methods,
the most usual trend-following device is the moving average, which may be
calculated and utilized in many ways.

Moving Averages

An average is merely the quotient of a sum divided by the number of its
terms. A 10-day average of a stock's closing prices would be the sum of its
last 10 days' closings divided by 10. A moving average simply adds a new
term periodically, such as daily or weekly, and at the same time drops the
oldest term so the sum of terms is still 10. Table 21-1 illustrates the computation of a 10-day moving average based upon the closing prices of a hypothetical stock.

The moving average can be for any length of time believed meaningful to
the chartist. Typical periods chosen are 3, 7, 10, 15, 20, and 30 days. A
comparison of a moving average chart with a chart of actual daily closes
will indicate that the moving average tends to smooth the more erratic action
of the prices themselves and thus better indicate the purported trend of the
price of the stock. The moving average will, by definition, lag behind the
actual prices and thus indicate to the chartist a change in the trend when
the moving average line crosses the line connecting the prices themselves.

---

[2]Alfred W. Cowles, "Can Stock Market Forecasters Forecast?" *Econometrica*, 1 (1933), 309–
324, and Daniel Seligman, "The Mystique of Point and Figure," *Fortune* (March 1962).

Table 21-1 Computation of a 10-Day Moving Average for a Hypothetical Stock

Date	Close (in dollars)	10-Day Net Change*	10-Day Total†	10-Day Average‡
3/15	29			
16	29¼			
17	29½			
3/20	29⅛			
21	29¼			
22	30½			
23	30¾			
24	31			
3/27	30¾			
28	31¼		300.38	30.04
29	30½	+1½	301.88	30.19
30	30¾	+1½	303.38	30.34
4/3	30⅞	+1⅜	304.76	30.48
4	30⅛	+ 1	305.76	30.58
5	30½	+ 1¼	307.01	30.70

*Difference (plus or minus) between latest close and the tenth close, counting back.
†Sum of 10 latest closes.
‡The 10-day-total column divided by 10. These figures in sequence make up the moving average.

Of course, the longer the moving averages, the smoother the line, and the greater the lag, the fewer the crossings.

In order to utilize the moving average to indicate the trend, and therefore trade with the market, all the chartist need do is decide how long an average to use and how to define a penetration. Short lengths of time used to compute moving averages will result in great sensitivity to price change and enable chartists to recognize price changes quickly. They will therefore enter a market immediately after the trend turns up and exit immediately after it turns down. If the market changes direction frequently and does not travel far, chartists find themselves entering and exiting so often that their profits, if any, are exceeded by the costs of trading. If they try to avoid this by extending the time period, they may find that a true move in the market is over before they have a chance to establish a position.

Other traders attempt to find significant changes and avoid whipsawing by demanding significant penetrations that they define in terms of the sharpness of angle or the length of time without another reversal. These devices have the same limitations as already described; that is, whipsawing is avoided only by missing large amounts of real market movements.

Still other followers of this method compute moving averages of different time lengths and attempt to attach significance to the crossing of one moving average line by the other.

Value of Trend Following

Those who use trend-following methods are at least forced to quantify their method. They must decide on the average lengths to utilize and what events induce market action. They can readily check their method in past markets without risking trading capital. The device will get them out of a market as well as into it. If there is a major continuous move in the market, the trader will profit by most of it and not lose much money before the abandonment of his position is indicated.

Like most simplistic methods, trend following does not thrust easy riches upon its advocates. The trader who believes that some big profits will ultimately justify the inevitable whipsaws all too often finds that the whipsaws overcome the large profits, if, indeed, there are any large profits. He may also find that his research in past markets was really inadequate, and that he is the victim of inadequate sampling, selective perception, or a failure to recognize the costs of trading including opportunity costs.[3]

CHARACTER-OF-MARKET ANALYSIS

Character-of-the-market analysis presumes that analysis of a market requires inputs somewhat more subtle than price or price and volume alone. It is presumed that price moves may be of good or bad quality and that the task of the analyst is to distinguish between the two by using inputs in addition to or in lieu of price.

Oscillators

Oscillators attempt to measure price changes rather than levels by measuring the distance price has moved over a given period. Computation can be simple or extremely complex, depending upon whether weighting techniques are used and whether factors other than price are blended together.

Regardless of their construction, all oscillators presume that a price may have risen too fast or too slowly in the time period selected and that a reversal becomes predictable. This device is therefore considered to be useful in identifying oversold or overbought markets which can be used as a guide to short-term trading. It may also indicate the exhaustion of a trend. In both cases, reversals are indicated ahead of changes of direction of actual prices.

The problems presented by oscillators are rather clear. The "signals"

---

[3]In addition to previous references, the reader might turn to Garfield Drew, *New Methods for Profit in the Stock Market* (Boston: Metcalf Press, 1966).

generated are difficult to quantify and so are affected considerably by the perception of the user. A trend that is supposed to be exhausted may sometimes continue far beyond what had been anticipated, so it is possible for many small trading profits to be followed by a substantial loss as a trend continues. Such a loss can exceed all the profits formerly generated or, worse, might precede the profits.

Volume

Without question, volume occupies more of the attention of technical analysts than any other factor with the exception of price. The heart of the analysis is an old market axiom, "Volume goes with the trend." Volume is supposed to increase on rallies in a bull market and to decline on reactions. In a bear market volume should increase on reactions and shrink on rallies. Heavy volume at the end of a considerable movement in prices is believed to indicate the end of that trend and the turning point in prices.

In precise form, the popular theory of volume may be stated thus: (1) the market is technically strong when volume increases on rallies and declines on reactions; (2) the market is technically weak when volume increases on reactions and declines on rallies.

If volume increases as prices advance, the theory is that demand is still greater than supply or, in other words, buying forces are stronger than selling forces. This is why traders like to see increasing volume on a rising market. On the other hand, in a bull market, if volume drops off as prices decline, this is a good sign. It indicates that the supply is falling off at lower prices and owners are unwilling to sell.

In a genuine bear market, volume is supposed to increase as prices drop, because supply is increasing and stockholders want to unload. This shows the market is weak. If volume drops off on temporary rallies, the market is still weak because no large amount of buying is entering the market.

This theory of volume probably obtained its first prominence in the early years of the Dow theory. William Hamilton, editor of *The Wall Street Journal*, gained great prominence in 1901 by identifying insider action in U.S. Steel merely by identifying price and volume action of the stock on the tape. Despite Hamilton's explanation of his approach in considerable detail, his thinking on the importance of volume was quite confusing because he stressed it in some editorials and minimized it in others.[4] There are, however, tape-watchers today who believe that by careful volume analysis along with observation of block trading they can identify the activities of arbitragers and other large traders accumulating and distributing their positions. The computers of regulatory bodies undoubtedly are set to identify strange changes

[4]One of his more complete analyses is contained in William Peter Hamilton, *The Stock Market Barometer* (New York: Harper & Row, 1922).

in volume patterns which may provide them with leads to inside trading and other abuses.

Technical analysts today still use volume for short-term analysis. Although it is still common to imply that price movements are more significant when combined with a high volume, it is difficult to quantify terms satisfactorily nor is it possible to find adequate correlation between price and volume to attribute real practical value to the relationship. It is possible to identify series of four and five consecutive major movements in the market with no perceptible correlation between volume and price.

On-Balance Volume

A refinement of the volume approach is the somewhat more complex concept of on-balance volume (OBV) usually applied to individual stocks. The assumption of those utilizing this device is that large traders with special information will accumulate stocks before a rise and distribute them before a fall. Technicians who believe this have attempted to uncover the quiet accumulation and distribution by noting whether greater volume is taking place on rising or on falling prices. The former would identify accumulation and the latter distribution.[5]

As is true with so many technical approaches, there is no statistical evidence that the method works. There is also considerable quarrel with the practice of defining volume as plus or minus depending upon the close for the day. It is possible, of course, for the bulk of the volume in a stock to be on the plus side only to have it close lower on a small volume late in the day. Nevertheless, all of the volume would be assigned to the minus side. In these days of high volumes combined with late tapes supplying often incomplete data, it would appear to be a formidable or even an impossible task to identify all volume in a stock as plus or minus over a long period.

Breadth of the Market

Many technical analysts stress the breadth of the market. This refers to the number of issues being traded. There are somewhat more than 1,500 stocks traded on the New York Stock Exchange. The number of these that advance or decline in a given day is considered by many to be significant. For example, if on a given day 600 advanced, 400 declined, and 200 remained unchanged, the market would be considered to be technically strong. Many consider these data more important than the averages, because they show what is happening to the supply and demand for all stock and not merely for a few high-grade blue chips. An example of extreme technical weakness in the market occurred on September 26, 1955, the first day the market was open

---

[5]Joseph Granville, *Granville's New Key to Stock Market Profits* (Englewood Cliffs, NJ: Prentice-Hall, 1963). This approach is discussed here in detail.

after the President Eisenhower's heart attack. On that day, there were 1,247 declines and only 38 advances, a situation without precedent.

An increase in the breadth or number of issues traded is considered by some as a favorable sign in a rising market and an unfavorable one in a falling market.

New Highs and Lows

Keen interest is shown by many in the number of new highs and lows being reported on the NYSE each day. One criticism made is that the averages represent a faulty sampling of the market and consist largely of a few blue-chip stocks. Hence, an average may make a new high or new low and yet not mean too much. To those who subscribe to this viewpoint, the number of new highs or lows attains much importance. For example, on a given day the market may show 10 new highs for the year, but 100 new lows. This would be interpreted as a sign of great technical weakness. On the day just mentioned, September 26, 1955, the market made one new high and 131 new lows for the year.

Unfortunately, this technical factor sometimes plays tricks on its followers. It has not been unusual for many new highs to be established just before a sustained drop in the market or for many new lows to be followed by a sustained rise in the market.

Short Interest

Short selling at the time it occurs is supposed to be a sign of technical weakness in the market, because the normal amount of stock offered for sale is augmented by that of the short sellers. Conversely, short covering is alleged to be a sign of strength, because the short sellers repurchase the stock previously sold. A large short interest is supposed to make the market technically strong, because short sellers must cover eventually, thus bringing buying power into the market. On the other hand, a light short interest makes the market weak, for this support is not under the market.

Too much reliance should not be placed on short selling and the short interest as technical factors. There are several reasons for this conclusion. First, the amount of short selling and the consequent short interest are rather small. Fewer than 1% of the shares outstanding in listed issues on the NYSE were held in short positions in recent years. Second, much short selling is done for technical rather than for speculative reasons. For example, it may have been sold short against the box for tax reasons or held against a long position by an arbitrager. In both instances, the short position will not be covered in the market and, hence, will create none of the anticipated strength from such buying. Third, speculative short sellers have no market judgment proved superior to that of long buyers. Large quantities of short selling have been identified at the bottoms of markets and have failed to appear at the tops of markets. There appears to be little correlation between the volume of short selling and the movement of stock prices, either for individual stocks or for the market as a whole.

Theory of Contrary Opinion

Some traders approach technical analysis from the standpoint of psychology. Their belief is that "the public is always wrong" and that success in forecasting stock prices is achieved by determining the buying and selling moods of the public and then doing just exactly the opposite. This, of course, is a very old theory, going back nearly 150 years to the days of Baron Meyer Rothschild, who operated on the basis of buying when others sold and selling when others bought. This theory is based on the analysis of mass psychology in the market. It stresses the fact that stock prices are determined by the emotional decisions of thousands of traders and investors who often trade without sound knowledge of the market. These errors of judgment are not confined to the general public but are often made by professional advisers and forecasters of the market.

On the basis of this premise, a successful trader on technical conditions would sell when mass optimism about stock prices was high and buy when it was low. He would be a good psychologist rather than a good economist. There is no little truth in the theory. The difficulty comes from the lack of precise measurements of public psychology. It is easier to indict the public for bad judgment after a market error than before.

There are those who have believed that the extremes of crowd psychology can be recognized and acted upon.[6] The contrarian does not look for daily trades based upon fragile differences of opinion. He waits for a strong consensus concerning price direction, or he might note increasing interest in a neglected stock or the ignoring of a formerly active stock. Furthermore, he ascertains whether the reason for a currently strong opinion is strong or weak as evidenced by the degree to which facts have been publicized and the degree to which "facts" are supported by evidence. The contrarian is looking for a widely held opinion with little support.

Like other technicians, contrarians have problems. How they identify and quantify the prevailing opinion, much less assess its quality? Having entered a trade where do they exit? Where is the evidence that the method works other than the unsupported representations of those who sell services based upon the method?

Behavior of Odd-Lot Public

A theory of technical analysis similar to the theory of contrary opinion is that of trading on the behavior of the odd-lot public. Garfield A. Drew has

[6]Humphrey Neill, *The Art of Contrary Thinking* (Caldwell, Ohio: The Caxton Printers, 1963).

stressed this aspect perhaps more than any other analyst.[7] Trading under this theory is dictated by changes in the volume of buying and selling of the odd-lot public. Elaborate indexes have been developed that measure these changes and signal market movements to be followed by more informed traders. Drew's theory is not based on the well-known axiom, "The public is always wrong," but upon the premise that the market can be forecast by watching for periods when the odd-lot public changes its on-balance buying to on-balance selling or vice versa.

Whether or not the actions of the odd-lot public can be used to predict stock price movements has been the subject of much controversy. C. O. Hardy concluded that any correlation between market actions and those of the odd-lot public would have slight forecasting value.[8] The odd-lot public may be wrong at times, just as professional traders are sometimes wrong, but it is not always wrong. And it may be right just often enough to make faulty any predictions based on its behavior. The actions of no class of traders are so consistent as to be infallible guides to market behavior. In addition, the behavior of the odd-lot public may be such as to indicate no trading signals at all.

Low-Priced and High-Priced Stocks

Another relationship watched by technical analysts is that between the actions of low- and high-priced stocks in bull markets. Briefly, the theory is that low-priced stocks, percentagewise, will show greater gains in a bull market than high-priced ones. The speculative public will purchase these in preference to the high-priced, sound blue chips, which appear to offer less opportunities for large profits. A point profile on a $10 stock is 10%, but is only 1% on a $100 issue. The theory of the uninformed public is that the $10 stock in a bull market is likely to go up 10% more quickly than the $100 stock.

Timing plays an important part in this theory. It is believed that in the early stages of a bull market, leadership is provided by sound investment stocks. As the market advances and the general public enters in large numbers, attention focuses more and more on the highly speculative issues which tend to be lower priced. At, or even before, the crest of the market, speculation in them is very intense. As the market reaches its peak, public confidence declines rapidly in the speculative issues, which drop with great speed.

Some services, such as Standard and Poor's, regularly publish indexes of both low-priced speculative stocks and high-grade investment issues. Technical analysts can thus watch the action of these two series.

[7]Garfield A. Drew, *New Methods for Profit in the Stock Market* (Boston: The Metcalf Press, 1966), esp. sec. VI.
[8]C. O. Hardy, *Odd-Lot Trading on the New York Stock Exchange* (Washington, DC: The Brookings Institution, 1939), p. 77.

Unlike so many other technical theories, this theory has often been well supported by facts. A close examination of charts of the action of low-priced and high-grade stocks since 1926 reveals that the low-priced stocks clearly outperformed high-grade stocks at the tops of almost every bull market. Such uniformity is rare for a technical factor.

Reaction to News

Some technical analysts are interested in the reaction of the market to good and bad news. If the market fails to react favorably to good news, it is believed to be a sign of technical weakness because it does not induce selling. Traders, however, would be wise to reject such a simple analysis with reservations. The market is often able to discount news successfully a considerable period in advance. The effect of the good or bad news has already been discounted by the market in such instances. No further action is to be expected. "Sell when the good news is out" was a market axiom long ago.

Value of Character-of-the-Market Analysis

Some serious problems are involved in determining the value of character-of-the-market analysis. First, there is a long list of such methods, by no means all of which were represented in the sampling offered above. Many others might have been mentioned, such as mutual fund liquidity as measured by their cash balances; *Barron's* Confidence Index, which is the ratio of the yields on the best-grade bonds relative to intermediate-grade bonds; ratios which indicate the difference in yields between a stock index and a bond index; and the action of stock exchange specialists. Some believe that specialists not only know what the market will do, but can themselves cause it to move. Those who hold this belief might consider that the short positions, accumulation, or distribution of stocks by specialists are far more important indicators than similar data about others. Tape reading is an approach also followed by many who believe that short-term price action and volume, particularly of large blocks, clearly indicate market direction.

It also appears clear that advocates of these analyses almost all utilize suspect statistical techniques. Terms are ill defined, such as "unusual strength," "good buying," "light volume," and "trend," which may well be the most overworked word of all. Samples are often small, if available at all. Selective perception is apparently rampant. Some methods are impossible to analyze because the user (particularly if he sells a service) often claims to have secret (proprietary) devices. It can always be said that there is no proof of anything, because those who have developed successful methods naturally keep them to themselves in order to avoid their destruction by widespread adaptation. They also point to examples of individual traders or groups that have made too much money over too long a period of time to attribute it merely to luck.

STRUCTURAL THEORIES

Structural theories include three methods popular among some traders: seasonals, time cycles, and the Elliott wave theory. There are many other structural theories which are obscure, arcane, and exotic, and, although somewhat interesting, have insufficient substance to warrant detailed discussion here.

The structural analyst does not rely upon daily charts to indicate patterns, nor does he construct indexes for predictive purposes. He believes that the study of historical performance will identify repeating price patterns in the market. The structural trader is searching for a far larger picture than the chartist. He believes that price patterns are rather regular and predict prices for long periods.

Seasonal Movements of the Market

The question is often asked: Does the market show a seasonal pattern? The answers vary. Theoretically, such a pattern could not exist if it were of any significant size. Let us suppose that stocks always rose strongly from November to December. To take advantage of this rise, well-informed traders would always buy in November in order to sell in December at a profit. This early action would entirely destroy the pattern.

There is no question but that there is a slight seasonal pattern, which can be explained. Using the Dow Jones industrial average as an example, studies found that over the period from 1897 to the present, the market has tended to go up in certain months. It is more likely to go up than down in January, July, August, and December. Hence, one hears of "the December rise."

One must not take these variations too seriously, nor can one use them as reliable indicators of profit-making opportunities. They are too small and too erratic to justify risking one's money on them. Even if the pattern were sharp enough to permit a profit, as indicated by the 30-stock Dow Jones average, traders have no assurance that there would be any profit in particular stocks they might own or that they could cover out-of-pocket and opportunity costs.

Let us take the month of December, a month of rising prices. At this time of year, income tax payers have typically sold issues carrying losses for the year, so that these losses could be established in computing capital gains taxes. They have now reentered the market to place idle funds at work. This continues into January. One could logically expect some improvement in prices at this time.

Actually, during the twentieth century the market has shown a gain from the end of November to the end of December in about three years of each four. Before one gets too excited about such a large favorable sample, however, remember that if one had traded all such moves, he would have been ahead only in one-half the years on the average and that most such rises were insufficient to cover the costs of trading, including opportunity costs.

Furthermore, it is necessary to choose the right stocks to reflect the rise. It is also difficult to separate the apparent seasonal rise from the long-term uptrend in the market which has lent an upward bias to all months.

Other seasonal observations have been no more encouraging. Observations of the market during election years, for example, indicate a rising market more often than not, but not by an overwhelming margin so great as to induce traders to wait four years for an imagined great opportunity. Other tendencies, such as for direction on Fridays (particularly downward), to be followed by a continuation of the same direction on the following Mondays, do not appear to offer sufficient attraction either.

The trader who turns to obviously seasonal companies, such as airlines, soft drink manufacturers, air conditioning manufacturers, or toy makers believing that their peak seasons will be followed by favorable movement of their common stocks is quite naïve indeed. Even one who believes the market to be almost completely inefficient could hardly believe that factors as obvious as this would not soon result in self-defeating prophecies.

It is possible that seasonal strength and weakness caused by tax or political considerations are adequate to warrant consideration by someone who is considering buying or selling securities anyhow, but hardly enough to appeal to someone attempting to use such seasonals in themselves as a means to achieve important gains.

The Elliott Wave Theory

There are almost as many specialized technical approaches to the stock market as there are writers on the subject, but one such approach that has created considerable interest has been the Elliott wave theory. R. N. Elliott believed it possible to recognize rhythmic patterns in stock prices. He believed that prices move in a five-wave sequence in line with the direction of the main trend and in a three-wave sequence during "corrective" movements against the main trend. Waves can be carried to subwaves of quite short durations (subminuette) and to long waves of 100 years or more (the grand supercycle). Considerable attention was drawn to this device by comments concerning its use by the well-respected *Bank Credit Analyst*.[9]

Elliott's wave counts are based on the interesting Fibonacci summation series. This series was developed about 700 years ago by Leonardo Fibonacci, an Italian mathematician. In this series, which begins with 1, 2, 3, 5, 8, 13, 21, 34, 55, 89, each number equals the sum of the preceding two numbers. The ratio of any number in the series to the next highest is 61.82, which has come to be called the "golden mean."

The series and its mean have attracted the attention of many people who

---

[9]See Hamilton Bolton, *The Elliott Wave Principle–A Critical Appraisal* (Montreal: Bolton, Tremblan, 1960); also Hamilton Bolton and Charles Collins, *The Elliott Wave Principle–1966 Supplement, The Bank Credit Analyst* (Montreal: 1245 Sherbrooke Street West, Montreal 109, Quebec, Canada).

form a virtual cult. The series has been applied to the population of animals, the growth of plants, and the formation of crystalline structures. The mean has been applied to many areas such as architecture, where it explains the measurements of the Great Pyramid of Cheops. Speculators have tried to apply both to price forecasting.

As is usual with so many technical approaches, it is difficult for one follower of a theory to see the same patterns in data that may be apparent to another. What looks like a wave to one follower of the theory might well not look like a wave to another. Some point to examples which were apparently predicted accurately by the theory as proof of its validity. Cynics point out that given a universe of numbers large enough, almost anything can be proved if successes are documented and failures are ignored or explained away.

Cycles

Anyone who charts the Dow Jones averages or any other broad stock market indicator can hardly miss the fact that stock prices have significant rises and falls over time. The tremendous movements of 1921–1929, 1929–1932, 1932–1966, 1973–1974, 1974–1976, and 1982–1987 are evident to the most naïve of observers. Equally evident is the fact that these movements, and the many which preceded them, have varied greatly in duration and intervals, and gave no apparent sign of their comings and goings. Nevertheless, the value of being able to anticipate such cycles is great enough to attract much effort. Accordingly, there are those who have offered evidence of all sorts of cycles ranging from duration of a few months to others of many decades.

A most obvious conclusion is that there is a correlation between stock market prices and business conditions. It is only one more step to attempt to develop a proxy for business conditions and use that as a guide to the direction of stock market prices. Attempts to utilize such thinking to anticipate stock market prices have not often led to encouraging results. Even a cursory study reveals that the stock market sometimes acts before a great economic change and sometimes after, as in 1929, but most often a few months before. At other times, it seems to ignore business conditions altogether for long periods.

Despite all of the exceptions, the analyst who accepts a correlation would seem better advised to use the stock market to forecast business conditions rather than the reverse. Although stock market cycle analysis is certainly an interesting exercise, it would not appear to offer a rewarding approach to the seeking of profits.

A FINAL COMMENT

Much of what has been said in this chapter is not too encouraging to the technical analyst. It was not intended to imply that the person searching for nonrandom elements in stock market data is wasting his time, but merely that the constant searching for such elements by so many students of the market has almost certainly caused an already efficient structure to become even more efficient. The computer, often offered as a device to find a way to beat the market, has probably made data even more readily, quickly, and accurately available and thus made the market that much more difficult to beat. It is quite possible that the Rothschilds, Baruchs, and Livermores would have found success more difficult now than in their simpler times.

Well-disciplined, thoughtful traders might well be able to realize above-average returns because of their skilled utilization of useful data properly organized. Insiders with legally useful knowledge might also do well. Some people might even have been blessed with some special touch just as some are born with great musical or artistic talents. Technical analysis unquestionably smooths and organizes data which may help investors make sound market judgments. The organized data, however, may well serve only to describe what markets have done and not what they are going to do. If long-term successful forecasting is really possible, the success may be the result of the investor's judgment and not the technical data, however well organized. The search for a simple, easily attainable mechanical system that will yield above-average returns from stock market forecasting seems doomed to fail.

22 Securities Options

Options for the purchase and sale of securities (calls and puts, respectively) have existed for many years. Reports of their use in England go as far back as 1694, some 80 years earlier than the founding of the London Stock Exchange. Indeed, one of the classic stories of speculative mania concerns the collapse of the tulip bulb market in seventeenth-century Holland and the particular disaster that befell the writers of put options. Options in other forms of business enterprise, particularly real estate, are much older still and are common today. Certainly, the typical sports fan knows precisely what a professional athlete means when he announces that he is "playing out his option" this year.

Puts and calls were widely used in this country in the 1920s, although largely by professionals. Their use, in fact, was generally associated with pool activities and manipulation, frequently involving "insiders." To a large extent, that unsavory reputation persisted through the years in the minds of both the public and the regulators.

From the 1920s until 1973 the securities options business was concentrated in the hands of a dozen or so small firms which eventually organized the Put and Call Brokers and Dealers Association. Their function was to facilitate option buyers and sellers ("writers") by locating and becoming the opposite side of a proposed transaction. Most of the larger retail-oriented firms also had small options departments that worked with their own customers and these other dealers to supply the requested options. Although some of these "conventional" (OTC) options are still traded, the business was too limited to withstand the onslaught of the listed options market in the 1970s. The specialized options dealer firms were either liquidated or merged into the rapidly growing options departments of the large full-service and institutional firms. Over-the-counter options now survive, and indeed are flourishing, primarily in the institutional debt market as the large bond dealers create puts and calls to hedge fixed income positions for their clients who became shell-shocked from the wild gyrations of previously tame bond markets in the period starting in the late 1970s and still continuing.

THE NATURE OF THE OPTIONS BUSINESS

Puts and calls, whether exchange-traded or conventional, have many similarities. A put gives the holder the right to sell 100 shares of stock at a fixed price for a fixed period. A call option conveys a similar right to buy. In order to obtain this privilege, the buyer (or "long") pays a consideration to the seller, or writer ("short"). The price per share at which the option may be exercised—the underlying stock being either bought or sold—is called the exercise or striking price, or simply the "strike."

Conventional options are individually contracted arrangements between buyers and sellers. Everything is negotiable—time span, premium, striking price, even the very stock itself. Because each contract is unique, there is virtually no liquidity. Should he wish to sell, the holder of an OTC option has to locate someone willing to take on the exact terms of the original contract, including the now shortened life span left from the original agreement.

The lack of any real visibility (no newspaper quotes or exchange tape) led to wide spreads between bids and offers, if there were any spreads at all. This made it extremely difficult to utilize options profitably, even when the trader's basic forecast proved correct.

There was virtually no institutional participation in the conventional options market. Outside of the essentially speculative nature of the market as it was perceived by investors, there was a major technical drawback. Over-the-counter option striking prices were reduced on ex-dividend date by the amount of the dividend; for example, a call with a 50 strike became one with a 49½ strike after going ex-dividend, a 50 cent dividend. This meant that the covered call writer (one who owned the stock and sold a call on that stock) effectively parted with the dividend if the option was exercised, as a lesser amount was paid. This factor removed one of the main reasons why a fiduciary, for example, might want to consider options in the first place. The designers of the listed option did not repeat this mistake. Listed calls are never reduced in striking price because of a cash dividend, making the position vastly more appealing to the total rate of return investment policy followed by many institutional investors. Listed options are, however, adjusted to reflect any property distribution such as new shares from a split or stock dividend, a spin-off of another company's shares, or a rights offering.

The formation of the CBOE in 1973 revolutionized options trading. Borrowing heavily from the commodities futures business of its parent, the Chicago Board of Trade, the CBOE created standardized, exchange-traded options with interchangeable features. All contracts of a specific kind on the same stock have identical expiration dates and striking prices, leaving only the premium to be negotiated in an open auction market. Options became, for the first time, truly liquid vehicles. It now became possible to *trade* puts and calls, either to claim a profit or to cut a loss. The complex and costly process of exercising options, while still available, is now utilized for only 5% or fewer of all options traded. The liquidity and visibility created by this market made possible strategies not even considered in the OTC options trade. Additionally, the market was used by institutional investors to a degree never before thought possible. Likewise, many individual investors were drawn to a concept previously regarded as an arcane art, practiced only by highly sophisticated professionals. But, this can be considered a mixed blessing at best, and there are doubtless many such traders who rue the day when they first thought they understood this market.

The CBOE's success was immediate and dramatic. The concept was quickly copied by the American, Philadelphia, and Pacific Stock Exchanges. An attempt to establish a second Chicago market at the Midwest Stock Exchange failed to develop sufficient activity, and its options facilities were merged in 1980 into those of the CBOE, its close neighbor in the Chicago financial district. The NYSE got off to a tardy start in options because many of its members were unenthusiastic about trading such exotic and speculative items. Finally, the Big Board opened trading in options on its Composite Index in 1983 and then equity options on, of all things, some select NASDAQ issues in 1985.

The options business has grown far beyond even the most optimistic of early growth projections. The key to this growth was clearly the previously mentioned ability to extract profits (or cut losses) through trading the contracts, as opposed to exercise or awaiting expiration, the only methods readily available in the OTC market. Starting with calls only on 16 different stocks and a volume of 1,119,177 contracts in 1973, the CBOE market expanded to 161 stocks and a volume of 148,968,845 puts and calls by the end of 1985. Add to this the Amex figures of 129 and 36,103,282 respectively for 1985, to say nothing of the other exchanges, and one can get some appreciation for the level of success achieved.

No such success can be without its drawbacks, and listed options are most assuredly no exception to this rule. The visibility and easy access to a hitherto largely unknown specialty drew substantial interest from a broad spectrum of the investing public, including many ill suited to the complexities and short-term nature of the game. The glamor of trading, for example, IBM at $150 per share was now available via the option proxy for a few hundred dollars or less to the small speculator who doubtless would have been better off with the purchase of an odd lot of IBM or some similar quality investment vehicle such as a mutual fund.

Thus, before embarking on further discussion on the uses of options, it may be well to state an elementary but easily ignored truth: *Most individual investors lose money trying to trade options in attempts to beat the market.* The differences between options and their underlying stocks are in kind, not degree. Stocks do not expire; options do. There are blue-chip stocks and there are options on blue-chip stocks. There are, however, no blue-chip options. Even though the underlying stock may trade actively, the market for certain of its options may range from thin to virtually nonexistent at times. Furthermore, like all major securities markets, this one too has become dominated by institutional investors and their brokers, as well as by professional trading firms. As these participants have difficulty achieving consistent profitability, there is small likelihood of the penny-ante speculator gaining much more than an occasional trading success, just enough to lure him back to the table—a strategy long found profitable by the casinos in Las Vegas and Atlantic City but rarely by those in front of the tables.

The commission costs of options trading can be steep. For example, most major retail firms charge a commission of about $50 to execute an order for two options at a price of $3 each (total $600) and, of course, about the same to liquidate the position. Thus the small trader who buys two such options and sells them at $4 (total $800) will have his profit halved by transaction costs. Of course, larger orders bring the percentage cost of commissions down considerably, but given the short-term orientation of the market and its participants, it should be apparent that commissions have a much more severe impact on options trading profits (and losses) than they do on routine stock transactions.

The following section provides a number of theoretical situations where the profit potential appears very attractive compared with the possible risk. The trader should bear in mind that some such trades may produce net losses when commissions are included. An interesting illustration of how the theoretical collides with the real may be illustrated with a fascinating position called a "butterfly spread." Although it takes a bit of work to follow, consider the following:

Long 1 XYZ October 70 call @ 1

Short 2 XYZ October 65 calls @ 3

Long 1 XYZ October 60 call @ 5

One notes that the $600 cost of the two long options is offset by the receipt of $600 in premiums on the short options. One would further note that a price decline below 60 would cause all options to expire, producing neither gain nor loss. Furthermore, any price appreciation above 70 would also produce neither gain nor loss because the profits on the two long calls offset the losses on the two short ones. Finally, if the market instead remains locked in a 60–70 trading range, the investor makes a profit, an apparently no-lose proposition.

When, however, the real world intrudes and one factors in commissions, the theoretical profits evaporate and the supposed break-even points show real losses out-of-pocket. Thus, to Wall Street cynics the butterfly spread is more appropriately called the "alligator spread" because the commissions "chew you up alive."

LISTED CALL OPTIONS

Owning a call option will generally prove profitable if the underlying stock rises in price. The owner, having fixed his or her purchase price, hopes the stock will rise fast enough and far enough to show a profit. The call buyer, if correct, stands to reap a handsome profit through leverage, the ability to make $1 do the work of several. If wrong, he faces the prospect of a total loss of his investment.

Listed options have, as noted, standardized striking prices and expiration months. For example, options on AT&T on the CBOE had expiration dates 90 days apart, on the Saturday following the third Friday of each January, April, July, and October. Other securities trade on a February–May–August– November cycle or one with expirations in March, June, September, and December. Only the nearest three months are available for trading at any time. As an experiment, the options exchanges shifted trading in a number of their most active options to a shorter-term cycle in 1985. In the experiment, an option will always be available for the current month as well as the month immediately following. In addition, the third month becomes the next expiration in the regular cycle and is available as the most distant choice. Thus, in January (all experimental choices were from this cycle) expiration months were trading with January, February, and April dates. This reflects the essentially short-term nature of this market and the dearth of activity in six- or nine-month options traded in the usual cycles.

Striking prices are set at 2½-point intervals up to 25 and 5-point intervals above that point. Lower-priced stocks will therefore have striking prices such as 17½, 20, and 22½, while higher-priced issues will have strikes like 40, 45, and 50. When a stock's market price moves to the next higher or lower level, new striking prices are ordinarily introduced two business days later, except in the case of options already in their expiration month. A stock trading at $26 per share is likely to have striking prices at 25 and 30. Should that stock advance to 30, new strikes would be introduced at 35, and so on.

The striking price represents the dollars per share a holder must pay in order to claim the shares. Except for adjustments caused primarily by stock dividends and splits, option contracts call for the delivery of 100 shares. A holder of an AT&T January 20 call, therefore, will have to pay a writer $2,000 to exercise that call. The call may be either traded or exercised any time until its expiration in January. Upon expiration it becomes worthless, whatever its previous value might have been.

If a trader had paid a premium of $250 to a writer for this AT&T January 20 call, it is apparent that he has a theoretical break-even point of 22½. That is, the stock could be purchased via exercise at 20 and immediately sold in the market for 22½. The $250 profit offsets the premium cost, making any higher price profitable. If, for instance, AT&T were to be at 25, the call would have to be worth at least the intrinsic value (market price of the stock less the call's striking price) of $500, doubling the trader's initial stake. If, on the other hand, AT&T were below 20 at expiration, the trader loses his entire capital commitment.

Although it's true that options speculators may cut their losses by trading a depreciated option prior to its maturity, the potential for a total loss may never be dismissed. Indeed, the *probability* of loss seems all too likely. In order to be successful the call trader must be simultaneously correct in three different ways:

1   Direction   The stock must go up, not down or sideways.
2   Time   The anticipated motion must take place prior to expiration.
3   Extent   The stock must rise over the striking price by more than the option's cost (the premium and trading costs).

A failure to judge any one of these correctly tends to negate good judgment on the other two.

Assuming the market price of AT&T shares to have been at 20 at the time the call was purchased, one can see that a 2-point price rise prior to expiration would have satisfied two of the three requirements and yet still have resulted in a loss of $50. This is exactly what makes options trading so exceedingly difficult, not just for the typical "retail" speculator, but for the seasoned professional.

Nevertheless, the possibility that AT&T might advance to 25 or even 30 creates interest for those with resources substantial enough to accept the possibility of a $250 loss versus the potential of doubling or quadrupling that amount. There are few securities-related investments that hold the promise for such returns on a short-term basis.

In the listed options market the premiums are determined by open outcry between buyers and sellers in an auction on the exchange floor. There are, however, a number of factors that either dictate or help define what that premium will be. First, there is the relationship between the call's striking price and the price of the underlying shares. In the example an "at-the-money" option was illustrated. When the stock's market price and the striking price are identical, it follows that the appreciation in the stock price is likely to be mirrored in the option's price unless the call is close to expiration.

When the call is "in the money" (striking price lower than the current market price of the stock), price changes of any kind are likely to be quickly transmitted to the premium because of arbitrage potential. For example, assume AT&T stock is @ 22 and an AT&T January 20 call is selling for $400 in October. If AT&T rises to 26, the premium must increase to at least $600. Were the premium to remain at $400, an arbitrager would simply: (1) sell the stock short @ 26; (2) buy the call for $400 and immediately exercise it; and (3) deliver the stock received via exercise to close out the short position. The net result of this would be a risk-free $200 profit ($2,600 short-sale proceeds less $2,400 in costs—exercise price plus premium). Naturally, there are many such traders actively seeking such opportunities, most of them working for brokerage firms or institutional clients where transaction costs are a negligible factor. The very activities of these professionals buying in the cheap market and selling in the dear quickly closes the gaps by forcing premiums up and share prices down until an equilibrium is reached.

"Out-of-the-money" calls, on the other hand, have no intrinsic value and represent a pure speculation on future price increases. If AT&T were @ 17, for instance, the shares could rise by 3 points prior to expiration and an AT&T 20 call would still be worthless. This lack of tangible value means that the premiums are largely determined by two other factors, present in all option pricing, which we have not as yet considered.

Logically, one would expect traders to be willing to pay more for a call on a volatile growth stock than for one on a stodgy public utility. Likewise, the potential for an anticipated price change is greater given a 4-month duration rather than a 3-week one. Relative volatility and time, therefore, are important components in determining what premium a buyer should be willing to pay or, alternately, what a seller should be willing to accept. Historically, IBM calls have regularly sold at higher relative prices than those on AT&T (or most other issues, for that matter). Considering only IBM calls, however, one will note higher premiums for more distant expiration months although the striking prices may be identical; for example, an IBM January 150 call might be priced @ $600 whereas an IBM April 150 call would surely sell for at least another $100.

Because the dollar price of out-of-the-money options is strictly determined by these two subjective factors, it is here that the market is most speculative, that the trader gets the occasional chance to run $50 into several hundred or even more. Generally speaking, most traders should not nibble at this "cheap" bait. The out-of-the-money call is cheap for a good reason; it may well be cheap in dollars, but this cheapness means the market accords it scant prospects for appreciation. Trading this type of option successfully relies more on the classic "greater fool" theory than it does on quantifiable risk. To the cynic, such options are the biggest sucker bet on Wall Street.

COVERED CALL WRITING

This strategy is the simplest, most conservative, and most widely used method of option writing. It is the only strategy that has met wide-scale institutional acceptance and the only one suitable for the typical retail customer. The strategy involves selling call options against holdings of common stock or equivalents, such as convertible bonds.

For example, suppose a customer buys 100 IBM @ 126 and simultaneously sells 1 IBM January 125 call for $800. The "covered call" so created has no margin maintenance requirement, thus allowing the premium to be applied against the cost of the IBM shares for a total cash investment of $11,800. If the market remains unchanged through January, rises by any amount, or falls by less than $1 per share, the call will be exercised generating a $700 profit. The investor will have sold stock @ 125 when it cost 126, a $100 loss. The option premium, on the other hand, more than offsets this amount.

Indeed, even if IBM should fall by fewer than 8 points, the overall position is still profitable at the option's expiration. A sale of the shares @ 118 results in an $800 loss, but at any price under 125 the call expires leaving the writer with $800 in premiums. Consequently, a sale of the stock at any higher price must show an overall profit even though the stock position itself may lose money. To illustrate further, a sale of IBM @ 122 registers a $400 loss on the stock but a net gain of $300 when the premium is included.

If this appears to be a virtually no-lose proposition, consider the possibility of IBM @ 150 just prior to the call's expiration. The option, of course, will be exercised at the agreed striking price of $125 and the writer's $800 premium will appear a poor bargain indeed. By the same token, had IBM fallen to 100, the loss on the shares would have substantially exceeded the cushion provided by the premium.

The writer need not feel restricted to writing "near" or at-the-money calls, as in this example. Writing out-of-the-money calls produces smaller premiums but allows for more gain through appreciation of the underlying stock. Writing deep-in-the-money calls forgoes any further profit due to appreciation but generates large premiums and consequently much downside protection. In the former instance the investor is likely to be rather bullish on the stock. On the same day IBM January 125 calls were selling for about $800, the January 135 calls were trading for about $288. Thus, buying 100 IBM @ 126 and selling a January 135 call creates the opportunity to make $1,188 by expiration. If IBM rises between purchase and expiration, the writer will realize whatever profit attends the stock plus the $288 premium. For example, a sale of the stock @ 130 yields $688. Above 135, of course, the profit ceases accruing as the call will be exercised. Because of the relatively small premium, the writer's downside break-even point is only about 123⅛.

An investor more concerned with market weakness might write a deep-in-the-money call to provide greater protection against a temporary decline. In this case the investor might buy 100 IBM @ 126 and sell a January 115 call for, possibly, $1,700. The writer is now protected against out-of-pocket loss unless IBM drops below 109, a 13% price decline. As long as the stock remains above 115, the option will be exercised and stock bought @ 126 will be sold @ 115, leaving the investor with an overall $600 profit.

Such calls thus appear to provide a wide range within which the investor might have a profitable transaction. In the given example, if IBM (1) advanced, (2) remained unchanged, or (3) dropped by fewer than 11 points, the position is profitable by $600. Indeed, unless the market price drops by more than 17 points, some profit is made. The major drawback is that it is often difficult to find a buyer. The typical call buyer is looking for leverage and limited risk, usually coupled with a minimal capital commitment. While a writer might therefore be delighted to sell this call for $1,700, the buyer might be more interested in one costing $600 or even $288.

Naturally, these illustrations deal with assumptions that do not prevail in reality. Commissions in fact generally make a 100-share, 1-call position economically unrewarding, although multiple positions fare much better on a percentage basis. Also, the examples assume that positions are maintained until just prior to expiration, something that infrequently happens. While uncommon in the U.S. markets, the European option permits exercise only upon expiration, and our theoretical examples illustrate this kind of option for convenience. In actuality, early exercises are not uncommon, particularly near ex-dividend dates when a number of arbitrage trading techniques are employed.

The conservative (and patient) investor may find covered call writing attractive on a total rate of return basis. That is, the return from premium income, dividends, and possibly limited price appreciation may exceed that of simply buying and holding a stock portfolio. For a while, this seemed a veritable sure thing as option buyers tended to overpay premiums. The market, however, responded as it normally does, becoming quite efficient. As more and more sophisticated analytical work was applied to the options market, it became less easy to find such overly generous premiums. Nevertheless, the strategy can still produce attractive results for the investor patient enough to develop a consistent course of action and knowledgeable enough not to regret the occasional large price gain forgone because a call was written too cheaply.

How attractive are "attractive results"? Most professionals feel that a pre-tax compound return of 12 to 18% is possible, depending on how aggressive the writer's program is. Recent inflationary rates aside, such rates are rarely seen except in highly speculative ventures. Over a 10-year period, a portfolio growing at an average annual rate of 15%, for example, will increase in value from $10,000 to about $51,000. The steady compounding effect of covered writing may not produce the dramatic home run occasionally hit by the speculative buyer, but neither does it produce the total wipe-out of invested capital often associated with such attempts to beat the market.

PUTS

The speculator looking for a profit on a declining asset may sell a security short. The process involves borrowing a security, selling it, and if the forecast proved correct, buying it back at a lower price later. In other words, the speculator is simply buying cheap and selling dear, but in reverse of the usual order. The unappealing aspect of all this is that if the security goes up instead of down, the potential loss is unlimited. This prospect is enough to dissuade all but the iron-willed from such a hazardous enterprise.

The put option, on the other hand, gives the possibility of profit on a declining stock but limits the trader's risk exposure to the cost of the option. Because the put option allows the holder to sell at a fixed price, it allows for a sort of retroactive short sale in which the trader only sells once the price objective has been achieved.

Assume a trader forecasts a price decline in the shares of XYZ Corp. from 50 to 35 and purchases one XYZ August 50 put for $300. If the market indeed falls to 35, the put will have to be worth at least its intrinsic value of $1,500, five times the original investment. At this point, the holder could either exercise the option, selling the stock at $50 versus a market cost of 35, or else sell the put to another at its appreciated value. This latter course of action would usually be favored if substantial time value remained in the premium.

If the market instead rose, the put holder's loss is limited to the premium. This factor may well be significant in the making of a successful trade because of the psychology of the short sale. The unlimited risk justly makes short sellers nervous and often forces them to cover prematurely when the market quickly rises after the short sale is made. In such a case the put premium can be regarded as having bought peace of mind as well as profit potential. Because the put holder knows he or she can't lose more than the option's cost, he or she is unlikely to be shaken out by short-term adversity.

Puts may also be used to limit risk on long stock positions. Suppose an investor likes the longer-term potential of CDE Corp., a volatile growth issue. Realizing that her timing might not be correct, the investor could buy 100 CDE @ 60 and buy one CDE October 60 put for $450. Her loss is thus limited to the $450 premium, as she can sell CDE at the same price for which it was purchased regardless of how low it may drop before the October expiration. Of course, if CDE rises as anticipated, the put will expire unexercised (or be sold at a loss by the holder), thus reducing the profit, but the cost of this "insurance policy" may be well worth it.

PUT WRITING

As call sellers are generally neutral to bearish on the underlying stock, it's logical to assume that put writers are neutral to bullish. As market prices increase, put premiums decline so that the seller may buy them back at cheaper prices or simply watch them expire. The put writer may also be looking to buy the shares at a cheaper price than the current market may afford. For example, suppose the investor would like to buy FGH at about $36 per share but the current market level is $39. By selling an FGH March 40 put for $400, the investor will indeed buy FGH at an effective cost of 36 as long as it remains below 40. That is, the option will ultimately be exercised and the writer will pay $4,000 for 100 FGH. Because the $400 premium was received first, however, the actual out-of-pocket cost is really only $3,600. If the market falls below 36, the investor will have paid more for the stock than it is currently worth, although this may not be a serious concern for the long-term holder. On the other hand, if the market rises above 40, the put will expire and the stock will not be purchased. The writer may be a bit disappointed, but will have the $400 expired option premium in pocket for his trouble.

STRADDLES AND COMBINATIONS

The ready availability of a wide variety of listed puts and calls makes it possible to structure positions that will be profitable regardless of the direction the underlying stock follows. A put and a call on the same stock with the same expiration date and the same striking price is called a "straddle." If the options' terms are not the same, the position is usually called a "combination" or simply a "combo."

Suppose MNO is a volatile issue, possibly one involved with a lot of takeover rumors. A speculator feels that the next move is likely to be sharp but its direction totally unpredictable. Thus the trader puts on a straddle by buying *both* a January 75 call and a January 75 put. With the stock trading at about 78, assume the options cost $500 and $200 respectively, or a $700 total. The holder will profit if the market rises to more than 82 or falls below 68; that is, the striking price plus and minus the *combined* premiums. Of course, if either of these price levels is reached, the trader will have to make a decision as to when the position is to be closed. If the market reaches 82 and looks as if it will continue higher, he should sell the put for whatever value (probably little) it retains and hold the call position or exercise it, depending on his forecast. The reverse is true if the market falls to 68 and appears to be headed lower. While the packaged position is called by a single name, it is composed of two totally independent contracts. Indeed, in rare circumstances the nimble trader may be able to trade each "leg" profitably. The break-even points are computed, however, on the assumption that this is a highly unlikely situation. At expiration the market is virtually certain to be either higher or lower than 75, meaning that either the put or the call will be a total loss. Thus the profit on the winning side must not only offset its cost, but also cover the expense of the losing side.

A common variation on this strategy is the combination with two out-of-the-money legs, for example, STU February 30 calls and STU February 25 puts when STU stock is at 27. As no intrinsic value is present in either option, the dollar price of this position is likely to be relatively inexpensive. Once again, the break-even points are found by adding the combined premiums to the call striking price and subtracting them from the put striking price. Because a similar vehicle has become widely used by traders of options on Treasury bond futures, the term "strangle" used by these traders to describe an out-of-the-money combination has also gained some currency in the stock option business.

SPREADS

Straddles and combinations are used in anticipation of sharp price moves by option buyers; the spread is typically designed to reward the trader in the event of a relatively limited price change. Spreads can be used in up, down, or flat markets, but generally they are most useful when no major price change is expected. If the market movement follows the spreader's forecast, the profit achieved will generally exceed that of an outright long or short option position. At the same time, if the forecast is incorrect, the loss potential is also less than that of a plain call or put. The drawback derives from the fact that the profit is likewise limited and often predetermined when the spread is placed. The spreader may thus outsmart himself and miss participation in a major move, another reminder that one cannot get something for nothing in the stock market.

There are many possible spread configurations. To illustrate how one common type works, assume a spread trader expects to see RST rise from its current price of 63 to 70. With a market price of 63 it is likely that RST calls will be available at striking prices of 60, 65, and 70. With a bullish move in mind the spreader might *buy* one RST January 60 call and simultaneously *sell* one RST January 70 call. The premium for the 60 call might perhaps be $500, whereas that for the 70 call might be only $100, as it is 7 points out of the money. The spread, the difference between the premiums, is thus $400.

The spreader's objective is to see this difference either widen or narrow. The position illustrated is said to be a "debit" spread, as the cost of the long option exceeds the premium received for the sale of the short one. A profit will be realized if a debit spread widens, and in this case that widening effect will be seen if the price of RST rises. For example, should RST reach 70 at expiration of the calls, the 60 call will be worth $1,000 but the 70 will be worthless. This means that the spreader has made $500 on the long 60 option and $100 on the expired 70 call which was sold short. In other words, the spread had widened from $400 to $1,000, and the trader had pocketed the $600 difference. It will readily be seen, however, that should RST have risen to 80, the profit would still not exceed $600, as every point of profit on the long 60 call will be offset by a point of loss on the short 70 call.

Had the market instead declined and remained below 60, both options would expire. The loss on the call at 60 would be reduced by $100 as the 70 also expires. In this case, the spread had narrowed and a loss resulted. From this, one can draw the conclusion that a bearish spreader might have done exactly the reverse of this example and sold the 60 call while buying the 70 call, producing a "credit" spread of $400. Credit spreads must narrow to prove profitable, and the maximum possible narrowing, of course, occurs if both options expire, the spread at that point being zero.

Another type of popular spread is the "calendar" spread. This strategy utilizes a certainty in options pricing, namely that a near term option loses its time value before a more distant contract. This is not to imply that profits are indeed certain, but rather that the usual phenomenon of the decay of time value is likely to lead to a profit given a relatively flat market.

Suppose in December XYZ shares are trading at 24. XYZ February 25 puts are priced @ $300 and XYZ May 25 puts are @ $425. A spreader forecasting a neutral market could buy the May put and simultaneously sell the February for a $125 debit. If the market remained unchanged through February, the February put will revert to its intrinsic value of $100 as the time value decays; that is, with virtually no time left before expiration no one will pay more than the actual worth of the put. On the other hand, the May put may have the same intrinsic value, but it still has 90 days to run. Thus, the spreader might be able to repurchase the February 25 put for about $100 and sell the May for about $300. While $125 is lost on the May put, $200 is made on the February, for a net profit of $75. Because the only cost in negotiating this spread is the debit of $125, the return on investment can be very attractive. A strong up move in the market, however, can spoil the strategy, as the February is likely to rise much more quickly than the more distant May option. Should this happen, a loss on the near option will usually exceed any profit derived from the more distant maturity. The strategy is best employed with stocks least likely to make sharp price advances when the market rallies.

Despite their apparent appeal, spreads are generally not good vehicles for the typical trader, even one experienced in options. For one thing, commission costs are at least doubled when compared with regular purchases or sales. Given the limited profitability of such positions to start with, the added transaction costs are likely to bite deeply into the profits if and when achieved. Add to this the probability that any profits are most likely to be treated as short-term capital gains, and one reaches the conclusion that these sophisticated devices are best left to the professionals.

INDEX OPTIONS

One of the most intriguing developments in a highly innovative field has been the introduction of options designed to mirror the price movements of various stock market indicators. Traders may now indeed "buy the market" without regard to individual issues. Likewise, investors may hedge diversified portfolios against broad market declines by buying puts or selling calls on an index, leaving their securities holdings undisturbed.

The concept was first approached through the use of stock index futures, which will be discussed later on. The futures idea has become enormously popular with institutional investors and brokers, but the trading mechanism and margin considerations of the futures market have made them less well received by the individual investor. On the other hand, options had already become established and familiar investment vehicles by the time stock futures were introduced. Most sophisticated traders were by then aware of the basic options strategies. In addition, options trade in the familiar ⅛ point variations used in stock trading, whereas futures pricing is rather different. Some investors find that it requires a good bit of study or experience before a futures price table is as easily readable as the more familiar stock market column. Finally, futures margins are substantially greater than premiums for index options; for example, $6,000 for a S&P's 500 futures contract versus a few hundred (or fewer) dollars for most index puts and calls.

The most popular of these index options is the one on the S&P's 100-Stock Index, usually referred to by its ticker symbol—OEX. The index itself is artificial, having been created to reflect price movements in blue-chip stocks because Dow Jones had refused to allow its familiar 30-stock industrial average to be used for this purpose. In fact, the contract was initially called the CBOE 100 and was later renamed when a licensing agreement was concluded with S&P's. Interestingly enough, an option on the S&P's 500 Index has been much less successful, while the futures contract on the same indicator has been one of the great success stories in the brief history of financial futures. The options on the futures contract have also proved to be successful.

First introduced in March 1983 the OEX immediately drew a number of competing contracts on other exchanges, but none has even approached its success. The next most popular index option is the Major Market Index (XMI), the Amex's equivalent of the Dow Jones industrials. The NYSE offers an option on its own composite index (NYA) and one with twice the dollar value of the NYA, the NDX. The latter was introduced in 1984 as an attempt to appeal to institutional investors desiring a larger contract as a hedging tool. In January 1985 the Philadelphia Stock Exchange introduced options on the 1,700-stock Value Line Index (XVL), a spin-off from the futures contract traded on the Kansas City Board of Trade.

USES OF INDEX OPTIONS

These contracts permit the trader to focus on major market moves without the risk of being wrong on individual stocks or industry groups. Many are familiar with the old saws, "You can't buy the market," and "There's no such thing as a stock market, only a market for stocks." These adages indicate that the investor must be selective, and in so choosing one issue, or even a few, runs the risk of having chosen incorrectly. The market as a whole rises, but the investor's particular holdings do not (or even decline).

If one has enough money, one can diversify away almost all of this type of firm-specific or industry risk. Diversification, however, is not effective against a general market decline. The systematic risk of any securities position is that an overall market decline sends most issues down. In effect, the baby and the bath water are both expelled.

One possible defense against systematic risk is the index option. Suppose a pension fund manager controls a sizeable blue-chip portfolio. He intends to stay fully invested, having long since given up on attempts to time major market moves. Indeed, the very cost of liquidating the portfolio and then reestablishing it might prove prohibitive even if his market judgment were correct. Fearing a sharp near-term drop, the manager buys NYA puts that best reflect his particular portfolio's volatility. If the market does in fact decline, the loss in portfolio value will be at least offset by the increase in the price of the puts, which will have likewise reflected market prices, going up in value as the market went down. Similarly, if the market instead rose in value, the options premiums would be lost but the portfolio would appreciate.

One of the major threats to modern institutional money managers has been the frantic scramble to climb aboard a rapidly accelerating bull market train. The explosive market rise of August 1982 well illustrates the danger of being caught with a large defensive or cash position. Those who thought the rally a mere flash in the pan paid heavily in opportunity losses as the market ran away from them.

Let's say, for example, that a mutual fund manager controls a stock portfolio of $70 million and is negative about the near-term course of the market. He has about $3 million of cash reserves, but is unwilling to liquidate his holdings or commit his reserves until the market direction becomes clearer. Feeling that the greater danger is to be caught underinvested, he buys 1,000 OEX May 175 calls for $400 each (total $400,000) when the S&P 100 average was at 177.

Now suppose the market surges by 10% to 194.7. The May 175 calls will be worth at least their intrinsic value of 19.7 points. The 1,000 call position would now be worth a minimum of $1,970,000, almost five times the original investment. If the calls retained a significant amount of time value, the manager could sell them and reinvest the proceeds. If they were near expiration, the calls would probably be exercised, also realizing cash to reinvest in stocks. Although equity prices would now be about 10% higher than before, the manager has an additional $1.5 million to invest in stocks.

Another possible strategy is the use of index options as proxies for the market by creating a sort of index fund. A manager attempting to duplicate the price action of the market might choose to keep his funds invested in essentially risk-free Treasury bills and reinvest the "income stream" (actually the accreted discount) in index call options. With the proper blend of these investments, the strategy should produce a close correlation with the chosen market indicator, but at a much lower cost because no actual stock purchases or sales are made. The strategy is even easier to implement through the use of stock futures instead of options. A number of institutional investors, however, have legal or procedural problems with futures trading, and this option–Treasury bill approach produces similar results without violating the fiduciary rules governing their investments.

The very success of these instruments has created new problems for the markets. As derivative products, options raise no new capital directly. Proponents of options trading have, however, been quick to produce impressive studies demonstrating that the options markets aid the capital formation process. These studies contend that the existence of an active and liquid options market allows risks to be laid off onto others so that underwriters and position traders are more willing to commit their own capital to help their customers raise theirs. Given the increasing size and speed of capital market transactions today, it is clear that there is much truth in this argument. Certainly few brokers are willing to commit several hundred thousand dollars of their own capital on a single trade without some form of risk transfer mechanism. Institutional investors, in fact, regularly demand this kind of service from their brokers, and it seems doubtful that the current level of institutional investment in stocks would be possible without the options markets.

Nevertheless, it can hardly be denied that many investors are simply betting on the course of the market when they might be investing in securities. Furthermore, the index options have cannibalized their equity options brethren in much the same manner that the latter siphoned money out of shares on the American and regional stock exchanges as well as the OTC market. Funds that might have been directed toward shares of smaller and newer ventures are instead diverted into options on the likes of IBM or GM, or worse yet, into parlays on the next major move in the overall stock market. It sometimes appears, as noted by the economist Henry Kaufman, that the critical capital formation process is being relegated to casinos.

Typically, Wall Street overdid a good thing and was soon awash in a flood of new options, mostly on segments of the market. By and large, these appear to have been introduced with little concern for their need or long-term viability. Rather, the impetus seems to have been provided by simple "metooism." Some have become virtually (or literally) defunct, such as Gaming Stocks (Philadelphia), Transportation (American), or Oil and Gas (American). Others continue to trade, but at volume levels so low as to preclude truly liquid transactions. Among these are Computer Technology (American), Oil (American), and the American Stock Market Value Index, the XAM. Occasionally, the Gold and Silver Index on the Philadelphia Stock Exchange becomes quite active, reflecting periodic spurts in the precious metals markets, but overall activity is little different from other subindexes.

HOW INDEX OPTIONS WORK

The dollar value of all major index option contracts is arbitrarily set at $100 times the current index level. For example, if the current OEX level were 167.95, the index is "worth" $16,795 and a full point move to 168.95 would represent a value change of $100. In this way the contracts may be traded in the familiar ⅛ point "ticks" or variations of $12.50, the same as for round lots of stock or for regular equity options. A premium quotation of 2½ would thus cost a buyer $250 ($2.50 × 100).

An exercise of a $17,000 package of 100 or more stocks would be totally impractical if physical delivery were required. Thus, all index options are settled in cash; no securities are delivered. If a short (writer) receives an exercise assignment, he delivers the in-the-money amount to the exercising long. For example, if today's OEX value were 165.50, a long exercising a December 160 call would receive $550 cash from the writer (5.5 points × $100).

Even though commissions are charged on the exercise of any index option, the long does not have to put up any additional funds or margin. In the example above, an exercise might carry a commission of about $35, leaving a net profit of $515. Conversely, an investor exercising a typical stock option such as a Texaco July 35 call would have to: (1) deposit $3,500, or $1,750 margin; (2) pay a commission, probably around $60; and (3) sell the shares to capture the profit, necessitating yet another commission of similar amount. In other words, unless a stock option is in-the-money by a significant amount, it often does not pay the retail customer to exercise. This is clearly less of a problem with index options, and has doubtless contributed to their popularity. As with stock options, however, well over 90% of all index put and call contracts will be offset with closing transactions or else will expire.

THE STANDARD & POOR'S 100 INDEX OPTION

This is by far the most actively traded index contract. Indeed, it is regularly the most actively traded of all options. For example, on November 21, 1984, the NYSE volume was an unexceptional 81,620,000 shares. The most actively traded security option that day was the IBM January 120 call with a volume of 8,179 contracts. On that day the OEX December 165 call had a trading volume of 39,399 contracts. In fact, 8 of the 10 most active contracts on the CBOE that day were OEX options, and 5 of the top 10 on the Amex were Major Market Index options.

The OEX is composed of 100 blue-chip favorites such as General Motors, IBM, Exxon, and Eastman Kodak. The index is weighted to give proportionate representation to market capitalization; that is, IBM carries more weight than B. F. Goodrich. The market value of each component share is multiplied by the number of outstanding shares. The total of these products is then divided by a "base value," arbitrarily selected as the aggregate value of the 100 component issues as of January 2, 1976. Finally, the resultant quotient is multiplied by 100 to give the current value. To give some idea of relative value, in December 1985 the OEX stood at about 196, the Dow Jones industrials were approximately 1475, and the S&P's 500 Index was at 202.

Market options were originally traded on a standard cycle with 90-day intervals separating expiration months, exactly as with standard equity options. It was quickly found, however, that hedgers and traders were far more interested in the next 90 days than in the next 6 months. Because the OEX was originally in the March–June–September–December cycle and the XMI traded in the January–April–July–October one, traders tended to shift positions from one index to the other upon the expiration of the current or nearest month. For instance, when the OEX December contract expired, the next available OEX was the March expiration, but the next available broad market option was the January XMI. Thus, most activity swung over to the Amex throughout January, back to the CBOE in February, and so on.

Because of the disruptive trading patterns so engendered, the exchanges agreed in 1985 to trade index options with expirations only in the current month and the two succeeding months. Thus, in April index options are available with April, May, and June expirations. Following the April expiration, trading will begin in July contracts and May becomes the current month. With trading in only the nearest three months possible, index options cannot be used to hedge longer-term price changes, and those interested in such strategies may find that index futures are fitting, as these contracts may have maturities a full year distant.

Striking prices are set at 5-point intervals with new ones added as the market moves up or down to the next level. For instance, if the index were currently at 167.85, striking prices would be available at 165 and 170, and quite possibly some others depending on recent price trends. If the index reaches 170, a new striking price at 175 would usually be added two business days later. This may not be done for all contracts, particularly those near expiration. The usual practice in this situation is to add the new striking prices only to the two following contract months.

THE MAJOR MARKET INDEX (XMI)

This is the second most actively traded index option. Its volume typically is something less than 20% of that of the OEX but is a substantial figure nonetheless. For example, in the week ending December 2, 1985, trading volume in the main index options was:

S&P 100	634,163
Major Market	105,076
NYSE	9,500
NYSE Double	10,543
Value Line	11,435
NASDAQ 100	1,355

The XMI is thus a strong second when compared to the competition. Its popularity stems from its blue-chip composition. Its 20 component issues include 15 from the Dow Jones industrials. It is thus hardly surprising that the correlation between the two measures is about 97%, closer than any other indexes.

Trading suffered at first when the expiration months were changed. It revived, however, following the introduction of a companion futures contract traded on the Chicago Board of Trade. The CBOT had lacked an equity-based competitor to the successful Standard and Poor's futures offered by its nearby archrival, the Chicago Mercantile Exchange. Trading in the futures has since shifted mostly to the larger "Maxi" XMI contract, but the viability of the basic XMI index seems assured.

OTHER INDEX OPTIONS

As the trading statistics indicate, none of the remaining index options even approaches the first two, but each has a niche and apparently enough volume to remain liquid and useful to both speculators and hedgers. The NYSE Composite and its larger Double variation reflect all common issues listed on the NYSE, making it somewhat less selective than the S&P 500 and much less so than the XMI.

The Philadelphia Stock Exchange's Value Line Average was spun off from the first stock index future, offered on the Kansas City Board of Trade. It has found a following among those more interested in a broader spectrum of the overall market. Its 1,700 issues show what is happening to OTC and Amex stocks as well as the blue-chip favorites, since the former issues are included in much greater number than in any of the other broad market gauges. Its use is usually favored in the latter stages of market advances after the better-known issues have achieved the bulk of their advances.

The NASDAQ 100 was introduced in 1985 by the Philadelphia Stock Exchange. Thus far it seems to have stalled at its current trading level. This is probably due mostly to the lack of major hedging interest among institutional investors, most of which do not have large holdings of OTC stocks and consequently little need to hedge a potentially adverse market move.

STOCK INDEX FUTURES

At one time there was little similarity between securities and futures (commodities) other than the fact that abrupt price changes in both present opportunities for speculators either to reap large profits or sustain equally large losses. Commodities brokers often occupied desks in conventional brokerage offices but usually talked about things that seemed foreign or arcane to regular stock brokers. They made investment decisions based on such curious terms as "the basis," or the current outlook for the soybean harvest.

The adaptation of the futures market to financial instruments in the 1970s caused a major change in the way futures trading was perceived. If it was possible to trade futures on the Swiss franc and GNMA pass-throughs, why not on stocks? Finally, trading in stock index futures commenced on February 24, 1982. The first stock future was the Value Line Index on the Kansas City Board of Trade, previously known as the mart for hard red winter wheat, the staple of America's bread-baking industry. A scant two months later the Chicago Mercantile Exchange began offering futures on the S&P 500, and the NYSE followed with a contract on its own Composite Index, offered on its subsidiary, the New York Futures Exchange.

The idea is not far different from the index options already discussed. The stock index future gives the investor the ability to hedge systematic risk, the risk that the entire market has a tendency to move in broad, overall swings. No matter how well chosen, the individual issue is not likely to be able to withstand a broad market decline. If it is indeed true that a rising tide lifts all boats, it is likewise true that a falling one has the opposite effect. The stock index future offers one means of hedging against, or profiting by, such swings without the need to select individual stocks.

It would be well first to distinguish between the index options already discussed and futures. Simply put, futures create the *obligation* to make or take delivery at some future date, while options create the *right, but not the obligation*, to do the same. Options require the payment of a nonrefundable premium; futures do not. Futures contracts are larger. Each of the major futures contracts is valued at $500 times the index value, whereas the most popular index options have a $100 multiplier. Unfortunately, understanding the differences has been further complicated by the introduction of options on the futures contract. These hybrids combine the limited-risk nature of the option with the profit potential of the futures contract. In the most basic of distinctions, however, it may be said that options provide a *range* within which (or outside of which) a position proves profitable, while a futures contract establishes a *price*.

All three of the first stock futures have succeeded, but the greatest success has been that of the S&P 500 contract on the Chicago Mercantile Exchange. In the last week of February 1986, for instance, S&P trading outpaced the NYSE Composite by about 450,000 contracts to 75,000, the Value Line bringing up the rear with a not unrespectable 26,000.

For institutional investors futures are generally considered to be more useful than index options because they are considerably larger and allow for a greater ease in hedging. Each of the major futures contracts is valued at $500 times the index, as opposed to the $100 which is more common to the index options previously discussed. Thus, if the S&P Index is at 225; the value of one contract is $112,500. A portfolio manager seeking protection against a temporary market decline could hedge a $1 million portfolio by selling 10 contracts, assuming the portfolio performed pretty much in step with the index (in other words, had a beta of about 1). A 10% market decline would also result in a similar decline in the short futures contract. Therefore, the paper loss in value on the portfolio has been largely, if not entirely, offset by a profit in the futures market.

Stock index futures are settled in cash and do not require the delivery of any stocks. Each full point of price change results in a $500 gain or loss. Futures trading is quite different from stock trading. For one thing, futures exchanges do not use the specialist system common to American stock exchanges. For another, the margining systems are quite different. Only a relatively small amount of securities trading is done on margin, and that at 50% of current market values. Long options must be paid in full, but that amount rarely exceeds several hundred dollars per option. All stock futures trading, on the other hand, is done on margin averaging less than 5% of current contract values. These amounts range from about $3,500 to $6,000 per contract. The major risk difference in the margining systems, however, is that with either a long stock or option position the original deposit represents the maximum possible loss, but with a futures position the loss can exceed the original margin commitment.

As with other futures contracts, the market cannot exist only for the hedgers. There must be an opposite side of every transaction. Stock futures have succeeded in developing a good deal of speculative interest, particularly from the floor traders or "locals" on each exchange. Other speculators are drawn by the usual appeal of any futures contract—low margin (great leverage) and the potential to make a quick killing. The fact that few of them do so does not seem to deter others from trying.

PROGRAM TRADING

The most recent and controversial development involving stock index futures is called program (or basket) trading. Basically, these are computer-generated arbitrages between a stock index future and a "basket" of shares from that index which have a closely correlated price action. The concept is fundamentally simple, although its implementation requires considerable skill and speed in execution.

First the trader identifies a group of stocks within one of the indexes that move closely in line with the value of the index. Then he or she awaits a situation where the index future sells either at a discount or a premium to the value of these stocks. If, for example, the futures rise to a meaningful premium over the stock value, the trader sells the futures short and buys the underlying securities, locking in a price differential between the two. Conversely, with futures at a discount the process is reversed. Because gaps between the two prices will be closed by other arbitragers buying in the cheap market and selling in the high, the position is essentially risk free.

Programs require split-second timing, as the gaps do not exist for very long. The mechanics of executing various stock orders almost simultaneously at different locations on the trading floor are obviously difficult, but the firms specializing in program trading have mastered them by such devices as preprinted order tickets that need only be time-stamped at point of entry. Because few firms have enough floor brokers to handle this quick flood of orders, $2 brokers are generally employed in addition to the firm's own personnel.

Program trading releases a huge order volume into the market in a very short time span and has a tendency to create wide price swings in the averages and the underlying stocks. This disconcerting, if not pernicious, phenomenon, has propelled the market up or down by unusually large amounts. Daily price fluctuations in the Dow Jones industrial average of 20 or 30 points have become rather commonplace, especially on the third Friday of the months of March, June, September, and December. This is because both index options and futures for that month expire, forcing an immediate alignment of closing prices with the actual indexes. For example, on March 24, 1986, the Dow was down 10 points from the previous day's close at 3:00 P.M., down 8 points by 3:30, and finished down 36 points. Some 57 million shares traded in the last half hour on that day, and a large portion of this was certainly attributed to program trading.

Partisans of such programs note that the effects on the course of the overall market are short-lived and relatively harmless. Others are not so sure. The price moves created by the programs occasionally give investors fortunate enough to own stocks a free ride, or at least a profit in about 30 minutes that might have otherwise required 6 months. The other side of the coin is more troubling. When programs force the market down, this may well discourage investors from committing capital. Prices fall not because of any fundamental weakness in the corporation's business but because the particular security has the misfortune to be included in someone's index basket.

Its very nature restricts program trading to the accounts of large institutional investors and brokerage firms. The SEC has given indications that it is concerned about the effects of such trades on the market. As it is difficult to demonstrate any significant public benefit from the basket programs, it appears likely that some restrictions will be imposed in the future.

23 Convertible Securities, Warrants, and Rights

CONVERTIBLE SECURITIES

Convertible securities appear to be highly attractive as investments. In some mysterious way they seem to have both the strength of a senior security and the speculative possibilities of a common stock. Everything in the financial world has its price, however, and the convertible security is no exception.

Nature

Convertible securities have so many special characteristics that it is desirable to discuss them at greater length than was possible in Chapter 2.

A *convertible security* is one that permits the holder, at his option and under certain conditions, to exchange such an issue for another security. Usually a convertible security may be exchanged for common stock in the same company, but there are some exceptions in which the holder may receive preferred stock and others in which the security received is an issue of another company. Holders of a convertible security may exercise this option of exchange to realize a profit, increase yield, avoid a call, or for any other reason they believe valid.

Convertible securities are, as a rule, either junior bonds or preferred stocks. Senior bonds, such as the first mortgage type, seldom carry the privilege. This section will deal mostly with convertible bonds. The same principles apply in general to convertible preferred stocks. Hence, a detailed treatment of both types of securities is unnecessary.

Importance of Convertible Security Financing

Although only an insignificant number of privately placed security issues have a conversion feature, public issues frequently have it. There is a substantial variation depending upon market conditions, but it seems likely that over 20% of all public offerings of corporate bonds and preferred stocks over time are convertible. The figure is much higher for preferred stock, usually exceeding 30%, whereas it is closer to 10% for bonds. Industrial corporations tend to use the conversion feature about four times as often as do utilities, banks, and insurance companies. This is true partially because industrials, as a group, find it more difficult to raise new capital than the other groups and partly because the public regards growth as more likely among industrial issues, which would tend to make the convertible feature more attractive.

The volume of convertible security financing is very large in the aggregate. During bull market periods especially, many such issues appear. In bullish years, issues of convertible bonds have totaled from $4 to $5 billion and then dropped to as low as $½ billion in bearish or dull years.

Reasons for Financing with Convertibles

Corporations never add extra features to bond indentures or stock contracts without a purpose. A number of reasons justify corporations in making certain issues convertible. A major reason is apparently to raise additional equity capital. This is particularly true for large corporations. We need a word of explanation at this point. For example, a given company wishes to raise a certain amount of new capital. It is believed that the time is not propitious to issue common stock, although the company might prefer this method of financing. It sells, therefore, an issue of convertible bonds expecting them to be eventually converted. The capitalization has changed from bonded indebtedness to equity capital. The company has, in effect, raised funds today at tomorrow's presumably higher stock prices. This is just the opposite of raising capital by selling common stock under a privileged subscription. In this instance the company raises equity capital by selling stock at less than today's stock prices, because the subscription price is typically under the market price by a substantial margin.

A second reason for convertible security financing is the desire to make the issue more salable or, in the words of the trade, to "sweeten" the issue. Debenture bonds and preferred stocks are often hard to sell. This additional feature often makes an issue an attractive one to investors who wish to combine speculation and investment in purchasing a single security. This reason seems particularly important in the financing of small unseasoned companies that tend to be the primary issuers of convertible securities. This reason is especially powerful during a weak bond market or during a bull stock market when so many investors are interested in common stocks.

Another factor in favor of this type of financing is that it can result in a lower rate of interest on the bonds or in a higher offering price, which means one and the same thing in terms of reduction of cost and risk incurred by the issuer. Again, it may be argued that the company benefits upon conversion, because fixed charges are then eliminated. A minor advantage, perhaps, is that conversion often results in additional stockholders for the company, an objective often of considerable importance in the eyes of corporate boards.

Everything is said to have its price. This can certainly be said of conversion security financing. If convertible bonds are held by those who are not common stockholders, there is always the possibility of a shift in voting control upon conversion. Extensive conversion dilutes the per-share earnings of the common stock, because more common shares are issued upon conversion. It also reduces the advantage to the corporation of trading on the equity, which means that the company is no longer borrowing money at a low cost but at the higher cost of common stock dividends. Conversion also increases the income tax load, because interest payments on convertible bonds are regarded as expenses, whereas dividends are not. Finally, a large convertible issue overhanging the market tends to depress the price of the common stock. To the extent that these disadvantages affect the corporation they also affect the common stockholders in the corporation.

Type of Companies Using Convertibles

All types of companies—large and small, strong and weak—use convertible security financing. Thousands of small and weak companies as well as companies that have long ago reached maturity use them. Even "growth companies" use them. As far as quality is concerned, however, by far the largest number of convertible issues are rated medium grade or lower.

One of the largest offerings of a convertible in history was an issue by U.S. Steel of $400 million of 25-year convertible debentures maturing in the year 2001. Interest was payable semiannually at 5¾% per year. At that time, interest on nonconvertible bonds of comparable quality was about 8¾%, so the company saved interest payments of about $12 million per year. The debentures, which had a face or par value of $1,000 each, were convertible into the common stock of the company at $62.75 per share. When the debentures were issued, the common stock of U.S. Steel was selling at about $55; thus conversion would become profitable if the common stock were to rise by about 14%.

Attraction to Investors

Convertible securities have an irresistible attraction to many investors, based on the natural desire to "have your cake and eat it too." First, some investors view a convertible bond as a very desirable security. It appears to give the safety of a bond plus the speculative possibilities of a common stock. As long as one holds on to the bond, one possesses a secure investment with a fixed return. If the company becomes very prosperous, one may convert the bond into common stock and benefit by the company's increased earning power.

A second reason for the convertible security's attraction is the suggestion that it is a hedge against inflation. As long as the price level remains stable, the bond can be retained. If further inflation occurs and the purchasing power of fixed interest payments declines, the rising dividends of stock obtained upon conversion will offset the increase in living costs. The principal will also rise if the conversion is effected.

In practice, the investor may be disappointed on one or both grounds. If the conversion clause is worth anything, it means that the purchaser of the convertible will have to take a smaller yield on the issue—the coupon will be less or the offering price will be higher. If the clause were added to the issue to sell it, obviously the company received more for the security than it would have otherwise. Again, the common stock may never rise enough to make conversion profitable.

However, in the bull market that started in 1949 and ran longer than any other of record, owners of convertibles obtained handsome profits because of the sustained and substantial rise in stock prices. This market benefited the holders of both convertible bonds and convertible preferred stocks. In those years the buyers of convertible bonds issued by AT&T, for example, were able to obtain almost immediate profits under the terms covering its large issues.

The Preemptive Right

Common stockholders are generally given the preemptive right to buy new convertible bonds whenever this privilege is accorded these security owners in purchasing additional common stock. The theory behind this is the same that underlies the granting of preemptive rights when additional common shares are to be issued.

Securities Given the Conversion Privilege

As already indicated, the practice is to give the holder of junior or unsecured bonds the privilege of buying stock rather than giving this privilege to the holders of well-secured issues. The debenture or unsecured bond is a favorite security to be made convertible. Nearly all industrial and utility issues are of this type, and some railroad convertible issues are still outstanding. Investment experts once believed that convertibles were weak securities and that the conversion feature merely was used to compensate for inadequate safety. That opinion is much less prevalent now, but investors should be aware of the relationship between bond quality and the conversion right when buying such securities.

The Conversion Period

This important part of the conversion feature indicates when the privilege begins and ends. Extreme variations are found in this respect as in most other features of convertible securities. The privilege may be limited or unlimited. If unlimited, it extends throughout the life of the bonds; if limited, there is a cutoff date, which is often from 10 to 15 years after the issue of the bonds. For preferred stock the privilege typically is unlimited.

The privilege may be delayed from a month to several years after the date of issue. Such delay permits the company to put the invested funds to work before it is necessary to issue more stock.

The Conversion Security

Any of a variety of securities may be the type of security received upon exercise of the conversion privilege. The usual provision permits the conversion of a senior security into common stock. This is the practice in the issue of utility and industrial bonds. In railroad finance, in some instances, bonds may be convertible into preferred stock. There are also examples of one class of common stock convertible into another—as Citizens Utilities A is convertible into the B stock.

The Redemption Clause

Convertible bonds frequently give the company the right to redeem or call the securities before maturity. If they are called by the company, the investor has no alternative but to turn in his security and receive cash. The call feature is typical of bond financing today. The advantages to the company are overwhelming; there are none to the investor. The provision has two effects upon the holder of a conversion issue: (1) it limits the possible profits to the holder, because the security may be called before the common stock has reached its highest point in a bull market; and (2) it may force the investor to convert when he would prefer not to do so.

The investor is usually given a reasonable notice that the company is to redeem the issue. The period is usually 30 days. The holder may convert until about 3 to 10 days before the call date.

Protection Against Dilution

An interesting problem relative to the conversion clause is that of dilution. This can take place when the company increases the number of shares without a corresponding increase in the assets or earning power of the company. Examples would include stock splits, stock dividends, issuance of new shares at less than the market price under a privileged subscription, issue of new convertible securities, merger, consolidation, and sale of assets. Most convertible issues have "antidilution" clauses that protect the investor, but there are exceptions. The investor should be certain that he is adequately protected against procedures that would dilute his conversion right.

Let us take an example. Let us suppose that a given bond with $1,000 par value can be converted into 10 shares of common stock. The company declares a 100% stock dividend. Each share of stock is now worth only half what it was before the dividend. Full protection against this dilution would be provided if the company were to change the number of shares receivable on conversion from 10 to 20.

Many other events may require an adjustment if a specified minimum level of dilution is exceeded. The level is specified when the convertible security is issued. Such events, other than stock dividends or rights offerings, include stock splits and special distributions of assets and indebtedness to stockholders.

The Conversion Ratio or Rate

The language of the financier and writer in the description of conversion security operations is often indefinite. There is no uniform terminology. Hence, one encounters such terms as conversion rate, conversion ratio, conversion price, and parity price often used interchangeably.

For the purposes of this description, the term *conversion rate* or *ratio* refers to the rate at which a $1,000 par value bond may be converted into shares of common stock. This ratio may be 10, 20, 25, or 50 shares, or any other rate set by the company. The ratio is definite and can easily be verified by examining the indenture. The formula for determination is to divide $1,000 in par value by the conversion price, which is described next.

The Conversion Price

This is usually defined as the amount of par value exchangeable for one share of common stock. For each such unit of par value surrendered to the company, one share will be issued. A few examples will clarify the definition.

Let us suppose that the conversion price is $50. This sum divided into $1,000 indicates that the holder will receive 20 shares upon conversion. Again, let us suppose the price is $100. The holder is entitled to 10 shares. Now, let us suppose that the price is $125. The holder will receive eight shares if he converts.

The simplest form of conversion contract has a conversion price that is constant throughout the conversion period. There are, however, issues in which the price changes during the conversion period. Two kinds of changes are common: (1) increasing the price with the passage of time and (2) increasing the price as the amount of conversion increases.

In the first situation, the conversion price might be $100 for the first five years, $105 for the next five years, $110 for the next five years, and $115 for the final five years of a 20-year issue.

In the second situation, the conversion price might rise with the volume of conversions. Thus the price might be $100 until 25% of the convertible issue had been converted, $105 until 50% was converted, $110 until 75%

was converted, and $115 for the remaining life of the issue. This form of step-up is much less common than the first, and both are relatively uncommon in convertible financing.

The effect of stepped-up ratios is a tendency to force conversion and a reduction in the dilution of the equity of other stockholders. The value of a conversion privilege falls on the date that a step-up in the conversion price occurs. It is as though the security sold ex-rights. An investor should be thoroughly familiar with the conversion clause in any issue he purchases or owns.

Uneven Conversion

A technical problem arises when bonds do not convert into an even number of shares of stock. Such a situation develops under some indentures when there are changing conversion terms. For example, a bond is convertible at $100, then at $105, then at $110. Let us suppose that a given investor is ready to convert when the price is stepped up to $110, which means that $110 in par value is exchanged for one share of common stock. On a $1,000 par value bond, such an exchange would result in the holder receiving nine shares with $10 in par value left over. What becomes of this $10 that is not converted?

There are four possible plans the company may use in the indenture. One permits the issue of warrants or scrip by the company; in this method, the company would issue a $10 warrant to the bondholder. This could be sold or used together with other scrip purchased to buy an additional share. This is fair to the investor and is the usual plan. A second plan would permit a cash payment by the investor. In our example, the individual could deposit $100 in cash plus the $10 in unused par value and secure another share. A third plan is one in which the company requires even conversion. In other words, the investor loses the unused portion of his bond unless enough par value is deposited to secure an even number of shares. In the present example, the holder would have to turn in $11,000 in par value or 11 bonds to obtain an even conversion of 100 shares. A final plan would be one in which the company would redeem in cash the unused part of the bond, in this case, $10.

Cash Payments upon Conversion

The typical conversion provision permits conversion of a bond into a certain number of shares of stock by simple exchange. However, some companies require the surrender of the convertible bond plus a payment of cash to obtain the additional stock. The leading exponent of this practice is AT&T. The conversion price on most post World War II issues has been $100, which means the holder received 10 shares for each $1,000 bond. However, the holder was required to pay additional cash per share. For example, in the

$637 million issue of 1955, the conversion price was $100, and the additional cash payment was $48 per share, making a total cost of $148.

The Adjusted Stock Price

Professional traders in convertible securities often go into very precise adjustments in making conversions. Profits are small and costs must be calculated within close limits. One such adjustment would be the computation of an adjusted stock price.

Because bonds are quoted by a different method from stocks, the stock price should be adjusted to obtain an equality with the convertible bond. The problem is to adjust the prices of the two securities. Recall that stocks are sold "flat" and bonds "with interest." This means that the stock quotation includes accumulated income, whereas the bond quotation excludes it. In buying a bond, one usually pays the quoted price plus interest. For example, if a given stock is quoted at 104, that is all that one pays, even though the company may be ready to pay a $1 dividend in a few weeks. If a bond is quoted at 104, one pays $1,040 plus, perhaps, $4, $10, or $15 accumulated interest.[1]

To place these two securities on the same basis, it is necessary to subtract the accumulated dividend on the stock; this, of course, is exactly what has already been done with the interest in the bond quotation. Accumulated dividends are figured on the basis of 365 days per year to the nearest $\frac{1}{8}$ point. Adjustment tables permit easy calculations for those who have access to them.

Let us take an example. A given stock pays a dividend of $6 per year. Two months have elapsed since the last dividend date. The current market price is 104⅜. If the dividend rate is $1.50 per quarter, or $.50 per month, it is obvious that dividends of $1.00 have accumulated. The adjusted stock price is, therefore, 103⅜.

Another example may be useful. A stock is paying dividends at an annual rate of $2.40; its market price is 40⅛. It went ex-dividend 20 days ago; find the adjusted stock price. The dividend rate is $.20 per month. Two-thirds of a month have elapsed, so a dividend of $.13 has accrued. The nearest fractional point is ⅛. Hence, the adjusted stock price is 40⅛ minus ⅛, or 40.

Conversion Equivalent

This may be defined as the adjusted price at which the stock must sell to be on an exact equality with the bond. If one disregards taxes and commissions, the stock received is worth exactly as much as the bond given at conversion; the investor would break even if he were to convert. Carefully note at this

---

[1]A small number of bond issues trade flat, that is, without accumulated interest. These issues are usually income or adjustment bonds or bonds currently in default.

point that the conversion equivalent is based upon the adjusted stock price
and not the actual market price.

This formula will permit easy calculation of the equivalent:

$$\text{Conversion equivalent} = \frac{\text{Market price of bond}}{\text{Number of shares received}}$$

Let us take a few examples. The bond is selling at 104½ and is convertible
at 100, or par for par. Ten shares are received upon conversion, so the conversion equivalent is found by dividing the value of the bond, $1,045, by 10;
the result is 104½. Accrued interest may be ignored because bondholders
who choose to convert their bonds lose their right to such interest. If bonds
are converted voluntarily, therefore, it generally behooves the bondholder
to do so immediately after an interest payment.

In a second example, the bond is selling at 104; it is convertible at 25.
The stock is selling at 28½ with a ½ point accumulated dividend. The investor
buys a bond and converts. What is his gross profit if taxes and commission
are disregarded?

The answer is $80, as the following solution will show:

$25 | $1,000
40 shares received

40 | $1,040
$26—the conversion equivalent

Market price of stock	$28.50
Less: Accumulated dividend	.50
Adjusted stock price	28.00
Less: Conversion equivalent	26.00
Profit per share	2.00
Multiply by 40 shares	× 40
Gross profit	$80.00

In other words, the stock costs the investor $26 per share or the conversion
equivalent. The stock, less the accumulated dividend, can be sold for $28.
Because he receives 40 shares upon conversion, his gross profit is $80. If
the adjusted stock price had been only $26, he would have neither lost nor
gained on the transaction, provided taxes and commissions were ignored.
Obviously, in practice, if the stock price rose above $26, the bond price
would rise also. A profit on conversion is extremely rare.

Valuation

Convertible bonds command a higher price than nonconvertible bonds that
are similar in all respects except convertibility because they derive their

value from two sources rather than one. Like any bond, they offer the buyer interest on his money with less risk than would be involved in buying equities offered by the same company. In addition, they offer the buyer the right to acquire the common stock and thus have value similar to that of an option. The first of these is called the bond, investment, or theoretical value. The second is called the conversion value, which leads to the premium paid for convertible bonds.

If the stock rises above the conversion price, the bond price will rise in sympathy. If the stock should fall, however, the bond price will not tend to fall as far relative to the stock as might be expected because it will be supported by its interest payments. In effect, the conversion value could be lost altogether because the public loses any hope of ever profiting by conversion, but the bond will still be expected to sell at a level comparable to bonds of similar quality that are not convertible. By computing bond value, the buyer of a convertible may estimate the risk he is incurring when he pays a premium for the conversion value.

Assume, for example, that a bond buyer buys the U.S. Steel convertible described above, but that he buys it in 1981 when it has a remaining maturity of 20 years. Assume further that interest rates have risen to 12% on non-convertible issues similar in quality to the U.S. Steel bond. If it is assumed that bond interest is paid at the rate of $57.50 annually (5¾% of $1,000), then the current bond value would be found by discounting the 20 annual $57.50 interest payments and the $1,000 principal to be received at maturity at 12%:

$$\text{Bond value} = \sum_{t=1}^{20} \frac{57.50}{(1.12)^t} + \frac{\$1,000}{(1.12)^{20}} = \frac{57.50}{.1037} + \frac{\$1,000}{7.4694} = \$533.19$$

Price Movements

Under certain conditions there is a close relationship between the price movements of a convertible bond and the security into which it is convertible. If the stock is selling below the conversion equivalent, there is no profit to be gained in converting the bond; hence, the price of the stock has comparatively little effect on the market value of the bond. Except for a premium based upon the possible optimism of buyers toward the short-term outlook for the stock, the bond will sell primarily on its merits as an investment issue.

Let us suppose, however, that the stock rises sufficiently to offer a profit to bondholders upon conversion. The conversion security is then said to exercise "sympathetic price control" over the market value of the bond. If the stock increases above the lowest conversion equivalent, the bond will automatically rise because of transactions by arbitragers. These arbitragers, who see a profit opportunity, will buy the bonds and convert into stock through an arbitrage transaction. Conversion equivalence will be maintained as the stock price rises further.

For example, let us suppose that the conversion price of a given issue is $100. The stock rises to $125. The bond will rise to at least 125, because 10 shares of stock upon conversion would be worth $1,250. In a situation such as this, the investor would need to be sure he converted the bond into stock if the company called the issue.

Rapidity of Conversion

The question here is how soon after a convertible issue is sold may the investor expect to realize a conversion profit. There are three possibilities: (1) quickly, (2) in a number of years, and (3) never.

There are few instances in which the investor may expect to realize quick profits. The conversion price is usually so high that there is no immediate chance of conversion at a profit. American Telephone & Telegraph convertibles have been a marked exception. Such issues permit an immediate profit as soon as the conversion privilege begins, which is typically in two to four months after the close of subscriptions for the issue. Investors know that immediate profits are possible at the end of this short waiting period. The result is a great stimulus to the sale of the convertibles. For example, in the $637 million issue of 1955, the earliest day of exchange was two months after the close of the subscription period. An immediate profit was possible. As a result, a total of $250 million was converted on the first day, with 295,000 of 525,000 subscribers taking advantage of this opportunity.

Typically, however, 2 to 4 years elapse before the common stock is high enough to permit profitable conversion. A bull market will shorten the period necessary. In many instances there is never the opportunity to gain a profit on conversion, and bonds will remain outstanding until called or retired. In such cases the issuer is said to have an "overhanging convertible" and finds itself paying interest on long-term debt, whereas it had anticipated conversion into equity within a reasonably short period.

In that convertible securities tend to sell at a premium, yield at least as much as the securities into which they are convertible, and frequently entail less risk, the incentive to convert is rarely present. Most conversions actually result from a call below the market price of the bonds. The right to convert expires a few days before the redemption date. The holder has little choice but to convert while it is still possible, so this series of events is commonly known as *forced conversion*. There are usually restrictions imposed upon a company to preclude it from calling a convertible too soon after it is issued. Typical restrictions provide for the passage of a specific number of years from the issue date and a share price trading at a substantial designated premium over the stated conversion price.

Arbitrage Profits

An arbitrage profit becomes possible in a convertible bond whenever the adjusted stock price is higher than the conversion equivalent by at least the amount of taxes and commissions involved in the transaction. Let us take a simple example. A bond is selling at 100 and can be converted into 10 shares of stock, the adjusted price of which is 104. The difference between the selling price of 10 shares of stock, or $1,040, and the cost of the bond, or $1,000, represents the gross profit from which must be deducted the commissions involved in the operation.

There are three ways in which to take advantage of such a situation. The first is to buy the bond at 100 in anticipation that it will rise to about 104 because of sympathetic price control. The price would be forced upward by speculators. After this happens, the bond could be disposed of by sale without any conversion. This method has an element of risk in that the stock may fall instead and the profit never be realized.

The second way is to sell the stock short, the technique of the professional. At the instant a professional arbitrager or bond trader sees a profit differential, he will buy the bond and sell short the number of shares to be received upon conversion. This operation guarantees him an immediate gross profit, which is the difference between the stock price, say 104, and the cost of the bond, or 100. Such opportunities exist only momentarily. The gain, however, is certain. This is an example of riskless or *bona fide* arbitrage.

The final method is to purchase the bond, convert into stock, and sell the stock. If the bond were purchased at $1,000 and the stock were sold at $1,040, there is a $40 gross profit. The danger of this method is that by the time the bond is purchased, delivered, and converted into the equivalent number of shares, the profit differential may have disappeared.

Interest and Dividend Adjustment

In some cases companies have made adjustments for accrued interest on the converted bonds or accumulated dividends on preferred stock when conversion takes place, but this is a rare practice today.

Convertible Preferred Stocks

The principles and practices governing the issuance of convertible bonds are applicable for the most part to convertible preferred stocks; hence, only limited discussion of them is necessary at this point. Historically, about one-third of all issues of preferred stocks tend to be convertible, although in recent years they have become less popular than convertible bonds. High interest rates combined with high corporate tax rates have encouraged corporations to issue bonds rather than stocks because the interest paid is deductible, whereas dividends are not. Furthermore, interest is a liability, whereas there is no legal obligation to pay dividends. Failure to pay preferred stock dividends, however, may lead to difficulty in offering securities successfully in the future.

Most buyers of convertible preferred issues are noncorporate buyers who cannot take advantage of the dividend exclusion from their income taxes, so the yields of convertible preferred and bond issues do not reflect the premiums which are usually built into the prices of the preferred issues. The tax position of the issuer therefore becomes more of a consideration than usual in determining which type of security will be issued. If the issuer pays no taxes, it might lean toward preferred, and if it does pay taxes, it will lean toward bonds. If it pays no taxes currently but anticipates that it will be doing so within the near future, it might issue a curious type of issue called a convertible exchangeable preferred stock. This is a convertible preferred which may be exchanged into convertible bonds at the discretion of the issuer.

In that bonds have a maturity date, there are instances of bonds without a call provision. Because preferred stock does not mature, it is usually necessary for the company to include a call feature if it expects to eliminate the issue efficiently in the future. Many convertible stock issues require the company to retire the issue through a sinking-fund provision.

Like the convertible bond, the convertible preferred has two elements of value: investment value and conversion value. The first is merely the price at which the stock could reasonably be expected to sell if it were not convertible. This price can be ascertained by comparisons with other preferred stock issues similar in all respects except convertibility.

Most convertible preferred issues are public issues rather than private placements. Industrials use convertibles much more extensively than do utilities or railroads. The life of the privilege is typically unlimited and the conversion ratio is fixed. In some cases, the conversion ratio may change over time, whereas in other cases, it might expire altogether. In some cases, the right to convert is not available immediately but is delayed. The buyer of such issues is well advised to be aware of the conversion provision. In practically all cases, the conversion security is common stock and the conversion price is constant.

Convertible preferred stocks, like convertible bonds, tend to become quite popular with investors during bull markets or anticipated bull markets. Such preferred issues will have to rise in sympathy with the underlying common stock and usually sell at a premium. Premiums for preferred issues tend to be smaller than for bonds. Even though preferred issues are widely referred to as quasi-debt, they are nevertheless fundamentally equity securities and therefore carry more risk than would bonds issued by the same company.

Examples of Convertible Securities

In the description of convertible issues, we believed it unwise to burden the reader with repeated examples of these securities. Eight typical issues are given at this point to indicate representative features of these bonds and stocks.

1   Occidental Petroleum. $6.25 Series J. Preferred stock is convertible into 1.25 shares of the common stock.

2 Ashland Oil, Inc.. $3.96 convertible preferred stock is convertible into common stock on a share-for-share basis.

3 GTE Corporation. $2 Series C. Preferred stock is convertible into .52 shares of the common stock.

4 Reading & Bates Corporation. $2.125 preferred stock is convertible into 1.3005 shares of the common stock.

5 Atlantic Richfield Company. $2.80 Series C. Preferred stock is convertible into 2.4 shares of the common stock.

6 K mart. 6s, 1999, are convertible into 28.17 shares of common stock per $1,000 bond.

7 Great Western Financial. 8⅞s, 2007, are convertible into 32.79 shares of the common stock.

8 Big Three Industries, Incorporated. 8½s, 2006, are convertible into 22.9885 shares of the common stock.

WARRANTS

A *warrant* is a security that gives its holder the right to buy a specified amount of another security, usually common stock, for a stated period of time and at a stated price. Warrants are, in effect, call options. Some warrants are issued individually, sometimes as compensation for underwriters or as part of a reorganization or acquisition, but more frequently as part of a package with preferred stock or, more often, with bonds. As part of such packages or units the warrants act as a "sweetener" or "kicker."

Nature

Warrants are similar to calls on common stock in that they allow the holders to buy common shares when they wish for a stated period at a stated price. Calls, however, are usually exercisable only for a few months and differ from warrants in the manner in which they are issued. Calls are created by a writer who may or may not own the related common stock and are sold through option exchanges or, infrequently, through dealers. Warrants are created by the company which issues the related securities. Warrants therefore create a cash flow into a company and dilute the outstanding stock, whereas calls do neither. Most warrants are detachable from their package after a specified time and may then be traded separately. Others are not detachable unless exercised or if the bonds to which they are attached are redeemed.

Like convertible bonds, the exercise price of a common stock into which a warrant is convertible is usually above the market price at the time of issue by about 15%. Unlike the holders of convertible bonds, however, the warrant holder who exercises a warrant must pay some cash for the stock acquired.

If bonds are converted, there is usually no payment of money involved unless there are provisions for rounding off into full shares in the event of uneven conversion ratios.

If the common stock that the warrant holder may acquire is split or if there is a stock dividend, protection against dilution is provided by a reduction in the exercise price in proportion to the split or dividend. This allows the acquisition of enough additional shares to compensate for the change in capitalization.

Exercise prices may remain constant or may change, usually by periodic increases. Most warrants have a life of 10 to 20 years, but a few are perpetual.

Value of Warrants

There are two basic elements entering into the value of a warrant. First is investment value, which has to do with the value of the stock that may be acquired. For example, if a warrant represents a claim on 10 shares of stock at $30 per share and the stock is currently selling for $35, the warrant has an intrinsic value of $50 (10 times $5) and must sell at $50 or more because of ever-alert arbitragers.

The other element of value depends upon the length of life remaining for the warrant. In general, the longer the remaining life, the higher the value of the warrant. If a stock were selling below the exercise price, a warrant with one day of life left would be regarded as worthless. If a stock were below the exercise price, however, and the warrant had a significant length of time remaining before expiration, its time value would result in a market value that could be substantial. The precise level would depend upon several factors, including the amount of time left, how far the stock was below its exercise price, how favorably the public judged the outlook for the stock and its dividend, interest rates, and general market conditions. Naturally, premiums tend to grow in bull markets and contract in bear markets.

Examples of Warrants

Most brokers can provide investors with long lists of warrants of current interest, but the following list indicates four typical warrants similar to the others which trade on the various exchanges or over the counter. The investor should always check conversion terms and trading bases in detail.

1 Atlas Corporation. Warrants allow the purchase of one share at $31.25 in perpetuity.
2 Bally Manufacturing. Warrants allow the purchase of one share of common stock at $40. Warrants expire January 4, 1988, but management may accelerate the expiration date.
3 Angeles Corporation. Warrants allow the purchase of one share of common stock at $21. Company extended expiration deadline from 1988 to January 15, 1991.

4   Horn & Hardart. Warrants allow purchase of one share of common stock
at $18.75. Warrants expire December 28, 1987.

RIGHTS OFFERINGS

Many investors from time to time receive rights to subscribe to stock or
bonds in the companies in which they have a stockholder interest. These
rights are options with some resemblance to call options and warrants. Like
the latter, they are issued by a company, but for shorter periods and under
different conditions. They offer the right to buy a stated number of shares
of stock or a stated par value of bonds at a predetermined price during a
specified period. Experienced investors are aware of the market and economic
values of such rights and the different ways in which they may be utilized.

Rights are issued to stockholders of record on a date set by the Board of
Directors of a company. They are in the form of stock, or bond, subscription
warrants. The stockholders may exercise these rights by returning them to
the corporation with the required funds to pay for the new security. If the
stockholders do not wish to exercise the rights, they may sell them in the
market. A considerable amount of trading in rights usually takes place during
the period in which they may be exercised.

PRIVILEGED SUBSCRIPTION

Rights are issued under a procedure known as a *privileged subscription*. This
procedure means that existing stockholders are given priority in subscribing
for the new shares at a price lower than the current market price. This privilege is widely considered a favor by the stockholders, but it may have much
less value than popular opinion accords it.

Legal Aspects of Privileged Subscriptions

The laws on privileged subscriptions have undergone a considerable change
over the years. Under the common law, the owners of a business have a
right to anything of value distributed by the corporation. This would obviously
include the issue of new stock with its claims on earning power, assets,
dividends, and voting power. These claims have been widely supported by
state laws and regulations that require, encourage, or at least permit preemptive rights. Encouraged by both the common law and directives of state corporation legislation, many corporate charters provide for preemptive rights
by shareholders.

There have been some exceptions to the broad principle of the preemptive
right. Although such a right has been attached to the issuance of new common
and most preferred stock, it has not been applied to debt issues unless they

are, in turn, convertible into equity. Furthermore, the preemptive right has usually been applied only to general distributions of stock to the investing public and not to more restrictive issues such as stock issued to employees under stock option plans, stock utilized for acquisition of other companies, or the sale of treasury stock that was reacquired from stockholders by purchase or donation.

There has been some trend away from using the privileged subscription both by some states that have reduced their pressure to utilize this means of financing and by corporations, some of which have even attempted to amend their charters to avoid having to offer the preemptive right.

The common law justification for the preemptive right has been altered by legislation over the years. A considerable variation therefore exists now among the several states. Some states, such as California, Indiana, and Pennsylvania, require the preemptive right only if it is specifically introduced into the charter, or articles of incorporation, by the founders. In other states a corporation may be formed and the founders are free to include or exclude the preemptive right in the charter as they see fit. States such as Delaware, California, Indiana, New Jersey, Ohio, and Pennsylvania permit a majority of the stockholders of a company to amend the charter and deny preemptive rights.

Although many corporations have amended their charters to permit the directors to issue stock without the preemptive right, this option is not always taken. Even some companies which formerly issued new stock through privileged subscription although it was not required by their charter provisions have abandoned this practice and no longer use rights.

The SEC has also recognized a changing concept with respect to the preemptive right. In earlier years, the SEC in interpreting the Public Utility Holding Company Act, held that stockholders were entitled to preemptive rights. In more recent years the Commission has not insisted on the principle when it appeared that the management could obtain funds on more favorable terms by selling stock under competitive bidding.

The right of stockholders to buy new stock before it is issued for cash to nonstockholders has often been justified by two arguments. The first is that each stockholder is entitled to preserve or maintain a proportionate voting interest in the corporation. A substantial block of new stock sold to outsiders might cause a marked change in the voting control of the corporation; control might shift from one group to another. Under the preemptive right, however, a given stockholder or group of stockholders could subscribe to new stock in proportion to current holdings and maintain the same degree of control as before. Rights offerings are accordingly popular among companies which are controlled by small numbers of stockholders who wish to avoid dispersing their control among new stockholders.

The second argument is that each stockholder is entitled to maintain a proportionate share in the assets of the corporation or, to put it another way, to maintain a proportionate share in the net worth or equity of the common stockholders. Stock issued under privileged subscription typically is sold at a price below the current market price. Thus book value of each old share is diluted and the stock tends to fall in value after the issue of new shares. The stockholder is entitled to protection against such decline. This protection is secured by the right to buy new stock before an offer to other purchasers and on more favorable terms than other purchasers.

The arguments supporting or objecting to the utilization of rights are not always easy to prove. The privileged subscription may be less of a favor to stockholders than is alleged. The absence of the preemptive right requirement obviously increases the freedom of directors in the method of issuing new securities, but whether this freedom is sound policy and fair to stockholders is likewise debatable.

Purpose of Issuing Rights

Rights are offered to stockholders when the directors believe this to be the best method of raising additional funds. Long-term, or capital, funds may be secured by selling common stock, preferred stock, or bonds. If a company wishes to secure more funds from common stockholders, it may issue rights even though the preemptive right is waived under the charter. The rights are a vehicle facilitating subscription to the new stock. The immediate recipients may sell their rights to others; but, ultimately, barring nonsense destruction of the warrants or a drastic decline of the stock price, these rights will end in the hands of individuals who will exercise them and buy the stock.

Pricing the New Stock

In all privileged subscriptions, the directors set a subscription price which is below the current market price of the stock at the time the rights are issued. This is not benevolence on the part of directors. Rather, it is part of a policy designed to make the new issue a success. No Board of Directors expects present stockholders to make a significant financial sacrifice by buying new stock above the market price. Indeed, they expect them to buy the stock only if the issue is made sufficiently attractive through a price discount.

The pricing of new stock requires exercising care. Decision on the exact subscription price may be deferred until a day or two before the public announcement, which follows the release of the issue by the SEC. The market price may be as much as 40% higher than the subscription price chosen, particularly if the issue is not underwritten, although the spread on a typical rights deal is usually much less than this. The offering price, of course, must equal or exceed the par value of the stock, if it has one. A substantial spread between market and subscription price is justified on two grounds. First, the risk is reduced that the market price will fall during the subscription period enough to jeopardize the success of the issue. Second, a substantial spread sweetens the issue, in the sense that it gives the stockholders the sense of a bargain and increases the willingness to accept the new issue.

ISSUING RIGHTS

Procedure

A number of steps must be followed by the Board of Directors in issuing rights. First, the directors must authorize issue of the new stock through a formal resolution. If the company does not have enough unissued stock for this purpose, an amendment to the charter by the stockholders will be needed before the additional shares can be issued.

Second, approval of the new issue by the stockholders is required. Usually, a special meeting of the stockholders is called. Approval by vote of holders of two-thirds of the stock present at the meeting is a usual requirement. Some corporate laws, however, permit authorization of new stock issues at a regular meeting of the stockholders.

In calling a meeting of the stockholders, the directors send them a special letter and a proxy statement with complete details of the proposed financing and its justification. The company also releases items to newspapers during the period before the stockholders' meeting in order to increase the likelihood of understanding and, hence, of acceptance of the proposal. Such proposals of directors are usually approved by the stockholders with a large majority vote.

The Securities Act of 1933 requires that all nonexempt issues be registered with the SEC before a public offering. A registration statement is prepared and submitted to the Commission. At the same time a preliminary, or "red herring," prospectus—minus some important items such as price—may be printed and released to the securities industry. The Act requires a 20-day waiting period before the public sale, although the period is considerably shortened in practice. Shortly before the end of this period, a decision is made as to the subscription price, unless such a decision was made earlier.

As soon as possible after an issue is released for sale by the SEC, the subscription warrants are issued. A date of record is decided upon by the directors prior to this time. Ordinarily, this date is the same as the date on which the registration is declared effective by the SEC. As soon as the stockholders of record on this specified date are properly identified from the stock record books, subscription warrants are prepared in their names and mailed to them. This is a complex and expensive process, because thousands of stockholders must be reached; commonly a company starts days ahead in preparing stockholder lists and then makes corrections up to the date of record from later information. In view of the short duration of the offering period in most rights distributions, companies begin mailing warrants within 24 hours of the date of record. Some large companies, however, may take one to two weeks to complete the process.

To avoid errors and possible loss by stockholders, subscription warrants are prepared to look like instruments of value, even though most are now in some form designed to be compatible with computerized accounting systems. Each warrant shows the number of rights represented by the warrant. Blank spaces permit the holder to subscribe for the new stock or endorse the warrant for sale of these rights. Warrants may be exercised by surrendering them to the company or to its subscription agent with the proper funds needed to buy the new stock. If the holder wishes to sell them, he may do so through any broker. Often the corporation appoints a bank or trust company to act as its agent; holders do business through this agent if they care to do so. Subscriptions are handled for a subscriber without cost. Some agents also arrange the sale of rights at no charge.

The stockholder receiving a warrant also receives detailed instructions from the company. Sometimes the instructions are printed on the reverse side of the warrant itself. This gives complete details on the number of shares that may be purchased, the subscription price, the date when the subscription period expires, how new stock may be purchased, and how the rights may be sold. In case the warrant does not represent the exact number of rights needed to buy an integral number of shares, additional rights can be purchased or the excess rights may be sold. For example, if the company were to require 20 rights to buy one new share and the stockholder had 25 rights, he could either sell 5 rights or buy an additional 15 rights in order to buy one more share.

As soon as stockholders receive their warrants, they are faced with the question of what to do with them. The company has provided the opportunity to surrender the warrant and subscribe for new stock. They may, however, prefer to sell their rights. Their decision may be based on any of a number of things, such as their investment funds, the merits of the stock as an investment or speculation, the size of their present holdings in the company, the relative merits in buying the stock or disposing of the rights, or their forecast of the market. A number of alternatives are open; these will be examined shortly.

Meaning of a Right

A *right* is the privilege attached to one old share of stock. Each outstanding share is given one right; the number of old shares and the number of rights are identical. Stockholders owning 10 shares will receive 10 rights. Those possessing 200 shares will receive 200. This is the so-called New York plan now generally used in privileged subscriptions.

Rights Needed to Buy New Stocks

The directors, in setting forth the terms of the privileged subscription, always state in clear language the number of rights needed to buy one new share. For example, 3, 5, 10, or 20 rights may be necessary. If the stockholder owns 50 old shares and 10 rights are necessary to acquire one new share, he may subscribe for 5 new shares.

A simple method is used by the company to decide how many new rights are necessary to subscribe for one new share. Let us suppose that a company has 1 million shares outstanding and proposes to issue 50,000 new shares. One million rights will be issued. The directors do not want to sell more than 50,000 shares. Hence they decide that 20 rights must be surrendered in the purchase of each new share. All of the rights will have been exercised by the time the offer of 50,000 shares is fully subscribed.

Trading in Rights

Rights on stock exchanges are usually traded as soon as registration of the issue is effective under the 1933 Act. The Department of Stock List announces when this activity may begin. Before trading is approved, the Department must be certain that all details of the new issue have been approved by the directors and by the stockholders, if required; that they have been effectively registered with the SEC; and that they are approved by any other governmental body with regulatory jurisdiction. Shares to be newly issued must be approved by the Department and the Board of Governors of the Exchange.

Rights are traded on a "when-issued" basis until they are mailed out to stockholders by the company. Thereafter they are traded "regular way." The period in which when-issued trading in rights continues will vary; it might be from one day to as long as five weeks. The deciding factor is how quickly the warrants can be processed and mailed to the stockholders. For the majority of smaller issues, when-issued trading is limited to one or a few days.

The original issue trades ex-rights usually on the first business day following the first day of trading in the rights, but not earlier than the fourth business day before the date of record. The stock is said to be selling "cum rights" or "rights on" before it goes ex-rights.

From this date until the end of the privileged subscription period, the rights are freely bought and sold separately from the stock. The stock transactions are ex-rights and the buyers and sellers understand that no rights go with it. Trading in the rights themselves continues until noon on the day when the right to subscribe expires.

The entire process of issuing rights typically takes seven to eight weeks. Typically, the process may involve the following steps. Three to four weeks before the issue date the underwriting syndicate is formed and registration documents are filed with the SEC and with corporation offices in any states in which the securities are to be sold. The latter process is referred to as "blue-skying." Any deficiencies in the registration documents are corrected, if possible, in a little under one month. One day before the issue, the subscription price is set and the final makeup of the underwriting group is determined. Rights are mailed to stockholders on the issue date and trade for about three weeks, at which point they expire. A closing date is set, usually one week later, on which trades are settled by delivery of certificates and payments are made for them.

The rights are mailed to all stockholders who are holders on a record date set by the directors of the corporation. In order for a person to be a holder of record on the record date, the stock must be bought in time to settle on or before that date. This usually means that it must be bought at least five business days previously. Stock bought only four days before the record date will settle one day too late to allow receipt of the rights. Such a transaction is designated as ex-rights.

Trading in rights on a when-issued basis takes place before they are actually mailed. When-issued contracts are settled by delivery of the rights, and payment therefore is made on a date fixed by a special ruling of the Exchange's Department of Stock List if the stock is listed.

Value of Rights

Many speculators and traders in rights use some formula to determine the theoretical value of such rights. The word "theoretical" should not be taken to mean unrealistic. Rights will tend to trade at levels almost precisely with the computed theoretical value. There is no reason for anyone to pay more for rights than they are worth, because they would merely allow purchase of stock at a level totaling more than would be paid on the open market not utilizing the rights. If rights were too cheap relative to the stock, profitable arbitraging would become possible, which would act immediately to bring the value of the stocks and rights into equilibrium. Two formulas have some use in figuring theoretical value: (1) before the stock goes ex-rights and (2) after it goes ex-rights. These are given below.

To find the theoretical value of one right before the stock goes ex-rights, the following formula is used:

$$V = \frac{M - S}{N + 1}$$

where V is the value of one right.
M is the market price of the old stock.
S is the subscription price of the new stock.
N is the number of rights necessary to buy one new share.

Let us take two examples and find the theoretical value of a right. First, a stock is selling at 40 in the market; it is offered to the stockholders at 30;

9 rights are necessary to subscribe for one new share. The value of the right is $1.

$$\frac{40 - 30}{9 + 1} = \$1$$

In the next example, the stock is selling at 95; the subscription price is 75; 7 rights are necessary to buy one new share.

$$\frac{95 - 75}{7 + 1} = \$2.50$$

The reader may be puzzled as to why the figure "1" is added each time, and may wish proof that the rights are worth the figures indicated. Let us go back to our first example.

Nine old shares worth $40 each	$360
Plus one new share contributing $30	30
Total value of 10 shares	390
Value of each of the 10 shares	39
Theoretical value of stock after subscriptions	39
Cost of the new share	30
Value received from old 9 shares	$ 9
Value received from each old share	$ 1

In other words, the company now has 10 shares outstanding instead of 9; there are $390 in assets and earning power behind each of the 10 shares of $39 each. The new share was purchased for $30. The stockholder realized $9 in value, but had to own 9 shares to obtain it. Each right was worth, therefore, $1.

A formula for finding the value of the rights after the stock goes ex-rights is as follows:

$$V = \frac{M - S}{N}$$

After the stock goes ex-rights, it is not as valuable as before; its market value falls approximately the amount equal to the theoretical value of the right. In our preceding first example, this new value is $39; the value of one right is still $1.

$$\frac{39 - 30}{9} = \$1$$

Market and Theoretical Values of Rights

In practice, the actual or market value of a right and its theoretical value are seldom precisely the same. The market value may fluctuate above and below the theoretical value. Actually, however, the market and the theoretical prices remain quite close together most of the time and most frequently trade at the precise theoretical value. Because the subscription price is well publicized and arbitragers ever watchful, it would be almost impossible for any significant deviation to exist for more than an extremely brief period.

An Illusion—The Privileged Subscription

Many stockholders are pleased to be invited to buy new stock at subscription prices substantially below the market price. The differential of, perhaps, $5 to $30 appears to be a genuine source of profit and the low subscription price a definite bargain. From a theoretical standpoint, there is no profit and the stock is no bargain. The "profit" made by buying the stock at the subscription price is exactly offset by the decline in the market value of the stock after the operation is ended. There are more shares outstanding and less equity behind each share. Theoretically, the company cannot earn as much per share as it did before and the stock will fall.

In the first example just cited, let us suppose that a stockholder had 9 shares worth $40 each and $30 in cash; his total assets are $390. If he were to buy the new share for $30, he would now possess 10 shares worth $39 each; his assets are still $390. If he were to sell his rights at $1 each, he would now possess 9 shares worth $351, his original $30 in cash, and $9 received from the sale of 9 rights; his assets are still $390. Either way he comes out with the same total assets in the end; there has been no real profit.

Actually, instances of losses because of privileged subscriptions are more common than those of profits. Rights are frequently sold through brokers who charge a commission for the transaction. In the case of low-priced rights, the commission can be a significant percentage of the value of the transaction. Sometimes customers neglect to sell their rights at all and thus their value is lost. If a stock yielding rights is held by a brokerage house, the rights might be sold by the broker in the absence of direction from a customer who cannot be contacted in time to give specific instructions.

In practice, stockholders often do not accept this analysis. Because many investors do not realize the effect of any issue of new stock upon per share earnings, dividends, and assets, they consider the proceeds from the sale of rights a real income or profit, even though the stock will probably drop in value. Other stockholders are of the opinion that the company will probably maintain the same dividend and hence the stock should go back to its original market price. They believe that companies that issue additional stock through privileged subscriptions are growing companies and will be able to put the new money to work to good advantage. The profits made from the sale of rights are considered by numerous stockholders as merely additional dividends or income from ownership.

Market Value of Rights

The most difficult problem connected with trading in rights is that they fluctuate constantly; they may be worth more at the beginning, in the middle, or at the end of the subscription period. The holder therefore has the difficult decision to make as to the timing of the sale of rights, if he wishes to dispose of them.

"Sell rights early" has for years been an axiom among speculators. It is based on the theory that rights are worth more when the plan is proposed or when rights are first available for sale than at the close of the subscription period when, it is believed, rights will be dumped on the market by holders who do not care to put up the cash to subscribe to new stock; this will force the value of the rights to a low level. The trouble with this theory is that if everyone follows it, it will not work out this way. If everyone sells at once, the rights will immediately touch bottom and will not go any further. This, of course, does not happen.

There is little published material to indicate at what point in the subscription period rights sell at their highest level. Dewing, an authority in the field of finance, made several unpublished studies many years ago. In a study of 191 privileged subscriptions of railroads, public utilities, and industrials from 1918 to 1929, he found that in 46% of the cases rights sold at their highest at the beginning of the subscription period, in 15% of the cases at the middle of the period, and in 39% of the cases at the end of the period.[2] Other studies by him in earlier years showed substantially the same distribution. It seems a fair conclusion, therefore, that the axiom "Sell rights early" is something less than a solid foundation for success in trading in stock rights. An important factor governing the value of rights during the subscription period is the trend of the market. A rising market will cause the rights to sell at their highest at the end of the period, and the reverse is also true. The trend, of course, will not be known until after the fact.

Alternatives Offered Holders of Rights

The holder of rights has a number of options. The first one is disposal in the waste basket, meaning no action. It is surprising how many stockholders take no action when receiving rights and how much money is lost this way each year. During typical subscription periods, from ½ to 2½% of the total rights offered are not exercised, thus resulting in losses to stockholders to-

[2]A.S. Dewing, *Financial Policy of Corporations* (5th ed., New York: Ronald Press, 1953), p. 1159.

taling hundreds of thousands or millions of dollars. Many companies go to great lengths to prevent this and often engage in an extended educational campaign over a period of years. Repeated attempts are made to get stock-holders to exercise or sell their rights, yet the irreducible minimum in losses appears to be about ½ of 1%.[3]

The option desired by the company is the surrender of the rights and subscription to new stock. Many stockholders, however, do not do this. It is not unusual for fewer than 40% of the original holders to exercise their rights and purchase new stock.

The third option is the sale of the rights on a when-issued basis. This is done through a contract handled by the broker. The Exchange determines when such trading may begin and when it terminates, as stated earlier. The Exchange also fixes the date when the rights must be delivered and payment made for them. This option is used by those who subscribe to the theory that rights sell at their highest when first announced. A heavy volume of trading takes place this way in privileged subscriptions of large companies.

The fourth option is to sell them the "regular way." This is done by selling the warrant when received by the stockholder. This is the simplest and cheap-est alternative and a highly popular one.

The fifth option is to sell the stock with "rights on," or "cum rights" as it is sometimes called. This means selling the stock before it goes ex-rights. Here the stock and the rights are both sold together. The action is based on the previously stated theory that one should sell rights early. After the stock goes ex-rights, it can be replaced at the pleasure of the former stockholder. It can now be purchased cheaper than when sold; the difference is a profit. In doing this, the owner should realize that he pays the regular selling and buying commissions on the stock. This makes it more expensive than merely selling rights the regular way. There may also be a capital gain tax conse-quence.

The sixth option is similar to the fifth. Here the stockholder sells the stock with rights on before the stock goes ex-rights. The difference is the method of replacement. In this instance the owner buys enough rights to replace the amount of stock sold. He does this on the belief that rights may be picked up cheaply in the market near the end of the subscription period. For example, he has 100 shares of stock. New stock may be purchased by the surrender of 10 rights for each new share. During the subscription period, 1,000 rights are purchased and used to buy the new stock. All the previously sold stock has now been replaced. The difference between the sale of the stock with rights on and the cost of the rights plus the subscription price is the gross profit on the deal.

[3]C. James Pilcher, *Raising Capital with Convertible Securities* (Ann Arbor: University of Mich-igan Press, 1955), p. 105.

Arbitrage in Rights

Some professional trading takes place in rights on an arbitrage basis. For example, a trader may find that rights are selling too low on the basis of the market price of the stock. He may then sell 100 shares short, buy enough rights to subscribe for 100 shares, purchase the stock, and cover by delivering the subscribed stock that he will obtain in due time. Such action reduces the market price of the stock and increases that of the rights; thus the two are kept on a parity with each other. This arbitrage requires close cost calculations as well as rapid and accurate calculations. Errors can cause quick and large losses. This is no business for an amateur.

Standby Underwriting

There will almost always be some rights not exercised in any subscription offering. As previously indicated, some rights will be lost or unused through ignorance or carelessness. Far more serious to the issuer is the possibility of the market price falling below the subscription price, thereby making subscription undesirable because the rights no longer have any intrinsic value. This could be avoided by setting the subscription price far below the current market price of the stock, but this would necessitate the issuance of so many new shares that it would entail considerable dilution of earnings on equity and also make it difficult for the issuer to maintain the payment of dividends at the same level as previously. Compensating for this problem by reducing the dividend paid per share might well be considered negatively by those evaluating the company's stock.

In order to offer the stock as little below the current market price as possible and still make certain of raising sufficient equity, it is usual for the issuer of a stock to make a standby arrangement with an underwriter who guarantees to purchase shares not taken up by present shareholders. Although it is highly unlikely, the amount involved could even be the entire issue.

In order to prevent the market price of the stock from dropping below the subscription price that would create their greatest risk, the underwriters are permitted to support (stabilize) the market price. If this is successful, the underwriter will acquire stock that is then reoffered to the public at a net price. Barring a continued drop in the market price of the stock, the underwriter can often realize income from the underwriting fee, which approximates 1% of the value of the issue profit on the sale of stock reoffered, and perhaps a profit on the rights themselves either by buying them from large stockholders below the going market price or by being credited with rights not utilized which allows the possible acquisition of stock below the going market price. Such stock can then be sold on a net basis to yield a profit.

As in most underwritings, the risk is generally spread among the members of a group who also realize any benefits. The fee, of course, will be divided among its members and any stock acquired is "laid-off" among the group's members who realize any profits or losses involved.

Long-Term Rights

When distinguishing between rights and warrants, it has been traditional to note that rights have a life of only a few weeks whereas warrants may trade for years or even perpetually. In recent years increasing use of a special kind of instrument has blurred this distinction.

Some companies have a declared dividend distribution of one or more rights which do not expire for many years. Such rights may not be exercisable, nor are actual certificates issued except under special circumstances. The special circumstances usually involve an attempt by an unfriendly suitor to absorb the company which has issued the rights. The rights may then become effective and allow their holders to acquire additional stock of the issuing company or stock of the acquiring company. The purpose is primarily to discourage attempts at acquisition or to make any acquisition difficult or unreasonably expensive. Such rights are, in effect, examples of so-called "poison pills" or "shark repellents."[4]

Taxes

Stockholders who receive rights eventually learn that they do not increase their total wealth by receiving them. They must sell their rights or subscribe to the newly offered stock merely to preserve the capital they already have. They may actually lose somewhat if they have to pay a commission on the disposal of their rights. In addition, they may discover that they have acquired a tax question that may require some time to answer or some cost if they pay a tax preparer on an hourly basis. These questions may concern holding periods, tax bases, or both.

Generally, the distribution of rights does not increase the gross income of the stockholder. The IRS agrees that no new wealth has been created. There are so many rules and exceptions concerning rights, however, that it is usually necessary to determine the tax treatment of any particular rights rather than rely on such general comments as can be offered here. For example, if stock rights have a fair market value of 15% or more of the value of the stock on which the distribution is made, the basis of the stock must be allocated between it and the rights if the rights are exercised or sold. If the market value is less than 15%, the stockholder may choose to elect allocation anyhow, but may also indicate the value of the rights as zero and leave the basis of the original stock unchanged. Any allocation is made as

---

[4]An example of such complex rights are those issued on February 24, 1986, by American Airlines. Their designated life was 10 years.

of the date on which the rights are distributed and not the record date. Exact allocations may be learned from most full-service brokers who gather such information for their clients.

Further questions might arise as to treatment of lapsed rights, taxable rights, information required on one's tax return, holding periods of sold rights and stock acquired by subscription, and the basis of stock newly acquired. Because such questions may require professional tax advice, inquiry of the IRS, or study of such sources as technical tax guides, it can be seen that receipt of rights may not be as beneficial as may first appear.

24 Sources of Information and Security Rating

The purpose of this chapter is to indicate a sampling of the sources of information available to the investor or trader. It is not meant to indicate everything that should be in the library of a professional security analyst. Some of the sources offer only purported facts, leaving interpretation to the reader. Some present interpretations in an effort to explain events that have occurred. Others offer forecasts. It is up to the individual to decide whether to rely on one's own judgments or to assume that one is better advised to accept the opinions of others. Investors may differ in their evaluations of the usefulness of sources, but most rely to varying degrees on some of the sources. The last section of this chapter deals with the subject of rating securities.

SOURCES OF INFORMATION

Newspaper Financial Pages

Without question, the first and most accessible source of information for nearly all followers of the market is a newspaper financial page. A well-edited financial page will summarize the chief business and financial news of the day and provide a substantial amount of interpretation. It is heavily weighted with "spot news," or current developments, and is often lacking in long-run interpretation. Such pages are typically the first source of information for anyone who wishes to keep abreast of current events as they affect the market. Price, volume, and other data of interest are presented in substantial quantity, but the serious researcher should realize that the need for speedy reporting of information precludes perfect editing. Those searching for "clean data" are advised to consider other sources.

Many large cities have major newspapers with financial pages ranging from excellent to poor. Many investors prefer to rely on a specialized financial newspaper such as *The Wall Street Journal* or the *Journal of Commerce*. Most students of the market utilize at least *The Wall Street Journal* supplemented by a good local paper if one is available.

News Ticker

The major financial news ticker service in the country is owned and operated by Dow Jones & Company, which also publishes *The Wall Street Journal*. This printing telegraph operates continuously throughout the day, and may be found in many brokerage houses. Its chief value is that it carries the leading spot news items of the day in the world of commerce, industry, finance, and politics. Because many spot news items are immediately evaluated by the market, the value of such a service is obvious. Sometimes this service is called the "broad tape"; it is often watched with the same concentration that characterizes the study of current price information. Many of the items appearing on the Dow Jones financial news ticker service eventually find their way to the financial pages of *The Wall Street Journal* and other publications.

The large press associations also have teletype and carry much financial news. At least one brokerage house has its own news ticker service and others carry news on multipurpose wire networks. Quote machines utilized by brokerage house sales personnel usually have the capacity to recover or monitor news beyond mere current price information.

Bank Letters

Several of the leading banks of the country release each month so-called bank letters, which are actually fairly large bulletins. Some are available free upon request to anyone interested in being placed on the mailing lists whereas others are subscription services. Their chief function is the interpretation of business and economic developments, often from a long-run point of view. Generally well edited, they give a more detached and objective interpretation of news than is often possible in the daily press. They do not deal primarily with the stock market, but aid one in understanding the basic and underlying currents of the business situation.

Among the best known of such publications are those published by Citibank, the Cleveland Trust Company, the Federal Reserve Bank of New York, and Security Pacific Bank of Los Angeles. There are also several excellent Canadian bank letters, that of the Bank of Montreal being a good example. Many of the Federal Reserve banks publish monthly bulletins that cover thoroughly and concisely the business conditions within their own districts.

Newsletters

Several newsletters have an extensive following. These reports, which go only to paid subscribers, summarize the latest news developments, particularly of a political character, together with an interpretation. Forecasts of coming political happenings play a significant part in the composition of such letters. *The Kiplinger Washington Letter, Babson's Reports,* and *Personal Finance Letter* are examples.

Financial Magazines

There are a number of financial magazines available. These vary widely in editorial approach, subject matter, and format. Generally, they stress the current business news and its effect upon the stock market and the business situation. Some give regular forecasts of the stock market with an evaluation of underlying factors of strength and weakness. A frequent feature is the selection of certain stocks that appear to be particularly promising investments or speculations. Other magazines are largely chronicles of financial news and make little attempt to advise the market trader or investor. Some periodicals are heavily weighted with stock and bond tables and earnings reports; others feature long articles on business conditions or case histories of leading corporations. No two of these magazines are exactly alike; each seeks to attract a particular audience. Students of the market will do well to examine a number of such periodicals and determine for themselves the contribution that each can make to their understanding of securities markets. Magazines and journals in this group include *Barron's, Commercial and Financial Chronicle, Dun's Review, Financial World, Forbes, Fortune, Investment Dealer's Digest, Money Magazine,* and *Nation's Business.*

There are a large number of journals available, some of which are quite scholarly. Examples include *Financial Analysts Journal, Journal of Futures Markets,* and *Journal of Money, Credit, and Banking.*

Other Magazines

Several magazines of a somewhat broader character than the group of financial magazines just examined are well worth reading by the investor or trader. Although not edited with this class of reader specifically in mind, they often contain carefully written articles on finance or the markets. Because the market is at all times sensitive to world events, political as well as economic, their interpretation of nonfinancial news is useful. Examples of such periodicals are *BusinessWeek, Time, Newsweek,* and *U.S. News and World Report.*

Federal Publications

The federal government and the Board of Governors of the Federal Reserve System release several publications of considerable value to the investor or speculator. The *Statistical Abstract* of the Department of Commerce is an annual volume which contains a great mass of statistical material on production, consumption, sales, employment, finance, population, taxation, prices, government expenditures, debts, banking, business conditions, and agriculture. The data are largely on an annual basis. For certain purposes the volume is invaluable.

The *Survey of Current Business,* also published by the Department of Commerce, is an unusual monthly periodical. The magazine is largely a tabulation of monthly business statistics that are covered both in the form of actual figures and as index numbers. Examples of topics covered include general business indicators, commodity prices, construction and real estate, domestic trade, employment and population, finance, international transactions, transportation and communications, and manufacturing. The publication also presents each month several outstanding articles on the banking, fiscal, and business situations.

Other useful publications among the large number published by the Department of Commerce include *Industrial Outlook* and *The Census of Business*.

The Board of Governors publishes two periodicals of significance to the student of economic conditions. The *Federal Reserve Bulletin,* a monthly release, emphasizes mainly the banking and financial conditions of the country; the banking statistics are particularly complete. The Board also publishes a monthly chart book covering the principal series of data in the *Bulletin*.

Another statistical service of the federal government is called *Economic Indicators*. Prepared by the Joint Committee on the Economic Report by the Council of Economic Advisers, it presents tables and charts on current economic conditions, such as output, income, and spending; employment, unemployment, and wages; production and business activity; prices; currency, credit, and security markets; and federal finance. It is very useful for those interested in the latest data on these series.

Yet another service of the federal government, called *Business Cycle Developments,* prepared monthly by the Bureau of the Census, provides data for those series most helpful in determining the peaks and valleys of economic fluctuation. It is a development following from the work of Geoffrey H. Moore and his colleagues at the National Bureau of Economic Research.

Corporations

The stockholders of corporations and the general public are furnished a great deal of information about corporate affairs. Many annual reports to stockholders are outstanding as sources of information. Stockholders of any company with securities registered for trading on a national stock exchange receive copies by mail routinely. They are usually available to inquirers by writing the secretary of the company. The reports vary widely in format, editorial treatment, presentation of figures on finances, and clarity. Much can be learned from these reports. One of the outstanding changes in these reports in recent years has been a genuine attempt to present the report in popular style easily understandable by the layperson. This is in distinct contrast to former reports, which were clear only to accountants and professional investors and often not even to them. Accounting terminology is also becoming more and more standardized, a reform much needed for many years. Even the appearance of the reports has been radically changed. The use of color and attractive design provides sharp contrast to the drab formats of a few years ago. Annual reports stand high as a source of information and cannot be ignored by any student of the market. Many of the corporations with securities registered for trading on a national stock exchange release quarterly reports of sales and earnings.

Trade Associations

Many of the large industries of the country have trade associations, often identified by such terms as "institute" or "advisory board." From time to time these associations prepare and release reports on their particular industries. Because these associations are the public relations representatives of their industries, it is also necessary to remember that they are presenting a certain point of view in the hope of its favorable acceptance. Examples of well-known trade associations are the American Iron and Steel Institute, American Petroleum Institute, Cotton Textile Institute, National Association of Wool Manufacturers, National Retail Dry Goods Association, National Brass and Copper Association, Edison Electric Institute, F. W. Dodge Corporation, and the Automobile Manufacturers' Association.

Trade Journals

There is a seemingly endless list of trade journals. These may be privately published or prepared by trade associations. Typically, they cover business conditions, production, sales, new developments, and personalities in their special fields. If well edited, they give a good presentation of the current economic situation in a given industry. A few examples are *Railway Age, Textile World, Food Industries, Electrical World, Machinery, Oil and Gas Journal, Chain Store Age, Iron Age, Steel,* and *Chemical and Metallurgical Engineering.*

Commercial Banks

A good customer of a commercial bank or trust company may often obtain valuable advice about the securities markets from the bank officers. Because banks are large holders of bonds, these officers are often particularly competent to advise on this class of investment. Many trust companies and trust departments, of course, are willing to handle customer investment portfolios on a fee basis.

Securities Houses

In many cases securities houses are the chief source of personal contact that their customers have for investment information and advice. Well-managed full-service organizations are in a position to give service to customers along many lines. Some customers consider personal conferences with officials and registered representatives useful for providing advice and information about buying and selling securities and other financial products. Many firms will examine without charge a customer's portfolio and advise as to its merits. Some will even prepare an elaborate financial plan, usually with a nominal charge. The broker, of course, hopes that such a procedure will result in more business; nevertheless, if such services are rendered in good faith, they may be of considerable value to the customer.

A good brokerage firm will ordinarily answer any reasonable query of a customer made by letter or over the telephone; in some instances a considerable amount of research will be undertaken to answer such requests. Many brokerage offices have stock and news tickers, and customers are encouraged to use them. A well-equipped firm will also have one or more of the statistical services; these may be used by customers, or a representative of the firm will secure such information as may be requested from them.

Firms differ considerably in the amount of research and publishing which they initiate themselves. Some of the larger firms have highly trained staffs that turn out a continuous stream of reports on the market, on corporations, on various industries, and on business conditions. These reports may take the form of market letters, industry reports, investor bulletins, special investigations of particular corporations, bulletins on how to trade or invest, reports on attractive stocks, studies of dividend-paying stocks, and so on. In recent years such reports have expanded greatly in number and scope; they also tend to stress the investment side of the market more than they did some years ago. If the firm is an underwriter of a new security issue, it can also supply the prospectus to interested customers.

Many years ago the market letter was the typical and often the sole release of the brokerage firm. It dealt with the day-to-day aspects of the market, largely from the standpoint of the in-and-out trader; it was often hastily and poorly edited and frequently was highly superficial. Although a number of firms still release such daily or weekly letters in mimeographed, multilithed, or printed form, they are considerably less important than they were at one time. The market analysis of a good financial page will contain about the same information.

Securities and Exchange Commission

The SEC in its Washington and regional offices receives from registered corporations a considerable amount of information useful to the investor. This takes the form of registration statements for securities being underwritten or sold, periodic reports to the Commission, and reports of companies registered on national securities exchanges. The reports are mandatory under the Securities Act of 1933, the Securities Exchange Act of 1934, the Public Utility Holding Company Act of 1935, and the Investment Company Act of 1940. These reports are available for public inspection; an extensive use of them is made by the various commercial statistical services, which secure primary data from them. The annual 10-K and quarterly 10-Q reports, which contain more detailed and probably less biased information than a company's own report to stockholders, are especially popular with professional researchers. Although these reports are also available to individual investors from the SEC and often from the issuing companies, most find it simpler to rely on secondary sources, such as a brokerage firm, a registration prospectus, or a securities manual.

The monthly *Statistical Bulletin* and the *Annual Report* of the SEC are invaluable aids for serious students of the securities markets and general economic activity analysis.

Chart Services

A number of chart services have attained popularity with market followers. These services have a great similarity in format and composition. Essentially, they seek to chart the stocks of many leading corporations of the country, largely those listed on the New York Stock Exchange. The number of charts varies from under 200 to over 1,000; each chart covers a number of years. They may cover earnings, dividends, volume of trading, prices, and price ranges. New additions appear monthly or bimonthly. Each chart in a given service is the same size as every other chart; this makes it easier to compare the performance of one stock with another. A feature of some of the chart services is a transparent work sheet, which may show, for example, the Dow Jones industrial average. This work sheet may be superimposed over the chart of any particular company, and a careful study may indicate how well that company's stock is conducting itself as compared with the market averages. The value of the services, therefore, is that the user may feel able to select certain stocks that apparently show promise as either investments or speculations or, conversely, to sell those already owned that are doing poorly in the market.

Advisory Services and Investment Counselors

The number of individuals and firms in the securities field that attempt to advise speculators and investors is legion. They vary from some of the most respected organizations in the field with excellent staffs and long records of reputable service to fleeting individuals or organizations that flourish with each market rise and disappear with each major decline. It goes without saying that a most careful investigation of such a service should be made by anyone before subscribing to it.

The Statistical Services

One of the most widely used sources of information available to securities owners is the statistical service. Among the best known organizations are Moody's Investors Service, Standard & Poor's Corporation, the Fitch Publishing Company, and the Value Line Investment Survey. In addition to security rating, which will be described shortly, these services gather and publish a vast amount of statistical information on corporate stocks and bonds.

Perhaps the best known of these services are the large manuals of corporation records. They are usually too expensive for the individual investor to purchase, but they are generally available at banks, libraries, and brokerage houses. The manuals are either bound or in loose-leaf form; in any case, they are kept up to date by frequent reports. For ease of reference the large annual volumes are often broken down into rails, utilities, industrials, governments, and banks and finance. The services report on nearly all large companies in which there is a definite investment interest. Typically, the report for a given company will contain a short description of the company's business, its industry position, its income account and balance sheet, its securities, the security ratings, the dividends and earnings per share, and the market price of the securities. The statistical information may be carried back from 5 to 10 years for comparative purposes. Monthly, weekly, or even daily supplements keep the annual volumes from becoming obsolete. They contain the latest figures on earnings, dividends, calls, rights, new offerings, ratings changes, securities which have matured, and so on.

Standard & Poor's, in addition to its basic *Corporation Records,* also publishes the *Standard Stock Reports* that are available in almost every brokerage house. A considerable amount of information is provided in summary form on one sheet that can be utilized in the broker's office or mailed to a client and then replaced in its loose-leaf binder. These popular summaries are often called "tear sheets."

The services also publish stock and bond surveys. There are separate reports for each, and publication is often once a week. A typical stock survey or report will contain such topics as the near-term prospect for stocks, the longer prospect, individual issues, business outlook, business, and the market stock groups. These reports also feature opinions on individual stocks, such as a general market opinion, fundamental position, dividend forecast, earnings prospects, recent developments, finances, recommendations for buying and selling. Such a service is therefore of a definitely advisory character.

The bond survey also keeps investors informed of the latest developments in the bond business, such as market outlook, construction activity, new offerings, yields, new government issues, and financing. All important factors, economic, financial, or political, that determine and affect security prices are discussed in the stock and bond surveys.

In summary, the statistical services gather and release a large amount of statistical information on nearly all important companies, listed and unlisted, together with analyses and interpretations of the positions of those companies and their securities. The reports are factual, analytical, and advisory.

Investment Company Manuals

Several organizations issue manuals and interim reports providing data on investment company portfolios and performance. Perhaps the most widely known is that of Arthur Wiesenburger and Company, *Investment Companies,* published annually. The periodic analyses of investment company performances and portfolios in *Barron's* and *Forbes* are also well known.

Forecasting Services

Perhaps the most recurrent question in the entire field of speculation is: What is the market going to do? Everyone would like to know the course of security prices; the answer would provide an invaluable road map to certain wealth. To provide such forecasts is a popular and profitable pursuit of many informational services, whether they be periodicals, advisory services, columnists, brokerage houses, security dealers, or forecasting services. The value of such advice depends, of course, upon its accuracy.

Many studies have been made of the reliability of financial services in forecasting the stock market, none of which has proved particularly encouraging. Two early studies received widespread attention. The first was made by a distinguished economist and statistician, Alfred Cowles III, and published in 1933.[1] He examined 16 financial services over a period from January 1, 1928, to July 1, 1932. In that period 7,500 recommendations were made on common stocks for investment. His conclusion was that the stock recommended by these services showed an annual record gain for the stockholders that was on the average 1.4% poorer than the average common stock.

In addition, Cowles investigated 24 financial publications and their ability to forecast the stock market during the same period. He found that during this four-and-a-half year period the group failed by 4% to achieve a result as good as the average of purely random performance. In other words, their forecasts were little better than those that could be expected from pure chance.

A second study of forecasting accuracy was conducted by the SEC in its study on stock trading on the New York Stock Exchange on September 3, 1946. On that day the market fell sharply; the average price decline of 945 issues in the 100-share market was $3.40. The bear market continued downward and the share prices did not rise again to the 1946 high until 1950. The SEC examined 896 different pieces of literature disseminated by 166 investment advisers, brokers, and dealers from August 26 to September 3, the week that immediately preceded the break. These were market letters, bulletins, news items, flash reports, and other forms of market comment.

A total of 489 forecasts was made on the long-term market outlook at that time. About 260, or nearly 60%, were bullish at the time without qualification;

---

[1]"Can Stock Market Forecasters Forecast?" *Econometrica* (July 1933), 314–16.

only 20, or 4%, were definitely bearish or advised selling at least part of holdings. The rest were cautious or uncertain.

Ninety-five forecasts were made on the day-to-day outlook; 55 were bullish, 34 were cautious, and 6 were bearish. As to the outlook for specific industries and companies at that time, 272 forecasts were bullish, 10 were bearish, 17 were mixed, and 13 were inconclusive.

A scholarly study by Brealey does not indicate that professional forecasters gain materially from their forecasting ability, particularly when they must make frequent decisions involving large numbers of securities. This might cause some discouragement among those who rely on investment companies, brokerage firm research departments, or investment advisory services as easy roads to wealth.[2]

SECURITY RATING

Nature

Security rating is a process by which a statistical service prepares various ratings, identified by symbols, which are indicators of the investment quality of the securities so rated. The best quality securities are rated A, the next best B, and the poorest C or D. Moody's, Fitch, and Value Line, just described, rate bonds in this manner. Standard & Poor's Corporation also rates stocks.

History

Four concerns which specialized in bond ratings have in the past achieved enough importance in the field of security ratings to be classified as historical leaders. The first security ratings were published by John Moody during 1909 in his analyses of railroad investments. This evolved into one of the two rating companies that now dominate the field, Moody's Investors Services, Inc., a division of Dun and Bradstreet, Inc. Moody was followed by Poor's Publishing Company, which entered the field in 1916, and the Standard Statistics Company in 1922. These two companies later merged into what is now the largest bond rating concern, Standard & Poor's Corporation, a subsidiary of McGraw-Hill, Inc.

The next company to enter the field was the Fitch Publishing Company of New York, which was established in 1924. Fitch remained firmly entrenched in the number three position, but more recently has been challenged

---

[2]Richard A. Brealey, *An Introduction to Risk and Return from Common Stocks* (2d ed., Cambridge, MA: The MIT Press, 1983), Chap. 3. The bibliography following that chapter provides the reader with a guide to further information on this subject.

by the recognition of two new companies by the SEC. Duff & Phelps of Chicago was recognized in 1982 and McCarthy, Crisanti & Maffei, Inc. of New York in 1984. The latter was acquired by the financial services group of the Xerox Corporation in 1985.

These five companies are the only ones with SEC recognition as national bond rating companies, but other services which rate securities, especially stocks, have become popular among individual investors. An example is Value Line Investment Survey.

From the first, security ratings were received with considerable enthusiasm by investors but were bitterly opposed by many corporations and investment bankers, who objected to inferior ratings for some of their securities that caused them to sell at higher yields. The fact that rating companies charged the issuer for the ratings was understandably disturbing to companies that received low ratings. Similar opposition characterized the early history of commercial credit ratings.

Use of Ratings

Many institutions and investors find the rating system a useful one. Banks, particularly the smaller ones, find ratings helpful in selecting their portfolios; the larger banks also use them as a check on their own investigations. Brokers generally employ them for investment opinions and as a service for their customers. Insurance companies use them in the purchase of their bonds, even though their own staffs prepare investment analyses. They are also used by trust companies, trust funds, investment companies, and endowed institutions as a significant type of information in security management. Although not too many individuals can afford the heavy expense of the complete services, unless they are relatively large investors, countless persons have access to them through banks and libraries and utilize them accordingly. They are also available through brokers.

The rating services have even been accorded public recognition by both federal and state banking authorities in evaluating bank portfolios. Some years ago the Comptroller of Currency issued a ruling that national banks could carry at cost only bonds rated at Baa or the equivalent; fractional write-offs were necessary for other securities. Later a retreat was made from the ruling, but the bond ratings of the services are still important in the management of bank portfolios; they would be even more so were it not for the fact that, in recent years, banks have held large amounts of government securities. Bonds rated at Baa or higher by Moody's and BBB or higher by Standard & Poor's are still generally designated as "investment grade," whereas those below are popularly referred to as "junk bonds."

The SEC uses the ratings of its recognized agencies to evaluate the bond assets of brokers and dealers registered with the agency, although this recognition is not required to enter the bond rating business and does not constitute approval.

Information for Ratings

The services apparently obtain their data for ratings from much the same sources described in the earlier part of the chapter, namely, such official and primary sources as annual and quarterly reports of companies and data filed with the SEC. Primary reliance, however, would appear to be on the financial statement; the services, of course, do not reveal how the information is obtained or used, except to release broad statements to the effect that information from "all sources" is considered.

Rating Symbols

The rating services employ nearly identical symbols; each symbol means approximately the same thing as do investment rating. These are tabulated in Table 24-1.

In the A group the services are uniform in their appraisals; each subgroup carries the same meaning. These are bonds of the highest grade; they are characterized by maximum safety as to principal and income. They are protected by ample assets; they have a large margin of earnings to protect interest payments; changes in business conditions have little effect upon their security. These are the "gilt-edged" bonds of the seasoned companies; they are characterized by low yields. Changes in interest rates are more important than changes in business conditions.

The B group might be called "business people's investments." They are attractive investments for those who are skilled in the purchase of investments; individuals who are willing to accept some uncertainty will receive higher yields than those who buy only A-rated issues. They are affected by some uncertainty as to interest, security, and stability; their values are influenced markedly by changes in business conditions. Since they are characterized by more or less uncertainty, they need very capable selection and management.

The C and D groups must be considered together, because neither the Moody Service nor Standard & Poor's has a so-called D group. Taken as a whole, the two groups range from outright speculations at the top with a poor statistical standing and great uncertainty down to worthless issues with no apparent value at the bottom. The issues in these two bottom groups are gambles at best; usually they are in default; only the most promising issues have any prospect of recovery. In no sense can either group be considered an investment.

The Rating of Bonds

Bond rating is considered a more scientific procedure than the rating of stock. A few fundamental factors are used in determining ratings. Chief among

Table 24-1 Comparative Bond Ratings of Five Statistical Services

Moody's	Standard & Poor's	Fitch	Duff & Phelps	McCarthy Crisanti & Maffei	Interpretation
Aaa	AAA	AAA	1	AAA	Highest grade
Aa1	AA+	AA+	2	AA+	
Aa2	AA	AA	3	AA	High grade
Aa3	AA−	AA−	4	AA−	
A1	A+	A+	5	A+	
A2	A	A	6	A	Upper medium;
A3	A−	A−	7	A−	sound
Baa1	BBB+	BBB+	8	BBB+	
Baa2	BBB	BBB	9	BBB	Medium; some
Baa3	BBB−	BBB−	10	BBB−	uncertainty
Ba1	BB+	BB+	11	BB+	
Ba2	BB	BB	12	BB	Fair; uncertainty
Ba3	BB−	BB−	13	BB−	
		B+	14		
B	B	B	15	B	Speculative
		B−	16		
Caa	CCC	CCC			
Ca	CC	CC	17		Speculative;
C	C	C			default imminent
	DDD	DDD			
	DD	DD		DD	In default; no
	D	D			apparent value

these are earning power, asset value, security of income, and stability of income. Certain intangible factors, such as management and company prospects, also play a part.

Moody Bond Ratings

The Moody's Investors Service at the present time rates well over 5,000 issues in the corporate and tax-exempt areas. It does not rate real estate bonds, obligations of financial companies, nonprofit corporations, issues sold privately, or issues of less than $600,000. Ratings are long-run judgments designed to show protection at the low point of the business cycle. They are not raised and lowered with changes in business conditions. The ratings are raised and lowered only when fundamental conditions affecting a particular issue change, such as when a borrower is gaining or losing ground in relation to other parts of industry or when the amount of debt is substantially reduced or increased.

The organization employs the usual tests of the ordinary income account and balance sheet analysis, but does not set up arbitrary standards in this analysis. The ratings are not mechanical ratings, the service believing that there are no mechanical means to true judgment.

In addition to the usual statistical analysis, the service considers nonstatistical factors, particularly long-run industry trends. Financial practices and policies are examined, such as a dividend policy in relation to financial needs. Another nonstatistical factor examined is the amplitude of cyclical fluctuations in the industry of the particular issuer. Intangibles, such as franchises, leases, and patents, are studied. Another factor is the indenture and its features, such as call feature, sinking fund, power of issuer to create additional indebtedness, after-acquired clause, indebtedness of subsidiaries, and right of the issuer to sell or lease its property.

The service stresses the fact that no single formula is used in rating bonds and that judgment plays a highly important part in the final determination of all ratings.

Standard & Poor's Bond Ratings

This organization determines its bond ratings on statistical tests and upon economic and trade developments. Prices are not a part of their rating system, but they are used to indicate whether or not a given issue requires a complete new study.

In their work of arriving at ratings of bond quality, the organization relies upon all information available about the company and the industry in which it operates. This information varies, of course, with industrials, public utilities, and railroads. The following material relative to the rating of industrial issues is illustrative.

Five major classes of information are evaluated in the rating of industrial bonds. The first is earnings. These are evaluated from the standpoint of earnings prospects, immediate and long term; present earnings; past record; reputation of products and position of company in trade; character of trade; and quality of management as indicated by reputation, earnings record, sales trend, operating ratios, efficiency, depreciation practices, and dividend policy.

Other factors included in analyzing industrial issues include protection from fixed assets, from net current assets, and from cash resources alone, and adequacy of working capital.

Fitch Bond Ratings

Factors considered by Fitch in its rating of bonds are similar to those of the two services just described. In addition to reliance upon the analysis of profit-

and-loss statements and balance sheets, the organization considers all factors bearing on immediate and more distant prospects of the issuer. The current position of the company is studied with special consideration to net working capital, floating debt, and approaching maturities of bonded debt. An examination is made of the nature of the industry in which the company is located and the position of the issuer in the industry. An important factor is the legal nature of the debt, such as the degree of lien, and whether the issue is a collateral trust issue or an unsecured issue. Guarantees, call provisions, and sinking-fund features have an influence upon ratings.

In addition, the service examines the outlook for prompt payment of the security at maturity, the possibilities of refunding, its banking connections, and financial plans for the future. Many ratios are used by the service, such as debt to equity capital and the current ratio. For industrials, stress is also placed upon such ratios as sales to inventory, operating ratio, depreciation, net available for common to invested capital, common profit margin, common earnings to property, and price—earnings ratio. Although statistics play an important part in arriving at ratings, this service also places much stress upon nonstatistical factors.

Duff & Phelps Bond Ratings

Although Duff & Phelps received SEC recognition only in 1982, the firm has been issuing ratings since the 1940s. Its ratings tend to be in line with those of Moody's and Standard & Poor's; but whereas its two largest competitors cover about 2,000 companies each, Duff & Phelps covers only about 400 and these are generally the largest issuers of bonds. The two large firms charge bond issuers for rating insertions, where Duff & Phelps charges both issuers and investors.

The firm has several other unusual practices. It allows personnel of issuers to meet directly with the rating committee. Its ratings tend to be more detailed than most, and it offers investors advice through general seminars and even a personal investment counseling service.

McCarthy, Crisanti & Maffei

McCarthy is the newest and smallest of the five bond rating firms. Although it rates about 400 to 500 companies, it utilizes fewer analysts than any of the other firms. It is the only one of its group that charges investors rather than issuers for its services.

McCarthy's ratings tend to be lower than those of its competitors. This, of course, does not endear the company to issuers who have to pay higher yields to compensate for the more conservative ratings because they imply higher risk.

This agency apparently meets rarely with issuers, even when issuing a rating for the first time. The other four agencies allow issuers to refuse or appeal a rating. McCarthy can afford a more independent attitude, of course, because the issuers are not paying for the ratings.

McCarthy concentrates only on large corporate issuers and leaves the rating of smaller corporations and tax-exempt issuers to the other rating companies.

Stock Ratings

Stocks are assigned formal rating symbols by only a limited number of companies. These are dominated by Standard & Poor's Corporation and Value Line Investment Survey.

Many have contended that stock ratings are not satisfactory, because stocks lack many of the characteristics of a good investment. They are unstable in price; their income is not secure; and their asset value is often not important. Since dividends are not fixed charges, it is impossible to estimate the number of times charges are earned, which is a basic factor used in determining the safety of a bond. The common stock is a residual legatee of a company's earnings; hence such earnings become highly conjectural. Stocks are therefore less adaptable to rating systems than are bonds. It is doubtful whether stock ratings have the validity that has become so accepted in the field of bond investments.

In contrast to its system of rating bonds, Standard & Poor's is frank to admit that its stock ratings are based on a formula, which is fully described in its *Stock Guide*. The formula judges the quality of common and preferred stocks upon two factors alone—earnings and dividends.

In the rating of stocks, the service discards the usual criteria used in the analysis of bonds, such as financial position, capital structure, cash resources, asset values, depreciation policies, and profit margins. It maintains that there are no common denominators for many of these elements in the rating of stocks. It is their contention that all of the elements that make for a high or low quality stock are ultimately reflected in per-share earnings and dividends.

Earnings are examined over the previous eight years. Earnings stability is a key factor in the earnings record. A basic score is given for each year in which per-share earnings are equal to, or greater than, those for the preceding year, whereas the score is reduced in any year where a decline takes place. The average of these eight annual scores becomes the basic earnings index. This stability index is then multiplied by a growth index, based on the square root of the percentage by which earnings increased between the base years 1946–1949 and the three most recent years. This stability of the particular company is compared with that of the general economy to see whether the company is doing as well as, better, or poorer than the economy as a whole.

Dividend stability is the other factor used in the formula. For determining this, a 20-year period is examined with weights increased for more recent years. The result is also multiplied by a growth factor similar to that for earnings, but for a longer period.

These two factors, earnings and dividends, are then combined into a single numerical rating. All stocks are then divided into seven classes, which range from highest to lowest as follows:

A +	Excellent	B +	Average
A	Good	B	Below average
A −	Above average	B −	Low
	C	Lowest	

The ratings are not market recommendations and do not indicate whether or not a given stock is overpriced or underpriced. They are not intended to be substitutes for analysis. Certain highly speculative stocks dependent upon unusual factors, such as airplane contracts, are not rated.

Value of Ratings

That rating, especially of bonds, possess a considerable value to the investment community would seem to be indicated by the extensive use made of them by many institutional and individual investors over a long period. Even organizations with their own extensive staffs utilize them in cross-checking their investigations. They are a quick, easy reference available to most investors; when used with care, they are a valuable source of information to supplement other data.

Limitations of Ratings

Certain limitations are evident in the ratings. Based as they must be on the element of judgment, especially as to forecasting the future, they must be considered as only tentative. The fact that many changes occur in the ratings indicates that finality is impossible. They cannot be used as a recommendation to purchase, because the ratings are not based upon price. An A-rated bond may or may not be a bargain at any particular quotation. Because of the great number of securities rated, it is doubtful whether the services can or do consider more than the chief factors in any one rating. For this reason the investor will do well to examine the primary sources of information on all investments that are purchased. Ratings, as far as they are obtained from statistical data, must look to the past. This immediately limits the value of ratings to some extent. Many of the strongest companies become insecure under the impact of economic change; for example, the railroads and the traction companies. On the other hand, many of the most promising industries rise from highly uncertain origins. Management is important in all companies, particularly industrials; it is often more important than assets or even past earnings. Yet its valuation without the most intimate study is often mere conjecture.

Glossary

Adjustment Bonds   *See* Income Bonds.

ADR   *See* American Depository Receipt; Automatic Dividend Reinvestment.

Advance-Decline Theory (Line)   A theory that maintains that there is significance in the number of price advances versus price declines relative to the total number of issues traded.

Allied Member   Partners or voting stockholders of member firms or corporations who are not personally members of an exchange; in the case of publicly held member corporations, a principal executive officer designated by the corporation.

All-or-None Underwriting   An underwriting that is canceled if the underwriter is unable to sell the entire issue.

American Depository Receipt (ADR)   A receipt that evidences shares of an alien corporation. Transactions in the ADR are made in lieu of transactions in the security itself, which is usually held by a trustee. The ADR is usually issued by a foreign branch of an American bank, most frequently the Morgan Guaranty Trust.

American Option   A put or call that can be exercised at any time prior to expiration. All listed options, including those on European exchanges, are of this type. *See* European Option.

Amex   American Stock Exchange.

Arbitrage   The simultaneous or closely related purchase and sale of the same or equivalent securities made in an attempt to take advantage of price differences believed to be unrealistic. May be in the same or different markets. May or may not entail risk; usually involves options or convertible securities.

Arrearage   Accumulation of undeclared or unpaid dividends that must be paid to holders of cumulative preferred stock before any dividends may be paid to common stockholders. May also apply to unpaid interest on some income bonds.

At-the-Money The exercise price of an option and the price of its underlying stock are equal.

Authorized Stock The maximum number of shares that a corporation may issue under terms of its charter.

Automatic Dividend Reinvestment A plan whereby stockholders or holders of mutual fund shares automatically reinvest their dividends in additional stock of the paying corporation.

Average (1) A stock market indicator based upon the mean of the prices of a number of stocks on a given market. May be a sample or all stocks. Divisor may be adjusted for changes in capitalization as is done by Dow Jones. (*See* Index.) (2) A trading technique of adding additional shares of stock to a position as the price of a stock moves favorably or unfavorably. The former is referred to as averaging with the market and the latter as against the market or as "averaging up" or "averaging down."

Back Office The operations department of a brokerage firm. Concerned with cashiering, margins, bookkeeping, and other nonsales functions.

Basis Point Generally applied to bond yields; 100 basis points equals one percentage point. *See* Point.

Bear One who believes that market prices will fall. A bear market is a declining market. A bear spread in commodities or securities is one that should yield a profit if the market falls. *See* Bull.

Bearer Bond A bond whose ownership is not registered by a transfer agent. The principal is paid to the presenter at maturity and interest is paid to presenters of coupons that are detached from the bonds. Since July 1983 they can no longer be issued in the United States, although many billions of dollars in bearer municipal and U.S. government bonds will remain outstanding until well into the twenty-first century. Still the preferred format for Eurobonds.

Best Efforts Offering A sale of securities by investment bankers acting as brokers rather than as dealers. Results are not guaranteed although such an offering may be all or none; that is, canceled if all stock is not sold.

Beta Risk Risk from one firm's stock from the standpoint of an investor who holds a diversified portfolio. Sometimes called unique risk or unsystematic risk.

Big Board New York Stock Exchange.

Block Positioning Temporary market-making in listed issues by nonspecialist exchange member firms, which risk their own capital to facilitate the execution of large block orders from customers.

Blue Chip Stock issued by a well-known company with an established record of making money and paying dividends.

Blue Sky State security laws particularly as applied to new issues of securities. Getting new issues approved by state security departments is referred to as "blue-skying." The laws themselves are often called blue-sky laws. Such laws also normally require registration of broker—dealers, representatives, and investment advisors doing business in a state.

Bond A long-term promissory note evidencing corporate debt. May or may not be registered. May or may not bear coupons. Interest normally paid semiannually. Face (par) value usually $1,000, but may be more or less. *See* Debenture.

Breadth Index The net number of securities on a given market that advance or decline on a given day divided by the total number of issues that traded that day. The divisor includes issues that close unchanged. Used by market technicians.

Breakpoint The dollar amounts of mutual fund shares that qualify a buyer for discounts. A sale by a salesperson of an amount just below a discount level is known as a breakpoint sale and is regarded as an unfair practice.

Brokers' Loan *See* Call Loan.

Bucket Shop A firm that executes orders after an unreasonable period of time or not at all. It attempts, in effect, to win what a customer loses. This practice is known as bucketing and is now illegal.

Bull One who believes that market prices will rise. A bull market is a rising market. A bull spread in commodities or securities is one that should yield a profit if the market rises. *See* Bear.

Buying Power The dollar amount of additional securities which could be purchased in a margin account without an additional deposit of funds. May vary with the securities to be bought because these may or may not have loan values.

Calendar Spread The simultaneous purchase and sale of options of the same class and with the same striking prices but with different expiration dates. The option sold has an earlier expiration date than the option bought. Synonymous with horizontal spread.

Call (1) The option to buy a share of stock at a specified price on or before a specified date. (2) The redemption of a preferred stock or of a bond before its due date.

Call Loan A loan usually made to a broker or specialist by a commercial bank with securities as collateral. Most such loans can be terminated by either party on 24-hours notice and hence are said to involve "call money." Call loans are more formally designated "brokers' loans." They should not be confused with loans made by brokers to customers.

CBOE *See* Chicago Board Options Exchange.

Certificates of Deposit (CDs) Negotiable notes issued by commercial banks or thrift institutions evidencing time deposits. Usually in minimum denominations of $100,000 with either a specified interest rate or a floating one. May be held to maturity or traded in the secondary market.

Chicago Board Options Exchange   The pioneer exchange dealing exclusively with listed options. Sponsored by the Chicago Board of Trade that incorporated many of the principles of commodity trading into options trading.

Churning   Excessive trading by one who controls a security or commodity account owned by someone else. The motivation is usually generation of commissions. Control may consist of a formal power of attorney or strong influence upon one relying on the churner's expertise and integrity.

Class   All call options or all put options on the same underlying security. All call options constitute one class. All put options constitute another.

Clearance   (1) Trade comparisons prior to settlement. (2) Actual delivery of securities or funds in the settlement of a trade.

Collateral Trust Bonds   Bonds secured by securities owned by the corporation that sells the bonds. The securities are usually stocks or bonds and are deposited with a trustee.

Combination   A market position consisting of the purchase or sale of both puts and calls with different exercise prices and/or expiration dates. *See* Straddle; Strangle.

Commercial Paper   Unsecured promissory notes issued by corporations, finance companies, bank holding companies, and various other financial institutions. It is sold at a discount (have no specified interest rate) in typical multiples of $250,000. Secondary market is generally not liquid. Tax-exempt municipal commercial paper has been offered by a number of major cities (e.g., Philadelphia).

Common Stock   Equity securities having last claim on residual assets and earnings of a corporation. Dividends usually paid only after preferred stock dividends paid. Usually have voting rights of one vote per share. Common stockholders normally have the power to elect directors, authorize new stock issues, and approve or disapprove of major corporate changes.

Consolidated Tape   The system of reporting trades made on various exchanges, indicating such data as the price of each transaction, the number of shares involved, and the exchange on which the trade took place. Network A emphasizes NYSE stocks and network B, Amex stocks. Both also report trades in their listed securities done on other exchanges.

Constant Dollar Plan   An investment formula plan whereby an investor keeps his investment in the various securities in his account constant by selling or buying various issues if prices move significantly.

Constant Ratio Plan   An investment formula plan whereby an investor keeps the ratio of his investments between the stock and bond portions of his portfolio constant by buying or selling if the ratio varies significantly.

Contractual Plan   A plan for making periodic fixed investments into a mutual fund. Such a plan normally designates a 10- or 15-year program and may involve a substantial prepaid load.

Conventional Option   An option sold or acquired through an option dealer rather than on an exchange.

Conversion   (1) A provision of a bond or preferred stock which permits it to be converted into another security, ordinarily common stock, at the discretion of the holder. May be forced by the call of a convertible issue. (2) An arbitrage technique wherein the trader simultaneously buys 100 shares of stock, sells one call option, and buys a put, creating a risk-free hedge and a locked-in profit due to premium differences between the options.

Conversion Parity   Conversion parity for a stock into which a bond is convertible is that price of the stock at which it would be equal in value to the bond.

Conversion Price   The par value of a convertible preferred stock or bond divided by the number of shares of common stock into which it may be exchanged at the discretion of the holder.

Conversion Ratio   The number of common shares into which one share of preferred stock or one bond is convertible.

Corporation   A business organization recognized as an artificial person with perpetual life and limited liability. Created under a charter approved by a state corporation commissioner. Rights are limited to those specified in the charter and bylaws. Controlled by voting stockholders who elect directors, who in turn select officers.

Covered Option   Call options sold by an investor against stocks he actually holds in his portfolio.

Cum Rights   A stock trading with "rights on"; that is, the purchaser of a stock will pay for and shortly receive a previously announced right with each share purchased. *See* Ex-Rights.

Cumulative   Usually applied to a preferred stock designated as cumulative preferred. Dividends must be declared and paid for current and previous years on such shares before common shares in the same company may receive dividends. *See* Arrearage.

Cumulative Voting   A form of corporate voting designed to give a group of minority stockholders a voice on the Board of Directors by allowing stockholders to cast all votes for one director or to divide their votes as they see fit. Each stockholder has the number of votes that equals the number of shares that he owns multiplied by the number of directors to be elected.

Dealer   A securities firm or individual acting as a principal rather than as an agent. A firm may act as a principal in some transactions and an agent in others. If so, it is known as a broker—dealer.

Debenture   A bond having no such specified collateral as a mortgage. It is secured by all unencumbered assets of the issuer.

Debit Balance   The amount owed to a broker by a customer in a margin account. Secured by securities held by the broker. Interest is charged at a level above the call money rate. *See* Equity.

Deficiency Letter   A letter from the SEC to one intending to issue new securities. It indicates the SEC's dissatisfaction with omissions, inconsistencies, or misstatements in the corporation's registration statement. Such deficiencies must be eliminated before issuance of securities is permitted.

Deliver versus Payment   A delivery requiring payment upon receipt of the security. In effect, a COD transaction.

Designated Order Turnaround   An electronic system devised by the NYSE to allow odd-lot orders and round-lot orders of up to 30,099 shares to be transmitted from brokerage firms directly to posts on the Exchange floor.

Development Bond   A bond sold by a government agency, the proceeds from which are used for economic development in a specified geographic area. Usually tax exempt.

Diagonal Spread   A position in options involving a purchase and sale of options of the same class but with different striking prices and different expiration dates. A diagonal bear spread involves purchase of a long-term option and the sale of a shorter-term option with a lower striking price. A diagonal bull spread would utilize a later option with a price lower than the earlier.

Direct Participation Program   Limited partnership organized to flow the benefits of certain investment characteristics through to the partners. *See* Tax Shelter.

Discretionary Account   An account for which trading decisions have been delegated to another, usually the registered representative of a brokerage firm. Authority may not be verbal but must be given via a general or limited power of attorney. The latter is often called a trading authority.

Discretionary Order   An order placed by one person, usually a registered representative, on behalf of another. In the securities area discretion occurs if any decision is made beyond price or time of execution. In commodities, decisions involving the latter two items may also be considered discretionary. Unauthorized discretion is a serious violation of good business practice.

Dividend   A distribution to stockholders declared by a corporate Board of Directors. It may consist of cash, stock, or property.

Dollar Cost Averaging   An investment formula plan whereby an investor invests fixed dollar amounts at fixed intervals. In that larger amounts are bought when the market is low than when it is high, the average purchase price will be favorable if the market trends are upward.

DOT   *See* Designated Order Turnaround.

Double Option An option to buy or sell but not both. Exercise of either the put or call causes the other side to expire. Rare in U.S. markets.

Dow Jones Averages Market indicators issued by the Dow Jones Publishing Company to indicate significant changes in industrial, transportation, utility, and composite groups of stocks.

Dow Theory The belief that the Dow Jones industrial and transportation averages under certain circumstances may indicate basic market trends when both averages break previously established high or low levels.

Down and Out Option Conventional call options that lose their exercise privilege if the underlying stock sells below a specified price.

Due Bill A document that specifies an obligation of one party to another arising from a security distribution, usually a dividend.

Due Diligence Meeting A meeting between corporate and underwriting officials in connection with a proposed securities issue. Primarily concerned with making certain that all information in the registration statement is accurate and clear. Normally held a week to 10 days prior to the offering date.

DVP *See* Deliver versus Payment.

Effective Date The date on which a security may be publicly offered. Assumes that all deficiencies noted by the SEC have been eliminated. Normally 20 days after registration statement is filed.

Efficient Market A market in which the prices or securities immediately reflect all available information. Prices are therefore in equilibrium.

Endorsement A guarantee that the terms of an option will be carried out. A conventional option is guaranteed by a NYSE member firm and listed options by the Options Clearing Corporation (OCC).

Equipment Trust Certificate or Bond A debt instrument secured by specific equipment such as railroad rolling stock. Generally regarded as a high-quality security. Ownership of the equipment is retained by a trustee until the debt is paid.

Equity (1) The share of security value in a brokerage account belonging to a customer. In effect, the difference between total value and debit balance. (2) The net worth section of a corporate balance sheet.

Eurobond A bond sold in a country other than the one in whose currency the bond is denominated.

Eurodollar A U.S. dollar on deposit in a foreign bank; usually, but not necessarily, a European bank. May be in a foreign branch of a U.S. bank.

European Option An option that can be exercised only on its expiration date, rather than on or before that date.

Excess Excess equity in a margin account; that is, the amount by which the equity exceeds the margin requirements. Can be withdrawn or used as buying power for additional positions.

Ex-Distribution   The buyer of a security selling ex-distribution has bought it too late to be entitled to a previously announced distribution such as spin-off stock.

Ex-Dividend   The ex-dividend buyer of a stock will not receive a dividend which has been declared because he purchased it too late to be of record on the record date. Most frequently four days before the record date. *See* Record Date.

Exempt Securities   Securities not subject to registration under the Securities Act of 1933 and most of the margin and other restrictions defined in the Securities Act of 1934. In general, these are government, government agency, and municipal securities.

Exercise   (1) The requirement by the buyer of any option that the seller must deliver or receive stock as specified in their contract. The seller of a call must deliver stock and the seller of a put must receive it. (2) The purchase of a stock by the holder of a warrant.

Exercise Price   The price at which an option is exercisable. Normally fixed but may vary with distributions such as stock dividends or cash dividends in the case of conventional options.

Ex-Rights   The ex-rights buyer of a stock will not get the right to subscribe to a forthcoming stock issue because he purchased the stock after the cutoff (ex-rights) date. The rights are said to be off. *See* Cum Rights.

Flash Prices   Prices of selected stocks indicated earlier than their normal position on a tape when transactions are reported six or more minutes late in order to give a better indication of what the market is doing.

Flat   A transaction usually involving bonds in which interest is not added to the purchase price. Typically involves income bonds or bonds currently in default.

Flower Bonds   A U.S. government bond sold at a discount but redeemable at par even if bought at a discount if used to pay estate taxes upon the death of the owner. No such bonds have been issued since 1971.

Fourth Market   Purchases and sales made directly between institutions which involve no brokers or dealers.

Front-End Load   A substantial markup over net asset value by a mutual fund charged to the purchaser under a long-term contractual plan at the beginning of the plan. Amounts to a prepayment of charges and is supposed to encourage the buyer to stay with his purchase plan.

General Mortgage Bond   A bond secured by all of a company's property.

General Obligation Bond   A municipal bond secured by the issuer's taxing power and good faith. Sometimes called a full faith and credit bond. *See* Revenue Bond.

Give-Up Diversion of commissions or markups from one broker or dealer to another at the direction of the customer paying the commission or fee.

Group Sales Sales of a new issue to large, usually institutional, buyers directly by the manager of an underwriting syndicate lessening the amount of an issue available to smaller buyers by other members of the selling group.

Guaranteed Account A brokerage account in which losses or margin requirements are guaranteed by another account.

Guaranteed Bonds Bonds guaranteed as to interest, principal, or both by a company other than the issuer. Most frequently utilized in the rail industry in the past. Guaranteed municipal bonds have become popular in recent years. The guarantor is an industrial corporation with a major stake in the construction of a new publicly financed facility.

Guaranteed Stock A stock whose dividends are guaranteed by a company other than the issuer. Usually preferred stock.

Hedge Protecting a long position in one asset while being short in another in order to reduce overall risk. In commodities one side of the hedge is in the cash market and the other in the futures market.

Hedge Clause A disclaimer on a market letter or research report in which the writer indicates that he is presenting his opinion in good faith, but cannot be held liable for errors or for reasonable misjudgment.

Hedge Fund An investment pool characterized by selling short as well as buying securities in the same industry.

High Yield Bonds *See* Junk Bonds.

Horizontal Spread *See* Calendar Spread.

Hypothecation The pledging of securities as collateral. The term is usually used in connection with brokerage firm margin accounts. *See* Rehypothecation.

Income Bonds Bonds which pay interest only if earned. Interest payments not made may or may not be designated as cumulative. *See* Flat.

Indenture The formal agreement between the issuer of a bond and its buyers which sets forth the terms of the bonds.

Index A measure based upon comparison with a base year which is normally designated as 100. *See* Average.

Index Option A cash-settled listed option based on an index or average.

Indication of Interest Indications by customers that they might buy a new issue when and if brought to market. Because registration statements are not yet effective, an order or purchase would be premature and probably illegal.

Individual Retirement Account   A retirement program which may permit an investor to set aside a limited amount toward retirement each year and deduct some or all of that amount from taxable income.

Insider   One who is restricted from some kinds of trading in a company's stock because he has access to privileged information. Obvious insiders are officers, directors, and any large stockholders, but the term may also include attorneys and investment banking personnel, among others.

Intermarket Trading System   An electronic network linking the floors of the NYSE or AEX with the floors of regional exchanges trading the same stocks in an effort to provide access to the most favorable prices.

In-the-Money   An option with intrinsic value. A call is in-the-money when the underlying stock is selling above the exercise price of the call. A put is in-the-money when the underlying stock is selling below the exercise price.

Intrinsic Value   That portion of an option's value attributable to its selling in-the-money as opposed to that portion attributable to time alone (extrinsic value).

Investment Advisor   A firm or person who manages the investments of others and is compensated for his advice. Registration is usually required under the Investment Advisors Act of 1940, which is administered by the SEC.

Investment Banker   A firm which advises other firms how to raise capital, arranges deals, such as acquisitions or disposal of property, or distributes new equity or debt securities. Although all investment bankers are underwriters, an underwriter is a narrower term than investment banker.

Investment Company   A company organized primarily to invest in the securities of other companies. Organized either as closed end or open end. Shares of closed end investment companies are traded like any other stocks either on or off exchanges. Shares of open-end companies are bought or sold directly from the company or its sponsors. Open-end investment companies and mutual funds are synonymous.

Investment Grade Bonds   Bonds rated Baa or above by Moody's.

Investment Letter   *See* Letter Security.

IRA   *See* Individual Retirement Account.

ITS   *See* Intermarket Trading System.

Junk Bonds   Bonds rated lower than Baa by Moody's.

Keogh Plan   A plan that allows self-employed individuals to set aside income up to a specified limit and invest it until retirement while deferring income tax on the funds. In effect, an individual tax shelter.

Lay-Off   Generally applied to a provision in a subscription (rights) offering of additional corporate stock in which the underwriter agrees under a stand-by underwriting agreement to buy any shares which are not taken up by the corporation's stockholders.

Letter Security   Privately placed securities, usually stock, requiring a letter from the purchaser indicating that the stock was purchased as a long-term investment and not for short-term resale. Letter may be required by the SEC or a state securities commissioner.

Leveraged Buy-out   A strategy used to acquire a publicly held corporation by offering to exchange the common stock for an amount of cash or debt greater than the market value of the shares. The company is then converted to private ownership. The buyers are usually the management of the corporation and the funds are typically generated through the issuance of low-rated debt backed by the stockholders' equity. *See* Junk Bonds.

LIBOR   The London interbank offered rate. Relatively short-term, fluctuating, borrowing rate prevailing in the London banking community. A common benchmark for pricing Eurobond issues (e.g., "35 basis points over LIBOR").

Load   The markup on the shares of most open-end investment companies. In effect, the amount paid by the buyer per share in excess of the current net asset value per share.

Loan Value   (1) The amount which can be loaned on a particular security. Percentage may differ on stocks and bonds of various types from as much as 95% on U.S. government bonds to zero on some over-the-counter securities. (2) The maximum that can be loaned on all of the securities in a margin account.

Long   The position of one who has bought and holds a security. A long position does not always result from a purchase because the buyer could be covering a formerly established short position.

Maintenance Call   A call issued for additional funds to the owner of a margin account. Almost always results from an adverse market movement. Sometimes referred to as a margin call, but margin calls may also result from the establishment of new positions.

Majority Voting   A form of corporate voting in which each director is voted upon separately. This may result in minority stockholders having no voice on the Board of Directors. Also called statutory voting. *See* Cumulative Voting.

Maloney Act   A 1938 law permitting the establishment of self-regulatory security broker—dealer associations. The major association resulting was the NASD.

Margin   (1) The funds required to be deposited by one purchasing securities. (2) The percentage of equity in an account owned by someone who has bought on credit.

Margin Account   A brokerage account which enables a client to borrow against eligible securities purchased in or deposited into the account.

Margin Call   A demand by a broker that a customer deposit additional funds either because additional securities have been bought or sold short (original, federal, or Regulation T call) or because there has been adverse market action (maintenance call). *See* Regulation T.

Market Maker   A dealer in over-the-counter stocks or a dealer in listed options who makes firm bids and offers rather than merely acting as a broker.

Member   An individual who owns a seat on a securities or futures exchange.

Member Organization   A member firm or member corporation. A member firm is a partnership with one or more partners or employees who are members of an exchange. A securities firm organized as a corporation is called a member corporation if one or more of its officers or employees is a member of an exchange.

Money Market   A financial market in which funds are borrowed or lent for short periods as distinguished from the capital market for long-term funds. *See* Money Market Instruments.

Money Market Fund   A mutual fund which invests its assets in money market instruments.

Money Market Instruments   Short-term debt instruments such as Treasury bills, bankers' acceptances, certificates of deposit, commercial paper, repurchase agreements, and certain Eurocurrency instruments.

Mortgage Bond   A bond which protects its buyers by giving them first claim on specified real assets of the corporation. In the event of liquidation, the owners have a general claim on all unencumbered assets if the mortgage is insufficient to provide them with the par value of their bonds.

Mutual Fund   *See* Investment Company.

Naked Option   An option written by one who utilizes collateral other than the security upon which the option is written.

NASD   *See* National Association of Securities Dealers.

NASDAQ   *See* National Association of Securities Dealers Automated Quotations.

National Association of Securities Dealers   An industry association of brokers and dealers who operate in the over-the-counter market. It regulates its members in a quasi-governmental manner. Created in accordance with the Maloney Act of 1938.

National Association of Securities Dealers Automated Quotations   A system for providing securities firms with prices of over-the-counter securities via an instantaneously updated display on a cathode-ray tube.

National Stock Clearing Corporation   A corporation jointly owned by the New York Stock Exchange, American Stock Exchange, and the NASD, which arranges clearing of transactions and deliveries of securities for the members. Including servicing by the Securities Industry Automation Corporation, the National Stock Clearing Corporation performs clearing functions for the NYSE, the Amex, many OTC trades, and some municipal bonds.

Net Change The amount by which the closing price of a security differs from its closing price on the previous day it traded.

Nine Bond Rule A NYSE rule that an order for fewer than 10 bonds listed on the Exchange must be filled on the Exchange if possible rather than being filled over the counter without being sent to the Exchange floor first.

No-Par Refers to stock with no specific value designated.

Nominal Quotation An approximation of a security's market value which does not purport to be a firm bid or asking price.

Nonclearing Member A member of an exchange who does not also belong to the clearing facility associated with that exchange. Trades of such members are cleared on the books of clearing members in return for a share of commission or a fee.

Nonpurpose Loan A loan against securities but not for the purpose of buying those or other securities on margin. Such loans are therefore not subject to federal or exchange margin requirements.

OCC *See* Options Clearing Corporation.

Odd Lot Listed shares of stock traded in an amount less than the number designated by an exchange as a round lot. The round lot is most frequently 100 shares, but on some exchanges may be 50, 25, or 10 shares for inactive or high-priced stocks.

Odd-Lot Theory A belief that the odd-lot trader is usually wrong when buying aggressively at market highs and selling aggressively at lows. Technicians who believe this utilize it as a timing device by acting opposite to the odd-lot customer.

Off-Board Over-the-counter transactions.

Omnibus Account An account carried by a member firm for a nonmember correspondent firm. The omnibus account represents the individual accounts of a number of the correspondent firm's customers.

On-Balance Volume A technical approach to market analysis that attempts to discern accumulation or distribution of stocks by large traders by comparing the volume of trading on rising markets with the volume on falling markets.

Open-End Investment Company A mutual fund. New shares are created in accordance with demand rather than being authorized and offered in a limited number as in the case of closed-end investment companies.

Open Interest The total number of outstanding options or commodity contracts indicated on the books of a clearing house. It is the total of either the longs or shorts that must be equal.

Option   A privilege sold by one party to another which offers the buyer the right to buy (call) or sell (put) a security at an agreed-upon price during a specified period or on a specified date. May be listed (exchange options) or traded over the counter (conventional options).

Option Class   All listed call options or all listed put options covering the same underlying security.

Option Premium   The price paid for a listed option.

Option Series   All options of the same class that also have the same striking price and expiration date.

Option Type   Options are of two types: puts and calls.

Option Writer   The seller of an option who guarantees performance by a deposit of cash, securities, or both.

Options Clearing Corporation   The issuer of all listed options. It is involved in all exercises because all call buyers who exercise their options obtain their securities from other members of the Corporation. Likewise put buyers who exercise sell their shares to other members of the Corporation. It is owned by the domestic options exchanges.

OTC   *See* Over the Counter.

Out of the Money   An option with time value but no intrinsic value. The current market price of the underlying stock is below the striking price of a call or above that of a put.

Over the Counter   Trading among firms usually by telephone in which orders are not filled on floors of exchanges. Firms may act either as brokers or dealers. Sometimes called "off-board."

P&S Department   *See* Purchase and Sale Department.

Par Value   The value of a security indicated on the certificate. In the case of a bond, it is synonymous with the face value. In the case of common stock, it is frequently an arbitrary number.

Point   (1) One dollar on a share of stock; (2) $10 on a bond; (3) one unit in an average. One percentage point equals 100 basis points.

Point and Figure   A technical device based upon the charting of price fluctuation emphasizing changes and amount of movement without regard to time or volume. Purports to indicate support and resistance levels. Sometimes called reversal charts.

Poison Pill   Any of a number of defensive tactics written into a corporate charter to fend off the advances of an unwanted suitor. Among these are provisions to create huge debt which a potential acquirer would be forced to assume in order to complete a take-over, and the issuance of long-term (10 or more years) subscription rights to create more new stock when any acquirer obtains a certain percentage of outstanding shares.

Portfolio Effect   The degree to which the variability or returns on a combination of assets such as stocks are less than the sum of the variations of the individual assets.

Post   *See* Trading Post.

Preemptive Right   The privilege given to corporate stockholders that allows them to participate in anything of value distributed by the corporation. Usually applies to the right to subscribe to new issues of a common stock on a pro rata basis.

Preference Stock   Essentially the same as preferred stock but junior to it. Issued by companies whose charters preclude issuance of additional preferred stock.

Preferred Stock   Stock which has a claim on a corporation's earnings, dividends, and assets ahead of the common stock but behind debt. Sometimes regarded as quasi-debt because of the pressure, if not obligation, to pay dividends. Dividends frequently are cumulative. *See* Arrearage.

Preliminary Prospectus   An early edition of a prospectus intended to inform interested parties about an unregistered new issue and not to be used as a selling device. Does not indicate price, offering date, and other information that will appear in the final prospectus. Sometimes called a "red herring."

Premium   The cost of a listed option.

Prerefunded Bonds   Municipal bonds which remain outstanding despite the fact that their redemption has been technically accomplished through the deposit of U.S. government securities into an escrow account. The technique is used by municipalities to lower borrowing costs when interest rates fall but outstanding issues cannot be redeemed yet because of call protection.

Price-Earnings Ratio   The current market price of a stock divided by its earnings per share.

Price Spread   Synonymous with vertical spread.

Prime Rate   The interest rate charged by banks to their clients with the best credit ratings.

Private Placement   The distribution of securities to a small number of sophisticated investors who usually must sign an investment letter. Such placements are usually exempt from SEC and state registration procedures.

Prospectus   A summary of the registration statement filed with the SEC for most new issues. The prospectus is partially a selling device and partially a means of making certain that buyers of new issues have had all essential information about the issue disclosed to them. *See* Preliminary Prospectus.

Proxy   A document giving a person the authority to act for another. Such documents are frequently used to delegate the authority to vote shares of common stock.

Prudent Man Rule   Restriction placed on fiduciaries under state laws requiring that they act for others in a conservative manner when handling funds belonging to others. Some states provide a special list of securities which may be considered. This is designated as the legal list.

Purchase and Sale Department   A department of a brokerage company which confirms sales and purchases to customers and compares trades with the brokers handling the other side.

Purpose Loan   A loan used to buy or maintain a security position or margin. Credit restriction usually more stringent than for a nonpurpose loan.

Put   An option to sell a stock at a fixed price for a stated period of time.

Pyramiding   Adding to positions by using profits or buying power gained from previously favorable market action. This is a narrower term than "averaging," which might involve additional deposits of capital.

Real Estate Investment Trust   An investment company which invests in real estate rather than securities.

Receive versus Payment   A sale of securities providing for payment immediately upon receipt instead of regular way.

Record Date   The date by which security holders must be registered in order to receive a forthcoming distribution such as dividends or rights or to have the right to vote at a forthcoming stockholders' meeting.

Red Herring   *See* Preliminary Prospectus.

Redemption   The retirement of bonds before maturity or preferred stocks on a call at a price designated as the redemption price. Calls are at the discretion of the issuer. Often used to force conversion. Also, the liquidation of mutual fund shares at net asset value.

Refunding   Retirement of securities utilizing funds gained from the sale of new securities.

Registrar   A financial institution selected by a corporation to record the issuance and the ownership of the corporation's securities. Not to be confused with the transfer agent.

Registration Statement   A document filed with the SEC by a company which proposes to issue new securities. Its primary purpose is to make certain that all essential facts are available to potential purchasers.

Regular Way Delivery   The usual day by which delivery of a security must be made by a selling broker or payment made by a buying broker. Five business days for stocks and bonds; one business day for options and U.S. government securities.

Regulation A Issue   New security issues partially exempt from SEC regulation primarily because of the small dollar amount of the issue ($1.5 million or less). All exemptions are not regulation A. Others include intrastate issues and government securities.

Regulation T The amount of credit which a customer may receive from a broker when trading securities. The percentage may vary as to the type of securities bought or sold short and may be raised or lowered in accordance with the current attitude of the Federal Reserve Board toward easy or tight credit.

Regulation T Call A margin call based upon federal requirements rather than those imposed by an exchange or a brokerage house.

Regulation U Similar to regulation T, but governs extension of credit by banks rather than by brokers.

Rehypothecation Borrowing by a brokerage company utilizing securities in margin accounts deposited by customers who have borrowed funds from the brokerage company. The latter is hypothecation.

REIT *See* Real Estate Investment Trust.

Restricted Account (1) A margin account with less equity than the current Regulation T requirement. (2) An account precluded from new transactions or placed on a cash-in-advance basis for making a practice of such activities as free riding.

Retained Earnings That part of corporate net income not paid out in dividends. The balance sheet figure is the total of all retained earnings during the corporate life.

Retention Requirement The requirement that a stated percentage of proceeds in liquidating transactions be kept in an undermargined account rather than being available for withdrawal.

Revenue Bond A type of municipal bond that relies upon revenues from income from a specified project for payment of interest and principal rather than a government body's taxing power and general credit. The latter (general obligation bond) is generally safer and yields less.

Reverse Split A reduction in a corporation's outstanding common stock accomplished by replacing outstanding common stock by fewer shares and increasing the stated or par value per share. Usually done when a corporation believes the market price of its stock is too low.

Rolling Over Substituting an option presently held with another with different terms such as a later date or a higher or lower striking price.

Round Lot A unit of trading designated by exchanges for listed stocks or bonds. Usually 100 shares of stock, but sometimes 50, 25, or 10. *See* Odd Lot. No standard terms for bonds, but U.S. government and municipal traders recognize $100,000 par value as standard round lots for most good securities.

RVP *See* Receive versus Payment.

Seat A membership on an exchange. There may or may not be an actual place to sit down.

SEC *See* Securities and Exchange Commission.

Secondary Distribution   A distribution of previously issued securities. Such offerings are handled off the exchange floors whether or not the stock is listed. Usually offered at a fixed price which includes compensation for sellers.

Secondary Market   The market in which stocks are traded after being issued in a primary market.

Securities Act of 1933   An act which attempts to make essential facts about securities available to potential buyers to whom the securities are being distributed. Administered by the Securities and Exchange Commission.

Securities and Exchange Commission   A U.S. government agency established in 1934 to regulate the issuance and trading of securities, securities markets; including options but not commodities, and personnel including investment advisers operating in the securities business.

Securities Exchange Act of 1934   Created the Securities and Exchange Commission, giving it the authority to regulate markets and securities industry personnel, supervise disclosure of essential facts concerning security distributions, and enforce credit restrictions dictated by the Federal Reserve Board of Governors.

Securities Industry Automation Corporation   An organization jointly owned by the NYSE and Amex to provide data processing, clearing, communications, and other services.

Securities Investor Protection Corporation   A corporation backed by federal guarantees that protects customers against losses of cash or securities suffered because of a broker's bankruptcy. Protection is limited to stated maximums. Funded by assessment of its members that include all exchange members and most NASD members.

Security   An investment contract containing the following elements: (1) a transaction in which money is invested; (2) the investment is in a common enterprise; and (3) there is an expectation of profit resulting from the efforts of others. Important examples of securities are stocks, bonds, and options. Commodity futures have been held not to be securities.

Segregated Securities   Securities held by a brokerage firm for customers, but which cannot be used for collateral by the broker because the customer has no loan outstanding against the securities.

Selling Group   An ad hoc group of security firms formed to sell a new security issue.

Serial Bond   A bond that matures at intervals stated on the bonds. Similar to a sinking-fund bond issue, but the latter does not indicate when specific bonds will mature. Typical of municipal general obligation issues and railroad equipment trust certificates.

Settlement Date   The date on which securities sold must be delivered or the date on which securities bought must be paid for.

Sheets Price quotations of over-the-counter securities issued by the National Quotation Service of the National Quotation Bureau, Inc. "Pink Sheets" indicate stock quotations; "Yellow Sheets," bonds.

Shelf Registration A form of registration whereby established issuers are allowed to preregister securities and await favorable market conditions before offering. Usually done under SEC Rule 415 and without the conventional investment banking syndicates. Instead, interested firms make bids to the issuer, which will sell to the most attractive proposal.

Short The sale of a security which is settled by the delivery of borrowed securities rather than by delivery of securities owned by the seller. The seller may wish to retain his securities for such reasons as tax advantage or control. He might not own the securities at all.

Short against the Box A short sale made by one who owns the security sold. The transaction is settled by delivery of borrowed stock. Usually done for tax reasons.

SIAC *See* Securities Industry Automation Corporation.

Sinking Fund A means of amortizing a bond issue by means of regular, usually annual, payments. The sinking fund may either accumulate in the form of high-grade securities or may be used for the periodic random retirement of the securities for which they are provided.

SIPC *See* Securities Investor Protection Corporation.

SMA See Special Memorandum Account.

Special Memorandum Account An account used to indicate the maximum excess and buying power available to a brokerage house client with a margin account. Sometimes called a Special Miscellaneous Account.

Special Offering A sale of a large block of previously issued stock, but unlike a secondary distribution, it is traded on an exchange floor. Rarely used in recent years.

Special Option An unexpired conventional option for sale by a dealer who acquired it from a seller who chose to sell before expiration.

Special Subscription Account An account opened for the purpose of acquiring stock issued by means of preemptive rights. The buyer can usually borrow more against his purchase in such an account than is possible in the general account.

Specialist An exchange member operating on an exchange floor as a dealer in some transactions and a broker in others. His function is to act to maintain a fair and orderly market in securities assigned to him and also to hold limit or stop orders for other brokers executing such orders when possible in return for part of the commission.

Specialist's Book The notebook utilized by a specialist in his function as a broker to keep a record of limit or stop orders left with him by other brokers acting for customers of brokerage firms.

Spin-Off   A stock dividend paid by one company in stock of another corporation rather than in its own stock.

Spread   (1) The difference between the price bid by a dealer in stock and the price which he asks. (2) The purchase of one listed option and the sale of another on the same stock.

Spread Option   The simultaneous purchase of a put and call or some combination of multiple puts and calls. In the conventional option market a spread is differentiated from a straddle in that the exercise price of the call is above the market and that of the put is below the market. *See* Spread; Strip; Strap.

Stabilization   Support of the market price of new security issues by the underwriting group in order to help sell the issue. It amounts, in effect, to a legal manipulation.

Standby Agreement   An agreement by an underwriter to purchase all shares in a rights issue not subscribed to by the public holders of the rights.

Stock   A certificate representing one or more shares of a corporation's equity.

Stock Dividend   A dividend paid in shares of stock rather than cash. It involves a transfer of retained earnings to the capital stock account and does not affect par value. A stock dividend paid in shares of another company such as a subsidiary is sometimes called a spin-off.

Stock Power   A separate form or a form printed on the back of a security which when executed allows transfer of the security by a third party. Frequently used when a security is pledged as collateral for a loan.

Stock Split   An increase in the number of corporate shares outstanding by means of a reduction in par value and a corresponding reduction in equity value per share.

Stopping Stock   A guarantee by a specialist that a limit order will be filled at a designated level or better. This gives a customer a chance to wait for a more favorable price at which to buy or sell while avoiding the risk of "missing the market." Not to be confused with a stop order.

Straddle   A combination option of one put and one call with identical exercise prices and expiration dates. The put and call are exercisable and can be traded individually.

Strap   A combination option consisting of two calls and one put.

Street Name   Securities owned by a customer, but held in the name of a broker, are said to be in street name. This may be done either because the securities are collateral in a margin account or to simplify trading. "Street" refers to Wall Street or more generally to the brokerage industry.

Striking Price   See Exercise Price.

Strip   A combination option consisting of two puts and one call.

Subchapter S A section of the Internal Revenue Code that allows small corporations to elect to be taxed as either individual proprietorships or partnerships rather than as corporations. Designed to avoid so-called double taxation.

Subordinated Debt Debt having a claim on assets only after more senior debt has been paid off in full. A common example is subordinated debentures.

Subscription Privilege The preemptive right given to corporate stockholders to buy a proportionate share of new stock or securities convertible into stock issued by a corporation before such new securities are offered to others. The subscription price is set below the prevailing market price.

Superrestricted A margin account with an equity so low relative to market value that it may be subject to added defined restrictions by the Federal Reserve System or by exchanges. Superrestriction, when imposed, is usually imposed when equity is less than 30% of market value.

Syndicate An ad hoc group of investment bankers grouped together to share the risk of underwriting and/or selling a new security issue.

Tax-Exempt Securities Often called municipal bonds but may be issued by any state, county, city, or other taxing government unit except the federal government. Exempt from federal income tax and from state income tax in the state where issued. Not exempt from capital gains, inheritance, or estate taxes.

Tax Shelter An investment or other means intended to reduce or eliminate taxes. Examples include tax-exempt municipal securities, interest or dividend tax exclusions, and limited partnerships in such areas as real estate, cattle raising, equipment leasing, oil drilling, research and development projects, and motion picture production. The latter are intended to reduce or defer taxes while held at the same time providing current income, a gain at the time of disposition, or both.

Tender Offer A public offer to buy shares from stockholders usually at a price above that prevailing in the open market. Usually applied to acquisition of shares in a company other than the one asking for tenders.

Third Market Trading in securities listed on exchange by nonmember firms over the counter.

Time Value That part of an option premium which reflects only its remaining life. Extrinsic value. See Intrinsic Value.

Tombstone Published advertisement listing the underwriters of a securities issue.

Trading Post A numbered location on an exchange floor where stocks of specified companies are traded.

Transfer Agent Usually a bank that serves a corporation by keeping a record of registered shareholders and making sure that old certificates are canceled and new ones issued when a change of ownership takes place. Not to be confused with the registrar.

Treasury Bills   Short-term obligations of the U.S. government issued for periods of one year or less. (Treasury certificates maturing in less than one year have not been issued since 1966.)

Treasury Bonds   United States government obligations issued for long periods typically 15–30 years.

Treasury Notes   United States government obligations issued for periods of more than one year but not more than 10 years.

Treasury Stock   Common stock that has been repurchased by, or donated to, or otherwise reacquired by the issuing firm. It receives no dividends and has no voting privilege.

Type of Option   The classification of an option as a put, call, or combination.

Uncovered Writer   One who does not own the stock for which he writes a call option. This is sometimes called naked writing. (See Naked Option.)

Underwriting   One of the functions of investment bankers. Involves the buying of new issues of securities from corporations and the reselling of such issues. May be done individually, but usually underwriting risk is reduced through formation of an ad hoc syndicate.

Uniform Gifts to Minor Act   State laws that make it possible for minors to own assets including securities without creation of a formal trust.

Up and Out Option   A conventional put option which expires if the market price of the underlying stock rises above a predetermined level.

Variable Spread   Offsetting long and short option positions in options of the same class and type, but with a mismatching number of contracts and involving different striking prices and/or expiration dates.

Vertical Spread   Purchase and sale of options with the same expiration date. A call bear spread consists of the option with the higher striking price on the long side and that with the lower striking price on the short side. A bull spread reverses these positions.

Warrant   Similar to a call option but exercisable over a much longer period ranging from one year to perpetuity. May be issued individually or in connection with a stock or bond offering in order to make the issue more desirable; in this case, the warrant is said to act as a "sweetener."

Wash Sale   (1) Security transaction involving no real change of ownership as in the sale of a stock by a man to his wife or a sale in one account and the purchase in another at the same time. (2) The repurchase within 30 days of a security sold at a loss. This usually has the effect of eliminating the deductability of the loss.

Work-Out Market   An over-the-counter market or option market in which a dealer's offer to buy or sell is not firm, but rather is subject to his ability to find a buyer or seller. The dealer is unable or unwilling to buy stock for his inventory or sell it either from his inventory or short.

Writer   A person or organization who sells a call or a put and thereby assumes the obligation to buy or sell a stock at the exercise price upon demand by the Options Clearing Corporation if the position is not offset before the expiration date.

Yield to Maturity   The internal rate of return of a debt instrument.

Zero Coupon Bond   A bond which pays no current interest. Such a bond sells at a deep discount from its redemption price. If taxable, interest is imputed.

Index